Marriages & Families

Marriages & Families

NEW PROBLEMS, NEW OPPORTUNITIES

Ernest Havemann

Marlene Lehtinen
University of Utah

Prentice-Hall   Englewood Cliffs, New Jersey 07632

Library of Congress Cataloging-in-Publication Data

HAVEMANN, ERNEST. (date)
  Marriages and families.

  Bibliography
  Includes index.
  1. Family life education. 2. Family—United States.
3. Marriage—United States. I. Lehtinen, Marlene, (date)
  II. Title.
HQ10.H36 1986   306.8   85-25689
ISBN 0-13-559030-2

Editorial/production supervision: Martha Masterson
Interior and cover design: Jayne Conte
Cover photo: Apple Computers
Manufacturing buyer: John Hall
Photo Editor: Lorinda Morris
Photo Research: Christina Carey and Teri Stratford

Chapter Opening Photos: 1. Hella Hammid, Photo Researchers;
2. Menschenfreund, Taurus Photos; 3. Hanna Schreiber; 4. Teri
Leigh Stratford, Photo Researchers; 5. Frank Siteman, Taurus
Photos; 6. Ed Lettau, Photo Researchers; 7. Mimi Forsyth,
Monkmeyer; 8. Michael Kagan; 9. Michael Kagan, Stock Boston;
10. Mikki Ansin; 11. David S. Strickler, Monkmeyer; 12. Stan
Levy, Photo Researchers; 13. IBM corporation.

Printed in the United States of America

10 9 8 7 6 5 4 3 2 1

ISBN 0-13-559030-2

Prentice-Hall International (UK) Limited, *London*
Prentice-Hall of Australia Pty. Limited, *Sydney*
Prentice-Hall Canada Inc., *Toronto*
Prentice-Hall Hispanoamericana, S. A., *Mexico*
Prentice-Hall of India Private Limited, *New Delhi*
Prentice-Hall of Japan, Inc., *Tokyo*
Prentice-Hall of Southeast Asia Pte. Ltd., *Singapore*
Editora Prentice-Hall do Brasil, Ltda., *Rio de Janeiro*
Whitehall Books Limited, *Wellington, New Zealand*

Contents

PART TWO

THE FEMININE AND MASCULINE ROLES

PART THREE

FINDING A MATE AND SEXUALITY

6 Sex: How People Feel, Think, and Behave 135

PART FOUR

CONFLICT AND ADJUSTMENT IN MARRIAGE

7 The Basic Source of Conflict in Marriage 167

8 The Fine Art of Getting Along Together 193

9 Decision Making and Communication 221

PART FIVE

THE COUPLES WHO STAY MARRIED: THE POST-HONEYMOON YEARS AND PARENTHOOD

PART SIX

TODAY'S MARRIAGES, DIVORCES, AND THE FUTURE

13 Where Today's Trends May Be Leading 321

Appendix A: Family Finances 355

Appendix B: Sexual Anatomy, Pregnancy, and Birth Control 371

References 381

Name Index 403

Subject Index 409

Preface

The title of this book summarizes the four chief aspects of its purpose, viewpoint, and content. First, of course, the title indicates that the book is designed for the college course in marriage and the family. To this bare statement we should immediately add that it is addressed in particular to students who are especially interested in knowledge that can be applied to their own marriages— or indeed to any of their human relationships—and to instructors who take a functional as well as scientific view of the course.

Second, the words *Marriages and Families* are in the plural to indicate our conviction that intimate human relationships in our pluralistic society must be discussed not as a matter that is the same for everyone but with a constant regard for individual differences among the millions of people who take part in these relationships. Third, the words *New Problems* are a recognition of the simple fact, so obvious from the divorce statistics, that marriages and families face many unprecedented difficulties in these times of rapid change. Fourth, the added words *New Opportunities* express our belief that today's male-female relationships offer more people more chances for self-fulfillment and mutual

growth than existed in the more stable but also more rigid past.

Hence the full title: *Marriages and Families: New Problems, New Opportunities.*

***

On the matter of pluralism, there seems to have been a sort of culture lag in both popular and scientific circles. At one time there may in fact have been a generally accepted pattern and set of norms for all marriages and all families, though we do not really know this and should probably be skeptical. If a single pattern ever did exist— despite all the individual differences that have now been so well documented by social scientists in all areas from inborn tendencies and capacities to socialization into varying cultures and subcultures—this pattern has now been shattered. At some point in the recent past, marriage changed "from institution to companionship," the famous observation of Burgess and Locke (see p. 13). When it did, the mold was broken. An institution imposes its own rules and encourages conformity. A companionship can be as varied as its partners care to make it.

Yet the habit of thinking about marriage and the family as being the same for everyone persists. Many people assume that what is true about one marriage (or one divorce) is true about all of them. Newspaper columns purvey advice intended for everyone. Parents continue to make generalities about whom to marry and how to stay married. Even social scientists have not been guiltless. As Marvin Sussman has pointed out, we have been quick to recognize and to study the whole gamut of plurality in religious, ethnic, and racial backgrounds—but have been slow to realize that there is likewise a vast diversity of male-female relationships and that the participants in all these varied relationships have "vastly different problems to solve and issues to face."*

The new problems that every male-female relationship is bound to encounter stem largely from the uncompleted transition from institution to companionship, which is difficult for men and women alike (as described in Chapters 1 and 2). The problems center in particular on today's changing sex roles and new and as yet vaguely defined roles wives and husbands can now play in marriage, as discussed in Chapters 2–4. The idea of companionship has changed what we look for in a partner and how we go about finding one (Chapter 5). It has altered our sexual expectations in the complicated, hopeful, but at present not altogether helpful way described in Chapter 6. It has led to more frequent divorce but also to frequent remarriage, as discussed in Chapter 12.

On the matter of new opportunities, our viewpoint is that the breaking of the old mold has at least produced an environment in which male-female relationships can flourish

as never before—even if many of them do not seem to be doing so at the moment. And here is where social scientists probably have the most to contribute. Chapter 7 discusses what social scientists have learned about conflict. Chapter 8 describes what we now know about adjustment, or the day-to-day process of getting along with a human being of the opposite sex. Chapter 9 talks of discoveries about decision-making and the fine art of communication. One measure of how much has been learned about intimate human relationships is the fact that these chapters could not have been written until recently.

Besides these chapters on what is now known about marriages and families in general, the book addresses itself to some specific concerns. Chapter 10 discusses the post-honeymoon years, parenthood, and retirement. Chapter 11 describes what has been learned about bringing up children. Chapter 13 talks about egalitarian marriage and some of the other lifestyles that are alternatives to conventional marriage—particularly the single life, which, now that pluralism has begun to be recognized, seems to be attracting more Americans now than in the recent past. This final chapter of the book also summarizes some informed guesses on where today's trends may lead in the future. Two appendices discuss family money management and the physiological facts about sex, pregnancy, and contraception.

The chapter order in which these topics are presented is of course the one we find most logical. But here too there will undoubtedly be individual differences. Many instructors will prefer some other arrangement or may want to omit some of the chapters. We have therefore written each chapter as a self-contained unit that can be understood without having read previous chap-

*Sussman, M. B. "Family systems in the 1970's: Analysis, policies, and programs." *The Annals of the American Academy of Political and Social Science,* 1971, 396, 40–56.

ters. Where cross-references seem to be helpful, they have been provided. An Instructor's Manual with Tests, expertly prepared by Mark Kassop of Bergen Community College, available to those who assign the book to their classes, offers many suggestions for using it to full advantage.

***

As will be quickly apparent, this is not a "preachy" book. Our concern for the pluralism of American society makes us unwilling to try to set rules for other people's behavior. Moreover we have kept pasted above our desks the warning of Arlene Skolnick that there is no other subject or college course that presents such a great temptation to over-generalize on the basis of one's own experiences (see p. 18). We were determined to resist the temptation—and have been able to help each other because the two of us are of different generations and from different family and marital backgrounds. Thus we have simply tried to present what is known—and to let students make their own choices.

More than 1/4 of the references are dated in the 1980s and 80% go back no further than the 1970s. This reflects the fact that conditions affecting marriages and families have been changing so rapidly that most of the current problems and opportunities could not be studied until recently because they did not exist.

On the other hand, many of today's difficulties and possible solutions were intuitively foreseen by scholars long before most of today's students were even born. Some of the early insights—such as those of Burgess and Locke, Clifford Kirkpatrick, Mudd and Hey, and in the sex field Kinsey—are as pertinent today as they ever were. We have tried to do justice to the ideas of these pioneers and to persuade students that there is always more continuity between past and present than new generations like to think.

Similarly we have avoided embracing new ideas just for the sake of their novelty, especially if they have not yet met the test of solid verification and replication. We have seen too many fads come and go—new revelations hailed as the great modern hope of humanity, only to be discarded a few years later. We are skeptical anyway of formulas for success. We have little faith in the ten easy rules for marriage (or sex, or quarreling, or being a parent). We do have an abiding faith in humanity—and in the knowledge social scientists have acquired about the ways in which human beings can understand and love one another.

***

We are indebted to the following reviewers of the manuscript, who have given us numerous valuable criticisms and suggestions: Ross A. Klein, Iowa State University, and Robert J. Stout, St. Petersburg College.

Ernest Havemann
Marlene Lehtinen

CHAPTER 1

Marriage in Today's World: How It Has Changed

Most people today, young and old, have mixed feelings about marriage. On the one hand, people are cynical and pessimistic. A public opinion poll in the 1970s found that 70 percent of Americans believed marriage was a weaker force in our society than in the past. A sizable number—35 percent—agreed with the statement, "You see so few good or happy marriages that you have to question it as a way of life" (Roper, 1974). Divorce has become so commonplace that "the silver screen and the tube constantly bombard us with intimate scenes from a marriage headed for the rocks" (Levitan and Belous, 1981). There are more unmarried adults and childless couples today than ever before—and one sociologist has told a congressional committee that if present trends continue "not one American family will be left" by the mid-1990s (Etzioni, 1978).

Yet Americans continue to flock to this "weak," "questionable," and perhaps disappearing institution. Close to 5 million women and men a year buy the license and take the vows (National Center for Health Statistics, 1984). Indeed more than 90 percent of the population winds up married (Bureau of the Census, 1984a), and an even higher proportion of young people—97 percent of 18-year-olds who took part in one survey—expect to join the club (Institute for Social Research, 1980). Moreover, people who are currently married seem to have a generally high esteem for the institution. One opinion poll found that nine out of ten were either very satisfied or mostly satisfied with their marriage, and the pollsters concluded that their findings "completely refuted . . . any belief that Americans do not place top priority on the family" (Gallup, 1980).

College students, by and large, share the mingled optimism and pessimism. Many young people take a dim view of their parents' marriage, as can be seen in the box on *Opinions and Experiences,** but this does not seem to make them any less confident that they themselves can find marriage a highly satisfactory way of life. Indeed one study found that 96 percent of students feel they are personally capable of building a good marriage (Whitehurst, 1977b).

Opinions and Experiences boxes are found throughout the book. In some cases, as in this first one, they are the spoken or written comments of social scientists on matters of special interest. In other cases they are reports of interviews the authors have conducted with people of all walks of life who have talked about their own experiences with matters discussed in this book.

Opinions and Experiences

SOME STUDENT VIEWS OF MARRIAGE

Luella K. Alexander, who teaches the marriage and family course at the University of South Florida, discusses some of the attitudes her students bring to class.

By rough count over the last few years, perhaps as many as 80 percent of my students have been disillusioned with their parents' marriages. They don't like what they have seen. In many cases the parents have been divorced. In others the students feel that the marriage, though it still exists, has brought very little happiness to either the mother or the father. It certainly hasn't been the kind of marriage that they themselves would want.

That figure of close to 80 percent can't be taken at full face value because part of it has to be attributed to the generation gap. Undoubtedly quite a few of these parents are perfectly happy by their own lights, but they do not seem happy to their children because they no longer feel in their forty's like doing all the exciting and glamorous things that twenty-year-olds enjoy. Like lots of partying and riding a motorcycle, just to mention a few aspects of the generation gap. But even allowing for misunderstandings, the fact remains that many of my students seem to have come from homes that would hardly inspire any great optimism about marriage.

Nonetheless, most of the students are optimists. The women, in particular, usually take the course to learn what they can about marriage because they definitely think of marriage as part of their own future. They may plan to have their own careers, but they also expect to get married. The men tend to be more skeptical, but probably this is because many of them still enjoy being footloose and fancy-free. I don't think they would take the course unless they too figured that marriage was somewhere around the corner. In general, the parents' failures—or what have been interpreted as failures—have definitely not scared off many of these students.

Courtesy of Mrs. Luella K. Alexander, University of South Florida

TODAY'S ATTITUDES TOWARD MARRIAGE AND THE FAMILY

Mixed feelings about the merits of marriage and the future of the family are by no means brand new. One scholar has traced harsh criticism of the family to as far back as the ancient Greek philosopher Plato and the early Christians. The people of Medieval Europe also held marriage and the family in low esteem, as did such eminent social commentators as Thomas Paine in the early days of our own nation (Pickett, 1975). Yet there have been enough optimists throughout history to keep marriage alive in every known society of every known period. As one social scientist has written:

> Marriage is one of the oldest, most universal, and most distinctive of human institutions. There is no record of any society, however simple its economic and political system, that does not have marriage as one of the key elements of its social structure.
> *(Fuchs, 1983)*

Eric Kroll, Taurus

A loving and optimistic start for one of the 2.5 million American couples who get married each year.

The conflict between pessimism and optimism is perhaps more widespread and insistent today than ever before. Many people seem convinced that *The Death of the Family* (the title of an influential book of the 1970s) is taking place under our very eyes. Yet people continue to marry, with every expectation that their own marriage will be happy, successful, and immune to whatever malady is plaguing marriage in general.

Why is marriage the subject of so much controversy—and regarded with such a strange mixture of cynicism and hope? Where are marriage and the family headed, and what lies ahead for the individuals who

are or will be engaged in them? How can we ourselves best avoid the disaster predicted by the pessimists and fulfill our own optimistic hopes? Answering such questions—by presenting the most pertinent and useful knowledge that sociologists and other experts on family matters have acquired—is the purpose of this book.

The Modern-day Family

It must first be noted that marriage and the family have been undergoing vast and unprecedented changes, all taking place at breakneck speed. Perhaps the most dramatic evidence is this startling statistic: As recently as the 1950s, the typical American family was composed of a father whose earnings provided the financial support, a stay-at-home mother, and at least one and often two or three or more children living in the home. That kind of family, which then made up 70 percent of all households, has now dwindled to a mere 15 percent (Yankelovich, 1981).

About 23 percent of today's households are not really families at all but are made up of one person living alone (Bureau of the Census, 1984a). Many young adults, still unmarried or having been divorced, have established their own home. Among older people, many widows and a smaller number of widowers have done likewise. Besides these one-person households there are also many single-parent families—headed by a divorced woman or sometimes a divorced man with children—and nearly 2 million households in which the two partners are living together without being married (Spanier, 1983). Many married couples have never had children, and in others the children have grown up. Even in families with children under 18 years of age, about half of all the mothers have jobs outside the home and contribute to the family income (Bureau of the Census, 1984a).

Thus the once-typical family of bread-winning husband, stay-at-home wife, and young children has been turned into a small minority by developments of the past three decades. We now live in "a more variegated society with many types of households, no one of which predominates" (Yankelovich, 1981).

Modern-day Society

Not only the family but all other social institutions have had to cope with the startling developments that have made the United States of the 1980s a far different place from the United States of the past—even the recent past. An *institution* is a part of the social system that helps meet the basic needs of society. The family is the institution that enables a society to survive by reproducing itself and training the new generation. The political institution, or government, maintains internal order and stability and protects the society against outside enemies. The economic institution produces and distributes the food, clothing, and other goods that society requires. The religious institution provides a set of shared beliefs and rituals. The educational institution offers the specialized training that individuals need to function as effective members of society.

Society's institutions have been affected in many ways by the sweeping developments of recent years. The economic institution has been revolutionized by twentieth-century technology (for example, computers and other electronic discoveries, medical techniques, communications satellites, the jet airplane, and space ships). The political institution has undertaken such new responsibilities as welfare, Social Security, regula-

tion of industry, enforcement of civil rights, and protection against pollution. The educational institution has expanded immensely to afford more years of schooling to greater numbers of students, particularly women and members of minority groups.

All these developments, coming in such rapid succession, have created problems as well as benefits. As Talcott Parsons (1955) has pointed out, "Major structural changes in social systems always involve strain and disorganization"—and no institution has been spared the strains and upheavals of the twentieth century. Today's economists sometimes throw up their hands when they contemplate such problems as inflation, recession, unemployment, and the question of how the industrial system can survive shortages of oil and other resources. Political scientists are baffled by overpopulation, international tensions, the threat of military conflict, and the question of how government can perform all the tasks it has undertaken without going bankrupt. The religious institution no longer has as much influence over the lives of as many people as it once did. The educational institution is embroiled in controversy over its standards and teaching methods and the question of how to handle such urgent problems as discipline, dropouts, and reading disabilities.

HOW AND WHY MARRIAGE AND THE FAMILY HAVE CHANGED

With all other institutions in turmoil, it would be strange indeed if marriage and the family had stayed firm in their 1900 pattern, untouched by the benefits and blissfully free

National Archives

This old photograph is awkwardly posed in the fashion of the day, but it tells a lot about the valuable part played by children in the family as an economic unit.

from the problems that are altering the rest of the social structure. Change in the family was inevitable as society changed.

In the early days of America, when the whole structure of society was far simpler, the majority of colonial families lived on isolated farms where they had to be almost entirely self-sufficient. They built their own homes, raised their own food, and made their own clothing and furniture (Adams, 1974). They conducted their own religious services. Often, because schoolhouses were rare, they tutored their own children in reading, writing, and arithmetic. They de-

vised their own recreation and provided their own security, symbolized by a rifle hanging over the fireplace (Kirkpatrick, 1963).

Many of these duties, of course, have now been shifted from the home and family to outside agencies—the local police force, the movie house and football stadium, the schools and colleges, the churches and Sunday schools. In these respects the family is no longer so essential as it once was. In a phrase that William Ogburn made famous in sociology, it has suffered a "loss of function"—so severe that Ogburn himself despaired of its future (Ogburn, 1933).

The Family of the Past as an Economic Unit

Of all the losses of function cited by Ogburn, perhaps the greatest force for change within the family has been the nation's changing economic structure, for one strong bond that helped hold families together in the past was the simple dollars-and-cents facts of life. Even as recently as the early years of this century—your great-grandparents' time—the family was an economic unit, a sort of little business firm. People could live much better if they were married and had children.

On the farms where so many Americans then lived, every member of the family pitched in. While the husband worked in the fields, the wife churned butter, baked the bread, and sewed the quilts. The children milked the cows, slopped the hogs, and helped with the plowing, and they were an asset in another important way. There were no such things in those days as Social Security and company pension plans. When people got old, their children supported them. If they had no children, they went off to the poorhouse—that is, if they were lucky enough to live in a county that even bothered to provide such a haven of last resort.

Thus the American man of a few generations ago could get along much better with a helpful wife and some strong and willing children than he could by himself. As for the woman, she had no real alternative. If she did not have a husband—and unless she was one of the very few women with enough education to become a schoolteacher or that new-fangled person known as a stenographer—she could only sit home and grow old. The "old maid" was dependent all her uneasy years for every meal, every piece of clothing, and every cent of spending money.

She lived first by courtesy of her parents, who often could not hide their disappointment in her failure to marry. After the parents' deaths, she was an unpaying boarder with a brother or a married sister.

Knocking the Economic Props out from Under

In dollars-and-cents terms, the family has been on the decline ever since industrialization created the first textile mills, which could turn out cloth that was much better and cheaper than anything that could be produced at home on spinning wheel and loom. Throughout the present century the decline has been rapid and drastic.

Bakery bread helped knock the economic props out from under marriage. So did the canning industry. Americans have moved by the millions from farms where they were self-sufficient by necessity into city houses too crowded together to accommodate even a chicken coop. They live near supermarkets that sell instant coffee, cake mixes, and frozen tv dinners. What the family needs nowadays, it buys.

Children began losing their economic value about the time families started moving from farm to city and were further downgraded with the disappearance of the wood stove and the rug beater. Except for single-parent families where an older child can provide valuable help, most people today have difficulty thinking up any chores at all to keep children busy and disciplined. Instead of being a financial asset, children are a liability. The Department of Agriculture estimates that it costs 15 to 17 percent of family income to bring up a child—meaning that a family earning $20,000 a year spends close to $60,000 to get a child through high school, with college expenses still to come.

Since the Social Security system was set up in the 1930s, most elderly parents are no longer completely dependent on their children. True, people past retirement age usually have a hard time getting along if they have to rely entirely on Social Security payments, and many do not have company pensions or other income. But being independent of one's children has become a matter of pride for older people—a sharp change from the attitude that prevailed until recently (Nye, 1967).

Fewer Children or None

If children have become expensive, they also have become a matter of choice. Birth control, as it happens, is hardly a new development in human history. It was mentioned in an Egyptian papyrus written about 4,000 years ago and was a topic of debate among Greek philosophers 2,400 years ago (Havemann, 1967). But the availability of effective methods to anyone who cares to use them dates back only a few decades. In the United States physicians were jailed for offering information on birth control as recently as the 1920s. Abortion except under special circumstances was illegal in every state until 1970 (Kogan, 1973).

Many people, of course, continue to oppose the practice of birth control. The majority of American couples, however, limit the size of their family, and today's birth rate is only half as high as in the early years of the century. Many young couples do not have any children at all: 42 percent of all wives between the ages of 20 and 24 are childless, and of wives aged 25 to 29 some 22 percent are childless (Bureau of the Census, 1983a). These figures are considerably higher than they were even ten years ago—and far higher than twenty or more years ago. Some of the young wives are merely

postponing childbirth, but others will never have children. Daniel Yankelovich, who has conducted many public opinion polls, has pointed out that in the decade of the 1970s ten million American men and women had themselves sterilized as an absolute guarantee against having children (or any more children) and has commented:

> Our studies show that, unlike most American women in the recent past, tens of millions of women no longer regard having babies as self-fulfilling. Large-scale and deliberate childlessness is a new experience for our society.
>
> *(Yankelovich, 1981)*

Many people now make the decision to have children only after long and thoughtful consideration. As one sociologist has put it, "Young people are gradually rejecting the myth of 'parenthood is fun,' and realizing that parenthood is a very serious business and one which ought to be undertaken only when people are ready to plunge in and do a good job" (Davids, 1971). A public opinion poll found that 51 percent of American adults consider two children the ideal family size. More than three children are considered ideal by only 17 percent, down from 38 percent forty years ago (Roper, 1980).

Today's Long, Long Lifetime

Today's small families are just one aspect of a modern phenomenon that has revolutionized living patterns and societies within the span of this century. The United States of 1900, like all previous societies throughout history, was characterized not only by a high birth rate but also by a high death rate. The average life expectancy was less than fifty years, meaning that more than half of all people born in the nation died before they reached their fiftieth birthday. People died young, leaving many children behind. Indeed a high birth rate was essential to maintaining the population.

Modern sanitation methods and medical science have now changed this pattern. Today's average life expectancy has jumped to 71½ years for white men and 79 years for white women, about six years less for blacks (National Center for Health Statistics, 1985). People live a long, long time but leave fewer children behind. Indeed today's lower birth rate is almost an essential in our society. Had the birth rate not gone down along with the death rate, we would face monstrous problems of overpopulation, overcrowding, and inadequate food supplies, as is actually happening in parts of the world where modern life-prolonging techniques have not been accompanied by smaller families.

This shift from a society where people were lucky to live more than five decades to a society where they can realistically expect to live seven or more has resulted in a new kind of world. It has changed the entire composition of our society. Where people of 65 and over were once rare, they now total nearly 26 million (Bureau of the Census, 1984b), and the number is growing all the time. People have to take a new approach to jobs, planning for the future, and retirement. The shift has greatly affected human motivation and many of our institutions—the economy, government, even education. Talcott Parsons (1955) called it "one of the profoundest adjustments human societies have ever had to make." Since he wrote those words the expectancy figures have jumped even higher.

Longer Marriages, Too

Certainly the effect on the institution of marriage and the family has been tremendous. Today's marriages, unless ended by divorce, last much longer than in the past. Moreover, a couple who stay married for a lifetime have many more years in which they are on their own, without children in the home.

Mary Jo Bane (1976) attempting to chart the course of a typical lifetime marriage today as compared with a century ago, arrived at these estimates: In the family of old, as shown in Figure 1-1, the marriage lasted only thirty-four years until the death of the

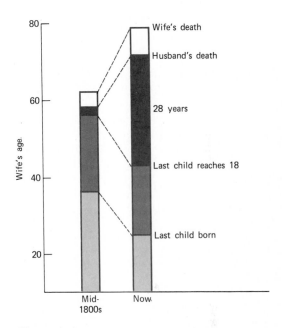

Figure 1-1
A WIFE'S LIFE SPAN, 100 YEARS AGO AND NOW
One spectacular way marriage has changed within the last century is apparent in this depiction of the more-or-less typical life span of women then and now if married to the same husband for a lifetime. The solid parts of the bars are the most significant, because they show the length of time wife and husband have together after the last child becomes 18 years old (Bane, 1976; National Center for Health Statistics, 1984).

husband. Because the wife bore children over a long period of time, there was at least one child under 18 in the family for about thirty-two of those thirty-four years. By contrast, today's marriage lasts nearly fifty years, and the husband and wife are in each other's company, without the responsibility of schoolchildren, for about twenty-eight of those years (National Center for Health Statistics, 1984).

The potential length of marriage today, with no children present during so many of the years, creates an entirely new situation, with new problems and new opportunities.

As one study has found:

> Marriage becomes more of a personal relationship between husband and wife, and less of a union of a mother and father preoccupied with the needs of their offspring. The prospect of fifty years with the same person increases tensions in marriage and makes it more likely that dissatisfaction will lead to divorce. Furthermore, in a rapidly changing society, the couple who seemed to be well-suited to each other in their early twenties may find themselves growing in different ways and at different rates later on.
>
> *(Skolnick and Skolnick, 1974)*

On the other hand, the added time has also created new satisfactions. During the child-rearing years, as one marriage counselor has pointed out, the marriage must to some extent "take a back seat to the children" (Figley, 1978). Once the children are on their own, the couple can again enjoy each other's company without distractions. Even after the age of sixty—despite the physical inroads of growing old—husbands and wives often find that "their sense of satisfaction with the marriage has absolutely soared" (Feldman, 1975).

The developments just described—the increase in life expectancy and length of marriages, the lower birth rate, and the decline of the family's dollars-and-cents value—have combined to create another striking change in our society. This is the almost unbelievable boom in the number of women who are not only wives but also paid employees in jobs outside the home.

The "working wife" (so-called to distinguish her from the housewife, though any housewife will tell you that she too has a full-time job) was once a rarity, usually holding some kind of menial job such as cleaning woman because her husband was sick or unemployed. Even as recently as 1940, only about one wife in seven worked outside the home. Since then the figure has soared to a clear majority, as shown in Figure 1–2. No other statistic shows the same steep rise, ex-

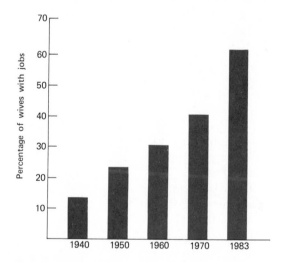

Figure 1–2
WIVES WITH JOBS: THEIR RAPID RISE IN RECENT DECADES
In every decade, the percentage of wives who work outside the home has steadily climbed, to the point where they are now the majority (Bureau of the Census, 1984a).

cept possibly the use of recent inventions such as television sets.

When wives first began this move into jobs outside the home, most were women who had no children or whose children had finished high school. Now, however, the move has been joined by 19.5 million women with children under eighteen years of age, including 8 million with preschool youngsters under six (Bureau of Labor Statistics, 1984). This of course creates a new problem for millions of families: how to provide care for these children while mother and father are away at work.

Presumably the figures for wives who work outside the home—often while their children are in the care of someone else—are still rising because today's young women are even more career-minded than older women. A public opinion poll at the start of the decade showed that more than two-thirds of all women under thirty hope to combine marriage and job. Only 27 percent would prefer to be housewives (Roper, 1980). Among college women these percentages are even more one-sided.

Many wives take jobs for strictly financial reasons. In families where the husband has limited earning power, the wife often has to take a job just to make ends meet. Eve.. when the husband has a reasonably good income, there may not be enough money for the family to live as well as it would like in our modern "affluent society," where most people have high expectations. Obviously, a family with only one breadwinner has to settle for a lower standard of living than is enjoyed by neighboring families with two breadwinners. One study has pointed out that "it is hard enough to keep up with the Joneses under normal circumstances, but when both of the Joneses are working it becomes virtually impossible" (Ross and Sawhill, 1975).

Thus a majority of working wives hold

Ken Karp

One of the 62 percent majority of American wives with jobs outside the home as she gets some help from her husband in leaving for work.

their jobs because they need or want the money. A public opinion poll has also found, however, that there are a fair number—14 percent—who say they work chiefly to have something interesting to do (Roper, 1980). This number is probably growing, since young women are especially partial to the idea of combining marriage and career. It must also be noted that women today are far better equipped to hold jobs than they were in the past, for the percentage with high school or college diplomas has risen rapidly (Bureau of the Census, 1982). Indeed more women than men now enter our institutions of higher learning. Women now have the skills required by the business establishment, especially in our new "service economy" in which "the hospital, the classroom, and the shopping center have replaced the coal mine, the steel mill, and the assembly line as the major work sites of modern society'' (Fuchs, 1983), though, as you will see in Chapter 3, women are still far from attaining equal treatment at work.

Divorce: From a Rarity to the Commonplace

Along with all these changes—and partly as a result of them—has come perhaps the most startling development of all. At one time there were entire towns and even small cities where not one person had ever been divorced, and where just the thought of such a thing would have created a scandal. But the number of divorces has risen rapidly throughout this century, as shown in Figure 1–3, and divorce is so commonplace today that you can undoubtedly name a whole list of friends and relatives who have gone through it. More than a million divorces a year are now granted in the United States, meaning that over two million people find their marriage was a mistake and call it quits.

Although many Americans still disapprove of divorce, mostly on religious or moral grounds or because they consider it unfair to children, a majority now regard it as a perfectly proper step to take, not to be condemned and indeed probably inevitable in many cases. A public opinion poll on this matter showed that 60 percent of American adults consider divorce acceptable when a marriage proves unsuccessful, while only about 23 percent are flatly opposed (Roper, 1980).

Thus for a majority of Americans marriage ''has lost its taken-for-granted, lifelong quality'' (Skolnick and Skolnick, 1974). The majority no longer enter marriage with a firm commitment to spend an entire lifetime together through thick and through thin, regardless of how bad the relationship turns out to be. Divorce is always available as a convenient escape hatch, if worse comes to worse. One authority on population trends

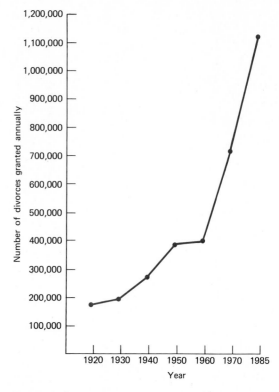

Figure 1–3
DIVORCE IN THE U.S.: UP, UP, AND WAY UP
The graph line shows how the number of divorces granted each year has climbed steadily throughout the 1900s—and with remarkable speed in the last two decades (National Center for Health Statistics, 1985).

has estimated that nearly half of all marriages of today's young adults will end in divorce (Norton, 1983).

THE NEW COMPANIONSHIP MARRIAGE AND WHAT IT MEANS

Most of the revolutionary social changes with which marriage and the family must now cope have been going on for many years, but the revolution was slow to arrive. Only in recent decades, as the pace of change quickened, did the revolution at last occur. Even today it is by no means complete. Many people, indeed, remain unaware of it.

Well into this century most marriages and families fell into a familiar and traditional pattern that had evolved over the centuries in the United States and in many other societies as well. The husband was in charge of the family's economic and financial affairs. The wife was in charge of the household and the care of the children. The family had a "rigid and inflexible role system" and a "clear-cut division of labor" (Gecas, 1979). Moreover, the husband was the undisputed boss. He made the decisions about where and how he would earn a living, where the family would live, and how it would spend its money. The wife was expected to follow along. She could make suggestions, plead, and even argue, but the husband always had the final word, by custom and even by law.

The family in its traditional form had the full support of society as a whole. Young people were encouraged to marry, to stay married despite any difficulties they might encounter, and to have children early and often. The family had the blessing of not only the church but the government, in the form of laws that made marriage easy and divorce as difficult as possible.

No doubt many couples managed to turn their traditional marriage into a happy and rewarding relationship, offering a great deal of affection, love, mutual respect, and self-fulfillment. But the rules did not demand or perhaps even encourage such a relationship. Whether a husband and wife liked each other and really wanted to stay together did not much matter. They were bound to each other by financial necessity, by the law, and by "public opinion, tradition, the authority of the family head, rigid discipline, and elaborate ritual" (Burgess and Locke, 1945). In many cases they did not know each other

very well or make much attempt to cultivate a friendship: "Their relationships were highly formal and often very superficial. They were held together by pressure from the outside, by the sense of duty imposed upon the partners, and by the fear of retribution if they broke up" (Mace and Mace, 1974). Regardless of how they really felt, their dealings with each other were "dominated by custom, ritual, and predetermined roles," and the family was "rigidly structured, legally fenced in, and often tyrannical" (Mace, 1975). Many couples never even thought of asking whether they were happy or unhappy. Why bother, since nothing could be done about it anyway?

"From Institution to Companionship"

Traditions die hard. Social readjustments take place slowly, like glaciers inching their way across the face of the earth. Though the society in which men and women live is drastically changed, the traditional pattern of marriage and family has by no means disappeared. Millions of Americans continue to view marriage just as our great-grandparents did, with the same sense of authority, discipline, and duty.

Yet at some time in our nation's recent past, a new and radically different kind of marriage began to emerge. At first to only a few people, then to thousands, now to millions and indeed most of us, marriage has been transformed as strikingly as a caterpillar turning into a butterfly (or, as the pessimists might prefer, a rose shriveling into a gnarled ball of soot with the coming of frost).

In a famous phrase coined by Burgess and Locke, marriage and the family have made a giant leap "from institution to companionship." That is to say, what holds a family together today is found "less and less in community pressures and more and more in such interpersonal relations as the mutual affection, the sympathetic understanding, and the comradeship of its members'' (Burgess and Locke, 1945).

The Burgess and Locke phrase, though it was dramatic and immediately captured the attention of social scientists everywhere, is not quite correct. Marriage and the family remain an institution, as they always have been and probably always will be even if they change form again and again in the future. It is more accurate to speak of a giant leap from traditional marriage to companionship marriage. The traditional marriage was ''essentially a power structure based on a system of authority and submission.'' The new companionship marriage represents an attempt ''to foster creative relationships in an atmosphere of love and intimacy'' (Mace, 1975).

To today's college students, the idea of marriage based on comradeship and intimacy may not seem very startling, but the idea would certainly have amazed your great-grandparents, who would have dismissed it as not only a violation of time-honored rules but a downright impossibility. The phrase ''from institution to companionship'' was not invented until 1945. Its full implications are still not understood by most Americans, who are in the puzzling position of taking part in a revolution without realizing what it is about or even that it is taking place.

The Rapid Rise of Companionship Marriage

The leap from traditional to companionship marriage has been very much like a rebellion that topples a dictatorship and replaces it with a democracy. In this case the rebellion has been a long drawn-out struggle fraught with hardships and producing many casualties. If marriage and the family strike some

observers as being in grave trouble and in danger of disappearing, one reason is that the revolution has been so difficult and is still incomplete. Marriage remains ''in a period of transition and readaptation,'' not yet sure how to foster comradeship, creative relationships, and human growth or how to function in general to meet the new needs of our greatly changed modern society (Crosby, 1975).

For one thing, the idea of companionship marriage is still by no means totally accepted. Most older people prefer to think of marriage and the family in traditional form. Only among younger people is there a clear majority who favor companionship marriage, and even among the very youngest adults millions still favor marriage as it existed in the past. This can be seen in Figure

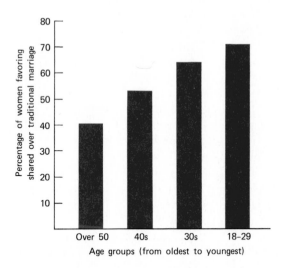

Figure 1–4
HOW COMPANIONSHIP MARRIAGE HAS FLOURISHED
The sharp recent rise in the popularity of companionship marriage is shown by the increasing height of the bars. Note that only a minority of women over 50 (far left) favor companionship over traditional marriage—but a large majority of women under 30 (far right) prefer the companionship type (adapted from Roper, 1980).

1-4, based on a 1980 public opinion poll that deserves special attention. In this poll, men and women of all ages were asked which of the following two kinds of marriage they would prefer as offering the most satisfying and interesting lifestyle:

1. A traditional marriage, with the husband assuming the responsibility for providing for the family, and the wife taking care of the house and children.

or

2. A marriage where husband and wife share responsibilities more: both work and both share homemaking and child-care responsibilities.

The two choices are hardly a full definition of traditional as opposed to companionship marriage—something that would be impossible in the brief questions of a public opinion poll—but they do point to what is perhaps the major difference. Thus the responses constitute at least a rough measure of how today's Americans feel about the two kinds of marriage that exist in the current period of transition. Of the people who made the choice, 45 percent of women and 46 percent of men favored traditional marriage, while 55 percent of women and 54 percent of men favored companionship marriage. The vote was close only because the pollsters interviewed women and men of all ages. As Figure 1-4 shows, a majority of women over 50 continue to favor traditional marriage. This number goes down steadily, however, in the lower-age brackets—to the point where women under 30 choose companionship marriage by an overwhelming margin of 71 percent to 29 percent. (The figures for men follow a similar pattern.)

What Companionship Marriage Means

It would be interesting to know what would have happened if the people who voted in this poll for "a marriage where husband and

Teri Leigh Stratford

A companionship wife and mother at her college graduation.

wife share responsibilities more'' had been asked to spell out exactly how they interpreted ''shared responsibilities.'' In all probability their answers would have varied widely. There is as yet no standard definition of this new-fangled idea of companionship marriage, which can mean different things to different people in our changing society. For every hundred people questioned, there might have been a hundred different answers. There are, however, a few general principles that seem to be characteristic of the idea of companionship marriage as most people view it. Among them are:

1. *Comradeship.* Companionship marriages tend to be based on love and friendship rather than on mere sexual

desire or economic convenience (Gordon, 1975). Husband and wife are much closer than in the more formal, arm's-length kind of traditional marriage. They seek ''trust, affection, affiliation, and. . . . psychological intimacy'' (O'Neill and O'Neill, 1973). They are concerned about communicating their thoughts and feelings. Table 1–1 indicates how strongly the idea of comradeship flourishes among people today.

2. *Partnership.* In the traditional marriage, the husband was not only breadwinner but also boss. The family was based on the notion that ''father knows best,'' as, considering the limited education of most women in the past, he often did.

Table 1–1

Marriage and Comradeship

HOW IMPORTANT ARE THESE ITEMS TO A HAPPY MARRIAGE?	PERCENTAGE CALLING THESE ITEMS VERY IMPORTANT	
	Women	Men
1. Being in love	89	87
2. Being able to talk together about your feelings	84	79
3. Partner's sexual fidelity	79	72
4. Both being able to see the humorous side of things	74	70
5. Having similar ideas on how to rear children	71	63
6. Keeping romance alive	71	73
7. Good sexual relationship	68	73
8. Having similar ideas on how to handle money	68	63
9. Liking the same kind of life, activities, and friends	64	62
10. Your spouse having an understanding of what you do every day (your work around the house or your job, outside interests, abilities, etc.)	63	59
11. Financial security	57	58
12. Having children	46	43
13. Having similar backgrounds	27	25

In a public opinion poll, people were asked to look at these thirteen items and say how important they considered each of them to a good marriage. The results show that nearly 90 percent of both women and men called ''being in love'' very important, but only a minority thought having children or coming from a similar background was very important. Note how many of the items considered very important by both sexes were related to comradeship, notably items 1, 4, 5, 8, 9, and 10 (*Roper, 1980*).

In companionship marriages there is a more equal kind of give-and-take. Husband and wife tend to consider themselves partners, not boss and hired hand.

3. *Individual identity.* People in companionship marriages no longer think of themselves as merely playing the assigned roles of husband-father and wife-mother. Women in particular, as is shown by the boom in working wives, have begun in increasing numbers to think of themselves as having careers and therefore identities outside the home as well as in it. Both wives and husbands think of themselves as individuals to a greater extent than in the past. They have "personal as well as family goals" (Seidenberg, 1973).

4. *Mutual self-fulfillment.* As noted earlier, it seems likely that many couples joined in the traditional marriages of the past never bothered to question whether they were happy or unhappy. In the companionship marriage "the happiness of the partners is a primary goal" (Keller, 1971). Happiness is often regarded in terms of self-fulfillment, with both partners helping each other toward this goal of growth and psychological wholeness. Marriage is viewed as "an exciting union which has as its main purpose the involvement of both partners in the adventure of actualizing each other's potential" (Otto, 1970).

WHAT KIND OF MARRIAGE DO *YOU* WANT?

Not everyone who favors companionship marriage would agree that all the four points just mentioned should be part of the definition, and some people would want to add other points. Indeed one reason for today's mixed feelings about marriage is that it is almost impossible to define male-female relationships in terms that suit everybody.

The two conflicting ideas of marriage—traditional versus companionship—vie for attention. All of us are pulled in one direction by the views of the past, in the opposite direction by new developments and attitudes. Even among people who say they continue to prefer traditional marriage, some of the notions of companionship marriage have taken hold. Even the most modern proponents of companionship marriage still have some lingering ties to tradition. Thus almost all male-female relationships are influenced to at least some extent by the four principles of companionship marriage, but also by the more rigid attitudes that prevailed in the past.

You yourself may be a firm believer in companionship marriage yet reject some or all of the four principles. On the other hand, you may agree in general with all four of the points mentioned yet also believe in many of the traditional ideas of marriage. (If a woman, for example, you do not want to work outside the home or to have your husband share the duties inside the home. If a man, you do not want your wife to work and do not expect to share household responsibilities.) You may like the general idea of companionship marriage but prefer to combine it with a large number of children. Or you may prefer the idea of traditional marriage yet not want any children at all.

The possible points of view about marriages and families are almost endless. Even people who share more or less the same viewpoint may do so for different reasons and with different shadings of meaning and emotion. Thus marriage in today's world is an individual matter. You cannot seek out some guru on a mountaintop and say, "Tell me, oh Master, what is the ideal marriage and how do I go about attaining it?'' You have to look into yourself and ask, ''What kind of marriage do *I* want?''

The Fallacy of ''The Ten Easy Rules''

Many people like to set themselves up as marriage gurus. We are swamped with advice from friends and relatives who believe they have all the answers. At this very minute, somewhere in our nation, some woman is telling a young friend, ''Don't marry him until he absolutely guarantees that you will have the final say on where to live.'' An older brother is telling a young husband, ''I wouldn't put up with that. If she does it again, walk out on her.'' These opinions are being handed down as gospel truth, though perhaps the woman giving advice has never managed to establish a satisfactory relationship of her own and the brother is having serious trouble with his wife. (It is a strange quirk of human nature that often the people who are the least successful in their own relationships are the quickest to counsel others, just as parents whose own children have given them the most trouble are the freest with dogma on child rearing.)

Newspapers and books are full of advice on how to get and stay married (or with warnings to avoid marriage like the plague). New books come out all the time with ten easy rules on how to win a mate, have a happy marriage twenty-four hours a day, solve arguments, attain sexual ecstasy, and live as luxuriously as a king and queen on an income that would doom other people to poverty.

Marriage, sex, and children are topics on which everyone is a self-appointed expert. As Arlene Skolnick has pointed out, ''In no other field of study is there such a great temptation to use one's own experience as a basis for wide-ranging generalizations'' (Skolnick, 1973). But the experience from which most advice givers generalize is woefully limited—to the particular kind of family in which they themselves grew up (maybe happily but maybe not), the particular way in which they themselves have tried to establish human relationships (with or without success), their own particular marriage (happy or not) with their own particular mate. They may or may not have learned very much from their experiences. Either way, the conclusions they have reached may be totally inapplicable to anybody else.

All Kinds of People: Cultural Pluralism

This is a big nation. We have about 167 million adults, people 18 years of age or older (Bureau of the Census, 1984b). To a greater extent than any other nation, moreover, the United States is what sociologists call *pluralistic,* that is, composed of many different groups with their own cultural backgrounds and traditions. In religion we Americans are Buddhists, Jews, Mohammedans, Shintoists, and Christians of numerous denominations, not to mention agnostics and atheists. Racially we are brown, black, white, and yellow. Our origins go back to such diverse homelands as England, France, Germany, Italy, Mexico, Poland, Puerto Rico, and China.

As is shown in the next chapter, all of us are influenced in important ways by the kinds of home and culture into which we are born. Some of us go through life without ever questioning the attitudes instilled in us in childhood. Even those who rebel never manage to shake the past off completely. In more ways than we ever realize, we are the product of our background. The family and culture into which we were born play a great part in determining our feelings about how men should behave, how women should behave, what we seek in marriage, how husbands and wives should treat each other, and how children should be brought up.

Our pluralistic society thus produces a vast diversity in attitudes toward marriages and families. What you think about relationships between the sexes is bound to depend to a large extent on your religious, racial, and national background. It is also influenced by the social class into which you were born, even though you may have moved or be in the process of moving to a different level of society, as determined by such factors as education and income. Social classes range from the lower-lower (illiterate or semiliterate people living in poverty) through the large and famous middle class (high school or college education, good incomes, and comfortable homes) and on to the upper-upper (the socially prominent people, like the Rockefellers, whose families have been wealthy for generations). The prevailing attitudes toward marriage and family vary greatly from one of these classes to another.

All Kinds of People: Individual Differences

Besides having pluralistic backgrounds, we differ in many other ways. The fact is that no two people are exactly alike. Evidence of a wide range of individual differences has been piling up ever since Sir Francis Galton, around a hundred years ago, began measuring people's size, strength, hearing ability, sense of smell, color vision, and ability to judge weights. We now know that wide variations are found in all kinds of human traits—intelligence, emotional reactions, motives toward achievement or dependence, sexual capacity and desire, even tendencies to be loners or to seek the company of other people.

These differences result partly from heredity. You carry around in the cells of your body and brain your own individual combination of genes—molecules of powerful chemicals, inherited in random combination from all your ancestors, that direct your growth from a single fertilized egg cell into a living baby with all kinds of specialized organs and muscles and glands, then later into a full-grown adult with your own individual kind of body build, complexion, eye color, brain power, and many built-in tendencies to behave in your own particular fashion.

The differences also result from learning—all the effects of your environment from birth onward, especially your experiences with other people. No two people have the same experiences. Thus even identical twins, who have exactly the same combination of genes, often have very different attitudes toward life and behave in very different ways. They look alike and we may not be able to tell them apart in photographs, but we can distinguish them quickly when we see them in action because twin A does not *act* like twin B.

All Kinds of Marriages

Because people exhibit such a wide range of individual differences and because attitudes toward relations between the sexes have been influenced by such pluralistic backgrounds there are all kinds of marriages and families. Indeed the use of either word in the singular is suspect. When a person says, "I'll tell you what I think about marriage," you have to be skeptical of whatever follows. If you do not mind being impolite and want to steer the conversation along more useful lines, you might ask, "Whose marriage?" The same goes for book or magazine titles like *The Death of the Family*. The question to ask is, Whose family is dead?

We have in the United States "a pluralism in family forms existing side by side,'' and the people in these various kinds of families have ''different problems to solve and issues to face'' (Sussman, 1971). Your own problems and issues, in everything from finding a mate to contemplating children, may be very different from those of the person sitting next to you in class, your neighbors, your friends, or even your brothers and sisters. Nobody else can tell you what best to do. The only thing that really counts is how you—a unique individual, with your own pattern of genes and your own background and experiences—think and feel about marriage.

What kind of marriage do you want? Are you sure you want to get married at all? How do you want to share the responsibilities and privileges of marriage with your mate? Or do you want to share them at all? What is your idea of fairness in marriage? Do you want children? How many? Do you want to think of divorce as an escape hatch if marriage goes bad? Or do you shun the very thought of divorce? Thinking of the period before your marriage (if indeed marriage is to occur), what kind of partner do you want to look for? What is your idea of the proper relationship, sexual and otherwise, between friends of opposite sexes?

These are the questions you have to ask. Only you can answer them.

THE SCIENTIFIC APPROACH TO MARRIAGE AND THE FAMILY

It would be misleading and unfair to suggest that the answers are easy to find. The giant leap from marriage as institution to marriage as companionship has been difficult for people of all ages and from all backgrounds, and it continues to be difficult. Companion-

ship marriage is more revolutionary than most people have ever imagined: ''It is a whole new way of life'' (Mace and Mace, 1974).

In our search for the answers, we are to a large extent on our own. Our society has not had much experience with companionship marriage and can offer us only limited help. In a sense we are like the Pilgrim Fathers who arrived on this continent knowing that life here would be very different, but not in what way it would be different or how they could best cope with it.

Of course the more you know about marriages and families—the ways they have been changing, the problems they face, and the opportunities they present—the better equipped you are to deal with the questions. And the more likely you are to come up with answers that will satisfy your individual needs, your partner's needs, and the obligations that you both feel to meet society's standards of responsible and ethical conduct.

This book and the course in which it is used are based on the assumption that the social scientists and other careful observers have discovered a great many important facts about marriage and the family, and that these facts can be of immense practical value in human relationships. The information you will find in the book and the course is a far cry from the off-the-cuff, overgeneralized, and often prejudiced opinions you are likely to get from friends, relatives, and magazine writers untrained in the social sciences. Instead, you will find a compilation of knowledge acquired by sound scientific methods, plus the observations and conclusions of people trained to look at society from an unbiased, objective viewpoint.

The book does not presume to tell you how to run your life. It merely presents what is known about marriages and families—or believed to be true by those who have devoted careful study to the subject—and leaves you to decide how to use the information, or even whether to use it at all.

Scientific Method

Much of the information in the book comes from sociologists, who have long been interested in marriage and the family as one of the basic institutions of human society. These scholars have made many studies of all aspects of the subject; for example, why people marry, how they feel about children, their sources of satisfaction and conflict, their sexual relationships, their financial problems and attempts to solve them, and their changing relationships as they get older.

Sociologists have also studied the reasons people get divorced and what happens to them afterward, as well as the trials and triumphs of people who choose to remain single or embrace some other alternative to marriage. They have viewed marriage and the family in the context of our society as a whole, for it is impossible to understand the changing circumstances of the family without regard to changes in other social institutions such as the economy, government, and education.

The information also comes from others who study marriage, the home, human relationships in general, or the cultural and psychological influences on human relationships. Anthropologists, who take a broad view of the many kinds of cultures humanity has created around the world throughout history, have enriched our knowledge of marriage and the family. So have psychologists interested in the way people behave as individuals and in their social relationships.

The book and the course draw heavily on the observations of marriage and family counselors, who have worked intimately with thousands of couples seeking to solve their marital difficulties. Counselors combine the scientific viewpoint with the practical experience of watching individual marriages improve or break up. Some counselors are psychiatrists or psychoanalysts, who add still another dimension to the search for truth.

The various specialists, well aware of the plurality and diversity of our society, have studied many kinds of people in many kinds of families: upper class, middle class, and lower class; those who married young and those who married later; childless couples and those with many children. They have examined the state of the family not only in the United States but in other nations, and not just in our own time but in the past. They have conducted public opinion polls and other surveys to determine how great numbers of people feel and behave. They have analyzed census reports about rates of marriage and divorce, size of families, and life expectancy. They have made many other kinds of studies, the results of which make up the content of this book and the course.

Facts and Informed Opinions

Most of the book is made up of information obtained through careful research. For example it has been well established, as reported near the start of this chapter, that a majority of Americans now believe that divorce is the best solution when a marriage has failed, whereas only a small percentage are flatly opposed to divorce. This information comes from a public opinion poll that surveyed a sample of Americans large enough and chosen in such a way as to be representative of the entire population.

The exact figures found in the poll—60 percent accepting divorce, 23 percent flatly opposing it—are subject to possible slight statistical error but can be taken at face value give or take a few percentage points. The figures tell you far more than you could learn from a casual attempt to tally the opinions of the people you happen to know. Depending on where you live and what kinds of acquaintances you have, you might conclude that almost everybody favors divorce, or that almost everybody opposes it.

A poll based on scientific sampling, it should be added, is far different from the so-called surveys often reported in popular magazines and books, which usually make no effort to find a group of people representative of the population as a whole. The next time you read that a magazine has discovered that 52.3 percent of all Americans believe so-and-so about marriage, or behave in such-and-such a manner, be on guard. Polls on sexual behavior are especially unreliable. One ''sex survey'' that became a best-selling book a few years ago claimed to be highly accurate because it had polled fully 3,000 American women. The 3,000 answers tabulated in the poll, however, were the only replies the author received to a barrage of questionnaires sent out to 100,000 women, who were hardly representative of Americans anyway, since most of them were readers of two publications of such limited appeal that they are read by only a fraction of 1 percent of the population. As a guide to how women in general regard sex, the survey was completely useless.

Even social scientists cannot always use the sampling methods of public opinion polls, which are very expensive. Instead they have to do the best they can with their available resources. Many of them are teachers in colleges and universities, and for reasons of convenience they often enlist students as the subjects of their investigations. Thus the college population has been more widely studied than any other group. (Since you are

yourself part of the college population, however, this is not entirely bad from your point of view.)

Unfortunately, many aspects of marriages and families do not lend themselves to specific research projects. Therefore the book also frequently reports the conclusions that the observers have drawn from such evidence as they have managed to gather. These conclusions cannot be scientifically proved. They are in a sense mere opinions; but they are informed opinions, reached only after intensive study and a great deal of careful thought. For example, the social scientists and family professionals who have counseled hundreds of couples, many of whom had problems in communicating with each other, are in a better position than most people to discuss the factors that can hamper or improve communication. Their conclusions may be mere opinions—and may in fact eventually prove to be wrong—but they are more likely to be useful than anything untrained friends can tell you from their own narrow experiences. Where the informed opinions reached by qualified observers are in conflict—as they often are in this complex field—the book presents both sides.

Interpreting the Knowledge

On the matter of studying and perhaps applying the facts and informed opinions presented here, a word of caution: There is a strong human tendency toward what social psychologists call conformity—to run with the herd, to think what everybody else seems to be thinking, to do what everybody else seems to be doing. We all have this tendency to at least some degree. Instead of looking into ourselves for guidance, we are tempted to look to others. Thus we are always in danger of being too impressed by studies and opinions of what seems to be the majority lifestyle. A public opinion poll reporting that most Americans now accept divorce—or that most young Americans now favor companionship marriage—may add impetus to such trends as well as report on them.

The information contained in the book will be most useful if kept in perspective. You must keep reminding yourself that this is a big and pluralistic nation, that individual differences prevail in all matters, and that lifestyles favored by the majority are not necessarily good for the dissenting minority. In most matters, it should be noted, even the people who are in the minority have a great deal of company. On divorce, for example, those figures of 60 percent accepting and 23 percent opposing seem overwhelming at first glance. But the 23 percent minority represents a great many people—more than 38 million adult Americans. Even an attitude held by only 1 percent of the adult population is a strong influence in the lives of nearly 1.7 million people.

What other people think, feel, or do is not really the crucial factor anyway. Even if you and your partner should happen to be a minority of two in the kind of relationship you want (a highly unlikely possibility), you must still go on the assumption that you are right as far as you are concerned.

A Word about Being "Modern"

There is also a strong human tendency to react to ideas simply on the basis of how new they are. Older people tend to be conservative, rejecting any idea they did not grow up with. They often view any change in public opinion or behavior as a sure sign that the world is going to the dogs. Younger people, on the other hand, have a way of embracing new ideas without questioning them or asking for proof. They often reject ideas just because they are old—even though, like the old-fashioned broom, they may still have their uses.

Both old and new generations lose a great deal because of this automatic reaction, pro or con, to "modern" ideas. Our world is constantly progressing (or so we have to hope). Useful new knowledge is being discovered all the time. Promising new ideas, worthy of everyone's attention, keep cropping up. On the other hand, the old saying that there is nothing really new under the sun contains a good deal of wisdom. There are more similarities between past and present—and the past has more guidance to offer—than new generations often like to think.

When living in communes became a fad in the 1960s, for example, it was popularly considered a brand-new development in human relationships. In truth, communes go back in the United States to the early days of the republic and were found elsewhere as long as 2,000 years ago (Fairfield, 1971). High divorce rates—probably a good deal higher than ours—existed in ancient Greece and Rome (Westermarck, 1925). For an interesting perspective on some other "modern" ideas such as living together before marriage and women's liberation, see the box on *Opinions and Experiences,* which you should read before going on to the next paragraph.

The woman whose words are reported in the interview was certainly not typical of the generation that went to college in the 1920s and 1930s, but neither was she entirely alone. There were quite a few others like her a half century ago, and indeed years earlier. Many of the questions, problems, and opportunities that are part of today's relationships between the sexes have been a matter

Opinions and Experiences

"GRANDDAUGHTER, LITTLE DO YOU KNOW!"

A woman who was in her 70s at the time gave this account of why there is a lot of truth in an old French saying.

I have a granddaughter in college. She's a grand-niece, really, but she calls me Grandma because her own grandparents are dead. And of course she considers me a terrible square, like everybody older than she is. She's thinking about getting married, and I offered to lend her a book that was a great help in my own marriage.* She took one look at the title page, which shows it was published in 1938, and cast it aside. "For heaven's sakes, Grandma," she said, "what could people possibly have known about marriage way back then?"

Everything seems new to my granddaughter. She's living with her young man, something she doesn't believe ever happened until the year before last. She's into women's lib. She plans to be a career woman, and she doesn't want children. All the things she thinks nobody ever dreamed of when I was a young woman. But it just goes to show that the French were right. *Plus ça change, plus c'est la même chose.* In English, "The more things change, the more they stay the same."

I lived with my young man too, while I was in college. Afterward, too, for four years in all before we got married. Not in the same apartment—because neither of us had enough money in those Depression days to live anywhere but with our parents. We "lived together"—that is, made love—in motels. There were a number of them on the outskirts of St. Louis that catered to the unmarried trade. If you had luggage, or any other indication that you planned to stay more than an hour or two, they wouldn't let you in.

I was also a women's libber—though the phrase hadn't been invented. I had my own career as a dress designer until I retired, and I usually made more money than my husband. We always shared whatever housework wasn't done by people we could hire. We moved from St. Louis to New York because I had better job opportunities there. My husband was willing to make the move even though he had to start over in a new kind of career. Or maybe *willing* is too strong a word. I admit I used a little pressure. I said, "I'm going—and I hope you come along." Over the years I made at least ten business trips to Europe alone, not to mention thirty or forty to different cities in the United States.

Like my granddaughter, I didn't want children. In fact, I never liked to be around children. My husband felt the same way, and so we stayed childless. Birth control isn't exactly brand-new either, you know, and it worked just as well in 1930 as it does now, if you were careful enough. Of course, we had to make an excuse to our parents, who, like most parents in those days, couldn't wait to have grandchildren. We told them I had a tumor of the womb and couldn't get pregnant. A downright lie, of course, but it made things easier.

I did everything my granddaughter does and wants to do in the future. I let her go on thinking how hopelessly old-fashioned I am because this seems to make her feel good, but little does she know.

*The book, which is still eminently worthwhile, was J. Levy and R. Munroe. *The Happy Family,* New York: Knopf, 1938.

of concern for a long time—at least to some Americans, and certainly to sociologists who could see the trends develop. As one scholar has written, "Most problems of our time have, in fact, also been problems in the past" (Anderson, 1980).

Thus numerous findings and informed opinions of the past are still pertinent.

Though most of the information in these pages is taken from studies made in the past few years, the book does not hesitate to report useful knowledge regardless of when it first appeared. For example this chapter has paid considerable attention to the giant leap from "institution to companionship" first noted by Burgess and Locke in 1945—which is still one of the keys to understanding and dealing with the problems and opportunities of marriages and families today.

SUMMARY

1. Most Americans today view marriage with mingled pessimism and optimism. Polls show that 70 percent believe it is a weaker force in our society than it used to be, and 35 percent agree that "you see so few good or happy marriages that you have to question it as a way of life." But 5 million people marry every year, and one poll found that nine of ten married people are either "very satisfied" or "mostly satisfied."

2. Criticisms of marriage and the family have been common since the time of the ancient Greeks, but "there is no record of any society . . . that does not have marriage as one of the key elements of its social structure."

3. A reason for today's confusion is the many rapid changes that have taken place in recent years, affecting the family and all other social *institutions,* that is, the parts of the social system that help meet the basic needs of society. The economic institution has been revolutionized by new technologies like electronics, the political institution by such new responsibilities as welfare and Social Security, and the educational institution by an influx of far greater numbers of high school and college students.

4. In marriage, one of the most dramatic changes has been the decline of the "typical" American family composed of a bread-winning father, a stay-at-home mother, and often two or three or more children living at home, from 70

percent of households in the 1950s to 15 percent today.

5. The family has suffered what William Ogburn calls "a loss of function" as many of the duties of the isolated farm household—providing much of its own food, clothing, religious services, recreation, and security, and often tutoring its children—have been shifted to other institutions.

6. Among the major changes that have affected the family is its decline as an economic unit. The American man of a few generations ago fared much better if he had a helpful wife and children to do some of the farm chores, churn the butter, and sew the quilts. Now most families have moved from farms to industrialized areas, and what the family needs it buys at a store. Children have become more of a financial liability than asset.

7. Other important recent changes are these:

> *Birth control* has greatly reduced the number of children in most families. A majority now consider two children the ideal number, and many families are childless.
>
> *Life expectancy* has jumped from an average of less than 50 years at the start of the century to 71½ years for white men and 79 years for white women, about six years less for blacks. There are now 25 million Americans aged 65 or older, and people must take a new approach to jobs, planning for their future, and retirement.
>
> *Longer marriages* have resulted from the higher life expectancy. A century ago the average marriage lasted only thirty-four years until the death of the husband. That figure has now jumped to nearly fifty years, in about half of which the wife and husband are together without responsibility for children. The long time span creates the danger of greater tensions, boredom, and a growing apart of the partners' interests. Many older

couples today, however, find that "satisfaction has absolutely soared" because the marriage no longer has to "take a back seat to the children."

A boom in working wives has resulted from economic developments, longer life expectancy, and the lower birth rate. In 1940 only one wife in seven worked outside the home. Now 53 percent do. Of working wives, 19.5 million have children under 18 years of age, including 8 million with youngsters under 6.

A sharp rise in divorces in recent years has raised the number granted each year to over a million. The best current estimate is that nearly half of today's marriages between young adults will end in divorce.

8. Until fairly recently, the *traditional marriage* prevailed. The husband earned the income and was in charge of all financial affairs. The wife was in charge of the household and the care of the children. The husband was the undisputed boss, and the relations between husband and wife were generally formal and "often very superficial."

9. Traditional marriage is still common and practiced by a majority of older Americans. But the prevailing form today, preferred for example by 71 percent of women under 30, is *companionship marriage,* described as an attempt "to foster creative relationships in an atmosphere of love and intimacy." The emergence of companionship marriage, first noted and described as a "giant leap" in 1945, has revolutionized marriage patterns and created "a period of transition and readaptation" with considerable confusion over attitudes and behavior patterns.

10. There is as yet no standard type of companionship marriage, and it takes many different forms. The following are general characteristics:

Comradeship. Companionship marriages are based on love and friendship rather than mere sexual desire or economic conven-

ience. The partners seek "trust, affection, affiliation, and psychological intimacy."

Partnership. Husband and wife consider themselves partners, not boss and hired hand, and there is a more equal give-and-take.

Individual identity. The partners have "personal as well as family goals." Many wives think of themselves as having careers and therefore identities outside the home as well as in it.

Mutual self-fulfillment. Wife and husband view themselves as "actualizing each other's potential," and "the happiness of the partners is a primary goal."

11. The conflicting preferences for traditional and companionship marriage exist side by side, pulling all of us in both directions at once. Even people who favor traditional marriage have adopted some of the notions of companionship marriage, and companionship marriages often show some traditional characteristics. In today's society we can take our pick of an almost endless variety of possible views, and marriage has become a highly individual matter where there are no standard guidelines or "ten easy rules" for success. We must ask, What kind of marriage do *I* want?

12. Our society is highly *pluralistic,* composed of many different groups of varied racial, religious, and cultural backgrounds. Since we are strongly influenced by our background, we 165 million adult Americans have many different views of how women and men should behave, what we seek in marriage, and how husbands and wives should treat each other.

13. We also display, as people do everywhere, many individual differences in intelligence, motives, emotions, and sexual desire.

14. The individual differences and cultural plurality create many kinds of marriages and families. We have "a pluralism in family forms existing side by side," whose members have "different problems to solve and issues to face."

15. Advice from relatives and friends is based on their own individual views and limited experiences and may not apply to our own problems and issues. Advice in popular marriage books and magazine articles usually assumes that all couples are alike and suggests formulas that are supposed to apply to everyone—an impossibility in our pluralistic society.

16. The information in this course and this book consists of the findings and views obtained by the scientific method—careful research and objective observation of many kinds of people and many kinds of marriages, performed by sociologists, anthropologists, psychologists, psychiatrists and psychoanalysts, marriage counselors, and others who have viewed the family and the home in the context of our society as a whole and in trends across many cultures and years of history.

17. Since many of the changes now affecting marriages have occurred only recently, most of the information comes from studies made in the past few years. Yet many older findings are still pertinent, for ''most problems of our time have, in fact, also been problems in the past.''

DISCUSSION QUESTIONS

1. How many families do you know that are made up of a bread-winning father, a mother who does not work outside the home, and at least one child living at home? How many families do you know that do not fit this once-typical pattern? How would you describe them?

2. How does your family depend on society's other institutions, political, economic, religious, and educational? Which of them would be the easiest for your family to get along without? Which would be the hardest?

3. Discuss the reasons families have fewer children now than earlier in the century. How do *you* feel about large versus small families?

4. What are some of the reasons more wives now work outside the home? How do *you* feel about working wives?

5. Would the ideal marriage relationship for you be traditional, companionship, or in-between?

6. Why are popular books and magazine articles about marriage and family issues likely to be unreliable? In view of what you now know about scientific methods, do you recall any books or articles that seem especially unsound?

CHAPTER 2

How the Family Always Changes and Always Survives

Many of the social developments described in Chapter 1 represent an unprecedented new stage in human history. But the fact that these developments are reshaping the institution of marriage and the family is hardly a surprise to social scientists. The institution has changed many times before. Indeed there has never been any such thing as *the* marriage or *the* family, following some immutable law of nature, accepted everywhere by people of all societies, and persisting unchanged as humanity moved from the caves (or the Garden of Eden) through the civilizations of the ancient Greeks and Romans, the turmoil of the Dark Ages, and the rise of our present era of science and industry.

Since history began, marriage and the family have taken many forms, radically different from one society to the next, radically different in the same society from one century to the next. Even today, although industrialization and the marvels of modern transportation have tended to erase many of the variations among human societies, scores of different kinds of marriages and families can still be found somewhere in the world. They represent many different kinds of female-male relationships, family living arrangements, and ways of regarding and treating children. Thus marriage and the family cannot be defined in any universal terms. They have always been whatever the members of any society decided they should be at that particular time and in that particular place.

THE FAMILY IN ITS MANY FORMS

Anthropologists and social historians have made many studies of how the family operates today in the industrial nations of the world, the developing nations, and the preliterate societies that still exist in remote geographical areas. They have delved into the workings of the institution throughout history—in our own colonial days, in Europe before the Industrial Revolution, and the ancient civilizations. Their findings, though so richly varied that they seem at first to defy any generalizations, can be summarized in a single sentence: It is virtually impossible to imagine any kind of marriage or family that has not already existed somewhere in the world at some time or another.

How Many Wives Should a Man Have? How Many Husbands Should a Woman Have?

In today's United States and in industrial societies in general, marriage is *monogamous*—one wife to one husband and vice versa. We usually think of any other arrangement as strange, barbarous, and immoral. A person married to more than one spouse at a time is guilty of *bigamy*, punishable by a prison sentence.

It was not always that way. The practice of *polygyny*, in which a man has more than one wife, has been approved at one time or another in most of the world's societies (Murdock, 1949). It goes back at least as far as biblical days, when King Solomon had 700 wives. Some of the kings of ancient African nations are believed to have had as many as 7,000 wives (though you have to wonder how anybody managed to count them all!). In the United States polygyny was practiced by Brigham Young and some of the early Mormons. In fact it was not completely outlawed until 1890.

A few societies—notably Tibet—have practiced *polyandry* (Stephens, 1963), in which a woman has more than one husband. Often these marriages were between a woman and a group of brothers, all of whom lived in the same household, with the eldest brother considered the head of the family and responsible for the children. In some cases, however, the wife never lived at all with her husbands. Instead, she continued to live with her own brothers and sisters, who helped her bring up the children of her polyandrous marriages.

Though having more than one spouse at a time may seem strange, quite a few people in the modern United States practice something very similar. Through divorce and remarriage they wind up with two and sometimes as many as a dozen partners in their lifetime. In this sense, there has been more polyandry in the United States than ever existed in Tibet, and more polygyny than ever took place in the old African kingdoms, where, after all, only the rulers and a few very rich men could afford a houseful of wives. Having a dozen spouses in a lifetime

is of course rare, but having more than one is not unusual at all. Millions of American men have had at least two wives, and millions of women have had at least two husbands.

Nuclear and Extended Families

Of the other forms that marriage and the family have taken, two more deserve mention. One is the *nuclear family,* the type now considered customary in the United States and other industrialized nations. The nuclear family is made up of the wife, the husband, and their children, if any, living together in their own residence. The husband and wife usually maintain close contact with their immediate relatives—their parents and the families of their brothers and sisters—and often with more distant relatives as well (Goode, 1963). But they main-

Elinor S. Beckwith, Taurus

One of today's extended families celebrates grandmother's birthday.

tain their own home and regard themselves as a more or less independent and self-sufficient unit.

The other type is the *extended family*, in which two or more generations occupy the same residence, often along with other relatives such as aunts, uncles, brothers, and sisters. The extended family may at one time have been the prevailing form. Indeed some sociologists believe that most of the world's goods were produced throughout most of history by groups of relatives who cooperated in seeking food or growing it or in working together to manufacture and sell clothing and other products (Parsons, 1955).

Extended families were once common in the United States, and the landscape is dotted by rambling old farmhouses obviously built to accommodate large groups of kinfolk who worked together to grow the crops. There are still many extended families, on a somewhat more modest scale, with grandparents, parents, and children living under the same roof.

The nuclear family, however, has been the prevailing form in the Western world for a long time. In England, the majority of families fell into the nuclear pattern as far back as the sixteenth century, long before the Industrial Revolution (Gordon, 1973). In the United States the nuclear family was in the majority as far back as colonial days (Crosbie, 1976). The rambling farmhouses were the exception, built by very wealthy extended families and made to last. The smaller and cheaper buildings that housed the majority of families, living in the nuclear pattern, have long since eroded away.

Most married couples would much rather live in their own household than with their parents, and parents feel the same way (Shanas et al., 1968). Historical evidence indicates that the two generations held similar views in colonial days and maintained their own homes whenever possible (Greven, 1966).

How Family Forms Are Shaped by Society

In taking its various forms, the family has always been strongly influenced by society as a whole. Indeed the family tends to take whatever form is best adapted to the realities of existence at that particular time and in that particular place. The extended family, for example, often represented an attempt to adjust to difficult economic conditions. One study found that Europeans who lived in extended families in the nineteenth century did so not by preference but largely because of a scarcity of land and housing (Habakkuk, 1955).

Where polyandry has flourished, it has been encouraged by special circumstances that made it possible and perhaps inevitable. The Tibetans, for example, practiced infanticide with most of their girl babies, so that there were never enough adult women for a one-to-one ratio between the sexes. Other polyandrous societies have been so poverty stricken that no one man was able to provide a living for a wife (Murdock, 1949). In one small society where polyandry has been common (the Nayar on the coastline of India), the men spent most of their time making war against their neighbors and were hardly ever home (Linton, 1936).

Polygyny, though often believed to stem from a male urge for sexual variety, has in fact been largely a response to economic conditions. Most societies that have practiced polygyny have lived barely at subsistence level, with food and other goods in extremely short supply. By marrying a number of wives, a man could acquire more hands to work for him, which made him wealthier, relatively speaking, and gave him greater prestige. In Madagascar, where both sexes had to work hard to scratch a living from the soil, the pattern seems to have been for a man to marry first for love, then take additional wives at his first wife's suggestion so that they could help her with her work (Linton, 1936).

The kind of polygyny and polyandry now widely practiced in the United States is at least in part a form of adjustment to today's social conditions. Many divorces and remarriages are the result of longer life expectancy and the fact that couples who got along well in their 20s may no longer have much in common in their 30s and 40s. The possibility of drifting apart as the years go on is increased by today's large number of couples whose partners work at different jobs, bringing them new experiences that may channel their interests and personalities in different directions.

Ken Karp

One of the 666,000 American men who are single parents enlists his children's help in preparing a meal.

Single-Parent and Blended Families

Though the nuclear family with or without children is the prevailing form in the United States today, several other types have taken shape. Largely because of the high divorce rate, we have a large number of single-parent families—usually a woman rearing her children without the presence of a husband, but sometimes a man maintaining a home for the children without the presence of a wife. The number of single-parent families is also increased to some extent by widows and widowers bringing up children, by women who become mothers outside of marriage, and by unmarried people of both sexes who adopt children. All told, the nation at last count had 5.6 million single-parent families headed by women and 666,000 headed by men (Glick, 1984).

Often the single-parent arrangement is temporary, since about three of every four divorced people and many widows and widowers remarry eventually. A remarriage may result in another common type of family that for lack of a better term is often called the *blended family*. This is a household made up of a husband and his children from a previous marriage, a wife and her children from a previous marriage, and younger children born into the present union. In speaking of their children, parents in blended families often distinguish among them as "his," "hers," and "ours." The special problems of single-parent and blended families are discussed in a later chapter.

TODAY'S ROADBLOCKS
TO HAPPINESS

Thus marriage and the family, as they have done so often in the past, are changing rapidly in today's changing society. They are taking new forms in response to modern social developments, and the new forms exist side by side with many of the old. We have in the United States today, besides the nuclear family, our own versions of polygyny and polyandry. We have extended families, single-parent families, and blended families. We also have, as you will recall from Chapter 1, traditional marriages, companionship marriages, and various marriages that fall somewhere between the two extremes.

All the change and variety are confusing and difficult to adjust to. The path to happiness and self-fulfillment in marriage is strewn with roadblocks—perhaps we should marvel not at how many of today's marriages fail but at how many succeed. Some of the most difficult obstacles are discussed in the following pages.

The Bewildering Array
of Choices

The traditional marriage certainly had its faults, but in one important way it was probably easier on women and men than modern marriage. It imposed well-known and clear-cut rules. It demanded automatic and unthinking obedience to its standards of behavior for husbands, wives, fathers, mothers, and children. People who took the rules for granted—as most did in the past—did not have to make any decisions because they had no choices.

This was of course rigid and constricting, but it was also comforting. Psychologists have shown that we human beings have a strong urge to know exactly where we stand, how other people are likely to treat us, and how we in turn are expected to behave. Traditional marriage provided this sense of certainty and security. Companionship marriages, on the other hand, can be as varied as their partners care to make them. There are no rules except those the partners set for themselves.

Thus, in your own marriage, you are likely to face a wide and potentially baffling range of options, of possibilities to be explored and decisions to be made. Moreover, you are surrounded by living examples of all the options, that is, by couples who still practice the most extreme form of traditional marriage, who have embraced the most extreme form of freewheeling companionship, or who have chosen one of the almost endless gradations in between.

You undoubtedly know people who have failed and been divorced (for reasons you can never fully know). Some of these divorced people have decided that marriage is a bad deal (for reasons that may or may not apply to you). Others have remarried and found happiness the second time (again for reasons you can never fully understand). You may know people whose unmarried lifestyles seem to argue that never getting married is best. (At least for them, but is it for you?) You may even know people who have opted for living in communes or group marriages.

All of us have all these options and as Jessie Bernard (1972) has said, "Options make great demands." They force us to make agonizing decisions, and afterward we may still wonder if our choice was wise: "Offer people marital options and they are exposed to conflict. No matter which option they choose, they wonder if they should have made a different choice. Some will run from one to another in the hope that some other kind of relationship will be better." It takes a good deal of self-awareness, self-esteem, and psychological strength to make up your mind and keep it made up.

Success Does Not "Just Come Natural"

The traditional marriage, it must also be noted, did not take much skill. Because the rules were clear cut, children learned early in life to recognize them and be prepared to behave, in adulthood, as husbands and wives were supposed to behave (Mace and Mace, 1975). They were like actors who had spent years memorizing a script and knew that no ad-libbing was permitted.

It takes a great deal of skill and ingenuity, however, to conduct the kinds of human relationships envisioned by companionship marriage. Comradeship and psychological intimacy have to be worked at, and they have their hazards as well as their advantages: "Studies of family interaction show that intimacy provides not only love and care, but often tension and conflict as well; and that these are inseparable parts of intimate relationships" (Skolnick and Skolnick, 1974). The two partners bare their souls and make themselves vulnerable. They risk rejection and disagreement. They must learn how to stay friends while quarreling.

Achieving fairness in marriage is also more difficult than following the old husband-dominated pattern. Just what does fairness mean? Can any human relationship be entirely fair? And where can today's couples find guidelines for the radical practice of approaching each other as equals? As one study has observed:

> It was much easier to maintain a marriage and to find peace in one's home as long as the man was dominant. There was no conflict about sex; women considered their sexual role merely as one of satisfying the needs of their husbands . . . As soon as one wants more than the other, the relationship becomes disturbed. The one who wants less feels imposed upon. . . . These difficulties, which discourage and demoralize husbands and wives alike, are partly due to this new relationship of equality, which developed as part of the democratic evolution. There is no tradition that teaches us how to live with each other as equals, in mutual respect and trust.
>
> *(Dreikus, 1968)*

The "Myth of Naturalism"

Social scientists pointed out a long time ago that the kind of marriage that has been developing in today's world requires what Foote and Cottrell (1955) call "interpersonal competence"; that is, skill at establishing and maintaining intimate relationships, achieving the spirit of fairness, solving the inevitable conflicts, making adjustments, communicating, and the like. (These will be discussed later in this book.)

Unfortunately, there is a lingering belief, surviving from simpler times, that everybody just naturally grows up knowing everything required for success in marriage. Our society goes to considerable trouble to try to teach everybody to read, write, and follow some of the basic rules for staying healthy. But, except in courses such as this one, it totally ignores training for interpersonal competence—which, as a result, is something that "the majority of Americans have never even heard about, much less mastered" (Mace, 1974).

Our society has simply assumed that everybody will fall in love and that love in itself is enough to guarantee a happy marriage. All people have to do, the popular belief goes, is follow their instincts—a totally false notion that Clark Vincent (1973) has termed the "myth of naturalism."

Many observers believe that this myth is the chief cause of marriage failures in today's confusing period of transition from tradition to companionship. They would like more young people to take courses on family life in the high schools and colleges (Glick, 1975). One study has urged that marriage education be considered at least as important as driver education, and preferably be made compulsory before a license can be issued (Roy and Roy, 1970).

Expecting Too Much

Along with the tendency to accept the myth of naturalism goes the tendency to expect too much from marriage. We may be cynical about marriage in general, but we are usually overoptimistic about our own. Like the young couple described in the box on *Opinions and Experiences,* we expect it to transform us, to lift us out of ourselves, to bring us ecstasies that life has otherwise denied us.

The overhigh expectations stem in part from the myth of naturalism. People have these unrealistic hopes because "instead of being trained in interpersonal competence, they were fed with romantic notions that being 'in love' would assure them of unending bliss" (Mace and Mace, 1975). Of the "romantic notions" one marriage counselor has written: "We are the most marriage-minded nation in the world. Our young and our not-so-young march down the marital aisle two by two, in an endless Noah's Ark flow, each couple bathed in a rosy haze of nervous anticipation and romantic love" (Albert, 1973). A sociologist has commented:

> Probably the most widely held and destructive myth is the quest for the *perfect* rela-

tionship. . . . [When this proves unrealistic] Americans take to the exits, not because they are anti-family, but anti-*their* family. Thus most divorced persons will try again, and many of those will risk a third time, restlessly looking for that Hollywood made-in-heaven marriage.
>
> *(Etzioni, 1977)*

To some extent, psychoanalysis and psychology have probably contributed to the problem, though often unwittingly. All the publicity about finding oneself through analysis, about attaining insights and creativity in encounter groups and consciousness-raising sessions, has perhaps tended to make us all a little too demanding of self-fulfillment and Happiness with a capital *H*: In today's marriages "the happiness of the partners is a primary goal although no one is very sure what happiness means nor how it may be achieved and sustained" (Keller, 1971). Indeed there can be a "tyranny behind the notion of fulfillment" when it sets too high a standard for "the goal of human happiness" (Epstein, 1974).

Expectations and Reality

Whatever the source of the overoptimistic expectations, they are bound sooner or later to clash with reality. Marriage is not a cure-all for psychological problems nor a guarantee of immunity from the disappointments that life is bound to bring us from time to time. Perhaps the wisest words ever written on this point come from a psychiatrist, John Levy, who counseled many married couples:

> Marriage is, in actual fact, just a way of living. We don't expect life to be all sunshine and roses, or even beer and skittles. But somehow we do expect marriage to be that way. People who are accustomed to bickering with everybody else are shocked

Opinions and Experiences

"THE PERFECT UNION, FREE FROM FLAW"

A perceptive uncle of the bride-to-be, who has watched her and her fiancé grow up, describes the young couple about to marry.

My niece Jane, sorry to say, did not have an especially happy childhood. She was the youngest in the family, and her older sister and two brothers were all very smart in school and socially successful. She often seemed to have the uncomfortable feeling of tagging along, small and incompetent, behind confident giants. She was fifteen, big for her age, and awkward when her sister got married—and I'm sure it was agonizing for her to look like a woman and be regarded as a child on such an occasion. She did not especially like college. She was homesick all through her freshman year, had some scholastic problems in her sophomore year, and went through the pain of falling in love and breaking up when she was a junior. She's always been shy and has had very few good friends.

John, her husband-to-be, has also had his share of problems. He was embarrassed as a boy and particularly during adolescence by an oversolicitous mother. He tried but failed to make his high school football and basketball teams. Being cast aside by his first steady girl was a shattering experience. So was the discovery that he was not good enough at mathematics to be an engineer. He seems to view his present job with mixed emotions and to worry about his chances of success. He told me once that he's been skeptical of human nature ever since his best friend in college borrowed thirty dollars from him and failed to return it, and I think he suspects that many of his colleagues at the office, even those who seem friendliest, would not hesitate to knife him if he stood in the way of their own advancement.

I would say that Jane and John are mildly disillusioned about everything in the world—including themselves—with one exception. They still have romanticized and overblown hopes for marriage. They'll tell you that theirs will be the perfect union, free from flaw and immune to adversity. They honestly believe that they will never disagree, will never quarrel, and will always live in a golden glow of mutual admiration and complete rapport. They expect marriage to be different from everything else in life—and infinitely better.

when they find that they bicker with their wives. Women who have found everything disappointing are surprised and pained when marriage proves no exception. Most of the complaints about . . . matrimony arise not because it is worse than the rest of life, but because it is not incomparably better.

(Levy and Munroe, 1959)

Levy went on to explain that marriages cannot be perfect because none of us is perfect. Being human, we have faults as well as virtues. We are at times gloomy, cranky, selfish, and unreasonable. We are a strange mixture of "generous and altruistic feelings" existing side by side with "self-seeking aims, petty vanities and ambitions, hostilities, resentments, and competitive attitudes" even toward those we love. We combine "love and courage" with "selfishness and fear."

Since we human beings are this combination of virtues and faults, human relationships are also an alloy of gold and tin. As David Mace (1975) has observed, "The average marriage is neither good nor bad but a mixture of desirable and undesirable components.'' It is a compound of joy and sadness, peace and turmoil, friendship and hostility. If we expect more than this, we are doomed to disappointment. In the words of another marriage counselor, ''Husbands and wives have to learn to cut back their unrealistic goals and be satisfied with what they have today—because today is all they have to live with'' (Phillips, 1980).

Cynicism and Choosing the Wrong Partner

Paradoxical as it may sound, while expecting too much of marriage we also expect too little. In our nation of hopeful cynics, often the accent is on the cynicism rather than on the hope. When people talk about marriage, they often do so disparagingly. Wives are referred to as ''the ball and chain,'' and people still laugh, as they have for generations, over the mythical magazine article called ''How to Be Happy though Married.'' This kind of cynicism is another roadblock to success in marriage, for even a semiserious assumption that marriages usually go sour can be a self-fulfilling prophecy.

Another barrier to success is careless selection of a partner. Too many people marry the wrong person for the wrong reason (Albert, 1973), and are therefore doomed from the start. This is such an important topic that it demands a chapter of its own. You will find a full discussion of finding the right partner—or the wrong one—in Chapter 5.

Life's Many Inconveniences and Crises

A final roadblock is that modern society operates in a way that can be highly inconvenient for marriage partners, especially when both have jobs outside the home and young children to care for. Society runs on a schedule, and all of us must conform. We have to show up for work on time and stay until the workday is over. Schools have their opening bells and dismissal bells. We have to make appointments, not necessarily from choice, to visit a doctor or dentist, get the car repaired, or have a service representative fix the refrigerator. It is the family, not the rest of society, that must somehow adjust.

Life, moreover, can bring disappointments, crises, even tragedies. Married partners as well as single people get sick, or injured in accidents. They may lose their jobs in a recession (as more than 10 million people did in 1982) or because of technological change. They may become alcoholics or develop a crippling mental disturbance that requires hospitalization. Their children may be born retarded or otherwise handicapped or may become juvenile delinquents or runaways. Relatives may cause trouble or need financial assistance that strains the family budget.

Trouble for Even the Most Successful

Even the most successful families seldom live through an entire lifetime unhampered by any of these possible burdens. In 1960 Mudd and Taubin began studying a group of 100 young families deliberately chosen as having the stability and strength to do well throughout life. In 1980, when these people were in late middle age, they were studied again. Their lives in the meantime had proved to be anything but trouble-free.

> Illness, accidents, death, financial reverses, dislocations, and relocations were mentioned freely. Husbands bring up ''oldest son's diabetes,'' ''pulling through bad auto accident,'' ''open heart surgery,'' ''being caught with another woman.'' The wives

mention . . . "death of a son after being shot," "responsibility of caring for an invalid mother and mother-in-law," "lawsuit against family business." Clearly these families had not been immune from the exigencies of ordinary living.

(Mudd and Taubin, 1982)

Despite the misfortunes many of the families had suffered, they continued by and large "to be optimistic, to consider themselves fortunate." Perhaps marriage, though it is no guarantee against adversity, can cushion the blow. A study made for the National Institute for Mental Health, comparing married couples with unmarried people, found that those who are married are more likely to cope successfully with life's hardships and less likely to succumb to depression. Apparently, the study concluded, they "have the advantage of being able to draw emotional support from their partners" (Pearlin and Johnson, 1977).

MARRIAGE AS AN OASIS OF INTIMACY IN AN IMPERSONAL WORLD

Despite all the roadblocks to happiness—and the rapid change and confusion—the family survives. True, it has abandoned many of the tasks it performed in the past. In Ogburn's phrase, mentioned in Chapter 1, it has suffered "a loss of function." It is no longer primarily responsible for conducting society's economic affairs (and thus earning a living for its members) or providing recreation, education, and religious training.

Yet, though the family performs fewer functions nowadays, it continues to serve the needs of society in essential ways—indeed, in ways that are perhaps more demanding and vital today than in the past. The family

is now a highly specialized institution, concentrating on a narrow range of tasks. Talcott Parsons (1955) has observed that it is "probably more specialized than it has been in any previous society." In other words, as the family's functions have declined in number, the importance of its remaining functions has been sharpened and magnified.

Modern Industrial Society: Efficient but Cold

One function of today's family has assumed deep significance because of the very nature of modern society. The pattern of life in all industrial nations tends to isolate individuals from friendships, emotional attachments, or any other kind of real intimacy with their fellow human beings. Even as a college student, you may already have sensed some of this impersonality of modern life, for, especially on large campuses, students sometimes feel that they are merely faceless names or numbers on an educational assembly line.

In the workaday world off campus, the great majority of human contacts are conducted without any trace of intimacy or emotional concern. People ride to work on a bus with silent strangers or encased in an automobile, driving over roads where everyone else is also hidden inside steel and glass, identified only by a license plate. To our government we are a Social Security number, to our bank another string of numbers printed in magnetic ink at the bottom of a check. We have never even met the people who grew our food, made our clothing, or built our automobiles and television sets. We know nothing about the sales clerks and cashiers with whom we do business, and certainly have no emotional ties to them. Our own job may require a high degree of self-discipline and emotional control. We are not supposed to be blue, cranky, angry, or fearful, or for that matter overcome by fits of generosity or kindness.

The impersonality cannot be avoided in an industrial society dedicated to efficiency. As Clark Vincent (1966) has pointed out, we may complain about our cold and arm's-length dealings with the anonymous supermarket cashier, the unsmiling bank teller, and the busy physician with an office full of patients, but how would we feel about waiting in line for an extra hour while every customer and patient received painstaking individual care?

The impersonality of industrial society is magnified by the restless character of the modern United States, where many of us move around too quickly to establish roots. To seek better jobs, or a better climate, or what we think will be better living conditions, we change our addresses in great numbers and with dazzling speed. Nearly half of us do not live today where we lived five years ago, and every single year finds 8 million of us moving at least to a new county, if not to an entirely new part of the nation (Bureau of the Census, 1983b). Because we figure that we will soon move away—or that our neighbors will depart—we are not likely to become close friends with the people living around us.

The Warmth of the Family as an "Emotional Balance"

Our industrial society is highly efficient—most of the time and for most people—at meeting our needs for food, shelter, clothing, and other material goods. It does very little, however, for such other human needs as affection, warmth, emotional support, and intimacy—the feeling of caring and being cared for. Only in marriage and the family are we likely to satisfy these needs. The

Frank Siteman, Taurus

An example of the family as an "oasis of intimacy and affection."

home is the one place where we can let our hair down, be ourselves, display our emotions, communicate our deepest thoughts and feelings, and hope to find genuine security, understanding, acceptance, sympathy, and support (Kirkpatrick, 1963).

In William Goode's (1964) phrase, the family provides an "emotional balance" that offsets the impersonality of the industrial society. It serves as a tiny oasis of intimacy and affection in an otherwise barren desert of casual relationships conducted without feeling or satisfaction. Thus the family alone meets some of our deepest psychological and spiritual yearnings. Indeed, as Talcott Parsons (1955) has pointed out, the major function of the family today is not to serve society as a whole but to operate in behalf of the human personality, nurturing a vital part of human nature that is neglected by other social institutions. The warm and close relationship inside the family and the cool and distant relationships outside it mean that a wife and husband "are thrown upon each other." They are more dependent emotionally on marriage and the family than ever before in history.

The extent to which husband and wife must rely on their marriage for emotional fulfillment accounts for many of the apparent contradictions that surround the question of whether the family is flourishing or dying. All of us, when we marry, have a great personal stake in the relationship. We depend on marriage and demand a great deal from it. Some of us succeed and attain a level of intimacy and happiness that was probably rare in the past. But if anything goes wrong we tend to be bitterly disappointed, with results that are apparent in the high divorce rate.

The Matter of Primary and Secondary Groups

The importance of the family as an emotional balance can be further emphasized by pointing out the difference between two widely studied types of social unit. A married couple and their children if any constitute a *primary group*, that is, the close-knit, enduring unit described long ago as based on "intimate face-to-face association and cooperation" (Cooley, 1910). The family is one of the few primary groups to which any of us is likely to belong. Our other contacts with our fellow human beings are largely conducted in some form of *secondary group*, a unit of a very different kind. Although you may already be familiar with these terms from introductory sociology, they are worth reviewing because of their special significance to marriage and the family.

One typical secondary group to which you belong is the class taking this course. You meet regularly with your classmates and instructor, but you do so only for a specific purpose and on a temporary basis. When the course is finished the class will disband, and you may never see the instructor or any of these particular classmates again. Though you perhaps have one or two close friends in the class, by and large you know little if anything about the other members of the group and have no emotional ties to them. If one of them dropped out, you would hardly notice. Even the instructor could be replaced by someone equally skilled as a teacher without any serious disruption to the group's activities.

In general, secondary groups are characterized by the fact that they come together for some definite and practical reason, such as acquiring an education in the classroom, doing the work that has to be done in an office, or enjoying the recreation afforded by a tennis club. The members interact in only limited fashion, without personal or emotional ties, often hardly knowing each other. The personalities of the members play little part in the interaction. Indeed the members are interchangeable, in that any one of them can be replaced by someone else without any sense of loss to the group.

You can belong to dozens of secondary groups in a lifetime—those already mentioned and others such as church congregations, alumni clubs, political parties, neighborhood associations, parent-teacher organizations, and groups that meet to play cards, tennis, or softball—without ever establishing any kind of intimate friendship with anyone. The family is one of the very few places where who we are is just as important as what we do, where our unique qualities and characteristics are understood and appreciated and we cannot be replaced by a substitute, like a cog being replaced in a machine.

MARRIAGE AS AN AGENCY OF SOCIALIZATION

Another essential service the family performs for society, and always has, stems from the very nature of humanity. A newborn is totally incapable of surviving on its own, totally unaware of all the knowledge and skills needed to become a full-fledged member of even the simplest society, much less a society like ours. If babies were left to their own devices—like spiders popping unattended from the egg—humanity and human societies would quickly disappear.

All human beings, from the moment of birth, begin by necessity a lifelong education in becoming members of their society. They learn to speak English (or Spanish or Chinese). They learn to eat with a knife and fork (or with chopsticks). They learn to drive on the right side of the road (or, in England, on the left side). They learn to be on time for school and for appointments (or, in some countries, that nobody is expected to pay much attention to clocks). They learn their society's laws and its informal rules about how people are expected to behave toward one another, express or hide their emotions, work and play, and feel about religion and politics.

This education in how to get along in society is called *socialization,* and its effects are so all-inclusive as to influence almost everything we think, feel, and do throughout life. As anthropologist Ruth Benedict (1959) has pointed out, "The life history of the individual is first and foremost an accommodation to the patterns and standards tradition-

ally handed down" in the society into which the individual is born.

The customs and beliefs of our society, learned through socialization, become our own customs and beliefs. It is through socialization that we acquire our notions of how we and other people are supposed to behave, how we should talk and dress, what we regard as right and wrong, even what we consider beautiful and desirable. We share these notions with the other members of our society and live accordingly—in a way that we find perfectly logical and natural, even though a person brought up in a different society might not understand or approve of our behavior at all.

The socialization process continues throughout life as we go to school, enter the job world, acquire new knowledge, meet new people, and have new experiences. Yet nowhere else does it have such great influence, especially in molding the way we behave toward other people and expect them to behave toward us, as in our early years in the family (Walters and Stinnett, 1971). The family into which we are born is the primary agency of socialization. Indeed it is the family that "is charged with transforming a biological organism into a human being" (Goode, 1964).

Socialization and Culture

As the primary agency of socialization, the family performs the task of preserving and passing along to new generations that important heritage known as *culture.* As used by social scientists, this term has a much broader meaning than in popular usage, where it usually refers to such intellectual and esthetic matters as literature, music, and the other arts. To social scientists a society's culture is its entire way of life. The term embraces all the physical objects that charac-

The family fulfilling its function of socializing the young into the traditions of the culture and subculture.

terize the society—the tools it uses and the things it produces; not just its works of art but its food, clothing, and shelter (and in our society such technological marvels as automobiles, telephone systems, television sets, and computers.) Culture also includes the society's knowledge and ideas—such things as its language, political system, patterns of family life, beliefs, values, and rules of conduct established by law or by custom.

Our culture regulates everything we do throughout life and creates an orderly society by providing shared, agreed-on standards of how we are expected to behave and how we can expect others to behave toward us. As a simple example of how the shared nature of culture brings order, try to imagine what our society would be like if we all

had a different system of telling what time of day it was, or if half of us insisted on driving on the left side of the road instead of the right.

Even societies that to us seem crude and barbarous—like cannibal tribes—have a culture that regulates the behavior of their members and enables them to live together. As one social scientist has said, people without culture "do not in fact exist, have never existed, and most important, could not in the nature of the case exist" (Geertz, 1968). Living together in a society requires a culture, and the transmission of the culture to new generations requires socialization.

Culture and Subculture

In a society as large and pluralistic as ours, it must be added, not every child is socialized to follow exactly the same rules and customs. Within the general culture of our nation, there are many *subcultures,* or variations in the way of life. Children are socialized into one kind of subculture if they are born on a farm, into another kind if they grow up in a small town, still another if they grow up in a big city. Some subcultures are characterized by their religious beliefs, others by customs and values brought to the United States by people from different racial and national backgrounds, still others by occupation or the particular geographical area of the nation.

The various social classes also constitute subcultures, each having somewhat different customs, accepted standards of behavior, and beliefs and attitudes. Indeed the class to which we belong—upper, upper middle, lower middle, upper lower, or lower lower—is determined more by our standards of behavior and attitudes than by our income or wealth. An eccentric and uneducated old prospector is considered a member of the lower class even if he has several hundred thousand dollars hidden under his kitchen floor. A well-educated elderly woman from a prominent family is considered upper class even after all her money is gone and she is dependent on the charity of relatives.

The different classes vary in many ways, and they socialize their children accordingly. Parents in the higher ranges tend to speak a richer language to their children, reason with them more, be more permissive, and use less physical punishment. Lower-class parents tend to speak a more restricted kind of language to their children, be more authoritarian, and punish more severely (Gecas, 1979). The socialization in upper- and middle-class families tends to turn out children who grow up with a strong desire for achievement and success (Rosen, 1956), who tend to be conservative in their political and economic thinking (Lane, 1959), but who are more liberal in their attitudes toward such matters as women's rights and the companionship form of marriage (Ditkoff, 1979). Women from families in the higher classes usually marry later than women from families at the lower levels, have their first child at a later age, and have fewer children in all. They are also less likely to get divorced (Spanier and Glick, 1980b).

Like Parent, like Child

Since socialization is a lifelong process, events after childhood may of course change us in many ways. It has been found, for example, that the number of children who favor the same political party as their parents drops from about 80 percent in elementary school to only about 55 percent in college (Goldsen et al., 1960). Going to college is one of the most influential of all factors in socialization after childhood, especially for those of us whose parents never went, for college-educated people tend to have different attitudes from noncollege-educated people on a wide range of topics (Feldman and Newcomb, 1969).

Yet so powerful is the effect of socialization within the family, in whatever the subculture, that most of us continue to resemble our parents to a remarkable extent. A public opinion survey in the 1970s found that fully 73 percent of young people aged 15 to 21 were in substantial agreement with their parents' values and ideals (Harris, 1971). Often our early socialization in the family affects us more than we realize, and more than some of us might like to think. Campus radicals, for example, might seem to be in active rebellion against their families and their early socialization. Yet a study of such students found that they and their parents were in fact more alike than different in numerous basic ways (Bem, 1970).

Why the Family Seems Here to Stay

Today's highly specialized family may concentrate on only two functions, but what other social institution, either now in existence or even imaginable, could perform these two essential tasks? What other primary group, in this society of secondary groups, could provide the emotional balance of affection, emotional support, and intimacy? And how else could children receive the crucial early months and years of socialization into our culture?

Thus, although some sociologists are pessimistic about the future of the family, the majority believe it "is a resilient institution that still maintains more strength than its harshest critics maintain" (Cherlin and Furstenberg, 1983). As John Crosby (1975) has observed:

No one can yet foresee what the structure of the future family system will look like because no one can know with certainty what the functions and needs of the future family will be. It is likely, however, that the needs for primary affection bonds, intimacy, . . . socialization of the young, and reproduction will not soon yield to obsolescence. To the extent that human needs will not change drastically, the family structure will not change drastically. . . . No amount of ridicule or rhetoric will suffice to kill the family until an alternative structure evolves that is capable of filling the basic needs . . . and is also sufficiently appealing for mass adoption. When and if such a "replacement" structure evolves, it will undoubtedly be commonly referred to as "a family."

The family may change form again in the future, as it has many times and in many places in the past, but it is so essential to both the human personality and the survival of society that it seems here to stay.

SUMMARY

1. Marriage and the family cannot be defined in any universal terms, for they have taken many forms in different cultures and different periods. It would be difficult to imagine any type of arrangement that has never yet existed somewhere at some time.

2. *Polygyny,* in which a man has more than one wife, has been approved at one time or another in most of the world's societies. Some societies have practiced *polyandry,* in which a woman has more than one husband.

3. The *nuclear family,* now customary in the United States and most other industrialized nations, is made up of the wife, the husband, and their children, if any, living in their own residence as an independent and self-sufficient unit.

4. In the *extended family,* two or more generations occupy the same residence, often along with other relatives, with everyone cooperating in farm chores or some kind of production. The extended family has been the prevailing form in many societies and was once fairly common in the United States.

5. The form taken by the family is always strongly influenced by society as a whole. The extended family has often represented an attempt to adjust to difficult economic conditions. Polygyny has thrived in societies where food and goods were scarce and men sought more help in scratching a living. Polyandry was common in Tibet because the Tibetans practiced infanticide with most girl babies and there were never enough adult women.

6. In our current society, the high divorce rate has produced many *single-parent* families headed by a divorced woman or man and *blended* families of remarried couples, their children, and their children from their previous marriage. We also have some extended families and family relationships ranging from completely traditional to full companionship.

7. Some of today's obstacles to successful marriage are these:

   a. The many choices now available "make great demands" and create conflicts: "No matter which option people choose, they wonder if they should have made a different choice."

   b. The traditional marriage, with its clear-cut rules, did not require much skill; but it takes considerable skill and ingenuity to succeed at companionship marriage, especially since there are no established guidelines to follow. "Intimacy provides not only love and care but often tension and conflict as well, and these are inseparable parts of intimate relationships."

   c. It is still popular to think that everybody just naturally grows up knowing everything required for success in marriage, a belief that has been called "the myth of naturalism.'' In fact, today's marriages call for ''interpersonal competence''—learned skills at conducting intimate relationships, achieving fairness, solving conflicts, making adjustments, and communicating.

d. Many people expect too much from marriage: ''Instead of being trained in interpersonal competence, they were fed with romantic notions that being in love would assure them of unending bliss.''

e. We tend to expect too much from marriage and are therefore disappointed. Marriages cannot be perfect because none of us is perfect. We have our faults as well as our virtues. We are a strange mixture of ''generous and altruistic feelings'' existing side by side with ''self-seeking aims'' and ''resentments and competitive attitudes'' even toward those we love.

f. We may also expect too little. A cynical attitude toward marriage and its chances of success can be a self-fulfilling prophecy.

g. Many people choose the wrong partner, dooming the marriage from the start.

h. Society sets schedules, for example, working hours, the school day, and appointments set by doctors, automobile mechanics, and appliance repair staffs. The family must conform, often at great inconvenience.

i. The family is always subject to crises and tragedies. Married people get sick or injured, lose their job, become alcoholics, or develop mental disturbances. Children may be born retarded or otherwise handicapped, or they may become delinquents. Relatives may cause trouble or need financial help. Even the most successful families seldom live an entire lifetime unmarred by a crisis or tragedy.

8. Although the family has suffered ''a loss of function'' because many of its former services have been taken over by other social institutions, it continues to serve two highly important purposes that could hardly be filled in any other way.

9. One of these functions stems from the nature of an industrial society, where the majority of human contacts occur without any intimacy or emotional concern. We conduct most of our affairs impersonally, with unknown sales clerks and cashiers. The family provides our ''emotional balance'' as an oasis of intimacy and affection in an otherwise barren desert of casual relationships conducted without feeling or satisfaction. The home is the one place where we can be ourselves, display our emotions, communicate our deepest thoughts and feelings, and hope to find genuine security and support.

10. The family provides emotional balance because it is a *primary group,* a close-knit, enduring unit based on ''intimate face-to-face association and cooperation.'' Our other human contacts are largely in *secondary groups,* whose members meet for a specific purpose (as in a classroom or business office) and interact in only limited fashion, without personal or emotional ties.

11. The family's other vital function, which it has served since the beginning, is to nurture and socialize the newborn. *Socialization* is the process of teaching children all the rules and customs of society, the ways people are expected to behave.

12. In socializing the young, the family preserves and passes along that important heritage called *culture,* meaning the society's language, political system, patterns of family life, beliefs, values, and rules of conduct—in sum, its entire way of life.

13. In addition to culture, the family passes along the ways of the particular *subculture* to which it belongs because of religious, racial, or national background, social class, and place of residence.

14. Socialization is a lifelong process, changing with new experiences, but early socialization into the family is such a powerful influence that most of us continue to resemble our parents to a remarkable degree.

15. Because the family serves the two vital functions of providing emotional intimacy and

socialization of the young, most scholars believe it is a "resilient institution" that is here to stay.

DISCUSSION QUESTIONS

1. Would you prefer living in a nuclear family or an extended family? Why?
2. Would you favor a law requiring marriage education before a marriage license is issued?
3. Why do couples often have unrealistic expectations about marriage?
4. Of which secondary groups are you currently a member? Have there been times when your family met needs that your secondary groups could not?
5. In what ways are your values and ideals similar to those of your parents? In what ways are they different?
6. Of the functions of the family—providing an "emotional balance" and socialization—which would be easier for another social institution to perform? Why?

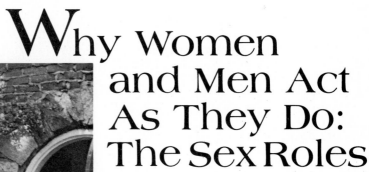

CHAPTER 3

Why Women and Men Act As They Do: The Sex Roles

The sexes have always been a mystery to each other (and sometimes to themselves). In many ways they seem almost exactly alike. They speak the same language, often in indistinguishable tones of voice. They get the same scores on intelligence tests. They sit side by side in classrooms and often work side by side at the same jobs, with equal efficiency. In other ways they seem as far apart, to themselves and to each other, as an aardvark and a zebra. Women throw up their hands and cry, "That's just like a man." Men shake their heads and mourn, "That's just like a woman."

Most people have always taken the similarities and differences for granted, as a simple fact of life. Certainly being "she" or "he" is one of the most clear-cut of all human traits. You knew which you were when you were a mere toddler, for even 3-year-olds have learned that females and males, though similar in some ways, are profoundly different in others.

In one respect the difference between "he" and "she" has a simple explanation. The sex to which you belong was determined nine months before you were born, at the moment of conception. If among the chromosomes you inherited you have what is called an X-X combination, you are female. If instead you have an X-Y combination, you are male. But what about all those tremendous differences in the way women and men act? Are they the result of those X-X and X-Y chromosomes? Or of something else?

In any discussion of marriages and families, the answer is vitally important. If the chromosomes decree that men are one breed of animal and women an entirely different breed— if the two have clashing personalities, interests, and goals in life—then like a dog and a cat they can never be real friends. About the best they can do, with care and luck, is manage to live in the same household without open friction.

They may cooperate to a certain extent, like a dog and a cat sharing the same water bowl. They may even play together at times. But they will never be intimates. And always, just beneath the surface, there will lurk a natural enmity that may break out at any time. If all this is determined once and for all at the moment of conception, we can have only the most modest hopes for happiness in marriage—and certainly companionship marriage would appear to be a contradiction in terms.

WHAT IS A WOMAN? WHAT IS A MAN?

There is no doubt that men and women, over the centuries, have generally thought of themselves as belonging to different breeds. As Tavris and Offir (1977) have said:

Throughout history the sexes have regarded each other less as fellow human beings than as alien and exotic creatures. . . . In every society, in every century, people have assumed that males and females are different not only in basic anatomy but in elusive qualities of spirit, soul, and ability. . . . Every society has distinguished men's work from women's work and created barriers between the sexes. Sometimes men and women have had so little to do with one another that one wonders how the population explosion ever managed to take place.

Those words are of course a generality. There doubtless have always been many individual differences in the ways in which particular men and women have regarded themselves and each other. By and large, however, people have always assumed that men and women display striking dissimilarities.

One indication comes from a study made in the 1970s in which people were asked to describe the typical traits of women and men. The subjects, both male and female, agreed in general that men tend to be aggressive, independent, dominant, competitive, logical, direct, adventurous, self-confident, and ambitious. Women were characterized as almost exactly the opposite—unaggressive, dependent, submissive, not competitive, illogical, sneaky, timid, lacking in self-confidence, and unambitious. Men were described as close mouthed and women as talkative, men as rough and women as gentle, men as sloppy in their habits and women as neat. It was agreed that men do not usually enjoy art and literature and cannot easily express any tender feelings, whereas women do like art and literature and find it easy to express their feelings (Broverman et al., 1972).

The "Masculine" Man and the "Feminine" Woman

People have assumed not only that females and males *are* different but that they *should* be different. In almost all past and present societies men have been expected to be "masculine" and self-reliant and women to be "feminine" and dependent (Barry, Bacon, and Child, 1957). Almost without exception men have done the fighting and women have cared for the children (D'Andrade, 1966).

Although some individual women have managed to achieve political power from time to time, there is no known case of a society controlled by women as a group (Bamberger, 1974). The old myths about the Amazons, a kingdom of fierce women who were supposed to have waged war against nations with male armies, are purely imaginary. In marriage, in particular, the male has usually been dominant, the female passive and nurturing. Marriages like those described in the box on *Opinions and Experiences* have been uncommon not only in our own nation but everywhere.

Being X-X (or X-Y) All Over

As to what part biology plays in making females "feminine" and males "masculine," we can start with the fact that women and men are biologically different not only in their sex organs but in every other part of the body. Every female cell—in bone, muscle, heart, and brain—contains the X-X chromosome pair. Every cell of the male body contains the X-Y pair. In some species of life the two chromosome pairs are enough to create startling physical differences. The male red-winged blackbird, for example, is a solid shiny black except for the bright red and yellow patches on his wings. The female

Opinions and Experiences

MEN WHO KEEP HOUSE

A newspaperman who has known many people of the entertainment world in New York and Hollywood describes some of the "reverse marriages" he has seen.

It is not at all unusual in the entertainment world for the wife to be the breadwinner and the husband the stay-at-home. I've watched it happen many times. Usually, to keep up appearances, the couple pretend that the husband is the wife's manager or public relations expert, or in some other way acts as the power behind the throne. But everybody knows that the wife has all the talent and could get along perfectly well by herself—except that she apparently enjoys the marriage.

There was one New York actress whose husband did everything that a faithful housewife is supposed to do—or was supposed to do before women's lib came along. In the days before she became successful enough to afford other kinds of help, he cleaned their apartment, did the shopping and the laundry, sent her clothes out to the cleaner, walked and fed the dog, and cooked all their meals. He had tried acting himself and knew he was never going to make it—so why not? He was a little self-conscious because of the tradition that a "real man" didn't do such things, but otherwise they seemed to be perfectly happy. They stayed married long after she got famous—until he died, as a matter of fact.

There is a movie actress whose husband did even more. He took care of their children from the time they were born. Diapered them, bottled them, saw that they took their naps, and later got them off to school. This couple always had enough money to hire servants and nurses for the kids, but I guess he liked it that way. No kids ever had a better "mother," I'll say that. The marriage may have been totally in reverse by the standards of the time, but it worked. They're still married, and I'd have to say they're just about the happiest middle-aged couple in Hollywood.

is not black at all. She is brown, with no wing patches but a heavily striped breast. Looking at the two of them, you have to wonder how they ever manage to figure out that nature intended them to get together.

Among human beings, there are some general differences in size, with the average male taller and heavier. Yet many women are bigger and heavier than many men, and there are no really pronounced differences at all in basic appearance. Except for their sex organs, boy babies and girl babies look alike. If they are wearing a diaper, it is impossible to tell them apart. Even when adult males and females are dressed alike in jeans and shirts, with hair the same length, it can be difficult at first glance to tell which is which.

The Male and Female Hormones

The chief physical difference between the sexes is invisible, lying in the hormones produced by the sex glands. The male glands produce large amounts of hormones called androgens and only small amounts of estrogen. The female glands do the opposite, producing large amounts of estrogen and only small amounts of androgens. This difference in hormones, which are circulated by the blood stream to every part of the body, undoubtedly has some effect on behavior. Indeed, the effects are apparent even before birth. All fertilized eggs, in the first stage of development inside the womb, start out to grow into females. In the case of X-Y eggs, the Y-chromosome then orders a flood of androgens, and this androgen bath switches the course of development into the formation of male sex organs (Money and Ehrhardt, 1972).

Some scientists believe that the two hormones may also act before birth to influence the nervous system, with androgens or estrogen "programming" the brain to operate in different ways. In one area of the brain that influences sexual behavior some significant differences have been found between male and female monkeys, presumably caused by the different hormones (Ayoub, Greenough, and Juraska, 1983). It has also been found that changing the balance of the two hormones, before or just after birth, can make male monkeys grow up acting like the females of the species and females acting like males (Bardwick, 1971).

With human beings, a study was made of some young women who had been affected by androgens before birth as an unexpected side effect of a new drug taken by their mothers. As a group these young women appeared to be unusually masculine in their behavior. As children they were tomboys, preferring baseball and football to dolls. In early adolescence they were not very interested in boys and felt uncomfortable acting as babysitters. They were not sure they wanted to get married or become mothers. A follow-up study made when they were 16 to 27 years old, however, found that they were no longer interested in sports and resembled any other group of women in dating and other behavior (Money and Mathews, 1982).

Biology Isn't Everything

All in all, it seems likely that the biological makeup of the two sexes creates some inborn tendencies to behave in somewhat different fashion. But biology, alone does not make men independent and aggressive and women passive and submissive. Whatever the effects of the X-X and X-Y chromosomes may be, there is ample proof that what they do to the human personality is by no means final and irreversible (Stoller, 1972).

The evidence started piling up a half century ago when Margaret Mead, an anthropologist, reported the unusual behavior of three native tribes with whom she had lived in the wilds of the South Pacific island of New Guinea. The men and women in these tribes undoubtedly were the same as the rest of humanity in the matter of X-X and X-Y chromosomes, estrogen, and androgen, but their notions of masculinity and femininity were altogether different from those that have prevailed in our society and most others.

In tribe 1, the Mundugomor, both men and women were aggressive to the point of outright violence. In fact they were headhunters and cannibals. The women—perhaps because pregnancy interfered with their normal warlike habits—disliked having and caring for their children, especially girl babies. In other words, both sexes were about as far-out "masculine" as the Billy the Kids and other outlaws of our own wild West— with the added unrefinement of eating their victims.

In tribe 2, the Arapesh, both men and women were highly "feminine." Both sexes shunned aggression, even any kind of competition for amassing possessions. Both were gentle, kind, passive, and warmly emotional. They both took care of and nurtured the children.

In tribe 3, the Tchambuli, by contrast, there were even more differences between men and women than in our own society. The members of one sex spent all their time applying cosmetics, gossiping, pouting, indulging in emotional outbursts, and taking care of the children. The members of the other sex had clean-shaven heads, scorned any ornamentation, were active and domineering, and provided most of the tribe's food and other necessities. But the last sentence describes how the women of this tribe behaved. The preceding sentence, about cosmetics and emotional outbursts, describes the men (Mead, 1935).

Anthropologists have since found a number of other places where there is hardly any difference in the behavior of the two sexes, or where the men seem feminine and the women masculine by our traditional standards (D'Andrade, 1966).

The Strange Case
of the Boy-Girls and Girl-Boys

In our own society, the most dramatic evidence that biology is not everything comes from a study of hermaphrodites, people born, through a strange flaw in the growth process, with some of the male sex organs and some of the female. Until the discovery of the X-X and X-Y chromosomes and how to spot them by looking at a cell through a microscope, there was no way of knowing whether hermaphrodites were female or male. Their parents and physicians could only guess. If they guessed male, then usually the female characteristics were removed through surgery and the baby was brought up as a boy. If they guessed female, the opposite kind of surgery was performed and the baby was brought up as a girl.

Researchers at the Johns Hopkins University managed to find a number of people born as hermaphrodites, in the days of guesswork, and gave them a chromosome test that proved whether they were biologically male or female. It turned out that some

who were brought up as boys had the X-Y combination and were in fact males, but that others had the X-X combination and were actually females. Likewise, some brought up as girls were X-X and indeed female, but others were X-Y and actually male.

As far as the behavior of these people was concerned, however, the facts revealed by the chromosome test did not seem to matter. Those brought up as girls acted feminine and those brought up as boys acted masculine regardless of whether they were X-X or X-Y—to such an extent that a "person meeting them socially or vocationally" would have had "no clues as to the remarkable contents of their medical histories" (Money and Ehrhardt, 1972).

THE NATURE
AND EFFECT OF
SEX-ROLE
SOCIALIZATION

For the chief reason men and women behave as they do, we must obviously look beyond biology and the chromosomes. We will find it, instead, in the fact that the socialization process takes very different forms for females and males almost from the moment of birth.

Suppose you hear that a friend or relative has just had a baby. Your first question is not "How much did it weigh?" Nor "Does it have a lot of hair?" Nor even "Is it normal and healthy?" Instead you are almost sure to ask, "Is it a boy or a girl?" This is also the first concern of the mother and father. The newborn's socialization will depend to a great extent on whether the answer to that all-important first question is "It's a boy" or "It's a girl."

To a physician or psychologist examining

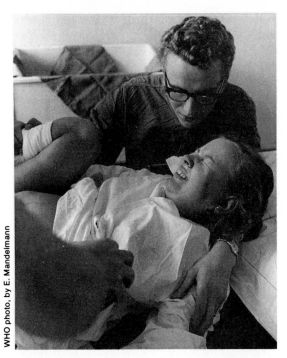

WHO photo, by E. Mandelmann

A husband supporting his wife through childbirth. Will it be a girl or a boy—and how will this affect its life?

babies at birth, a boy and girl usually seem exactly alike in every respect except their sex organs. But they do not seem alike to their parents. This was shown in a study of parents interviewed on the first day of their newborns' lives. Half the babies were boys, half girls. Tests at the hospital where they were born showed that as a group the boys and girls were remarkably alike in every measurable trait. They could not be distinguished by appearance, muscle tone, reflexes, or even size. Yet the parents of the boys thought their babies were outstandingly strong, firm, hardy, alert, and well coordinated. The parents of the girls described their babies as smaller, finer featured, softer,

and less inclined to pay attention (Rubin, Provenzano, and Luria, 1974).

The researchers who made the study concluded that the physical traits and personality characteristics of babies are mostly "in the eye of the beholder." It so happens that the eyes of most beholders look at males and females very differently, and treat them differently, from the cradle on. Males are socialized into one pattern, females into another.

Socialization and Status

Among the things socialization teaches us is our *status,* meaning the position we occupy in society. Status depends on many factors. One is age. (Babies have one kind of status in society, schoolchildren another, and so on for young adults, the middle-aged, and old people.) Other factors are position in the family (mother, father, or child) and occupation. Still another, of special concern to us here, is sex, for males occupy one kind of status, females a very different kind.

In most societies throughout history, males have had a privileged status. Females have seldom shared equally in society's esteem, praise, and rewards. They were treated as the inferior sex in ancient Egypt, Greece, and Rome, and on our own continent by the Indians (Tavris and Offir, 1977). Though the kind of work done by the two sexes has varied from society to society, the jobs assigned to men have always been considered more important (Goode, 1964). In fact, sexual discrimination may have been humanity's first form of social inequality (Robertson, 1977), practiced before people ever thought of discriminating against one another on the basis of race or social class.

How Society Assigns Roles

We also learn through socialization that a person in a particular status is expected to behave accordingly, to act out the *role* that society considers appropriate. The term *role* is borrowed from the theatrical world, where the playwright's script dictates the behavior of a Hamlet or a Lady Macbeth, giving them the same words to speak and actions to take regardless of who happens to be playing the part.

Like the playwright's script, society prescribes the role that each of us is expected to play in our dealings with others. A college professor—any college professor—is assigned one kind of role. A student—any student—is assigned another. The student, for example, is expected among other things to take a certain number of courses, get a certain grade level, refrain from cheating on examinations, and maintain certain standards of personal conduct.

One way to describe the difference between status and role is this: You occupy a status but play a role (Linton, 1936). The two, however, are closely related, for the role you are expected to play is determined by the status you occupy. The roles played by a professor and a student in the classroom, for example, are different than they would be in some other setting where they occupy a different status, such as if both were members of a volunteer ambulance corps or a little-theater group.

Society exerts a great deal of pressure for the proper performance of the role it has assigned to us. When we play it as society expects, we win acceptance and approval. When we play it badly, we run into the powerful force of disapproval, criticism, and sometimes outright rejection. Thus, like actors who will be acclaimed if they speak Shakespeare's words well but fired if they ad lib, we have every incentive to go along with the role that society has assigned to us.

The Female Role and the Male Role

The *sex roles,* or behavior considered appropriate for women and men, can vary considerably from one culture to the next, as Margaret Mead's study showed. Whatever they may be, they are taught by society from the cradle on. It is our sex-role socialization, much more than biology, that makes us act feminine or masculine.

Until very recently in our own society, the female and male roles were clear-cut. Women were brought up to be feminine, meaning dependent, submissive, and noncompetitive. Men were brought up to be masculine, meaning independent, dominant, and highly competitive. As a result the two sexes often did seem like two different creatures, having very little in common.

In marriage, the feminine woman took for granted that she would be the passive, dependent, nurturing housewife and mother. The masculine man expected to be the strong, independent breadwinner, provider, protector, and boss. This is why the traditional marriage, tailored to that kind of sex-role socialization, was often such an arm's-length arrangement, a little like the strained relationship between a dog and cat.

The Continuing Power of Tradition

There were always rebels, of course. History tells us that many women of the past objected strenuously to the role assigned them by society. Today's feminist movement, often called women's liberation, is merely a modern version of a long struggle for women's rights that dates back to before the Civil

War, when it was led by such famous early *suffragettes,* or advocates of letting women vote, as Susan B. Anthony and Lucy Stone. We can assume that there probably were also many husbands of the past who hated being so all-fired masculine and aggressive and wished instead that they could be more tender, express their emotions, and explore the path of genuine companionship.

Most men and women, however, played out their roles uncomplainingly. Indeed they usually had no real alternatives. In the days before coeducation and jobs for women, it took an exceptional woman to visualize any role for herself except housewife and mother. It also took an exceptional man to embrace the wild and unpopular theory that the two sexes might be basically more alike than different, and therefore deserving of equal status in society. (Lucy Stone's husband, Dr. Henry Blackwell, was one such person.)

Today many people have begun to question the old sex roles and search for new ones. A public opinion poll showed that by the start of this decade a majority of Americans—about 56 percent—were convinced that men act in masculine ways and women in feminine ways largely because of the "way they are raised and taught to act" rather than because of "basic physical differences between them." In other words, the majority agreed that the behavior of the two sexes results from socialization rather than from biology. Moreover, parents had begun to treat girls and boys much more equally than in the past. The poll showed a sharp increase in the number of mothers who asked their daughters to help with such traditionally male tasks as household repairs and mowing the lawn, and their sons to help with such traditionally female tasks as cooking and laundry (Roper, 1980).

Despite these changes, however, it is still difficult to cast off the old sex roles and find new ones. Since traditions die hard, sex-role socialization continues in many ways to follow the pattern of the past. There are still powerful forces at work pushing females in the direction of being feminine and males in the direction of being masculine.

Socializing without Knowing It

Even when cooing to a baby in the crib, it has been found, parents use one tone of voice toward a girl and a different one toward a boy. Fathers playing with the baby are cautiously gentle toward a girl, more roughhouse toward a boy (Weitzman, 1975). Mothers display many differences in behavior. Even on the first day of life, they generally feed boys more than girls (Lewis and Als, 1975). They dress the two sexes in different clothes, even if the two happen to be twins (Brooks and Lewis, 1974). They look at a girl baby more than a boy and talk to her more (Goldberg and Lewis, 1969).

Even parents who say they believe in treating the two sexes equally seem to fall into many habits that differentiate between boys and girls. Some convincing evidence comes from an ingenious experiment with a group of young and theoretically liberated mothers. All these women claimed that boy and girl babies were alike and that they would treat the two sexes exactly the same. Indeed almost all of them said that they themselves encouraged their own girls to be rough-and-tumble and their boys to play with dolls. Yet their conduct in the experiment showed otherwise.

Half the women were introduced to a 6-month-old named Adam and observed while playing with him in a room that contained a train (typically a male toy), a doll (typically female), and a toy fish (neuter). These mothers usually handed Adam the train. The other half were observed while playing with six-month-old Beth. These mothers usually handed Beth the doll, and afterward some of them remarked what a sweet and uncomplaining little girl she was. Actually, as you have probably guessed, there was really only one baby. (It happened to be a boy.) But six-month-olds look so very much alike that none of the mothers caught on. They gave "Adam" the traditional treatment for a boy, "Beth" the traditional treatment for a girl (Will, Self, and Datan, 1974).

Many other studies have likewise shown that parents, though they may not realize it and may stoutly deny it, tend to foster the traditional sex roles. Lenore Weitzman (1975) has summed up the evidence in these words:

> Research . . . indicates that sex-role socialization begins before the child is even aware of a sexual identity: before he or she can have an internal motive for conforming to sex-role standards. It also indicates that cultural assumptions about what is "natural" for a boy or for a girl are so deeply ingrained that parents may treat their children differently without even being aware of it. Wittingly or unwittingly, parents encourage and reinforce sex-appropriate behavior, and little boys and little girls respond to parental encouragement and rewards.

For the Child, Feminine and Masculine on All Sides

Parents, of course, are not the only influences in the lives of their children, but all the other factors that help socialize youngsters have also been found to teach the traditional sex roles. Television shows and books for children often reflect traditional attitudes. In nursery schools, attended by children of 3 to 5, teachers have been found to pay considerably more attention to the boys. They talk more to boys, give them more individual instruction and help when needed, and reward them more frequently for their accomplishments (Serbin et al., 1973).

The teachers in elementary schools, though most of them are women, also give boys more attention, encouragement, and praise. They seem to take for granted that boys often call out an answer without first raising a hand but usually criticize girls who do this. Like parents, they often are unaware that they are treating the two sexes differently (Sadker and Sadker, 1985).

Children's toys often fall into the traditional pattern. When a sociologist sent assistants to a number of stores to ask for help in selecting a present for a 5-year-old relative, the suggestions turned out to depend largely on whether the child was said to be a niece or a nephew. More than 70 percent of the time, the salesperson's recommendation for a girl was a doll, tea set, nurse's kit, or something equally feminine; for a boy a racing car, construction set, gun, or army truck (Ungar, 1982).

Getting the Message Early

All in all, the various agencies of socialization make young children extremely conscious of their sexual identities. Boys quickly discover that they are male, girls that they are female. Both learn very early in life that society in general assigns very different statuses and roles to males and females. Even before they are of kindergarten age, and increasingly thereafter, they tend to try hard to win society's approval by living up to the roles:

> Even the preschool boy seems to be constantly asking himself, "How masculine am I?" Even the preschool girl wants to know, "How feminine am I?" Their feelings

about how well they are living up to their sex roles begin to play an increasing part in their self-evaluation and their feelings of self-esteem.

(Kagan, 1985)

Children also seem to understand that society has assigned males a higher status and with it greater privileges and opportunities (Beuf, 1974). Thus a considerable number of kindergarten girls often wish they were boys, but the boys agree almost unanimously that they have no desire at all to be girls (Ollison, 1975). Still, though girls may envy the male role, they seem to be just as eager to be feminine—and thus win society's approval—as boys are to be masculine. If they do happen to stray from their assigned roles, society tries to force them back, as in the case of the former tomboy quoted in the box on *Opinions and Experiences*. What with the rewards for doing what one is expected to do, and the penalties for failure, few girls insist very long on being tomboys or boys on being sissies.

HOW THE SEX ROLES CREATE PROBLEMS FOR WOMEN

By the time we become adults, most of us have had a long education in the traditional feminine and masculine roles. Attitudes learned over such a long period tend to have a life of their own. Thus even women who have become ardent advocates of the liberation movement, deploring the old female sex role and status as unfair and demeaning, sometimes think or act in a traditionally feminine way almost as if by reflex action. Even men who heartily approve of the liberation movement are bound to show lingering traces of the old masculine standards.

It may be, as some scholars believe, that the traditional sex roles served a useful purpose and that today's society would be better off if everyone continued to play them as in the past. Or it may be, as others believe, that the roles are just a useless relic of humanity's past, like the vermiform appendix of the digestive system. At any rate, they continue to help shape our feelings and our behavior, especially on all matters related to marriage and the family. Like the human appendix, they can cause a great deal of trouble.

One problem is the fact that the sex roles are assigned strictly on the basis of biology, as if all males were exactly alike because of that X-Y chromosome pair and all females were cut in the same mold because of the X-X chromosome pair. Actually, as social scientists have been discovering ever since the time of Francis Galton a century ago, human characteristics can be very different from one person to the next. Sir Francis found that human beings, both male and female, show a wide range of individual differences in such matters as size, physical strength, sense of hearing and smell, and ability to judge weights. It has since been established that people also range from very low to very high in intelligence and in tendencies to be emotional or stolid, extroverted or introverted, or happy or sad, as well as in many other traits.

As Roger Brown (1965) has pointed out, there is a large "overlap" between the sexes in almost all human traits. For example, though men are physically bigger and stronger than women on the average, many women are bigger and stronger than many men. Males and females simply do not fall into two neat and separate categories. Therefore sex-role socialization is likely to be "an anxiety-producing process for boys and girls because it requires them both to conform to rigid sex-role standards that are

Opinions and Experiences

A TOMBOY AND HER HORRIFIED PARENTS

A young New Jersey woman describes the trials and tribulations of her childhood struggle against the female sex role.

I grew up on a suburban dead-end street, just two short blocks, where all the other kids my age were boys. Until I started kindergarten, I wasn't really sure there were any other girls in the world.

Naturally I became a tomboy. Like all the boys down the street, I had a lot of toy trucks and fire engines, a fire helmet, a tricycle, and some guns. Later, a ball and bat and a basketball, things like that. I was one of the fellows. I got dirty. I got my clothes torn. I even had a few fights. Once I broke my arm in a game of cops and robbers.

Maybe it was the broken arm that scared my mother. Or maybe it was just the matter of going to school and growing up. At any rate, my parents started to worry about me. All of a sudden they were trying to turn me into a "lady."

One Christmas I wanted a set of racing cars, but I didn't get it. My mother wanted me to get interested in doll houses, stuffed animals, sewing, and cooking sets. I came home one day covered with dirt and with my legs scratched up from playing football—and my mother was as angry as I've ever seen her. She said if I ever played any kind of sports with boys again, I could just start looking for another home—with somebody who didn't mind that the whole world considered me crazy.

They finally convinced me that a tomboy is a freak of nature and a disgrace to her family. Or maybe it was the other girls in school, who also thought I was strange. Probably both. By the time I started high school, I was as quiet, dainty, and ladylike as any girl you ever saw. You would never have guessed that, allowed to go my own way, I would probably have been trying out for the football team. Or maybe going to a school for racing drivers, if there is such a thing.

often in conflict with their individual temperaments or preferences'' (Weitzman, 1975b). This section of the chapter discusses the special problems that the traditional sex roles create for women. The following section gives equal attention to the problems they create for men.

The Age-old Game of Putting Women Down

In almost all societies throughout history, playing the feminine role has meant accepting an inferior status. The United States, from the very beginning, has been no exception. In the colonial days of our nation, there were far more men than women among

the early settlers (Stencel, 1979). Yet neither the scarcity of available wives nor the housewife's enormous economic contributions in those days ''seem to have given her any substantial status or authority.'' Indeed the husband had all the legal power, including control of any personal property the wife might possess. The husband could apprentice the children as he saw fit, even over the wife's objections, and could decree in his will where they would go after his death (Crosbie, 1976).

The law that prevailed in most colonies and states until the middle of the nineteenth century even exempted a husband from any prosecution for beating his wife, provided only that the beating did not endanger her

Library of Congress

Some of the forerunners of today's women's liberation movement.

life. The nation did not regard women to be capable of voting until the Nineteenth Amendment took effect in 1920. (The Declaration of Independence proclaimed only that "all men are created equal," begging the question of women's position in the emerging nation.)

Language patterns handed down from the past clearly reflect the low status of females. Fourth of July orators extol the virtues of our forefathers, making no mention of our foremothers, and many similar examples are common in everyday speech:

> When a woman marries, the couple is pronounced "man (the human being)" and "wife (the possession of the man)." . . . When a woman goes to work she is part of "manpower." If she is injured on the job she is entitled to "workman's compensation." If she is physically abused she is "manhandled." . . . Daily, women open letters addressed to "Dear Sir." They are called "gals" or "girls" by their employers until they are in their eighties. . . . If they do something dumb, they are told they behaved "just like a woman." If they say

something intelligent, they are told they "think just like a man."

(Allen, 1980)

Equal Jobs, Unequal Pay

In employment women have made notable strides in recent years. During the 1970s many moved into jobs where only a few had worked in previous years—for example, into work as accountants, computer scientists, operations researchers, insurance agents and brokers, and sales representatives for manufacturers. The number holding administrative and managerial posts rose from 1.4 million to 3.2 million (Department of Labor, 1983). Some of the largest gains, in percentage, are shown in Table 3–1.

In all positions of high prestige and salary, however, women are still greatly outnumbered by men. They are in the majority only in the less highly regarded professions that pay less—as librarians, registered nurses, social workers, and elementary schoolteachers—and in clerical and service work. The

Table 3–1

Some Big Job Gains for Women

OCCUPATION	1972	1981	PERCENT-AGE INCREASE
Engineers	9,000	68,000	656
Lawyers	12,000	79,000	558
Carpenters	5,000	21,000	320
Police officers	11,000	29,000	164
Pharmacists	16,000	39,000	144
Physicians	34,000	62,000	82
College teachers	130,000	206,000	58

In recent years the number of women in professional and skilled jobs—many of them once considered open only to men—has risen dramatically. Shown here is a representative sample *(Department of Labor, 1983)*.

five jobs at which the largest numbers of women are employed are secretary, bookkeeper, sales clerk, cashier, and waitress.

In earnings, women continue to lag far behind. In 1982 the median* salary of women employed full time was $13,600, for men $21,600 (Department of Labor, 1983). Thus women earned only 63 percent as much as men, a figure that has risen only slightly in the last twenty years. An explanation comes from another recent study, which found

> that employed women work fewer hours than men, even if both hold full-time jobs; that adult women are clustered, in higher proportion than men, in lower paying occupational categories; and that even within the same broad occupational category (e.g., the professions, sales jobs) women earn less than men
>
> *(Greenberger and Steinberg, 1983)*.

---

*The median is the halfway point. Half of all employed women earn less and half earn more.

Should men be paid more than women? Many companies seem to think so. There is a general belief among employers, who are mostly male, that women workers are less reliable than men. Women are supposed to be less interested in their jobs and inclined to loaf, waste time at the water cooler, call in sick, and quit to get married or have babies. But a study found that women actually work harder than men, putting in an average of about 12 percent more effort. They take less time away from the job on such interruptions as coffee breaks, talking, and getting back late from lunch—35 minutes a day compared with 52 minutes for men (Institute for Social Research, 1977). It has also been found that women, rather than losing more days because of illness than men, have an absentee rate that is if anything slightly lower (Suelzle, 1970).

The Psychological Putdown

To the 43 million women who hold jobs and especially the 6 million who support themselves and children under eighteen years old (Department of Labor, 1983), the unequal pay standards are a serious handicap. Another aspect of being female burdens every woman whether she works or not. This is the fact that the feminine role is frequently viewed with disrespect and even contempt. To be feminine may mean to be warm and nurturing, even ''sweet'' and lovable, but it also, in the eyes of society as a whole, means to be helpless, flighty, unpredictable, and more than a little bit silly.

How many cartoons have you seen in which women faint at the sight of a tiny mouse, run their automobiles into trees, or make stupid remarks about football and baseball? In the comic strips, how many times have you seen Blondie go berserk at a bargain sale, spend too much time dressing for a party, or hopelessly mismanage the family checking account? Of course Dagwood does some pretty dumb things himself. Americans have the fortunate gift of laughing at everything, including themselves. But society seems to laugh at women more than at men, and often in less kindly and forgiving fashion.

Most of the people who create the nation's humor are men, socialized into the masculine role, and the masculine role has traditionally included a certain amount of contempt for women: "A tendency to disparage women and female things is built into masculinity" (Skolnick and Skolnick, 1974).

Some dramatic evidence of this male attitude comes from a study in which fraternity men at a Southwestern university were asked to compare the two sexes. Most of the men agreed that women are just as intelligent, imaginative, and responsible, but in most other respects they took a very dim view of females. By substantial majorities, ranging from 64 to 83 percent, they maintained that women demand more attention, complain more, and are more concerned about "keeping up with the Joneses," more vicious in gossiping about other people, less capable at financial matters, less stable, and less logical (Ross and Walters, 1973).

The Female Inferiority Complex

As a result of the psychological putdown, many females have a built-in inferiority complex. This can be observed even among small children. In a study that asked kindergarten pupils which of their parents was smarter, over half the little girls replied that naturally their fathers were more intelligent (Ollison, 1975). Later, as the years pass, girls tend to move even more toward an increasing esteem for males and a lower opinion of themselves (Mendelsohn and Dobie, 1970).

By adolescence the female inferiority complex is well established. A study in Baltimore found that fully 71 percent of high school boys considered it "great" to be a male, but only 54 percent of the girls felt that good about being a female. The girls were much more inclined to be self-conscious, worry about their appearance, and have a low opinion of themselves. The study concluded that during the teen years "boys feel more favorable about being a member of their own sex and they certainly do not wish to behave like the less favored sex." On the other hand many high school girls "view their own sex with displeasure," and far more of them sometimes try to act like males, perhaps out of envy (Simons and Rosenberg, 1975).

By the time women enter college, many of them have learned to expect the worst. College women seem to have lower expectations than men about not only their class work but their future life in general (Frieze, 1975). When they do succeed, as when they make a good grade, they cannot bring themselves to believe they earned or deserved it. When they fail, even if through no fault of their own, their lack of self-confidence leads them to take the full blame and feel miserable (Tavris and Offir, 1977).

On Being Young and Beautiful

Another problem created by the feminine role can best be introduced by citing an experiment in which college men were asked to judge the quality of an essay supposedly written by another student. Some of the men were led to believe that the author was an extremely attractive woman, others that the author was a woman who was not at all attractive. A third group was told only that the author was a woman but nothing about her appearance. How do you suppose they graded the woman's essay? You would be right if you guessed that they gave the highest marks when they thought the author was attractive, the lowest when they thought she was unattractive, and in-between marks when they knew nothing about her appearance (Landy and Sigall, 1973).

Of course physical attractiveness plays a part in all human relationships, regardless of sex. As you know if you have taken a psychology course, most of us tend to form an immediately favorable opinion of attractive people and assume that they have many other good qualities besides their looks (Berscheid and Walster, 1978). But attractiveness is considered far more essential for women than for men. As one psychoanalyst has put it:

> As a rule, men don't have to be physically attractive to succeed in life. But . . . the male sex has imposed standards of attractiveness on females that do not apply to men themselves—thereby adding still another hardship and handicap, . . . It is young women, not young men, who straighten their hair, paint their faces, pin back their ears by surgery, and discard their glasses. . . . The fact that the Hollywood standard is not reachable by most women only adds to the self-hate which most women feel while growing up.
>
> *(Seidenberg, 1973)*

Even "those rare women who happen to look like the current beauty ideal feel insecure about their looks . . . [and] great beauties are notoriously afraid of aging" (Stannard, 1973). Indeed society seems to set a double standard for the sexes on the matter of age as well as looks. Women are considered old long before men. The emphasis on youth and beauty makes many women, as they move into middle age, "experience anxiety and a sense of diminished self-esteem" (Bell, 1970).

The Perils of Being Passive and Dependent

Besides asking women to be young and beautiful, the traditional sex role calls for them to be passive, dependent, and thoroughly reconciled to an inferior status in society. The feminine woman is not supposed to be ambitious or competitive. True, starting in her teens she is permitted and even encouraged to compete against other females for the attention of males, but she is not expected to engage in any other kind of rivalry. In particular, though she can compete *for* males, she must never even dream of competing *against* them. Being a winner—though an essential ingredient of the masculine role—is foreign to the feminine role.

Being so sweetly passive has some grave psychological dangers. The feminine role discourages women from becoming self-reliant and expressing their own personalities (Block, Von Der Lippe, and Block, 1973). Indeed Alexandra Symonds, a psychoanalyst, has pointed out that the "compliant, dependent, self-effacing personality" prescribed by the feminine role is likely to be accompanied by "neurotic needs and vulnerabilities" (1974). An especially unfortunate case she encountered is reported in the box on *Opinions and Experiences,* which will serve as an eloquent summary of the problems that the traditional sex roles can create for women.

HOW THE SEX ROLES CREATE PROBLEMS FOR MEN

The difficulties attached to the traditional feminine role have produced bitter complaints for many years. Much less has been said and written about men. But sociologists are well aware that the traditional masculine

Opinions and Experiences

A YOUNG WOMAN DOOMED BY THE ROLE SHE LEARNED

A psychoanalyst describes a young woman caught in the trap of the dependency into which she had been socialized.

Ellen, an intelligent girl who did well in school and had a special interest in art, was faced with the choice of colleges. At one college she would be able to continue in art, but would not know any of the students. At the other college the art courses were poor, but her boyfriend would be there. He was a boy she had clung to almost all through high school but whom she did not really love. They fought constantly but stayed together because Ellen was afraid to be alone and on her own.

I saw in this young girl all the signs of how her life would develop over the next ten years.

She distrusted her own judgment, was terrified of being alone, and considered having a boyfriend far more important than anything else. She would no doubt marry this boy or someone like him, place all her expectations in his achievements, and expect him to take care of her, and repay her for her unlived life. . . .

[She would] be an unhappy, angry, critical wife and mother; all of this to avoid the path of self-sufficiency, independence, and the discovery of her own identity. I have seen many women and girls enmeshed in this sequence, and it is a sad waste of human life. Everyone suffers, not only the depressed, angry, dependent woman but her husband, her children, and everyone else who becomes involved.

Reprinted with permission of the publisher, Agathon Press, Inc., from Symonds, Alexandra, The liberated woman: Healthy and neurotic. *American Journal of Psychoanalysis*, 1974, 34, 177–83.

standard also presents its difficulties, and they have become increasingly concerned with the fact that sex-role socialization may create heavier burdens for men than most people have ever stopped to think:

> There has been a growing awareness that the traditional pattern of sex-role differentiation has costs for men as well as women. . . . It is a strain to have to act tougher, stronger, more dominant, and more competent than one really is inside. It is also a strain to have one's masculine status constantly dependent on success at work and providing well for a family of dependents.
>
> *(Skolnick and Skolnick, 1974)*

The problems for males begin in early childhood. The traditional standards hold that it is shameful for a male to be "tied to his mother's apron strings." Yet in childhood boys as well as girls are closely bound to the strings, for the mother, or some other caretaker who is almost always a woman, is the most important person in the baby's life.

For girls, the strings are viewed as appropriate. But boys must somehow break away, and the break does not come easy:

> There is a good deal of evidence that girls have an easier time learning their feminine identity than boys do learning a masculine one. . . . The girl becomes a woman just by growing up, but the little boy becomes a man by proving to himself and to others that he isn't female.
>
> *(Skolnick and Skolnick, 1974)*

Proving One's Manhood

From the beginning, and continuing throughout life, boys have to demonstrate that they are strong, independent, competitive, and aggressive: "The real man must prove his masculinity" by facing and succeeding in all kinds of "financial, intellectual, sexual, and physical tests" (Stevens, 1974). At different ages and in different subcultures, the tests may vary. Boys may have to prove themselves by being athletic or by being tough, men by making a lot of money or by being a man's man in whatever way this is defined by their associates. But in one way or another the burden of proof is always present.

At many levels of our society, especially among the college educated, being a successful breadwinner often means a constant and painful struggle to get ahead in the world. Masculinity is measured in economic terms: a good job, a high salary. Men often become embroiled in this struggle, work hard at it, and deny themselves leisure and pleasures in their effort to get to the top, without ever asking whether this single-minded pursuit of success is in tune with their own innermost feelings and needs. They do what the masculine role says they should do, and they sometimes discover that their achievements, however impressive to others, give them very little personal satisfaction or sense of self-fulfillment (Zinberg, 1973).

The Trouble with "Playing It Cool"

Also built into the masculine role is a stern requirement to be totally logical. Males are supposed to be cool and rational, analyze their problems as dispassionately as computers, and act from their heads and not from their hearts. They are not supposed to get rattled, be emotional, or show any signs of fear. "Flighty" behavior is strictly for women.

But emotions cry out for expression, and the feelings that men most carefully hide—their tender and vulnerable feelings—are as powerful as any others. Suppressing them poses a double difficulty. In the first place, emotions are a natural part of the human makeup, and any command to sacrifice them is in effect a command "to transcend your humanity." In the second place, the attempt is doomed to failure anyway: "Since it is impossible to program out all emotions, even the most extreme he-man can only approximate the stereotype" (Stevens, 1974). Thus every man—aware of the stirrings of the softer and weaker side he tries so dutifully to hide—is bound to have some secret fears about his own masculinity.

"Playing it cool" can also be a serious barrier to relationships with the opposite sex, especially to any kind of satisfactory adjustment to companionship marriage. The demands that society now places on men in this regard are hopelessly inconsistent. On the one hand men are taught that "to be masculine is to be inexpressive," in other words, that they must either censor out any emotions or hide them from the world. On the other hand companionship marriage requires them to show and share affection, which in turn requires "the ability to communicate and express feelings" (Balswick and Peek, 1971). This is almost as impossible as being at the same time good-natured and cranky, or happy and sad.

Indeed the demands on men to be inexpressive tend to deny them close relationships of any kind, even with other men:

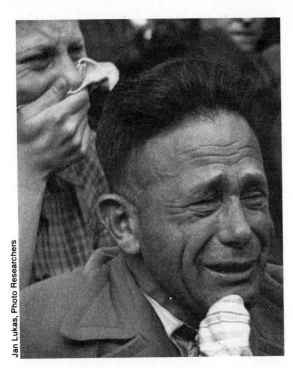

Men *do* have emotions—and sometimes display them despite all the rules of masculinity.

Men joke . . . with each other about masculine fears and feelings of inadequacy, but they rarely express their personal feelings directly. . . . Intimacy which is not hidden behind aggressive and competitive behavior is avoided, and when it occurs observers often wonder about homosexuality. Women, relatively free of this accusation, and usually less emotionally constipated than men, can at least relate to each other; men are prohibited from relating to anybody.

(Stevens, 1974)

For an interesting (and sad) comment from a man who discovered very late in life that he had many acquaintances but few friends, see *Opinions and Experiences.*

The Burden of Being Superior

If the masculine role has its drawbacks, it would also seem to have at least one clearcut advantage. Men are socialized to regard themselves as the superior sex, and surely superior is better. Or, on second thought, is it? As an approach to this question, you should read the box titled *An attack on male superiority* before going on to the next paragraph.

Most students who encounter the words in the box for the first time are thoroughly surprised to learn they were written not in these days of women's liberation but more than a century ago, and not by a woman but by a man. If you too were startled, let the feeling subside. Then, once you have got used to the idea, take another look at the last sentence in the box.

Many social scientists have pondered the question of how men are affected by being placed in a position of superiority "without any merit or any exertion" of their own. The answer seems to be that, while the superior status has its obvious advantages, it can also be a burden. Robert Seidenberg, a psychoanalyst, has made these observations (1973):

Ironically, it is quite probable that men become victims of their own advantages. An unearned superiority is thrust upon them. This places a constant burden of proof upon them which causes distortions of character and personality which are tragic to behold. The man is placed, often through no need or desire of his own, in a position of proving why he, of two people, should automatically be the standard bearer of the family. Often, to prove his doubtful superiority, he must resort to psuedo self-enhancement such as uncalled-for bravery, cunning, tricks, and outmoded feats of

Opinions and Experiences

"WHERE ARE MY FRIENDS NOW?"

A Chicago businessman, a year after retiring from his job, describes his surprising discovery about his life as one of the most popular members of his firm.

I'm gregarious. I've always been gregarious. My wife too. There have been very few evenings in our life when we sat down alone to dinner. We always had people in or we were out in a group, at somebody else's house or a restaurant.

I've been a golfer all my life and I spent my weekends at the club. I had lots of golfing companions. Afterward we played bridge or stood at the bar playing liar's poker, and then our wives joined us for dinner, eight or more of us at the table.

When I traveled, I never lacked for companionship at the end of the day. I could always round up a group to meet for drinks, eat, and knock around for the evening. I never once, when I was on the road, sat down for a meal alone. In fact I feel uncomfortable without at least a half dozen people around.

Two things have happened to me. One is that I've got a bad shoulder and can't play golf any more. The other is being out of the business world. I didn't realize how many of my friendships were based on my job. That's what we fellows had in common. We had the same business interests. We could do each other favors. We talked the same language.

If you ask me where my friends are now, I have to say that I don't know. They gradually dropped out. Oh, I see some of them once in a while. But not very often. My wife and I are pretty much alone now.

At first I was angry with my old friends. I thought, why did they drop me? Except for golf, I haven't changed. Why should a man become a social leper just because he doesn't go to the office every day?

Then I began to realize that I've done the same thing, many and many a time. My friends were always business associates. When I changed jobs, I changed friends. Especially—and I'm ashamed of this, now that I think about it—every time I moved up the ladder. When an old friend couldn't keep up with me, in salary or title, I didn't find him very attractive any more. I was living in a different pasture.

I guess that's the way it goes. I did it and now it's been done to me.

courage. . . . Men ultimately suffer the corruption of unearned victories and ascendancy. Their personalities become warped by the myth of their own dominance and superiority.

Can it really be just as burdensome to be superior as to be inferior? Certainly there is evidence that many men, pushed by the demand to prove themselves, set goals in life that they cannot possibly attain. One study of male seniors in a Midwestern university, for example, found that many of them planned high-level and difficult careers even though they had not done well in their classes and had not received much encouragement from their teachers, counselors, or friends. Since their ambitions apparently exceeded their abilities, the study concluded, these men ran a considerable risk of "dissatisfaction and frustration with their chosen careers" (Stake and Levitz, 1979).

CHANGE, TURMOIL, AND NEW OPPORTUNITY

The idea of male superiority, of course, is now being challenged as never before in our society's history. Indeed, many forces push

Opinions and Experiences

AN ATTACK ON "MALE SUPERIORITY"

The following are some famous words written about the assumption that all men, because they are male, are better than all women. As you read them, try to guess who the author may have been. Perhaps one of the leaders of today's women's liberation movement?

All the selfish propensities, the self-worship, the unjust self-preference, which exist among mankind, have their root in . . . the relation between men and women. Think of what it is to be a boy, to grow up to manhood in the belief that without any merit or any exertion of his own, though he may be the most frivolous and empty or the most ignorant and stolid of mankind, by the mere fact of being born a male he is by right the superior of all and every one of an entire half of the human race. . . .

Even if in his whole conduct he habitually follows a woman's guidance, still, if he is a fool, he thinks that of course she is not and cannot be equal in ability and judgment to himself. . . . If he is not a fool, he does worse—he sees that she is superior to him, and believes that, notwithstanding her superiority, he is entitled to command and she is bound to obey. What must be the effect on his character?

Believe it or not, the words were written by John Stuart Mill, a British philosopher, in 1869. Reprinted from his Three Essays, *London: Oxford University Press, 1966, pp. 522–23.*

us in a very different direction from the traditional sex roles. One such force is the educational system, in which females and males sit side by side as equals in the classroom, learning the same things and being graded by the same standards. Another is the vast migration of women into the occupational world. Still another is that giant leap in marriage "from institution to companionship."

The signs of change are all around us. The status of females is different from what it was at the start of the century, even from what it was a mere decade ago. In great numbers, people are questioning sex-role standards once considered graven in stone. Today's college women take a more liberated view than their mothers—and a much more liberated view than their grandmothers—on such issues as education, jobs, freedom, independence, dating practices, and marital relationships (Slevin and Wingrove, 1983). The trend toward liberalized views began in the 1960s, picked up speed in the 1970s, and has continued in the present decade (Thornton, Alwin, and Camburn, 1983).

Men as well as women have changed their attitudes (Gallagher, 1979), and in many ways the two sexes have begun to think in terms of the likenesses between them rather than the differences. A survey of 4,600 students at Eastern colleges found that both women and men were interested in having a successful career but also in close family ties. Both placed "time with spouse" at the top of their list of life priorities, and a third of them said they would prefer not to work, if possible, while their children were under five. In general the two sexes seemed "very similar in life goals, career values, and self-concepts," indicating that we may be "entering a new era with a dramatic convergence in the goals and attitudes of women and men'' (Zuckerman, 1984).

This is a confusing period, however, and we all are pulled in different directions by the conflicting attitudes that exist side by side in today's world. Both men and women display many inconsistencies in their views and behavior as they vacillate between old but not yet completely discarded roles and new but not yet thoroughly established roles. Though the two sexes now look at each other differently, they still do not know quite what to make of what they see. It is not at all surprising that people are plagued by disorganization, confusion, and a great deal of self-doubt. Yet the transition is under way, leading to standards and roles that none of us can as yet foresee.

The Female Status: Going Up

At this point in the transition period, how much has the status of women changed in our society? The people best qualified to answer that question would appear to be women themselves—and it turns out that a majority, though only a bare majority, now believe they enjoy more esteem as individuals in their own right than they did in the past. Figure 3–1 illustrates the results of a 1980 public opinion poll on this point. The figure also presents the results of a similar poll taken in 1970, when considerably fewer women felt their position in society had improved.

It is important to note, however, that the 1980 poll showed about one woman in five convinced that females receive less respect today than in the past. The responses of these women indicate a considerable dissatisfaction with the present situation. This dissatisfaction undoubtedly stems in part from some of the matters mentioned earlier in the

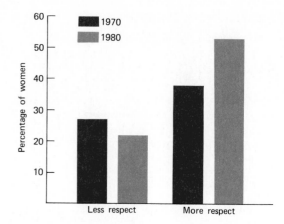

Figure 3–1
HOW WOMEN THINK
SOCIETY TREATS THEM
In polls taken a decade apart, American women were asked whether they felt females were "looked on with more respect as individual human beings" than ten years earlier. In 1970, only 38 percent of women agreed; by 1980 this number had grown to a majority. The percentage who felt women enjoyed less respect than in the past showed a drop. The figures do not add up to 100 percent because a substantial number of women—21 percent in 1980—felt the situation had not changed (adapted from Roper, 1980).

chapter, for example, unequal pay scales and the continuing psychological putdown that women often suffer. It may also stem in part from increased expectations on the part of today's women. Having tasted some of the fruits of improved status in society, they may find it difficult to be content with what still seems a meager share.

As to how much the status of women actually improved, if at all, there is simply no way to make any kind of accurate measurement. It is worthy of note, however, that young women today appear to have higher career ambitions than in the past, which may indicate a growing belief that some of the barriers against women are breaking down. Women college students began to outnumber men in 1979 and have been increasing their lead ever since (Bureau of the Census, 1984d). Women have been starting their own business firms at a "phenomenal rate," to the point where more than 3 million of them are now owners or sole proprietors (Naisbitt, 1982).

Further change seems to be on the way, for most Americans now favor, or at least say they favor, a higher status for women. If anyone might be expected to object, it would logically be men, eager to preserve their position of dominance and superiority. Yet, as Figure 3-2 shows, about two men out of three say they support change and improvement, and only about one in four expresses opposition. The figures for women are almost exactly the same: 64 percent in favor

One of the women who now make up half of all the enrollment in medical schools.

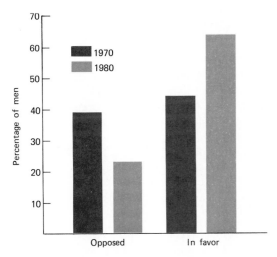

Figure 3-2
HOW MEN FEEL ABOUT WOMEN'S RIGHTS
In a 1980 poll, nearly two-thirds of American men said they favored "efforts to strengthen and change women's status in society"—up from a minority just a decade earlier. Only about one out of four said they opposed such efforts—down from about two out of five in 1970. The figures do not add up to 100 because some men in both polls said they were not sure (Roper, 1980).

and 24 percent opposed, with the rest undecided.

It may strike you as strange that a substantial minority of women would be against change, but it must be remembered that some of the most impassioned opposition to the liberation movement and the Equal Rights Amendment has come from women who believe on religious or philosophical grounds that the traditional sex roles and status are the natural order of things, or who, happy with their present lifestyle, believe that any change would do them more harm than good. The number of women opposed to change is considerably smaller among those under thirty (16 percent), the college educated (18 percent), and black women of all ages (14 percent).

Masculinity, Femininity, and Androgyny

To what extent have society's attitudes toward sex roles changed? Where do they stand at this point in the transition period? Some answers to these questions have been provided by a test devised by Sandra Bem, a social psychologist, to measure how people rate according to the conventional standards of masculinity and femininity.

When 2,000 students in junior colleges and universities took the Bem test in the 1970s, about a third of the men scored as definitely masculine and about a third of the women as clearly feminine. Some students scored in the near-masculine or near-feminine range. A few—less than 10 percent—wound up on the "wrong" side of the dividing point; that is, a few male students had feminine scores, and a few women had masculine scores. Nearly a third of both sexes showed a nearly even balance between masculine and feminine, or a neutral score. These students were classified as *androgynous*—a word that derives from a combination of the Greek *andros,* for man, and *gyne,* for woman.

The androgynous students, both male and female, had some of the personality traits that have traditionally been considered characteristic of men and others considered characteristic of women. In some situations they acted in typically masculine ways, in others in typically feminine ways. They would have been hard to tell apart on the basis of their behavior and interests.

Bem believes that androgynous people probably enjoy better mental health because they can be more flexible in dealing with the many kinds of situations that life and human relations are likely to present from time to

time. When circumstances dictate, they can be gentle, understanding, and sensitive to the needs of others, that is, feminine. When it seems desirable, they can be forceful, self-sufficient, and willing to take risks, that is, masculine.

A study of college women has found higher levels of self-esteem among those who scored as androgynous on the Bem test than those who scored as feminine (Kimlicka, Cross, and Tarnai, 1983). Another study, this one of high school seniors, showed greater self-esteem for both females and males classified as androgynous (Lamke, 1982).

Push-Pull between Old and New

The number of college women classed as androgynous grew rapidly in the 1960s. College men were later to start but caught up in the 1970s and are now generally more androgynous than women (Heilbrun and Schwartz, 1982). The high figures today are dramatic evidence of how rapidly sex roles have been changing. If a representative group of older people took the test, they would undoubtedly show far more men high in masculinity, far more women high in femininity, and not nearly so many in the androgynous range.

Making the choice between masculinity, femininity, and androgyny is not easy. It is particularly troublesome for the young. Reggie Gray (1979), a social worker who has done considerable counseling among young women aged 16 to 20, has found that many of them are thoroughly confused by "growing up in a society of contradictory messages" in which "new concepts of a socially acceptable woman's role," with new definitions of "right and wrong, good and bad, ladylike and unladylike," continue to "coexist with the more traditional views."

These young women are likely to view the

emergence of new roles for females as a great opportunity but also as a threat, since it seems to pose the danger of ''direct competition with men,'' the possibility that success in the competition will result in being criticized and shunned not only by men but by other women, and doubts and uncertainties about ''giving up the protected, secure, and familiar traditional position of women.''

For teenage women, living through what is at best a difficult period of search for self-identity, the strain of making the choice adds another burden to the usual ''insecurity, loneliness, anxiety, chaos, and confusion'' (Gray, 1979). Adolescent boys, also struggling to attain self-identity, undoubtedly suffer in a similar way from the push-pull between old roles and new.

The roles into which we are socialized, or which we choose to adopt after much conflict and soul searching, help determine our conduct from childhood to the grave. They influence our expectations of other people and what other people expect from us. Moreover the roles played by women and men intermesh and interact. Any change in the female role inevitably affects the attitudes and behavior—indeed, the very lives—of men. Any change in the male role is bound to affect the attitudes, behavior, and lives of women (Harrison, 1978). Thus, the sex roles—old, new, or in between—shape all our relationships with members of the opposite sex and our entire approach to the institution of marriage and the family. The next chapter discusses the way the changing roles operate for better or worse among husbands and wives.

SUMMARY

1. Our society and most others have assumed that men and women are different and should behave accordingly. Men have been expected to be masculine and self-reliant and women to be feminine and dependent.

2. In part the differences between the sexes depend on biological factors: the X–X (female) or X–Y (male) chromosome pairs we inherit, and the resulting differences in the body's supply of the hormones called *estrogens* (female) and *androgens* (male). Mostly the differences are learned through socialization, for parents tend to treat boys and girls differently, and expect them to act differently, from birth on.

3. Evidence of the importance of socialization comes from studies of other societies where both women and men act feminine, or both act masculine, or the women are highly masculine by our standards and the men are highly feminine. Evidence also comes from studies of *hermaphrodites,* or people born with some of the external sexual characteristics of both sexes. Those who were actually X–X female but brought up as boys behaved in a masculine fashion. Those who were actually X–Y male but brought up as girls acted feminine.

4. Our society, like most throughout history, has accorded males a higher *status,* or position in society, than females.

5. A person in a particular status is expected to behave accordingly—to act out the *role* that society considers appropriate. All of us are under considerable pressure for the proper performance of the role assigned to us.

6. Until recently in the United States, the female and male roles were sharply differentiated and children were socialized accordingly. The ''feminine'' woman grew up expecting to be a passive, dependent, nurturing housewife and mother. The masculine man expected to be the strong, independent provider, protector, and boss.

7. These traditional sex roles have now been challenged, but socialization continues in many ways to follow the pattern of the past. Even parents who believe the two sexes should be treated equally still tend to fall into many habits that differentiate between girls and boys, beginning in the cradle.

8. Many other influences on socialization—for example, toys, tv shows, and teachers—also tend to follow the traditional pattern. Children get the message early, and even preschoolers seem to be asking, "How feminine am I?" or "How masculine am I?"

9. In adulthood even women who have become ardent advocates of liberation may think or act in a feminine way almost as if by reflex. Even men who heartily approve of the liberation movement are bound to show lingering traces of masculine standards.

10. Traditional socialization is likely "to be an anxiety-producing process for boys and girls because it requires them both to conform to rigid sex-role standards in conflict with their individual preferences."

11. Some of the chief problems the traditional sex roles create for women are these:

a. They assign women an inferior status. Women suffer a psychological putdown that may result in a lifelong inferiority complex.

b. Working women hold few positions of high prestige and salary, and they earn only 63 percent as much as men.

c. Along with the feminine role goes a demand to be young and beautiful—a standard that does not apply to men.

d. The "compliant, self-effacing personality" expected of women tends to produce "neurotic needs and vulnerabilities."

12. The chief problems for men are these:

a. Men have to prove their masculinity by passing all kinds of "financial, intellectual, sexual, and physical tests."

b. The demand to "play it cool"—suppressing any tender and vulnerable feelings—denies the importance of emotions and creates a barrier to personal relationships, especially with a woman.

c. The assumption that men are superior to women imposes "a constant burden of proof" that causes "distortions of character and personality."

13. The traditional sex roles are now being seriously challenged by such developments as equal education for the sexes, the move of women into the work force, and companionship marriage. New ideas of equality have emerged, making this a confusing period of transition in which both sexes are pressured by new and old.

14. Today, women and men may both be highly masculine, highly feminine, or in between. Especially among the young, many now can be classed as *androgynous,* meaning that sometimes they act in feminine ways and sometimes in masculine ways. Androgynous people seem to enjoy better mental health because they are more flexible. Depending on circumstances, they can be gentle, understanding, and sensitive to the needs of others, or forceful, self-sufficient, and willing to take risks.

DISCUSSION QUESTIONS

1. If you wanted to avoid socializing a child into a female or male role, how would you go about it?

2. What if anything could our society do to increase the number of women in occupations of high prestige, power, and pay?

3. In what ways have you observed that females are encouraged to be concerned about their physical appearance?

4. In families you know, how much time do fathers spend with their young children?

5. Have you observed any differences between men who seem to follow the traditional masculine sex role and men who do not?

6. Discuss ways in which changes in the role of men have affected the role of women, and vice versa.

7. Have you observed any differences in the ways people talk and act toward girl babies and boy babies?

CHAPTER 4

Roles in Marriage: Harmony or Clash

There is a popular notion that any two people can have a deliriously happy marriage if only they are head over heels in love with each other. The widespread appeal of the idea is demonstrated by the romantic legend of Cinderella, which, in one version or another, has been handed down for countless generations in societies almost the world over. The poor little stepdaughter, forced to toil as a humble servant to her wicked family, meets the handsome and gallant Prince Charming. They fall in love.

No matter that Cinderella has been socialized to feel at home among the kitchen ashes, seems never to have spent a day at school, and would have no idea how to behave in the pomp and circumstance of the royal court. No matter that Prince Charming has grown up in an entirely different culture and acquired its education, tastes, and manners. No matter that the two of them know nothing about each other's attitudes toward the proper roles for wives and husbands. No matter that all they have in common is the glass slipper and the foot that fits it. Love conquers all and they live happily ever after.

Cinderella is a delightful story and probably all of us believe in it a little, even though we are long since past the innocent and trusting days of childhood. At least we would like to believe it. If you are a woman, what

could be nicer than to be whisked off by a Prince Charming into happy-ever-after land? If you are a man, what could be more welcome than the one woman in the land with glass-slipper perfection?

Alas, things do not work out that way in real life. We marry not mythical Prince Charmings and Cinderellas but other human beings very much like ourselves. Our partners, like us, have their faults as well as their virtues, their good points and their bad. Above all, they have their own firm attitudes about the way people should behave, both in general and in the marriage relationship. How well the marriage turns out has little to do with royal blood or shoe size. It depends to a large extent on the roles that we and our partners have learned or decided to play, the roles we expect our partners to play, and the question of whether these roles and role expectations harmonize or clash.

ARE THE TWO SEXES MOVING CLOSER TOGETHER OR FARTHER APART?

The traditional sex roles, though they may have limited the opportunities for really close relationships between the two sexes, also minimized the danger of clash. The matter of how to behave in marriage, and what to expect from your partner, was predetermined. Both partners were socialized to play by the rules of the institutional marriage. If they were unhappy with this arrangement, their quarrel was more with the institution of marriage than with each other.

Today the situation is altogether different. Although some people are still highly masculine or feminine by traditional standards, others have moved all the way to total androgyny, recognizing no differences at all in the way men and women should behave or be treated. What happens if a highly feminine woman falls in love with a man who has embraced androgyny and wants no part of the traditional masculine role? Or if a thoroughly masculine man falls in love with a woman who refuses to play the feminine role?

There are also many people who fall somewhere in between all-out masculinity or femininity and all-out androgyny. These men and women have rejected some parts of their traditional sex role but still cling to others. Their view of proper behavior for the opposite sex has likewise changed to a certain extent but not in toto. There are far more possible gradations between the two extremes than any test could measure— about as many as the shades between snow white and ebony black. In addition, there are many people, confused by changing sex-role standards, who are not exactly sure about the role they want to play or expect their partner to play, and who may change their mind from time to time. Only an exceptionally lucky couple can hope to find their attitudes toward marriage roles in full agreement on every detail, and even the couple blessed with this harmony today may no longer possess it tomorrow.

Why Men Worry

Some of the best evidence of today's confusions comes from studies of Ivy League seniors made by Mirra Komarovsky in the 1970s. She found that both male and female students, by and large, had been strongly influenced by the swing from the traditional sex roles toward androgyny. In their minds, both sexes tended to believe that women deserve an equal status in society and should play a more active and independent role. In their hearts, however, they still clung to many attitudes characteristic of the traditional roles. Both the men and women expressed general agreement, for example, that the ideal male-female relationship calls for the man to be at least somewhat dominant, a little more self-assured and aggressive than the woman.

The Komarovsky studies were particularly enlightening about the doubts and worries of the male students. In theory, the men tended toward a belief that the sexes are equal. In practice, they tended to be uncomfortable in the company of women who were in fact their equals—or superiors—in intelligence and education. About 30 percent conceded that when facing such a situation they had felt intellectually insecure or under strain (Komarovsky, 1973). As a consequence some had simply decided to avoid women who threatened their egos. ("If a girl knows more than I do, I resent her." "I enjoy talking to more intelligent girls, but I have no desire for a deeper relationship with them. I guess I still believe that the man should be more intelligent.")

Other men had mixed emotions. They wanted intellectual equality and companionship with women, but at the same time they found the idea threatening. (One man conceded that the idea of intellectual equality, though attractive, made him "nervous and humble.") The strains were neatly summed up in these words by one male subject:

> Despite my egalitarian proclamations, tugging at my psychic strings is the thought that I am really most comfortable in a situation where my fragile sense of security is not threatened by a woman, where I can maintain a comfortable dominance. Thus my basic insecurity conflicts with my liberated conscience, making me feel like a double-talking hypocrite.
>
> *(Komarovsky, 1976)*

Why Women Worry

College women also have their problems. For one thing, since our society is by no means unanimous about the proper role for females, women who would like to reject the traditional role cannot help worrying about the consequences. They are bound to wonder how society in general, and men in particular, will react if they insist on being independent, ambitious, and competitive. One clear indication comes from a mid-1970s study at a New Jersey women's college noted for its strong emphasis on courses and issues related to the liberation movement. The study found, as might be expected, that a considerable majority of the women at this college were deeply convinced that a wife's career is as important as the husband's career, and that both should contribute equally to family finances. Most of the women wanted to work all through life, believed their husbands should share in the housekeeping, and had no patience with the traditional belief that "the most important thing for a woman is to be a good wife and mother." Yet, at the same time, they feared that few men would want to marry a woman who held such liberated views.

Since most of the students wanted not just a career but also marriage and children, they were caught up in uncertainty and inner conflict and appeared to be "experiencing considerable anxiety about their futures" (Parelius, 1975). Their worries were probably justified, for many men continue to dislike the idea of a wife who is dedicated to a career. A survey of college men in the early 1970s showed that more than half of them would want their wives to abandon any outside work either immediately upon marriage (13 percent) or as soon as a child was born (41 percent). Another 42 percent expected their wives to stay home and take care of the children at least through the early years. Only 4 percent were willing to have their wives pursue a career continuously (McMillin, 1972).

Roles, Privileges, and Obligations

The possibilities of conflict between the roles and role expectations of wives and husbands were first pointed out many years ago by Clifford Kirkpatrick (1963), at a time when the traditional sex roles were just beginning to be seriously challenged and marriage was starting to shift "from institution to companionship." These changes, Kirkpatrick noted, were making it increasingly possible for both sexes to choose the roles they wanted to play in marriage, but the new options gave no guarantee of harmony or happiness. Instead they might produce misunderstandings and disappointments for partners who had reached different conclusions about the roles they wanted to play and expected their partners to play.

Kirkpatrick was aware that the changing sex roles made many kinds of marriage possible—indeed that the marriages of the future might take an almost infinite number of variations. But he foresaw that marriages would more or less resemble one of three distinct types, characterized by the basic nature of the role played by the wife:

1. *The housewife-mother.* This is the traditional role, central to institutional marriage. The woman who plays the role to the hilt abandons all thought of job or career, at least after the first child is born. She goes along completely with the traditional notions of femininity. She keeps the house, takes care of the children, and provides the emotional support and encouragement that hold the family together and helps her husband work more efficiently in the outside world. In return she receives economic security, respect as a wife and mother, loyalty, and sentimental gratitude from her husband and children.

2. *The partner-wife.* This is the role associated with companionship marriage. The woman who plays the role to the hilt shares responsibility for earning a living and representing the family in the outside world. She abandons such traditional feminine privileges as chivalry and alimony in case of divorce. In return, she expects to enjoy independence and an equal voice in how the family money should be spent and the household duties divided (or perhaps turned over to paid helpers), where the family should live, and how the family should conduct its social life.

3. *The ornament-wife.* This role occurs only infrequently, but the fact that it exists at all gives it considerable influence in people's attitudes toward marriage. The ornament-wife is a product of the affluent society, found only among the very wealthy or young people not yet faced with financial responsibilities. She might best be described as a party girl or a social butterfly. In her purest form she is the pretty young wife of a rich man who provides her with a life of luxury and leisure. Like the Bible's lilies of the field, she toils not and neither does she spin. But she has one definite obligation, which is to remain eternally young, slim, bright, alert, and sexy—constant fun to be around, an ornament to be shown off to her husband's friends and business associates. Although ornament-wives are rare, they beckon seductively from the society and entertainment pages and sometimes from the movie or television screen. Everyone knows that such a role* is possible and is likely to think about it at times.

The Danger of Expecting Too Much

All three of Kirkpatrick's basic types of possible roles for wives have advantages and disadvantages. Each carries its own privileges but also its own obligations. Whichever role the wife chooses, she agrees in effect to fulfill the obligations in return for receiving the privileges. The husband, in turn, agrees in effect to play a complementary role, meeting his own obligations and enjoying his own privileges. To achieve a harmonious relationship, the partners must follow a sort of unspoken contract about the roles they will play, the roles they expect each other to play, and the rewards and duties that go along with the roles.

Yet most people, Kirkpatrick found, have a strong tendency to expect too many privileges and accept too few obligations. In sur-

*Kirkpatrick's own term for this role, coined before the phrase "from institution to companionship" became famous, was *companion wife.* We have changed his terminology because companion wife now sounds like the role associated with companionship marriage.

veys of his students he found that the women, when thinking about marriage, had a strong tendency to yearn for the advantages associated with all three possible roles. They expected to enjoy many of the privileges of not only housewife-mother but partner-wife and ornament-wife. They were not prepared, however, to meet the obligations of all three. The male students were just the opposite. They expected their future wives to fulfill at least some of the obligations of all three roles, but they were unwilling to offer the corresponding privileges. In other words the two sexes, each in different ways, seemed to want the best of all three types of marriage.

The conflicting expectations that Kirkpatrick found among his students continue to flourish today. Most people have never thought about the different types of marriage, the different roles wives and husbands can choose to play, and the privileges and obligations that go along with the roles. Thus it often happens that a woman, without ever intending to be selfish, enters marriage fully believing that she is entitled to have her husband support her (the housewife-mother's privilege). Even if she works outside the home, she may feel no real responsibility for the family finances. At the same time, even if she intends to be a full-time housewife-mother, she may still take for granted that she should enjoy independence and an equal voice in how the family spends its money and where it lives (the partner-wife's privilege). She may also expect her husband to entertain, flatter, and spoil her (the ornament-wife's privilege).

A man may hold different but also inconsistent expectations. He may want his wife

Teri Leigh Stratford

A partner-wife and her husband share some of the obligations of the two roles.

to be at the same time submissive and supporting (a housewife-mother), ready to pitch in and bolster the family budget (a partner-wife), and totally devoted to fun and games (an ornament-wife). A good example of this kind of inconsistency is presented in the box on *Opinions and Experiences,* reporting the comments of one of the Ivy League students who took part in the Mirra Komarovsky surveys. Note that this man starts out by saying he would never be satisfied by marriage to a housewife-mother and instead wants a real partner, yet goes on to demand that his future mate behave exactly like a housewife-mother.

Kirkpatrick, after pondering the conflicting expectations of his male and female students, expressed the melancholy opinion: "It is no wonder that arguments rage as to who gets cheated in marriage." Other studies have reached similar conclusions. Helena Lopata (1972a), for example, has found that in today's confusing period of transition it is highly unlikely that any two people will agree on the proper roles for husband and wife, and therefore most partners make demands on each other that are "mutually inconsistent."

Other Sources of Conflict

Even when the two partners are consistent in their attitudes toward the privileges and obligations of the roles, they face other possible sources of conflict. One, of course, is that the partners may disagree about the proper roles for husband and wife. The woman who wants to be a partner-wife with her own career may find that her husband expects her to be a housewife-mother, or the woman who has no interest in a career and wants to be a housewife-mother may find that her husband expects her to be a partner-wife.

Another possible difficulty is that circumstances may force the partners into uncongenial roles. A couple who would prefer a more or less traditional marriage, with the woman in the role of housewife-mother, may find that the wife has to take an outside job because the family needs the money. Or a couple's preference for a completely companionship marriage may be thwarted when the wife decides that she must give up her career and stay at home because she has no other way of taking care of children born early in the marriage or because she feels an obligation to be with the children.

Given the possible conflicts in roles and role expectations, it is not surprising that they are a frequent cause of dissatisfaction in marriage. Indeed the presence or absence of such conflicts seems to represent one of the chief differences between happy and unhappy marriages. One indication comes from a study that compared a group of couples whose marriages apparently were going smoothly with another group who were experiencing so many problems that they had sought counseling at the University of Pittsburgh School of Medicine (Frank, Anderson, and Rubinstein, 1980). The attitudes of these two groups toward some of the roles possible in marriage were measured by asking them whether they believed that the wife, the husband, or both should engage in such activities as the following:

Care for the home, cook, and shop.

Make major family decisions.

Have a career.

Have responsibility for care of children.

Have interests and activities that do not include spouse.

Determine how money is spent.

Opinions and Experiences

I WANT A WIFE WHO REJECTS THE PASSIVE FEMININE ROLE—AS LONG AS SHE'S JUST LIKE THE GIRL WHO MARRIED DEAR OLD DAD.

These are the words of a man who, as a college senior a few years ago, was asked what kind of wife he hoped to marry.

I would not want to marry a woman whose only goal is to become a housewife. This type of woman would not have enough bounce and zest in her. I don't think a girl has much imagination if she just wants to settle down and raise a family from the very beginning. Moreover, I want an independent girl, one who has her own interests and does not always have to depend on me for stimulation and diversion.

However, when we both agree to have children, my wife must be the one to raise them. She'll have to forfeit her freedom for the chil-

From M. Komarovsky, "Dilemmas of masculinity: A study of college youth." New York: W. W. Norton & Co., Inc., 1976

dren. I believe that, when a woman wants a child, she must also accept the full responsibility of child care. . . .

Biology makes equality impossible. Besides, the person I'll marry will want the child and will want to care for the child. Ideally, I would hope I'm not forcing her to assume responsibility for raising the children. I would hope that this is her desire and that it is the happiest thing she can do. After we have children, it will be her career that will end, while mine will support us. I believe that women should have equal opportunities in business and the professions, but I still insist that a woman who is a mother should devote herself entirely to her children (Komarovsky, 1976).

The subjects were then asked whether, in their own marriages, these things were in fact being done by the wife, by the husband, or by both.

In marriages that were going smoothly, it was found, there was substantial similarity between the partners' notions of the proper behavior for husbands and wives and the way they were in fact behaving. Among the couples who were having problems, on the other hand, there was considerable discrepancy. In other words, the partners in the troubled marriages were experiencing a good deal of conflict between their feelings about the roles and the way they were actually playing the roles, as the marriage had turned out. This difference between "happy" and "unhappy" couples was apparent for both husbands and wives but was especially characteristic of the wives.

HOUSEWIFE-MOTHER OR PARTNER-WIFE: PROS AND CONS

As in the study just cited, a number of other investigators have found that wives are especially likely—much more so than their husbands—to experience and suffer from conflicts about roles and role expectations. The reason seems to be that there is a far sharper contrast between the role of housewife-mother and the role of partner-wife than between the complementary roles played by their husbands. A woman who stays home as a housewife-mother has a very different lifestyle from the partner-wife who works at a career. In either case, however, the husband almost always spends much of his time and energy at a job of his own. His lifestyle in general is not necessarily affected very strongly by the role played by his wife.

Many women, regardless of which role they have chosen or been forced into, seem to find the role unsatisfactory and to regret the way they are living their life. One indication comes from a 1980 public opinion poll. Of the women in the survey who were not employed outside the home (and who thus were playing the role of housewife-mother) three out of every ten said they would rather be working. Of the women with full-time jobs (characteristic of the partner-wife role) exactly the same 30 percent said they would rather be staying at home (Roper, 1980). Similar results were obtained in a 1983 poll (Dowd, 1983). Perhaps these findings can be explained in part by the old adage about the greener grass on the other side of the fence. But they also reflect the fact that the two roles have a profound effect on the way a woman lives, that each has great advantages and grave disadvantages, and that having to choose between them (or being pushed into one instead of the other) can lead to serious doubts and regrets. Thus it is important to examine the pros and cons of the two roles, starting with the housewife-mother.

The Housewife-Mother's Advantages

Despite the rise in popularity of companionship marriage, the housewife-mother role is certainly not obsolete in today's society. Many women still favor it, perhaps as a result of their socialization along traditional lines, perhaps as a considered and deliberate choice. Of women of all ages and from various subcultures, surveyed in the 1983 opinion poll, a majority of 47 percent said they would rather stay home, with 45 percent preferring an outside job and the rest undecided. Of women under 45 years old the number who said they would rather stay home was smaller but still represented a substantial minority of about 40 percent.

One advantage of being a housewife-mother is that it constitutes a lifestyle for which most Americans have been prepared by the socialization process. The housewife-mother is spared the difficulty of breaking away from the traditional feminine role. Usually she has the full support and approval of her parents (or, if not her parents, at least her grandparents). Moreover, she enjoys security and the right to be supported and protected.

There is no doubt that great numbers of women find the housewife-mother role a source of considerable happiness and self-fulfillment. In an important large-scale study of housewives in the Chicago area, for example, Helena Lopata (1972a) found that many of them regarded their role as "self-expressive and creative," a chance to create a richer and more varied lifestyle than could be attained in most jobs available in the business world. They enjoyed the freedom and challenge of "being one's own boss." (As one woman put it, "A homemaker is not responsible to anyone higher up. She makes her own decisions on her own.") They thought of themselves as being high-level executives who brought a great deal of skill and learning to a job in which they functioned as business managers, dietitians, interior decorators, and often gourmet chefs. They saw their relationships with their husbands "not as a struggle for authority but as a process of developing interpersonal depth suited to the unique needs of both personalities."

As for the job of bringing up their children, they were aware of the responsibilities and worried about providing the kind of psychological environment in which the children would thrive. But they thought of motherhood as "a process requiring active leadership," a challenge to be faced and surmounted. They enjoyed warm relationships with the children and found this a source of great satisfaction. Among their triumphs they mentioned such matters as these: "Children, hearing their joys." "My biggest thrill was to hear my daughter say 'Thank you, mummy.'" "It is satisfying when you teach your child to do something and then see the progress."

All in all, Lopata found, women who enjoy the housewife-mother role are "happy that they are appreciated or needed and that the family is pleased with their efforts." Many of them are also engaged outside the home in an "expanding involvement in political, economic, religious, recreational, and educational roles." The satisfactions inside the home and the activities outside it were especially characteristic of the college women in her sample. The higher a housewife-mother's education, Lopata found, "the more convinced she is that the role calls for a great deal of knowledge and the more able she is to bring new ideas into the home and go out in search of them." The women with less education took a more restricted and less creative view. Although they were generally reconciled to their role, they found it less gratifying.

The Burden of Being Dependent

Even at best, it must immediately be added, being a housewife-mother produces problems as well as satisfactions. For one thing, the woman who assumes the role takes a high-risk gamble. Her entire way of life will depend largely on her husband. It is mostly his actions, not hers, that will determine where and how the family lives, how much money they have and how they spend it, and their status in the community. To a very considerable extent the housewife-mother gives up control over her life and places it instead in the hands of her husband, whose future is often unpredictable.

In more than half of first marriages, the husband is not yet 24 years old (Bureau of the Census, 1985). He may be just out of school or at most just getting started in today's complex and rapidly changing occupational world. There is no way of knowing how he will turn out.

No matter how well the housewife-mother thinks she knows this man on whom her fate depends, she may also be in for some surprises about his personality. The way we select our mates, as will be seen in the next chapter, often leaves us unaware of many of their traits, especially of how they will behave in the day-to-day intimacy of marriage or in reacting to an unexpected crisis. And people do change. One study of women and men, first when they were in their teens and later when they were thirty, found some truly remarkable transformations. Some of the subjects who seemed most promising at eighteen—poised, self-confident, and popular—turned out to be surprisingly disappointed and discontented, not nearly so self-fulfilled or successful as would have been expected. Some who were the most troubled, unpopular, and despondent at eighteen—including several who were expelled from school for failing grades and misbehavior—were living far richer and more productive lives than could ever have been predicted (Macfarlane, 1963).

The housewife-mother simply has to take her chances and hope for the best. The observations in the box on *Opinions and Expe-*

Opinions and Experiences

THE BRIDE DOESN'T KNOW

These observations were recorded twenty years ago but still apply to many of today's marriages.

When I hear young brides say "I do," I always admire their gallantry. Though they never seem to recognize it, they are among history's most reckless and intrepid gamblers.

What does the bride know of her future? Very little. She is putting her faith in the hands of a man who may rise to be president of a corporation or may turn out to be a chronic failure, fired from one job after another. He may buy her a fine home in the suburbs or keep her living in a rented city flat. He may even take her to live in Turkey or Tokyo. He may decide to change careers—and instead of being the wife of a businessman she may suddenly find herself the wife of a preacher, high school teacher, or army officer.

What does she really know of her husband? Not much. She has never seen him at a break-fast table, or when he was ill, or at his job, or when forced to meet a crisis. She does not really know how he prefers to spend his spare time. She does not know for sure whether he wants children, or how many, or how he would feel about disciplining them.

He may turn out to be a money-grubber who talks business during every waking hour, or he may turn out to be a charming but improvident playboy. He may take to spending his weekends on a golf course or tennis court, leaving her to fend for herself. He may acquire interesting friends or dull ones. He may prove to be sweet and easy-going or sour and hot-tempered.

Marriage counselors say that one of the most frequent complaints they hear from young wives is that sad, sad comment, "He's just not the same man I married." He is the same man, all right—but the bride didn't know it. She never really had a chance to find out.

Adapted from an unpublished report by E. Koenig, 1962.

riences no longer apply to all marriages, but they are still true for many brides.

The Burden of Housework

The role of housewife-mother has another built-in disadvantage. Though it is free from the pressure of competition, it is certainly not easy. Housewives work hard. One study found that their job keeps them busy an average of fifty-five hours a week, which is longer than their great-grandmothers worked a half century ago. True, they have more labor-saving appliances in the house than in the old days and spend less time preparing meals, but they devote more hours to their children and to such newly complicated chores as shopping for all the modern family's needs. Even the laundry takes more time today despite electric washers and driers, for families own more clothes and keep them cleaner (Vanek, 1974).

To many women the nature and demands of the job come as a shock. When they first become housewives and find themselves at home all day, they are often distressed by the extent to which they are suddenly isolated from the companionship they formerly enjoyed with fellow workers or classmates (Holmstrom, 1973). Moreover, the Lopata (1972a) study showed that more than half of them felt they had never received adequate training for the job. Many had trouble moving from the business world, where they were told what to do and when to do it, into the responsibility of having to plan, organize, and perform on their own. Once they became mothers, they were especially plagued by feelings of responsibility and being tied down.

If some women find the housewife-mother role rich in satisfactions, others find that they hate it. They do not consider themselves very good at taking care of a home. Without the social contacts and regular paychecks provided by a job, they tend to lack a sense of personal worth and accomplishment (Ferree, 1976). They are forced to judge their status in society by the position occupied by the men in their lives—their husband and their father (Van Velsor and Beeghley, 1979). Even this attempt to "borrow" status may backfire, for a woman married to a highly successful man may only feel more insignificant by comparison. Thus, as a group, housewives tend to have unusually low self-esteem (Macke, Bohrnstedt, and Bernstein, 1979).

Many sociologists have explored the complaints of unhappy housewives. These women often feel that "the low-status, technically undemanding position" of the housewife does not match their educational and intellectual attainments (Gove, 1972). They resent the monotony of their day-after-day routine of making beds, cooking, and cleaning up, and the fact that their work, because it is unpaid, also seems unappreciated. They find, in Jessie Bernard's words, that housework is "an uncongenial occupation" and a "dead-end job with no chance of promotion," the equivalent of "requiring all men upon marriage to give up their jobs and become janitors, whether they like janitor work or not" (1972).

Public opinion polls indicate that more of today's women rate the housewife's work as dull and boring (34 percent) than as interesting (20 percent). Just as Helena Lopata found that some college women take special delight in the housewife-mother role, it has been found that college women are also prominent among those who despise the role the most (Yankelovitch, 1981).

The Partner-Wife's Advantages

The partner-wife, working at an outside job, escapes the danger of feeling isolated inside the home and tied down to its responsibilities. In theory at least, her contribution to the family budget gives her the same voice as her husband in deciding how the family will live. Studies have indicated that working wives indeed do have more decision-making power than housewives (Bahr, Bowerman, and Gecas, 1974), in particular over the important matter of how the family income should be spent (Hoffman and Nye, 1974). In the all-out form of companionship marriage, the partner-wife may even spend her spare time apart from her husband, pursuing her own interests. She enjoys freedom and independence, plus the sense of accomplishment derived from her performance in the business or professional world.

A recent public opinion poll showed that by far the majority of working wives feel that their job does not interfere with their ability to be a good wife and good mother—indeed that their work makes them a more interesting person in the eyes of the husband (Roper, 1980). Their husbands seem to share the view that the job does not interfere, for a recent large-scale survey found that they were just as happy and well adjusted in the marriage as the husbands of housewife-mothers (Locksley, 1980).

One unusual and interesting study compared the two types of husbands by looking

Ken Karp

A partner-wife with a successful career—and obviously happy about it.

for signs of any stress they might be suffering, as indicated not only by interviews about possible marriage difficulty but by their medical histories and various physical and psychiatric tests. The study indicated that husbands of working wives certainly experience no more stress than husbands of housewives, and if anything seem to be freer from stress (Booth, 1979).

Women who have achieved substantial success in a career appear to be particularly happy in the role of partner-wife, as indicated in a survey of wives holding such professional jobs as psychologist, writer, professor, actress, sculptor, and dean of a law school. To the question "Do you think that having a career has been detrimental to your family?" the forty women surveyed responded with a unanimous and enthusiastic "Not at all!" The study found that these professional women believed "they were able to give of themselves more because they were happier and exhilarated by their work. Their self-image was more positive and they enjoyed being with their children more than when they had not been outside the home pursuing a career." Many of them felt that their work had also created greater interaction between the members of the family, with the husband spending more time with the children and the children learning to accept responsibility for helping take care of the home (Clinch, 1975).

Even without reaching the professional ranks, many working wives seem to enjoy an increased sense of satisfaction because of their job. They feel they have attained their own position in the world, through their own efforts. Thus, at least in that large part of our society regarded as middle class or higher, these women tend to judge their social status to a considerable extent by the prestige of their own job (Philliber and Hiller, 1979), rather than as something acquired secondhand from their husband and father.

The Partner-Wife's Job Problems

So far so good. But the partner-wife role also has its disadvantages. A job outside the home makes rigid demands for promptness and efficiency, and the partner-wife is bound to have days when she would like to shed these obligations, sleep late, and enjoy what looks to her (at least on such days) like the unpressured contentment of the housewife-mother.

Even on good days, her job may leave something to be desired. Because of the various kinds of discrimination against women mentioned in Chapter 3, she may have to settle for work that does not fully utilize her education and abilities. Even if she manages to find a position that requires as much talent as her husband's job—or more—she usually earns less money (Bane, 1976). Thus the working wife is seldom a true fifty-fifty partner in the financial sense.

Some women, of course, actually earn more than their husbands. But this is unusual and occurs chiefly in very low income families where the husband, for one reason or another, has little or no earning power. In families where the husband earns $10,000 a year or more, a large majority of working wives make less money than their husbands, in most cases substantially less (Bureau of the Census, 1984c). Often the working wife and her husband both regard her paycheck as just a bonus to the family income, a fact that may greatly reduce the satisfaction she gains from working (Gove, 1972).

Socialization's Pull and Guilt Feelings

The partner-wife faces numerous other problems. She may still feel the pull of traditional socialization and worry about losing her femininity. She may miss the children she has been too busy to have—or, if she has children, wish that she could spend more time with them. She may wonder whether her family or her job is more important, and whether in her attempt to have both she is perhaps failing to do justice to either of them.

Worries of this type were apparent even in the study of the forty professional women who were so enthusiastic about the role of partner-wife. They reported unanimously that they had experienced conflicts between having a career and being a wife and mother, and all but one of them admitted feeling

guilty at times about neglecting the family. The guilt feelings were particularly troublesome to wives in the early years of trying to combine family and career (Clinch, 1975).

Partner-wives with less interesting and challenging jobs are probably even more inclined to question their lifestyle, and the number of working women worried about meeting the needs of their family is undoubtedly very high. Note, for example, that there is another side to the recent public opinion poll in which a majority of working wives said they believed their job did not interfere with being a good wife and mother. The poll also showed, it must now be added, that a substantial minority feared otherwise. Of those who gave a direct yes or no response, 16 percent—a figure that translates into 8 million women—expressed agreement with the statement "I feel I would be a better wife if I didn't work." An even larger number, 25 percent, said "I feel I would be a better mother" (Roper, 1980).

The Partner-Wife and Housework

It may be true, as dissatisfied housewives often suspect, that a job outside the home is more challenging and less monotonous than housework and babysitting. Even on this score the partner-wife faces a problem. The house has to be kept going. The meals have to be cooked. The children need care. So what does the partner-wife do when she gets home from her job? The answer is that during a considerable part of her "spare" time she does housework. One study found that working wives spend an average of slightly more than 28 hours a week taking care of their homes and children (Pleck, 1975). Another study put the figure at nearly five hours a day (Walker and Woods, 1976).

All this housework comes on top of a work week that may run as high as thirty-five hours or more for a partner-wife with a full-time job. As a result, it has been found, working wives generally suffer a serious "overload" of obligations. By and large they have less free time than their husbands to relax and enjoy themselves, or even sleep. Often they feel they are fighting a nerve-wracking—and losing—battle against the clock (Robinson, 1977).

Many partner-wives start out with the idea that, since they and their husbands will both be working, both will share equally in taking care of the house, the cooking, and eventually the children. But things seldom work out that way. Only slight differences have been found in the way household chores are divided in various kinds of families. Regardless of whether the wife stays home, works part time, or works full time, she usually does the bulk of the chores that have traditionally been considered feminine.

She does most of the cooking, washing of dishes and clothes, housecleaning, and child care. Her husband generally confines himself to such traditionally masculine (and less time-consuming) tasks as taking out the garbage, mowing the lawn, and taking care of the automobile (Beckman and Houser, 1979). A study made in the mid-1970s found that the husbands of working wives devoted an average of only an hour and thirty-six minutes a day to household work—exactly the same amount of time spent by the husbands of housewives staying at home (Walker and Woods, 1976).

The division of housekeeping chores along traditional masculine-feminine lines seems to occur in all kinds of households. It is common in families where the wife holds a high-level professional job and is highly committed to her career (Beckman and Houser, 1979), and it is by no means rare even in cases where a well-educated working wife is the chief breadwinner because her husband

is less successful (Ericksen, Yancey, and Ericksen, 1979). A study of couples living together without being married has shown that these women likewise perform most of the chores most of the time (Stafford, Backman, and JiBona, 1977). College couples living together usually fall into the same pattern, even though both may carry exactly the same load of classroom work (Alexander, 1981).

One particularly interesting example of the customary division of household labor—which you may find amusing or may find sad, depending on your point of view—has been reported by a young woman who lived in a commune that began in the 1960s with noble resolves about creating a "brave new world." Among other things, the members were determined to abandon any old fashioned notions about the proper roles of men and women. They started with the ideal of doing whatever jobs they felt like doing, regardless of sex. Somehow the old pattern soon prevailed. True, the women and men alike shared the farming chores that supported the commune. But when the day's work in the fields was done, the women found themselves cooking supper while the men took naps or sat around talking. The women also wound up doing the cleaning and the laundry (Leder, 1969).

Why Don't Husbands Do More of the Work?

Because of the way household chores get piled on top of the hours spent at outside work, the partner-wife with a full-time job has been called "the most overcommitted and disadvantaged" of all women and, "according to some radical feminists, the most enslaved" (Beckman and Houser, 1979). Many voices have been raised in bitter complaint. Pat Mainardi (1970) has termed the division of household labor a form of exploitation, suffered by women day in and day out. Margaret Polatnick (1973) contends that men deliberately burden their wives with responsibility for child care as a scheme to maintain their power over women.

Other sociologists, however, have suggested that the division of labor may simply represent an attempt to make the household run as efficiently as possible. Many women, probably because of the way they have been socialized, shun such tasks as taking care of the lawn and the automobile. But they are skilled in the traditionally feminine tasks, while many men are all thumbs at cooking and cleaning. Perhaps, as some suspect, this awkwardness of husbands is mostly a pose, adopted in a deliberate or unconscious attempt to avoid jobs that their socialization has taught them to consider inappropriate for men (Rapoport and Rapoport, 1975a). The fact remains, however, that most wives seem to prefer doing the tasks themselves, and doing them right. A national survey in the 1970s found that only 19 percent of wives wanted their husbands to give them more help (Robinson and Robinson, 1975).

Many studies have shown that women are far more interested in the home, and far more concerned with its appearance and its smooth operation, than are men. One study of how people relate to their environment found that sex differences are prominent even in childhood. Girls tend to stay close to home, boys to roam greater and greater distances away from it. With similar play materials at hand, girls tend to build houses and decorate the interiors, boys to construct far-ranging projects like towns and highways (Hart, 1978).

Throughout life women appear to consider their home an expression of their own personality, a place to find privacy and relaxation, entertain guests, and enjoy their possessions. Men are much less likely to have

such feelings (Saegert and Winkel, 1978). Among the elderly, widows who move into smaller quarters usually try to take along as much of their furniture and other possessions as possible. A widower is usually content to have an apartment almost completely bare except for such essentials as a bed, a place to store clothes, and a table and chair for meals (Howell, 1976).

A Possible Answer from Boston

Some valuable insights into the problems of the partner-wife and her husband come from Laura Lein and her associates (1979), who made an in-depth study of couples living in the Boston area, with both spouses holding jobs and preschool children in the home. Lein found that the partners in these marriages tended to be strongly influenced by their early socialization into traditional sex roles. The wives generally felt responsible for care of the house and the children, and in some cases they were actually reluctant to surrender any of this responsibility to the husband. The husbands thought of themselves as the breadwinner and regarded their job and their paycheck as "their primary contribution to the well-being of their family."

In some cases the partners engaged in a sort of play acting that helped them both feel they were fully living up to the traditional roles. Both carefully distinguished between what they considered a responsibility and what they felt was only "helping out." No matter how important the wife's paycheck was, they assured each other that the husband was responsible for the family income and the wife's job merely a bonus. When the husband spent time on the house or children, he was merely lending a hand in meeting the wife's obligations. This little game seemed to ease the discomfort that both felt

A modern father who doesn't mind taking his children to a playground.

when their behavior violated the traditional roles.

The study also found that the husband's and wife's social networks—that is, their relatives, friends, and fellow workers—tended to support their faithful performance of the traditional roles and frown on any violations. The husbands in particular were under considerable pressure from their friends and coworkers not to act "effeminate or weak" by undertaking housework. One father, who frequently took a young son to the neighborhood playground, reported that his behavior was considered strange even by the mothers who used the grounds: "I heard one woman whisper to another, That poor little boy. His mother must be dead—it's always his father who brings him here."

This sort of social pressure—or perhaps just the fear of it—seemed among other things to make it difficult for the fathers to express affection for their children in public. If anyone was looking, they were loath to hug or kiss a child. Thus, the report concluded that men's failure to take more part in housework and care of the children is, "not simply the result of personal weaknesses or lack of commitment to family life," but a reflection of deep-seated attitudes toward roles and role expectations instilled by socialization and supported by what appear to be society's expectations.

Is Help on the Way for the Partner-Wife?

Whatever the reasons, there is no question that today's partner-wife does typically have an overload of time-consuming obligations. As was pointed out many years ago, she really occupies two roles: She functions both as a member of the paid labor force and, in her hours away from the job, as a housewife-mother (Myrdal and Klein, 1956). She will continue to bear the overload unless and until her husband also undertakes to play a dual role, assuming greater responsibility for the house and children as well as for his own breadwinning activities (Young and Willmott, 1974).

One view of the problem is that it represents a "psychosocial lag" between the changes taking place in masculine and feminine roles (Rapoport and Rapoport, 1972). Switching from housewife to working wife means an abrupt shift into a new role with clear and definite rules such as the working hours and standards of performance set by the employer. There are no such rigid rules to guide a woman in her other role as wife and mother or to regulate what part her spouse should play in household and family affairs in his role as the husband of a working wife. Here the couple find themselves on their own, and it is perhaps not surprising that men's role in the family has changed more slowly than women's role in the work force.

There are some indications that the gap may be starting to close and that the partner-wife of the future may find her husband relieving her of more of her present responsibilities. Although a 1976 study found that that the husbands of working wives devoted no more time at all to care of the house and children than did other husbands, a 1979 study of a representative sample of U.S. families found that this may be changing.

The 1979 figures showed that the husbands of working wives had moved ahead of other husbands by 1.8 hours a week of housework and 2.7 hours of child care. Although these are small amounts, especially when converted into minutes per day, they were described as the first indication "that men are beginning at last to increase their family work when their wives are employed" (Pleck, 1979). As yet, however, the dual roles played by the partner-wife, with their dual obligations, can be a severe disadvantage. We can speculate that this is one of the chief reasons so many working wives—fully 30 percent of those employed full-time—would rather be staying at home.

HOW MUCH HARMONY, HOW MUCH CLASH, AND HOW MUCH HAPPINESS?

Although the changing sex roles can cause difficulties, today's marriages also provide opportunities for a kind of intimate harmony that was probably rare in the days when the sex roles were more rigid, as large numbers of blissfully married people would be glad to attest. The question now becomes, Does marriage today, by and large, produce happiness or unhappiness?

Life in general has always been surrounded by dangers and difficulties. Yet, insofar as human happiness can be measured, it appears that Americans are blessed with a good deal of it. Perhaps the best evidence comes from a public opinion poll of the mid-1970s. In this survey 40 percent described themselves as "very happy" and another 51 percent as "fairly happy," leaving only 9 percent who said they were "not too happy" (Gallup, 1976).

Surveys of this kind, of course, are not entirely satisfactory. Happiness and unhappiness are the haziest of words, meaning different things to different people. Whether you feel good or bad about life may depend on the mood of the moment. Moreover, some people might be ashamed to admit even to a faceless poll-taker that they had failed at the good old American custom called the pursuit of happiness.

Nonetheless, the mid-70s poll is one of the best large-scale studies offering a clue as to how Americans in general feel about themselves and their lives. It seems remarkable that only nine out of a hundred should have called themselves not very happy, for at the time the people were questioned quite a few of them must have had headaches, sore feet, dentist appointments, unpaid bills, or final exams lurking in the future.

Happiness in Marriage

If Americans in general are pleased with life, what about married people? Are they happier than most or less happy? Again we have to rely mostly on what people say about themselves, but again the evidence seems convincing. Although some Americans find marriage disastrous—and at any given moment some are in the process of getting divorced—the majority are more than content. A public opinion poll at the start of the decade found that nine married people out of ten report being mostly or very happy with their family life (Gallup, 1980).

An earlier poll comparing married with single and divorced people is illustrated in Figure 4-1. Note that about 60 percent of wives and husbands described themselves as "very satisfied" with their life—as opposed to just moderately or not at all satisfied—compared with around 50 percent of single or widowed people and less than 40 percent of divorced people.

Eric Kroll, Taurus

One of the reasons married people, in general, say they are happier than others.

Figure 4-1 also shows some interesting sex differences. There were considerably more very satisfied men than women among the single, divorced, and widowed people. In the married group, slightly more wives than husbands reported being very satisfied. Other studies have also found that wives generally are somewhat more likely to say they are happy than are husbands, and they are far more likely to do so than are women who are single, divorced or widowed (Glenn, 1975).

Is Marriage Good for Men?
Is It Good for Women?

A good deal of evidence, however, indicates that marriage is in fact more closely associated with the general well-being of men than of women. Compared with bachelors, married men rate considerably higher on many

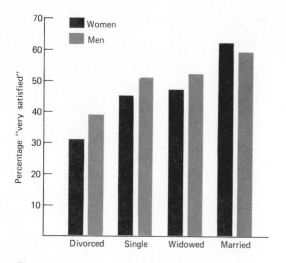

Figure 4–1
MARRIED IS HAPPIER
In a mid-1970s public opinion poll a substantial
number of married men and women reported that
they were "very satisfied" with their lives. Only
a minority of divorced people were "very satisfied,"
while the single and widowed fell in between (data
from Roper, 1974).

measures of physical health (Verbrugge, 1979). Their death rate is lower, especially from causes related to psychological stress—like suicide, accidents, and alcoholism (Gove, 1973). They are less than half as likely to be hospitalized in mental institutions (Rushing, 1979). On all these matters, married women are also better off in general than unmarried women, but to a much lesser extent.

In many ways wives actually seem to be at a disadvantage in comparison with unmarried women. It was noted a half century ago that they seemed more likely to display signs of neurotic behavior, that is, to worry, suffer from hurt feelings, cry easily, and sometimes feel self-conscious, grouchy, guilty, sad, or miserable (Willoughby, 1938). The findings have been confirmed many times since. One study showed that married

women are more likely than unmarried women to suffer such psychological symptoms as nightmares, dizziness, fainting, and nervous breakdowns (Srole, 1962). Another showed that wives are 25 percent more likely than single women to have irrational fears (for example of storms, diseases, and dying), more than 50 percent more likely to be depressed, and nearly 300 percent more likely to suffer from a severe neurosis (Knupfer, Clark, and Room, 1966).

The Married, the Unmarried, and the Marriage Gradient

Comparisons between married and unmarried people have to be viewed with reservations because of the *marriage gradient,* which is the tendency for men to "marry down" and women to "marry up" (Centers, 1949). Many studies have shown that in general the husband not only is several years older than the wife but also has a somewhat better education and job status and often comes from a family of higher social standing.

The effects of the marriage gradient have been described by Jessie Bernard (1972) in terms of the diagram in Figure 4–2, showing that the two groups least likely to marry are the men who are at the "bottom of the barrel" in desirable qualities and the very superior women who constitute the "cream of the crop." Among the men there undoubtedly are many who are handicapped by poor physical or mental health and who thus help account for the unfavorable comparisons found between bachelors and married men. The top-level women likely to remain unmarried probably enjoy superior physical and psychological health and thus help account for the unfavorable comparisons between married women and the unmarried.

The fact remains, however, that wives

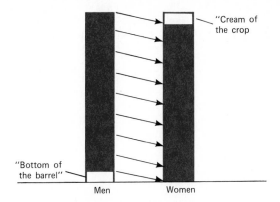

Figure 4-2
THE MARRIAGE GRADIENT AND THE PEOPLE IT KEEPS SINGLE
Because men tend to marry down and women tend to marry up, people in the two areas in white are often unable to find mates—and are permanently consigned to the ranks of the single (after Bernard, 1972).

seem to be at a disadvantage by comparison with husbands as well as when measured against unmarried women. Many studies have shown that more married women than married men suffer from psychological disturbances of all kinds, from the mildest to the most severe. One study found that they were more likely to feel inadequate, anxious, and about to have a nervous breakdown (Gurin, Veroff, and Feld, 1960). Another study found that 46 percent more wives than husbands suffered from depression and 83 percent more from irrational fears (Knupfer, Clark, and Room, 1966).

Indeed almost all the evidence gathered in recent decades shows that married women display more psychological disturbances than married men (Gove, 1972). They are more likely to experience everything from mild neurotic symptoms to such crippling ailments as schizophrenia, and they are more likely by 25 to 35 percent to become patients in a mental hospital.

HIS MARRIAGE AND HER MARRIAGE: GETTING THEM TOGETHER

The preceding section poses a puzzling contradiction. When wives and husbands are asked how satisfied they are with marriage, both report a good deal of happiness, wives even more than husbands. Yet wives seem to suffer to an unusual extent from psychological disturbances that make people uncomfortable and unhappy. They certainly display a lower level of mental health than unmarried women. Even if this comparison is discounted because of the marriage gradient, the fact remains that in general they have more psychological problems than married men, and this cannot readily be explained. Why then should the nation's wives call themselves so happy?

This intriguing question has been the subject of considerable speculation and debate. It relates to a larger argument that has been going on for years as to who has the harder time of it in life and in marriage—men or women, husbands or wives.

Jessie Bernard's Theory: The Brainwashed Wife and His-and-Her Marriages

One possible answer comes from Jessie Bernard (1975), who suggests that wives' "self-reported happiness seems almost like one of the symptoms" of psychological disturbance. That is to say, wives are not really all that happy; they have just been so thoroughly brainwashed by conventional attitudes toward sex roles and marriage that they think they are. In truth, marriage is "destructive" to wives and their lot in life is "dismal."

Bernard has coined the term "his-and-her marriages" to describe the contrasting benefits and burdens for men and women. The husband's marriage, she finds, is such a blessing that men "can hardly live without it." It is "one of the greatest boons" that the human male has ever known:

> There is no better guarantor of long life, health, and happiness for men than a wife well socialized to perform "the duties of a wife," willing to devote her life to taking care of him, providing, even enforcing, the regularity and security of a well-ordered home. . . . Marriage is more comfortable than bachelorhood; sex is always available; responsibility is a rewarding experience. It is reassuring to have a confidante. And then there is love, friendship, companionship.
> *(Bernard, 1975)*

In the wife's marriage, on the other hand, there are fewer benefits and "excessive costs." The wife has to be "more accommodating" and make the "greater adjustment." She is especially handicapped if she becomes a housewife, for "the nonspecialized and detailed nature of housework may actually have a deteriorating effect on her mind." Whatever role she plays, marriage thrusts "such profound discontinuities into the lives of women as to constitute genuine emotional health hazards." One shock is the realization that husbands do not necessarily live up to ideals of the masculine role as instilled by socialization:

> Girls are reared to accept themselves as naturally dependent, entitled to lean on the greater strength of men; and they enter marriage fully confident that these expectations will be fulfilled. They are therefore shaken when they come to realize that their husbands are not really so strong, so protective, so superior. Like children who

come to realize that their parents are not really omniscient—or, actually, all that powerful—wives learn with a shock that their husbands are not truly such sturdy oaks. They can no longer take it for granted that their husbands are stronger than they. . . . For some it becomes a full-time career to keep the self-image of husbands intact.
> *(Bernard, 1972)*

Norval Glenn's Theory: His Marriage and Her Marriage Are Both Okay

A very different theory comes from Norval Glenn (1975a), who believes that Bernard's interpretation is "biased and propagandistic," not so much "an objective assessment of the evidence" as a "plea for reform." Glenn agrees that the facts about mental health indicate "marriage is more stressful to American women than it should be," but he maintains that marriage provides women with psychological benefits that more than make up for the psychological costs. He believes "it is likely that women, as a whole, exceed men in both the stress and the satisfactions derived from marriage." Hence he finds no contradiction between the fact that more wives than husbands usually describe themselves as happy and the fact that more wives than husbands suffer psychological disturbances.

On the whole, Glenn concludes, the findings of social science "strongly suggest that American marriage, in spite of its many limitations, is typically beneficial to both husbands and wives." In other words, the husband's marriage and the wife's marriage may provide different benefits and extract different costs—like two different kinds of insurance policy—but both are worth the price.

Happiness, Mental Health, and Individual Differences

What has been said in this chapter about happiness and mental health, and the theories interpreting the findings, concern marriages in general and what social scientists have learned about them by studying large groups of people. The facts and theories are important to an understanding of trends and changes in today's relationships between women and men, but they by no means indicate that all marriages are destined to fall into any particular pattern.

In applying the facts and theories to our own relationships we must keep them in perspective. They are useful guidelines to some of the possible problems, costs, and benefits of marriage. They do not mean that we ourselves will necessarily face any given problem, have to pay any given cost, or receive any given benefit. In terms of our own relationship, they are no special reason for either pessimism or optimism.

The figures on mental health, for example, do not mean that every wife is more psychologically disturbed than her husband, nor even that every wife is disturbed at all. On the matter of the most drastic kinds of disturbance—so crippling as to require hospitalization—the difference between wives and husbands is substantial in percentages but small in actual numbers. A study of people admitted to state mental hospitals in Tennessee over a ten-year period showed that the rates were only 392 per 100,000 population for married women and 291 per 100,000 for married men (Rushing, 1979). The actual number of people suffering from less serious problems is difficult to determine, since psychiatrists and other authorities disagree on where the line should be drawn between mental health and psychological distur-

bance. Even by the most rigid standard, however, the number is certainly a minority (President's Commission on Mental Health, 1978).

Many factors help determine whether we will achieve happiness and self-fulfillment in marriage or will be discontented and perhaps psychologically disturbed. Individual differences play a great part. Some people, because of inherited traits or the way their experiences have molded them or both, have a generally positive and cheerful attitude toward life. They are enthusiastic, confident, flexible, and capable of coping with almost any situation that arises. In other words, they bring to marriage a great deal of what is known as mental health. Others are inclined toward unhappiness and neuroticism. They are likely to display psychological disturbances in all their relationships, their jobs, and their feelings about themselves. Naturally, this tendency is likely to affect their attitudes and reactions to such a basic and intimate relationship as marriage and the family.

Happiness and Roles

Above all, happiness and psychological well-being in marriage seem to depend on how successfully the individual couple manages to handle the possible conflicts between roles and role expectations discussed in this chapter. Despite the difficulties in this transition period of changing sex roles, most couples succeed well enough to find a reasonable amount of happiness and self-fulfillment in their marriage. Some people, however, find the role they are called on to play in marriage so uncomfortable as to produce various kinds of psychological disturbance, or at least to exaggerate preexisting tendencies in that direction.

For two reasons it is the wife whose well-being is most likely to suffer from role conflicts. One is the fact, already mentioned, that becoming a housewife-mother or a partner-wife has a profound effect on a woman's entire lifestyle. The other has been suggested by Walter Gove, who has made many of the statistical analyses showing that wives in general have poorer physical and mental health than husbands. Gove's explanation for his findings is that there are unusually severe strains in the role—or dual role—that women find themselves playing in marriage (Gove and Tudor, 1973).

We can assume that many married women who display poor mental health are found among the 30 percent of stay-at-home wives who would rather have outside jobs, that is, the housewife-mothers who hate housework and would much rather be enjoying a career as a partner-wife. This source of serious dissatisfaction was noted many years ago by Clifford Kirkpatrick (1963): "Many a capable woman, with talents fully equal to those of her husband, has become a neurotic housewife obsessed by envy of the woman who is a marriage partner." We can also assume that the same thing is true among the 30 percent of working wives who would rather be staying at home, that is, partner-wives who would prefer to be housewife-mothers. These women may not especially like their outside jobs. Or they may be concerned about the effects on their marriage and children. Or they may despair of catching up with all the time-consuming obligations of their dual roles in the work world and the home.

Men, though less affected by the role they play in marriage, are not totally free from the strains. The husband of a housewife-mother may be under considerable stress from his obligations to take care of the family's income and general welfare and to live up to the traditional ideal of the strong and dependable male. The husband of a partner-wife may have trouble breaking away from the male role into which he has been socialized. He may feel like less of a man because his wife works, and especially if he attempts to play a part in the unfamiliar domain of housework and child care.

Finding Your Own Solution

If there are many possibilities for conflict, there are also many possible solutions. Today's marriages are not all cut from the same cloth. The roles played by wives and husbands are not inflexible. Because a woman stays home and takes care of the house and children, for example, does not necessarily mean that the couple follow all the rules of traditional marriage. They may behave in many of the ways characteristic of companionship marriage. They may enjoy a great deal of comradeship and intimacy, share an equal voice in family decisions, and maintain a strong sense of individual identity and independence. Similarly the working wife may find ways, satisfactory to both her and her family, to combine her outside job with what was the woman's role in the traditional marriage. On the matter of sharing housework and child care, the couple is free to experiment along any lines that both consider fair and reasonable.

In this period of change and confusion, there is no formula for success. Couples have to work out their own solutions, in whatever way they find possible and rewarding. As Helena Lopata (1972) has put it, "Each marital team has to work out its own pattern, meeting individually defined needs and requirements." Attempts to find a suitable pattern often continue throughout life, for the needs and requirements change as we ourselves change. The many problems and opportunities are discussed throughout the book.

SUMMARY

1. Today's marriage partners may hold different, and possibly conflicting, views on masculinity, femininity, and androgyny.

2. The possibilities of conflict were foreseen many years ago by Clifford Kirkpatrick, who suggested that marriages would take three distinct forms characterized by the basic nature of the role played by the wife:

  a. *The housewife-mother.* This is the traditional role. The wife abandons all thought of a career, at least after a child is born. She keeps the house, takes care of the children, and provides emotional support and encouragement. In return she receives economic security, respect as a wife and mother, and the gratitude of her husband and children.
  b. *The partner-wife.* This is the role associated with companionship marriage. The partner-wife shares responsibility for earning a living and abandons such feminine privileges as chivalry. In return she expects to enjoy independence and an equal voice in family decisions.
  c. *The ornament-wife.* In purest form, the ornament-wife is the pretty young wife of a rich man who provides her with leisure and luxury. Her obligation is to remain eternally young, bright, and sexy—fun to be around and an ornament to be shown off to her husband's friends and business associates. Ornament-wives are rare, but everyone knows such a role exists and is likely to think about it at times.

3. Kirkpatrick found that his women students tended to hope for the advantages and privileges of housewife-mother, partner-wife, and ornament-wife but were not prepared to meet the obligations of all three. The men expected their future wives to fulfill at least some of the obligations of all three roles but were unwilling to offer all the corresponding privileges. "It is no wonder," Kirkpatrick concluded, "that arguments rage as to who gets cheated in marriage."

4. Two possible sources of conflict are these:

  a. The partners may disagree about the proper roles for husband and wife; for example, a woman wants to be a partner-wife with her own career but her husband wants her to be a housewife-mother.
  b. Circumstances may force the partners into uncongenial roles; for example, a couple who prefer a traditional marriage with the woman in the role of housewife-mother may find that the wife has to take an outside job because they need money.

5. Many people, especially women, seem unhappy with the role they have chosen or have been forced into. Opinion polls have found that 30 percent of women not employed outside the home (housewife-mothers) would rather have jobs. The same percentage of women with full-time jobs (partner-wives) would rather be staying at home.

6. Many women continue to favor the housewife-mother role, which has these advantages:

  a. Women with this lifestyle are spared the difficulty of breaking away from the traditional feminine role.
  b. Many find that running a household and raising children give them considerable happiness and self-fulfillment: "They are happy that they are appreciated or needed and that the family is pleased with their efforts."
  c. Many, especially the college educated, find another source of satisfaction in activities outside the home—with political, religious, and recreational groups.

7. The chief disadvantages of the housewife-mother role are these:

a. Women with this lifestyle are almost entirely dependent on their husband, who controls where and how the family lives, how much money they spend and how they spend it, and their status in the community.

b. They usually work longer hours than they would at an outside job—according to one study, fifty-five hours a week.

c. Many women are surprised and distressed by their isolation from the companionship they formerly enjoyed with classmates or fellow workers.

d. Without the social contacts and paychecks provided by an outside job, they may lack a sense of personal worth and accomplishment. And many women—34 percent, according to one opinion poll—consider the housework dull and boring.

8. Partner-wives enjoy these advantages:

a. Many of them consider their outside job a source of increased satisfaction. They feel they have attained their own position in the world, through their own efforts.

b. They escape the danger of feeling isolated inside the home.

c. Their earnings give them more decision-making power than housewives enjoy, especially over how to spend the family income.

d. Most of them feel that their outside job does not interfere with being a good wife and mother; in fact, that their work makes them more interesting to their husband.

e. They can regard their social status as won through their own efforts, rather than as something acquired secondhand from their husband.

9. Partner-wives face these disadvantages:

a. On bad days, when they would like to escape the outside job's rigid demands for promptness and efficiency, they envy what they envision as the unpressured contentment of the housewife-mother.

b. Since women have trouble finding high-prestige jobs and earn less money than men, they are seldom true fifty-fifty partners financially.

c. Many of them still feel the pull of traditional sex-role socialization and worry about losing their femininity. They may miss the children they were too busy to have or wish they could spend more time with the children they do have.

d. They generally suffer an overload of responsibilities. One study found that they work an average of twenty-eight hours a week, on top of their hours at the outside job, taking care of their home and children. The husbands of partner-wives spend no more time helping with these chores than the husbands of stay-at-home wives.

10. One reason husbands offer so little help with housework is that women are far more interested than men in the appearance and smooth operation of the home and often prefer to do the work themselves in the interest of efficiency. But the chief reason seems to be that men generally have been socialized and are under pressure from other men to shun housework lest they seem "effeminate and weak."

11. There are some indications that the male attitudes are changing and that husbands are beginning to be more helpful.

12. About nine in ten couples report being mostly happy or very happy with their family life. As a group they appear to be more satisfied with their life than single or divorced people.

13. By and large, married men seem to fare better than married women on measures of physical and mental health.

14. To explain why wives seem to have more psychological problems than husbands, Jessie Bernard has distinguished between "his marriage" and "her marriage." The "his marriage" is such a boon that men "can hardly live without it," but the "her marriage" is an "emotional health hazard" because the wife is forced

to be "more accommodating" and make the "greater adjustment."

15. Norvall Glenn agrees that marriage is more stressful to women than it should be, but he maintains that marriage provides women with psychological benefits that more than make up for the psychological costs and that wives experience not only more stress but more satisfactions. Marriage, he concludes, "is typically beneficial to both husbands and wives."

16. There is no magic formula for avoiding the possible conflicts in the roles played in marriage and establishing a harmonious and mutually rewarding relationship: "Each marital team has to work out its own pattern, meeting individually defined needs and requirements."

DISCUSSION QUESTIONS

1. Of Kirkpatrick's three roles in marriage— the housewife-mother, the partner-wife, and the ornament-wife—which is most desirable to you?

2. Why do women generally experience more role conflict than men?

3. Why do you think the division of housekeeping chores along traditional masculine-feminine lines occurs in partner-wife as well as housewife-mother households?

4. Discuss the reasons marriage may be more closely associated with the general well-being of men than of women.

5. Do *you* think that marriage is more of a benefit to husbands or to wives?

6. In families you know, how has conflict over sex roles occurred and been resolved?

CHAPTER 5

Meeting and Falling in Love: The Hazards and Rewards

To the great majority of us, the nine of ten Americans who are or will be married, finding a mate is probably the most important step we will ever take. The way men and women meet, start spending time together, fall in love, and eventually marry—if it results in the right mate—can be a greater source of happiness than getting the right kind of education or finding the right job. Finding the wrong mate can mean spending your years with "a lifelong enemy" (Kirkpatrick, 1963).

True, it is relatively easy nowadays to end a bad marriage through divorce, but divorce can be a painful and sometimes expensive experience. Many couples, shunning divorce for one reason or another, wind up spending an entire lifetime of mismatched misery. Thus the process of finding a mate deserves to be given the most serious consideration, to be viewed with respect, and a certain amount of awe, to be studied and worked at.

Mate selection is especially crucial in a society as pluralistic as ours. By the time Americans are old enough to marry, they have been socialized into a bewildering variety of patterns that determine how they will behave in marriage and how likely it is that any two of them will be lifelong enemies or fit together in like-minded harmony. They have learned to play sex roles ranging from extreme femininity or masculinity to total androgyny, to hold various views of their own proper behavior in marriage, and to have various role expectations for their partner. In addition, they have learned many different ways to play their other roles in society—as son or daughter to their parents; as student or worker; as friend, neighbor, and member of the community. They have varying ideas about the role they should play as parent to their own children.

Socialization also creates many other individual differences in personality and behavior. People acquire widely varying attitudes toward religion, politics, sexual behavior, and such issues of the day as nuclear energy, military policy, taxes, welfare, abortion, and the death penalty. They have different values. (For example, some value accomplishment and wealth, others leisure and the simple life.) They have different tastes in food, clothing, and recreation.

Inborn characteristics also contribute to the broad range of individual differences. People vary in intelligence, physical stamina, and tendencies to be calm or emotional, outgoing or introverted, gloomy or optimistic. Anyone starting on a serious search can be sure of finding a proper fit somewhere in the midst of this diversity, but the selection cannot be left to luck. If our society simply put the names of all men and women of marriageable age into a computer, which then picked out pairs at random, the results would be disastrous.

THE AMERICAN SYSTEM OF "GETTING TOGETHER"

Some sociologists believe that the way we Americans go about finding our mates is in fact no better than a random matching of names in a computer bank. Our system has been called "universally haphazard," meaning that too often it brings people together by sheer chance when in fact both would be much better suited to different partners (Glick, 1975). One critic has suggested that most women and men, far from taking a sensible approach to the search for a mate, "stumble into the union as though blindfolded and temporarily deranged" (Lederer, 1973). Some have even claimed, after examining our nation's high divorce statistics, that the system actually encourages bad choices, creating a situation in which marriages, though popularly said to be made in heaven, often "appear to have been made on the battlefield" (Raths et al., 1974).

But the system, though it has its failures, is the only one we have. Indeed most sociologists would probably agree that our particular kind of society could hardly find an adequate substitute (Lowrie, 1948). We must take the system for granted and ask, How does it operate? Why does it often fail? How can we make it work for us?

Whatever It Is, We Do It Early and Often

Our system is so loosely organized and so much a matter of individual choice that it does not even have a name. A few decades ago, it was generally called dating, with a date defined as an agreement, made in advance, to go out together on a particular occasion, such as to the movies or to a high school or college dance. Dating, in this sense, has certainly not disappeared, and neither has the term. Nowadays the two sexes frequently meet in such a casual way that they hardly think of themselves as having anything so cut-and-dried as a date. They simply engage in what is now often called getting together; that is, they gather in groups at some sort of hangout or party, then more or less naturally wind up in pairs. This informality is thought of by many people as a brand-new development; but, as can be seen in the box on *Opinions and Experiences,* some forms of getting together have been going on for a long time.

In one or another of its various forms, dating or getting together is an established American custom. As shown in Figure 5–1, most young Americans start in their very early teens. Eventually nearly all young people date, usually frequently and with many partners. Nor is the practice confined to the young. It is also common among people who remain unmarried in their late 20s and their 30s, and at even later ages by people who are single because of divorce or the death of a mate. It is one of the most widely observed of all our social customs.

Other Systems of Choosing a Mate

So thoroughly accepted is our system that it is difficult for Americans to imagine a society where it does not exist. Yet in most societies of the past, and in many societies even today, the relations between the unmarried have been much more restricted. Young people met only people of the opposite sex carefully screened by their parents, usually in the presence of chaperones who carefully supervised what they did after meeting.

Opinions and Experiences

HOW TIMES HAVE CHANGED—OR HAVE THEY?

In 1975 a former teacher, now dead, taped these recollections of her high school students' dating habits a half century ago.

Around 1930 I was teaching English in a little town of 3,500 people in the Midwest. Since I was just out of college and looked even younger than I was, I had a lot of opportunities to get close to my kids.

People say times have changed, but dating in our school was just as informal then as it's said to be now. The way it often happened was that two girls went out for a walk in the evening, hoping that two acceptable boys would pick them up in a car. You didn't need a driver's license in those days, and many of the boys were using the family car even when they were high school freshmen.

Or the girls and boys would arrive separately at a basketball game, or sometimes at a dance or a church supper or a spur-of-the-moment party at somebody's house. Then they'd pair off, and the boy would walk or drive the girl home. Sometimes they got together at a picnic, or on one of the hills that were good for sleds in the winter, or a carnival when one came to

town. They always found one way or another to meet. It wasn't until they were juniors and seniors and some of them were pretty well committed to going together that they made the kind of date where the boy went to the girl's house to take her out to the movies or for an auto ride.

I suppose young people today think they discovered sex, but it wasn't exactly a secret in 1928. One year there were nineteen girls in our graduating class—and under their robes four of them were pregnant. Some of the kids came to me for advice when something bothered them, and I heard quite a few of the problems that are supposed to be so "modern" in today's world. One boy was worried about homosexual feelings—and he did decide later, in college, to go in that direction. One girl was worried because she and her boyfriend had got into oral sex and she thought it might be a perversion. There wasn't as much open talk about sex in those days and unfortunately not nearly so much information available. I didn't know myself what was and wasn't a perversion. But otherwise I can't see that times have changed so much.

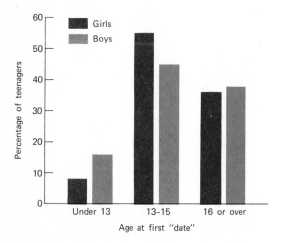

Figure 5–1
GETTING TOGETHER AT AN EARLY AGE
A poll of American teenagers in the late 1970s showed that well over half of both sexes had gone on some kind of "date" before their sixteenth birthday —some even before they were thirteen. Among those not dating until they were sixteen or older were a considerable number of 16-to-18-year-olds who had not yet dated at all at the time the poll was taken (after Gallup, 1977).

Combining college work and the modern practice of "getting together."

Most marriages of the past were based not on mutual attraction but on much more practical considerations. In Europe in the 1880s, according to one of the first social historians, nine out of ten marriages took this form (Nordau, 1884). The chief practical consideration usually was how the marriage would affect the financial interests of both families, and often marriages were arranged by the parents on both sides without much, if any, regard for the opinions of the bride and groom. Arranged marriages are still customary in parts of the world. Though this may seem incredible to Americans, the young people in these societies do not necessarily hate the idea, as evident in the box titled *Letting one's parents choose one's mate*.

Even in the United States, until little more than a half century ago, there was no such thing as today's free-and-easy approach. The process of finding a mate was called courtship—a term that now has a curiously formal and old-fashioned flavor—and courtship was indeed a formal and carefully supervised activity. A young man did not "go calling" on a young woman without first seeking the permission of her parents, and the very act of going calling implied intentions of marriage. As the description of an old-time courtship in the box on *Opinions and Experiences* makes clear, this form of finding a mate often led to marriage without much opportunity for the two young people to get to know each other. In a very real sense they might remain relative strangers until the wedding ceremony was performed.

Opinions and Experiences

LETTING ONE'S PARENTS CHOOSE ONE'S MATE

These are the comments of three girls in India in defense of the practice of letting one's parents select one's mate.

[The American system of finding a husband is] humiliating. It makes getting married a sort of competition in which the girls are fighting each other for the boys. And it encourages a girl to pretend she's better than she really is. She can't relax and be herself. She has to make a good impression to get a boy, and then she has to go on making a good impression to get him to marry her.

In our system . . . we girls don't have to worry at all. We know we'll get married. When we are old enough, our parents will find a suitable boy, and everything will be arranged. We don't have to be in competition with each other.

How would we be able to judge the character of a boy we met and got friendly with? We are young and inexperienced. Our parents are older and wiser, and they aren't as easily deceived as we would be. I would far rather have my parents choose for me. It's so important that the man I marry should be the right one. I could so easily make a mistake if I had to find him for myself.

From D. R. Mace and V. C. Mace, "Marriage East and West." 1960

How Our Modern System Began

The present system of dating or getting together began around 1920, at the time of the social upheaval associated with the First World War. It was the result of many factors. One was the increased industrialization of the United States and the concentration of population in cities rather than on farms and in small towns. Another was the expansion of education, which resulted in keeping many more young people in high school and college, along with a trend toward coeducational schools in which male and female students attended classes side by side.

Men and women began to go to school together for increasingly long periods. Afterward they often worked together in factories and offices as women entered the world of business and industry. Inventions such as the movies gave them a place to go, the automobile a way of getting there together in privacy, and the telephone a way to converse without their parents' supervision. In the fast-moving new American society the old customs of courtship in the parlor broke down. Parents lost control of the process (and were probably happy to get rid of the responsibility). In finding a mate, people were increasingly on their own.

WHAT THE SYSTEM CAN ACCOMPLISH FOR THE INDIVIDUAL

The way we go about seeking our mates, though often resulting in mistakes and failures, seems to many students of the family to represent an almost inevitable outcome of the American emphasis on independence and freedom of choice. It may be, in fact, that today's many failures are due not so much to the system itself as to the fact that people have not yet learned to use the system to the best advantage.

Opinions and Experiences
THE DAYS WHEN MEN CAME A-COURTING

An elderly woman who lived all her life in St. Louis gave this account of how people found their mates in 1905.

Like all the other girls in our neighborhood, I only went to school for a few years. I think I was about twelve and had finished the sixth grade. Then I stayed home to help with the housework. There was a lot of work in those days. We made our own soap and canned fruit and vegetables, and we made most of our clothes. We baked bread, of course, and we had a chicken coop in the back yard. Monday I scrubbed clothes on a washboard, and on Tuesday we ironed. . . . I did try a job for a while, at a place where they made ready-to-wear dresses, but I didn't like it. I was always a homebody.

I never knew any boys very well. In fact, we didn't know many people—just our neighbors on the block, and some relatives we went to visit in other parts of the city on Sundays, taking the streetcar. I met my husband-to-be because he was our mailman, also he lived in a boarding house on the next block and went to our church. We talked sometimes when he brought the mail or we were leaving church, but I never really thought much about him until he asked my father if he could come calling on me.

He would come over in the evening, after supper, and we all sat around in the parlor—he and I, my mother and father, and my brother and two sisters, sometimes also a bachelor uncle who spent a good deal of time at our house. The older folks did most of the talking, especially when my uncle was there.

Everybody took for granted that we were going to get married, and after a while he proposed to me and I said yes. We didn't know each other very well. In fact, we hardly spent any time alone together until after we were married. But I knew I loved him, and he loved me.

I sometimes worry that I wasn't the right wife for him. He was very scholarly and always reading, even the encyclopedia. He really should have been a teacher or something like that, but he never went past the sixth grade either. I wasn't much of a reader, and a lot of times what he was talking about went over my head. But I did keep a good house for him and I was a good cook, and I know I was a good mother to our three children. I think he was happy. I'm only sorry he didn't live to see the children graduate from college, which was always his ambition.

It's different nowadays, isn't it? All the girls and boys I grew up with married people from our neighborhood, or friends of relatives in other parts of the city. Those were the only people you knew. But my oldest son married a girl from out in the suburbs whom he met in college. The other boy teaches in California and married a girl who grew up in San Diego. My daughter went to work in Chicago and married a man she met in her office, and he's from South Carolina.

Theoretically, at least, our methods can perform a number of useful and indeed essential functions, not just in finding marriage partners but in contributing to the development of the individual as a member of modern society. These individual benefits are so important—and so frequently ignored—that they deserve special mention.

Leaving the Nest

Growing up from childhood to adulthood, if it is to be successful, must necessarily include the gradual emancipation of children from parents. The children must eventually become independent, leave home, and establish lives (and usually families) of their own. When this emancipation does not occur, the results are painfully apparent in the form of a 40-year-old "mamma's boy" who is still so tied to his mother's apron strings that he cannot make a decision on his own, or a grown woman who submerges her own interests and continues to live at home, still a child to her parents.

In simple societies, the move from childhood dependence to full adulthood presents few problems. Children begin helping with the work of the community as soon as they can; and one day, without strain or fuss, they quietly become self-sufficient and start rearing their own family. There is no such thing as the difficult period of transition that we call adolescence. Many societies do not even have a word meaning adolescence, and the term was largely unknown in the Western world until the Industrial Revolution got under way.

In our society, however, the situation is entirely different. Education for full adult participation in a highly industrialized nation takes time, and thus many of the responsibilities of adulthood are long delayed. Millions of young women and men are still going to school—and usually are still financially dependent on their parents—at an age when most people throughout history have been entirely on their own.

Though full emancipation is impossible for most young people in their teens, at least dating serves as one important step in that direction. It represents an acknowledgement, by both children and parents, that the time has now come for young people to begin to establish their own social lives, and embark on a series of relationships that will eventually lead to marriage and the creation of a new family. The first date is often the first significant milestone in the transition from dependent child to independent adult. (For some comments on this point by teen-

agers, see the box titled *Teenagers, parents, and dating*.

Acquiring Social Skills

Most early teenagers are uncomfortable in social situations, especially around members of the opposite sex. They tend to be bashful and tongue-tied, not knowing quite what to say. At the opposite extreme, they may be overaggressive and blustering. Many studies have shown that they enter the world of dating with a certain amount of fear and trembling. The high school girls quoted in *Teenagers, parents, and dating* agreed unanimously that their first dates were "full of apprehension and often painfully awkward," and many of them felt similarly uncomfortable each time they dated a new partner. Other studies have indicated that high school students of both sexes often consider themselves failures at dating, do not know how to act on dates, and frequently experience more fear than pleasure (Williams, 1949).

Even college students often feel uncomfortable. In a recent survey, 23 percent of college women reported problems with unwanted pressure to engage in sex, 22 percent with lack of suitable places to go on a date, and 20 percent with communication. Of the men, 35 percent reported problems with communication, 23 percent with places to go, 20 percent with shyness, and 17 percent with lack of money (Knox and Wilson, 1983).

Yet dating, though it may be difficult at the start and for years afterward, gives young people a chance, away from what they conceive to be the critical eyes of adults, to take their first faltering steps toward a more sophisticated and successful form of social behavior. They can make mistakes together and learn from the other's reaction that mistakes are not necessarily fatal.

Opinions and Experiences

TEENAGERS, PARENTS, AND DATING

A sociologist who studied 15- and 16-year-old high school girls in a California suburb recorded these comments on dating, parents, and life in general. Representative statements made by a number of the girls have been put together as if spoken by a single voice.

My mother told me I couldn't go out with boys until I was 16. But when I was 14 I just told her, "Mom, I'm going out with Joe tonight." I didn't get out that night, but the next weekend I did. You can't ask your parents. You just tell them.

When one parent says no, I ask the other. It always starts a family fight between Mom and Dad. It doesn't always work and I end up staying home, usually cleaning house. Sometimes it works, though. It helps if I say that all my friends are going; if I name a whole group of girls that are going, my mom usually lets me go too. Also, I plead for my older sister when she wants to go out. That way, when my time comes, I can go too.

Of course, I try to pick out boys that I know they will say, yes, I can go out with. And I tell the boy to be sure to make a good first impression. I expect him to come to the door when he takes me out, because that's what my parents expect. If he wants to make points with my parents, he'd *better* come to the door. Then, if he shakes hands, my father is automatically in love with him. My dad thinks that's cool. . . . But if my parents didn't like the boy and I really did, I'd stay with him. I'd sneak to go out if they tried to stop me.

Dating is a good experience because you are meeting more people and you learn to get along with them better. It's fun. It's nice to talk to a guy. It's different than with girls—something different to relate to. It makes me feel good. It's exciting. It's scary.

You have a different relationship with all your friends than with your family. Friends are someone you can talk to. I can't talk to my parents. They don't understand. If I had a problem with a boy, they would say, "Oh, that's not important. There are other boys."

With friends you can discuss things and don't have to keep everything to yourself. You have the same problems as they do. You can identify with their experiences because you have more in common. It relieves you. You don't sit there all closed up inside. If I didn't have friends to talk to, I'd be a very closed-up person. The best part about school is being able to communicate with other kids—just meeting other people and seeing how they react to things.

As I get older, I can see how my parents feel—and how different I am. My views are different. I used to think my parents were always right, but now I don't. My mother thinks she knows what is best for me, but she doesn't understand my point of view. Her way of thinking is different; she's narrow minded.

But they don't really govern what I do, and they know it. I came home late last Friday night. My father said, "I have to assume you don't care about us—but I'm not going to punish you because it won't do any good." He has a way of trying to make me feel guilty, but in the end I usually get away with it.

I realized I was growing away from my parents when I found I couldn't stand to talk to them. What I really want is to go away to college—to get away from them and see what kind of person I am. I can't wait to go to college and they know it.

From D. M. Place, The dating experience of adolescent girls, *Adolescence* 1975, 10, 157–174

Learning to Get Along with the Opposite Sex

Many people grow up believing in *stereotypes* about the sexes, a stereotype being a shared belief that all members of the same group behave in the same manner. Thus large numbers of boys who arrive at the dating age—and a smaller though still significant number of girls—believe that women are just naturally illogical, impractical, and emotionally flighty, while men are logical, practical, and able to control their emotions (Ditkoff, 1979).

Since stereotypes totally disregard individual differences, they are always wrong. (It is definitely not true, for example, that all redheads have hot tempers or that all fat people are jolly.) The stereotypes about the sexes are especially misguided in this period of rapidly changing sex roles, for there is no such thing in our present society as a typical woman or a typical man. There are in fact far greater variations within each sex than between the sexes.

It is true, however, that the continued pull of traditional sex-role socialization usually makes adolescent boys in general somewhat unlike adolescent girls in general. In many cases, the sexes tend toward different patterns of attitudes, values, interests, and tastes. Indeed a male and female socialized into the extreme forms of masculine and feminine roles seem to differ almost as much as two people brought up in entirely different cultures.

If young people are to get along together, they must learn to discard the stereotypes, recognize and understand any differences that actually do exist, and make adjustments. In fact two people attempting to establish any kind of continuing relationship— even a nine-to-five acquaintance with a fellow worker—must engage in a good deal of mutual accommodation. The process of dating or getting together makes it possible for this accommodation between the sexes to be made gradually. The process also gives both sexes an opportunity to learn about individual differences, for going out with a number of people offers ample proof that no two are exactly alike.

Acquiring Self-awareness

You can gain another great benefit from dating or getting together or whatever you choose to call it, especially if you engage in it as a college student during the years between adolescence and full adulthood. These years are in some ways an awkward period of marking time, but they also present a unique opportunity to learn more about yourself as well as about the opposite sex. Never before and never again will you be so free to examine your own personality, discover who you are and what you want, and develop a keen sense of self-awareness. This exploration of the self can be greatly facilitated by contacts with the opposite sex.

Through the high school years you were kept busy playing roles assigned by society. You were socialized into not only some kind of sex role but also the role of a child expected by your family to behave in a certain pattern and the role of school pupil in relation to your teachers. After college, you will again be under pressure of the various roles that go along with whatever status you occupy in society, for example, the role of employee or boss, of good citizen or criminal, of rich person, poor person, or something in between. All these roles make rigorous demands. Society has definite expectations of how you should play the roles, and usually you find yourself behaving as the expectations dictate.

Even in college you are subject to pressures from your instructors and fellow students to follow certain standards of behavior, but the role of college student is more loosely defined than most. Indeed one of the difficulties of being a student, as you may at times have complained, is that you can never be quite sure how you are supposed to act. Your instructors probably seem to have certain expectations, but these expectations often vary from class to class. One instructor may want you to learn the facts and figures in the course almost by heart. Another may gloss over the factual details and emphasize the broad principles and the importance of independent and original thinking. In the personal philosophies instructors exhibit in the classroom, they may reveal a wide range of opinions, pro and con, on everything from politics to religion and from women's liberation to smoking pot.

As for how your classmates view your behavior, there may be almost as many different expectations as there are students. Most campuses today are truly melting pots, bringing together many diverse people with diverse and conflicting values. On any given campus you can usually cast your lot with serious scholars or people who view education as a lark, students interested in art or athletics (or sometimes both), people who hope to become everything from entertainers to engineers, conservatives and radicals, the religiously devout and the outspokenly atheistic. You have an almost endless array of friends to choose and roles to adopt or to reject.

Dating or getting together increases the opportunity to make choices. You can write your own scenario for how you will meet members of the opposite sex, how you will behave, and how you will expect them to behave. You are free to date, feel no vibrations, and never date that person again. Or to get together, enjoy the experience, and

continue the relationship, developing it in any way you and your partner find congenial and rewarding. Never again will you be quite so free to learn about yourself and another human being.

The college years offer the perfect opportunity to ask some important questions: Who are you? What are you really like (as opposed to what your parents, teachers, and childhood friends expected you to be)? What do you want out of life (as opposed to what other people seem to think you should want)? How congenial do you find the traditional masculine or feminine role or its new alternatives? What kinds of people do you truly enjoy being around? What kind of marriage partner (if any) do you truly want? Being what you are, how can you achieve your own individual kind of self-fulfillment?

The answers, of course, are not easy to find. Social scientists learned long ago that complete self-awareness is an elusive goal that none of us may ever quite reach. But here is your best chance to move a little closer.

GETTING TOGETHER AS A PRELUDE TO MARRIAGE

The first contacts between the sexes are usually conducted in a spirit of fun and games. Certainly the large numbers of girls and boys who begin dating or getting together before they are sixteen have no immediate intentions of marriage. Many older people, including college students, also date casually, with many partners and no thought of serious commitment. Indeed, one reason our system is so popular is that it provides a good deal of fun. Even serious dating—what is sometimes called going steady, or confining one's attentions to a single partner—does not always lead to permanent commitment.

Most college students can look back to at least one occasion when they were convinced they were in love but eventually broke off the relationship. Even couples who have reached the stage of becoming formally engaged to marry often break the engagement—according to one study, in as many as half of all cases (Burgess and Wallin, 1953).

Yet the ultimate result, sooner or later, is almost always marriage. Thus, in the last analysis, our system is a matching-up process—a trial-and-error procedure that, ideally, enables two people who are suited to partnership to discover each other and their compatibility. As a prelude to marriage, the system serves a number of important functions.

Striking a Bargain: Exchange Theory

We Americans generally take an idealistic and romantic view of our system of searching for a mate. We do not like to think that the search bears any resemblance to shopping for a bargain in the marketplace, and particularly not to the kind of financial haggling that takes place in some other societies. Students are usually horrified to learn that in the African nation of Kenya one of the burning political issues has been the high price that the parents of young women charge to give them away as brides (Lord, 1970). Or to learn of a case in Sicily, reported by a social observer who grew up there, in which plans for a marriage collapsed because the father of the boy insisted that the bride bring two brooms to the marriage, one for the kitchen and one for the rest of the house, and the girl's father refused to supply more than one (Cammalleri, 1984).

Yet the plain truth is that a certain amount of bargaining does take place in our system. Indeed one widely held sociological view, called exchange theory, holds that all social relationships are governed by the rewards they provide and the costs they charge. According to this theory, all of us seek out companions who have the qualities and resources to give us the maximum amount of pleasure, and whose less desirable traits or demands on us cause a minimum of pain (Huston, 1974).

All of us have something to offer as a prospective marriage partner but also certain drawbacks, and how the pluses and minuses balance out is bound to influence what kind of mate we are likely to attract. Take for example the case of a young man who is physically attractive, kind, and generous but does not have much intelligence or education and seems stuck in a low-level job. This man may dream of marrying a television star who lives a glamorous life in Hollywood, but he will almost surely have to settle for a woman of somewhat less glittering status.

In our system, a young man soon learns what kinds of women are attracted to his particular qualities and what kinds find him not worthy of consideration. A young woman learns the limits of the range of men who are likely to regard her as a possible wife. Just as it is not really true that any American can become President, so is it impractical to think that anybody can marry anybody else. You have to go out shopping in the marriage market, looking for the best possible partner to whom your own qualifications entitle you. The realistic approach is to keep your "eyes wide open for a good bargain at a price that can be paid" (Kirkpatrick, 1963).

How Cold-Blooded a Bargain?

Lest the application of exchange theory to the search for a mate sound discouragingly cold-blooded, it should be pointed out that financial considerations and social climbing do not seem to play a very important part in most people's thinking. The bargains most Americans seek are in basic personal qualities rather than in cash payments or an extra broom for the household. In one public opinion poll women said the qualities they admired most in a man were, in order, (1) intelligence, (2) sensitivity to the feelings of others, (3) a sense of humor, (4) gentleness, and (5) self-control. Men placed these same five traits at the top of the list of qualities they admired most in a woman, though in slightly different order (Roper, 1980).

College students seem to agree to a considerable extent. A survey at a Southwestern university found that both women and men judged prospective partners mostly on the basis of emotional stability, dependability, pleasing disposition, intelligence, and feelings of mutual attraction, with such factors as "good financial prospects" and "favorable social status" far down on their lists (Hudson and Hoyt, 1978). In a study at two Florida universities, none of the factors associated with money or social standing turned up among the qualities most admired by students, which again proved to center on personality and character (Hansen and Hicks, 1980).

Learning about Each Other

To the extent that our system is a bargaining process, it serves to bring women and men together who seem to have some matching qualities—at least at first glance—and therefore a chance of becoming genuine partners. But what are these two people really like? When dating or getting together becomes serious, it helps answer this question. It performs the all-important function of enabling the two people to get to know each other in the very deep and realistic way that is essential to successful marriage.

Getting to know another person takes time

and a variety of experiences. For one thing, social psychologists have clearly established that human behavior and human personality are not necessarily consistent. Depending on the situation and the other people in it, a person may be aggressive on some occasions but meek and submissive on others, quiet or boisterous, generous or selfish, kindly or hostile, even honest or dishonest. Which is the real personality? You cannot know from what you see solely in a classroom, or at work, or around a few chosen friends. Instead you must make observations over a period of time and a wide range of situations.

Moreover, when a woman and a man first meet, they are usually careful not to reveal too much about themselves. They may even do considerable play acting, trying to impress each other rather than to reveal their true selves. Closer involvement tends to strip away the artificial aspects of their behavior. They begin to see each other for what they really are, with faults as well as virtues. They learn how to cope with quarrels, resentments, and jealousies. Even if they have a tendency to be blinded by infatuation and to see more good qualities in each other than actually exist, their vision may be helped by the more down-to-earth reactions of the other people with whom they come in contact.

At least this is what the system should accomplish. And dating or getting together today is certainly much franker and more self-revealing than in the past. A study once made of a group of women who got married around the year 1900 found that only about a third of them had ever talked to their husbands-to-be about such basic matters as religion or the husband's job plans, only about a fifth of them about handling the family's money or having children, fewer than one in ten about whether the wife should or should not work. Among women of the next generation, those who married around 1925, slightly more than half had talked about having children, but fewer than half had talked about religion, the husband's job, or money (Koller, 1951).

Nowadays there is considerable exchange of many kinds of information and opinion, particularly among the college educated. This was shown in a study of Boston-area college students who had been going together for an average of eight months, were dating each other exclusively, but did not in most cases have any definite plans for marriage. Some of the topics they had discussed openly and candidly are shown in Figure 5–2. Note that many of these women and men had fully disclosed their innermost thoughts and feelings, and nearly all of them had displayed at least some self-disclosure. In addition to the topics shown in the figure, most of them had also discussed such matters as

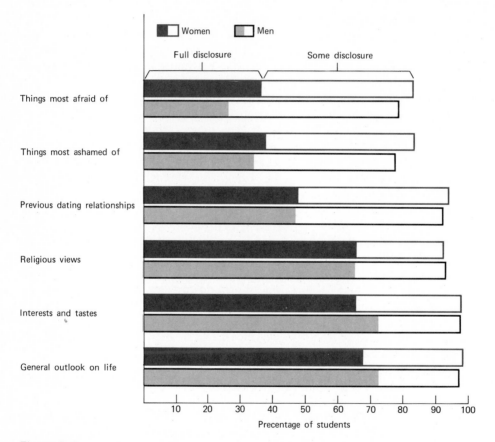

Figure 5–2
SELF-DISCLOSURE AMONG COLLEGE COUPLES
The bars show the remarkable extent to which today's college couples talk frankly about some of their intimate problems, experiences, and attitudes. The two sexes are about equally open on most matters, but men appear more reluctant to admit fears and the traits they are most ashamed of—perhaps because of the continuing pull of traditional sex-role socialization (after Rubin et al, 1980).

their political views, feelings toward parents and friends, accomplishments and other things they were proud of, and thoughts about the future of their relationship. The social scientists who conducted the study concluded that today's students seem to have moved a long way toward an "ethic of openness."

Finding a Suitable Partner

Free and open discussion is essential if our system is to fulfill its most important function of all—which is of course to bring together a woman and man who are suited to each other in deep and basic ways. It should prevent marriages between those with such deeply ingrained and persistent conflicts—in personality or in roles and role expectations—that they are doomed to failure. Any discussion of finding the right mate must begin with a word of caution. The old notion that there is one ideal mate somewhere in the world for each person, as has often been assumed by the writers of romantic fiction, is just a fairy tale. Indeed many psychiatrists believe that almost any two people who are emotionally mature can manage to get along in marriage, that it makes little difference whether, from a large field of eligibles, you pick partner A, B, X, Y, or Z (Levy and Munroe, 1959). Waiting and hoping for the dream person to come along can blind us to the opportunities we actually encounter in life. There is also such a thing as being too critical, that is, expecting a prospective mate to possess more virtues and fewer faults than is humanly possible.

Yet it is extremely difficult for two people to succeed in marriage if they have profound differences in attitudes and personality. The importance of harmony rather than clash in roles and role expectations was emphasized in the preceding chapter. Other factors can also make a great difference. It would be un-

likely to find a happy marriage between a devoutly religious person and an outspoken atheist; an ambitious seeker after material goods and someone who wants to live a life of ascetic contemplation; or a hot-tempered, violent person and one who views any sign of hostility with distaste; or between people whose IQs are as far apart as 140 and 80. No doubt you can expand this list yourself, perhaps from actual experience with couples who have failed.

Our system of getting together, by introducing us to many members of the opposite sex, makes it more likely that we will eventually reach some kind of happy fit with a suitable person. In simple mathematical terms, you have a better chance of finding someone with whom you can hit it off in marriage if you get to know fifty people than if you meet only one or two. This is especially true if you are an unusual person—for example, a man who wants to reverse the old sex roles and stay at home keeping the house and caring for the children while your wife earns the living; a woman who seeks such a husband; a person dedicated to unusual religious or philosophical beliefs; or someone with out-of-the-ordinary tastes and interests. If only 1 or 2 percent of Americans are like you in ways of great importance to you, it may take considerable searching to find a suitable partner.

FALLING IN LOVE

To most people the most important part of finding a mate is falling in love—a term that defies definition. Dictionaries call love a "passionate affection for one of the opposite sex" or "becoming enamored of and sexually attracted." But to anyone who has been in love, these definitions are totally inadequate—a pale and washed-out attempt to describe something that is bold and vivid be-

We can't define love, but we can certainly recognize it.

yond compare. Science, alas, can add little of value to the dictionary definitions. Indeed, no one can tell you what love is like. To know what it is, you have to experience it. Even then you do not understand what it is—except one of life's most glowing and overwhelming emotions. Years ago there was a popular song called "What Is This Thing Called Love?" The question was not answered in the song and in fact cannot be answered. We know it when we feel it, but we cannot describe it or even know whether how we feel is the same as other people feel.

This indefinable thing called love is a powerful force in our lives. Love is the theme of much of our literature, many of our movies and television shows, many of our songs. We are socialized from early childhood to expect to fall in love. The idea of a lifetime without it, for most people, is inconceivable.

Young women and men do as they were socialized to do—or perhaps as some innate quality of human nature demands. As they proceed through adolescence, they fall in love. Sometimes they fall out of it. Eventually, in most cases, they find themselves so deeply in love with someone that marriage is the only logical outcome. When people are asked to name the reasons for marrying, they place being in love at the top of the list by a wide margin (Roper, 1980). Thus our system of dating or getting together is not just a search for one's own identity and a suitable mate but a search for love.

Some Clues to the Meaning of Love

Although love defies definition, social scientists have come up with some valuable clues to its delights and dangers. In the first place, as anyone who has been in love might guess, it has been found that love is very different from any other kind of human relationship. Compared with people who are merely friends, those who are in love have much stronger feelings of close affiliation and need. They have been found to agree wholeheartedly with statements such as "It would be hard for me to get along without X" (with X, of course, being the partner). They also feel protective and helpful, and they agree strongly with statements such as "I would do almost anything for X" and "One of my primary concerns is for X's welfare." Finally, they feel a unique intimacy and are deeply absorbed in the relationship. They agree strongly with statements such as "I would greatly enjoy being confided in by X" and "I feel that I can confide in X about virtually anything" (Rubin, 1970).

Being in love has a profound effect on how you feel about yourself and the world. In one survey, the results of which are shown in Figure 5-3, college students reported that some of their sensations were upsetting, such

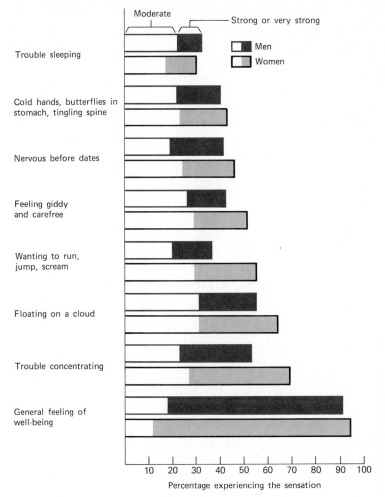

Figure 5-3
HOW LOVERS FEEL
Students at a state university in the Midwest were asked about the sensations they experienced while they were in love. The bars show the number who reported moderate or strong sensations, as opposed to none or slight. The differences between men's and women's responses are discussed in the text.

Are Women More Romantic than Men?

as having trouble sleeping and trouble concentrating. But the most widely experienced sensation of all was a pronounced feeling of well-being, reported by over 90 percent of both men and women. Sensations of floating on a cloud, feeling giddy and carefree, and wanting to run, jump, or scream—all of which would seem to indicate extreme joy— were also reported by many of the students (Kanin, Davidson, and Scheck, 1970).

One of the interesting aspects of the survey illustrated in Figure 5-3 is the differences found between men and women. For all the sensations associated with love except trouble sleeping, women proved more likely to have experienced the feeling and to have experienced it more strongly. This was particularly true for feeling giddy and carefree, wanting to run, jump, or scream, floating on a cloud, and having trouble concentrating.

In the same study students in love were asked to describe their partners and their relationship, and again some sex differences were found. In general, the women took an extremely rose-colored view, much more so than did the men. They gave their partners higher marks for being free of such defects as irritability, stubbornness, moodiness, or a quick temper. They were also considerably more likely to say that they could not possibly have a better relationship with anyone else.

Does this mean that women tend to fall in love more deeply than men, that they are more "romantic," as the old stereotypes maintain? Perhaps. But the study also produced evidence that in at least one important respect women are far more practical and realistic. As is shown in Figure 5–4, the study

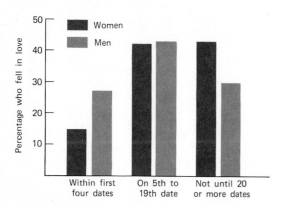

Figure 5–4
WHO FALLS IN LOVE FASTER—WOMEN OR MEN?
When students were asked how quickly they had fallen in love, nearly twice as many men as women reported that it happened within the first four occasions of dating or getting together. Far more women than men took twenty or more dates to make up their minds (Kanin, Davidson, and Scheck, 1970).

found that women students were significantly less inclined to display romantic impetuousness by falling in love at first sight. They were much more likely to find themselves in love only after a more prolonged acquaintance, providing time to discover whether the partner was indeed as lovable as first impressions might indicate.

There is no clear-cut answer to the question of whether women or men are more romantic. All of us, men and women alike, have acquired such strong hopes for love and romance that we tend to leap at every opportunity. A study of fifth-graders once showed that even though the majority had never even dated, 80 percent of the boys and 94 percent of the girls claimed they already had "sweethearts" (Broderick and Fowler, 1961). Exactly what the word *sweetheart* means to a 10-year-old or 11-year-old is difficult to say, but its use by these children makes clear that the thirst for romance is ingrained early and deeply.

Because of the different ways the sexes are socialized, it is perhaps inevitable that romanticism should take somewhat different forms for women and for men. Women are probably more romantic in some ways, men in other ways. Even these differences may be in the process of disappearing as sex roles change.

Tempering Romance with Realism

Though we are all romanticists at heart, we are not completely carried off our feet. We do look at the facts. Love does not turn us into such wide-eyed admirers of our partners that we can see only shining virtues, a total absence of anything remotely resembling a defect. Indeed it appears that if anything we become less idealistic and more realistic as a love affair progresses. At a state university in the Southwest, a study was made of men and women who were in various stages of being in love. It turned out that those who were just "casually involved" had a greater tendency to idealize their partners than those who were "moderately involved," and those who were "moderately involved" were in turn more inclined to idealize their partners than those who were "seriously involved" (Pollis, 1969).

Another study, made at a Florida university, also showed that students of both sexes tend to become more realistic with age and experience (Knox and Sporakowski, 1968). From the freshman to the senior year, there was a sharp and consistent decline in the number who agreed with such romantic notions as these:

> When you fall head-over-heels in love, it's sure to be the real thing.
>
> Love at first sight is often the deepest and most enduring type of love.
>
> Common interests are really unimportant. As long as each of you is truly in love, you will adjust.

The phrase "love is blind," introduced by the fourteenth-century poet Chaucer, is an established part of our folklore. Like so many other old adages, it does not stand up under scientific examination.

HOW LOVE STARTS, PROGRESSES, AND SOMETIMES DISAPPEARS

By the time people reach college age, most of them have been in love and have fallen out of love, many of them more than once. Many of them are or soon will be in love again. These facts raise some interesting questions: What is it that brings a particular man and a particular woman together? Why do some couples soon part and others find themselves in love? Why do some love affairs break up while others end in marriage? The questions are difficult to answer. What social science has learned is certainly not the last word (which indeed may never be written), but it does offer some valuable guidance.

To a considerable extent, the possibility that any two people will ever fall in love is determined by chance (Cameron, Oskamp, and Sparks, 1977). There can be no partnership between a woman who never travels outside her native state of California and a man who never travels outside his native state of Ohio. Even a woman and man who grow up in the same community have a much greater chance of falling in love if they happen to choose the same college than if they go to campuses a thousand miles apart. The possibilities of getting together may also depend on such chance factors as having a mutual friend, working for the same company, or even taking adjoining seats in a bus.

There are also some social rules that govern the possibility of partnerships. One is the rule of *exogamy,* or marrying outside the immediate social group. Some societies, usually to extend their influence and wealth, have required their members to marry people from a different tribe or village. In our society, exogamy takes the form of forbidding marriages between people related by blood, up to and including first cousins.

Another rule, called *endogamy* works in the opposite fashion. Some societies, usually to preserve their solidarity, have required that marriages take place only between fellow members of the tribe, village, or other group (Fairchild, 1964). In our society, many families try to enforce a kind of endogamy by pressuring their sons and daughters to marry partners of the same religion or ethnic background. Seventeen states had laws actually prohibiting interracial marriages until these laws were declared unconstitutional by the Supreme Court in 1967.

How Like Attracts Like: The Principle of Homogamy

Even without any formal rules of endogamy, there is a strong tendency—in love as well as in the old saying—for birds of a feather to flock together. It is mostly in the storybooks that the prince falls in love with Cinderella, or Lady Chatterley with her gardener. When such events occur in real life—when the heir to a European throne marries a commoner, or an American heiress her chauffeur—the incident is considered so unusual as to make newspaper headlines.

Why are people attracted to one another? Studies have found a number of important factors. In general, we like people whom we consider physically attractive. We are also attracted to people whom we consider competent, though not so frighteningly competent that they make us feel inferior. Although popular literature and songs often speak of an instant surge of attraction toward a stranger, in fact we tend to like people whom we have known for a long time. The more familiar we are with them, and the more chance we have to get used to them, the more likely we are to be attracted to them. Since feelings of attraction are not likely to flourish unless reciprocated, we tend to like people who show that they also like us.

Above all, however, we have a strong tendency to be attracted to those who think and feel much as we do. We like people who have similar values and attitudes—toward politics, religion, social problems, economic issues, recreational activities, and lifestyle in general. Thus we usually fall in love with and marry partners who resemble us in these important respects (Coombs, 1966). This tendency, *homogamy,* is a powerful force in bringing some people together and keeping others apart.

The principle of homogamy makes marriage likeliest between a woman and man from the same kind of subculture, for socialization tends to produce similar attitudes among people of similar ethnic and religious background and social class. As one study summarized the facts, "Catholics tend to marry Catholics; whites, whites; persons of Greek descent, other Greek-Americans; and members of the upper-middle class, others in the same class" (Blau, Beeker, and Fitzpatrick, 1984).

Even among those socialized to think

Laimute E. Druskis, Taurus

The college experience: a powerful modern force in the workings of homogamy.

more or less as we do, we seem to search for those who resemble us the most. Thus people who marry show an even greater similarity in values and attitudes than is generally found among those from the same kind of background (Schellenberg, 1960). Married people also tend to be similar in age, with the husband usually about two years older. They resemble each other in intelligence as well as in height, weight, complexion, and color of eyes (Spuhler, 1968).

There is some evidence that those who were the first-born in their families are likely to pair up with other first-borns, and later-borns with other later-borns (Ward, Castro, and Wilcox, 1974). So strong is the tendency for like to choose like that there are even similarities in physical attractiveness (Berscheid and Walster, 1978). A study made on college campuses in New England and the Midwest found significant relationships in the physical attractiveness of students and their friends of both sexes, with the greatest relationships between partners who were going together and considered themselves "committed" (McKillip and Riedel, 1983).

Homogamy, Birthplace, and Social Class

At one time the workings of homogamy produced many marriages between men and women of the same birthplace, that is, those who grew up in the same small town or big-city neighborhood. Today the place of birth and growing up has less influence. Love affairs now tend to spring up between people who find themselves moving in the same circles when they are adults, in geographical locations that may be far removed from their original homes. Work brings many people together. For college students, the campus is an important factor. As far back as the 1940s, a study found that 43 percent of women graduates of the University of Maine were married to Maine graduates (Lamson, 1946). The influence of the campus as a meeting place—and in establishing its own kind of homogamy—is doubtless even greater today because more people go to college.

The effect of social background has also changed. Even as recently as three decades ago, 54 percent of married couples came from families of the same social status (on the broad spectrum from lower-lower to upper-upper) and another 40 percent from a class just one step above or one step below (Roth and Peck, 1951). Today's young people are less concerned with family origins. Most of them appear to regard themselves as not so much born into a social class as establishing their own status. But homogamy still operates in respect to education, which is one of the characteristics that determine social class. Census figures show that nearly half of all married couples have exactly the same educational level (Rawlings, 1978), and many others resemble each other fairly closely.

Do Opposites Attract?

The evidence on homogamy strongly bears out the birds-of-a-feather adage. But what about another old and established piece of folk wisdom which holds that, especially when it comes to falling in love, opposites attract?

This possibility has been intensively studied by Robert Winch (1958) and has led to what he calls the theory of *complementary needs,* holding that love does have a way of bringing together people who are very different in some basic way. The theory does not deny the importance of homogamy. Winch agrees that we narrow the field of eligibles by selecting possible partners who are similar in such respects as attitudes, education, intelligence, and the other characteristics that have just been discussed. From within this field of eligibles, however, Winch contends that we are most likely to select as our final choice a person who is unlike us in important psychological ways and can thus meet some of the psychological needs for which we hunger, either consciously or unconsciously.

Consider, for example, the case of a young man who is inclined to be domineering. Given a choice between two young women equally suitable in other respects, the Winch theory holds, he is more likely to select the one who tends to be submissive rather than the one who is just as strong-minded as he is. Her need to be submissive fits in with his need to be dominant. The two needs complement each other like two halves of a pair of scissors.

Similarly, Winch holds, a very nurturant type of woman—the ''mothering'' type—is likely to select a man who tends to be dependent and likes to be mothered rather than one who resembles her in being a strong source of help and sympathy to others. People who are strongly motivated to achievement—getting ahead in the world—are likely to select partners who would just as soon sit back and enjoy basking in the success vicariously. Hostile people tend to select partners who find some masochistic satisfactions in being treated badly (Winch, 1958).

The theory of complementary needs has been a matter of much debate. Some investigators, on the basis of studies of couples who were going together or were married, have concluded as did Winch that complementary needs are often apparent. Others have reported that they were unable to find any evidence to verify the theory (Murstein, 1972). At the moment, the theory can perhaps best be considered an interesting possibility. Perhaps some of us are inclined to search for a partner with complementary needs, but others are not.

How Love Grows Deeper: The Wheel Theory

The question of how love affairs develop, from an initial mild attraction to a deep and intimate relationship and eventually marriage, has also been the subject of many sociological investigations. In the last analysis, perhaps every love affair is unique. Yet it appears that all of them seem to thrive under certain conditions and to wither under other conditions.

One interesting and widely discussed description of the course of true love, as it progresses when all goes well, comes from Ira Reiss (1960). He calls his views the *wheel theory* because he sees love's progress as resembling a wheel rolling downhill, with one forward motion leading to the next and the next and the next, and the momentum gradually increasing. The wheel can be thought of as having four spokes, as illustrated in Figure 5–5; or the spokes can be thought of

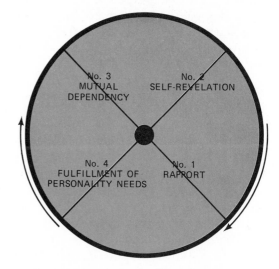

Figure 5–5
LOVE'S WHEEL AND HOW IT TURNS
The wheel starts in motion when two people meet and find they have rapport. For what the other spokes in the wheel mean, see the text.

as four stages through which a successful love affair progresses, with each stage fostering the next.

When a man and woman first meet, the possibility that they will fall in love depends on what Reiss calls *rapport.* If they feel comfortable together, at ease, and eager to learn more about each other, the wheel has made its first forward turn. In this matter of rapport, homogamy plays a great part. The two people are likely to feel good about each other if they come from similar social and cultural backgrounds, have similar educations, and above all share similar attitudes on issues that are important to them.

Rapport leads to further acquaintance and to *self-revelation,* in which the two partners begin to disclose what Reiss calls their most intimate "hopes, desires, fears, and ambitions." This in turn leads to *mutual dependency,* the point at which they come to need each other as companions, listeners, and, to a greater or lesser extent, as sexual partners. Finally, as the wheel keeps turning, they arrive at the point of *fulfillment of personality needs,* where each finds that the other serves in a most soul-satisfying way to provide some of the deep kinds of support and comfort they have always sought in human relationships.

As for what kinds of personality needs people seek to fulfill, Reiss has found that both women and men place high importance on such matters as "someone who loves me," "someone to confide in," "someone who respects my ideals," and "someone who shows me a lot of affection." To a somewhat lesser extent, they stress such matters as "someone who appreciates what I want to achieve," "someone who gives me self-confidence in my relations with people," and "someone who understands my moods." (To this list, followers of Winch might want to add "someone who has complementary needs.")

As Reiss points out, the needs that seek fulfillment resemble the factors that originally caused rapport because they too are influenced by background and socialization. Therefore the wheel tends to keep turning, leading to even greater rapport, self-revelation, mutual dependency, and fulfillment. If the wheel's progress is interrupted, however, it can reverse course, turn backward, and end the relationship. This can happen at any point. Either partner or both may find that they do not approve of the other's self-revelations, or may experience only frustration at what should be the stage of mutual dependency, or may find that they do not really fulfill each other's personality needs.

Why Couples Marry or Break Up

An indication of why some couples go on to marriage while others break up has been provided by a study of people who were brought together by a computer dating service (Sindberg, Roberts, and McClain, 1972). Like all such dating services, this one tried to match men and women for age, race, religion, education, interests, and attitudes. Thus, all the couples introduced by the service exhibited a great deal of homogamy. As the wheel theory suggests, they should have felt considerable rapport at their first meeting. Indeed some of the couples fell so deeply in love that they eventually married. Others, however, despite the careful matching, simply did not hit it off together.

To try to learn why, the investigators studied couples who married as a result of the computer matching. Then they studied other partners to whom these men and women had also been introduced by the computer service and whom they had dated briefly and unsuccessfully. As a result of this comparison, the investigators were able to draw up the list of factors, shown in Table

Table 5-1

Some Factors Favorable and Unfavorable to Marriage

FAVORABLE

A strong desire by both partners to get married soon.

Similarity between partners in the tendency to think abstractly or concretely.

Similarity between partners in the tendency to approach life with a sober attitude or a happy-go-lucky attitude.

Similarity between partners in the tendency to be confident or apprehensive.

A tendency by one partner to be witty, the other to be placid.

UNFAVORABLE

A large difference in amount of interest in sports.

A large difference in height.

A very large difference in tendencies to be dominant or submissive.

A very large difference in tendencies to be controlled as opposed to undisciplined.

A markedly greater interest by the man in the fine arts and music.

A greater need for affection on the part of the man.

A much higher tendency by the man to be tense as opposed to relaxed.

R. M. Sindberg, A. F. Roberts, and D. McClain, "Mate selection factors in computer matched marriages." Journal of Marriage and the Family 1972, #34, pp. 611–614.

In a study of computer dating, couples who eventually got married tended to display the "favorable" characteristics. Those who never progressed beyond a few dates, even though they seemed to have a great deal in common, displayed the "unfavorable" characteristics.

5-1, that seemed to determine whether closely matched couples would go on to marriage or would part after only a few dates.

The list deserves careful study. Note especially the importance of a strong desire, on the part of both partners, to marry soon. It appears that women and men who are eager for marriage, even though they have not yet chosen a partner, are especially likely to fall in love when they have the opportunity. The other favorable factors that characterized the couples who married, and the unfavorable factors that distinguished those who broke up, also offer some valuable clues to the chances that any given couple will or will not progress from initial meeting to love to marriage.

When Love Affairs End

Shakespeare said, "The course of true love never did run smooth"—and millions of people can testify that Shakespeare was absolutely right. Even the deepest and most intense love affairs, those in which Reiss's wheel has turned many times, have a way of coming to an end.

In a study that followed the progress of young people who were going together—about half of them college students—it was found that nearly half broke up within the next two years (Hill, Rubin, and Peplau, 1976). The most frequent reason was that they had become bored with the relationship. Other reasons often cited were differences in interests, backgrounds, or attitudes toward sex, or the fact that one of the partners either desired more independence or became interested in somebody else. Usually one partner took the lead in breaking off the relationship. In 51 percent of the cases it was the woman and in 42 percent the man. In the other 7 percent of cases, the desire to end the relationship was mutual.

It is interesting to note that women were more likely to make the break even when they considered themselves more involved in the relationship than the man. The study suggested that perhaps women have "greater interpersonal sensitivity and discrimination," have higher standards for falling and staying in love, and tend to reevaluate a relationship more carefully as time goes on.

Shirley Zeiberg, Taurus

Proof, as the text explains, that Shakespeare was right.

When circumstances demand, they are willing to break off even a very meaningful relationship, whereas men who are deeply involved find a break more difficult. Indeed, the men in the study seemed in general to be hit harder by the breakup than the women. The men were more likely to feel unhappy, lonely, and depressed, though they were less inclined to feel guilty.

Among college students, the study indicated, breakups are especially likely to occur at the end of a school term, as in the spring, around the first of the year, or when a new term begins in the fall. Apparently the changes in living patterns at such times help cause the break or serve as an excuse for a partner who has already made the decision.

Some of the breakups were quite casual. The woman and the man simply went back to their separate homes at the end of the col-

lege term and never got together again. In general the breakups seemed much less agonizing than a divorce would probably have been later on—partly, at least, because getting together, breaking up, and finding new partners is such an accepted practice in the dating system.

Sometimes, of course, the end of a love affair represents a personal tragedy causing intense unhappiness that persists for a long time, as it did in the case described in the box on *Opinions and Experiences*. But to most of us, falling in love, falling out, and falling in again seem to be a customary and perhaps essential part of searching for a mate. In general, the harm done by a broken love affair seems to be outweighed by the value of the experience. Even the most painful breakup can be an education in human relations and a step toward finding a more

Opinions and Experiences

A WOMAN WHOSE HEART WAS BROKEN

These are the words of a woman who lives in a small Indiana town.

I had a passionate love affair from the time I was about seventeen until I was twenty-three—almost six long years in which I hardly thought about anything else. We grew up together here in this town and went off to the same college. We even tried to take the same classes so that we could be together as much as possible. We were inseparable. The few times we were apart—as when we went on vacations with our families—we exchanged letters every day. I doubt that any two people were ever more head-over-heels in love.

There was no doubt in our minds that we wanted to get married and would do it as soon as possible. We were ready any time after our senior year in high school, but our parents wanted us to wait. They believed firmly that no couple should get married until they are self-supporting.

After graduation I came back here to teach in the high school. My boyfriend went to the city to work on a newspaper. But we still saw each other almost every weekend and wrote to each other almost every day. It was just a matter of a little more time until I could find a teaching job in the city or he was making enough money for both of us.

What happened? Well, frankly, I got dumped. By mail, which is the worst way. I got a letter out of the blue one day saying that he was sorry, but he had found somebody else. That was the end of it.

I can't describe how I felt. I cried all that day and most of the night. In the next six months, I lost twenty pounds. Yes, I thought of suicide. As far as I was concerned, my life was over anyway. I spent more than a year of total despair before I finally began to snap out of it, even a little bit.

Funny how what seems like an unbearable tragedy can turn out for the best. Here I am now with a husband I dearly love and the two greatest children in the world, living in the house of my dreams in the town I've always felt was home. I'm a small-town girl at heart, and this is what I've always wanted.

My ex-boyfriend was different. He was always restless and ambitious, and he said he never wanted to have children, though I didn't take him seriously at the time. He and his wife have lived in Chicago and New York, and now they're in Europe somewhere; he's a foreign correspondent for his newspaper. I couldn't live like that. We would never have made it together. As terrible as I felt at the time, I know now that it was better to break up then than to get a divorce later. . . . For one thing, if I had been trying to act happy in some big city like New York or Paris, I would never have met my husband. I might still be just another lonely divorcee.

suitable partner for marriage, as the box also indicates.

WHERE THE SEARCH GOES WRONG

Much more painful than the love affair that is broken off is the one that leads to a broken marriage. The real failure of our system of finding a mate is measured by our high divorce statistics. Though people have a great deal of freedom in getting together and usually many chances to find the right partner, they often fail. Why does our system result in so many errors? What goes wrong? Obviously, there are many pitfalls, and knowing what they are may help us avoid them. Thus this final section of the chapter is devoted to what seem to be the most common mistakes.

The Missed Opportunity

One of the most frequent problems is that many people engage in dating or getting together not too much but too little. In high school and college, and later in a job, you are literally surrounded by people of the opposite sex. Somewhere in this big field of possible partners, surely there is someone suitable. But to find this someone you have to work at getting around, making acquaintances, and learning more about them. Many people never make the effort.

There are many reasons for dating too little. Even sexual urges, ironically, can be one of them, as the case described in *Opinions and Experiences* suggests even though it had a happy ending. But the chief reason seems to be that it takes a good deal of self-confidence to grasp the opportunities, and many people lack the courage to try. Counselors in marriage and dating are constantly amazed to find that even the most intelligent, capable, and attractive people often have inferiority complexes that make them hesitate to attempt approaches for fear of rejection (Kirkpatrick, 1963).

Among young people, including students who go to college right after high school, the lack of self-confidence seems to vary somewhat by sex. Male students often shy away from contacts with the opposite sex because they have such low opinions of themselves in general (Glasgow and Arkowitz, 1975). Women are more likely to be handicapped by the fear that they lack the necessary social skills. For whatever reason, failures to participate fully in dating or getting together are so common that family specialists at some colleges have established classes that attempt to teach a more effective approach, apparently with considerable success (MacDonald et al., 1975).

Getting Committed While Too Young

Some people fail to take advantage of our system because they close out their options too soon. They pair off in high school and never get to know any other possible partners. Both may change greatly after they first become committed to each other. The time may come when they no longer have much in common. Yet the relationship persists anyway, almost as if by force of habit, and eventually winds up in a marriage between two people who in effect made the contract in a dim, dark past when they knew very little about themselves or each other.

In the decade after leaving high school, people often change in many ways, sometimes to a spectacular degree. Students who are shy, withdrawn, and hopeless about the future—and who therefore cling to others with the same traits—may blossom into self-confident and cheerful adults. On the other hand, many of the leading lights in high school, socially skillful and popular, lose their zest and turn sour. There are slow bloomers and those who seem to bloom too fast and quickly fade away (Macfarlane, 1963). The years may also bring many new attitudes toward roles and role expectations.

Those who go to college are especially likely to change, for the college experience has been found to result in dramatic shifts in interests, tastes, values, and many basic attitudes (Freedman, Carlsmith, and Sears, 1970). These changes tend to be long-lasting (Newcomb, 1963), often persisting throughout life. Thus two people who are very similar when they first arrive on the campus may be totally unlike by the time they leave.

Opinions and Experiences

THE WRONG WAY TO FIND A MATE

An Illinois insurance agent talks about some advice he would like to give his children but probably never will.

When I look at my two young sons and realize that just ten or twelve years from now they'll be starting to go out with girls, I think of all the things I did wrong at that age. I could be the old voice of experience and give the kids some good advice, though I doubt that I'll ever have the nerve. But maybe they won't have the same problem I did.

My problem was that I've always had a terrific sex drive. I didn't go with girls for the fun of dating, or to get to know them better, or with any thought of trying to find a suitable wife. I went with them purely and simply to satisfy my sexual urges.

In fact, I've really only gone around with two girls in my entire life. I found a sex partner in high school and was devoted to her until after our sophomore year in college together. Then she left school and I found another girl who liked me sexually, and now this girl is my wife. Oh, I spent a little time with a few other girls, but nothing to speak of. If a girl didn't want to go to bed with me, and quick, I didn't have time for her.

I couldn't help it—but I realize that it was a crazy way to select somebody to spend your life with. Think of it. There were only two women I ever did more than pass the time of day with. What are your chances of finding the right person if you narrow the field to just two people in the entire world?

As it turned out, my wife and I get along beautifully. We think the same way. We have the same tastes. She has more good qualities than I ever dreamed of, and I love her more every day. But I was just lucky. If I ran my business the way I went about getting married, I'd have gone broke long ago. You might say that all I did was buy two lottery tickets in the marriage sweepstakes, which sure isn't the sensible way to do things.

The danger of growing apart is even greater when one partner goes to college—thus encountering a new form of socialization—and the other does not. (One well-known example is the high rate of unhappiness and divorce among physicians and the women who dropped out and went to work to help send them through medical school.) The risks are greatest of all when early commitment leads to early marriage. The divorce rate among women who marry at 18 or 19 is 50 percent higher than for women who marry in their 20s (Spanier and Glick, 1981).

Dating's Little White Lies— and Some Bigger Lies as Well

Another reason our system often fails to bring the right two people together is that the partners are not completely honest. There is always a temptation, when people first meet, to put one's best foot forward. The partners may give the appearance of virtues they do not actually possess. They may conceal such traits as selfishness, stinginess, a bad temper, or a strong urge to dominate.

Sometimes the deception that takes place

during dating springs from innocent motives. The partners may simply be over-polite. They want to get along. They want things to go smoothly. So they cater to each other's preferences and avoid disagreements. Avoiding controversy is common in all kinds of social relationships. When it is practiced by prospective mates, unfortunately, it can lead to a marriage in which unexpected differences suddenly become apparent.

Sometimes the deception is deliberate, an attempt by one partner to use the other for personal advantage in such matters as ego satisfactions, prestige, sex, entertainment, or money. Sometimes both may be exploiting each other, often for different reasons. Among men who are dating, exploitation often takes the form of pretending a non-existent affection and involvement for sexual reasons. Among women, it often takes the form of encouraging the man for the sheer sake of having a companion who will take them places, or perhaps in the hope he will offer marriage.

Exploitation is especially likely to occur when the partners differ in how committed they are to each other. One of them may want very badly to maintain the relationship, while the other is only mildly concerned or even indifferent. In such a situation, the person with little or nothing at stake can very easily exploit or dominate the partner who has a great deal at stake. The unfair and often cruel advantage that a less committed partner has over a more committed partner has been studied for a long time and is known to sociologists as the principle of "least interest" (Waller, 1938). In the dating or getting together process, it has been found, men are more likely to display "least interest" than women (Eslinger, Clarke and Dynes, 1972). The "least inter-est" pattern may continue into marriage, with unhappy results.

Closing Your Eyes to the Facts

Sometimes our system fails because the two partners simply refuse to admit the truth. They can see that they have sharp differences of opinion. They observe many things about each other that they dislike, but somehow they manage to ignore all these matters. Our system has fulfilled its function of helping them get to know each other, and what they have learned clearly shows that they are mismatched, but they persist in going ahead anyway.

Often they continue the relationship in the mistaken belief that marriage can somehow work miracles. This belief is often expressed in our literature. A confirmed Don Juan, after years of cynical conquests of the women he meets, falls in love with a beautiful and virtuous librarian and is instantly reformed into a faithful husband and father. A hard-bitten prostitute nurses a dying artist back to health, marries him, inspires him to greatness, and spends the rest of her life tire-lessly doing good deeds for the poor. The idea is appealing—but it happens only in the story books. In real life, the people who expect marriage to change their partners are doomed to disappointment (see the box on *Opinions and Experiences*).

People do change, of course; but change takes time. It is not an instant miracle produced by saying the magic words "I do." Usually it is the result of many experiences with many people. Marriage is only one such experience, and marriage partners have far less influence on each other than most of them would like to think. What you see during dating or getting together is very much what you get in marriage, which is all the

Opinions and Experiences

"I THOUGHT HE WOULD CHANGE"

The director of a family counseling service in New York State describes one of the mistakes people often make in choosing a mate.

People who come for help bring us many different kinds of problems—but the most common one crops up so frequently that we are always waiting for it. Time after time we are consulted by a woman who complains that her husband gambles, or drinks, or has a bad temper, or refuses to hold a steady job. We ask, "Did you notice this before you were married?" And usually she replies, "Yes, I noticed it—but I thought he would change." We hear those words, *I thought he would change*, or *I thought she would change*, over and over again, like a stuck record.

more reason to use the system to take a long, hard look.

Ignoring the Question of Roles

The one thing above all that has caused failures in the past—and still constitutes a common and serious risk—centers on sex roles, marriage roles, and role expectations. The way these roles are established through socialization, have changed in recent years, and are still in transition has not been widely understood or even considered by most people. It is no exaggeration to say that you, after reading the early chapters of this book, know more about these roles than 99 percent of all the people who have ever been married.

Until family experts began studying the socialization process and the pressure to play roles exerted by society, many aspects of male and female behavior and of relationships between the sexes were shrouded in mystery and misconception. Since women and men searching for a mate did not even know about roles in marriage, they could hardly discuss the question of whether their attitudes might produce harmony or clash.

Not that it is easy to find a perfect fit in these days of rapid change. It is difficult even to describe where institutional marriage ends and companionship marriage begins, much less to make a clear-cut choice between them or foresee all the day-to-day adjustments that the choice will demand. And all of us are torn to some extent between the traditional sex roles and new roles that are as yet not clearly defined. Even if a couple agree that she intends to be a partner-wife and he desires a partner-wife, they must still work out the details of exactly what the term means to them and how they will cope with such issues as the working wife's overload of work. But knowing about the problems, which is something that few people did in the past, is the first step to solving them.

SUMMARY

1. Most marriages throughout history have been based not on mutual attraction but on the financial interests of the couple's families, who often arranged the wedding without consulting the bride or groom. The American system, by contrast, gives young people a free hand to en-

gage in dating or "getting together" as they please.

2. Though the system has its critics, who believe it often brings couples together through sheer chance, it can actually perform a number of important functions. It starts young people on the road to emancipating themselves from their parents and preparing to establish lives of their own, teaches them social skills and how to get along with the opposite sex, and helps them acquire self-awareness and a sense of their own identity. Ideally, it enables two people well suited for partnership in marriage to discover each other and their compatibility.

3. One explanation of how partners choose each other is *exchange theory,* which holds that we seek out those whose traits give us the maximum amount of pleasure and cause minimum pain. In other words, we go shopping for the best possible partner to whom our own characteristics entitle us.

4. Financial considerations and social climbing do not play an important part in the thinking of most Americans. Instead most people admire intelligence, sensitivity, sense of humor, gentleness, and self-control.

5. When a woman and man first meet, they are usually careful not to reveal too much of themselves. Closer involvement in getting together strips away the play acting, and, ideally, they see each other as they really are. Today's young people, when they get serious about a relationship, usually disclose their innermost thoughts and feelings about religious views, philosophy of life, interests, tastes, and fears.

6. To most people, the most important part of finding a mate is falling in love—a term that defies definition. When people are asked to name the reasons for marrying, they place being in love at the top of the list by a wide margin.

7. People in love have strong feelings of close affiliation, need, and joy. They describe themselves as floating on a cloud, giddy, carefree, wanting to run, jump, or scream—though they

may also have trouble sleeping, have butterflies in the stomach, and feel nervous before dates.

8. Women who are in love take an extremely rose-colored view of their partners, in whom they see no signs of stubbornness, irritability, or quick temper. Men are less "romantic" in this respect, but they are much more likely to fall in love at first sight.

9. The old adage that love is blind is untrue. People temper romance with realism and are not blinded to the facts about the partner's personality.

10. One of the social rules that helps determine who will fall in love and marry is *exogamy,* or the requirement of some societies that its members marry people from a different tribe or village. In the United States, exogamy takes the form of forbidding marriage between blood relatives, up to and including first cousins.

11. The opposite rule is *endogamy,* or the requirement to marry within the group. Many U.S. families try to enforce a kind of endogamy by pressuring their children to marry partners of the same religion or ethnic background.

12. Many studies have shown that people also have a tendency toward *homogamy,* or attraction to others of the same social and religious background, with similar values, attitudes, tastes, and interests.

13. The *theory of complementary needs* holds that we narrow the field of eligibles through homogamy, but then tend to select someone who is unlike us in important psychological ways and can thus meet some of the needs for which we hunger, consciously or unconsciously. Thus a domineering man tends to favor a submissive woman rather than one just as strong-minded as he is.

14. The *wheel theory* of how love grows holds that the progress resembles a four-spoked wheel rolling downhill. The first spoke is a feeling of *rapport,* or being at ease and comfortable together. Next comes *self-revelation,* in which the two begin to discuss their most intimate "hopes, desires, and fears." The third spoke is *mutual dependency,*

in which the couple come to need each other as companions and listeners. The final spoke is *self-fulfillment,* where each finds that the other provides the most soul-satisfying kind of support and comfort. If all goes well, the wheel keeps turning, with increasing speed. However, it can stop, turn backward, and end the relationship if something goes wrong at any of the four stages.

15. A couple are most likely to marry if both have had a strong desire to marry someone soon and find similarities in their thinking, attitude toward life (happy-go-lucky or sober), and tendency to be confident or apprehensive, and if one is witty and the other placid. They are least likely to marry if there are large differences in height, interest in sports, tendency to be controlled as opposed to undisciplined, and leaning toward dominance or submission, and if the man is more tense and has a greater need for affection than the woman.

16. Many love affairs break up usually because the two people become bored or find differences in interests and attitudes, or because one of them either wants more independence or becomes interested in someone else. Often the split is made casually and without much pain, although some people are deeply hurt. Men seem to be hit harder than women and to feel unhappy, lonely, and depressed. Women are more inclined to feel guilty for the failure.

17. Divorce often represents a failure to find a suitable partner. Among common reasons for the failure are these:

Lack of self-confidence makes many people hesitate to make acquaintances and learn more about them. They lose opportunities because they date not too much but too little.

Getting committed while too young is a mistake made by couples who pair off in high school and let the relationship persist even though they change afterward and no longer have much in common.

Lack of honesty by one or both, in an effort to put the best foot forward, sometimes hides aspects of personality that will crop up after marriage and distress the other person. The deception may spring from the most innocent motives, like over-politeness to keep things going smoothly, or it may be a deliberate attempt to exploit the partner.

Refusal to admit the truth may keep a couple together even when they see things about each other that they dislike, often in the mistaken belief that marriage will set everything straight.

Ignoring the question of roles was once the chief cause of mismatches, for few people understood the nature or importance of sex roles, marriage roles, and role expectations. It is still common, and people often enter marriage with only a hazy notion of how the partner feels about such issues as traditional versus companionship marriage, what exactly is meant by these terms, or the privileges and obligations of the partners.

DISCUSSION QUESTIONS

1. Describe the most common patterns of dating or getting together that exist in your community.

2. How would you feel if your parents selected a marriage partner for you, as happens in arranged marriages?

3. What qualities do you think are the most important to look for in a prospective marriage partner?

4. Discuss the reasons men and women tend to become more realistic and less romantic with increasing age and experience.

5. Describe couples you know whose similarities illustrate homogamy. Describe couples whose differences indicate complementary needs.

6. How may dating a very small number of people reduce your chances of finding a suitable marriage partner?

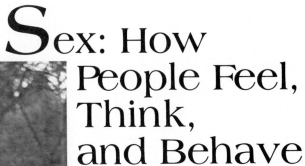

CHAPTER 6

Sex: How People Feel, Think, and Behave

A half century ago any visitors from outer space might have had a difficult time figuring out how we Americans produce our babies. They would have found virtually no mention of sex in our newspapers, magazines, or books. In the movies, they would have seen that males and females became attracted to one another, but apparently only for the sake of a brief and antiseptic kiss just before the film ended. They would have found nothing about sex taught in the schools, even medical schools.

Visitors today would get a far different impression. Many of our novels and movies now make it seem that the human race is programmed by nature to spend most of its time in bed or getting there. The paperback racks are full of manuals presenting step-by-step formulas for more and better orgasms. Our visitors would be forced to wonder not how we reproduce but how we ever find time to do anything else.

But appearances can be deceiving. As research scientists discovered when they began a serious study of sexual behavior in the 1940s, the America of the past was by no means so sexless and proper as it pretended. And today's America, despite the more free-and-easy atmosphere spawned by the well-publicized "sexual revolution," is by no means so totally preoccupied with sex as our literature and films might indicate.

AMERICA'S SEXUAL REVOLUTION

The sexual revolution reached its peak from about 1965 to 1975 and has since been on the wane. The annual Yankelovich polls of public opinion have shown a consistent trend toward conservatism since 1976 (Yankelovich, Skelly, and White, 1983), and there have been numerous other indications that great numbers of Americans found the footloose and emotionless sex advocated by the revolution unsatisfactory. As one therapist has described the situation at the height of the revolution, "We have been liberated from the taboos of the past only to find ourselves imprisoned in a 'freedom' that brings us no closer to our real nature or needs" (Marin, 1983). Today's tendency is to return to such traditional values as personal commitment and fidelity. In a survey made in the 1970s 23 percent of Americans said they would welcome less emphasis on marriage, but more recently this figure has dropped to only 15 percent (Gallup, 1978, 1980).

The sexual revolution, of course, changed the United States to a spectacular degree. Older people, who grew up when sex was spoken of only in whispers, if at all, can hardly believe their ears and eyes—and often they take what they hear and see as a sure sign that the nation is well down the road to damnation and ruin. Younger people can hardly imagine the secrecy and ignorance in which sex used to be shrouded. The situation described in the box on *Opinions and Experiences* sounds like something that happened a thousand years ago, yet it accurately depicts the experiences of millions of people who are still alive.

Sex Through the Ages

To a social historian, there is nothing surprising or even unusual about the recent swings in attitudes toward sex. Studies of cultural standards around the world, past and present, show that almost everything about sex has been eagerly embraced by some societies and condemned by others. Homosexual acts were punishable by death among the ancient Hebrews but accepted and even admired by the ancient Greeks. The early Christians held that the noblest form of sexual behavior was abstinence, but at about the same time the Romans were indulging in their famous orgies in the Colosseum.

In England at the time of Queen Elizabeth, sex was treated ''with a frankness and frequently with a ribaldry that has no parallel in Western history.'' A little later, under Queen Victoria, sex was treated ''with such great circumspection that among some groups of these very same Englishmen one would hardly have known that coitus ever took place,'' and any falls from propriety ''were the cause of great scandal and disgrace'' (Ehrmann, 1964).

Similar differences can still be found today. A group in New Guinea considers sexual activity a sin, engaged in only out of the duty to create a new generation—and people in the Polynesian Islands consider it a fine and laudable art worthy of being taught from

childhood on. A number of cultures, for example in the Gilbert Islands of the South Pacific, condemn to death any couple found to have had sexual relations before marriage, but the Lepcha people in India are happy to see their 12-year-old daughters having intercourse because they believe it helps the girls mature (Gagnon, 1975). There are societies in Africa and India that even approve of intercourse between a young sister and brother (Stephens, 1963).

How Our Sexual Revolution Began

The revolution in the American sexual climate, like most social changes, sprang from many sources. In part it resulted from the same factors that produced the modern system of dating or getting together, chiefly the increasing industrialization of the nation and the concentration of population in cities. In part it reflected the views of Sigmund Freud, with his emphasis on sexuality as a human motive—views that gained more popular acceptance in the United States than in his native Europe. It depended to some extent on increased availability of effective techniques of birth control.

American participation in World War I, in 1917 and 1918, also played a considerable part. Serving in the armed forces brought many American men from the upper and middle classes into close association with men of the lower social classes, who had much more permissive standards of sexual behavior. It also introduced many Americans to the more permissive attitudes of some of their European allies. In actual behavior a great change took place in the years immediately after the war. Various forms of ''petting'' became a popular pastime among young people. The number of young people

Opinions and Experiences

SEX EDUCATION A HALF CENTURY AGO

A man who went to college in the 1920s and 1930s once taped these recollections of how much he was able to learn in those years before the sexual revolution.

I came from an average home—and in the average home sex was never mentioned. Except that boys were always warned against masturbation, because masturbation was supposed to drive you crazy. When I was in the eighth grade one boy did go crazy, more or less. He jumped up in class one day and asked for permission to go outside and cast stones at the devil—which the teacher, who probably was completely flabbergasted, granted without asking for any further explanation. The word around town was that, sure enough, masturbation had eaten his brain away. Nobody seemed to suspect, as people would immediately figure today, that his problem was *worry* over masturbating.

Girls apparently weren't even warned. I suppose most adults in those days didn't know that women could masturbate—or, if they knew, they weren't going to admit it.

There were a few books about sex that got passed around: *What Every Boy Should Know* and *What Every Girl Should Know.* But they didn't say much, except that venereal disease was a bad thing and that you shouldn't have too much sex anyway. I firmly believed for a long time that a man is capable of only so many

orgasms in his life, and if you use them up when you're young you won't have any left.

In the city where I was going to college, a visiting lecturer once rented a theater and promised to tell all about sex, but all he did was try to sell a book on how to avoid premature ejaculation. I was going with a girl and we were having sex, and I had no way of knowing whether I was guilty or not of premature ejaculation; so I bought the book. Believe it or not, I spent an hour every day in the bathtub sitting first in hot water and then in cold, alternating the temperature every fifteen minutes, which was what the book advised.

There was no lack of pornography, of course—what we called French postcards and comic books that were "dirty" versions of the strips in the newspapers. Sometimes we got films to show at the fraternity house. So we learned that people could do all kinds of things to and with one another; but we never knew what was normal and what was not, and we had our worries.

Or maybe I worried more than most. Once I had an angry red spot down in the pubic area and I was sure it was a syphilitic chancre. I got up my nerve and went to a doctor—a doctor who didn't know me, in a different part of town. He got a great laugh out of it. My "chancre" was a pimple from an ingrown hair. Would you believe I was a college sophomore at the time and that's all I knew about sex?

---

who had intercourse before marriage increased (Simon, Berger, and Gagnon, 1972).

But revolutions, though they always have complex causes, usually do not erupt unless they have a leader. In this case, as so many, the mantle of leadership fell on a previously obscure person—Alfred Kinsey, a university professor who was in part a product of social change and in part the instrument of change.

The Revolution's Unlikely Leader

Kinsey was about as unlikely a candidate for leader of a sexual revolution as could be imagined. In his youth he was an Eagle Scout. As an adult he was deadly serious, hard working, an upright and even prissy kind of man. He never smoked or drank un-

til in his later years when his physician recommended a little alcohol for a heart
condition. His favorite entertainment was
inviting friends to his house to sit on stiff
chairs and listen to his collection of classical
records, preceded by his own dry and formally delivered program notes.

His chosen field was zoology, his specialty
the life cycle of the gall wasp—a little insect
that lays its eggs in the bark of trees, causing
unsightly swellings. Since gall wasps are of
interest to only a minority, there was no indication when Kinsey was in his early 40s
that his name would ever be a household
word.

What got Kinsey interested in studying
sex was the fact that his students sometimes
asked him for advice. Though zoology is supposed to be about reproduction as much as
anything else, he found he was unable to answer many of their questions. With his usual
thoroughness, he tried to find the answers
in the university library. There too he was
frustrated. He found plenty of philosophical
discussions of how people should behave sexually but almost nothing about how they actually do behave. The few studies he did find
were based on only a small number of cases.
Since he himself had once studied no less
than 150,000 individual gall wasps before
venturing to make any generalizations about
the species, he was hardly impressed.

So Kinsey set out to fill what he saw as a
great gap in human knowledge. The difficulties were staggering. People were reluctant to talk about their sex lives. In the first
six months of trying to find willing subjects,
Kinsey and his associates rounded up only
sixty-two, mostly students and faculty members. Even when he discovered better ways
of persuading people to volunteer information, he ran into other problems. In several
cities the police got after him, and in one rural area the local sheriff. Many people tried

to pressure his university to stop him, fire
him, or both.

It was probably Kinsey's stern personality
that carried the day. He went about his work
with "a near-puritan rigor" (Foote, 1954).
Only the most prejudiced person could possibly have imagined that he took any pru-
rient interest in his subject. He managed in
his dead-serious manner to get the cooperation of church groups, women's clubs,
business clubs, and PTA groups. Over the
next ten years he and his associates interviewed 5,300 men and nearly 8,000 women.

Kinsey conducted more than 7,000 of the
interviews himself, thus getting a liberal education in the many diverse forms that sexual behavior takes. Doubtless much of what
he heard shocked him at first, but he wound
up with a great deal of sympathy for people
who told him about activities that he once
would have considered outrageous. For example, he listened without a trace of disapproval to the most lurid experiences of the
many prostitutes who gave him their life histories. In areas outside sex, however, he remained strait-laced to the end. He could
never forgive the prostitutes for staying up
most of the night, getting up late, and in
general living a life of what struck him as
self-indulgent indolence.

The Two Kinsey Reports

The first of the Kinsey reports, *Sexual Behavior in the Human Male,* was published in 1948.
It appeared without any fanfare. Book reviewers generally ignored it. The *New York
Times,* considered a liberal newspaper, refused to run an advertisement for it. Nonetheless, the book sold 265,000 copies and its
message—notably that the male sex drive
starts earlier, lasts longer, and is stronger
than most Americans had been willing to admit—was in one way or another heard

around the nation. The message was not always welcomed, and many people reacted with downright shock. One elderly woman wrote an angry letter to Kinsey berating him for wasting his time in proving what every woman had known all along, which is that "the male population is a herd of prancing, leering goats" (Gebhard, 1981).

By the time the Kinsey report on women was published five years later, the nation was ready for it. This book, *Sexual Behavior in the Human Female,* was one of the most widely covered news stories of all time. Almost every newspaper and magazine printed detailed summaries, using such terms, once foreign to their pages, as *orgasm* and *masturbation.* The Kinsey reports paved the way for a frank discussion of sex unprecedented in our nation's history. They also provided a great deal of sex education. Although they are based on information gathered four decades ago, they remain one of our best sources of knowledge, covering more aspects of sexuality in more detail than any study made since.

A Word of Caution on Sex Surveys

All sex surveys, it should be pointed out, have an inherent weakness. They can study only self-reports of sexual activity, which means they must rely on their subjects' honesty and the accuracy of their subjects' memories. It is quite possible that the continuing influence of sex-role socialization tends to make males exaggerate their sexual activity and females play it down. Moreover it is difficult to study a representative sample of the population, since many people refuse to discuss such matters at all.

Kinsey was aware of these problems and acknowledged that his results were only "approximations of the fact," though he felt they

were "probably fair approximations" (Kinsey et al., 1948). His sampling methods were certainly not perfect, but the large number of people he studied made up in part for this defect. Through long experience interviewing so many subjects, he and his associates were confident they could quickly spot a subject who was trying to falsify.

Some of the most widely publicized surveys of recent years have no real claim at all to being scientific. The studies reported by magazines are usually based on the responses of their own readers, who constitute a small and special group interested in the subject matter and viewpoint of that particular publication. Even the most impressive-sounding books are often statistically unsound. A frequently cited study called *Sexual Behavior in the 1970's,* commissioned by *Playboy* and advertised as a thorough updating of the Kinsey reports, used a sampling procedure that has been termed "the poorest of the major studies" made in that decade (Reiss, 1976).

The constant flood of books and articles claiming to be the last word on sexual behavior is interesting as one aspect of the sexual climate, but it seldom has any scientific value. The latest so-called scientific survey may serve to introduce you to some new viewpoints held by some people somewhere, but it is probably statistically inaccurate and certainly worthless as personal guidance. Be especially suspicious of any findings that differ sharply from the figures presented in this chapter, which come from studies that used the best possible methods.

THE NEW PERMISSIVENESS

The most striking feature of the sexual revolution is the permissiveness so readily apparent in today's society. Magazines are

The cover and an inside page of a pamphlet that could not have been published a few decades ago.

An example of the new permissiveness created by the sexual revolution: on openly gay couple are hardly even noticed by other pedestrians.

filled with articles on every conceivable aspect of sex. Bookstores stock volumes of advice written by everyone from eminent physicians to former prostitutes. Supreme Court decisions on obscenity have legalized what was once outlawed as pornography, and X-rated films portray every kind of sexual activity that is humanly possible—and even, thanks to the technical tricks of the movie studio, some that are hardly likely in real life.

Some of the pioneers in the birth control movement went to jail for their beliefs. Now information is available in almost any library and the equipment in almost any drugstore. Abortion, though still a hotly debated issue, is legally available in many places and sometimes provided at government expense. Such practices as oral sex, for which even married couples sometimes went to prison in the past, are generally accepted. Most people are no longer horrified when a prominent American, male or female, acknowledges homosexual activity, which was also a criminal offense in the past.

Old Restrictions and the Double Standard

The restrictions of the past made sex not only unspeakable, at least out loud, but also to some extent unthinkable and "dirty." This attitude did not necessarily deter males from going ahead anyway. Kinsey found that well over half masturbated before they were 14, and 92 percent by the time they were 19.

Over half engaged in intercourse by the time they were 16, and 72 percent by the age of 19 (Kinsey et al., 1948). But the stigma was there, and these activities were secret and often guilt-ridden. In fact the atmosphere of shame has not entirely disappeared. Masters and Johnson, who are among today's most prominent sex researchers, have reported these words from a troubled husband:

> For a long time I believed that the act of intercourse was dirty. My whole experience with it—not being married—meant being reminded that it was all dirty. And since I couldn't understand how it could be dirty only if it was out of marriage, I thought it was more or less dirty even when you were married.
>
> *(Masters and Johnson, 1976)*

The effect on women was considerably greater. At one time many American females, especially in the middle class, were socialized to believe that "a nice girl" simply did not have any sexual desires. In marriage, sex was considered by many just a rather unpleasant duty, performed to indulge the husband's more bestial nature. As evident in some of the medical literature of the past, a woman discussing sexual matters with her physician might report how many times her husband had "used" her within the past month.

There was in essence a double standard of sexual behavior, with one set of rules for males and another for females. Women were definitely supposed to remain virgins before marriage. Although men too were theoretically expected to refrain from sex outside marriage, society managed to look the other way when they strayed. Thus the 72 percent found by Kinsey to have engaged in intercourse by the age of 19 did so mostly with prostitutes or with a small pool of "bad

girls" who were available for experimentation (Miller and Simon, 1974). Of the women studied by Kinsey, only about 18 percent had experienced intercourse by 19 (Kinsey et al., 1953).

Today's Attitudes

Many of the old attitudes have now been discarded by most people. As early as the 1960s sociologists noted that "many influential people are moving away from the view that sexual morality is defined by abstinence from nonmarital intercourse toward one in which morality is expressed through responsible sexual behavior and a sincere regard for the rights of others" (Kirkendall and Libby, 1966). In marriage, it has been observed that "sex now represents a delight instead of a duty, and even a form of play" (Gagnon, 1975).

Charles Westoff, who has made a number of careful statistical studies, has reported "clear evidence" that by and large married couples now engage in intercourse more frequently than in the past. Undoubtedly one reason is that modern contraceptive methods reduce the risk of an unwanted pregnancy. Westoff suggests that the increase may also reflect the fact that sex "is becoming perceived as a more natural, less taboo subject." The sexual revolution has created "a developing emphasis on the woman's right to personal fulfillment," and the female's "traditional passive sexual role may be giving way to more assertive sexual behavior" (Westoff, 1974). Other observers have also noted a strong tendency for women to participate in a very different way from the days when they might speak of being "used" (Bell and Bell, 1972). The tendency appears to be greatest among women of greater education and of less traditional attitudes toward sex roles.

Attitudes toward Premarital Sex

When George Gallup took his first public opinion poll of attitudes toward premarital sex in 1969, he found that 68 percent of Americans considered it morally wrong. But the latest Gallup poll (1985) shows that only 39 percent still think it is wrong, 52 percent disagree, and the other 9 percent have no opinion. The only group that continues to consider it wrong is people aged fifty and over (56 percent). Of young adults, aged eighteen to twenty-nine, a mere 18 percent find it wrong. Other polls have shown that the groups most tolerant of premarital sex, besides the young, are the best educated and those with a high family income (Singh, 1980). Some of the arguments most frequently cited by college students in favor of engaging in premarital sex—or abstaining from it—are presented in a box on *Opinions and Experiences*.

Although most Americans now appear to accept premarital sex in general, another poll taken in the late 1970s found that a considerable majority—63 percent—said it was morally wrong for teenagers to have sexual relations (Yankelovich, Skelly, and White, 1977a). On the other hand, another poll taken at about the same time found that 77 percent of adult Americans favored sex education in the public schools, with 69 percent agreeing that this should include information on contraception. Indeed 56 percent were in favor of making birth control devices available to teenagers of both sexes (Gallup, 1978).

Even parents who are permissive in general, however, may take a stricter view of their own children's activities. A study in the late 1960s found that 97 percent of the mothers interviewed wanted their daughters to refrain from premarital sex, even though 30 percent of these mothers had themselves engaged in it. Of the fathers studied, 90 percent wanted their sons to refrain, though 51 percent of these fathers had not done so themselves (Wake, 1969).

What's Happened to the Double Standard?

The double standard has certainly not disappeared. Many people continue to oppose premarital sexual activity for females but condone it for males, and many parents take a far stricter stand toward their daughters than their sons.

Even in the most casual forms of dating or getting together there continues to be a tendency for women to play a passive role, waiting to be asked. "When it come to pursuing men, women still have a long way to go before they can feel comfortable," a hesitancy that is compounded by a tendency for men to be embarrassed and fearful when women take the initiative (Safilios-Rothschild, 1977). As for actually making sexual advances, a study of college women in the 1970s found that about two-thirds were loath to attempt this (Burstein, 1975). One reason, again, is that many people continue to have a double standard of proper sexual conduct for females and males.

In many respects, however, the double standard is less prevalent and influential than in the past. The attitudes held by and toward the sexes have shifted toward greater equality. In actual behavior the sexes have moved much closer, as is clearly shown by recent findings on the sexual activity of unmarried people.

Opinions and Experiences

THE PRO AND CON OF PREMARITAL SEX

These comments were recorded over the years from students in a marriage and family course. Although the same or similar opinions have been presented from time to time by students of both sexes, the particular speaker quoted here is identified by an *M* for male or *F* for female.

Student Arguments in Favor

F: If you love someone, you want the relationship to be as emotionally deep as possible, and making love is the deepest form of emotional expression.

M: Sex is a pleasure, perhaps the greatest of pleasures. It's recreation. It's fun. It feels good. And it's better to have it than to think about it all the time and never get any studying done.

F: If you plan to marry someone, you want to be sure that the two of you are sexually compatible. Also, you want to be sure you really know your partner, and having sex is one way of learning more.

M: Having a good sexual relationship is something you have to learn. A couple who develop their sexual skills before marriage are almost bound to have better sex after marriage, or at least have it sooner than couples who wait.

F: A lot of students think there's something wrong with you if you don't. Call it peer pressure or whatever; you have to keep up with your friends.

M: I intend to be married for a long time, and I intend to be faithful; but I would like a little variety before I take that step.

Arguments Against

M: I'm not about to do something that goes against my religious and ethical principles. I've seen too many people, men and women both, who did it and suffered terrible feelings of guilt. You read about the rise in campus suicides, and I think guilt over sex may be one of the causes.

F: The greatest reason to abstain is the danger of pregnancy. What do you do if that happens? Quit school and get left out of all the things your classmates are doing? What about the effect on the father, and on your and his parents? Or even the child? How good a parent can you be if you're young, troubled, and strapped for money?

M: Having sex is too much of a commitment. It cuts off the opportunity to get to know someone who might be a much better partner. And you might wind up getting married just because the girl feels she has to marry a man after she's had sex with him, and because you feel obligated to her.

F: There's the danger of losing your reputation, or having your parents disapprove if they find out. And how can you be sure that the fellow, even if he says it will make no difference, will actually respect you as much?

M: I'd worry about marrying a woman who had premarital experience, even just with me. I'd wonder if she'd be faithful to me.

F: You'd always be running the risk of venereal disease. Just reading about herpes, which can't be cured at all, is enough to stop me.

Sex before Marriage

Among males, the number who engage in sexual intercourse before marriage has not changed very much since the time of the Kinsey surveys, which set the figures at 72 percent by the age of 19. The most recent study showed that 78 percent of unmarried men in the United States have experienced intercourse by the age of 19, with the proportion about equal for whites and blacks (Zelnick and Kantner, 1980). The rate among unmarried women, however, has risen sharply. From the 18 percent found by Kinsey for women who were 19 or younger, the number has now risen to 40 percent of white women and 58 percent of black women (Pratt and Bachrach, 1984). Among unmarried women in their 20s, the figure now stands at 82 percent (Tanfer and Horn, 1985).

The new findings indicate that the double standard has lost its influence in at least one important respect. To a considerable extent, young men no longer gain their sexual experience with prostitutes or "bad girls." Perhaps the ranks of the "bad girls" have thinned, or perhaps young men no longer seek them out. Men and women meet on a more equal basis and decide together whether or not to have intercourse.

One of the side effects of the recent rise in the number of young women who engage in premarital intercourse has been a sharp increase in teenage pregnancies. Of all unmarried young females between 15 and 19 years of age, 11 percent of the whites and 26

percent of the blacks become pregnant (Pratt and Bachrach, 1984). The pregnancy rate per 1,000 teenagers is much higher in the United States, 83 for whites and 163 for blacks, than in other industrialized nations, where it ranges from 14 in the Netherlands to 45 in England and Wales. The abortion rate is also much higher in the United States (Alan Guttmacher Institute, 1985).

The high rates are attributed to the fact that teenagers here "are less likely to use contraception, and among those who do use it, they are less likely to take the pill." One study found that about one sexually active young woman in four never uses any form of birth control, and only about one in three always does so (Zelnick and Kantner, 1980). Teenagers having their first experience are unlikely to take any precautions—less than half the time—probably because the experience is an unplanned, spur-of-the moment decision for more than four out of five young women and three out of four men (Zelnick and Shah, 1983). Some findings indicate that teenage pregnancy may not always be unwelcome for the mother-to-be. One study of young women who had babies while still

One of many thousands of teenagers who become pregnant in the United States every year.

Patricia Angre, Photo Researchers

in school found that many of them were in love and fully expected to marry their partner—and considered the child another bond to the man (Scott, 1983).

Sex in College

It is difficult to make generalities about the sexual behavior of unmarried college students. The amount of sexual activity varies from one campus to another, depending on the general atmosphere, the nature of the student body, and whether most of the students live at home and commute to the campus or come from faraway places and live in dormitories or off-campus housing. Even on the same campus, the amount of activity may vary substantially over a period of years. Thus what is true on one campus may not be at all true of another campus, or even of that same school in a different year.

Certainly the amount of sexual activity on the campus increased dramatically during the sexual revolution. One series of surveys at a big-city university indicated that only about 19 percent of the women students had engaged in intercourse in 1958, but this number rose to 29 percent in 1968 and then jumped to 62 percent in 1978 (Bell and Coughey, 1980). At a state university in the South, the number of women students who had experienced intercourse rose from 29 percent in 1969 to 57 percent in 1975, then to 64 percent in 1980. The figures for male students started at 65 percent in 1965 and reached 77 percent in 1980 (Robinson and Jedlicka, 1982).

During the present decade, as the revolution has waned, the increase seems to have leveled off (Gerrard, 1982). Indeed the amount of activity has probably dropped. A number of sex counselors in colleges have reported a decline in promiscuity and a growing concern for commitment, marriage, and children (Stern, 1983).

Many studies have shown that the number of college students who engage in intercourse rises steadily from the freshman year to the senior year. One study made about a decade ago found that the number more than doubled among women and nearly doubled among men (Simon, Berger, and Gagnon, 1972). The figures also rise with increasing romantic involvement. Of women students, 50 percent had engaged in intercourse when merely dating, but 67 percent when going steady and 76 percent when engaged to be married.

Living Together on the Campus

Like the number of students having intercourse, the number of students who live with a member of the opposite sex also varies greatly from campus to campus. At some schools, especially small colleges where most students commute to the campus, the number may be close to zero. At others, especially large universities that draw students from a wide area, the number may be high.

No nationwide college sampling has ever been made on this matter of *cohabitation,* that is, living together in a sexual relationship. The studies that do exist have naturally been made on campuses where cohabitation was sufficiently widespread to attract attention. One such study, at a state university in the West, found that 18 percent of the women and 29 percent of the men had cohabited at one time or another (Henze and Hudson, 1974), with the higher figure for men presumably indicating that some were living with a nonstudent.

A study at a state university in the East found that 33 percent of the students had cohabited, with the figure almost exactly the

Hugh Rogers, Monkmeyer

A neighbor drops in on one of the couples living together in college.

same for women and men. At this university the arrangement was usually short-lived. Asked about their longest period of cohabitation, 31 percent of the women and 50 percent of the men reported less than a month, 75 percent of the women and 82 percent of the men less than six months. Possibly because the arrangements tended to be so temporary, many of the students were repeaters. More than 40 percent of the women and 62 percent of the men had cohabited with more than one partner (Peterman, Ridley, and Anderson, 1974).

Cohabitation on the campus is usually accompanied by strong feelings of affection and even love, but when it occurs during the early college years it is not necessarily considered to be any kind of permanent arrangement, especially by the men. Among seniors, cohabitation seems to take on more of the characteristics of a trial marriage, to turn into actual marriage if everything works out.

Why "Cohabitors" Break Up: A Possible Answer

As to why living together should so often be abandoned, and so quickly, a possible clue comes from a study made in Colorado, in which the subjects were both students and nonstudents. An attempt was made to compare couples who were cohabiting with similar couples who were merely going together. In many ways the two kinds of couples were very much alike. They showed no great differences, for example, in home background, income, or religious attitude. Moreover, both kinds of couples considered themselves highly involved in the relationship and happy with it. In some respects, however, there were marked differences between the two kinds of couples.

The going-together pairs were in close agreement on such matters as expectations of marriage and feelings of need and respect for each other. The couples who were living together displayed much less agreement. In particular, the women were considerably more likely to be thinking of eventual marriage than their male partners, only 17 percent of whom expressed intentions of marrying. Moreover, the men tended to display a low level of need and respect for the women they were living with. The psychologists who conducted the study concluded that the living-together couples lacked many of the mutual feelings considered essential to any good relationship between the sexes, and that one reason may have been differing motives for the living arrangement (Lyness, Lipetz, and Davis, 1972).

Does Cohabitation Result in Happy Marriages?

In the United States the number of couples living together without marriage now stands at around 2 million, and it is expected to reach about 3.5 million by the end of the decade (Glick, 1984). These are remarkable figures, considering that there were only about a half million such couples as recently as 1970. The rise in cohabitation has been so rapid that there has not yet been time to

determine exactly what its effect will be on marital happiness and the divorce rate.

In the days when cohabitation was rare, many sociologists theorized that it might produce happier marriages in the long run. It seemed only logical to believe that a trial period of living together would reveal any drastic incompatibilities and limit actual marriage to partners who had proved their ability to get along (Trost, 1975). It was also thought that living together could serve as effective training for marriage (Macklin, 1972).

These theories have not been borne out by the research done since the number of cohabitors began to grow. One study of couples who had lived together before marriage found that their divorce rate was just as high after four years as among other couples who had not been cohabitors (Bentler and Newcomb, 1978). A recent study found that couples who had lived together seemed no more satisfied with their marriages than other couples, and if anything were less satisfied (DeMaris and Leslie, 1984). It will be some years, however, before all the facts are available.

Some Other Results of the Sexual Revolution

Along with different attitudes and behaviors related to sex before marriage, the sexual revolution produced many other changes, for example, a sharp increase in sexual activity among people who are separated or divorced. It also produced a great deal of discussion about various practices that can generally be classifed under extramarital sex. One such practice, widely publicized in the 1970s, was "swinging," in which married couples arrange to engage in sex with other couples, exchanging their mates at meetings of four or more people. Another was living in group marriages or in sexually permissive communes in which each woman considered herself married to all the men and each man considered himself married to all the women.

Even at the height of the revolution, however, all forms of extramarital sex were far less common than the publicity might have indicated. The number of people who have engaged in swinging, for example, was never more than 1 percent and possibly no higher than half of 1 percent (Bartel, 1971). An overwhelming majority of Americans, despite all the recent changes, have always placed a high value on sexual fidelity in marriage.

In a 1980 public opinion poll a list of matters that might be considered basic to a good marriage was shown to a representative sample of men and women, who were asked to pick out the items they considered most essential. Sexual fidelity was termed very important by 72 percent of men and 79 percent of women—more than chose financial security, having similar ideas on how to handle money or rear children, being able to see the humorous side, or liking the same kinds of friends, activities, and lifestyles (Roper, 1980).

Another poll, conducted in the early 1980s, surveyed only couples living in metropolitan areas, where sexual infidelity is most likely to occur. Of these couples 75 percent of husbands and 84 percent of wives said they considered it important to be monogamous, and only 11 percent of the men and 7 percent of the women disagreed, with the others neutral. Among couples married for ten years or more, 30 percent of the husbands and 22 percent of the wives had actually engaged in extramarital activity (figures not very different from those found by Kinsey in the 1940s). Often the incident was casual and occurred more or less by chance. The sociologists who conducted the study concluded, "Husbands and wives may indulge their curiosity or succumb to a moment of romantic temptation, but they will nevertheless continue to regard these acts as out of bounds" (Blumstein and Schwartz, 1983).

Indeed the sexual revolution probably never progressed as far as has often been assumed. It certainly produced a great deal of confusion over moral standards. A public opinion poll in the late 1970s found 61 percent of Americans agreeing that "it's getting harder and harder to know what's right and what's wrong these days." But the poll also showed that most Americans definitely disapproved of pornographic movies, nudity in movies or on bathing beaches, and prostitution. More considered homosexual activity morally wrong than accepted it, and only a bare majority considered cohabitation acceptable, while 76 percent agreed that "permissiveness had led to a lot of things that are wrong with the country these days." The poll also found that, while 41 percent felt they themselves had become more permissive about sexual matters in recent years, 15 percent said they had turned more conservative (Yankelovich, Skelly, and White, 1977a)—one of the first indications that the revolution had started to produce a backlash.

PLURALISM IN ATTITUDES AND BEHAVIOR: THE FORGOTTEN MESSAGE OF THE KINSEY REPORTS

Many of the popular beliefs about sex—and much of what is written about it—assume that all people are alike in attitudes and behavior. Many sex manuals, for example, purport to describe what (all) women like, what (all) men like, and how (all) people should go about having sex and how often. The new breed of experts spawned by the sexual revolution assumes that everyone has now been stripped of all inhibitions, uncovering a universal and infinite capacity for sexual performance and delight. We are bombarded from all sides by advice on how (all) men and (all) women can be aroused to sexual fervor, how (all) people can produce the best orgasms, and how sex in general can be made a constant delight (for everyone).

The assumption that all people are alike blithely ignores what was without doubt the chief contribution of the Kinsey reports, yet one that has somehow been forgotten. Kinsey spent most of his time studying and describing the vast pluralism of our society in sexual matters, differences in attitudes and behavior that he found to exist over a range of remarkable variety. The situation today is almost as if the revolution had seized on his work as a command for more and better sexuality while completely overlooking his plain and simple message that there are about as many different kinds of sexuality as there are people.

Differences in Desire and Capacity

Just as people come in various shapes and sizes, the Kinsey reports showed, they arrive at maturity in an endless variety of sexual patterns. This is especially true, he found, of desire and capacity. Some people, men and women alike, can be aroused to a high pitch of excitement by the mere thought of a member of the opposite sex. Others can hardly be aroused at all. Some get nervous and cranky if deprived of sex for a day. Others are perfectly happy to go without it for weeks, months, or even a lifetime.

Kinsey measured individual sexual capac-

ities by the number of orgasms that people experienced, and he found a range so enormously wide as to be almost unbelievable. Among men, for example, he found that for those in their late teens, 20s, and early 30s the median number* of orgasms per week was about two. At one extreme there were some men that age who were never having an orgasm. At the opposite extreme, there were some who were having as many as four a day, day in and day out (Kinsey et al., 1948).

Among women, the differences proved even greater. Some of the women interviewed by the Kinsey staff had never in their life experienced any kind of sexual excitement, much less an orgasm. At the other extreme there were women whose desires were so frequent and intense that they could be satisfied only by masturbation—in one case as many as thirty or more times a week, each time with as many as a hundred orgasms in quick succession (Kinsey et al, 1953).

Differences in Female Response

Kinsey concluded that all women, even those at the lower end of the range he discovered, are capable of responding to the point of orgasm under the proper conditions—though some of his subjects never discovered it or took many years to learn. He found one woman, for example, who was married for twenty-eight years before she experienced her first orgasm. He also found a number who had been divorced and remarried three or four times before they finally wound up with a partner with whom they managed to attain orgasm.

At the upper end of the range, he found some women so responsive that they had or-

---

*In any distribution, the median is the halfway point; 50 percent of cases are above this point and 50 percent below.

gasms almost immediately—in intercourse, within fifteen to thirty seconds. Under the most favorable circumstances, indeed, he found that most women respond more quickly than is generally assumed. In masturbation, which is the most efficient way to produce female orgasm, he found that nearly half of all women reach climax within three minutes, and another fourth of them in four or five minutes. Only about one in eight requires more than ten minutes. (Sexual intercourse is less likely than masturbation to produce an orgasm for a woman because it does not provide as much sustained stimulation of the *clitoris,* a small structure of tissue at the top of the vaginal entrance, which is richly supplied with nerve endings and is the focal point of sexual sensations.* Moreover intercourse provides other kinds of physical and psychological stimulation that are in some ways distracting.)

Thus women vary widely in their ability to achieve orgasm in intercourse. On the average, Kinsey found, a woman is likely to reach orgasm about three-fourths of the time and to fail on the other occasions. But some women never experience orgasm in intercourse and some do so rarely, while others do so always. The ability to achieve orgasm is lowest among young and inexperienced women and usually increases later.

Multiple orgasms in women is another topic that has been widely discussed in recent years. Again there are many individual differences. Kinsey found that about one woman in seven regularly experiences multiple orgasms. The number may be anywhere from two to a dozen during intercourse—or in masturbation, as has been said, in some rare cases as many as a hundred, over a period lasting as long as an hour. Some women respond with multiple orgasms during intercourse on some occasions even though they do not have orgasms at all on other occasions. Most women do not experience multiple orgasms, even when stimulation is intense and prolonged.

What Causes the Differences?

The individual differences found by Kinsey still prevail despite the sexual revolution and the present swing of the pendulum back toward more conservative standards. A recent survey, designed by sex researchers and conducted by a polling organization among a representative sample of women and men, found a wide range of attitudes, preferences, and practices—from a "pansexual" group of 20 percent of the subjects who consider sex very important and engage in it frequently and in many ways to a "nonsexual" group of 13 percent who "have no interest in sex" and are "unaroused by even the most erotic sexual stimulation" (Ubell, 1984).

Though such a wide range of sexual capacity, desire, and responsiveness seems startling at first glance, it is really not surprising in view of what is known about other individual differences. Human intelligence, it has been found, ranges from IQs of below 20 to above 180. Even in such a simple physical trait as height, people vary from about three feet to about eight. (The "experts" who offer the same kind of sex advice to everybody would hardly open a clothing store that stocked only one size—or would they?)

Like intelligence and height, sexual capacity and desire are determined in part by inherited physiological factors. In the human body there is an almost infinite variety from one individual to another in the sen-

*Diagrams of the female and male organs will be found in an appendix on sexual anatomy, pregnancy, and birth control.

sitivity of the nervous system (Gellhorn and Miller, 1961) and the size and activity of the glands that help regulate emotions and behavior (Williams, 1956). The particular nervous pathways that control sexual behavior seem to comprise a complex network that extends from the lower part of the spinal cord to the topmost areas of the brain (Whalen, 1976). Some of these far-reaching pathways may have been programmed by heredity and others established by learning, and some are influenced by glandular activity in ways that have thus far defied analysis (Beach, 1976).

Thus to some extent our own individual pattern of sexuality appears to depend on the mysterious workings of physiological factors that are inherited and more or less set at birth like the color of our eyes and the shape of our nose. It also depends on socialization, as indicated by the great variety of sexual practices observed in cultures around the world and from one period of history to another. We are influenced by our society's laws and taboos and by what it finds right and desirable in general, as well as by the attitudes and practices of the particular subculture in which we have grown up. In these changing times, we are pulled in many different directions by many conflicting forces—to cite the most extreme example, between the old belief that sex is "dirty" and the sexual revolution's propaganda urging us all to be "sexual supermen and superwomen" (Lydon, 1968). Small wonder that there is such a great pluralism of sexuality in our pluralistic society.

Even what is considered sexually stimulating is influenced by socialization. Most American men regard the female breast as erotic, but such an idea is regarded as childish in other places such as the South Pacific island of Magaia (Marshall, 1972). Even within our society, people differ greatly in their preferences: for certain types of body build or faces, certain kinds of environment (from a candlelit room to a deserted stretch of beach under the noonday sun), certain types of clothing, certain parts of the body.

It would be impossible to trace all the origins of any individual's sexual attitudes and behavior, which are shaped in subtle ways by all kinds of experiences with other people while growing up. We somehow begin in early childhood to acquire an array of desires and preferences, as well as strong feelings about what is distasteful. Our sexuality is influenced by the varied aspects of the personality we develop, the attitudes and moral standards we have accepted or rejected, and our social relationships—the ways in which we have learned to regard our parents and brothers and sisters, establish friendships, and view marriage and other human interactions. Some people, in fact, have learned to value sexual experiences less for the physical gratification they provide than as acts of communication, friendship, or even hostility. (Most rapists are driven less by sexual passion than by a hatred of the opposite sex.)

We're Us—and We're Stuck with It

To the extent that an individual's particular pattern of sexuality is determined by learning and socialization, it is subject to change. The Kinsey subject who had her first orgasm after twenty-eight years of marriage probably is a good example of how childhood training and society's taboos can inhibit sexual response, and of how a person can break out of the inhibitions and learn to relax and enjoy it. Similarly, some forms of unsatisfactory sexual behavior have been eliminated through various forms of therapy.

Masters and Johnson, for example, have reported good results in helping women who were unable to reach orgasm and men who thought they were impotent (Masters and Johnson, 1970).

Changed circumstances sometimes produce an unusual surge in sexual activity. The Kinsey interviewers found a number of men, for example, who suddenly became capable of performing far beyond what they believed to be their limits when they found a new partner. One man, who was having intercourse the more-or-less average twice a week with his wife, became separated from her, met another woman, and found himself eager to enjoy sex every day. Such increases in activity, however, are almost always temporary. Within a few months, the man was back to his former rhythm of twice a week (Gebhard, 1980).

Sexuality is also reduced at times by unfavorable circumstances or physical conditions. Many people find that they have less interest in sex when they are worried about their classes or their jobs, suffering bouts of depression, or just plain run down physically. Women often have a lowered interest during the years when they are under the constant psychological and physical strains of caring for young children. On the other hand, most couples find that their sexual activity is at a peak when they are on vacation, away from their usual problems and tensions and feeling physically rested.

Changes in desire and capacity, however, ordinarily occur only under special circumstances and to a limited extent. A man whose sexual pattern calls for an orgasm every two weeks may see a pornographic movie, marvel at the studs on the screen who seem able to perform at any time and in any place, and wish for a moment that he could follow their example—but this wistful urge is doomed to

failure. A woman who is able to respond to the point of orgasm once a month cannot force herself to do so every week, much less every night, no matter how hard she tries. And women and men who crave sex every day find it difficult to reconcile themselves to once or twice a week no matter how many cold showers they take or how many inspirational books on will power they read.

The Differences as a Source of Trouble

The wide range of differences often causes problems. It is rare indeed to find a couple who are so closely matched in capacity, desire, and responsiveness that they always feel like having sexual relations at exactly the same moment—and to whom the experience is always equally satisfactory. It is not at all rare to find couples who are strikingly mismatched, one person with a strong and insistent sexual appetite and another with less than average.

In the past, differences in sexuality often resulted in intense unhappiness and sometimes tragedy. For example, the Kinsey researchers found a 1943 incident in which a state supreme court was asked to rule on the case of a 42-year-old man who had been committed to a mental hospital as a sexual psychopath. The record showed that the man was "mentally bright, capable and a good worker." Yet the court ruled that he belonged in a mental institution because he was guilty of seeking intercourse with his wife three or four times a week. Although this is an above-average frequency, it is by no means rare, but the wife, her lawyers, and the various judges seemed to find it totally incomprehensible and depraved.

This kind of tragic misunderstanding

probably could not occur today. If nothing else, the lawyer for the "sexual psychopath" could cite Kinsey's figures to show that his behavior was well within the normal range. But the differences in desire and capacity still trouble many relationships, even among college students who have chosen to live together without marriage. One study of such relationships found that 70 percent were troubled by the fact that one partner had a higher interest in sex than the other, or that the times when they felt an interest did not match. In nearly two-thirds of the relationships, the woman was troubled by failure to reach orgasm as often as she would have liked (Macklin, 1972).

In marriage, one partner may accuse the other of being "oversexed" and may be accused in turn of being "undersexed," though if the two were matched with different people the "oversexed" partner might be considered rather tame and the "undersexed" partner might have the stronger appetite. ("Oversexed" and "undersexed" are meaningless terms that depend on where the accuser and accused happen to fall in the wide range of differences in capacity and desire.)

Even when an ideal matching does occur, it does not necessarily last forever. The male sex appetite is at a peak in early adolescence and begins a pronounced decline in the late 20s. The more-or-less "average" man who seeks an orgasm about once every three days in his youth is likely to slow down to about once every four or five days by the time he is 40, and to about once a week by the time he is fifty (Kinsey, 1948).

No such decline occurs among women, who if anything show increased sexual desire as they get older. (Older wives who do not understand the life cycle of the sex appetite often worry that their husbands no longer find them attractive or are having affairs,

when in fact the husbands are merely showing the effects of age.)

Pluralism in Sexual Expression and Moral Standards

Aside from capacity and desire, there is also a vast pluralism in many kinds of attitudes toward sex and sexual expression. People vary greatly in what they have learned to like or dislike about sex. Some people enjoy sex most when it is surrounded by an aura of romance. They are inspired by soft music, candlelight, and poetic conversation. Some regard it as an urgent physical desire that demands to be satisfied as quickly as possible, without any nonsense. Some go about it in a spirit of humorous play, turning it into a rowdy frolic akin to a childhood pillow fight. Some may do all these things at various times, depending on their moods.

Human ingenuity at performing intercourse, finding substitutes, and engaging in sexual play seems to have been almost boundless as far back as history goes. Every possibility was explored long ago. It can safely be said that a modern couple who pride themselves on discovering something new in sexual behavior would be humbled by a visit to any library that has a collection on sex through the ages. They would find their supposed "invention" described in full detail—and possibly with some embellishments they never dreamed of—in a book written centuries ago. Or they would find it illustrated in an ancient painting.

The sights, sounds, odors, and forms of touching that can turn people on are almost endless. But what arouses one person to ecstasy may leave another person totally unmoved, annoyed, or even disgusted. Thus, people who read a sex manual or watch a pornographic movie usually react with mixed emotions. They may be favorably inclined to some of the activity but find other parts incomprehensible or perverted. Some people approach sex with a sort of uninhibited abandon. Others approach it shyly and may even be embarrassed by nudity.

Moral standards, though generally ignored in books and magazine articles, play an important part in determining sexual behavior. Kinsey found that among the unmarried women in his sample who had remained virgins, almost nine out of ten listed moral objections as a reason—far more than mentioned fear of public opinion, pregnancy, or venereal disease (Kinsey, 1953).

The standards people acquire of what is right or wrong about sexual activity in general, or about any particular kind of activity, vary considerably. These standards are often a matter of intense personal conviction, and it has been found that people who violate their own firmly held beliefs sometimes suffer strong pangs of guilt or remorse (Christensen and Gregg, 1970).

Differences by Social Class

Variations in forms of sexual expression seem to depend in part on the particular subculture into which a person has been socialized. Kinsey found a number of such differences between the less-educated lower classes and the better-educated middle and upper classes. Men of the lower classes were more likely to frown on masturbation but feel free to indulge in premarital sex and experiences with prostitutes. Although they expressed great contempt for homosexuality, more of them actually took part in homosexual activities. Married couples in the lower classes tended to take a direct and matter-of-fact approach to sex, without "petting" or foreplay, even kissing. Many of them avoided nudity.

Subsequent studies have verified that sex in lower-class marriages tends to be a more or less mechanical process without much display of affection (Pierson and D'Antonio, 1974). Wives often regard it as "a man's pleasure and a woman's duty," into which they enter not so much in expectation of enjoyment as because they believe their husband will seek intercourse elsewhere if they do not provide it (Rainwater, 1972).

Many lower-class husbands do nothing to dispel this attitude. Among men who had never been to college, one survey found that only about one in seven felt any responsibility at all for his wife's sexual satisfaction (Masters and Johnson, 1966). This probably explains another of Kinsey's findings, which was that lower-class wives were considerably less likely to attain orgasm in intercourse. In the fifth year of marriage, the number of wives who never experienced orgasm was nearly twice as high among those with only a grade-school education as among those who had been to college.

Some Differences between Females and Males

Do men and women in general have different patterns of sexuality? Certainly not in one basic physiological way. As Masters and Johnson have established, all the bodily processes that take place during sexual stimulation and orgasm are almost exactly alike, even though men produce an ejaculation and women do not (Masters and Johnson, 1966). Yet men and women do appear, by and large, to display some differences in approach and attitude. In most societies throughout history, men have been the aggressors in sexual matters (Collins, 1971). In our own society in general "male patterns are characterized by a capacity to treat sexuality as an end in itself, whereas female patterns are less directly sexual and more typically an outgrowth or expression of some more encompassing emotional or social commitment'' (Walshock, 1973).

In one way or another, many males get the idea early in life that sex is a kind of contest to be enjoyed for its own sake and that ''scoring'' is something to be bragged about to one's friends, since it is admired and envied by the young male subculture. One survey found that college men are likely to report their first experience at once, often to a considerable number of their friends, and to expect praise and congratulations (Carns, 1973).

Mirra Komarovsky (1976) found those who remain virgins are likely to be troubled by feelings of inferiority, as if they had suffered a humiliating failure. On the other hand a young man who has great success at scoring may become an egotist who believes he is blessed with an unusual degree of physical attractiveness. He may think of himself as ''a real cock-of-the-walk'' whose mere ''physical presence and virility'' are so rewarding to women that he need not bother to display any other virtues such as sensitivity or understanding (Murstein, 1974).

Since men tend to regard ''sexuality as an end in itself,'' they often have their first experience with a woman for whom they have no particular affection and whom they may never see again. One study of college students with sexual experience found that the first partner of 46 percent of the men was a pickup or casual date, a woman to whom they had no emotional attachment, or in some cases a prostitute. At the time the survey was made, fewer than one out of twelve of the men had a continuing relationship with the first partner (Simon, Berger, and Gagnon, 1972).

For college women, the first experience usually resulted not from a direct search for sexual activity but as the by-product of a close relationship. As shown in Figure 6–1, about four out of five women were in love with their first partner, usually to the point of planning marriage. Only one in twenty had no emotional ties at all. Moreover, it has been found that college women, unlike men, do not ordinarily brag about their first experience. They are much less likely than men to talk about it at all. If they do mention the incident, they are likely to wait longer and confide in fewer of their friends (Carns, 1973).

Studies have also shown that the amount of satisfaction women receive from premar-

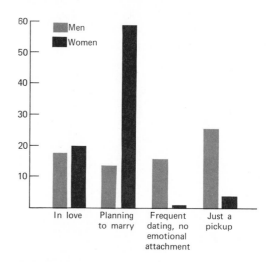

Figure 6–1
SEX AND LOVE:
THE MALE-FEMALE DIFFERENCE
College students who had experienced sexual intercourse were asked how they felt about their first partner. Note how many more women than men were in love at the time or even planning marriage—and how many more men than women had their first experience with a pickup or someone else to whom they had no emotional attachment. The figures for men and women do not add up to 100 percent because some first partners fell into categories not shown here (after Simon, Berger, and Gagnon, 1972).

ital intercourse depends on how strongly they feel about their partner (Ehrmann, 1964) and how well they feel the relationship is progressing (Murstein, 1974). The "one-night stand"—sex with a person never met before or known only casually, then quickly dropped and never seen again—is much less common among women than men. This appears to be true not only in the United States but also in other nations such as Germany and Norway (Luckey and Nass, 1969). Women who do go in for one-night stands often find them unsatisfactory, a sort of necessary evil (see, for example, the box on *Opinions and Experiences.*)

At least some of the differences between women and men may be disappearing because of today's changing sex roles and the move toward androgyny. Some observers have already found indications of a trend for men to consider sex an expression of affection rather than as a mere matter of scoring and for women to think of sex as something to be valued for its own sake (Carns, 1973). But the attitudes instilled by traditional sex-role socialization and the double standard are difficult to cast aside even for people who have come to believe most strongly in equality of the sexes. As one sociologist has said, "The two sexes haven't had time to learn to live in a truly equal relationship. We may be theoretically liberated—but our personal relationships can be quite different" (Schwartz, 1979).

THE KEY TO SEXUAL FULFILLMENT

In view of the pluralism in desire and capacity, moral standards, and preferences for various forms of sexual expression, it seems almost a wonder that any two people should ever manage to establish a satisfac-

tory relationship. It is difficult for two people near the opposite extremes of the range of sexual appetite to understand each other's desires. It may be difficult for people socialized into different subcultures to reconcile their very different attitudes and approaches. At least to the extent that sex-role socialization produces differences between females and males, it may indeed be difficult for any man and any woman to fully comprehend each other's feelings.

Kinsey, on the basis of his thousands of case histories, concluded that about two-thirds of all marriages of the 1940s ran into sexual difficulties, at least at one time or another and in some cases from beginning to end. Whether this is still true is not known. Perhaps the present-day freedom in sexual information and discussion has reduced the number of problems. On the other hand, some investigators believe that today's permissive atmosphere may only have replaced one uncomfortable set of guidelines with another that is equally demanding and troublemaking:

> Many of the obstacles to sexual life are not merely the function of repressive attitudes. . . . They are grounded in the complexities of human nature and in the everyday difficulties of living together. And all these natural—one is almost inclined to say "eternal"—difficulties are intensified by the disappearance of traditional sex roles, the proliferation of sexual choices and styles, the permission to introduce, in public life, the full range of sexual fantasies to which we are prey and heir.
>
> *(Marin, 1983).*

The Realistic Approach

Perhaps the first step in achieving genuine fulfillment is to forget everything you may have read and start over with a realistic and

Opinions and Experiences

SEX WITH A STRANGER

A California woman in her late 20s discusses the problem of being single and having a strong sexual appetite.

I was married in college, but it didn't work out. The only good thing about it was that my ex-husband and I both have high sex drives and we put them together beautifully. We had a really fantastic sex life but soon discovered we had nothing else in common. I'm divorced now and playing the field.

Which means that, things being the way they are, I've had my share of one-night stands. I don't recommend them. For one thing, I don't think many women can enjoy sex unless they really like the man and feel close to him. I'm as liberated as any woman, and I don't have any moral qualms, but I don't get turned on by the idea of sex with just anybody.

Even if I like the man a lot—if he talks well and has a good sense of humor—I'm usually disappointed. It's difficult to have successful sex with a stranger. If the two of you don't know each other very well, you can't talk intimately. He doesn't know what you like, and you don't know what he likes.

Certainly men aren't at their best on one-night stands. They're worried about how they're going to perform. It's like they're taking an exam to prove their masculinity rather than having fun. And I'm afraid most men aren't very good at sex anyway. They may be good guys, but they're bad lovers. You run into an awful lot of thirty-second wonders. In fact, they don't seem to know much about sex—like even where the clitoris is. That's hard to believe but it's true. I suppose they're too proud to find out. I just can't imagine the average man, with all his pride in knowing it all, going up to another man and asking, "Hey, do you know where it is?"

The sex part of the singles life isn't what it's cracked up to be. I really miss the kind of sex I had with a man I was living with and loved at the time—when I understood everything about his tastes and he knew everything about mine, and even if it didn't work 100 percent every time we could make up for it.

---

down-to-earth approach. Establishing a good sexual relationship is not easy, natural, or automatic. It is not something that can be accomplished by any two strangers who happen to meet in the night. Even some of the lower animals, untroubled by the complications of human pluralism, have to learn. If a male and female monkey are raised in isolation, never seeing any other members of their species engage in sexual activity, they have no idea what to do when they first see each other (Leuba, 1954).

For human beings, the search for sexual identity is immensely puzzling and difficult. In most other forms of behavior we have clear guidelines; like when to show up in the classroom or at work, which side of the road to drive on, or even how to take out a marriage license. In sex conflicting guidelines exist side by side. The suggestions we find depend on whose book we read, and we can never be sure whether they are true in general, much less if they apply to our individual situation. If we seek advice from our friends, we are never sure they know what they are talking about or even if they are telling the truth. (Exaggerating sexual exploits has been common among men and seems to be increasing among women.)

The search is especially puzzling for young people, who must try to establish their sexual identity at the same time they must face all the other problems of entering adulthood. Despite today's permissive atmosphere—or perhaps because of it—their task is beset by embarrassment, confusion, and self-doubt. They find that "coping with sexual development remains a lonely and overly silent experience" (Simon, Berger, and Gagnon, 1972).

For many young people, the first sexual experience is not nearly so glorious as advertised. Some unusual and interesting evidence comes from a study made in Denmark, a nation that has been tolerant of premarital sex for a long time. One would suppose that sex would come natural in Denmark if anywhere; but only 26 percent of the young women and men in the survey reported that their first experience had been generally satisfactory. About 21 percent had viewed it with mixed emotions, and 54 percent had negative feelings (Hessellund, 1971). Note these comments from the negative side:

By men

> Happy to have tried it but disappointed that the experience was not greater.
>
> I was disappointed.
>
> Very awkward. Everything went wrong. . . .
>
> It was a great disappointment. An enormous failure. I was afraid of the next time and did not make new attempts for the following two years.

By women

> It was definitely no experience. Neither I nor my partner got an orgasm.
>
> It was unpleasant. . . . It hurt.
>
> I was curious and excited but it was horrible.
>
> I was disappointed, pessimistic.

An unhappy introduction to sex, however, did not prove permanently damaging to these young Danes. At the time they were interviewed, when their average age was 23, all but a few were either married or had established some other kind of sexual relationship. The lesson the study has to tell us is this: It is probably as unrealistic to expect glorious success in one's first attempts at sex as in one's first attempts at playing the piano. Indeed not all of us will ever in our lives attain the kind of glorious, mind-boggling success described in many sex manuals any more than all of us will play piano concertos with a symphony orchestra.

The Fallacy of the Sex Manuals

There would be no point here in summarizing the advice contained in the sex manuals for example, in listing the possible positions in intercourse and all the techniques of foreplay. For one thing the bookstores and movie theaters are flooded with such information, and anyone interested in exploring the subject has probably long since done so. For another it is doubtful that the books and movies ever teach anybody anything new.

If we have a natural taste for any particular kind of sexual activity, we are likely to discover it for ourselves, without the need for instruction. If there is something we have not thought of, it is probably because we are not really interested. Reading a sex manual, or for that matter an elaborate pornographic description of sexual behavior, is like reading a fancy cookbook. The recipes may sound ingenious—but, for our own palates, would the results be worth the trouble?

Sex manuals and other forms of specific sexual advice can in fact be harmful rather than helpful. Even the best of them, produced by serious writers in a serious attempt to help their readers, tend to ignore individual differences. Many of them tell more about the interests and hangups of the writer than about the subject matter. And the writer's tastes may be totally different from those of the reader. Anyone who takes a sex manual too seriously, accepts it as the final truth on attaining happiness, and feels compelled to follow its advice to the letter can get into trouble—as did the woman who tells her story in the box on *Opinions and Experiences*.

Another fault of many manuals is that they turn sex into a problem in mechanical engineering, like the difficult task of putting together a stereo set that arrives unassembled from the factory. Often they make sex seem like work rather than pleasure—a job requiring rigorous training and constant dedication. For some people the techniques are unsuitable anyway. The authors of recent manuals have become more and more hard-pressed to go a step beyond anything written by last year's authors. As a result, many of the techniques now recommended constitute totally uninhibited experimentation that not everyone can be comfortable with.

Some people are quiet and reserved about sexual matters. The all-out abandon urged by many manuals is foreign to their personalities. Such people are much happier if they forget about the experimentation and approach sex with their customary shyness and a minimum of attempts at fancy play, particularly since too much attention to technique may turn sex from a spontaneous expression of love into a merely mechanical performance that they find distasteful (Vincent, 1956).

The Importance of Being Yourself

Although Shakespeare's famous words "to thine own self be true" were not intended as sexual advice, they just happen to be better advice than will be found in most sex manuals. It really does not matter what other people recommend, or what they are doing, or how they feel. The only thing that matters to any of us, as we seek as much sexual fulfillment as we are capable of, is how *we* feel. Fulfillment is possible for all of us—whatever attitudes and tastes we may have acquired, and wherever we happen to fall on the range of desire and capacity from low to high—provided we are willing to accept ourselves as we are and act accordingly. For some words of wisdom about this first step toward sexual happiness, see John Messenger's comments in the box on *Opinions and Experiences*.

In marriage some couples will gladly embrace what Messenger calls the push of today's propaganda toward "a hyperactive sex life," a type of relationship that in fact existed in some marriages long before the sexual revolution. Other couples will place much less emphasis on sexual activity. As long as they are doing what they honestly feel like doing, the choice does not matter. Paul Gebhard (1982) has said:

> If there is one thing that we at the Institute for Sex Research have been absolutely sure of, from all the marriages and other relationships we studied, it is that the amount of sex bears no relation to happiness. A couple can be just as happy having sex once a month, if that is what both of them prefer, as every night in the week.

A recent large-scale survey reached the same conclusion: "People who have sex infrequently are just as likely to have a long-lasting relationship as those who have sex often" (Blumstein and Schwartz, 1983). Another suggestion that sexual fulfillment depends on individual feelings, rather than arbitrary standards, comes from a sociologist who has done considerable marriage counseling:

Opinions and Experiences

WHAT YOU LEARN CAN HURT YOU

A married woman in her 40s describes an unhappy experience that could happen to anybody of either sex at any age.

You're listening to a person whose life was almost ruined by a book. It sounds funny—even I have to smile when I look back—but it certainly wasn't funny at the time.

It was a sex manual that a friend of mine was reading. I borrowed it from her and read it with horror. Not for what the book said, but for how ignorant my husband and I had been.

We had been married for nearly fifteen years at the time, but we were kindergarten kids in the matter of sex. We had never done anything that the book recommended. It was one of those books that are very big on techniques and refinements, lots of variety and fancy play.

What mostly threw me was that the book said a woman should have multiple orgasms, that if she didn't she was missing the whole meaning of sex. I'd never had that experience in my life. I'd never even heard of it. I felt like a total failure, an ignoramus. I was ashamed of myself and angry with my husband. I went through a depression so deep I can't even describe it.

Should I tell my husband? I worried over this for a week and then instead I went to a marriage counselor. When I explained my problem he asked, "How was your sex life before you read the book?" I told him I had thought it was fine. He said, "And it probably was—until you let somebody else tell you how to live it. Forget about the book. And forget about multiple orgasms. Some women have them and some don't, and either way nobody can change it."

So our marriage has been back in business ever since. I suppose the author of that book would say my husband and I are in a rut—but that happens to be the way we like it.

Fortunate couples in their sixties will tell you that their sexual relationship gets better every year [though probably] no one under thirty really believes this statement. We tend to think in terms of quantity (how many times a week?), just as we measure the success of a meeting in terms of attendance. People in their sixties and seventies are talking about the quality of their relationship.

(Vincent, 1956)

Two Barriers: Lack of Information and *Mis*information

There are, however, a number of more or less mechanical aspects of sex that are important to consider, because fulfillment can be made unnecessarily difficult by lack of knowledge and a number of false notions that have somehow gained wide acceptance. The following facts, all firmly established by research, may be useful, though of course any that violate your moral or religious standards (or even your tastes) should not be applied.

Clitoral versus vaginal orgasm   The idea that only stimulation of the vagina can produce a true orgasm, and that a response to stimulation of the clitoris is an inferior substitute, was popularized by Sigmund Freud and still troubles many women, though many researchers have proved it false. The clitoris is by far the most sensitive female sex area and serves as the powerful little generator for the female orgasm. The vagina is only sparsely supplied with nerve endings

Opinions and Experiences

"IN YOUR OWN WAY AND AT YOUR OWN CHOOSING . . . "

John Messenger, an anthropologist who has studied sexual practices in many cultures, discusses what he considers one of the most important things he has learned.

The trouble with the recent sexual climate in the United States was that all the propaganda pushed us in the direction of greater sexuality. In the past we were asked to conform to a code of sexual behavior that was so strict as to be entirely unrealistic. But the sexual revolution asked us to conform to a pattern that was equally unrealistic and perhaps even more dangerous because it demanded a level of interest and performance beyond most people's capacities.

I myself like to think that sex should be enjoyed for the sheer magnificence of it, that this is what sex is all about. But sex can be magnificent only when you engage in it in your own

way and at your own choosing—as much or as little of it as you please, and according to your own tastes and preferences. All the solid research ever done shows that no two people are alike in how they feel about sex, how much capacity they have for it, or what they like and don't like. The kind of sexual behavior that is successful for one person can be absolutely devastating for another person.

Certainly the idea that everybody has to lead a hyperactive sex life to be happy is nonsense—and dangerous nonsense at that. It is perfectly possible to be a 30-year-old virgin and yet completely fulfilled as a human being, leading a joyful and useful life. In fact I have known some priests and nuns, vowed to celibacy, who appeared to be among the brightest, liveliest, and most thoroughly contented people I have ever met.

Courtesy of Dr. John Messenger, Ohio State University.

and produces very little sensation. Orgasm during intercourse occurs chiefly because of indirect stimulation of the clitoris through movements of the lips of the vulva, as well as by pressure from the man's body. Some women find it completely impossible to achieve orgasm through intercourse, yet they have strong and sometimes multiple orgasms in response to clitoral stimulation.

The false lure of mutual orgasm   Perhaps the most damaging of all the myths is the idea that intercourse is satisfactory only when both partners achieve orgasm at exactly the same moment. The mutual orgasm, though it can be a rewarding experience when it occurs, is unlikely to happen very often, and there is no effective way of seeking it. A re-

lated myth, entirely false, holds that mutual orgasm is also essential for the conception of a child.

Sex during menstruation and pregnancy   Many people have the idea that sexual activity should be avoided when a woman is menstruating. Actually it can do no damage to either partner, and some women find that their desires peak during such periods. Intercourse is also harmless during pregnancy, except possibly during the final stages. (The physician who will conduct the delivery is the best source of advice.)

Male fears of failure and impotence   Many men, partly as a result of today's sexual atmosphere, have acquired what is called *per-*

formance anxiety. They are so eager to please their partner and bring her to climax that they worry about failure, especially since intercourse does not always produce the female orgasm no matter what the male does. Therapists have a high rate of success in treating performance anxiety by encouraging a more relaxed and realistic attitude toward the possibility of "failure."

Closely related to performance anxiety is the concern experienced by many men over *impotence,* or the inability to have an erection. True impotence, caused by organic or glandular abnormalities, is extremely rare. But what is called secondary impotence, caused by anxiety or temporary physical conditions such as fatigue or too much alcohol, is common. Most men have experienced secondary impotence on occasion and nothing is more likely to produce another episode than worrying that it may occur again. As in the case of performance anxiety, therapists are very successful at treating it.

Premature ejaculation This term is difficult to define. Strictly in the biological and medical sense, there is no such thing, except in cases where excitement or anxiety causes the male to have an orgasm before intercourse actually begins, with resulting sensations that are physiologically and psychologically unsatisfactory. The natural male pattern seems to be to experience orgasm very quickly. Kinsey found that about three-fourths of the men he studied took no more than two minutes, with many taking only a minute or less. (Kinsey also noted that our closest relatives in the animal kingdom, the apes, usually have an orgasm within ten or twenty seconds). But most therapists agree with Masters and Johnson that ejaculation is premature if the man does not wait long enough for his partner to have an orgasm 50 percent of the time.

In consideration of the partner, most men in the middle and upper classes try to prolong intercourse, with varying success. Masters and Johnson recommend practicing the so-called "squeeze technique," described in the appendix, as the most effective method of learning control.

"Oversexed" and "undersexed" partners As noted earlier, it is rare to find a couple who have exactly the same level of sexual appetite and capacity, and even this unusual and fortunate pair is unlikely to remain in perfect unison as the years go on. Moreover, though the two appetites may happen to be perfectly matched in general, they will not always be aroused simultaneously. Thus in any relationship there are bound to be times when one partner wants sex and the other does not.

Sometimes the eager partner, out of deference to the other's feelings, can back off without undue disappointment or discomfort. But this is not always easy, and it may be almost impossible. The problem is especially burdensome in cases of drastic mismatch, say with one partner preferring intercourse four times a week and the other once a week. The only workable solution is for the partner with the less frequent desires to accommodate the one with the stronger appetite.

Some women find intercourse emotionally gratifying even when they have no burning desire; and some men are able to maintain an erection long enough for their partner's climax, and enjoy the sensations, without any intention of achieving orgasm. But intercourse is not actually necessary for sexual gratification. As is shown by the large number of lesbian women and gay men who have established satisfactory long-term relationships (Blumstein and Schwartz, 1983), the penis is not essential to female fulfillment, nor the vagina to male fulfillment. A physically and emotionally gratifying orgasm can be provided for either sex through stimulation by hand or mouth. The type of stimulation that works best is a matter of individual preference. Many women, for example, find that direct manipulation of the clitoris is irritating rather than pleasant, and that stroking of the area around it is much more effective.

The Magic Word: Communication

The only way for a couple to find out what works best in their relationship is to discuss it. Indeed the whole secret of attaining sexual happiness seems to be communication. What do you like to do, and how do you like to do it? How often, and when and where? What do you dislike, and how intensely? Your sexual partner cannot know unless you say, and you cannot know how best to please your partner unless you are told.

Masters and Johnson have termed open discussion of sexual preferences the "absolute cornerstone" of a successful relationship (Masters and Johnson, 1972). Paul Gebhard has stated:

> The chief stumbling block to fulfillment is the fact that couples don't talk enough about their feelings. Even couples who have been married for 20 years, and know each other's preferences in food, reading, and music like the backs of their hands, often hesitate to tell each other what they like, dislike, or view with indifference in sexual matters.
>
> *(Gebhard, 1982).*

Unfortunately, candor about sexual matters does not come easy for most people, even in these post-revolution days. In some ways, indeed, the sexual revolution may have made communication more difficult. In view of the popular "myths of sexual supermen and superwomen," it may be difficult for more or less average women and men to concede that they are not constantly preoccupied with sex and do not always find it an earthshaking event. They may feel compelled to feign a greater interest and delight than they actually experience.

In this respect the revolution has probably put more pressure on women, who are now supposed to be sexually liberated for the first time and eager to make the most of it, than on men, who were never under such severe restraints in the past. In another respect, however, frank communication is perhaps more difficult for men because it conflicts with the traditional sex-role standard maintaining that males are born experts in sexual matters. Clark Vincent (1976) has written:

> If a wife asks her husband to scratch her back and he complies, she does not hesitate to give him instructions: "Not so hard; now over to the left, under the shoulder blade; slow down . . . easier; over to the center . . . there." She can give her husband ten or twelve sets of instructions and it does not bother him. Why? Because no one ever told him that expertise in back-scratching has anything to do with masculinity. There is no threat to his male ego. . . . Now suppose the same wife is trying to derive some sexual pleasure from intercourse. Do you think she can give twelve instructions to her husband as to how to give her sexual pleasure? She is lucky if he will accept two. This is because males in our society learn at a very young age to equate "masculinity" with "knowing all about sex." . . . To learn something about a subject, you have to admit you do not already know everything there is to know—but for the male to admit there is something about sex he does not know is for him to question his own masculinity.

In view of changing attitudes toward sex roles, these words are probably less generally true now than when they were written. And perhaps the trend toward androgyny will make it easier in the future for both sexes to express their true sexual feelings, preferences, and even doubts. If so, sexual fulfillment will become a reality for more and more people, for open communication, and a willingness to learn and to please, can do miracles.

Possibly some couples will find that they are hopelessly mismatched and had better give up. If, for example, one partner is at the very top of Kinsey's range of sexual appetite and the other at the very bottom, the differences may be insurmountable. The majority of couples can find fulfillment together through frank expression in combination with those other virtues of sympathy, understanding, tolerance, and affection, especially since giving sexual pleasure can be as great a joy as receiving it.

SUMMARY

1. In the first part of this century the United States seemed to be a sexless society. Sex was never written about and seldom spoken about, except in whispers. It was considered "dirty," and certainly a "nice girl" was never supposed to have any sexual desires. The well-publicized "sexual revolution," which reached its peak in the 1960s and 1970s changed these attitudes completely.

2. A majority of Americans no longer consider premarital sex morally wrong. In the 1940s only 18 percent of women had experienced sexual intercourse by the age of 19, but the number has now risen to 40 percent of white women and 58 percent of black women. The figures for men have changed only slightly, because even in the 1940s about 72 percent of teenage males had experience, usually with prostitutes or a small pool of the community's "bad girls."

3. The rise in female sexual participation has produced a sharp increase in teenage pregnancies. Of all unmarried women aged 15–19, about 11 percent of whites and 26 percent of blacks become pregnant because one sexually active young woman out of four never uses any form of birth control, and only one in three always does.

4. Sexual activity in college varies greatly from one campus to another. Various surveys have reported rates at the start of the 1980s as high as 64 percent of women students and 77 percent of men. In the present decade, as the sexual revolution has waned, the numbers have apparently dropped and there has been a decline in promiscuity and a growing concern for commitment.

5. Living together, or *cohabitation,* also varies from one campus to another. It is usually accompanied by strong feelings of affection and even love, but among students in the early years it is not necessarily considered any kind of permanent arrangement, especially by the men. Among seniors living together appears to resemble trial marriage, expected to turn into actual marriage if all goes well.

6. In the United States, the number of couples living together without marriage is now around 2 million, and it is expected to reach 3.5 million by 1990. Studies have found no indications that couples who marry after a period of cohabitation are any happier or have a lower divorce rate than others.

7. Despite today's permissive atmosphere, recent surveys have found that close to 80 percent of Americans consider sexual fidelity very important in marriage. A majority disapprove of prostitution, nudity in movies, and pornography.

8. One result of the sexual revolution was a flood of books and magazine articles prescribing sure-fire methods of attaining sexual ecstasy.

Much of this literature assumes that all people are alike in attitudes and behavior and have an infinite capacity for sexual performance and delight once stripped of their inhibitions. Actually there is a vast range of individual differences in feelings, desires, and capacity, and there are about as many kinds of sexuality as there are people.

9. The striking nature of individual differences—and their great influence on sexual behavior—was pointed out by the famous Kinsey reports, which were based on interviews with over 13,000 women and men in the 1940s and remain one of our best sources of knowledge about sexual behavior.

10. Kinsey found that some people, male or female, can hardly be aroused at all, others by the mere thought of a member of the opposite sex. Some get nervous and cranky if deprived of sex for even a day. Others are perfectly happy to do without sex for weeks, months, or even a lifetime.

11. The wide range of differences depends in part on inherited physiological factors, for example, the sensitivity of the nervous system and the size and activity of the glands that help regulate emotions and behavior. It is also influenced by socialization, the attitudes and rules of the culture and subculture, the moral standards we have acquired, and our social relationships and the way we view them.

12. The differences often cause problems because a couple are rarely so closely matched in desire and responsiveness that they always feel like having sexual relations at exactly the same moment. One study of college students who were living together found that 70 percent were troubled by one partner's having a higher interest in sex than the other.

13. The bodily processes occurring during sexual stimulation and orgasm are identical in the two sexes, except that men produce an ejaculation and women do not. But men have traditionally tended to regard sexuality as an end in itself—a matter of "scoring." Women have tended to regard it as "an expression of some more encompassing emotional or social commitment," and the amount of pleasure they receive seems to depend on how strongly they feel about their partner. Today's trend toward androgyny may be leading men to a greater regard for sex as an accompaniment to affection, and for women to begin to value it for its own sake.

14. Sex manuals suggesting techniques of foreplay and sexual intercourse are seldom helpful—and may actually be harmful—because they usually ignore individual differences in sexual capacity, attitudes, and moral standards.

15. What other people are doing, how they feel, or what they recommend really does not matter. What counts is how *we* feel. Fulfillment is possible for all of us, wherever we fall on the range of desire and capacity, provided we accept ourselves as we are and act accordingly.

16. The only way a couple can find out what works best in their relationship is to tell each other what they like, how they like it, when, where, and how often. Masters and Johnson have called open discussion of sexual preferences the "absolute cornerstone" of a successful relationship.

DISCUSSION QUESTIONS

1. Is there still a double standard of sexual behavior, with one set of rules for males and another for females? Give examples.

2. Discuss the pros and cons of premarital sex.

3. What are some of the reasons more couples are living together without marriage? How do *you* feel about cohabitation?

4. Why are the terms *oversexed* and *undersexed* meaningless?

5. How do you feel about the statement "The amount of sex bears no relation to happiness"?

6. Why is good communication between partners related to sexual fulfillment?

The Basic Source of Conflict in Marriage

You may think it odd that a book on marriage should discuss conflict and quarrels before it discusses the ways in which people can get along with one another and live happily together. You may even feel that the chapter order of this book is pessimistic because problems are found here in Chapter 7, and adjustment and harmony are held back until Chapter 8—but the arrangement does not imply that marriage is more plagued by conflict than blessed by a mutuality of interests and emotions.

The chapter order is simply dictated by the fact that we cannot understand what is known about how two people can find happiness in marriage without first exploring the reasons some marriages fail. And we cannot be happy in our own marriages unless we are prepared to admit that no two people can live together for any length of time without running into problems—indeed without experiencing numerous disagreements, hurt feelings, and angry outbursts.

Marriages are an odd mixture of delight and disillusionment. You can expect to have times when you and your partner experience almost unbelievable ecstasies of intimacy and communion, and other times when you feel like strangers. You will have days when you consider your partner the most lovable person on earth, and other days when you come close to hating your partner.

Though this bittersweet combination sometimes comes as a shock to people who expect to "live happily ever after," it is hardly surprising in view of human relationships in general. Children have mixed emotions about their parents, and parents have mixed emotions about their children. Sisters and brothers love each other but quarrel. All of us sometimes like and sometimes despise our friends, our instructors, the people who work next to us on our jobs, and our bosses.

Countless studies have shown that quarreling in marriage is also inevitable. It cannot be avoided—and, in the opinion of most scholars, it should not be avoided. When we start a marriage, the question is not whether to quarrel or not to quarrel but how the quarrels will turn out. In fact people who stay married and regard themselves as extremely happy together are not very different from most of those who wind up so unhappy that they get divorced (Bernard, 1970). Both kinds of couples may face much the same problems and have the same kinds of clashes. Yet some couples manage to work through the problems, surmount them, and even profit from them, while others throw up their hands and call it quits.

Why should this be? Why, if quarreling is bound to take place, should it sometimes result in such bitterness and misery? Is there any way we can guarantee a happy ending for our own quarrels?

There is no magic answer—but we do have some clues about the reasons couples quarrel and the kind of basic conflict that is most devastating. This chapter presents some of the pitfalls that have been discovered, and the following chapter discusses some possible ways of avoiding the pitfalls.

WHY EVERYBODY FIGHTS

Psychologists and sociologists have known for a long time that the notion of "living happily ever after"—a marriage without bruised feelings or disagreements—is a myth. We human beings are just not built that way. We are never completely and uninterruptedly happy about anything. We do not get along perfectly at all times with anybody. And marriage is the most demanding and difficult of all human relationships, particularly under today's conditions.

The family, as pointed out earlier in the book, is an oasis of intimacy in an impersonal world—one of the few places we have close emotional ties and can find warmth and a sense of intimacy and belonging. We desperately depend on our partner for basic psychological satisfactions that cannot be found elsewhere. So we demand a lot of marriage and of our partner, and when anything goes wrong we tend to be bitterly disappointed and inclined to fight back.

Social Pressures on Marriage

Adding to the chances of conflict is another social development: Just as society has turned marriage into our one emotional haven, it also makes this haven difficult to maintain. Husbands and wives, in their daily activities, usually are forced to lead very dif-ferent lives. If both have jobs, their work is usually in different places and of different types. If the wife is a housewife-mother, not employed outside the home, she is busy all day with responsibilities revolving around the house and the children.

Either way, husband and wife spend their days apart, in different environments, doing work that makes different kinds of demands and may produce different moods and emotional needs (Feldberg and Kohen, 1976). In the time they have together, after meeting all their daily obligations, they may naturally have trouble achieving the kind of rapport and intimate understanding that both expect from marriage.

The family is subject to many other pressures from the outside world. Of all social institutions it is the least powerful—the one that must adapt to all the others. Business firms set their own working hours, and employees have to show up when the schedule dictates. A husband and wife who both have jobs may have such different schedules that they are left with very little time to spend together. Or an employer may require that one of them move to a different city, thereby disrupting both their lives. A housewife-mother has to cope with the schedules of schools, libraries, stores, doctors, and dentists. Even churches hold services only at appointed hours.

Financial pressures often add to all the others. It costs a great deal of money to establish a home, even a small and modest apartment. Children are more expensive than is generally realized. A couple's income goes up and down over the years. So do their expenses, particularly if they decide to have a number of children. There may be periods of what has been called the "life cycle squeeze," when there is painful pressure from needs and wishes that family income simply cannot meet (Wilensky, 1963). This is especially true of families in which the husband bumps into his income ceiling early in life and the wife is busy with many children. The husband may be forced to moonlight on a second job—a drastic strain on the marriage relationship—or the wife and even some of the children may have to take jobs against their own wishes and best interests (Gove et al., 1973).

Clashes over Basic Roles and "Tremendous Trifles"

Not all the pressures come from the outside. Many of them develop out of the very intimacy of marriage. Whenever you rub two sticks together you get friction, and often you get smoke and sometimes fire. Quarrels, open or concealed, are produced wherever people are rubbed together—in classrooms, business offices, basketball courts, and meetings of the town council or United Nations general assembly. And nowhere else in our society are personalities rubbed together so constantly and abrasively as in marriage.

All of us are different. We glory in our own opinions and habits, which we consider completely sensible, and find many of the ideas and actions of other people annoying, just as they in turn often find ours repugnant. Of course, the principle of homogamy, as explained in Chapter 5, tends to bring people together in marriage who are generally similar in backgrounds and attitudes. But no two people are completely alike, and even the best-matched husband and wife are almost sure to have as many differences as similarities.

Some clashes may stem from basic differences in attitudes toward sex roles, for example, how well the partners agree on whether the wife should be a housewife-mother, a partner-wife, or both, and to what extent. There are also many possible sources

of disagreement in the various other attitudes, values, and habits we have acquired from our socialization into the particular subculture and the particular home in which we were brought up.

Some of us have turned out to be gushy and sentimental, some cool and taciturn. Some of us like to visit our parents at every possible opportunity. Some of us have no desire at all for close relations with our parents. Some of us are shy and some revel in nudity. Some of us expect presents on our birthdays, and others would be embarrassed. We may like the Christmas tree heavily ornamented or adorned with nothing but lights and a little tinsel, or we may think Christmas trees of any kind are silly.

These are small matters, perhaps, but they can cause clashes. Sociologists have recognized for many years that many problems arise over what have been called the "tremendous trifles" of marriage. In this large and pluralistic nation there are millions of disagreements every year—spoken or unspoken—over such "tremendous trifles" as the big breakfast versus the small, the fresh orange juice versus the frozen, the open bedroom window versus the closed, the soap placed parallel in its dish versus crosswise. A wife who grew up in a home where neatness was paramount can hardly become reconciled to a husband who leaves wet towels on the bathroom floor, and her happy-go-lucky husband can hardly become reconciled to her fussiness. The spendthrift husband irritates the financially conservative wife. And so it goes.

When disagreements do arise, they are more difficult to resolve in the primary group of the family than in the secondary groups to which we belong. In secondary groups, our role is clearly defined and there are usually rules for settling any differences. The teacher or the boss may be authorized to settle the conflicts, or we may have to abide by majority vote or arbitration, or the group may agree to disagree and quietly break up. In the family, however, there are no established guidelines for how we should behave, how our partner should behave, or how to conduct or decide the quarrels.

Usually conflict means that one partner's behavior has in some way violated the other partner's hopes and expectations (Patterson, Hops, and Weiss, 1975). But often it is difficult to pin down exactly what these hopes and expectations are and in what way they have met with disappointment. Indeed the problem may lie not so much in what the partner has actually done as in the way the behavior is interpreted (Lazarus, 1971). We may feel dissatisfied for reasons we do not understand, or we may cause our partner unhappiness without being aware of it. We may quarrel without quite knowing what we are quarreling about. The dissatisfaction, the unhappiness, and the quarreling are made more intense by our great personal stake in the primary group of the family.

Our Changing Moods

Many married couples, especially in the early years of marriage, are puzzled by the fact that the "tremendous trifles" often seem to act like time bombs that go unnoticed most of the time, quietly ticking away, then explode, suddenly and without warning. Husband and wife seem to be in tune most of the time. Then one day they are out of tune. Their differences in tastes and habits, usually too trifling to worry about, suddenly loom tremendous indeed—and husband and wife find themselves wondering if they really have anything in common at all.

All of us have our moods, our ups and downs. One day we are talkative, the next day withdrawn. Sometimes we feel reckless and sometimes we feel cautious. One day we are jolly, the next day pessimistic. At times we can remember only pleasant things about our mate and at other times we can remember nothing but trouble. A husband who reports on Wednesday that he lost a big bet on a baseball game may find his wife completely unconcerned, though she might have been upset and angry had he done so on Tuesday or waited until Thursday.

Studies have shown that most of us tend to have ups and downs in many respects that can affect marriage—not only mood but wakefulness or sleepiness, interest or lack of interest, efficiency, and ability to think straight (Keeney and Cromwell, 1979). The patterns seem to depend on many kinds of bodily processes that operate on rhythms that vary from person to person.

One of the best-known differences is between "day people" (wide awake the moment they arise, full of energy all morning,

Mimi Forsyth, Monkmeyer

A frequent trouble in marriage: a "night person" wife is still wide awake while her "day person" husband sleeps.

then gradually winding down until they can hardly hold their eyes open at 10 P.M.) and "night people" (loath to get out of bed in the morning, never fully awake until the sun goes down, then ready to go full speed long past midnight). When a day person marries a night person, the possibilities for friction are endless, as indicated by the cases described in the box on *Opinions and Experiences*. But, as the box also shows, it is often possible to make satisfactory adjustments.

Most physical and emotional ups and downs are less pronounced and persistent than the differences between day people and night people, and usually they cause only temporary trouble. But it often takes time for the newly married to learn that they both have their changing moods, and that the mood of the moment, though it may make everything seem hopeless, will pass.

Some people, it must be added, are more changeable than others. As Clifford Kirkpatrick (1963) pointed out, a man with a chameleonlike wife may sometimes feel "married to a harem rather than to one person." A wife may say of her husband, "I'd be happy to spend a half hour every afternoon getting in the mood to welcome Harry home from work, except that I never know which Harry to expect."

Some Comforting Statistics

If you ever find yourself worrying that you and your partner are in terrible trouble because everything about your marriage is not going smoothly, you can take comfort in the statistics a number of researchers have produced. In one study couples were asked, "Even in cases where people are happy there have often been times in the past when they weren't too happy—when they had problems getting along with each other. Has this ever been true of you?" As Figure 7-1 shows, there were many *yes* answers even

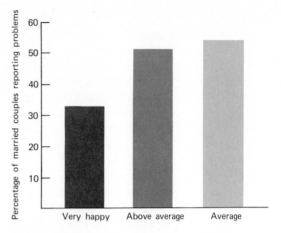

Figure 7-1
EVEN THE HAPPILY MARRIED HAVE PROBLEMS
A study of nearly 2,000 couples who said their marriages were at least average in happiness showed that nearly half of them (44 percent) admitted having problems. Couples who called themselves "very happy" were less likely to have problems than those who merely called themselves "above average"; and the "above average" were a little less likely than the "average." But even among the very happy about one couple in three admitted to problems (after Gurin, Veroff, and Feld, 1960).

from couples who considered themselves very happy, above average, or at least average in happiness.

Note that the question suggested problems that went on for a period of time. Had the couples been asked whether they ever had brief disagreements, the *yes* answers would probably have been close to unanimous. The couples who admitted having problems were then asked what their difficulties were all about. It turned out that their answers could in general be put into three categories.

One type of answer mentioned problems with the overall relationship between husband and wife ("We just don't get along." "We don't share the same interests.") Another took the form of complaints against the spouse ("My husband doesn't spend enough time with me." "My wife is too extrava-

Opinions and Experiences

A DAY AND NIGHT DIFFERENCE

Some of the difficulties in a marriage between a day person and a night person—and some satisfactory solutions—are illustrated by these comments from people who have been through such a marriage.

The Complaints

By a wife: This mismatch affects us when it is my bedtime. We've had many arguments about this. I feel so alone when I go to bed by myself. He is frustrated if he goes to bed early—because he's not ready. . . . And on Saturdays when I'm doing all the housework in the morning, it makes me think of him as very lazy because he sleeps until noon.

Another wife: We do not seem to agree on the time for sexual activities. I am really tired at night and go to bed for rest, not sex. In the morning, when I am rested and feeling great for a new day, is when I enjoy sexual activity the most. My husband wants to sleep in.

A husband: Differences between us still create some problems even after 27 years of mar-

riage. I do not try serious discussion with her in the morning and my wife refrains from such in the evenings.

Some Adjustments

A wife: On weekends I use the mornings as my private time. I enjoy solitude then and read, fool around, or stare into space. Mark finds the same freedom at night after I have gone to sleep. We go to bed at the same time but after I'm asleep he prowls, plays the piano, eats, watches tv, etc. Conflict arises only if he wakes me up.

Another wife: The mismatch has little effect on us . . . because of our similar goals and values. . . . We compromise so that our differences are equalized. For example, Ken will stay up late to help me or for social events. I, in return, will get up early for church, even though I may want to sleep, because of the values and goals we have. Working to balance our differences is important.

B. N. Adams and R. E. Cromwell, Morning and Night People in the Family: A Preliminary Statement, *Family Coordinator,* 1978, 27, pp. 5–13.

gant.'') The third category blamed neither the relationship nor the spouse but the situation in which the couple happened to find themselves. The villain in this third category was outside influences, including financial difficulties, jobs that interfered with the marriage, and complaints such as ''The children take up so much time'' or ''My in-laws nag us.''

In this regard the answers showed some significant difficulties between the very happily married, the average, and another group of couples who admitted that they were not too happy. As can be seen in Figure 7–2, the

very happy couples were troubled mostly by situational problems—outside factors that got in the way of the marriage. The unhappy couples were much more likely to complain about their spouses or the marriage relationship.

The Special Problems— and Advantages— of the College Educated

One other finding of the study illustrated in Figures 7–1 and 7–2 deserves particular mention: the fact that college-educated cou-

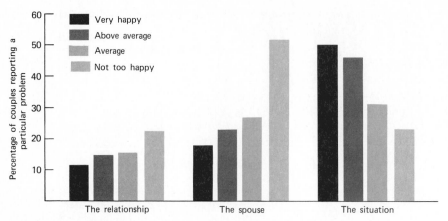

Figure 7-2
THE KINDS OF PROBLEMS FACED BY THE MARRIED
When married couples were asked to describe their problems, the kind of
difficulty they mentioned most prominently turned out to depend significantly on how happy or unhappy they were. Note how complaints about the
relationship or the spouse rise steadily from the "very happy" to the "not
too happy"—while complaints about the situation (or outside factors such
as money and in-laws) show exactly the opposite pattern (after Gurin, Veroff, and Feld, 1960).

ples who took part in the survey proved to
be a special kind of group. They showed a
different pattern from those who had only a
high school education and a very different
pattern from couples who had never gone
past elementary school. You might find it interesting to guess the results. Would you
suppose that the college-educated couples
were more or less happy than the others?
How would they compare when asked questions about how adequate they felt as marriage partners, such as this question asked of
women: "Many women feel that they're not
as good wives as they would like to be. Do
you feel this way a lot of times, or only once
in a while?"

As it turned out, the college-educated
couples were by far the most likely to report
feelings of personal inadequacy in marriage.
Fully 63 percent of them conceded that they
occasionally or often felt that they were inconsiderate to their partners, did not provide
enough companionship, or were poor providers or poor parents. (Only 55 percent of

the high school subjects reported such feelings of inadequacy, and only 44 percent of
the elementary school couples.) The college-
educated couples were also more likely to report that they had experienced problems in
the marriage.

All this sounds like bad news for college
students. At this point you might be inclined
to mourn your own chances of success in
marriage. But hold on. The study produced
another finding that is perhaps the most important of all. It turned out that far more of
the college-educated couples were thoroughly enjoying their marriage. About 60
percent of them described themselves as very
happy, compared with 46 percent of high
school couples and only 38 percent of elementary school couples.

The figures, though obtained a quarter of
a century ago, are still valid. A recent study
again found that college-educated partners
are much more likely than others to feel unhappy and inadequate at times, yet enjoy
more happiness and satisfaction at any given

moment (Locksley, 1982). At first glance the findings seem inconsistent. How can people be more problem ridden, more given to feelings of inadequacy, and still be happier in their marriages? The answer probably is that college-educated people have a higher degree of involvement in their relationship and indeed in life itself.

They seem somehow to be aware, even if they have not taken a course such as this one, that marriage can be an oasis of intimacy in a desert of impersonality. They recognize its importance and its potential for happiness. At the same time, they tend to be realists. They are aware of the problems and accept that nobody is or can be perfect. They acknowledge their own faults.

Perhaps they worry more about how well they and their marriages are doing because, as the authors of the 1960 study suggest, they have "an investment in life, a commitment to change, and an optimism about the possibility of change." Yet despite their worries, or perhaps even because of them, they are happier and more hopeful about the future.

IS QUARRELING GOOD OR BAD?

If it were possible to judge a marriage just by counting the number of arguments between husband and wife—no or few quarrels meaning a happy marriage, many quarrels an unhappy one—then we would have to say that marriage in the United States today is in terrible shape, far less happy than it was a few generations ago. By and large, American couples seem to have more quarrels than their great-grandparents did, and many more than married people do even today in societies where the general pattern of marriage resembles the traditional American pattern of the past.

But the reason our great-grandparents seldom quarreled had nothing to do with being happy or unhappy. Their lives together were peaceful and unmarred by conflict (on the surface) because there was simply no point in quarreling. In the old-fashioned, male-dominated marriage the husband never had to argue because he got his own way automatically. The wife seldom bothered to argue because there was no way she could win.

The "Peaceful" Family of the Past

An extreme form of male-dominated marriage is described in the box on *Opinions and Experiences* by a man who grew up in the Sicilian culture. In the United States, few husbands have ever been quite so clearly and arrogantly the lord and master. But certainly the man of the house, just a few generations ago, was often the unchallenged, unquestioned, unyielding boss. His welfare was paramount and his word was the law. His wife would never have thought of asking him to do the shopping, help with the housework, or take care of the children. The household revolved around him, run for his special benefit on a schedule designed to suit his convenience. His wife cooked the food the way he liked it. She took what money he felt like giving her and spent it as he commanded. She kept the children quiet while he was napping and out of his way altogether when he was irritable.

The husband was so firmly entrenched as boss that his wife knew full well that any complaint she made would only provoke him into behaving worse than ever. The safest course was to avoid crossing the tyrant and to keep him as quiet and content as possible. There were many families in those days, it is safe to say, where the surface was so placid that the neighbors considered man and wife ideally mated, yet where the husband never had the faintest idea of what his wife was

Opinions and Experiences

MARRIAGE MACHO STYLE

A man who is now a U.S. citizen recalls what marriage was like in the Sicilian village where he grew up in the 1930s.

In our village no self-respecting husband would think of hurrying home after work. He considered it a matter of honor to stop at the tavern for a few glasses of wine with his friends—and to stay as long as he pleased.

His wife, meanwhile, had not been out of the house all day except to shop for food. She had been scrubbing the floors, washing, ironing, mending her husband's socks, and shining his shoes. Toward late afternoon she had started work on a big supper—homemade pasta, chicken cacciatore, pastry for dessert. Then, after carefully scrubbing herself and the children to look their most presentable, she nervously awaited her husband's return.

Courtesy of Salvatore Cammalleri.

Unless he was in an exceptionally good mood, he would make a point of scorning the meal she had cooked. This again was a matter of honor. He would try a spoonful and push the dishes away, crying "Slop!" His wife, wringing her hands, would try to calm him. "Please! What would you like? Just tell me. I'll have it ready in a minute. Whatever you like."

His ego bolstered by this little game, the husband would leave immediately after the meal and go to his club, to spend the evening playing cards and drinking with the other men of the town. When he got home, if his wife happened to wake and ask where he had stayed so late, his answer was invariably, "It's none of your business"—which in fact was only too true in this kind of marriage.

---

really like as a human being, and where the wife in truth hated the very sight of her husband.

The Dead Hand of Tradition

Many people are still influenced in a strange way by the patterns of the past, for the tradition of maintaining peace at any price has not entirely disappeared. In many families the attempt to keep up the appearance of unbroken harmony has been passed along from great-grandparent to grandparent and on down the line. It continues to affect some members of today's newest generation even though it is no longer appropriate at a time when women and men are approaching a more equal footing.

This is because the children of homes where disagreements never broke into the open, no matter how fiercely they may have been boiling under the surface, are often ill equipped for candid and outspoken give-and-take in marriage. They grow up with a tendency to keep their emotions and hostilities in check, following the example of their parents. They may actually be afraid to argue.

Probably this is especially true of women. A woman who was brought up in a home where her parents seemed all sweetness and light, never raising their voices to each other, may prefer to endure almost any inconvenience or humiliation rather than start an argument. If she and her husband do get into an argument, despite her reluctance, she may find the experience shattering. She may find it difficult to forgive her husband for shouting at her; or she may be so shocked by her own anger and hostility, and so ashamed of it afterward, that she will never again dare to stand up for her rights (Duvall and Hill, 1960).

Quarreling Too Little

Not quarreling can get to be a habit. Often the habit begins before marriage, when many couples tend to be overpolite. They want to get along. They want things to go smoothly. So they cater to each other's preferences to avoid disagreements. Then, after marriage, a big and deadly serious problem comes up—one about which both are highly emotional. An attempt to discuss it results immediately in hurt feelings, resentments, and a good deal of vindictiveness. Instead of continuing with the quarrel and attempting to resolve it, they back off—partly from force of habit (Strong, 1975), partly because they are afraid of the strong feelings they perceive in themselves and each other.

Fear of conflict seems to stem from the fact that many of us have psychological quirks that make us feel inadequate and insecure, not sure whether we actually have any rights or how vigorously we are entitled to defend them. As one psychologist who is also a marriage counselor has said: "Many people, because of their inferiority feelings, are masochistic in their marriages. They put up with much more than they should" (Phillips, 1982). Another psychologist-counselor has observed: "Marital partners are afraid to be aggressive with each other. Some of us can tell the boss off, but never our spouse" (Burton, 1973).

All in all, the strange fact about quarreling is that there probably is not too much of it in marriage but too little, even today when give-and-take is more common than in the past. Disagreements, when dealt with honestly and constructively, are helpful rather than harmful, far better than any repression of one's feelings (Martinson, 1960). An open expression of discontent is often helpful and seldom harmful: "The danger for a marriage is much greater from apathy than it is from aggression. . . . In every case I have known, a proper aggression brought respect rather than retaliation. It is only when the aggression is useless, circular, brutal, or old-hat that the spouse really rejects it" (Burton, 1973).

SOME SPECIFIC SOURCES OF QUARRELS—AND WHY THE SPECIFICS DON'T MUCH MATTER

Because quarreling is so often repressed, some marriages go along for years in apparent harmony then suddenly break up, still without the exchange of harsh words that might have indicated a break was imminent. A husband is surprised to come home and find that his wife has moved out. A wife is amazed to find a note from her husband, saying that his lawyer will soon be in touch. Sometimes the husband or wife simply runs away and disappears, without any explanation. There are enough such runaways, indeed, to support a small industry of detective agencies that specialize in finding missing persons. Until recently, these agencies were mostly asked to find wandering husbands. Now, perhaps as another sign of the growing equality of the sexes, they are often asked to trace missing wives.

Usually, however, both husband and wife know when a marriage is in serious trouble. They may not argue openly over what is bothering them, or they may not argue very effectively, but they know full well that something is wrong—and they usually believe they can name it. Most couples who go to marriage counselors for help start out by listing specific disagreements that have caused serious trouble.

Money, Children, Sex, and Sex Roles

For many years studies have shown that two of the most common sources of quarrels are money matters and disagreements over children, including how many to have and how to discipline them (Blood and Wolfe, 1960; Roper, 1980). Some studies have found that arguments over sex were also high on the list of complaints (Scanzoni, 1975). Wives, particularly in lower-income families, have often complained about the husband's failure to support the family or his tendency to refuse to let her make her own decisions and in general to demand that she cater to his own selfish wishes (Goode, 1956). Husbands have often complained that the wife was suspicious, jealous, and nagging and failed to provide affection and companionship (Levinger, 1966).

In recent years two new sources of conflict seem to have cropped up. One concerns the division of household tasks, a problem that results from today's changing sex roles and the partner-wife's overload of obligations. The other is leisure activities, which presumably have become more important because of today's shorter work week. A large-scale study of over 1,500 wives and husbands in the mid-1970s found that household tasks and recreation topped the list of conflicts (Chadwick, Albrecht, and Kunz, 1976). In an even more recent public opinion poll 43 percent of women and 44 percent of men said they disagreed frequently about what to do with their leisure time, what to watch on television, or how to spend vacations (Roper, 1980).

A study of conflicts reported by married students at the University of Arizona is of special interest. Of the men and women who took part in the survey, 88 percent said they considered their marriages above average in happiness, and only 2 percent were either "quite unhappy" or "extremely unhappy." Yet they listed many conflicts. Heading the list, for both men and women, were sexual problems, followed by communication, recreation, money, friends, in-laws, and children (Gruver and Labadie, 1975).

Some of the problems of these married students appeared to be caused by the special pressures of college life. Many felt, for example, that they simply did not have enough time for communication, recreation, or friends. Why sex should have headed their list—mentioned by nearly two-thirds of both women and men—is something of a mystery. It may be that many of today's young people suffer from unrealistically high expectations created by the sexual revolution, as suggested in Chapter 6.

The Symptom but Not the Disease

Much of the popular advice about marriage assumes that happiness depends on solving all the individual and specific disagreements. Couples are urged to avoid quarrels over money by setting up a budget, having a joint checking account, or using other systems designed to ensure peace and harmony on the financial front. They are advised to budget their time outside the home—X number of hours for the wife to spend with her friends, Y number of hours for the husband with his. They are also advised to try to find forms of recreation that they enjoy equally and can share.

When the first marriage counselors started their practice, many of them were inclined to take the same approach to disagreements. They took specific conflicts seriously and tried to deal with them one at a time. They soon discovered, however, that usually the disagreement was merely a symptom and not

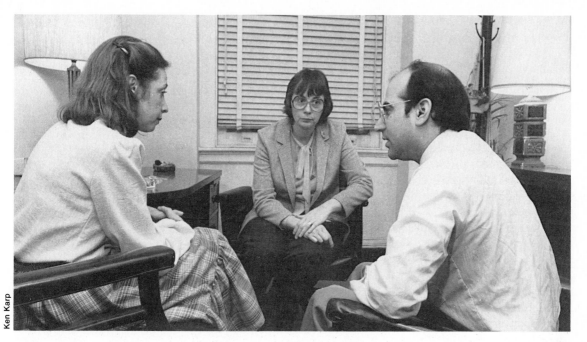

A marriage counselor (center) and two clients: Will they find that their disagreements are the disease or merely the symptoms?

the disease. Even if a symptom such as problems with sex or money could be persuaded to go away, a new one immediately cropped up (Burton, 1973). The early counselors were like physicians trying to lower a fever with aspirin while the patient was dying of pneumonia.

Disagreements over money, in particular, usually turn out to play far less part in marital unhappiness than is generally believed. One counselor has said: ''Money is sometimes a battleground—but not the battle. It may be the chief topic of conversation when people come for help, but after the first few interviews it usually drops out completely.'' Indeed finances are likely to cause real trouble only when a couple either come into a great deal of money, as by winning a lottery, or meet with some kind of financial catastrophe (Burton, 1973).

Disagreement Is All in the Mind

Specific disagreements, it would appear, are all in the mind—or rather in the two minds that go to make up the marriage. A couple who are not getting along can always find something to quarrel about, and if they stop fighting over that issue they will manage to find something else. And a couple who are getting along well can be happy even though they have numerous possible sources of serious disagreement.

One marriage counselor has reported working with a California couple who thought they were in trouble because the wife was addicted to the demanding and time-consuming sport of skiing, while the husband hated the very sight of snow. After the marriage as a whole was put on a healthy basis, their total difference of opinion on skiing did not bother them at all. This same counselor has also reported a similar experience with a wife who was a rabid Republican and liked to sit reading poetry or listening to music, married to a rabid Democrat who read nothing but history and liked to take long walks (Phillips, 1982).

Just as differences of this kind do not doom a marriage, it seems that the kind of "togetherness" often urged by popular magazines does not necessarily help. There is no evidence that couples are made any happier if they have an intense interest in each other's jobs, have a great deal of leisure time to spend together, or actually spend their spare time in close-knit family activities.

Recreation in which husband and wife participate jointly—such as playing games, visiting friends, or going on a camping trip—does seem to be related to happiness at certain periods in the marriage, particularly the early years. But apparently it does so chiefly because it helps husband and wife learn to communicate and establish a more intimate relationship (Orthner, 1975). No form of deliberate "togetherness"—even on such important matters as sex, money, or children—is enough in itself to make marriage a success (Burton, 1973).

WHAT CONFLICT IS REALLY ABOUT

If couples are not actually at odds on the specific issues that loom so large in their thinking, then what *do* they quarrel about? The answer is that they quarrel over their relationship. Something that is difficult to understand or put into words has gone wrong. They are vaguely unhappy with themselves, with each other, and with the marriage. They do not really know what the problem is. They cannot define it. Yet they assume, in this age of science, that cause and effect are always linked. So unhappy couples look for a cause—some specific cause, something they can put their finger on.

This "something" is always easy to find. A social historian who made a search for the strange reasons sometimes given for breaking up marriage found a case of a woman who received a divorce because her husband did not get home until 10 o'clock one night, then kept her up talking. Also in the records is a case of a woman who got her divorce because her husband never offered to take her out for an automobile ride (Westermarck, 1925). When a marriage has gone sour, almost anything can serve as a convenient explanation.

The Lost Oasis of Intimacy

What is fundamentally wrong with unhappy marriages—the basic conflict that drives couples apart and often into divorce—was discovered long ago by two of the noted pioneers in marriage counseling, Emily Mudd and her colleague Richard Hey of the Philadelphia Marriage Council. Mudd and Hey talked to many couples whose marriages were in trouble. Most couples began with the usual complaints: money, children, in-laws, sex, all the other specific disagreements. But it almost always turned out that these were only pinpricks on which the couples had focused what was really a general dissatisfaction with their entire relationship (Hey and Mudd, 1959).

In case after case, among couples of all ages and incomes, with no children or many, it soon became apparent that the real conflict lay in their relationship as a whole. Mudd and Hey concluded that the basic conflict in an unhappy marriage takes four interrelated forms:

1. Husband and wife both are lonely. They feel alone with their problems, misunderstood, unable to explain their anguish or find sympathy.
2. Both feel rejected and therefore unwanted and insecure.
3. They suffer from lack of communication. They cannot talk candidly about their problems and face the problems together.
4. They have experienced a loss of perspective. They have forgotten all the things they once liked about each other, the things that brought them together and gave them pleasure. They have lost their joy and optimism. They feel helpless and hopeless about the future.

What Mudd and Hey learned about unhappy marriages might be summarized by saying that the partners have failed to turn their relationship into the oasis of intimacy they hoped for. They are not communicating their deepest thoughts and feelings. They are not being and revealing themselves and displaying their emotions. Because they are dealing with each other at arm's length, rather than as close and trusting friends, they have not found the genuine security, sympathy, and support that everyone needs and that marriage promises. They are not intimate companions but strangers, even enemies.

"He (She) Doesn't Love Me"

Some further light on the basic conflict comes from an unusual study (Mathews and Mihanovich, 1963) made in an attempt to discover some of the differences between unhappy and happy couples. The sociologists who conducted the study did not ask their subjects to recite their problems. Thus they avoided the usual list of specific complaints

that couples ordinarily take to marriage counselors on the first visit. Instead they drew up a list of their own, containing 400 possible sources of conflict, and asked their subjects to check the ones they had found troublesome.

As might be expected, unhappily married subjects checked far more items than the happy. But the important finding concerned the kinds of problems that were characteristic of the two groups. Some of the items checked far more frequently by the unhappy subjects are listed in Table 7-1, which deserves careful study.

Note that all the items in Table 7-1—problems that loomed so large among the unhappily married but bothered only small numbers of the happy—fall into the pattern described by Mudd and Hey. The problems reveal feelings of loneliness, rejection, and lack of communication. The unhappily married couples were characterized by feelings of neglect and "lack of affection, understanding, appreciation, and companionship." The partners had withdrawn into their shells. Even worse, they had fallen into the practice of belittling each other. (Large numbers of the unhappily married checked items such as "Mate magnifies my faults," "Mate criticizes me too much," and "Mate makes me feel worthless.") Instead of lending support, they attacked and undermined each other's self-respect.

Nowhere on the list in Table 7-1 is there any mention of such specific conflicts as money, children, sex, or recreation. The basic conflict that makes marriage unhappy has very little to do with such symptoms and everything to do with a general illness centering on lost intimacy and lack of mutual acceptance. Perhaps the attitude of the unhappily married can be summed up in a single sentence: "He (she) doesn't love me—and I have stopped loving him (her)."

Table 7–1

The Real Causes of Unhappiness

	Percentage of couples with the problem who are	
	Unhappy	Happy
Partners don't think alike on many matters	50	11
Partners say things that hurt each other	45	12
My mate rarely compliments me	42	13
My mate has little insight into my feelings	40	6
I keep things to myself	39	14
My mate takes me for granted	39	9
I desire more affection	38	12
I have to give in more than my mate does	38	10
I often feel unloved	35	3
I need someone to confide in	34	6
My mate can't accept criticism	34	9
My mate is stubborn	32	8
My mate does not enjoy many things I enjoy	32	6
My mate is often moody	31	9
I can't talk to my mate	31	5

Listed here are fifteen problems that were reported frequently by unhappily married couples and significantly less frequently by the happily married. For a description of the study of nearly 1,000 men and women from which the figures come, see the text *(Mathews, V. D. and Mihanovich, C. S. New Orientations on Marital Adjustments.* Marriage and Family Living, *1963, 25, pp. 300–304).*

The Vicious Circle

Marriage is probably the most complex of all human relationships. The pattern in general, and the way it varies from moment to moment, depend on a whole host of inter-

actions between wife and husband. The relationship is affected not only by the way the wife behaves toward the husband but by the way she responds to his behavior, and in turn by both the husband's actions and how he responds to her actions.

The partners relate to each other in different ways at different times and under different circumstances, even in a single day. On some topics the wife may be frank and outspoken, the husband unwilling to express his opinions. On other topics the husband may be outspoken and the wife silent. Thus, the marriage ebbs and flows in accordance with the many aspects of the two personalities. It is also influenced by the relationship as a whole, which has a sort of life of its own and helps determine how the two partners behave and respond (Miller, Corrales, and Wackman, 1975).

When this complicated relationship goes well, it resembles a snowball rolling downhill. The path may be bumpy, jarred by disagreements and quarrels. But in general the relationship seems to grow almost of its own accord in awareness, intimacy, and affection. In one way or another, even by the manner in which they quarrel, husband and wife manage to reassure each other that they value the relationship. Despite their inevitable disagreements, they make it clear that they like themselves and each other. They build each other up by exchanging tokens of love and respect. The way they behave and respond in the relationship leaves no doubt that they enjoy being married to each other and would not have it any other way.

But the relationship can also move in the opposite direction. One problem can lead to another, starting the couple on the path to serious conflict. If one partner starts to go into a shell, hiding intimate feelings and withholding affection, the other is likely to react by doing the same. If one partner lashes out, putting the other down, the other is likely to retaliate. Both sense and aggravate the hostility. Harsh words lead to more harsh words (Jourard, 1964). Feelings of rejection crop up and multiply. The unhappy marriage gets to be a vicious circle.

The partners caught in the vicious circle cease to be lovers or even friends. They are open or secret enemies, watching each other suspiciously, expecting rebuff and criticism. They are ready to fight at the drop of a hat and try to protect themselves by delivering the first blow. They will argue over anything and everything, often as viciously as they know how. A seventeenth-century English dramatist wisely wrote that "heaven has no rage like love to hatred turned," for couples locked in the basic conflict are so hurt and disappointed over the path the relationship has taken that they hate each other more than they sometimes realize.

THE FALLACY OF FORCING YOUR MATE TO CHANGE

All this is not to say that specific disagreements are unimportant. Even the "tremendous trifles" can loom as huge obstacles to happiness, and more serious conflicts can be devastating. Somehow we have to resolve them, perhaps in the ways described in the next two chapters, or learn to live with them. Marriage counselors often take a sort of dual approach to disagreements plaguing their clients, trying to remedy the specific ones while at the same time pointing a way to escape from the basic conflict over the lost oasis of intimacy.

In some cases, where the partners are so mismatched that their differing desires and interests are almost bound to clash, the basic conflict seems unavoidable and there is no apparent way to reverse the vicious circle. (For some valuable comments on this point, see the box on *Opinions and Experiences*.) But in many cases couples who might be capable of considerable success somehow get started on the circle, often because they let minor disagreements turn into a major disaster.

One significant fact counselors have learned is that many disagreements, especially those that are likely to get a couple started on the vicious circle, can best be described as an attempt to play God. This misguided attempt begins with the fact that all of us glory in the habits and actions our socialization has produced. We tend to think that we are absolutely right about everything—our tastes in food and clothing, the way we spend or save money, the time we like to go to bed and get up, our approach to sex. We cannot understand why anyone else would have different preferences.

If we want to be harsh on ourselves, we can say that we are self-centered. But being "self-centered" in this manner is only human. It is in truth very difficult for those of us who like country music to understand why anyone should prefer symphonies. If we like our steaks well-done we find it hard to understand why anyone should like them bloody rare. The trouble is that in marriage—that oasis of intimacy in which we have such a great personal stake—we are likely to consider any behavior unlike our own as a personal insult. Thus, we have a strong—and sometimes fatal—urge to remake our partner in our own image. If our wife has a misguided taste for the television programs on Channel 2, we feel we have to convert her to our own much more logical preference for Channel 4. If our husband likes to sleep late on Saturday morning, we

Opinions and Experiences

HOW MARRIAGE FOR THE WRONG REASON BREEDS CONFLICT

Two therapists discuss marriages they have seen where basic conflict and eventual failure seemed inevitable.

How well people fit together is a major determinant of how gratifying their relationship will be and how long it is likely to be sustained. A relationship of any substance or duration is likely to be one between two people who connect at many levels—who enjoy commonality of needs, interests, values, goals, expectations, "turn-ons," and of course such fundamentals as language and educational levels.

People enter into romantic relationships primarily out of a variety of near-universal needs—intimacy, closeness, sexual gratification, a family—and out of more narrow and idiosyncratic ones, such as status, recognition, and validation. These [latter] are the needs many confound with love, thinking "I love you" when they mean "I need you." In these cases the reason the relationship began in the first place may be the very lethal microbe which eventually kills it.

From Lynch, C. and M. Blinder, The Romantic Relationships: Why and How People Fall in Love, the Way Couples Connect, and Why They Break Apart, *Family Therapy*, 1983, 10, pp. 91–104.

For example, a woman may marry so that she may quit an onerous job, be psychologically indulged, and have a family. And in return she may at first be very content to live docilely in the shadow of the powerful man she chose to provide these things. At the time of their marriage, her husband too may have a need for a family, especially one within which he can enjoy the feeling of total control, the prerogative to make the financial and social decisions, and the freedom to devote himself to his career provided by a live-in helpmate. Thus the doctor marries his nurse, the lawyer his secretary.

For a while they seem perfectly compatible. In time, however, she becomes more assertive and challenges their implicit marital contract. Dormant issues such as her anger over never having choices now surface. She is more likely to demand the space to explore who she is. Should the relationship not be sufficiently flexible to accommodate these changes, it will break apart as each seeks to meet his or her needs elsewhere.

---

feel almost obligated to educate him in the obvious advantages of being up and about.

Why Aren't You like Me?

If you happen to see *My Fair Lady* on the late night television movie, you will hear the male star sing "Why Can't a Woman Be More Like a Man?" a song that contains a good deal of wisdom. What the singer really means is "Why can't *she* be more like *me*?"

This is a sad refrain that has been voiced by countless husbands—while their wives have been equally unhappy in wondering "Why can't *he* be more like *me*?"

A more or less typical couple caught in the urge to remake each other in their own images might feel like this: The wife has decided that she will go out of her mind if her husband ever again leaves beard stubble in the wash basin, forgets her birthday or their anniversary, lends money to an old college chum who has never yet repaid a debt, or drinks a little too much at parties and tells the same corny jokes he has been telling since year one. The husband has decided that he will go out of his mind if his wife ever again nags him about dropping cigarette ashes, spends too much money buying him a birthday present that he really does not need, invites her no-good brother over for expensive meals, or holds long telephone conversations while he is trying to listen to the stereo.

The trouble is that these complaints center on deep-seated personality traits. The husband, being the way he is, cannot remember to clean the wash basin, thinks that birthdays and anniversaries are unimportant, cannot say no to a friend who asks for a loan, and gets a tremendous kick out of being the life of the party. The wife, being the way she is, cannot abide the thought of ashes on the carpet, enjoys buying presents, loves her brother despite his faults, and would much rather talk with her friends than listen to music.

The two people are what they are. They cannot change their habits and preferences, even on these relatively minor matters, without making a superhuman effort entailing considerable self-sacrifice and painful withdrawal symptoms. And it seems pertinent to ask, Why should they change? Does anyone—even a marriage partner—have a right to demand that they change?

The Shoulds of Forcing Change

There is at least some reasonable doubt about the correct answers to those last questions. Yet attempts by marriage partners to change each other go on all the time. Often the changes demanded by husbands and wives concern much more basic matters than those just described. A man marries a shy wife and decides that he must help turn her into a stunning social success, something that she has absolutely no desire or talent to be. A college woman marries a man with less education and sets about improving his grammar, knocking off his rough edges, and teaching him how to behave like a "gentleman."

Our friends and parents often encourage us in this hopeless attempt to turn our mates from what they are into what they are not. A mother tells her married daughter, "Tom's getting too fat. You ought to put him on a diet." The father says, "Tom doesn't have enough ambition. You ought to light a fire under him." A friend says, "Tom ought to carry a lot more life insurance for your protection." Meanwhile Tom is hearing from his side of the family and his friends: "I know Joan is tired when she gets home from work, but she should keep the house a little neater." "I don't see why Joan needs a car to get to work; she could take the bus." "Joan ought to look a little better, considering all the money she spends on clothes."

A good deal of popular thinking about marriage is based on the notion that we can create any change in our partners that we set our mind to. When the attempt fails, as it almost always does, we are likely to be enraged at our partners for their stubbornness and at the same time flushed with guilt for our own ineffectiveness. No one can be so frustrated and full of despair as a wife who believes she *should* be able to make her husband clean out the wash basin, *should* be able to make him remember her birthdays, and *should* be able to make him behave better at parties—unless it is the husband who believes that he *should* be able to make her drop her no-good brother and *should* be able to keep her off the telephone when the stereo is on.

Maslow's B Love and D Love

A valuable insight into the urge to remake our partner comes from psychologist Abraham Maslow (1968), who suggested that there are two very different ways in which people can love one another—or think they love one another. One way he termed D (for deficiency) love, in which our feelings are self-seeking and demanding. A husband who has only D love for his wife wants her chiefly as an adjunct to his own personality. He thinks of her as a piece of clay he can mold to his own convenience, someone he can exploit and dominate for his own selfish ends.

Maslow's other way is B (for being) love, in which our regard for the other person is unselfish, admiring, and respectful. A wife who feels B love for her husband relishes him just the way he is, with his faults as well as his virtues. She accepts him as a unique human being. She does not attempt to interfere with his expression of his own personality. She does not demand that he change. She can put up with what by her own standards are defects because they are simply a part of this human being for whom, on the whole, she has such great outgoing affection.

As an example of the difference between B and D love, Maslow used the homely example of the relations between a pet owner and a dog. The owners of show dogs, he suggested, are the D lovers of the pet world. They are not so much interested in the dog itself as in the blue ribbons and ego trips that the dog can produce. Thus they are constantly striving to change the dog's basic nature through selective breeding, tail cropping, ear cropping, and clipping the coat—all designed to produce animals that will be artificially beautiful and will bring great honor, though they may lose all their value as companions in the process. The B lovers of the pet world can be just as happy with

any old mutt of mixed parentage, dubious beauty, and sloppy behavior, as long as the dog is a happy and affectionate companion.

The B and D Mixture

If you have taken a psychology course, you probably know that Maslow is most noted for his *theory of self-actualization*. Maslow believed that human beings are innately inclined to seek beauty, truth, goodness, and the fullest possible development of their unique potentiality for perfection and creativity. Given the opportunity, his theory holds, they strive for a kind of self-fulfillment that puts them in tune with the meaning and mystery of life. They become self-actualizers who cheerfully accept themselves and others and the realities of existence. They are spontaneous and full of good humor. They rejoice in the experience of living.

Maslow recognized, however, that most people never attain self-actualization. The way they are brought up may warp their development. Or they may be too busy trying to satisfy more urgent motives for food, shelter, sex, and security. Social pressures may force them off the path to the ideal. Only a few people surmount all the obstacles and become such true self-actualizers as Albert Einstein, Helen Keller, Eleanor Roosevelt, and Albert Schweitzer, to name some of the people cited by Maslow.

Total B love is as difficult to achieve as complete self-actualization. Most of us will always feel a mixture of B and D love—toward ourself, our friends, and especially our mate. A certain amount of D love does not doom a relationship. As long as there is more B than D, a marriage usually thrives despite the inevitable disagreements and some attempt to manipulate and dominate. One research project has shown that very happy couples display about twice as much B love as D love (Shostrum, 1967).

Trying to force a partner to change is an example of D love at its worst, and it lies at the very heart of the basic conflict that can doom a marriage. When we try to force change we are seeking to get our own way, to run the show, to control our partner. The attempt is always self-defeating. You cannot browbeat a wife into changing her ways. (If anything, you will only make her more stubborn about resisting change.) You cannot shame a husband into dropping his bad habits. (If anything, you will only drive him deeper into his addictions.) One reason is that demands for change are in the last analysis a form of criticism. When we say to our partner, "You'll have to do things differently; you'll have to change," we are in effect saying, "I'm not satisfied with you the way you are." We attack the partner's self-esteem.

Indeed the basic conflict in marriage often turns into an exchange of insults. The two partners call each other stupid, sloppy, careless, unaffectionate, demanding, extravagant, thoughtless, and generally obnoxious. All these insults may contain a kernel of truth, for all of us are at times and to a certain extent stupid, sloppy, careless, and all the rest, including obnoxious. But we are not about to change—except perhaps slowly and gradually as we get older and wiser—and neither is our partner. All of us hate to be reminded of defects of which we are already too painfully aware.

HOW TO STAY FRIENDS WHILE FIGHTING

People being what they are, and marriage being what it is, quarrels are inevitable: "Marriage, the most intimate and demanding of all adult human relationships, has conflict as an inescapable part of its nature" (Duvall and Hill, 1960). "If we want the flavor and richness of a real marriage in a real world, we have to accept jolts and risks as a part of our experience" (Levy and Munroe, 1959).

In our overpolite society, open expression

Marilyn M. Pfaltz, Taurus

These two people must have quarreled many times over the years—but have obviously remained good friends.

of conflict is probably a release that all of us need. In most of our social relationships we must display an artificial and often hypocritical friendliness and tact. The male breadwinner and the working wife are expected to give service with a smile, to be deferential to their boss, customers, and even underlings. The housewife-mother feels obligated to be polite to her neighbors, her neighbors' children, and the salespeople who pester her constantly by telephone. Hardly an honest emotion is ever expressed. We have many acquaintances and few friends. Thus we need someone with whom we can have a rich, full meeting of real selves, no matter how much turmoil the confrontation creates.

Out of quarreling—once we have given up the futile attempt to remake each other into something we are not—can come the true spiritual union that only marriage provides. Once husband and wife have fought it through, and learned in the heat of battle to respect each other's individuality and desires, the "tremendous trifles" never seem quite so tremendous again.

The two can find ways to make the minor allowances, fine-tuned adjustments, and compromises that make life smoother. They can learn to appreciate the sincerity of each other's feelings, even if they find the feelings different from their own. They can even start changing in ways that bring them closer together—not out of duress, which never works, but because they want to, which does.

Are There Rules for Fighting Fair?

Popular books on marriage and psychology often set forth formulas for handling conflict—rules for fighting fair, like the rules that govern boxing matches. But conflict in marriage is not a prizefight designed to determine a winner and a loser. In fact, because every time you quarrel you are in essence attempting to force your partner to give you something that is beyond your partner's capacity to give, you cannot possibly win. The best you can hope for is a tie.

Thus the rules have dubious value. Clifford Kirkpatrick (1963) once collected some of the more common ones and appended his own funny-sad explanations of why they seldom work:

Never get angry at the same time. Try telling this to a couple engaged in a quarrel. The wife will say, "I'm not angry. It's him." The husband will say, "I'm not angry, It's her."

Even while quarreling, think of pleasant things about the marriage. "I'd be glad to," says the angry spouse, "but I'm too mad just now."

Heap coals of fire on your partner's head by being so nice that only a moral imbecile would fail to respond in kind. The partner will be quick to say, "I see through that one."

Arouse jealousy. You may seek more appreciation—but you are sure to get hatred instead.

Let the husband be boss one week, the wife have her own way the next. The aggrieved partner will vow, "You just wait until I'm boss next week."

Have your friends or relatives serve as arbiters. But who will decide, "Whose friends? Whose relatives?"

Kirkpatrick found it "naive" to think that conflict in marriage can be controlled through any such list of rules hung on the kitchen wall and consulted every time a disagreement arises. About all anyone can do to help you is offer some clues to the difference between constructive quarreling, which is good for the soul and helps the relationship grow in intimacy and awareness of each other's needs, and destructive fighting, which starts the vicious circle. Techniques of quarreling—which are easily forgotten anyway in the heat of battle—are not very important. What really matters is the spirit in which conflict is approached.

Some "Helpful Hints"

As a guide to approaching quarrels in the proper spirit, Kirkpatrick (1963) offered what he called some "helpful hints," by no means guaranteed to produce results but at least a step in the right direction. They include the following:

1. Keep the quarrel within bounds—that is, confined to a single specific issue, giving both partners a chance to express their feelings, release their tensions, clarify the problem, and find a solution to which both can agree.
2. Make clear that disagreement on one issue does not mean that you reject your partner in all respects—in other words, avoid the charge that "the trouble with you is you're no damn good."
3. Assume that the marriage is intact and will survive—at least until "the failure is clear and the suitcases packed."
4. Never quarrel in public—so that you don't have to win the argument to impress your friends or relatives.

Kirkpatrick also urged partners to spend some time studying their own desires and needs, exploring their feelings, and revealing these deep-seated aspects of their personality, but at the same time preserving a certain amount of privacy and independence. He felt that brief vacations from the marriage, especially when the relationship was going smoothly, might help both partners "restore novelty and appreciation." He also suggested an occasional exchange of roles—for example, with the breadwinner-husband caring for the children and the housewife-mother taking a temporary outside job—as an aid to understanding the partner's problems. If a quarrel could not be resolved, he recommended professional help, such as marriage counseling.

Another set of suggestions, also consid-

Ken Karp

A suggestion often made by counselors: a husband switches roles with his wife and takes care of the baby.

erably more helpful than those usually found in popular writings, has been drawn up by Evelyn Duvall and Reuben Hill (1960). Their advice includes the following:

Spell out exactly what you don't like and how you want things changed.

Get it out. Don't let it fester.

Stick to the point and avoid side issues.

Stay with it until you thrash things out.

Go on to some simple next step for improvement.

Attack the problem rather than each other. It is especially damaging to blame a partner for faults that cannot be helped—for example, if a wife makes fun of her husband's salary, which is almost surely the best he can manage, or if a husband jeers at a sterile wife's inability to have children, an unavoidable handicap about which she is already deeply sensitive.

Avoid dragging in your relatives.

It must be emphasized again that the suggestions by Duvall and Hill and by Kirkpatrick are merely helpful hints, which may relieve conflict if you can remember them and apply them. They are not an ironclad formula that must be followed to the letter because it is the only sure guide to successful quarreling. As in so many aspects of human relationships, there are no "ten easy rules" that will guarantee the outcome. When conflict occurs, and tempers run high, the rules are likely to be forgotten anyway. Kirkpatrick pointed out that even the most sensible suggestions "work best when least needed"; in other words, they sound better when all is calm than in the heat of battle. (Just as people who swear never again to lose their

temper have no trouble sticking to their vow until something makes them mad.)

From the Mouths of Babes: The Best Advice

Perhaps the best clue to successful quarreling can be discovered by watching children at play, for children have the happy gift of quarreling bitterly and then making up without reservations or resentment. You will not have to watch long to see two youngsters hurl insults, perhaps even exchange blows, part forever, and ten minutes later go back to playing together as if nothing had happened. Two boys aged 5, getting together on a summer morning, know they are almost bound to engage in a bitter quarrel before the long day's end, probably several bitter quarrels, yet they greet each other with the deepest affection. And after each fight they renew their acquaintanceship with the same eager warmth. Johnnie may have a black eye, but ask him who his best friend is and he will unhesitatingly name the neighbor boy who inflicted the damage.

Young children, of course, have never heard of any rules for fighting fair, except possibly not to bite or kick in the groin, which are rules that they sometimes ignore. They do not stick to the issue (and in fact often would be hard pressed to name the issue). They have no hesitancy about attacking each other's personal appearance, character, honesty, mother, father, sisters, and brothers. They do everything wrong. Yet they do have one saving grace which makes all else unimportant: They know they are friends. They like each other. They are committed to each other. They need each other. They would be broken-hearted if either had to move away.

They quarrel. Their relationship is beset

by conflict all the time. But they never get into the basic conflict and the vicious circle. They never have the feelings that Mudd and Hey found so devastating—they never feel lonely, misunderstood, rejected, unwanted, and insecure. They would never dream of thinking the fatal thought: "He (she) doesn't love me—and I have stopped loving him (her)."

SUMMARY

1. Quarreling in marriage is inevitable because quarrels flare up whenever people are rubbed together, and nowhere else are two personalities rubbed together so constantly and abrasively as in marriage.

2. Many disagreements occur over "tremendous trifles," that is, minor differences in tastes and habits like neatness, eating preferences, and what to watch on television.

3. Disagreements are more difficult to resolve in the family than in secondary groups. In the secondary groups to which we belong, there are usually clear-cut rules for settling disputes. In marriage there are no established guidelines, and we have more at stake in the family "oasis of intimacy" because we desperately depend on our partner for psychological satisfactions that cannot be found elsewhere.

4. The "tremendous trifles" act like time bombs, and go unnoticed most of the time, then suddenly explode. One reason is that we have changing moods, ups and downs that swing from jolly to cranky. Two people can be out of synchronization; one common way is if one is a "day person" and the other a "night person."

5. All couples, even those who consider themselves the happiest, report disagreements. There is a difference, however, in the kinds of disagreements reported by happy and unhappy couples. Happy couples are troubled mostly by situational problems—such matters as financial pressures, in-laws, and lack of time. Unhappy couples complain about their partner or their relationship.

6. More college-educated people than others are likely to report problems in marriage and to concede that they sometimes feel they are inconsiderate partners and poor providers or parents. Nevertheless the college-educated are more likely than others to say they thoroughly enjoy the marriage. The reason seems to be that they have a higher degree of involvement in their relationship.

7. Couples today seem to have more quarrels than in the past. Traditional marriages seemed unmarred by conflict—on the surface—because the husband got his way automatically and the wife could gain nothing by arguing.

8. The tradition of maintaining peace at any price has a lingering effect because people brought up in homes where disagreements never broke into the open are often unprepared for and afraid of candid give-and-take. Thus, there probably is not too much quarreling in marriage but too little, because an honest and constructive attempt to deal with disagreements is far better than repression of feelings.

9. Some common sources of quarrels are money matters, different ideas of raising children, sex, sharing of household chores, and leisure activities. But the specific nature of quarreling is just the symptom and not the disease. An unhappy couple can always find something to fight about. Happy couples stay friends even when they have many possible sources of serious disagreement.

10. The basic conflict that drives partners apart is dissatisfaction with their relationship as a whole. The partners have lost their perspective and optimism and cannot communicate. Both feel lonely, misunderstood, rejected, unwanted, and insecure. In effect they are saying "He (she) doesn't love me—and I have stopped loving him (her)."

11. Once basic conflict has started, both partners sense and aggravate the situation. If one goes into a shell or lashes out, the other retaliates by doing the same. Harsh words lead to more harsh words. Feelings of rejection crop up and multiply. The relationship becomes a vicious circle.

12. The happy couple, by contrast, support each other by enchanging tokens of love and respect. Even by the manner in which they quarrel, they manage to reassure each other that they value the relationship, which seems to grow almost of its own accord in awareness, intimacy, and affection.

13. Many of the conflicts that get a couple started on the vicious circle spring from attempts to change one's partner into one's own image—in all sorts of habits, tastes, and preferences. Such attempts are dangerous because the demands for change are a form of criticism. They seem to say, "I'm not satisfied with you the way you are."

14. Attempts to force change are an example of what Abraham Maslow has called D (for deficiency) love, in which feelings are self-seeking and demanding. This is in contrast to Maslow's B (for being) love, in which regard for the other person is unselfish, respectful, and admiring.

15. Although popular books on marriage often suggest rules for fighting fair and handling conflict, the techniques for quarreling are not important, and they are easily forgotten anyway in the heat of battle. What really matters is the spirit in which conflict is approached. Constructive quarreling helps the relationship grow in intimacy and awareness of each other's needs. Destructive fighting starts the vicious circle of the basic conflict.

Discussion Questions

1. What are "tremendous trifles" and why are they more difficult to resolve in the primary group of the family than in secondary groups?
2. In marriages that you know, are the happiest couples troubled mostly by situational problems? Do the unhappy couples complain more about each other and the marital relationship?
3. Do you agree that couples who rarely quarrel are happier than couples who argue often? Why?
4. If not money, children, sex, or sex roles, what is the *basic* conflict in unhappy marriages?
5. How is a husband who is trying to force his timid wife to become a social butterfly demonstrating D love?
6. What is the difference between constructive quarreling and destructive fighting?

CHAPTER 8

The Fine Art of Getting Along Together

Unhappy couples may think they have their own unique problems and quarrels, but their difficulties usually revolve around the same basic conflict. Happy couples, on the other hand, have no such thing as a basic source of satisfaction. The people who manage to get along together have many different kinds of personality, relationship, and lifestyle. They may be rich, poor, or in between. They may have many children, no children, or in between. Their sexual relationship may vary from intense to almost non-existent.

Thus it is more difficult to make any general statements about happy couples—and how they got that way—than about the conflict ridden. The ways in which men and women manage to get along together, make the necessary adjustments, and love each other throughout life (even at times when they are beset by the inevitable quarrels discussed in the previous chapter) are so varied as to almost defy description.

It is easier to list the things that seem to have little or no effect on how well couples get along than to name the things that do. It has been found, for example, that many matters generally believed important to happiness are actually not important at all. Family income and job prestige seem to have little effect on marital satisfaction (Jorgensen, 1979). Indeed, there are indications that wives tend to be less rather than more satisfied if the husband's job, although it provides a high standard of living, also makes great demands on his time and energy (Burke, Weir, and DuWors, 1980). Couples who live in run-down housing in poor neighborhoods seem to be just as capable of a satisfactory marriage as those who live in luxurious surroundings (Chilman, 1978).

Studies have also shown that a number of matters generally considered an invitation to trouble do not really reduce the chances of a successful marriage. For example, couples do not necessarily have any special trouble getting along together even when a working wife moves ahead of her husband in job prestige (Richardson, 1979). Nor does choosing a mate from outside one's own social class usually interfere with satisfactory adjustment. Men who marry down or marry up seem to be just as happy as any others. Among women, marrying down seems to be unfavorable only for those with strong ambitions for social status, and marrying up only for those who have little concern with status and would rather have the husband devote his energies to his family rather than to his career (Jorgensen, 1977).

Making adjustments and getting along together seem to be a fine art rather than a science. Nonetheless, a great deal has been learned about the ways the art can be practiced. This chapter discusses some of the matters that have been found especially important to the adjustment process. The first is what might be called the spirit of fairness.

PLAYING FAIR IN MARRIAGE

Even in the simplest business relationship, happiness on both sides depends to a great extent on how fair the two parties consider the arrangement. If you feel that your employer is paying you fairly, and the employer feels that you are doing a fair day's work, then all is well. If either you or the employer feels cheated, you are in trouble. In the intimate relationship of marriage, fairness is so obviously important that most people would say they are willing and eager to be fair in every respect. Yet this goal, though so generally accepted, seems difficult to attain in actual practice. The feeling of being treated unjustly is one of the most common problems of all found by marriage counselors, and also crops up frequently among married people who are in individual psychotherapy (Gass, 1974).

A wife may say, "He spends more time with his friends than he does with me. It just isn't fair." Or "We always spend our vacations where he wants to go." Or "He regards all the money he makes as his, but my pay is supposed to go into the household fund." A husband may say, "She doesn't understand that I need to relax on my weekends; I don't have the energy to turn our apartment into a dream house, and anyway I don't care how it looks." Or "I pay the rent and everything else, but she's used her paychecks to buy herself a new car." Or if they have children, "The kids come first, and I'm supposed to make do with whatever little time she has left over."

Many complaints about unfairness, it must be pointed out, are themselves unfair. Many husbands and wives imagine that they are being unjustly treated even when an impartial observer, say a marriage counselor, can find no grounds for complaint. This seems to be because many of us have grown up with a strong tendency toward nagging worries about being cheated—of giving more than we get, of being "taken" by salesmen, coworkers, and even our own friends, relatives, and spouses. We are what psychiatrists call "injustice collectors," a term so eloquent that its meaning leaps immediately to mind. Perhaps the widespread existence of this attitude is inevitable in our society, as suggested by the marriage counselor quoted in the box on *Opinions and Experiences*.

Yet, though many of us may exaggerate the shabby way we are being treated by the world in general and our mate in particular, there is no question that complaints of unfairness in marriage are often based on actual fact. Fairness is difficult to establish and practice. It is especially difficult today, when the sex roles are changing so rapidly and new and unfamiliar forms of marriage relationships are still in the blueprint stage. But it is essential to successful marriage—probably the first step of all in making satisfactory adjustments.

Defining *Un*fairness: This Is Easy

A grossly unfair marriage is easy to spot. The Sicilian husband described in the preceding chapter and his American counterparts were tyrants who made no attempt at fair play. They ran the show, issued the orders, and demanded obedience and servitude. Their marriages were like the relationship between a high-and-mighty, insulting boss and a downtrodden worker afraid of losing the job.

There are still marriages that are com-

Opinions and Experiences

"A BUNDLE OF QUIVERING SUPERSENSITIVITIES"

Clinton Phillips, a California marriage counselor, describes what he believes to be a major problem in most marriages.

One big trouble with marriage—certainly middle-class and upper-class marriages, the kind that most college students will have—is that the very nature of modern society keeps all of us in a constant state of anxiety. We adults, meaning everybody over 18, are the products of a system that makes us much too touchy, too quick to take offense, too slow to forgive.

Ours has been a nation of constant striving and progress. The immigrant who arrived penniless and unable to speak a word of English was followed by a son who finished grammar school and earned good pay in the steel mills. The son's son finished high school and made big money selling insurance. The son's son's son—or maybe the daughter—has now been graduated from Harvard Law School.

So nobody is satisfied. At no point can a man or woman say, "This is it. I have now attained my goal. This is where I stop and enjoy my success." The day after a man is made assistant sales manager he starts pining for the job of manager. The day after a woman becomes a college dean she starts thinking about being president.

Even aside from our jobs, our puritanical consciences tell us we should be able to do anything we set our minds to. We should all be as funny as Woody Allen, as smart as Margaret Mead, as attractive as Robert Redford, and as athletic as Martina Navratilova. We can't live up to these standards. So we feel inadequate and jumpy. We expect criticism and can find it in the most innocent remark.

A husband and wife are watching tv, and on the screen comes Liza Minelli, dressed to the nines. The wife says, "Isn't that a beautiful fur coat?" She is just making conversation. She never expects to own a coat like that and may not even want one. But her husband, well aware that some men do manage to buy fur coats for their wives, thinks she is insulting him. Or the husband says, "Wow, can she sing!" This time the wife, who incorrectly thought in high school that she might have the making of a voice, is insulted.

Behind our thin skins we are a bundle of quivering supersensitivities, awaiting the lash. When it comes—or when we think it comes—we exaggerate the pain. We cannot fight and forget because the blows cut too deep, right to the core of our shaky self-esteem. Some psychologists and psychiatrists would say that all this is neurotic, that "healthy" people should be able to recognize their own worth without constant reassurance. I disagree. I think society does this to us. It is the price we pay for progress, democracy, and the Puritan heritage.

Courtesy of Dr. Clinton E. Phillips.

pletely one sided. The husband refuses to let his wife take a job, however much she might like to. He gives her only as much money as he chooses and expects her to do miracles with it in running the house. He makes all the decisions about where they will live, their social life and vacations, and the purchase of such items as automobiles and tv sets. He also decides how many children the wife will have and how she must rear them.

Less frequent, but not totally unknown, are marriages in which the wife takes over with an equally high-handed disregard for fair play. One therapist has reported the case of a woman who convinced her husband he was so totally incompetent that he should sign the house over to her and let her run all their financial affairs. She worked while he stayed home and tried to manage on the allowance she gave him (Melville, 1973). The therapist, incidentally, discovered that the man was as competent as anybody else, except perhaps in his self-effacing role in the marriage.

Defining Fairness: This Is More Difficult

Though unfairness can be obvious, fairness in marriage is as tricky to recognize and describe as it is to attain. One reason is that personal attitudes about fairness are as pluralistic and subject to individual differences as everything else. A relationship that one couple consider perfectly fair might seem completely one sided to a different woman or a different man.

Note the marriage described in the box on *Opinions and Experiences*. To people who have totally rejected the traditional sex roles, this relationship of Jeanne and Ronald will seem distressingly similar to the old-fashioned, male-dominated arrangement of the past (as indeed it did to the counselor who describes it). It might be said that the wife is saddled with all the boring routine—the housework and cooking, responsibility for the children, even serving as typist for her husband. He has all the freedom from menial chores and annoyances—and all the opportunities for soul-satisfying work and study. She gives. He gets. Yet as the interview makes clear, the relationship is working and there is no complaint of unjust treatment.

We can make a few assumptions that will explain the success of the Jeanne-Ronald marriage. In all probability, Jeanne does not see housework, cooking, and children as a bore. She actually enjoys all these activities. She would rather be doing these things than working at a career or on a Ph.D. She may in fact believe that Ronald gets the worst of the bargain because he has to work so hard on his job and his studies. She is happy to help out at the typewriter, for she feels that Ronald works not only for self-fulfillment but for the good of the family.

Whether or not we approve of the Jeanne-Ronald relationship, it contains a lesson for

One form of fairness in marriage: sharing the duties on a family ranch.

Mimi Forsyth, Monkmeyer

Opinions and Experiences

IS THIS MARRIAGE FAIR?

A Florida marriage counselor reported these observations of a couple in their early 30s—not people he was counseling, just next-door neighbors whom he regarded as good friends.

Ronald is the most ambitious man I know. He works hard as a junior executive with a chemical company, and on the side he's getting a Ph. D. On weekends you can usually find him in his back yard under a beach umbrella, hitting his books or scribbling on a yellow legal pad. That's his dissertation, which he has been writing and rewriting for months. His two young sons may be out there too, and maybe some of their friends; but Ronald is off in another world, paying no attention. When the kids get in trouble, it's Jeanne who comes out of the house and sets things straight.

Along toward late afternoon, Ronald comes back down to earth and plays with the boys for a while. Or maybe he takes the family to the beach. Sometimes he cooks hamburgers or steaks on the grill. And he does mow the lawn—when he can't get one of the neighborhood teenagers to do it—and grow a few flowers and tomatoes. But that's about it. Ronald is not what you would call the world's most helpful husband. I'm not sure he even knows how to turn on the vacuum cleaner or the washing machine.

Jeanne does it all. Her house is spotless. The kids are always neat. When we go over there for dinner, she serves an elegant meal. On days when Ronald is at work and the boys are playing somewhere else, we can hear her typewriter going. She's typing Ronald's dissertation or his business reports.

My own wife is a career woman. She teaches sociology at the university while I do my counseling in my office downtown. She's thoroughly emancipated. And I was a firm believer in women's liberation long before the term was invented. So we sometimes think we ought to talk to Jeanne and Ronald and set them straight. The only trouble is that we both agree they're the happiest couple we know, next to us. How can you knock success?

---

us. Fairness is largely a state of mind. As long as we ourselves feel that our partner is treating us fairly, then the relationship is fair—no matter what particular form the relationship takes or what anyone else might think about it. A fair marriage can be defined in only the most general terms, that is, as one in which both partners feel they have an equal opportunity to express themselves and satisfy their personal needs. The specifics of what it means to express oneself and satisfy one's needs have to be left up to each individual.

Fairness as a State of Mind

The statement that fairness is largely a state of mind deserves further comment. Let us start by making some other reasonable assumptions about Jeanne and Ronald. Because they are both so content with their relationship, we can assume that they display a good deal of mutual respect. They appreciate each other's virtues. They value each other. Jeanne does not regard herself—nor does Ronald regard her—as nothing more than a sort of super-servant hired to keep house and baby-sit. She does not re-gard her typing, and nor does he, as a me-nial chore. Ronald, in turn, does not regard his career as something demanded by an ex-pensive and ungrateful family.

Thus, although the Jeanne-Ronald rela-tionship may take much the same outward form as marriages of the past, it is entirely different in spirit. Jeanne does not live in fear and trembling lest she offend her lord and master. Ronald does not regard Jeanne as an inferior to be ordered about, treated with a mixture of contempt and indulgence, and punished when slow to jump at his bid-ding. The two partners approach each other with a sense of equal integrity and worth that was rare in the days when both husbands and wives accepted ''obey'' as a part of the mar-riage ceremony.

What Would Be Fair in These Cases?

The spirit of mutual respect is the secret of avoiding feelings of unjust treatment, which otherwise could hardly be avoided in the course of a marriage lasting over a long pe-riod. Life itself, unfortunately, is not always fair. There are almost bound to be times in any marriage when one partner or the other gets the dirty end of the stick—not through the other person's fault, but simply because circumstances have worked out that way.

For some examples of situations where to-tal fairness is impossible, consider the fol-lowing cases. Note that the two partners to the marriage are called only A and B. In one of the cases, as it happened, A was the hus-band and B was the wife. In the other two, A was the wife and B the husband. But the sex of A and B should not count in judg-ments of what is fair and what is unjust; the

cases can best be considered without regard to who is the husband and who is the wife.

Case 1. A and B were married right after college. They have no children. Both had jobs at the time of the marriage, but A be-came dissatisfied with the type of work and has returned to college for intensive train-ing in another field. The course keeps A busy from morning to night. B now pro-vides the couple's full support and also does most of the work of taking care of their apartment, meals, and the rest of the es-sential daily chores.

Case 2. A, in a moment of carelessness, drove through a red light and was seriously injured in a crash. After a long spell in a hospital, A is now recovering at home but still needs nursing care. The couple has gone heavily in debt for the medical bills. They are still paying for help during the daytime when B is at work. In the hours at home B serves as nurse as well as house-keeper and cook.

Case 3. A and B live in a big-city apartment near the offices in which they have been working. A's company is now moving to a suburb that is more than an hour's drive or bus ride away. A enjoys the job and wants to keep it. The couple does not know what to do. Is it fair that A should spend more than two hours a day commuting to work? Or should they move, and if so, where?

Sometimes You Just Can't Help Being Unfair

If any of these three cases had resulted in a lawsuit by A against B or vice versa and you were a juror, you would have a hard time deciding the rights and wrongs. In case 1, A's career ambitions have certainly put a burden on B; on the other hand, is it fair to ask A to give up these ambitions? In case 2, A was to blame for the automobile accident that is causing the trouble; but nobody except a psychotic bent on suicide deliberately runs a car into another, and surely the accident was not deliberate. Anyway, A has suffered just as much as B—in fact, because of a guilty conscience, probably even more. In case 3, plagued by the commuting problem, a Solomon would despair of finding a fair solution.

Sometimes couples try to find some kind of mechanical formula to work out problems such as these. The problem of job moves may be tackled by one partner's saying, "Last time I moved for you. Now it is your turn to move for me." One couple actually tried to figure out, by measuring the miles, where they could establish a home exactly halfway between the two places where they worked. If this last idea strikes you as carrying the idea of fairness a bit far, you are in good company. The social scientist who reported the incident termed it a matter of "going to such extremes" as to make "a parody" of attempts at absolute equality (Gass, 1974), for it is not the specific solutions but the spirit of fairness that counts—the feeling on both sides that they are working as partners toward their individual and mutual fulfillment and are willing to share the inevitable hardships they will encounter.

Time—Thank Goodness—Cures Many Ills

The attempt to acquire and preserve the spirit of fairness can be made much easier by taking a long-range view of marriage. Though there are times when circumstances put especially difficult burdens on one of the partners, circumstances have a way of changing. At the moment, the mixture of obligations and advantages of marriage may

be much worse for A than for B. But there will surely come a time when this will change. It helps if both parties think in terms of sharing fairly in both the opportunities and the duties that will occur over a lifetime—or at least over a period of three years or five or fifteen.

Taking the long-range view is not easy. It is especially difficult for young people, who often find it hard to imagine that they will ever be 30 years old, much less 40 or 50. But, as any older person can testify, nothing in life stays the same for very long. People's desires, tastes, and ambitions change. They change jobs. They move to new apartments or new houses, new neighborhoods, new cities. They get sick and get well again. In large numbers, they have children, and then the children also change, grow up, and leave home. The family's income and expenses go up and down.

Playing fair in marriage has been found to revolve to a great extent around the key word *tolerance* (Rapoport and Rapoport, 1975a), mostly tolerance for circumstances when there is no question that you are contributing more to the marriage than you are getting back. If you and your partner have established the spirit of fairness, this too will pass. Indeed there will doubtless come times when the shoe is on the other foot and you are getting more than you give. To couples who understand the secret of fair play in marriage, it all balances out in the end.

DRAWING UP A CONTRACT: DOES IT HELP?

Recently there has been considerable discussion about attempts to ensure fairness in marriage by drawing up a written agreement before the ceremony takes place. Some prospective brides and grooms have sat down, often with a lawyer, and worked out a contract defining the rights to which each of them is entitled and the duties and obligations each is expected to fill. How many such contracts have been signed is not known. Probably the number is small, but the marriage contract is an interesting idea that deserves discussion pro and con.

The "Unwritten Contract" of Marriage

The very act of getting married, it should be pointed out, creates a contract of sorts, although most people never realize this. The bride and groom are never told that they are acquiring any rights or assuming any duties and obligations. They sign no promises. Nonetheless the ceremony creates an unwritten contract between them containing some definite promises, on both sides, that the state courts stand ready to enforce if necessary.

The unwritten contract cannot be broken at the mere whim of one party or the other. It can be dissolved only by a ruling of the divorce court, which will then also rule on such matters as alimony, child custody and support, and how the couple's property should be divided. The unwritten contract even specifies some of the roles that husband and wife agree to play. By long-standing tradition, the husband is designated head of the family. He keeps his name, and the wife changes hers to his. He decides how and where to work, and his wife is obligated to go with him. He arranges for the family income and manages its money and property. In turn, he is responsible for supporting his wife and any children they may have. The wife is responsible for taking care of the house and the children (Weitzman, 1975a).

The Rebellion against the Unwritten Contract

To many women today, the unwritten contract is a distasteful reminder of the traditional male-dominated marriage and the status differences created by the traditional sex roles. The contract appears to give the husband all the privileges and only one obligation, that of supporting the family (an obligation that is in itself distasteful to liberated women because it implies that wives are incapable of supporting themselves). The contract makes no provision for fairness either in spirit or in actual conduct. In the words of one woman who has studied the legal aspects of marriage, it is "archaic . . . the 200-year-old vestige of an extinct social structure" (Weitzman, 1974).

The move toward written contracts, drawn up to the specifications of the individual couple, is in large part a rebellion against the traditional legal view of marriage. This rebellion, like so many other things generally believed to be completely new, actually goes back a long way. As early as 1855 a marriage agreement was drawn up by Lucy Stone, who became a pioneer in the women's rights movement after working her own way through college when her father refused to send her. The agreement between Lucy Stone and her husband-to-be stated that it represented a protest against "such of the present laws of marriage as refuse to recognize the wife as an independent, rational being, while they confer upon the husband injurious and unnatural superiority, investing him with legal powers which no honorable man would exercise and which no man should possess" (Davidson, Ginsberg, and Kay, 1974). Among other things, the agreement specified that Stone would keep her maiden name—a clause that is often included in "modern" marriage contracts.

For an example of a modern written agreement, see the box titled *A famous marriage contract,* which is a condensed version of a document signed by two young people before their 1972 marraige. Note that the bride and groom, with the help of a lawyer, tried to define in black and white some general feelings about their future relationship—such as their intention to continue to pursue their own careers, friendships, and family ties rather than abandon all outside interests in favor of togetherness. They also set down rules for conduct in such matters as religion, birth control, and the sharing of household expenses and household tasks. Sex is mentioned in a clause agreeing to avoid infidelity.

Some couples have drawn up contracts that are even more specific and detailed. They have attempted to set rules for sexual behavior in the marriage, relations with each other's parents and other relatives, and the division of property in case of a divorce. Some contracts even set a time limit, often five years or ten, after which the contract expires unless both parties wish to renew it, either in the original form or with revisions.

Are Husband-Wife Contracts Legal?

Although the word *contract* has a nice legal ring to it, there is considerable question about the actual legal standing of a written agreement of this kind. Even if drawn up by a lawyer—and filled with *whereases* and *party of the first parts*—a marriage contract will not necessarily be enforced in court. At one time the courts generally regarded such contracts as totally void, on the ground that they violated public policy. Now the legal establishment takes a more liberal view of provisions for dividing a couple's assets in case of divorce. But some provisions would probably

still be rejected because they conflict with the unwritten laws of marriage. For example, the courts would hardly accept a notion that the husband should be free from responsibility for supporting his wife, nor any agreement that the husband would pay the wife for taking care of the house or the children.

Thus, the chief value of a marriage contract probably lies in whatever it can contribute to the getting-to-know-you process described in Chapter 5. Writing an agreement demands serious discussion of attitudes toward marriage—of such questions as careers, handling money, household arrangements, parenthood, indeed, all the couple's "ideals and aspirations" (Weitzman, 1974). This in itself may be valuable, even if the agreement itself has no legal standing. As one lawyer has said: "The most important effect of a marriage contract is to help people define how they want to behave. There is no use entering one if you expect to seek a judge's assistance to assure compliance" (Fleishman, 1974).

The Pro and Con of Contracts

As to whether a contract is on the whole helpful or harmful, this is a matter of opinion. Some students who hear about the idea for the first time find it "radical" but attractive, as did the student quoted in the box titled *Yes, I definitely want a marriage contract.* The reasons given by this student, it should be pointed out, are much the same as those cited by social scientists who favor contracts. Note especially the last paragraph of the box. Many sociologists agree that the greatest value of attempts to draw up a contract may lie in preventing marriages between people who are in fact incompatible but might never discover it in time unless they sit and try to put their feelings into writing (Sheresky and Mannes, 1972).

Opinions and Experiences

A FAMOUS MARRIAGE CONTRACT

These are excerpts from an agreement drawn up by a young couple named Harriett Cody and Harvey Sadis. The agreement was first published in *Ms.* magazine and has been widely reprinted and studied.

Harriet and Harvey desire to enter into a marriage relationship, duly solemnized under the laws of the State of Washington, the rights and obligations of which differ from the traditional rights and obligations of married persons.

Harriett and Harvey affirm their individuality and equality in this relationship. The parties reject the concept of ownership implied in the adoption by the woman of the man's name; and they refuse to define themselves as husband and wife because of the possessory nature of these titles. Therefore the parties agree to retain and use the given family names of each party. The parties will employ the titles of address, Ms. Cody and Mr. Sadis, and will henceforth be known as partners in this relationship.

The parties have strong individual identities with their own families, friends, careers, histories, and interests, and do not view themselves as an inseparable couple who do not exist apart from each other. Therefore the parties agree to allow each other as much time with other friends individually as they spend with each other.

The parties freely acknowledge their insecurities about sexual relationships beyond the partnership. Therefore, the parties agree to maintain sexual fidelity to each other.

The parties agree to respect their individual preferences with respect to religion and to make no demand on each other to change such preferences.

At this time, the parties do not share a commitment to have children. The parties agree that any children will be the result of choice, not chance, and therefore the decision to have children will be mutual and deliberate. Further, the parties agree that the responsibility for birth control will be shared.

Harriett and Harvey value the importance and integrity of their respective careers. . . . Should a career opportunity arise for one of the parties in another city at any future time, the decision to move shall be mutual. The overall advantage gained by one of the partners in pursuing the new career opportunity shall be weighed against the disadvantages, economic and otherwise, incurred by the other.

The parties agree to share equally in the performance of household tasks, taking into consideration individual schedules and preferences.

The parties agree that the income derived by one of the parties will be the separate property of such party. In order to avoid the commingling of the separate assets, the parties agree to maintain separate bank accounts.

The parties agree to share responsibility for the following expenses, which shall be called living expenses, in proportion to their respective incomes: (1) mortgage payment or rent, (2) utilities, (3) home maintenance, (4) food, (5) shared entertainment, (6) medical expenses. Other expenses shall be called personal expenses and will be borne individually by the parties.

Ms. Magazine. June, 1973. Used by permission.

Opinions and Experiences

"YES, I DEFINITELY WANT A MARRIAGE CONTRACT"

These are the views of a University student asked to discuss in a final examination the reasons for approving or rejecting the idea of signing a written contract before marriage.

I can see why the idea of a marriage contract strikes many people as radical. It was not until recently that there was any reason for a contract, because society laid down a made-to-order blueprint of the roles that a husband and wife were supposed to play. Before birth control, a couple did not even have any choice about whether to have children or how many.

Things are different now. I would not want to get married without a firm agreement on whether to have children and, if so, how many, how soon, how they would be cared for, how they would be socialized, and how they would be disciplined. I would want to know how each of us feels about the other's parents and the question of whether they would live with us in their old age.

I would want an agreement on handling money, preferably with each of us contributing to the general household and living expenses and to a joint bank account for vacations taken together and joint entertainment, but also having bank accounts of our own. I would want an agreement that neither of us would take a job in a different city unless we could come to a joint decision that this was best. I would want us to respect each other's feelings about sexual permissiveness outside the marriage.

Mostly I would hope that we could make a firm agreement on our goals in life—educational, financial, spiritual, religious, and all the many other important facets of human existence. If a wife wants material possessions and the husband wants to give all his earnings to a campaign to save the blue whale, there are bound to be problems. If one person wants many outside relationships and interests, while the other wants total togetherness, again there will be trouble.

The value of putting all this down in black and white is that you are forced to define and reveal your feelings and expectations. Too many people enter into what is supposed to be the most important, dynamic, and long-lasting relationship of their lives with little or no planning. They never discuss children, for example, until after the marriage or even many years later—when a crisis arises (perhaps the sixth pregnancy) and it is too late. I would prefer to have the opportunity to get to know my future spouse's feelings in advance. Writing a contract will help us understand ourselves and each other and will protect us against having unexpected conflicts crop up later on.

Two people trying to draw up a contract may discover that they cannot agree, that they are really incompatible. But I would rather know about the incompatibilities beforehand than discover them in a more painful way later on.

Other students reject the idea of marriage contracts completely, as can be seen in the box titled *No contract—stifling . . . too much of a business deal.* Many social scientists agree with the arguments presented in this box. Sociologists have suggested that no fixed contract can possibly "assure maximum happiness and minimal annoyance in the fu-ture," which depends not on advance planning but on "continuous readjustment (Azrin, Naster, and Jones, 1973). It has also been suggested that contracts stipulating what will happen in case of divorce "are basically pessimistic documents . . . that expect the worst outcomes rather than stability and success" (Wells, 1976). One sociologist

Opinions and Experiences

"NO CONTRACT—STIFLING . . . TOO MUCH OF A BUSINESS DEAL"

Another University student, responding to the same examination question, is dead set against the idea.

When I first heard in class about marriage contracts, I thought they were an excellent idea. But, after thinking it over, I have changed my mind completely. A contract is too much of a business deal. It almost becomes a matter of "I'll give you this if you'll give me that." Love and giving should be voluntary and reciprocal. If you give with no strings or contingencies attached, you get back understanding and love without demanding it.

There is also the fact that no relationship stays the same over the years, and no set of rules can possibly apply to every situation that might arise. I do believe that every couple should sit down from time to time, discuss their present feelings and commitments to each other, and reevaluate their marriage. But a legal contract, rather than helping them grow and adjust, would be stifling. The two partners might be inclined to rely strictly on the written rules—thus giving up the kind of deep communication that a marriage needs and the understanding that comes from discussing new ideas and new points of view.

When a couple feel that they have to draw up a contract and make it into a legal document, I think this is a sad commentary on their relationship. There should be more faith and trust—and less reliance on legalizing everything they have said to each other. What happens if one of them breaks the contract or is thought by the other partner to have broken it? Should they prosecute?

(Gass, 1974) believes that the contracts place far too much emphasis on the "specifics and too little on the feeling of fairness," which, as you will recall, was the theme of the first section of this chapter.

HOW GETTING ALONG DEPENDS ON WORDS AND DEEDS

The chapter turns now to an entirely different but equally important subject. This is the matter of whether the two partners in marriage feel loved and appreciated and are therefore encouraged to offer more love and appreciation in return. Like the belief that our partner is treating us fairly, the feeling of being loved and appreciated is essential to a good marriage. But the things that make us feel that way and therefore get along with each other—or that make us feel unloved and unappreciated and therefore create the basic conflict—cannot be expected to happen spontaneously, just in the normal course of events. To achieve them we have to work at them, far more than is generally supposed.

Perhaps the best way to approach the subject is to imagine a college classroom in which a woman named Smith sits near the front and a man named Jones near the back. In this course there are many class discussions. Smith takes frequent part and lends a lot of humor to the discussions, because she has a way of making everybody laugh. Jones does not speak up very often—but, when he does, he has a way of putting into a few well-chosen words an idea that gets to the very heart of the discussion.

Smith greatly admires Jones's gift for

analyzing problems. She also happens to think that he is extremely attractive. She likes the way he looks and the tone of his voice. Jones greatly admires the way Smith can bring wit to her classroom remarks. He also happens to think that she is extremely attractive. He likes the way she looks and the tone of her voice.

Does this sound like the beginning of a beautiful romance? Not necessarily. Let us further imagine that Jones, from his seat at the rear, is one of the first out of the door after class because he must hurry to another building that is some distance away. Thus Jones and Smith never run into each other except sometimes in the hall on the way to the class. When they do, they merely nod and say hello.

There is no way in the world that Smith can have any idea that Jones harbors all those favorable notions about her. There is no way that Jones can imagine what an impression he has made on Smith. The way things stand, they will finish school and go their separate ways, never knowing they felt a mutual admiration that might have led to a rewarding friendship, perhaps even a delightful marriage.

There is a moral to this story—of such extreme importance that it deserves exploration in depth.

You Have to *Do* Something

As the case of Smith and Jones clearly demonstrates, two people cannot get together in the first place unless they *do* something. Thoughts and feelings, if never acted on, mean nothing. We cannot know that somebody likes us unless that person behaves as if liking us. Note these eloquent words about the crucial role of behavior:

How should one know that he is loved but by the way people act toward him: what they say, how they look, how they touch—in a word, what they *do*? Attention, praise, spoken niceties, and physical contact have been demonstrations of love for years. Who cares if someone loves them if they never receive evidence through attention, contact, or the spoken word?

(Madsen and Madsen, 1970)

What is true about getting together in the first place is equally true about getting along together once a relationship is established. Getting along together depends to a far greater extent than generally realized on deeds and words—on the exchange of visible, unmistakable signs of affection and mutual regard. As one student of marriage has put it: "Marital happiness does not occur by chance. A happy husband and wife are happy because of what their partner says and does" (Knox, 1972). How can a husband and wife arrange matters so that what each of them says and does makes the other happy?

Married Life Can't Be All Roses

We must approach the question of happiness in marriage with realism and caution. That is, we must recognize that there never yet has been a marriage in which everything the husband said and did pleased his wife, or everything the wife said and did pleased her husband. All marriages entail differences of opinion, differences of tastes, disagreements, and quarrels. No marriage is all roses all the time.

A group of social scientists at the University of Oregon went to some trouble to determine just how often a more-or-less typical husband and wife are likely to do something that either pleases or displeases the other partner. They found a group of couples ranging from 22 to 57 years of age, married anywhere from three to twenty-six years, having anywhere from no children to three. These couples, all of whom seemed to have reasonably stable and successful marriages, were asked to keep score over a period of two weeks.

Among other things, the scorecards bore out everything that has been said in this book about the inevitability of disagreements. For an average day in which the couples spent a little more than five of their waking hours together, the average wife reported that her husband had said or done five things that displeased her. The average husband reported that his wife had done six (Wills, Weiss, and Patterson, 1974).

These figures may inspire you to a little speculation. Does the difference between five offenses by husbands and six by wives mean that husbands are in fact better behaved? Or does it only mean that wives are more tolerant about judging their spouses' behavior? Any such speculation, though interesting, is only a sidelight. The important thing is that both husbands and wives were found to rub each other the wrong way not just occasionally but several times a day.

The Thorns Do Hurt: Why Displeasing Actions Loom Large

Besides showing that marriage is never all roses, the study also showed that the thorns in marriage cause considerable pain. This was apparent from a running record that the couples kept of how they felt in general about their relationship with their spouse during the fourteen-day period. The way they rated the relationship, on a scale ranging from "extremely pleasant" to "extremely unpleasant," rose and fell from day to day and from one hour to the next. What influenced the rating the most, an analysis showed, was the displeasing actions of their partners (Birchler, Weiss, and Wampler, 1972).

Displeasing behavior, indeed, seemed to account for about 65 percent of how the partners felt about the relationship at any given time. The partner's pleasing actions accounted for about 25 percent, and the rest depended on whether they were having good or bad experiences outside the relationship, as at the job or with neighbors.

Doing things that displease the partner was found to be common in the happiest of marriages as well as those on the verge of breaking up. In good marriages, however, the number of displeasing acts was very low in porportion to acts that give pleasure. In poor marriages it was much higher. Of all acts that produced feelings one way or the other, only 5 percent were displeasing in the successful marriages they studied, but 25 percent in distressed marriages. It seems clear that holding offensive acts to a minimum—or at least to a low number in relation to pleasing acts—is a great help in getting along together.

Actions That Please: The "Instrumental"

Even in distressed marriages pleasing actions outnumbered displeasing acts by three to one. This was because, any two people living together, regardless of whether they feel happy or unhappy, are simply bound in the normal course of events to cooperate and help each other in numerous ways. They have to earn a living. Their money has to be spent on necessities such as food, clothing, shelter, and transportation. They have to prepare and eat meals, keep their clothes clean, and maintain a place to live. To do all this, they have to exchange a great many *instrumental* favors, that is, actions that enable them to do what has to be done if they are to survive and keep functioning.

The exchange of instrumental favors can be observed most clearly in a marriage where the man is the breadwinner and the woman is a housewife-mother. At the very least, the husband brings home the paycheck on which the family's survival depends. In addition, he may take out the garbage, walk the dog, read the children a bedtime story, wash the car, mow the lawn, go shopping with the wife on Saturday morning, take the family to a movie on Saturday afternoon, and watch over the children on nights when the wife has a bowling league. The instrumental actions performed by the wife—in keeping house, cooking, and caring for the children—are so familiar that they hardly require mention, and are too numerous to list anyway.

In a marriage where both husband and wife have jobs, the pattern of doing what has to be done to earn a living and maintain a livable home may be quite different. Yet in any kind of living arrangement that two people share, there are tasks to be done. When one partner performs any of these tasks—especially if the job is done well and cheerfully—the other partner is the beneficiary of a friendly and pleasing act. As to whether these instrumental favors are fully appreciated, more will be said later.

Actions That Please: The "Affectional" or "Expressive"

In a very bad marriage, the only pleasing actions may be of the instrumental type. But in most marriages—and to a pronounced extent in very good marriages—there is also a concern for the partner's feelings, an exchange of emotional support, and words and gestures of acceptance and approval. These actions, large and small, are described as *affectional* because they indicate affection and warmth. They are also sometimes called *expressive* because they are an expression of emotion.

An affectional (or expressive) act can be a mere friendly touch on the arm. It can be a good-morning or a good-night kiss. It can be the words "I love you" or "You look lovely in that dress" or "You look extra handsome tonight." It can even be an expression of concern such as "You seem distracted. Is something wrong?" Any word or deed at all that shows warm regard and interest in the partner's well-being can be described as affectional.

Unlike instrumental actions, affectional actions are not essential to survival or to a couple's daily well-being. They are luxuries rather than necessities. The rent *has* to be

Ray Ellis, Rapho Photo Researchers

An affectional action that pleases the wife even after all the years.

paid, the food *has* to be bought, the garbage *has* to be taken out, the children (if there are any) *have* to be put to bed. But the pat on the arm, the expression of concern, the compliment, and the words of affection can wait. Thus, even in the best marriages affectional actions occur much less frequently than instrumental actions.

Yet affectional actions are one of the secrets of getting along together. It has been known for a long time that happy and unhappy couples are pretty much alike in the exchange of instrumental favors but very different in the way they behave at the affectional level (Kotlar, 1962).

How to Please a Wife

For some practical information on how affectional and instrumental actions affect happiness in marriage, let us take a further look at the study made at the University of Oregon. As was said, the researchers (Wills et al.) asked a group of married couples to keep a tally of pleasing and displeasing actions by their partners and a running record of how happy they felt about the relationship at any given time. It should now be added that the researchers also explained the difference between instrumental and affectional actions and asked their subjects to list all pleasing or displeasing actions in one of these two categories. As a result, the scores kept by husbands and wives offer some valuable information on what kinds of actions are most important in fostering happiness.

For wives, it turned out that their husband's pleasurable instrumental acts did not make much difference. If the husband took out the garbage or walked the dog, this was fine, but it did not have any significant effect on how happy the wife felt about him. Much more important, from the wife's viewpoint, were affectional actions. When the husband

provided the pat on the back, or the words of praise, or even the courtesy of asking what the wife thought and felt about matters at the moment, the wife's happiness in the marriage tended to get a nice, healthy boost.

To the husband who wants to please his wife, the message seems clear: Do not rely too much on performing such traditionally masculine tasks as driving the nails and edging the lawn. Concentrate instead on words and gestures of affection. One good "You're marvelous" is worth a dozen repairs of worn-out appliance cords.

How to Please a Husband

For husbands, the study showed exactly the opposite: Their wife's pleasurable affectional acts did not make much difference. If the wife hugged the husband, or sat on his lap, or told him how good looking he was, this was fine, but it had little effect on how happy he felt about the marriage. Much more important, from the husband's viewpoint, were instrumental actions. What the husbands really liked was for the wife to cook a great meal, or sew on a button, or get the family car down to the garage for repairs.

To the wife who wants to please her husband, the message is this: Do not rely too much on words and deeds of affection. Though many men are exceptions, most husbands are a lot more impressed by efficiency than by a pat on the arm.

Is What Pleases Us Changing?

As one research group has summarized the findings, "Affectional actions are important to females, while a good meal is still the way to a man's heart" (Weiss, Hops, and Patterson, 1973). But this is of course only a generality. There are as many individual differences in what people find pleasing as in everything else. The preferences we display are at least in large part the result of social-ization into the traditional female and male sex roles. Perhaps the ways in which hus-bands and wives can best please each other are currently changing along with the changes in the sex roles. Doubtless many women—especially younger women—place more value on instrumental actions than the Oregon study indicates is true in general. Likewise doubtless many men greatly value their wife's affectional behavior.

But old traditions and habits die hard, and the findings of the Oregon study probably still apply to the majority of marriages, even among the newest generations of brides and grooms. Indeed they point to an ironic source of a basic misunderstanding that pre-vents many marriages from being as happy as they might otherwise be.

If You Do What the Sex Roles Say, You're in Trouble

By tradition, a woman is supposed to play the affectional role in marriage. She is so-cialized to provide the emotional intimacy and support. The man is supposed to play the instrumental role. He is socialized to earn the living, handle the money, be inde-pendent and aggressive, and serve as the family's buffer against anything that threat-ens it.

Yet the message of the Oregon study is that husbands and wives can best please their partners by doing exactly the opposite of what they have traditionally been socialized and expected to do. The wife is most appre-ciated for instrumental behavior that she has been taught is not appropriate to her role—and that she herself does not particularly value when it is displayed by her husband. The husband is most appreciated for affec-tional behavior that goes counter to the role

he has been taught—and that he himself does not especially value on the part of his wife.

Just how foreign the display of affection is to many husbands was shown by a funny-sad incident that occurred in the Oregon study. On the final days of the record keep-ing, husbands were asked to make a delib-erate effort to increase their affectional behavior. Most of the wives reported that this had indeed happened, but one wife said there had been no change at all. The hus-band, asked why he had not obeyed instruc-tions, said, "What does she mean I didn't show more affection? I washed her car, didn't I?"

As that comment shows, even the defini-tion of affectional behavior can separate the sexes. All in all it appears that the traditional patterns of socialization contain a built-in in-consistency that could hardly have been bet-ter calculated to cause problems in marriage. The ideal products of the system—the 100 percent feminine woman and the 100 per-cent masculine man—are not soul-mates but strangers.

DO–IT–YOURSELF MARRIAGE COUNSELING

Everything that has just been said about the pleasing actions that make for a happy mar-riage—and the displeasing actions that cause unhappiness—is of special significance be-cause it is the basis of a form of marriage counseling that has become widely practiced in recent decades. The method is usually called *behavioral counseling,* because it empha-sizes the way husband and wife act toward each other—the words and deeds that we have been talking about. It is also sometimes called *reciprocal counseling,* because it tries to help couples create a snowball effect in which pleasant actions by one partner inspire the other partner to reciprocate, that is, to return the favor. The basic assumption is that the husband's friendly words and deeds make the wife feel good, and she therefore responds with friendly words and deeds of her own. Her behavior in turn makes the husband feel good, and therefore his behavior becomes even more pleasing—and so on and so on toward ever higher levels of mutual gratification.

In the previous chapter, you will recall, the basic conflict in unhappy marriages was characterized as a vicious circle in which feelings of lost intimacy and lack of mutual acceptance become aggravated and multiplied. The end result was described as the hopeless attitude "He (she) doesn't love me—and I have stopped loving him (her)." Behavioral (or reciprocal) counseling tries to encourage exactly the opposite kind of interaction. Its goal has been described as the feeling by both husband and wife that "I am trying to make him (her) as happy as I can because he (she) is trying to make me happy" (Azrin, Naster, and Jones, 1973).

Behavioral counseling will be discussed at some length, because many of its principles and techniques can be practiced without the help of a counselor. Using the ideas presented in this final section of the chapter, you should be able to apply some do-it-yourself counseling of your own. The ideas can be helpful not only in rescuing a troubled marriage but in making a good relationship even better or in starting a new relationship off on the right path.

A WORD ON COUNSELING IN GENERAL

First it should be pointed out that there are many kinds of counseling. Some counselors concentrate on individual psychological problems troubling the husband or wife or both. Some try to help couples gain insights into the reasons for their unhappiness in general or on specific problems. Some try to offer emotional support by serving as a sympathetic, objective peacemaker. There are numerous other approaches. Moreover, some counselors prefer to meet with just one of the partners, some with both partners but in separate sessions. Some meet with both partners at once, and some with a number of couples attending in a group. Counselors called family therapists work with the entire family, including the children.

Despite the differences in theory and methods, there is considerable agreement among counselors about what they try to do for their clients. Most would probably agree in general with the following list of goals, which were given priority in a survey of members of the American Association for Marriage and Family Therapy:

1. To help all members of the family achieve an increased sense of independence and self-responsibility.
2. To foster the sharing of feelings and the frank discussion of conflicts, with the aim of finding mutually agreeable rather than one-sided solutions.
3. To encourage members of the family to listen to one another carefully and with full attention—accepting the speaker and the message as worthwhile and important even during disagreements.
4. To encourage flexibility—a willingness to change behavior and relationships to meet new situations.
5. In general, to create an atmosphere in which husband, wife, and children offer one another emotional support and nurturance, bolster one another's self-esteem, and can deal even with conflicts in a respectful and loving way. (Sprenkel and Fisher, 1980)

In attaining such goals, all counseling methods have proved reasonably successful. They seem to be most effective when the counselor sees not just one partner but both, either in a meeting with the two of them or in a group of couples (Cookerly, 1973). For couples who are having sexual difficulties, a combination of marriage counseling and sex therapy is often successful, with the sex therapy especially helpful to the wife and the general counseling to the husband (Hartman, 1983).

Any legitimate counseling, regardless of what technique it uses or what theory it is based on, has been found to help about two-thirds of the men and women who try it (Beck, 1975). Therefore a couple having difficulties with their relationship, but preferring to stay together if possible, are well advised to seek help. Indeed counseling can be useful even when divorce is inevitable, in preparing both partners to handle the difficulties created by the end of a relationship.

Unfortunately, most states permit anyone to set up shop as a counselor, without regard to training, experience, or ability. One way to be sure of finding a qualified person is to call the American Association for Marriage and Family Therapy at 202–429–1825, or write to the association at 1717 K. Street N.W. #407 WASHINGTON, D.C. 20006. The particular school of thought to which the counselor belongs need not be considered. The behavioral school is discussed here not because it is the only effective method but because of its do-it-yourself possibilities.

Goodbye Ulcers, Hello Orgasm: A Successful Case of Counseling

As an example of how behavioral or reciprocal counseling works, consider the case of Mr. and Mrs. B, who showed up at the psychological clinic of Pennsylvania State University with a story of deep trouble. Mr. B, a 31-year-old graduate student, was nervous, had ulcers, felt sexually unfulfilled, and was having trouble concentrating on his classes. Mrs. B, 30, felt unloved, neglected, sexually unfulfilled, and lonesome for the family and friends she had left behind to accompany her husband to the university. They had been tensely and unhappily married for seven years.

Their counselors began by asking them to list some of the things they wished the partner would do. As it happened, both mentioned a number of "little things" they would enjoy—having the partner do small favors, pay compliments, make affectionate remarks, even write notes of appreciation and endearment. (Many of these "little things," you will observe, fell into the category of affectional behavior. Others were instrumental.) In addition, Mr. B asked for a quiet, trouble-free period of a half hour or so each day when he got home from school, to give him a chance to relax and unwind. He also requested more sexual responsiveness. Mrs. B asked for more conversation between them—a period of at least fifteen minutes a day when Mr. B would listen with interest to her concerns. She also asked for changes in Mr. B's approach to sex.

The counselors suggested that they try to please each other in these various ways, meanwhile keeping a record of how often they felt the partner had done so. On the matter of the "little things," one good turn led to another very quickly. The "little things" got done and were reciprocated. The snowball effect sought in behavioral counseling was soon apparent. Mr. B got his chance to unwind after school, not always but often enough to help. Mrs. B got her daily conversation periods, not always to her complete satisfaction, but in a far more gratifying way than in the past.

Listening with interest to each other's concerns: a step often urged by behavioral counselors.

Their sexual difficulties were complicated by the fact that Mrs. B turned out to have some physical problems and that both needed help in learning how to please each other. But even in this area they got along much better, and Mrs. B was able to reach orgasm in intercourse for the first time. The couple's scores on tests measuring adjustment and happiness went up. Mr. B's ulcers became less troublesome and he finished his classes successfully (Wieman, Shoulders, and Farr, 1974).

Why Exchanging Favors Works

To understand why the case of Mr. and Mrs. B is important to everybody who wants to get along better with a partner, it is necessary to know something of the theory on which behavioral therapy is based. The theory is that our behavior is determined in large part by the way we are rewarded or punished by the people around us. When our actions are rewarded by other people with praise or other pleasing responses, we tend to repeat them. When our actions are punished by rejection, we abandon them. In other words, we learn to do what works best for us. We try to behave in ways that will bring us acceptance and praise. We try to avoid behavior that will bring us rejection and criticism.

Behavioral (or reciprocal) counseling attempts to encourage a greater exchange of the rewards that all of us seek in our human relationships. The husband is urged to do more things that reward the wife, and the wife to do more things that please the husband. The more rewards they exchange the more they like each other—and the more they like each other, the more they feel like pleasing each other, which results in an even richer exchange of mutual rewards. Behavioral counseling is in a way a modern application of the old saying: "You scratch my back and I'll scratch yours."

A Barrier to the Exchange

The idea of exchanging favors and rewards is so simple and commonsensical—and seems so obviously likely to lead to greater happiness for both partners—that you may wonder why it is not universally practiced. The answer is that most of us have been socialized into doing exactly the opposite. We have been taught that human relationships are controlled not by rewards but by punishments.

When we are children, our parents often use punishment or the threat of punishment to control our behavior. True, wise parents also mold us through affection and the reward of praise for good behavior; but even the wisest parents use punishment at times, and this is what we best remember. We are small, helpless, and utterly dependent. Our parents have the authority and the force. We soon learn that there are dozens of actions that can only bring us punishment ranging anywhere from a harsh word of disapproval to, in some families, a severe beating.

The schools also try to control us through punishment—the threat of a failing grade or of suspension. So do our employers. We soon learn that if we arrive late or make a bad mistake we can expect at least to be bawled out, perhaps even fired. And we learn that society as a whole will punish us if we drive too fast or without a license, create a public nuisance, or do any of hundreds of other things prohibited by law.

The use of force and punishment is everywhere around us, all our life from the time we start toddling into the family living room. Without ever realizing it, we become experts ourselves at dishing out punishment to anyone who displeases us (Weiss, Hops, and Patterson, 1973). We get into the habit of acting toward other people like a parent toward a balky child, a teacher toward a disobedient pupil, or a policeman toward a speeding motorist.

Exchanging Punishments Instead of Favors

Because of our training, what happens in marriage often turns into an exchange of punishments rather than favors. Let us consider, for example, the case of a wife who was highly annoyed because the family den, in which she and her husband usually spent their evenings, was always left in a mess. Her husband scattered his newspapers, magazines, and books all over the floor and the top of the television set, and there they stayed when he went to bed. The husband, in turn, was highly annoyed because his wife was often in a sour mood and had the habit of swearing at the children when they misbehaved.

These complaints were taken to a marriage counselor, and we will see later how they were dealt with in accordance with the principles of behavioral counseling. For the moment, however, the important thing is to note how disagreements of this kind are often handled (or to be more accurate mishandled) by partners who fall into the pattern of behaving like a parent, schoolteacher, or police officer.

What often happens, students of marriage have observed, is this: The wife annoyed by the messy den first asks her husband to straighten up before he goes to bed. The husband annoyed by his wife's behavior toward the children asks her to stop swearing at them. Nothing happens. The husband continues to leave the den in a shambles. The wife continues to swear at the children.

After a while, the more-or-less polite requests give way to punishment. The wife annoyed by the messy den starts to complain, loudly and often. She may throw out the husband's magazines and books. She may refuse to talk to him and reject his sexual advances. The husband annoyed by his wife's swearing may throw a temper tantrum, storm out of the house for the evening, or stop doing whatever chores he has been performing.

Both types of behavior represent an attempt to force change through punishment. The angry wife and angry husband are saying in effect, "Yes, I'm being as unpleasant as I possibly can—and I'm going to keep it up until you change your ways." This tactic usually fails. Even if it works on some particular matter, such as getting the den straightened up, it is likely to lead to future trouble. The husband or wife punished for bad behavior, and thus forced to change, is likely to retaliate the next time a disagreement occurs (Patterson, Hops, and Weiss, 1975).

When Displeasure Feeds on Displeasure

As stated earlier, acts that displease a partner have a great effect on how husbands and wives feel about a marriage. Perhaps because such acts are remembered longer, they do more to spoil happiness than pleasant actions do to create happiness. Moreover, it has been found that unpleasant actions by a husband are particularly likely to lead to similar behavior by the wife, and vice versa. Because of our training, most of us are quicker to return an insult (which almost always makes a deep and lasting impression) than a favor (which may go unnoticed).

For this reason, the tendency to force change through punishment is especially likely to cause trouble. Over a period of time, the exchange of punishments often seems to intensify, becoming more and more harsh (Patterson, Hops, and Weiss, 1975). The

more time a couple spend being unpleasant to each other, the less likely they are to engage in pleasant exchanges, such as friendly conversation and sexual intimacy (Stuart, 1969). They become less and less likely to have fun together in shared recreation (Birchler, Weiss, and Wampler, 1972).

This is one reason the "tremendous trifles" mentioned in Chapter 7 often play such a big part in marital conflict. The inevitable disagreements that crop up in marriage may be minor in themselves. But a disagreement over a messy den or yelling at the children can start a vicious circle of punishment, retaliation, and an ever-intensifying exchange of unpleasant behavior. Displeasure feeds on displeasure. Many couples who are in an advanced stage of conflict—feeling hostile toward each other, showing a pronounced mutual lack of respect—probably reached that point as the result of a series of small annoyances over simple and unimportant acts (Wills, Weiss, and Patterson, 1974).

How Behavioral Counselors Try to Change the Pattern

What behavioral counselors try to do is turn the pattern of displeasure feeding on displeasure to one of pleasure feeding on pleasure. They use every device they can think of to increase the exchange of rewards and cut down the exchange of punishments. For some examples, let us return to the case of the wife upset by the messy den and the husband angry about the wife's sour moods and swearing at the children. Here, the counselor discovered that the husband greatly enjoyed reading novels and the wife relished desserts and wanted her husband to spend more time at mutual activities on weekends. These little preferences were immediately put to good use in the counseling.

The husband was told to be alert to occasions when his wife was in a good mood and at such times to kiss her, caress her, tell her that he liked her when she was pleasant, and talk about plans for the weekend. When she was in a sour mood, he was told to ignore her completely.

Since the couple disagreed about other household matters as well as the messy den—including the question of who should feed the dog—they were both told to make out a list of daily responsibilities. Neither was allowed to go to bed until all the chores were finished, and if the husband slipped on the matter of straightening up the den he was penalized by not being permitted to read his novels. The wife was told to use milder words instead of swearing at the children, with the penalty of having to pass up dessert if she failed (Knox, 1972).

Simple Agreements as Steps to an Important Goal

Sometimes behavioral counselors even ask couples to draw up an agreement: I will do so-and-so for you if you will do so-and-so for me. A wife for example, might agree to wear a dress her husband likes in return for his taking her out to dinner. (These agreements are a little bit like the marriage contracts discussed earlier in the chapter, except that they apply only to a small number of actions and are supposed to be revised constantly as the couple find new ways of pleasing each other.) Sometimes the counselors themselves reward the husband and wife, as by reducing the fee charged for a session at which progress is reported. Or they may "punish" the couple by canceling the reduction if the couple slip back into their old ways.

Your first impression of these techniques may be that they are too mechanical, perhaps even childish. It does seem absurd in a way to ask a husband to reward himself by reading a novel when he straightens the den,

or to penalize a wife for "bad" conduct by taking away her dessert. But something has to start the snowball of mutual exchange of pleasures, and behavioral counselors have found that this is one way to do it.

The goal, of course, is not mechanical at all. The goal is to create a spirit of good will that makes both partners eager to please each other and grateful for the pleasures—and insofar as is humanly possible, to add to the good feeling by avoiding actions that the partner dislikes. This spirit of good will, as explained earlier, represents the deep-seated feeling by both husband and wife: "I am trying to make him (her) as happy as I can because he (she) is trying to make me happy."

"Love Days" and "Fantasies"

To foster mutual good will, some behavioral counselors ask couples to hold what they call "love days" (Patterson et al., 1975). One day a week the husband devotes himself to doing as many favors and being as affectionate as he possibly can. On a different day, the wife takes over and devotes herself to pleasing the husband in every possible way.

Some counselors encourage the husband and wife to sit down, separately, and write out a list of everything they think their partner would do in an absolutely perfect marriage. They are urged to be completely selfish in making out the list, indeed to indulge themselves in spinning their "fantasies" about an ideal mate. Usually husbands and wives hesitate, because they are afraid their partners will consider their requests unreasonable. But, once they let themselves go, their "fantasies" often turn into a helpful guide to the exchange of favors.

The husband's fantasies may not seem so outrageous to the wife as he feared. Her fantasies may not seem totally unreasonable to him. Often, with the help of the counselor, a compromise can be reached, and the couple learn that what once appeared to be impossible wishes can be fulfilled at least in part. The exchange of information about fantasies, plus the idea of trying to fulfill the partner's desires in return for having your own desires fulfilled, has frequently been found to create the attitude: "If you want it, you can get it" (Azrin et al., 1972)—an attitude which, when willingly held by both husband and wife, is almost a sure guarantee of happiness in marriage.

Counselors using the fantasy technique have found that often sexual overtures are mentioned. The wife wishes that the husband would always make the first approach. The husband wants the wife to make it. Thus their sexual relations have fallen victim to the unspoken words "You go first." "No, you go first." Both have been unwilling to change. This problem has often been resolved by working out a simple compromise. Couples usually find it easy to settle on a time table, with the husband making the first approach on this many occasions, the wife on that many. When they do, a mutual source of annoyance readily gives way to a mutual source of pleasure—indeed, of two-way fantasy fulfillment.

The Lesson of Behavioral Counseling

The results obtained in one study of behavioral counseling, including the couples' listing of "fantasies," are shown in Figure 8-1 which is especially interesting because of the speed with which improvement occurred. After a single week—only two hours of counseling—the couples in the study rated themselves about 24 percent happier on the average than when they first sought advice. By the end of the counseling process—eight hours in all, over a period of three to four

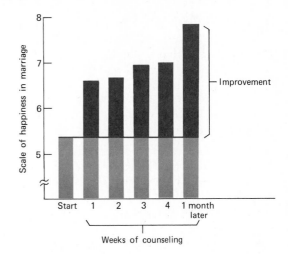

Figure 8-1
HAPPINESS THROUGH THE EXCHANGE OF PLEASURES
The bars show the rapid results obtained in a study of twelve couples who received marriage counseling of the behavioral (or reciprocity) type. The colored portion of the bars shows how their average happiness ratings improved almost immediately—and continued upward as they applied more and more of the techniques they had learned. (Azrin, Naster, and Weiss, 1972).

weeks—they reported that they were about 32 percent happier. The improvement continued after the counseling stopped. When they were again questioned a month later, their happiness scores were up by nearly 50 percent. All but one of the subjects reported at least some improvement.

Any state of mind as vague as happiness in marriage is of course difficult to measure. The couples' own reports of an increase in happiness may not have been entirely accurate. Moreover any attempt to measure the results of marriage counseling may be colored by the fact that people who seek counseling usually want and expect improvement—an attitude that may serve as a self-fulfilling prophecy, producing changes that are not necessarily the result of what happens in the counseling sessions. Nonetheless, Figure 8-1 offers strong evidence that behavioral counseling can improve marriages in a hurry and possibly start a snowball effect that will continue after counseling ends.

The lesson of all this is that it is just as easy to exchange rewards as to trade punishments. Perhaps it is actually easier to please a partner, do favors, engage in "love days"—and have the partner appreciate these actions and respond in kind—than to go the other route of displeasing the partner and suffering retaliation. Certainly the principles of behavioral counseling are worth trying. What can you lose?

SUMMARY

1. Many traditional marriages, in which the husband took advantage of his position and became a tyrant, were obviously unfair. But fairness in marriage is more difficult to recognize and describe because fairness is largely a state of mind and attitudes toward it are highly pluralistic. A fair marriage can be defined in only general terms as one in which both partners feel they have an equal opportunity to express themselves and satisfy their personal needs.

2. One key to playing fair in marriage is *tolerance,* especially for circumstances when you are contributing more to the marriage than you are getting back. (An example might be during a long illness of one of the partners.) At such a time the mixture of obligations and advantages might be much worse for the husband than the wife, or vice versa. But circumstances will change, however, and couples who understand the secret of fair play know that everything will balance in the end.

3. Marriage contracts are an attempt to ensure fairness by drawing up advance agreements defining the rights to which each partner is entitled and the duties and obligations each is expected to fulfill. Some contracts have specified detailed rules of sexual behavior, relations with

each other's relatives, and division of property in case of divorce. Some even set a time limit, usually five or ten years, after which the contract expires unless the partners choose to renew it.

4. There is considerable doubt as to whether a marriage contract could be enforced in court, especially if it conflicts with the unwritten contract that has been considered implied by the license and ceremony. The chief value of a marriage contract probably is that writing an agreement demands serious discussion of attitudes toward jobs and careers, handling money, household arrangements, and parenthood. Thus it helps a couple decide in detail how they both want to behave.

5. Like the belief that our partner is treating us fairly, the feeling of being loved and appreciated is essential to a good marriage. Getting along together depends on deeds and words—the exchange of visible, unmistakable signs of affection and mutual regard: "A happy husband and wife are happy because of what their partner says and does."

6. The exchange of evidence of affection and regard is especially important because everybody is bound to say or do things at times that displease the partner. One study found that husbands and wives in successful marriages do about a half dozen such displeasing things on the average day. These displeasing things have a strong effect on how the partners feel about the relationship at any given time.

7. In successful marriages, the proportion of displeasing acts to acts that give pleasure is low (about 5 percent). In poor marriages it is much greater (about 25 percent).

8. There are two types of actions that please or displease. One is *instrumental*—the practical, everyday actions, like earning a living or maintaining a home, that enable the couple to do what has to be done if they are to survive and keep functioning. The other is *affectional,* also called *expressive,* meaning all the large and small things that demonstrate affection and warmth, like a pat on the arm, a compliment, or even an expression of interest.

9. Happy and unhappy couples are alike in the exchange of instrumental favors, but the happy ones exchange many more expressive favors.

10. Possibly because of the continuing pull of traditional sex roles, wives are not especially impressed by such pleasurable instrumental acts as taking out the garbage or walking the dog but are delighted by such affectional actions as a pat on the back or words of praise. Husbands are less impressed by affectional acts than by such instrumental ones as cooking a great meal or getting the family car to the garage for repairs.

11. Thus husbands and wives can best please their partners by doing exactly the opposite of what they have traditionally been socialized and expected to do, which is for the husband to be instrumental and the wife to be affectional. All this may now be in the process of change because of new attitudes toward the sex roles.

12. There are many forms of *marriage counseling*, but in general all of them seek to (1) help members of the family achieve a sense of independence and self-responsibility, (2) foster the expression of feelings and frank discussion of conflicts, (3) encourage family members to listen to each other attentively and be flexible in changing behavior and relationships, and (4) lead family members to bolster each other's self-esteem, provide emotional support, and deal with conflicts in a respectful and loving way.

13. One form of counseling, called *behavioral,* is of special interest because its techniques can often be applied on a do-it-yourself basis. Behavioral counseling emphasizes the way wife and husband act toward each other, the words and deeds that please or displease. It is sometimes called *reciprocal* counseling because it tries to help couples create a snowball effect in which pleasant deeds by one partner inspire the other partner to reciprocate by returning the favor. The husband is helped to do things that the wife finds rewarding,

and the wife to do more things that please the husband.

14. The theory is that the more rewards they exchange the more they like each other, and the more they like each other the more they feel like pleasing each other. The goal is to create in both partners the feeling that "I am trying to make him (her) as happy as I can because she (he) is trying to make me happy."

15. In dealing with an unhappy marriage, behavioral counseling usually finds the opposite pattern. The partners are trying to force each other to change and abandon annoying habits through punishment. They are saying, in effect, "I'm being as unpleasant as I possibly can, and I'm going to keep it up until you change your ways." This tactic always produces retaliation instead of change, and behavioral counseling tries to reverse the vicious circle by suggesting any alternative that might possibly succeed.

DISCUSSION QUESTIONS

1. How does our society create "injustice collectors"? In marriages you know what are some of the issues of unfairness complained about by injustice collectors?

2. Why is it important to take a long-range view of marriage when assessing the issue of fairness?

3. How do *you* feel about marriage contracts? Would you want to write one before marriage?

4. Are instrumental or affectional actions more important to you?

5. If you were having marital problems, would you want to seek help through some form of marriage counseling?

6. Of the two methods used to promote change in a partner—punishment or rewards—which do you use more frequently?

CHAPTER 9

Decision Making and Communication

All day long, though you may never stop to think about it, you face one decision after another. What are you going to wear today? Are you going to study between classes or spend the time with friends? Where are you going to eat lunch? What are you going to do about your laundry? Your plans for the evening? For what hour will you set the alarm clock?

In this pluralistic society that offers so many possibilities and alternatives, some of the decisions can be agonizingly crucial. Your future may depend on whether you continue on your present course of study or switch to something else, on whether you stay at your present college or move to any one of many other campuses or drop out, which of all the possible kinds of job you seek, and what part of this widespread nation you choose as a future home. Often you find yourself pulled in two directions at once, and sometimes in several different directions.

In marriage, the decisions become still more difficult and potentially far-reaching, since now they concern not just one person but two. If there are children in the family, the wishes and welfare of both generations must be considered. The *decision-making process*—what the partners in marriage decide to do and how they go about making the choices—affects everything discussed in the

previous two chapters and is a major factor in determining whether wife and husband find themselves embroiled in the basic conflict or successful at the fine art of getting along together. Therefore this chapter discusses the process at considerable length. And since decision-making in the family depends on some kind of exchange of views between husband, wife, and children, the chapter also pays special attention to *communication*.

WHO MAKES THE DECISIONS?

In the traditional family of the past, before marriage made the giant leap "from institution to companionship," few couples devoted much thought to the decision-making process, which traditionally was left to the husband. The family lived in whatever kind of residence the husband felt he could afford, in whatever location he found convenient. He also generally handled all financial matters and set the pattern of spare-time activities, in which he might or might not decide to include his wife. One important matter, the size of the family, did not call for any planning or decision-making at all in those days before birth control was widely practiced.

Even today, most couples begin their life together without any serious attention to the decisions they must make. They are unaware of how many choices they will face or of how each choice, like a turn taken at the first crossroads in a long journey, may set the entire course of their marriage. Usually they do not even have any clear idea of how they will go about making the choices. Except for their relationships with the families in which they grew up, almost all their experience has been in secondary groups with well-established guidelines for making decisions, for example, in a classroom or job where the teacher or boss does the deciding, or in organizations where decisions are made by majority vote. In the new primary group of the family, there are no such guidelines for who will decide what.

Setting the Rules in Marriage

Some of the questions married couples face are listed in Table 9–1. In addition to those very practical matters is the more subtle problem of deciding how the two partners will behave in their day-to-day interaction. It has been recognized for a long time that people engaged in any kind of relationship must from the start attempt to establish rules that govern the way they act toward each other. Many of the decisions made by the new marriage partners, whether they realize it or not, result in such long-lasting rules.

The partners decide whether to talk to each other spontaneously, with a great deal of frankness and self-disclosure, or to keep their distance and talk only about neutral and "safe" topics like the weather. They set a pattern of encouraging or avoiding open displays of affection. They set rules for their conduct within the residence, even about such "tremendous trifles" as whether the window shades are kept all the way up or

Table 9–1

Decisions, Decisions!

Where will we live—what town or city, house or apartment?

Will we rent or try to buy?

How much can we afford to pay for housing?

Do we need insurance? What kind? How much?

How much can we spend on food? Clothes? Transportation? Entertainment?

How will we spend our evenings and weekends? Our vacations?

How often do we want to see our relatives?

Do we want children? How soon? How many?

Do we want to start a savings program?

In handling the household chores, who is responsible for what?

These are some of the most pressing questions that face the newly married couple and that will continue facing them for many years. Their happiness will depend to a considerable extent on the decisons they make—and, even more, on how they go about making them.

half-way down. They establish rules for sexual behavior, for example, when and where sexual relations are considered proper, what kinds of behavior are acceptable or distasteful, who is expected to make the first move, and how openly husband and wife can discuss their likes and dislikes (Haley, 1963).

Agreement, Disagreement, and the Question of Power

Reaching agreement on the rules is made easier by the fact that the workings of homogamy in mate selection usually bring together marriage partners with similar backgrounds. But no two people have received exactly the same kind of socialization. They have acquired many different attitudes, interests, and tastes. Moreover the two families in which they spent their childhood may have had very different rules and customs about a host of matters: eating habits, neatness, recreation, styles of conversation, the proper sex roles for women and men, and in particular the way a husband should behave toward a wife and a wife toward a husband. Men and women entering marriage may expect to live by the same rules they grew up with but find that the partner has equally strong expectations of living by a different set of rules.

Although there are bound to be many disagreements, those about the exact nature of the rules are not necessarily fatal. Often they can be resolved through compromise and minor adjustments on both sides. What is more dangerous is a struggle over the question of whether, when compromise is difficult, the wife or the husband has the right to set the rules. One study of decision making cites this very simple example:

> A wife could insist that her husband hang up his clothes so that she does not have to pick up after him like a servant. The husband might agree with his wife that she should not be his servant . . . but he still might not agree that she should be the one to give him orders about what to do about his clothes.
>
> (Haley, 1963)

It is disagreement over who sets the rules that is most likely to start the vicious circle of the basic conflict. Many unhappy couples seem to be locked in bitter competition over the right to make decisions. A particularly apt figure of speech that has been used to describe their plight is the difference between horizontal movement and vertical movement. Happy couples move horizontally, together and with mutual respect, cooperating toward mutually agreeable rules and mutually beneficial goals. Unhappy couples move vertically, seeking superiority

over each other (Mozdzierz and Lottman, 1973). They are fighting for the top rung on the ladder. Often, in the heat of this no-holds-barred battle, they try to bolster their own ego by tearing down their mate's ego.

In any competition, the issue of power arises. All of us like to have our own way, and when we have the power to enforce our wishes we are likely to use it, often without much regard for the wishes of anyone else. Many social relationships are influenced by the matter of who has and who does not have power. For an example, we can consider a filling station where three men work—all the same age, with the same intelligence and education, all equally pleasant and likeable. We can be pretty sure that the one who happens to own the station will use his power to keep most of the proceeds and to fob the more disagreeable jobs off on the other men.

Thus students of marriage have been interested for a long time in the matter of power. How much does the husband have? How much does the wife have? How do the partners choose to exercise their power? At what point does the attempt to exercise power begin to endanger a marriage?

The Once "All-powerful" Male

In marriages of the past, between a man playing the traditional masculine role and a woman playing the traditional feminine role, all the trappings of power were on the side of the husband. As the sole breadwinner in the family, he held all the financial power. His position was further bolstered by the accepted notion of male dominance and by the law, even by the wife's promise to obey that was part of the marriage ceremony.

Human relationships built strictly on power are likely to be unhappy ones, like the dealings between a jailer and a prisoner, or between an army of occupation and the people it has conquered. Potentially, at least, the traditional marriage had many of the injustices and tensions of a master-slave relationship. The husband who exercised his right to be an autocrat may have enjoyed his power to command, but he lived in fear of a slave uprising. His wife may have been secretly contemptuous of her strutting master, but she worried about her survival (Schwartz, 1980).

Even then, however, it seems likely that husbands in general were not quite the lords and masters. True, there must have been some husbands who wielded their power vigorously and even cruelly, as some masters have done wherever slavery existed. But there must also have been many who did not choose to exercise their power at all. Likewise there doubtless were wives who hated their master and sabotaged him at every opportunity. But there also must have been many who, as some slaves have always done, took affectionate care of an incompetent and sometimes alcoholic master and actually ran the plantation, all the while keeping up the appearance of meek servitude.

Among all the theoretically powerless wives, moreover, there surely were many who found methods of getting their own way to a far greater extent than their husbands ever suspected. Even the most downtrodden housewife, it has been pointed out, had (and still has) a few concealed weapons at her disposal. She could give her husband the choice of a congenial home or a crabby one, a neat house or a sloppy one, the food he liked or leftovers, a warm or ice-cold sexual companion (Safilios-Rothschild, 1976).

She could also call on such stratagems of the weak as coaxing, flattery, and tears. She could conspire with the children, for children too, though they seem to have no power at all over their parents, have their own ways of making their desires felt. Though in the-

ory the old-fashioned husband had as much power as an Ivan the Terrible, we have to wonder how effectively he could use it.

The Problem of Measuring Power

How power was held, exercised, and sometimes neutralized in marriages of the past is of course mere speculation. Indeed, we cannot be entirely sure about present-day marriages. Power is difficult even to define, much less measure. One social scientist who tried to study it by listening to actual conversations between wife and husband found he was dealing with events so complex that they posed an almost unanswerable question: "Does power reside in the person who wins in a disagreement, or in the person who decides who wins, or in the person who decides who decides?" (Ryder, 1970). Even if you do manage to find the answer, how can you be sure which partner is doing which?

The partners themselves do not always seem to know. One study found that wives usually believe the husband has more power than he himself claims to possess, and husbands usually believe the wife has more power than she sees herself as having (Heer, 1962). Another study, this one of families with children, found that in only 24 percent do all the members agree even about who is responsible for deciding how disputes are settled (Larson, 1974).

Two Important Studies of Decision Making and Power

Despite the difficulties, the search for knowledge about the decision-making process and its relation to power has been conducted by many students of the family over the years. Most investigators have drawn up a list of matters that frequently call for family deci-

Margaret Durrance, Photo Researchers

How did this couple decide on skiing as their leisure activity? By mutual agreement? Or did one partner exercise power?

sions, then have asked whether husband or wife usually has the final say on each matter. One classic study (Blood and Wolfe, 1960) used these eight items:

1. What car to buy.
2. Whether or not to buy life insurance.
3. What house or apartment to live in.
4. What job the husband should take.
5. Whether or not the wife should work.
6. How much money the family could afford to spend on food.
7. What doctor to call in case of illness.
8. Where to go on vacation.

Some 900 wives in urban and rural areas in and around Detroit were asked on how many of these items they usually or always made the final decision, on how many their husband did, and on how many the decision was made just as often by one partner as by the other. The study found that decision making was dominated by the husband in 25 percent of the marriages and by the wife in 3 percent. In the other 72 percent, both partners had about equal say. The most common pattern was a division of responsibility, with the wife usually or always deciding some matters, such as the food budget and selection of a doctor, and the husband deciding others, such as the purchase of a car and life insurance.

Another group of investigators (Centers, Raven, and Rodrigues, 1971) tried to explore a wider area of decision making by adding six other items:

1. What people you go out with or invite to your house.
2. How to furnish and decorate the house.
3. Which television or radio programs to choose.
4. What to have for dinner.
5. What clothes you will buy.
6. What clothes your partner will buy.

This study questioned both husbands and wives, more than 700 of them living in the Los Angeles area but representative of all city-dwelling couples in education and income. About 10 percent of the couples agreed that the husband's wishes dominated the decision making, 4 percent that the wife was dominant, and 86 percent that the partners had about equal say. As in the previous study, it was found that couples often made a his-and-hers division of responsibility, with the wife usually deciding some matters and the husband deciding others.

The "Resources Theory" of Power

Why should one partner in marriage ever have greater power over decision making? One explanation, *resources theory,* has been proposed by Blood and Wolfe (1960). In marriages of the past, they suggested, the husband had the right to be dominant—even autocratic if he so chose—simply because the traditional sex roles assumed that men were considered superior. Our culture gave power to "a competent sex over an incompetent sex."

Changing sex roles and the rise of companionship marriage, however, have turned the two sexes into equals, at least potentially. Power is now allocated to "a competent marriage partner over the incompetent one, regardless of sex." Thus, the right to make decisions depends on the resources each partner possesses, that is, on such matters as the husband's and wife's education, job prestige, and family background (Blood and Wolfe, 1960).

There is considerable evidence supporting the resources theory. For example, Blood and Wolfe found that the amount of control the husband holds over decision making is closely related to his occupation, income, and family background: "The higher the husband's social status, the greater his power." The husband's power is also greater when he is considerably older and better educated than his wife. Wives with small children in the home, and therefore clearly dependent financially, have less power than wives without children.

Other studies have produced similar findings. Working wives in general usually have more voice in decision making than housewives (Bahr, Bowerman, and Gecas, 1974). In particular, because working wives contribute to the family income, they take more part in the important decision of how the income will be spent (Hoffman and Nye, 1974). A job has been found to increase the wife's power most markedly in low-income families where her financial contribution may spell the difference between poverty and comfort.

Many sociologists have helped expand the resources theory as originally proposed by Blood and Wolfe. It has been pointed out that the two partners have a number of resources, in addition to financial and social position, that give them bargaining power (Safilios-Rothschild, 1976). For example, they have varying capacities to provide companionship, sexual fulfillment, affection and emotional support (the affectional or expressive actions whose importance was discussed in Chapter 8), and various personal services that help keep the family and household functioning (the instrumental actions).

It has also been pointed out that power depends on how much each partner values the resources possessed by the other (Blau, 1964). Thus a wife who greatly enjoys a high income and social prestige is likely to show greater deference toward a successful husband than is a wife who cares very little for money or social standing. A husband who values emotional support is likely to show more deference toward a wife generous with affectional actions than is a husband who has fewer emotional needs.

Moreover, the amount of deference may depend on how the partner's resources compare with what might be available elsewhere (Heer, 1963). Husbands and wives who feel they have no alternative to the marriage—that in fact they would be worse off financially and emotionally if they were living alone or married to someone else—are likely to concede power even when they do not especially admire or value their partner's resources.

Personality factors also play a part in determining which partner has how much decision-making power. Some people have grown up with a strong need to be dominant, and they seem determined to get their own way regardless of whether or not they deserve it. On the other hand some grow up with a strong tendency to be submissive and deliberately avoid the exercise of power (Winter and Stewart, 1978). In the past and to some extent even today, sex-role socialization has affected the balance of power in marriage by encouraging domination among males and submission among females. It is worthy of note that a long-term study of married women with children showed that 66 percent of them agreed in 1962 that the husband should make "most of the important decisions in the life of the family," but when the same women were questioned a few years ago the number had dropped to 28 percent (Thornton, 1980).

POWER AND VIOLENCE

The discussion of how power affects decision making in marriage would not be complete without mention of physical violence, which occurs more frequently than many people realize. Until recently social scientists who specialize in study of the family generally ignored the topic. Indeed, the word *violence* did not appear in the title of even a single article printed in one of their leading publications, *The Journal of Marriage and the Family*, in the entire thirty years up to 1970 (O'Brien, 1971). Now, however, the topic commands considerable attention. Perhaps the scholars of the past, like most people, preferred to avoid such a dark and unpleasant issue. Or

perhaps violence in the family, like violence in general, has become increasingly prominent in our society.

At any rate, references to the battered wife and the abused child are now commonplace, not just in scholarly articles but in newspaper headlines. Many cities have set up shelters to provide battered wives with safety and medical care. Other places are attempting to reduce child abuse by providing nurseries where parents can leave their children during periods of family crisis that might lead to violence. Many telephone books list, right at the front, "hot-line" numbers that victims of abuse can call for help.

Some Startling Estimates

Police records on family violence show only the tip of the iceberg, since most cases are never reported. A survey of a national sam-

A mother and her son consult with a social worker at a shelter for battered wives.

Bettye Lane, Photo Researchers

ple of wives and husbands indicated that some kind of physical violence had occurred in 16 percent of couples within the past year, and in 28 percent at some time in the marriage. Wives committed the violence about as often as husbands. The women, however, were more likely to use indirect methods like throwing an ashtray or a vase. Men were more likely to use their fists, and 4 percent of the wives reported getting "beat up" at least once within the year (Straus et al., 1980). That would indicate that about 2.5 million wives a year are seriously abused. Among couples living together without marriage, the proportion of violent incidents seems to be even greater (Yllo and Straus, 1981).

There is also considerable use of physical force on college campuses among couples who are not married but "going together." In a study made at a university in the Northwest, nearly 25 percent of students reported incidents of physical abuse. In about two-thirds of the cases, both partners used force (Henton, 1982). In similar studies, 21 percent reported violent episodes at a college in Minnesota (Makepeace, 1981) and 23 percent at an Eastern university (Matthews, 1984). On the Eastern campus the most common forms of violence were shoving, kicking, and hitting with the fist. Many of the students said the incident was caused by either the belief that the partner was getting interested in someone else or by frustration due to poor communication. Only 31 percent said the relationship was damaged by the incident, and 43 percent said it was improved.

The Wellsprings of Violence

Why do partners resort to violence? One reason, it appears, is that many people have learned to accept a certain amount of phys-

ical force in family life. Children who have been physically disciplined by their parents tend to use force themselves as adults, and those who have seen their parents strike each other tend to repeat the behavior in their own marriage (Kalmuss, 1984). Violence is particularly likely to erupt in a person who has been drinking (Riggs, 1981) or under severe stress (Straus, 1980).

There has been considerable publicity about *catharsis theory*, which maintains that tendencies to violence can be kept from exploding into actual use of force by releasing them in other ways, such as watching television shows or engaging in shouting and name calling. One advocate of this theory has urged married people to get rid of their "pent-up hostilities" by being totally "vicious" in arguments (Bach, 1973). But there is very little evidence to support the catharsis theory and a great deal that indicates exactly the opposite.

Watching violence on the screen has been found to encourage aggressive behavior rather than neutralize it (Steuer, Applefield, and Smith, 1971). And a study of marriage partners has shown that verbal fighting and the use of physical force go hand in hand, as shown in Figure 9–1. Contrary to catharsis theory, aggression of any kind seems to breed further and even greater violence.

Why Husbands Batter Their Wives

Husbands seem most inclined to use the power of physical force when they feel powerless in other ways, in other words, when they feel they have not earned a legitimate voice in family affairs. One study of husbands who had used physical force against their wife showed that:

> 44 percent were seriously dissatisfied with their jobs.

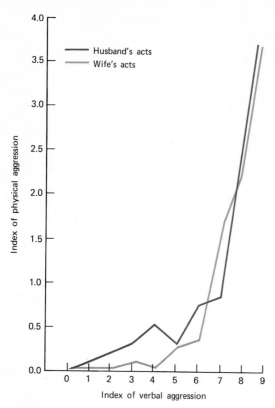

Figure 9–1
HARSH WORDS AND VIOLENT ACTIONS
The two graph lines were obtained by studying how often and how intensely a group of wives and husbands engaged in verbal aggression (shouts, insults, name-calling) and the amount of physical aggression they practiced. As the level of verbal aggression rises, the level of physical aggression rises even faster (Straus, 1974).

> 44 percent had started but failed to finish high school or college.
>
> 56 percent had less education than their wives. (O'Brien, 1971)

It has also been found that many wife beaters have a record of poor job performance (Hornung, McCullough, and Sugimoto, 1981). All in all it appears that violence is often the reaction of a man who feels he has not in any other way earned the right to control his wife and children and who therefore finds his masculinity threatened (Whitehurst, 1974).

The feelings that lead to violence, however, need not be caused by actual failure. Success and failure, power and powerlessness, are relative matters. A man who appears perfectly competent to other people may feel in his heart that he has failed to live up to his own possibilities. His self-image may be so fragile that it is threatened by any sign of independence on the part of his wife. This is probably one reason violence occurs at all levels of society. It has been suggested that many husbands at the upper levels feel threatened by today's changing sex roles and that indeed their violence may be one of the "short-term consequences of women's move toward equality" (Yllo, 1985).

Many researchers believe higher status for women will eventually result in less violence by husbands: "The more equality you have in a home, the less likelihood there is of physical abuse of any members" (Straus, 1981). This trend may already be under way. One study showed that wives with the greatest resources—in such matters as education, job possibilities, and actual income—are the quickest to leave husbands who use physical force (Pagelow, 1981). Another study found that the number of wives severely beaten by their husbands was about three times higher among those who were highly dependent than among those who enjoyed a great deal of financial independence (Kalmuss and Straus, 1982).

The Millions of Abused Children

Almost as common as violence between marriage partners is the abuse of children by parents. One estimate is at least 1.5 million incidents a year (California Commission on

Crime Control, 1981). Another study has set the figure even higher: at least 1.7 million cases a year of violent assault against children aged 3 through 17, plus an undetermined but undoubtedly large number against babies under 3 (Straus, 1980).

Abuse has been found to occur most frequently in families where the husband has recently been out of work (Gil, 1970) and grew up in a home where violence occurred (Straus, 1980), and it often goes hand-in-hand with excessive drinking (Wertham, 1972). It is found almost as often among the well educated, with jobs at the upper prestige levels, as in families with less education and less important jobs. But income makes a sharp difference. In families earning no more than $9,000 in 1976, the rate of abuse was 75 percent higher than in families with a more adequate income (Straus, 1980).

One explanation of child abuse, it has been suggested, is that most parents, at one time or another, have problems coping with their children. Their feelings of frustration and powerlessness may turn to anger, and their anger to physical punishment—sometimes more severe than they would ever have planned deliberately: "Is there any mother or father who has not been provoked almost to the breaking point? . . . How many parents have not had moments of concern and self-recrimination after having, in anger, hit their own child much harder than they expected they would? How many such incidents make a 'child abuser' out of a normal parent?" (Zalba, 1971).

Since our society has generally accepted the spanking of children by their parents—and until recently the use of corporal punishment in the schools—it is perhaps all too easy to cross the fine line between proper discipline and abuse. Studies indicate that parents who have clearly abused their children are pretty much like any other parents except in that one respect (Gil, 1970).

Sexual Abuse and Incest

Sexual abuse of children, by parents or other relatives, is also considerably more common than generally believed. The number is difficult to estimate, but one recent study managed to come up with a good approximation through careful interviews of a large group of representative adult women. A surprisingly large number, 12 percent, reported at least one experience before the age of 14, and 16 percent by the age of 18 (Russell, 1983).

Even more common is sexual abuse by someone outside the family. The interviews with adult women indicate that 20 percent had been abused in some way by an outsider by the age of 14, and 32 percent by the age of 18. Boys as well as girls can be victims, and the abuse can range from exhibitionism by an adult or fondling of the child to sexual intercourse and forcible rape. It includes an estimated 300,000 girls and boys who have somehow become engaged in prostitution or "kiddie pornography" (Kempe and Kempe, 1984).

One form of child abuse is incest, or parent-child sexual relations, usually between father and daughter, sometimes between father and son or brother and sister, and rarely between mother and son. One estimate is that about 2 million of the women in our nation have been victims of incest by the father or stepfather (Kempe and Kempe, 1984). The victims often suffer psychological damage that cripples them for life. A study of female prison inmates found that 36 percent of those convicted of felonies and 52 percent of those convicted of prostitution had a history of incest (Hinds, 1981).

At one time it was generally believed that incest occurred almost solely in the poorest of families, often between a father and daughter who were both of subnormal intelligence. This has proved completely untrue. Incest is found at all levels of society.

If anything, it is more common in well-to-do families (Kempe and Kempe, 1984).

Fathers who commit incest with a daughter are often introverted and socially isolated men with no meaningful relationships outside the family. Often their conduct is encouraged in one way or another by a wife who is highly dependent, worried about the marriage, and frantic to hold her husband for the financial and emotional support he provides. As one scholar has said, after studying many cases, "We have simply not seen an innocent mother in long-standing incest" (Kempe, 1980).

Jealousy: "The Green-eyed Monster"

One other aspect of violence deserves mention: jealousy, which has been recognized for many centuries as a powerful human emotion that sometimes leads to murder. Shakespeare based his tragic *Othello* on the theme of jealousy, which he termed "the green-eyed monster." Milton called it "the injured lover's hell," and Dryden "the jaundice of the soul." Today's newspapers often carry stories of killings committed in a jealous rage, sometimes by people who had never before shown any inclination to violence.

Anthropologists have observed that jealousy is found in all societies, including those where adultery is an accepted part of the culture, although its extent varies from one society to another and even from one individual to another within the same culture. Apparently it is particularly common and intense in societies with a tradition of machismo, where the male sex role demands a great display of virility and pride (Stephens, 1963).

Jealousy has been described as "a state of tension, unresolved and tormenting, which is no doubt why it provokes people to do things like kill each other and, with us milder

types, throw shoes at the wall" (Durbin, 1977). Because it takes so many forms—ranging from mild and temporary discomfort to prolonged and murderous anger—it is difficult to study. In what is probably its most common form, the husband is made jealous by another man who seems attractive to his wife, or the wife by another woman. But husbands are also frequently jealous of the time and affection the wife devotes to their children, and either partner may be jealous of the importance of the other's job, parents, or friends of the same sex. Even when jealousy does not lead to violence, it often provokes many conflicts in marriage.

The generally accepted theory is that jealousy springs from the very nature of a two-person relationship in which the partners are associated so intimately and on which they depend so greatly. A group of only two people, a *dyad,* is potentially unstable because the group will be destroyed if either person leaves it. Any larger group, even if just three people, is less fragile because it can survive the departure of one of its members (Simmel, 1950).

People who are low in self-esteem—dubious about their own attractiveness and worth—are especially likely to consider the marriage dyad fragile and consider it threatened by any sign that their partner may have outside interests. This leads to a whole new aspect of decision making and power struggle.

THE IMPORTANCE OF SELF-ESTEEM IN MARRIAGE

The part self-esteem plays in marriage can be best understood by examining the probable fate of two students, both extremely low in feelings of self-worth, who find themselves on the same campus. Mr. A considers himself physically unattractive—skinny and awkward in movement, with too large a nose and too small a chin. He does not think of himself as a good student and does not have much hope of a successful career. He also regards himself as tongue-tied in conversation, no good at making jokes, and generally dull as well as selfish, touchy, and bad tempered. One day, despite his misgivings, he starts to talk to Ms. B, and to his great surprise she seems interested.

Ms. B also has grave doubts about her physical appearance, which she finds distressingly plain and a little too plump and dumpy. She does not consider herself intelligent or clever at small talk, and she believes she has some defects of character that make her lazy, rather messy, self-centered, snide toward other people, and given to daydreaming rather than getting her work done. She feels she would be a poor wife or mother and has no real hope of ever marrying, until she meets Mr. A and finds that for some strange reason he seems interested in her.

The low opinions that Ms. B and Mr. A have of themselves may or may not be justified. In all probability their self-images are much worse than the actual facts would dictate, for people with low self-esteem always tend to exaggerate their faults. But the truth hardly matters, because both of them feel unlovable. What is likely to happen if that spark of interest develops into marriage?

The "Pseudomutual" Relationship

One possibility is that they will both walk on eggs throughout their married life, carefully steering away from words or actions that might threaten the fragile relationship they have so miraculously found. They will do a great deal of play acting. Mr. A will hide any urges he may feel to be selfish, thin-skinned, or angry. Ms. B, now Mrs. A, will try to suppress any tendencies to be self-centered

or critical. In their decision making, they will avoid any expression of their own true wishes. Instead, they will try to guess what the other partner wants and defer to it. The rules they set for their marriage will be designed to prevent conflict and preserve the appearance of harmony. They will avoid even talking about matters on which there is a chance they might not see eye to eye.

Since each believes the other has been fooled into the marriage, both want desperately to preserve the illusion. They cannot risk being honest and revealing how unworthy they know in their hearts that they are (or, more accurately, that they think they are). They will manage to keep the relationship going at any cost, even the cost of suppressing their own true individuality. They will never do or say anything that might change the partner's mistakenly high regard for them.

All in all, they will not be true partners in any sense of the word. They will be engaged not so much in a relationship as in a game of deception, played by two frightened people clinging to what seems their one chance of a lifetime to enjoy acceptance. The arrangement has been called *pseudomutuality* (Wynne et al., 1958), a kind of overdependent togetherness without any genuine intimacy.

When Pseudomutuality Fails and Conflict Takes Over

Even pseudomutuality may be impossible for Mr. and Mrs. A. Such partners often find themselves bitterly disappointed in marriage, become frustrated and angry, and are quickly drawn into the basic conflict that turns love into warfare. For one thing, the marriage is based on a false assumption. Virginia Satir (1967), a family therapist who stresses the importance of self-worth, has pointed out that people with low self-esteem usually disguise it. They act more confident than they really are, especially when trying to impress someone else. Mr. A probably married Ms. B in the belief that she was a strong person who would take care of him and provide the courage that he himself lacked. Ms. B probably married him for the same mistaken reasons. But the intimacy of marriage makes it difficult to conceal weakness, and people without a sense of self-worth are suspicious anyway. On the one hand they have "high hopes" about what to expect from others, but on the other hand they have "great fears" that make them "only too ready to expect disappointment and to distrust people" (Satir, 1967).

Moreover those with low self-esteem are unduly sensitive to criticism and the threat of rejection. Of course all of us judge ourselves to a considerable extent by the way other people react to us. Our sense of self-worth is built up by acceptance and praise. It is weakened, at least at times, by failure and criticism. But a confident person "can weather many failures," while a person with a poor self-image "can experience many successes yet feel a gnawing doubt about his own value" (Satir, 1972). Indeed, such people may discount even the most sincere praise and interpret the most harmless remark as a sharp-edged criticism. Since they are secretly critical of themselves, they expect criticism and often imagine it.

In whatever decision making they attempt, Mr. and Mrs. A are on dangerous ground. They are so dependent on each other yet so distrusting that the slightest difference of opinion, real or imaginary, strikes them "as an insult or a sign of being unloved." Their false pride and fear of criticism force them to fight for what little sense of individuality they possess. They have to respond to any apparent criticism with a countercriticism. Their decision making becomes a question of "who is right" and "who will win." They are now caught in the vicious circle of the basic conflict, or what Satir prefers to call the "war syndrome" (Satir, 1967).

How Self-esteem Is Torn Down and Built Up

Our society is full of people like Mr. and Mrs. A. In fact, there is at least a little of Mr. and Mrs. A in all of us. The reason seems to lie in the widespread tendency to try to control human relationships through criticism and punishment rather than through praise and rewards, as described in Chapter 8.

The criticism that all of us have so often experienced would not be so devastating to self-esteem if it was directed only to one specific action—if, for example, parents always said, "We love you. We know you are a marvelous child. But we don't approve of what you did to your little brother's toys." Unfortunately, however, many parents (and in marriage many wives and husbands) have a way of making criticism sound like an attack on the entire personality. Instead of saying, "I don't like what you did just now," they say: "You're bad." "You're selfish." "You're careless." "You make me sick." Often it seems that people accept us, if at all, only when we behave exactly the way they want us to behave. They are quick to reject us when we do anything they dislike (Rogers, 1953). At times we are almost bound to ask ourselves, "Am I a worthy human being or a monster?"

Yet self-esteem is essential to happiness, in marriage and in life in general. Virginia Satir, from her many years of practicing and teaching family therapy, has reached this conclusion: "From all the day-to-day experiences of my professional and personal living, I am convinced that the crucial factor in what happens both inside people and between people is the picture of individual worth that each person carries around." In working with a family, Satir (1967) always attempts to raise the confidence of all members. She believes that people can learn to feel better about themselves at any age.

All marriage counselors, whatever methods they use, try in one way or another to bolster self-esteem. For example, the exchange of rewards encouraged in behavioral counseling is specifically designed not only to foster mutual pleasure instead of punishment but to build up the partner's feelings of self-worth—which thrive on gestures of affection and approval, especially from those to whom we are closest, and wither under disapproval and ridicule.

Psychotherapists who treat personal problems not necessarily related to marriage also strive to make people feel better about themselves. Most psychologists would agree that a person who has developed high self-esteem can cope successfully with difficult situations that might shatter someone with a poor self-image, since the amount of anxiety and stress we suffer depends not so much on life's events as on the way we view ourselves and our experiences (Lazarus, 1978).

Self-esteem and the Happy Family

People with high self-esteem can enjoy a marriage free from the deception, suspicion, and fears that plague Mr. and Mrs. A. They are "real and honest to and about" themselves and each other. They are "loving, playful, authentic, and productive." They are "willing to take risks" and can "accommodate to what is new and different." The rules they set for their relationship are "flexible, human, appropriate, and subject to

change" (Satir, 1972). Untroubled by feelings of inferiority and guilt, they are not neurotically dependent on each other but can make their own decisions and act on their own, with each exhibiting "basic integrity as an individual" (Ammons and Stinnett, 1980).

A strong sense of individuality and self-worth has been found helpful not only in coping with stress but in forming good personal relationships (Frank, 1975) and achieving sexual fulfillment (Barton, Kawash, and Cattell, 1972). A study of exceptionally happy and "vital" marriages found that the partners all tended to have this kind of strength. In addition, they were committed "to developing and sustaining a vital marriage relationship," which they regarded as "one of their most important life goals." They had a psychological need "to be understanding and supportive," which increased "the likelihood of husband and wife mutually reinforcing each other's positive self concept." They viewed sex as an important part of the marriage and a means of "sustaining the dynamic intimacy" that both desired. All in all they had learned to "pull together" and had mastered "the art of losing themselves in the relationship without losing their sense of self in the process" (Ammons and Stinnett, 1980).

COMMUNICATION: BRIDGE OR BARRIER?

Just as fish are born to swim and moles to burrow in the ground, we human beings seem born to communicate with each other. The ability to speak and understand language depends primarily on a part of the brain that is larger in human beings than in any other living creature (Geschwind and Levitsky, 1968). This unique brain structure

Ken Karp

Partners who have found approval and self-esteem in marriage—and are there-fore "loving and playful."

has enabled us to develop an infinitely var-ied communications system that is humani-ty's most distinctive and perhaps most complex achievement.

Language is a versatile tool that enables us "to inform listeners, warn them, order them to do something, question them about a fact, or thank them for a gift or an act of kindness." We use words to convey our ideas and our wishes to the people around us, and we expect these people to understand our in-tentions and "act accordingly" (Clark and Clark, 1977). We can express pleasure, sym-pathy, and love—or dissatisfaction and re-sentment. In marriage, communication is the tool we use, for better or worse, in han-dling our disagreements, making our deci-sions, and setting our rules. It plays an important part in drawing the partners closer together or pushing them apart.

Communication and Happiness

Sociologists have observed for many years that the ability to communicate is closely re-lated to how satisfied people are with their marriage. A study made in the 1960s com-pared one group of presumably happy part-ners with another group who were having difficulties and had sought counseling. It was found that the happily married conducted more conversations, appeared to understand each other's statements better, and were quick to appreciate the inner feelings that lay behind the words. They seemed to respond not just to the words but to the way in which the words were spoken (Navran, 1967), that is, to such other tools of communication as tone of voice, gestures, and "body language."

Many subsequent studies have produced similar findings. It has been shown that marriages tend to be extremely happy when both partners are skillful at communication (Corrales, 1974). Indeed self-disclosure, which is one aspect of effective communication, bears an almost straight line relationship to happiness: For most couples, satisfaction with the marriage rises or falls along with the amount of "communicating about fears, problems, self-doubts, feelings of anger or depression, and aspects of marriage perceived to be bothersome to one or both partners, as well as openly sharing positive feelings about the self and other" (Jorgensen and Gaudy, 1980). Of all the things you could possibly know about a couple, the best clue to how happy they are is their ability (1) to express affection and understanding and (2) to use communication as a problem-solving tool to resolve disagreements and make decisions (Snyder, 1979).

Why Communication Is Important

Why is communication so important? The reason lies in a fact already discussed in Chapter 8: If you want to establish a relationship—and to preserve and nurture it—you have to *do* something. Note once again these comments quoted earlier but well worth repeating:

> How should one know that he is loved but by the way people act toward him: what

Mimi Forsythe, Monkmeyer

Open and honest communication: one of the best of all possible clues to the happiness level in marriage.

they say, how they look, how they touch—in a word, what they *do*. Attention, praise, spoken niceties, and physical contact have been demonstrations of love for years. Who cares if someone loves them if they never receive evidence through attention, contact, or the spoken word?

(Madsen and Madsen, 1972)

Many people, unfortunately, fail to provide the attention or the words. They overestimate the amount of understanding that can exist without clear communication:

> One of the most impossible hurdles in human relationships . . . is the assumption that you always know what I mean. The premise appears to be that if we love each other, we also can and should read each other's minds.
>
> The most frequent complaint I have heard people make about their family members is, ''I don't know what he feels,'' which results in a feeling of being left out. This puts a tremendous strain on any relationship. . . . People tell me they feel in a kind of no-man's-land as they try to make some kind of bridge to a family member who doesn't show or say what he feels. . . . Many people who are accused of this are often feeling very strongly, but are unaware they aren't showing it.
>
> *(Satir, 1972)*

Husbands in particular seem inclined to hide their feelings, probably because of the continuing influence of the traditional sex role calling for men to be the strong and silent partner. Misunderstandings often occur because the husband does not express his emotions and wishes, and the wife does not even know that he has such feelings (Shapiro and Swensen, 1969). One study found that many wives ''want their husbands to be more vulnerable and share more intimately with them. The emotional equality they seek

is of the deepest, most open, fully sharing, personally respectful, and accepting sort. . . . Husbands still prefer to give less of this than their wives would like'' (Hawkins, Weisberg, and Ray, 1980).

At one time the quality of communication in marriage seemed to vary by social class. Mirra Komarovsky (1967) found in the 1960s that men low in education and income had a ''trained incapacity to share'' because their socialization had taught them that ''feelings were not named, discussed, or explained.'' More recently it has been observed that educational level may no longer make much difference. At all levels, both husbands and wives now seem to prefer open communication and self-disclosure (Hawkins, Weisberg, and Ray, 1977). And you need not be a trained orator, gifted with an eloquent vocabulary, to express your feelings. Indeed too much skill at stringing words together can lead to an overintellectual approach and an attempt to ''establish your self-worth by using big words'' (Satir, 1972).

Just as effective communication appears to be a basic ingredient of a successful marriage, one large-scale study has found that faulty communication is the chief cause of failure (Mace, 1975). A number of methods have been developed for teaching the necessary skills. One of the best known is the Minnesota Couples Communication Program (Miller, 1976), which is usually presented to groups of five to ten couples who meet for four sessions lasting three hours each.* One study of the results found that participants, when tested just after completing the program, showed substantial increases in both openness of communication

---

*Information on sessions that may be available near your home can be obtained from Interpersonal Communications Programs, Inc., 1925 Nicollet Avenue, Minneapolis, MN 55403, phone 612-871-7388.

and feelings of satisfaction with the relationship. Six months later they seemed to have abandoned use of the techniques of communication they had learned, but they continued to feel that their relationship had improved (Wampler and Sprenkle, 1980).

How Talking to Each Other Affects Everything Else

The study of couples who took the Minnesota Couples Communication Program raises an interesting question. Why did training in communication help these people feel better about their marriages even after they apparently forgot or discarded what they learned about talking to each other? The answer seems to be that communication influences and in turn is influenced by the partners' attitudes toward decision making and the establishment of rules for their differences of opinion and their feelings about power, the self-esteem that they each bring to the marriage, and the way the relationship operates to build up or tear down self-esteem.

A change in any one of these matters can have a powerful effect on all the rest, just as a complex chemical compound can be transformed by changing just one of its molecules. Certainly self-esteem and self-disclosure are interdependent, for it has been found that people who are high in one are also high in the other (Shapiro, 1968). And self-disclosure helps the family achieve emotional intimacy and thus perform its function as ''an oasis of intimacy'' in today's otherwise impersonal society.

The couples who took the communication program may have gained a greater sense of self-esteem and become more honest about revealing their innermost feelings. Or they may have changed their approach to decision making. Or the mere act of taking the course may have enhanced their commitment to the marriage and their desire to be understanding and supportive. Even a temporary change in their methods of talking to each other could have served in numerous ways to alter the entire pattern of their relationship.

Is Communication Cause or Effect? Help Or Hindrance?

Some social scientists question whether the quality of communication—for example, the faulty communication that has been found characteristic of unhappy marriages—is a cause or an effect. Philip Brickman (1974), for example, has suggested that the ability to communicate is a valuable and sometimes essential tool in resolving disagreements and making decisions but is not ordinarily the source of the disagreement.

A case in point would be a man who wants his wife to be a housewife-mother but is married to a woman who wants to be a partner-wife. Their disagreement over whether or not she should take an outside job is clearly a conflict between their opposing views of the proper sex role for women. It does not in any sense stem from the way they communicate with each other, though open discussion of the problem may help them resolve it.

It has also been pointed out that in some cases frank discussion and honest expression of feelings, far from improving a relationship, can actually make matters worse (Levenson, 1972). An example would be a marriage in which neither partner has a particularly high regard for the other but both prefer staying together to any of the alternatives. The wife considers her husband unaffectionate, self-centered, and engrossed in his work and hobbies to the exclusion of all else; yet she likes their children, the home he has provided, and the outside interests she has developed, and she is afraid of striking out on her own. The husband considers his wife dull, inefficient, and inattentive; yet he likes the security of marriage and dreads the expense of a divorce and a new start. In this kind of relationship, which occurs frequently enough to have acquired the name *utilitarian marriage* (Cuber and Harroff, 1965), what could be gained by blurting out the unhappy truth?

Even in a more intimate and affectionate relationship some forms of frank communication can do more harm than good. It can be damaging to the partner's self-esteem if a wife or husband is brutally frank about negative feelings and quick to express dissatisfaction and criticism without balancing them with positive comments and praise. Feelings that the partner would find perfectly acceptable in private can be embarrassing if expressed in the company of relatives or friends (Jorgensen and Gaudy, 1980). Though some of the popular advice urges us to "let it all hang out," communication and self-disclosure seem to work best when kept in perspective as one of the many elements that are mixed together in marriage and that can either help or hinder one another in shaping a satisfactory relationship.

Some Guidelines to More Effective Communication

Many marriage counselors have drawn up lists of the ineffective forms of communication they have observed while listening to conversations between a wife and a husband. Some of the most frequent and perhaps most serious errors are described in the box on *Opinions and Experiences*. Unfortunately it is easier to point out mistakes than to suggest more effective methods. But counselors generally consider the following to be steps in the right direction:

1. *Being a good listener.* This means being willing to devote sincere attention to the partner's comments, wishes, and complaints. The good listener does not interrupt or break off the conversation by changing the subject or walking away. Instead the good listener tries to understand what is being said, take it seriously, and come to a mutually agreeable decision.

2. *Giving feedback.* Since it is impossible to conduct a conversation with a statue, mere listening is not enough. It is also important to show that you are listening and reacting. Thus feedback is an essential part of the kind of give-and-take discussion that can lead to a more intimate and solid relationship. It can be provided by repeating the partner's statements ("You're saying that you're upset because I was late.") or asking questions ("Are you saying that you wish I would straighten out my closet?"). Even nodding the head is body language that says you are paying attention and giving thoughtful consideration to your partner's words.

3. *Establishing eye contact.* Looking each other in the eye is a special form of body language that demonstrates attention. It also helps create a feeling of intimacy by serving "as a mutually understood signal that the communication channel between two people is open. While eye contact is sustained, the actions of either partner are automatically defined as relevant to both of them" (Rubin, 1973).

4. *Saying what you think and feel.* Counselors often urge partners to make frequent use of the word *I*, as in "I think this about the situation" or "I feel this way right now." When you concentrate on

Opinions and Experiences

SOME COMMON ERRORS IN COMMUNICATION

Many marriage counselors have drawn up lists of the ineffective forms of communication they have observed while listening to the conversations of wives and husbands. Some of the most frequent and perhaps most serious errors are listed here.

1. *Interrupting.* The wife starts to say, "I think the best way to settle this argument would be to" and the husband breaks in with, "Let me tell you what I think." Interrupting shows an unwillingness to listen and a lack of support.

2. *Arguing over the facts.* The husband says, "You promised me you'd pick up my shirts on the way home." The wife says, "I did not promise. I said I'd do it if I could get off work a little early." There is no way either of them can change the way the other remembers what was said, and arguing about it can only result in anger.

3. *Blaming each other.* The wife says, "You shouldn't have yelled at me just because I was a little late." The husband says, "I wouldn't have yelled if you had been on time." Here, both partners are in effect claiming, "I was right and you were wrong." Why argue over who was to blame? How can the argument solve anything? (A variation of this error is excusing one's own conduct by launching a countercriticism, as when the husband says, "You always leave the bathroom in a mess," and the wife says, "Your closet is always messy, too.")

4. *Attacking the personality instead of the deed.* One of the partners, upset because the

other wants to stay home and watch a television program rather than go out for the evening, cries out, "You're just totally selfish." This kind of name calling ignores the specific incident that caused the complaint and instead attacks the personality and character of the partner. It tears down self-esteem—and it makes the whole disagreement hopeless by implying that the problem is so deep-seated that nothing can ever change.

5. *Making the partner feel guilty.* This error is similar to the previous one. A partner says, "You just don't care about me. You keep hurting my feelings and you don't give a damn." This kind of complaint accuses the other person of being insensitive and impossible. Where do you go from there?

6. *The shotgun approach.* One of the partners says, "You're always badgering me and you kept me waiting this morning and you forgot to call the plumber." This immediately throws the discussion into utter confusion because it is impossible to deal with more than one disagreement at a time.

7. *Mind reading.* The husband says, "You think I spend too much time in my workshop," or the wife says, "You think I spend too much money on clothes." Since neither is qualified as a mind reader, how do they know? Why not ask what the other person is thinking?

8. *Sending mixed messages.* One of the partners, unwilling to express feelings honestly, says "All right, if that's what you want go ahead and do it" but at the same time sighs and shakes the head. Which message is the other person supposed to believe—the words, which say one thing, or the body language, which says the opposite?

Largely adapted from Thomas, Walter, and O'Flaherty, A Verbal Problem Checklist for Use in Assessing Family Verbal Behavior, *Behavior Therapy,* 1974, 5, pp. 235–236 and Lester, Beckham, and Baucomb, Implementation of Behavioral Marital Therapy. *Journal of Marital and Family Therapy* 1980, 6, pp. 189–199.

expressing your own thoughts and emotions, you avoid three errors: (1) trying to read your partner's mind, (2) blaming your partner, and (3) attacking the partner instead of the specific problem that has arisen.

Consider, for example, the case of the partner who was upset about not going out for the evening and complained, "You're totally selfish." Those words constituted a guess about the partner's motives, a placing of the blame, and an attack on the partner's personality and self-esteem. It would have been more constructive—and more correct—to say, "I really wanted to go out tonight and I'm feeling disappointed because you don't want to go."

5. *Being generous with praise.* Unfortunately most of us are more likely to speak up when we are displeased than when we are pleased—another example of the tendency to control others through criticism and punishment. In many marriages the only serious conversations take place when the wife or husband has a complaint. Their communication will be much more satisfactory if they frequently "tell each other what they like about the partner, what the partner has been doing well, and what the partner says that is helpful" (Lester, Beckham, and Baucomb, 1980). Being generous with praise builds up self-esteem and a spirit of good will that makes husband and wife eager to please each other and grateful for the pleasures received. It also makes it easier for them to accept disapproval on the inevitable occasions when they do something that displeases the partner.

Perhaps the secret of communication in marriage can be summed up as the ability to convey in one way or another, through words or body language or even touching, the clear message that "I love you. I admire and respect you. I may disagree with what you want to do now, or I may even hate something you just did, but that doesn't change my high opinion of you; so let's work together to find a solution and make a decision we can both gladly accept."

SUMMARY

1. Most couples start marriage without realizing how many decisions they will face, or how the choice they make may affect the entire future course of the relationship. From the beginning, every decision helps set long-lasting rules for speaking frankly or talking only about safe topics, encouraging or avoiding open displays of affection, and their behavior in general toward each other.

2. Disagreements over the exact nature of the rules are inevitable but can usually be resolved through compromise and minor adjustments on both sides. But disagreements over who sets the rules—in other words which partner is in control—may create a power struggle and lead to the basic conflict.

3. Power in marriage is difficult to define or study. Family members, if asked who is responsible for deciding how disputes get settled, usually disagree on the answer. Wives usually believe the husband has more power than he himself claims, and husbands believe the wife has more power than she thinks.

4. Couples often make a his-and-hers division of responsibility, with the wife usually deciding some matters and the husband deciding others.

5. *Resources theory* holds that power resides in the partner with the most to offer. In traditional marriages, the husband held the power because men were considered superior to women. In today's companionship marriages, power is allocated to "a competent partner over the

incompetent one, regardless of sex.'' The husband's power over decision making depends on his occupation, income, and family background. Working wives usually have more voice than housewives, especially in deciding how money will be spent.

6. Power is closely related to violence in the family. It is estimated that about 2.5 million wives a year are seriously abused by their husbands, and violence is even more likely to occur in couples living together without marriage. It also occurs in couples going together in college, where surveys have found that about one-fourth of students have experienced violent episodes.

7. Violence is especially common among husbands and wives whose parents practiced severe physical discipline, or who watched their parents strike each other. It is encouraged by drinking and stress. Husbands who beat their wife tend to be those who feel they have not in any other way earned the right to power—men who actually are or consider themselves failures in life.

8. Child abuse is also common. One study has set the number of violent assaults at 1.7 million a year against children aged 3 through 17, plus a large number against babies under 3. It is found just as often among well-educated parents as those with less education, but it is 75 percent higher in very low-income families than in families with a more adequate income.

9. Sexual abuse, ranging from exhibitionism by an adult or fondling of a child by an adult to sexual intercourse and forcible rape, also happens frequently. In one study of representative women, 12 percent reported at least one incident of abuse by a parent or other relative before the age of 14, and 16 percent by age of 18. Even more of the women reported sexual abuse by an outsider.

10. It is estimated that about 2 million women have been victims of incest, a form of sexual abuse, by their father or stepfather. The victims often suffer crippling psychological damage. Incest occurs at all levels of society. The fathers are often introverted and socially isolated men with no meaningful relationships outside the family.

The mothers often encourage the behavior because they are highly dependent, worried about the marriage, and frantic to hold onto the husband for the financial and emotional support he provides.

11. Violence may spring from jealousy, which is found even in societies where adultery is an accepted part of the culture. Jealousy seems to stem from the very nature of a two-person group, or *dyad,* where the partners are deeply dependent on each other and the relationship, which is potentially unstable because it is destroyed if either person leaves it.

12. People with low self-esteem, dubious about their own attractiveness and worth, are especially likely to feel jealous at any sign the partner may have outside interests. Indeed self-esteem is essential to happiness in marriage (and in life in general).

13. When two people with low self-esteem marry, their relationship is likely to be one of *pseudomutuality,* a game of deception in which both suppress their own true individuality and try never to say or do anything they feel might change the partner's mistakenly high regard for them.

14. It is difficult to acquire self-esteem because of the widespread tendency to control human relationships through criticism and punishment rather than praise and rewards. Criticism is not destructive to self-esteem if directed only to a specific action. Unfortunately, parents—and later marriage partners—seldom say merely, ''I don't like what you did just now.'' Instead their criticism becomes an attack on the entire personality: ''You're bad.'' ''You're selfish.''

15. Psychotherapists and marriage counselors all try to bolster self-esteem. The exchange of rewards encouraged in behavioral counseling is intended not only to foster mutual pleasure but to build up the partner's feelings of self-worth.

16. In happy marriages both partners have a strong sense of individuality and self-worth. They are real and honest to and about themselves, willing to take risks, and able to accommodate to new and different situations.

17. Happiness in marriage is also closely related to the ability to communicate. Happy partners hold more conversations than unhappy ones, understand each other's statements better, and are quick to appreciate the feelings behind the words. They use communication to express affection, resolve disagreements, and make decisions.

18. Couples who have taken communications training find their relationship improved even if they forget the specific techniques they have learned. Apparently they had become more honest about revealing their innermost feelings or changed their approach to decision making and had therefore gained in self-esteem.

19. Counselors suggest that communication can be improved by being a good listener (devoting serious and respectful attention to what the partner says), giving feedback that indicates a reaction, establishing eye contact (which helps create a feeling of intimacy), saying what *you* feel and think about something that has bothered you (rather than attacking the partner for it), and being generous with praise.

20. Some common mistakes are interrrupting, arguing over the facts, blaming each other, attacking the personality instead of the deed, making the partner feel guilty, and sending mixed messages (saying one thing but with facial expressions or gestures that say the opposite).

DISCUSSION QUESTIONS

1. Why has it been said that unhappy couples, when in disagreement over who should make decisions, move vertically and that happy couples move horizontally? Give examples of couples you know who are moving vertically and others who are moving horizontally.

2. Utilizing resources theory, discuss the factors that affect the power balance between husbands and wives in marriages today.

3. How is resources theory related to family violence?

4. Describe the type of family in which incest is most likely to occur.

5. Why do people with low self-esteem get caught up in the basic conflict? How is self-esteem related to happiness in marriage?

6. Of the eight common errors in communication, which do you make the most frequently? What are the results?

CHAPTER 10

Parenthood, Middle Age, and the "Golden Years"

One thing that comes to all marriages is birthdays. The young bride and groom (and older ones too) watch the years go by, and usually they become parents and watch the children grow up. Early youth gives way to a transition period, during the 30s and early 40s, in which people are neither still very young nor yet middle aged. At 45, by Census Bureau definition, they officially enter their middle age, though some still feel youthful on that birthday and others have thought of themselves as starting to get old long before then. At 65, by most standards, they become senior citizens, joining the growing ranks of the elderly in our society.

Not all brides and grooms, of course, are together throughout this long span of years. Divorce ends close to half of all first marriages and even more remarriages. Many people die before they reach old age, some even before middle age, and their partners either wind up their years as widows and widowers or remarry and start over. Our society today has no standard life cycle that applies to everyone who marries. Instead we have a whole variety of possible cycles that may include a broken marriage, a period of varying length living alone again (often as a single parent), remarriage, and possibly a second divorce and second remarriage (Norton, 1983).

Nonetheless about 70 percent of the people who get married will wind up living with their partner until "death do us part," if not in their first marriage, then in a remarriage (Glick, 1984). The number of people living together as husband and wife now stands at about 106 million, or nearly two-thirds of all adults (Bureau of the Census, 1984a). Since birthdays bring changes, there are considerable differences between the 20 million married people who are in their 20s, the 23 million between 35 and 44, and the 14 million elderly over 65.

GROWING OLDER IN THE TRADITIONAL MARRIAGE

Human development, so rapid and striking in the early years of life when a helpless infant quickly blossoms into a walking, talking, thinking schoolchild, slows down as time goes by but never really stops. Psychologists have shown that we human beings continue to profit from new experiences, learn, and change—sometimes in a spectacular way—for as long as we live.

For example, one study that followed children from birth through their teens, then observed them again when they reached the age of 30, found that many of them had turned into completely different people. Some of the most promising teenagers, successful in school and their social relations, well poised and self-confident, had become "brittle, discontented, and puzzled." Others who seemed maladjusted at 18—failures in school, unpopular, and despondent—had changed to "wise, steady, and understanding parents who appreciate the complexities of life and have both humor and compassion for the human race." Among the events in life that had helped transform them were a meaningful job, marriage, and especially parenthood, with its responsibilities and opportunities (Macfarlane, 1963).

Another psychologist measured a number of the characteristics and opinions of newly married men and women, then again twenty years later. The study found that the two decades had changed a majority of these people's attitudes, interests, values, and personality traits (Kelly, 1955).

When Middle Age Meant the Marital Blahs

Studies made a few decades ago, before marriage had made the giant leap "from institution to companionship," painted a dismal picture of marriage during the many long years after the glow of the honeymoon had worn off. One famous investigation, which looked at a group of young people first in 1936, again about four years later, and finally after they had been married for about twenty years, found a significant decline in their shared interests, beliefs, and values, accompanied by a drop in feelings of companionship and displays of affection (Burgess and Wallin, 1953).

In another notable study, made in the 1950s, sociologists interviewed a thousand wives of all ages, married for varying lengths of time. They found what they called a "corrosion" of many marriages with advancing years, shown most clearly by the fact that 52 percent of wives in the first two years of marriage were "very satisfied" and none seriously dissatisfied, but of those married for around twenty years only 6 percent were very satisfied and 27 percent were "conspicuously dissatisfied." The researchers concluded that

> the first two years of marriage are a honeymoon period which continues the romance of courtship. With the birth of the first baby, satisfaction with the standard of living and companionship declines. In subsequent years, love and understanding sag too. If children do not come, their absence is an alternative source of dissatisfaction. . . . Much of the decline in satisfaction reflects observable decreases in the number of things husbands and wives do with and for each other. . . . As individuals, middle-aged husbands and wives may find satisfaction elsewhere—in friends, the husband in his work, the wife in her children—but they seldom find as much in each other.
>
> *(Blood and Wolfe, 1960)*

The Masculine Role as a Problem for Husbands

One prominent cause of the "corrosion" the years brought to wives and husbands in the past was the feminine and masculine sex roles that went along with the traditional marriage. The dependent, passive, home-oriented female and the independent, aggressive, inexpressive male did not have much in common. They lived in two different worlds—the wife absorbed in housework and children; the husband in his job, his fellow workers, and his other outside interests. For a brief time, while flushed with the warmth of falling in love, they could imagine they were two kindred souls. Sooner or later, however, they were almost bound to discover that they were in many ways strangers.

The difficulties that growing older created for men thoroughly socialized into the masculine role have been described in these terms:

> The "male mystique" requires men to be strong, aggressive, unemotional, and tough, all characteristics which may be called into question during the decades when the male is confronted with the beginnings of bodily decline, career stagnation, and drastic changes within the family unit. . . . Males who adhere to the masculine role description may find themselves, in mid-life, questioning their achievements and accomplishments and bemoaning the inadequacy of their familial and other interpersonal relationships. . . . Conflict for the mid-life male and his spouse may be accentuated by his adherence to the rules of the "masculine mystique." If he feels that he must maintain the "macho" image of a strong, aggressive, unemotional male, then communication with his spouse about his difficulties will be difficult and resolution of his midlife crisis may be impossible.
>
> *(Cohen, 1979)*

The Feminine Role as a Problem for Wives

For the feminine woman, dedicated to the role of housewife-mother, one of the greatest difficulties was that the satisfactions she gained from the role were destined to end. For years she was busy and gained a sense of achievement at the job of raising the children; but the children eventually grew up, finished school, and left home to establish a life of their own. A large part of her life went with them. In many cases she had invested herself completely in the children and was unprepared to play any other role (Bart, 1975) and she was overwhelmed by the crisis of the "empty nest." She was especially likely to be unhappy and depressed if she felt that the children to whom she had devoted so much attention were not doing very well (Spence and Lonner, 1971).

Some housewife-mothers tried to fill the void by taking a job outside the home, for the first time in many years and perhaps for the first time ever. Often their abrupt entry into the marketplace was a painful event. Their homemaking skills were not very useful. By the work world's standards they lacked training and experience. They were used to setting their own pace and own standards in the security of the home and were unprepared for the demands of time clocks and schedules. They found themselves confronted by an entirely "different value system" (Nye and Berardo, 1973), and whether they found satisfaction or grief in the job depended on how well and how quickly they could adjust. Some managed. Some did not.

The Strange Midlife Reversal of Sex Roles

A handicap for both wives and husbands in a traditional marriage was the fact that the standard sex roles have a way of doing an about-face with the passage of time. Men tend in midlife to become less aggressive and competitive and take on some of the characteristics of the feminine role. Women, at the same time, become less dependent and submissive and begin to display many masculine traits (Zube, 1982).

This shift in long-standing attitudes and behaviors was especially upsetting to the partners in a traditional marriage. The husband, in particular, was likely to have difficulty adjusting to the changes in his wife, which usually took place at the same time he was experiencing the many self-doubts that usually afflicted the masculine male in middle age. As one sociologist has stated, the wife's growing tendency to be less passive and submissive meant that her interests had moved "outward, away from dependency on her husband, away from providing nurturance and support for him, so that the source of his recognition, affection, and sense of value" threatened "to disappear" (Brim, 1976).

One study found that about 80 percent of men reported experiencing turmoil in their early 40s (Levinson et al, 1976). Small wonder because a man that age, while trying to cope with the changes in his own personality, may also be confronted with other "challenges to the stereotyped male role as he is faced with the independence and departure of his children, the possible dependencies of his aging parents, and the growing assertiveness of his wife" (Cohen, 1979).

Marital Happiness and the U-shaped Curve

For many years it was generally accepted by family experts that happiness in marriage, if charted in a graph beginning with the ceremony and continuing on to old age, would take the form of what statisticians call a U-shaped curve. The graph line would start at a high level of happiness in the early months or years, then begin a sharp decline as soon as a child was born, remain at low ebb during all the years when the children were growing up, and start back toward its original high level when the children left home—immediately for the husband, later for the wife after she adjusted to the empty nest (Rollins and Feldman, 1970).

Of course, happiness is difficult to measure. It is especially difficult to compare different age groups, who have grown up under varying circumstances in our rapidly changing society and whose feelings, at their particular period in the life cycle, are affected by many factors besides the marriage relationship. Moreover the studies that led to acceptance of the U-shaped curve have been criticized on statistical and other grounds (Shram, 1979). Whether or not the U-shaped curve was ever typical, certainly marriages of the past experienced difficulties and disappointments in the posthoneymoon years, and many of the problems stemmed from the very nature of the traditional marriage and traditional sex roles.

Posthoneymoon Happiness in Modern Marriage

Today, of course, numerous kinds of marriages exist side by side. Some are thoroughly traditional, some all-out companionship, and many in between the two extremes. There are also numerous varieties of sex roles. Some women and men are highly feminine or masculine, some totally androgynous, exhibiting an equal number of the traditionally feminine and masculine traits; and many are somewhere in between, playing roles that are various mixtures of the traditional and the androgynous.

Since the sex roles play such a large part in adjustment to growing older, it is difficult to make any valid generalizations about what is now happening to marriages after the honeymoon years. Some couples, it seems clear, continue to suffer the same "corrosion" of their relationship that was found in surveys made a few decades ago. Others cope successfully with the problems and consider their marriage happier than ever.

One student of the family, writing about wives, has said that "for women the question of whether middle age is a crisis or [merely] a transition cannot be answered satisfactorily in the abstract and for all women" (Targ, 1979). The same thing could be said about men and about the marriage relationship. Surveys showing that X percent of couples are happy in the posthoneymoon years and Y percent unhappy tell us less about the effect of aging than about the many different ways people regard their string of birthdays.

If any generalization has a claim to validity, it is the suggestion that companionship marriages fare better than traditional marriages as the years roll by. One recent study found that the couples most likely to maintain the vitality of their relationship are those who treat each other as equals, have avoided struggles over power, and have established democratic and affectionate bonds with their children (Mudd and Taubin, 1982). Other research has also shown that the most successful couples treat each other with mutual respect and understanding, seek to accommodate each other's wishes rather than fight for their own way, and frequently express their appreciation and affection (Ammons and Stinnett, 1980).

THE JOY AND PAIN OF BEING A PARENT

Of all the events in the early years of marriage, the most momentous for most couples is becoming a parent, which brings new and often unexpected pleasures, duties, responsibilities, worries, and satisfactions. Without knowing quite why, most people want and welcome children. A 1974 survey by the Institute of Life Insurance found that 90 percent of young adults hoped to become parents. That number has probably declined somewhat, and for various reasons some people do not ever carry out the desire, but today's most authoritative estimate is that 75 to 80 percent of today's young women will eventually have at least one child (Bloom and Trussell, 1983). Most of the women expect to have two children (Bureau of the Census, 1983a).

In any given year, about 3.7 million babies are born in our nation (National Center for Health Statistics, 1985). Some of them, as in the days before birth control methods became generally available, arrive without planning or by accident. Most of them, however, represent a deliberate decision by wife and husband to undertake parenthood for the first time or to add to the size of the family (Commission on Population Growth, 1972).

Deciding to have a child is a lifelong commitment with far-ranging consequences. Short of suicide, it is about the only possible human action that is irreversible. You can always change your school, job, residence, church, or politics, and if a marriage goes bad you can get a divorce; but once you have a child, you are a parent forever. How do people go about making this crucial decision?

Why People Want or Don't Want Children

Young women—potential future mothers—seem to form strong feelings about children very early in life. By the time they are old enough to get pregnant, most of them apparently have already decided whether or not they want babies, and if so how many. Their attitudes are presumably the result of socialization, but which particular forces contribute to the socialization is something of a mystery (Pilliber, 1980). There is some evidence that college women who express a desire for children are more likely than others to report an affectionate early relationship with their mother and tendencies to prefer the feminine sex role and reject the philosophy of the feminist movement (Gerson, 1980).

Of women who decide against children, about a third have been found to be among those who make up their mind early. The rest do not rule out a pregnancy until after they are married. Perhaps they arrive at the decision after a series of postponements made for various reasons (Houseknecht, 1979b). It may be that they are reflecting the wishes of the husband, which at least one study has found to be a strong influence on the size of the family (Marciano, 1979).

Of the women who decide on parenthood, a majority prefer small families. A 1985 opinion poll (Gallup) found that 60 percent favor having only two children, and only 11 percent favor four or more. Especially likely to opt for small families are younger women and those who have at least some college education (Bureau of the Census, 1983a). The small-family women tend to be more interested in careers than the others (Scanzoni and McMurry, 1972) and to have a companionship marriage and more democratic relations with their husband (Scanzoni, 1976).

The Mixed Emotions of Parenthood

When college women are asked to discuss their attitude toward children, some express many of the same favorable feelings as the young wife quoted in the box titled *"We don't want to miss the experience."* Others express the kind of antipathy found in the box titled *"A terrific grandmother but never a twenty-four-hour-a-day mom."* Still others are not quite sure which way they lean and find themself pulled in both directions.

Making the decision is not easy, and arriving at a decision based on full understanding of the pros and cons is harder still, for the pleasures and problems of parenthood, and how you yourself are likely to

react to them, are difficult for any nonparent to imagine, much less predict. Having a child, perhaps more than any other of life's events, creates complex and sweeping changes in the roles wife and husband play in the marriage and in their lifestyle. New parents are usually prepared for the happy changes; they have seen many infants in other people's baby carriages and television commercials, where they are invariably cute, sweet, and thoroughly adorable. There is another side to parenthood, however, that only experience can reveal:

> Rearing children is hard work; it is often nerve-racking work; it involves tremendous responsibility; it takes all the ability one has (and more); and once you have begun you cannot quit when you feel like it. It would be helpful to young parents if they would be made to realize all this before they enlist.
>
> *(LeMasters and DeFrain, 1983)*

Bringing a newborn home from the hospital (where almost all births in the United States take place) means a sudden plunge into a new world of inescapable demands for food, diaper changing, and cuddling—demands on a twenty-four-hour-a-day schedule that shows no respect for usual bedtimes, sleep, or work routines. To many new parents, the experience comes as a shock. In the words of parents who took part in one study: "I knew our lives would be different when my wife got pregnant, but I didn't realize how much." "We had no idea that a baby would bring so many changes" (Miller and Sollie, 1980).

Many of the mothers in the study reported problems in coping with the unexpected events, as indicated by these comments: "One of the hardest adjustments for me was the unpredictableness of my day. I couldn't be sure of anything—that I would

Opinions and Experiences

"WE DON'T WANT TO MISS THE EXPERIENCE"

A young married University student talks about parenthood.

I certainly want the opportunity to become a mother—and this is a decision I've had plenty of time to consider because my husband and I have discussed the pros and cons many times.

We know that the decision isn't easy, and we sympathize with people who have come to the opposite conclusion. We have thought long and hard about the sacrifices we will have to make—emotional as well as financial—and the changes that children will make in our relationship and lifestyle, but we don't want to miss the experiences of caring for, loving, and shaping a child.

I plan a career after college. But when we decide the time has come to have our children I will gladly stop my job, for I feel that only a mother can give children the kind of full-time care and attention they need. My own parents provided me with a good, strong, open family life; and I hope I can do as well. I know that bringing up children can be a scary thing and that a mistake can bring heartbreak, but my husband and I are willing to learn whatever we need to equip us for this awesome task. We welcome the responsibility.

Opinions and Experiences

"A TERRIFIC GRANDMOTHER BUT NEVER A TWENTY–FOUR–HOUR–A–DAY MOM"

Another young married University student takes a very different view.

I have no future plans to include children in my life, and fortunately my husband agrees with me. My priorities are getting my degree and having a career in teaching and research. Children would handicap these plans. I think they would also interfere with my relationship with my husband, which is far more important to me than motherhood. For one thing, he and I are mountain climbers. Our trips mean a great deal to us but would be dangerous or impossible for children.

Perhaps this sounds self-centered, but I have another reason. I simply can't stand to be around children for any length of time. They're too messy and noisy, and their incessant needs and demands are too much for me. I would probably make a terrific grandmother but never a twenty-four-hour-a-day mom, which I just couldn't handle emotionally. Perhaps if more people would honestly evaluate their "frustration potential," they too would remain childless and the rate of child neglect and abuse would decrease.

be able to take a nap after her next feeding, that I would have time to clean the house [or] fix supper." "Because an infant is so demanding, there are days when one wished the baby did not exist." "My baby is a new individual in my life whom I love dearly, but . . . I am finding it difficult to cope with boredom and lack of intellectual stimulation in my life. (Some suggestions that have helped new mothers cope are listed in the box on *Opinions and Experiences.*)

Like the mother who "loved her baby dearly but," most parents soon come to view the new arrival with mixed emotions. They feel exhilarated and fulfilled. At the same time they are surprised and pained by the difficulties and disruptions to their usual schedules. They miss the leisure hours they had previously spent together, and they have trouble adjusting to their new life as parents rather than just husband and wife. The changes and demands may shake their confidence and self-esteem (Cowan and Coie, 1978). As one study has concluded, "The arrival of a child is a happy event, but one that puts unanticipated strains on the marriage" (Campbell, 1975).

How Parents View the Advantages of Having Children

What do parents, after they have had time to adjust to the experience, find to be the good and bad of having children? The best evidence comes from a study by Lois Hoffman (1975) based on a representative sample of 2,000 wives and husbands polled by the Institute for Social Research. First the advantages: The study found that four were mentioned far more frequently than any others. Listed in order, with the percentage of parents who spoke of them, they were as follows:

Primary group ties and affection, 63 percent Included in this category were all parents who gave responses indicating "that children satisfied their desire for love and the feeling of being in a family." To put this another way, the husbands and wives found that children enhanced the important function of marriage and the family, mentioned in Chapter 2, as an "oasis of intimacy."

Alice Randell, Photo Researchers

Two of the chief reasons nearly 80 percent of Americans want children: group affection and stimulation and fun.

Stimulation and fun, 58 percent Some of the typical comments about children in this second most frequent category were these: "They bring a liveliness to your life." "We love playing with them." "They're fun." "They're so funny." "They keep you young." "They make you forget your worries." "We love just watching them grow— it's like a built-in change so that each year is a little different from the one before."

Expansion of the self, 34 percent Included in this category were parents who felt that children provided them with a rich new learning experience, enhanced their sense of having a purpose in life, and evoked "previously untapped dimensions of personality." A number of these parents also considered children "a way of reproducing oneself, having one's characteristics reflected in another who

Opinions and Experiences

HOW THE NEW MOTHER CAN COPE

These twelve suggestions are designed to help the first-time mother adjust to the sudden change in her life.

1. The responsibilities of motherhood are learned—so get informed.
2. Seek help from husband, friends, and relatives.
3. Make friends with other child-rearing couples.
4. Don't move as soon as the baby arrives.
5. Don't overload yourself with unimportant tasks.
6. Get plenty of rest and sleep.
7. Don't be a nurse to others.
8. Don't be overconcerned about keeping up your appearance.
9. Confer and consult with others and discuss problems and worries.
10. Don't give up on your outside interests, but cut down on your responsibilities and rearrange your schedule.
11. Arrange for baby sitters early.
12. Get a family doctor early.

From B. K. Schwartz. "Easing the Adaptation to Parenthood." *Journal of Family Counseling*, 1974, 2, 32–39.

will live longer, and thus attaining a kind of immortality."

Adult status and social identity, 21 percent   The responses in this category indicated a belief by many parents, especially young wives, that "parenthood establishes a person as a truly mature, stable, and acceptable member of the community and provides access to other institutions of adult society." To many people, having a child seems to represent the final step in growing up and fulfilling one's destiny as a human being.

How Parents View the Disadvantages

Besides the advantages, parents were also asked to list the disadvantages of having children. They mentioned three problems by far the most frequently:

Loss of freedom, 51 percent   Children *do* "get in the way." They "tie parents down." Once they are on the scene, mother and father can no longer go where they please and when they please, especially not on the spur of the moment as before.

Financial costs, 42 percent   Children are a great deal more expensive than most people realize. The exact figures are difficult to calculate because prices of food, clothing, medical care, and all the other needs have a way of varying from year to year (usually in an upward direction). You can get an approximate figure by applying the Department of Agriculture's rule of thumb that a child takes 15 to 17 percent of family income. If you expect to have family earnings of $25,000 a year, you will spend about $4,000 a year on a child, or a total of $72,000 by the time the child is 19 years of age and out of high school. After that, of course, may come college, with costs that are impossible to predict.

Parental worries, 31 percent   Mentioned by the parents were concerns about the child's health, welfare, and safety—the traditional things that bother a mother and father when children are out of sight or seem to be running a fever—and about the state of our "troubled world" and the threats posed to the child's future by such problems as drugs, crime, nuclear war, and overpopulation. Some parents were also worried about their own ability to do a good job of bringing up a child.

How Parenthood's Joys and Pains Add Up

Being a parent is not entirely a bed of roses, nor entirely a bed of nails. Some parents find the advantages well worth the disadvantages. Others feel the opposite—including those who decide to remain childless. Which viewpoint a person will take depends on a complex array of individual differences in inborn characteristics and socialization.

What about the majority opinion? At one time it was generally accepted that couples who have children are less happy with their marriage, by and large, than other couples, both those who have never had a child and those whose children have grown up and left home. Many studies have found less satisfaction among couples with children (Feldman, 1971; Campbell, 1981). Very few studies have produced contrary findings. In recent years, however, there has been considerable doubt about the extent and significance of any differences between parents and nonparents.

A New View of Happiness and Dissatisfaction among Parents

One new view has been proposed by Norval Glenn and Sara McLanahan (1982), who analyzed a series of opinion polls made in the 1970s by the National Opinion Research Center. Like most previous investigators, they found that children seem to have a negative effect on marital happiness. They also found that the negative effect is apparent among parents "of both sexes and of all races, major religious preferences, educational levels, and employment status." Though the decline in happiness appears to be widespread, however, it is "rather small."

Quite possibly, Glenn and McLanahan suggested, the slightly lower level of happiness among parents has a simple explanation. Much if not all of it may be due to the fact that "the presence of a child or children deters many unhappily married persons from divorcing," at least until the children are older. Without the children, these couples might long since have parted and no longer have been included in any survey of married people.

This possibility was also mentioned by Karen Renne (1970) in her survey showing greater happiness among childless couples than parents. Unfortunately we have no evidence to show how valid it may be, because no survey has attempted the almost impossible task of identifying couples who stay married only for the sake of the children and measuring their influence on the results.

Being a Spouse *and* Parent Takes Time and Energy

Another possibility suggested by Glenn and McLanahan (1982) is that today's attitudes toward self-fulfillment may cause some people to be especially disturbed by the responsibilities of parenthood. In our present American society, they point out, "values are highly individualistic and hedonistic" and marriage is expected to be the partners' chief "source of companionship," providing "a high degree of emotional and sexual intimacy." Thus the roles that husband or wife are expected to play toward each other may be "in some respects inconsistent" with the role of parent, or at least "the demands made on time and energy by the two roles" may be too strenuous for some people.

Some support for this last suggestion comes from a small but exceptionally detailed study by Sharon Houseknecht (1979a), who surveyed fifty wives who were childless by choice and fifty mothers carefully matched in every other respect. Like Glenn and McLanahan, she found a difference— though only a small one—between the two groups. She also found that the difference seemed to be due largely to only one of the factors that indicate happiness in marriage. The mothers reported less "cohesion" in the marriage; that is, they less frequently exchanged stimulating ideas, engaged in outside interests, or worked together on joint projects with their husbands. There were no significant differences between the two groups in satisfaction with such other matters as expressions of affection and sexual relations.

The Bright Side of Parenthood

Regardless of how parents compare with the childless, or why, there is no doubt that having children has its rewards. Some convincing evidence comes from a public opinion poll of the late 1970s (Yankelovich, Skelly, and White, 1977b). In this large and representative sample of American parents of children under 13 years of age, 90 percent reported that the family was "doing well."

Among the satisfactions reported by the parents were the way the family members worked together (by 80 percent), the way they had managed to handle the problems in their life (79 percent), the time spent with the family (73 percent), and the fun and enjoyment provided by family life (73 percent). By and large the parents were confident in their role, with 63 percent reporting that they felt good about the way they were handling the job of bringing up the children and only 36 percent saying they were worried.

From a long list of specific matters that might cause worry, the subjects were asked to name the ones they had found troublesome. Among those most frequently named were giving in to children too often (by 37 percent), too much violence on television (34 percent), too much junk food (33 percent), and not being able to spend enough time with the children (32 percent). This last problem was especially common among working mothers (41 percent compared with only 19 percent of stay-at-home mothers).

Even couples who had specific worries, however, were apparently happy about the decision to become parents. An overwhelming 90 percent of all the subjects said they would again have children if they had their life to live over. Even among the single parents in the sample, faced with bringing up the children alone, 73 percent said they would do it again. These figures may be inflated by the fact that people have a tendency to answer polls in a way that justifies their actions; nonetheless, 90 percent of all parents and 73 percent of single parents are impressive numbers.

The Special Case of the One-child Family

Some couples make a compromise between childlessness and all-out parenthood by having only one child. Such couples are only a small minority, about 13 percent (Bureau of the Census, 1984a). One reason seems to be that the "only child" has long been thought of as spoiled, selfish, unsociable, and neurotic (Fenton, 1928). It was found years ago that many parents have their second child not so much out of real desire as in the belief that they "must have a second to save the first" (Solomon, Clare, and Westoff, 1956). One recent national survey found that 67 percent of people think being an only child is a disadvantage (Blake, 1981). Another survey showed that fewer than 2 percent think one child is the ideal number (Davis, 1983).

When only children are asked how *they* feel, they report a number of disadvantages. In one such study, the two chief problems mentioned were "not getting to experience a brother or sister relationship" and pressure to succeed: "I'm glad my parents are interested in what I do, but I often wish they had another kid to think about so they would get off my back once in a while." Ninety-eight percent of the subjects also thought there were many advantages: "I was never compared to a brother or sister." "My life was more private than if I had siblings—I had my own room." "I got most of the things I wanted, like band instruments." "The one-child family is a small deck, which makes it hard to get lost in the shuffle" (Hawke and Knox, 1978).

The opinions are many, but the facts are few. For one thing, being an only child or part of a larger family is just one of a myriad of factors that can affect happiness, psychological well-being, self-esteem, and success. For another, only children grow up in many different kinds of homes, with parents who have differing reasons for limiting family size. Researchers who have attempted various types of studies are virtually unanimous in agreeing there is no reason to "believe that only children, as a whole, differ to any substantial degree . . . in any way which

would generally be considered undesirable. . . . If reluctance to have an only child is based primarily on fear that he or she will be unusually likely to become a maladjusted and unhappy adult, we believe that the best available evidence indicates that the reluctance is ill-founded" (Glenn and Hoppe, 1984).

The Special Problems of One-Parent Families

There is one group of parents who face even more than the ordinary difficulties: the women and men who are bringing up children alone, usually as the result of divorce. Around the start of this decade nearly 6 million single mothers and over 700,000 single fathers were raising children under the age of 18 (Bureau of the Census, 1982). These figures are expected to increase substantially by 1990.

Virtually all the single fathers and most of the single mothers are full-time jobholders as well as parents, and they have no partner to

Ken Karp

A woman bringing up children alone may "face special and sometimes debilitating problems—but she also has her satisfactions.

help them meet the demands and responsibilities of the two roles. They have to find somebody to take care of the children during their working hours or else pay the high fees of a day-care center. If their children are of school age, they cannot stay away from work to be available during school vacations (Harriman, 1982). They often feel socially isolated and lonely (Schlesinger, 1980). Eventually most of them meet a prospective new partner and enter a dating or getting-together period, thus adding still another role to their already overburdened life.

Single mothers, especially those with children of preschool age, "face special and sometimes debilitating problems." One of the most common is severe financial pressure. Their median family income is less than half that of married couples with children, and for more than 3 million it is below the figure set by the government as the poverty level (Bureau of the Census, 1985).

Do You Want a Girl Baby or a Boy?

Many studies have shown that couples approaching parenthood for the first time have an overwhelming preference for a boy. Then, if they have a second child, they want a girl (Fidell, Hoffman, and Keith-Spiegel, 1979). Until recently they could only hope. Now techniques have been developed that can deliver a boy or girl baby to order—not always, but about 75 percent of the time.

The new techniques are based on the fact that male sperm cells with a Y chromosome, which will produce a boy if they fertilize the mother's egg cell, differ in several ways from sperm cells with the X chromosome that produces a girl. They are slightly heavier, are stronger swimmers, and have a different electrical potential. These characteristics make it possible for laboratory technicians to separate a sample of the father's semen into two parts, one with mostly Y cells and the other with mostly X cells, that can then be used to artificially inseminate the mother.

What would happen if large numbers of people took advantage of the techniques and started controlling the sex of their babies? Some social scientists find the possibility frightening. By creating a society with more males than females, it could seriously upset the balance that now exists. Even if it did nothing more than lead to a preponderance of two-child families in which a male was the first born and a female the second, it could place women in the inferior position of "chosen to be second" and "institutionalize a big brother, little sister relationship" (Steinbacher, 1984).

The question is how many couples would go to the trouble of using the techniques, especially for the firstborn. One survey of 2,000 couples who had asked laboratories for information about the techniques found that almost all of them already had two children or more, all or mostly of one sex, and wanted to have one more of the opposite sex to complete the family (Chico, 1985). Perhaps the new methods will be used mostly to create a balance in individual families, not an imbalance in society.

THE GROWING PAINS OF MIDDLE AGE

As parents or as childless couples, married people eventually begin, in their mid 40s, to spend about two decades of life in the bittersweet period of middle age. Aside from what happens in marriage, these middle years bring their share of problems to all of us as individuals (as indeed do all periods of life). One scholar has compared middle age to the lobster's shedding of its shell—a time of great vulnerability to pain and destruction, though also an essential stage in growth

(LeShan, 1973). Some observers have found it a period of turmoil and unhappiness and others have regarded it as a blissful opportunity, as shown by the sharply contrasting quotations in the box on *Opinions and Experiences.*

One problem is declining physical vigor and health, likely to be experienced by most people and especially by men. The middle-aged man, more than his wife, is subject to heart disease, ulcers, cancer, and many other complaints "ranging from baldness to prostate trouble" (Berland, 1970). Even people who escape any symptoms of their own note that some of their friends and former classmates are dying, and so "illness and death become more personal" (Kerckhoff, 1976).

Job Problems, Boredom, and Divorce

Husband and wife alike, if both work outside the home, often find that their job has come to a dead end. They have progressed as far as they can. Middle-class workers who have attained some kind of managerial position find that younger people are getting the promotions and passing them up. They begin to question their ability to compete and suffer what has been called "career discontent" (Tarnowieski, 1975). Many of them give serious thought to moving elsewhere, even to a new type of work, and some of them actually do.

Men in blue-collar jobs have perhaps even more serious difficulties: "They find their jobs unsatisfying, and they have nowhere to go with their problems. They have less information about the options open to them," and even if they had the knowledge, they would still lack "the financial or educational resources" to grasp the opportunities (Farrell, 1975).

The middle-aged may also feel trapped between job and marriage: "The world of work and the world of the family have different and competing expectations, and it often seems impossible to meet the demands of both realms." People sometimes feel "squeezed, pressured, disappointed, exploited, and exhausted" (Kerckhoff, 1976). They may also complain of boredom with the monotony of both a job and a marriage that have become routine, and sometimes the result is a middle-age divorce. About 85,000 divorces a year are granted to couples who were married for twenty years or more.

The Bright Side

Though middle age is a critical and difficult period of adjustment, it has its advantages. LeShan (1973) has called it a "wonderful crisis." Many studies, both old and new, have found that people in midlife can discover new and unexpected satisfactions. They often describe themselves as "no longer 'driven' but as now the 'driver'—in short, 'in command' " (Neugarten, 1968). For men the advancing years and decline in aggression and competitiveness can mean "regaining lost and hitherto undeveloped capacities for relating, enjoying, and knowing" (Gutmann, 1975). For both sexes the years can mean a keener appreciation of life and of each other. A public opinion poll of women in the 1970s found that those over fifty reported the most trouble-free marriages. Indeed 42 percent of them "could think of absolutely no subject of controversy" in their relationship, compared with 24 percent of wives in their 20s, 22 percent in their 30s, and 26 percent in their 40s (Roper, 1974).

One study found that the love partners feel toward each other, far from declining, actually increases in middle age. The older people in this survey expressed many highly romantic notions: They believed in "love at first sight" and agreed that "love comes but

Opinions and Experiences

THE PRO AND CON OF MIDDLE AGE

Two opposing views of the quality of life in the middle years—optimistic and pessimistic—are eloquently presented in these quotations.

Youth is a silly, vapid state;
Old age with fears and ills is rife;
This simple boon I beg of Fate—
A thousand years of Middle Life.

Carolyn Wells, 1900 from *Idle Idylls*, Dodd, Mead & Company

[In the middle-aged man] the hormone production is dropping, the head is balding, the sexual vigor is diminishing, the stress is unending, the children are leaving, the parents are dying, the job horizons are narrowing, the friends are having their first heart attacks, the past floats by in a fog of hopes not realized, opportunities not grasped, women not bedded, potentials not fulfilled, and the future is a confrontation with one's own mortality.

M. W. Lear, Is There a Male Menopause? Copyright © 1973 by the New York *Times* Company. Reprinted by permission.

[The challenges of middle age] are the greatest opportunity one has ever had to become most truly alive and oneself. If ever there is to be a moment that belongs to us, it is now, in our middle years. . . .

"Middlescence" is the opportunity for going on with the identity crisis of the first adolescence. It is our second chance to find out what it really means to "do your own thing," to sing your own song, to be deeply and truly yourself. It is a time for finding *one's own* truths at last, and thereby to become free to discover one's own identity.

Eda LeShan, from *The Wonderful Crisis of Middle Age*, 1974, Warner Paperback

If you are between 35 and 55 years old, you may belong to the *caught generation*—caught in between the demands of youth and expectations of the elderly. The respect you were taught to give your parents may have been denied to you by your children. . . . As a child you were taught to be seen and not heard; now as a parent you may feel you are to be neither seen nor heard.

From Clark Vincent, Prerequisites for Marital and Sexual Communication. E. A. Powers and M. W. Lees, eds., *Process in Relationship*, 2nd ed., 1976 Reprinted by permission of the author.

once in a lifetime" and that "a loveless marriage is tragic" (Knox, 1970). It may be that the all-consuming love of the young is replaced by a more placid kind of affection and companionship, but even this change may increase satisfaction with the midlife relationship. LeShan (1973) has observed:

One of the most valuable attributes of marriage is that one's partner can truly be one's best friend, and friendship was never more important. If one defines a friend as someone who loves you in spite of knowing your faults and weaknesses, and has ever better dreams for your fulfillment than you have yourself, it can surely be the foundation for what each of us needs most in middle age—permission to continue to quest for one's own identity.

Getting Along without Children or Youth

Recent studies have shown that the empty nest no longer holds terrors for wives born since 1940 (Borland, 1982). These women are far less dependent than previous generations on their children, and if anything they thrive after the last child has left home. One study found that empty-nest wives were happier than those of similar age who still had children present, with 48 percent calling themselves "very happy" and most of the others "pretty happy" (Glenn, 1975b).

As Richard Kerckhoff (1976) has concluded, middle-aged people have "a lot going for them." He points out:

> The middle years can be a time of recognition of our value, not just a time of doubt about our worth. They can be for many a time of reassessment, of withdrawal from energy-consuming activities to which we were never really committed, and of focus on those things in life which we now feel sure are worthwhile. There is some room for contemplation and for feelings of satisfaction in the lives of middle-aged people—time for learning from past experiences, for taking stock and for finding perspective. Middle-aged people, studies indicate, may feel squeezed by being in the middle, but they may, in addition, feel their own importance. They often know that they are the nation's decision-makers; they set the tone for life in this society. Society depends on middle-aged people's leadership and productivity. . . . It is not so much what happens to us in middle age as it is what we do with what happens to us; that's what counts. We all experience some kind of crisis in this as in other ages—but how do we use the crisis?

MARRIAGE AND THE ELDERLY

Old age, like adolescence, is in a sense an invention of modern society. True, throughout history there have always been some people, born with unusually rugged bodies, who lived for many decades, but not until the discovery of modern techniques of sanitation and medicine did large numbers survive into their 50s and 60s and longer. Now nearly, 26 million Americans—15 percent of the adult population—are 65 or over, and the number is increasing (Bureau of the Census, 1984b).

Like middle age, old age is difficult to define. It is often thought of as beginning at 65, which until recently was the customary retirement age. Many people, however, still think of themselves as in the prime of life at 65, and the age at which an employer can force retirement has been raised to 70. When elderly people are asked when old age starts, they often say 80 (Starr and Weiner, 1981).

The way people age, and how they feel about it, shows a wide range of individual differences. Some look and feel old while still in their 50s, and others are still hale, hearty, and active in their 80s. Inherited physical traits probably account for most of these differences, and lifelong patterns of nutrition and other factors that affect health for the rest.

Can You Be Happy Though Old?

In some societies, particularly in the Orient, the elderly are held in high regard and even venerated, but in today's United States old age has a bad name. Younger people await it with a certain amount of dread, considering it to be a period of loneliness, depression, outmoded ideas, forgetfulness, and senility. Even physicians often hold these views and tend to brush aside complaints of physical problems that could be successfully treated if taken seriously (Goodstein, 1981). The elderly themselves sometimes fall for the propaganda and create their own problems through a futile attempt to look and act young.

In actual fact, as has been shown in a number of studies, old people are by and large reasonably happy, cheerful, optimistic, and self-reliant. One of the first large-scale surveys, of 70,000 elderly in all parts of the nation, found that fully 87 percent were thoroughly satisfied with their circumstances and lifestyle (Neugarten and Weinstein, 1964). Far from feeling isolated, older people seem to be less troubled by loneliness than the young, with only 13 percent of them complaining of this problem compared with 65 percent of younger people (Harris, 1975). Those who have arrived at old age clearly find it quite the opposite of what young people expect it to be.

The elderly who remain in good health, without the chronic ailments and decline in eyesight and hearing that sometimes result from aging, are especially likely to be happy (Quinn, 1983). Even those with physical problems tend to be content with life if they feel they are still useful to a spouse who is in similar condition (Pollock, 1980). Income is also important, and by and large older people are better off financially than is generally believed, thanks to Social Security, savings, and often help from children (Harris, 1975).

The Golden Years of Marriage

Of the Americans 65 and over, about 14 million are married and living with their spouse (Bureau of the Census, 1984a). In general these are the most fortunate of the elderly. They are better adjusted, in better health, and less likely to feel lonely than the others (Falk, Falk, and Tomashevich, 1981). The death rate among them is lower (Atchley, 1972).

What about the quality of marriage in old age? Perhaps the best evidence comes from a study of 400 wives and husbands made in the 1970s. Of these elderly spouses, 45 percent called themselves very happy, 50 percent happy, and only 3 percent unhappy. About 53 percent said that the marriage had improved with the advancing years, and 55 percent that it was now happier than it had ever been before. Asked to name the most troublesome aspect of the relationship, 36 percent could think of nothing at all (Stinnett, Carter, and Montgomery, 1972).

Subsequent studies have also shown that older people generally consider the marriage to be just as happy as when they were younger, or even more so (Foster, 1982). Elderly couples tend to communicate better and feel more intimate and committed (Lingren et al., 1982). They feel they have acquired the important ability to provide companionship and understanding (Zube, 1982). Their sexual life may decline in frequency and intensity; but if they enjoy general good health, it can endure into the 80s and beyond (Masters and Johnson, 1966). The elderly wife quoted in the box on *Opinions and Experiences* is by no means unusual.

Most elderly couples live near at least one of their children and make frequent visits, and they often give or receive help or do both (Shanas, 1980). Of the 70 percent who are grandparents, many find this a new source of joy, in some ways better than being a parent because the responsibilities are less urgent (Robertson, 1977). Strangely, however, many studies have demonstrated that elderly people's emotional well-being and satisfaction with life are not affected much if at all by their relationships with children and other relatives (Lee and Ellithorpe, 1982). The explanation may be that elderly couples are generally so self-sufficient and pleased with their life together that they do not need support from others.

Opinions and Experiences

A WIFE WHO FOUND OLD AGE LESS TERRIFYING THAN ADVERTISED

A woman in her 70s describes a pleasant surprise that the years have brought to her and her marriage.

My husband and I dreaded getting old. Both of us were born when our parents were well into their 30s, and they seemed aged and infirm when we were still in our early middle years. They were in poor health, for one thing; and I suppose their aches and pains made them cranky and difficult to be around. They seemed to lose all concern for the world around them, including us and our children; and we found it almost impossible to maintain any common interests or communication.

For many years we helped support them and pay for the physicians and hospitals they needed. My husband, though he was our sole wage earner, never complained; but it was a terrible financial burden at a time when he was just really getting started toward any kind of success. This was in the days before Medicare and all the other government help that's available now, and the bills kept us poor and left us saddled with debts that it took a long time to repay. As we ourselves started to think about getting old, our first thought was the terrible fear that we might wind up needing that kind of help from *our* children.

We also thought of old age—probably all young people do—as a time when all affection and sexual passion had cooled and a husband and wife would no longer feel any trace of the love that brought them together. We expected to be no more than two people who happened to live in the same house, on friendly terms if we were lucky, but as enemies if we too grew cranky and difficult. We actually talked seriously, when we were in our 50s, about saving ourselves and our kids from pain and sorrow by committing suicide at 65.

Well—thank goodness!—it hasn't been like that at all. We're both in pretty good health. Our spirits, if not our bodies, haven't withered but blossomed. We're smarter and happier than we ever were, and we've learned to take joy in all the little pleasures of life that we never even noticed when we were younger. Like reading the morning newspaper, I mean. Or watching a rainstorm or a bird outside the window. Or eating a meal as simple as an apple and cheese.

We may have developed a few crochets, but our kids don't seem to find us cranky or difficult. We make frequent visits back and forth and always have a great time, and we're friends with their friends as well. We don't *feel* old or out of place when we're around them, and nobody seems troubled by any generation gap.

Above all, my husband and I love each other more than we ever did before. We've found that it takes time to develop true understanding and intimacy of body, mind, and soul. We don't make love as often or feverishly as when young, of course, but we enjoy it a lot more. When we started, we were both shy and unsure of ourselves. Now we have confidence in ourselves and each other. We know all our little quirks, and we relish them. My husband is not only my lover but also my best friend—and I'm his.

The Problem of Retirement

People of all ages have problems, of course, and the elderly are no exception. One survey found that only about half of them considered their health good to excellent, and only 40 percent were free from financial worries (Pollock, 1980). Although younger people also complain of physical ailments and money problems, the elderly are clearly worse off on both counts. Good to excellent health, for example, is reported by about 87

Nancy Durrell McKenna

Grandparenthood: a new source of joy that is in some ways better than being a parent.

Ken Karp, Sirovich Senior Center

The retirement years: one of life's most difficult adjustments, but not without its pleasures.

percent of the population as a whole (Department of Health, Education, and Welfare, 1978).

Another common and serious problem is retirement from the job world—the abrupt shift from what may have been a half century of life in the well-defined role of worker and wage earner, enjoying the company and regard of colleagues, to the totally new and vague role of a leisured person without duties, schedules, pay, workplace companions, or visible accomplishments. Retirement is a wrenching experience that brings many changes and produces a great deal of stress (Goodstein, 1981). It has been called the most difficult adjustment that the older family will ever face (Atchley, 1977).

The number of retired people has grown rapidly along with increased life expectancy, and it will rise still further in the future. So will the length of time that most people can expect to spend in retirement—in many cases, to as much as a fourth of a lifetime (Kovar, 1980). So, along with the increase in the employment of women, will the number of "dual-retired" couples (Keith and Brubaker, 1979) in which husband and wife will have to make the transition from workplace to leisure at about the same time. Women, it appears, may find retirement even more stressful than men. A study of retired teachers and telephone workers found that the women tended to feel lonelier and more depressed than the men and took longer to adapt to the change (Atchley, 1976).

In the past, the traditional sex roles into which most women and men were socialized, and the fact that most women were housewife-mothers, made retirement especially difficult. The husband was used to being away from home all day and establishing his self-esteem as the family's provider. The wife was used to her own daily routine—and gaining her own satisfactions—in running the household. On retirement the husband found himself at home throughout the day and sorely in need of some way to feel useful. Wives often feared that the husband, with time heavy on his hands, would intrude into their domain (Fengler, 1975), and indeed this frequently happened. One study found that

men tend not to understand that their wives have a personal life organized around the central fact that men are not there during the week days; and many women accordingly find it difficult to incorporate a masculine presence around the house for more than the accustomed times. One wife is reported as saying, "I married him for better or worse—but not for lunch."

(Rapoport and Rapoport, 1975b)

In today's more androgynous times, this burden on the retirement years appears to be easing. Recent studies have shown that older women, by and large, do not feel particularly possessive about their household domain (Keith and Powers, 1979). Often, indeed, they welcome their husband's participation (Hill and Dorfman, 1982). The more androgynous view may well be "associated with greater happiness and higher morale among older couples" (Keith and Brubaker, 1979).

The Cruel Blow of Widowhood

Unfortunately, the marriage that prospers into old age, surmounting the problems of retirement and achieving greater happiness than ever before, must inevitably end in sadness when one of the partners dies. Since women live seven years longer than men, on the average, usually it is the wife who survives and faces the new crisis of widowhood. There are now about 11 million widows in our nation, most of them elderly. Indeed half of all women over 65 are widows (Bureau of the Census, 1984a).

Psychologists have long recognized that the death of a spouse is the most stressful of all possible events (Holmes and Rahe, 1967). Newly widowed women usually face many other problems besides their grief. They must find new friends and activities, and often they find themselves short of money and are forced to move to less expensive housing. Thus they "must forge a total emotional, financial, and social reorganization of their lives, at a time when their resources for such a task are generally inadequate" (Hiltz, 1978). Note the large number of new widows who reported the problems listed in Table 10-1, problems that persisted even a year later.

During the shock stage immediately after the husband's death, many widows "tend to

withdraw from reality; they are characterized by an unresponsiveness to human relationships and may even be hostile to well-meaning attempts to help." They display an almost childlike dependence and desire "to have someone take care of them." If their mother is still alive, they often turn to her for emotional support and nurturance. The mother can be especially helpful, during this crisis period, if she herself is a widow and has been through the same experience (Bankoff, 1983). Indeed, any widow, whether a relative or not, may become the best source of comfort (Silverman and Cooperband, 1975).*

Some time after the initial shock has subsided, widows then enter a difficult transition period when they face "the task of rebuilding their lives as single rather than as married persons." The widow "now needs assistance in returning to a normal social life" (Bankoff, 1983). She must "establish new role relationships if her life is to be a satisfying one" (Hiltz, 1978).

She is unlikely to retain close ties to the friends and relatives who were part of the social life she shared with her husband and instead turns for support and intimacy to new people, especially women who are also widows or otherwise single. Indeed close relationships to old married friends and relatives can be a handicap in making new acquaintances and establishing a new lifestyle (Walker, MacBride, and Vachon, 1977), which is an arduous task at best.

Many widows continue to suffer feelings of social isolation and loneliness. Yet in large numbers they manage somehow to "develop

---

Table 10-1
The Widow's Problems

	Following husband's death	One year later
Emotional upset	80	68
Managing finances	68	51
Friends	53	49
Finding a job	49	39
Relations with family	39	32
Living quarters	32	31

The six difficulties most often reported by women whose husbands have died are listed here in order of the percentages of widows who named them shortly after the death. The final column shows the percentages who continued to have the problem a year later (R. Hiltz, *Widowhood: A Roleless Role, Marriage and Family Review*, 1978, 1, pp. 1-10. NY: Haworth Press).

---

*Help for the newly widowed, from women who have been through the experience, is offered by the Widowed Persons Service of the American Association of Retired Persons. Information can be obtained by writing to WPS-AARP, 1909 K Street NW, Washington, D.C., 20049. The service is available to widowers as well as widows.

satisfactory friendships, weather the transition period, and solve its problems creatively." The women most likely to achieve a successful adjustment "tend to have a higher education, a comfortable income, and the physical and psychic energy needed to initiate change" (Lopata, 1972b), a fact that gives college women a great advantage in this difficult period.

The Plight of the Widowed Man

There are of course widowers as well as widows, but not nearly so many—not quite 2 million. Like widows, most of them are elderly. Since there are about ten times as many widows as widowers of 65 and over, the widowers have a far better chance of remarrying, and many of them do. Those who do not seem to experience even more problems and stress than the nation's widows and to be much less successful at making any kind of satisfactory adjustment.

One dramatic indication of the widower's unhappy lot comes from a study of the death rate among 4,000 Maryland residents who became widows or widowers in the 1960s and 1970s. For the widows, the rate was only slightly higher than for other women carefully matched in age, race, education, and other factors that might affect health. For the widowers, however, it was shockingly higher. Among those aged 55 to 64, for example, it was 61 percent greater than in a similar group of married men (Helsing, Szklo, and Comstock, 1981). The researchers concluded that women are "more resistant to the stress of widowhood," apparently "more adaptable" and with a greater "sense of survivability."

Remarriage was found to produce a sharp increase in the widowers' chances of survival. Among those 55 to 64, for example, the death rate was only half as high for those who remarried as for those who did not—a statistic that may remind you of Jessie Barnard's statement that marriage is such a blessing to men that they "can hardly live without it." Moving into a retirement or nursing home had the opposite effect, tripling or even quadrupling the death rate.

An interesting sidelight to the Maryland study was the surprising finding that the effects of a spouse's death on the health of the survivor became apparent only with the passage of time. It is popularly believed that many widows and widowers die of grief and quickly follow their spouse to the grave, but the study produced no evidence that this is true. To the small degree that the death rate rose among widows, and to the considerable extent that it was higher among widowers, the effects showed up only over the long term. The researchers concluded that it is not the immediate shock of grief but the continued "stressful life situation of the widowed that seems hard on people."

Being a forlorn widow or widower, often for many long years, is an unfortunate ending to marriage. It is the price we must pay for the blessings of today's long lifetime and the companionship and intimacy of a good marriage.

SUMMARY

1. Traditional marriages tended to show "corrosion" as time went on, with the partners having fewer shared interests, beliefs, and values, and less likely to display affection and feel a sense of companionship. Middle-aged couples seldom found much satisfaction in their relationship and many were seriously dissatisfied.

2. The masculine man, as he encountered the beginnings of physical decline and stagnation or boredom at his job, was likely to question his achievements and deplore the inadequacy of his

family relationships. His macho standards made it difficult for him to talk to his wife about his difficulties.

3. The feminine woman, who had devoted herself to caring for the children, found it difficult to adjust to the "empty nest" period after the children had grown up and left home.

4. Both partners found themselves puzzled by the midlife reversal common in people who have played the traditional sex roles, which is for men to become less aggressive and competitive and take on some of the feminine characteristics and for women to become less dependent and submissive and display masculine characteristics.

5. Companionship marriages fare much better in middle age. Studies show that the happiest couples in midlife are those who have treated each other as equals, with mutual respect and understanding, and have sought to accommodate each other's wishes rather than fight for their own way.

6. The most momentous event in most marriages is the birth of a child, which brings new and often unexpected pleasures, duties, worries, and satisfactions. Childless couples are more common now than in the past, but it is estimated that 75 to 80 percent of today's young women will become parents.

7. Parenthood creates complex and sweeping changes in a couple's lifestyle and the roles the partners play. The parents usually come to view the new arrival with mixed emotions. They feel exhilarated and fulfilled, but they are pained by the demands of parenthood and the disruptions to their usual schedules, and they miss the leisure hours they formerly spent together.

8. The advantages of parenthood mentioned most often by mothers and fathers are (a) an increased sense of family ties and affection, (b) the stimulation and fun provided by children, (c) a sense of having a new purpose in life and new dimensions of personality, and (d) the feeling that parenthood is the final step in growing up and fulfilling one's destiny as a human being.

9. The disadvantages mentioned most often by parents are (a) loss of freedom, (b) financial costs, (c) and worries about the child's health, welfare, and safety.

10. To most parents, the advantages seem to prevail. Polls have shown that 90 percent of them report that the family is "doing well," also that 90 percent say they would have children again if they had their life to live over. Even among single parents, faced with the job of bringing up the children without a partner, 73 percent say they would do it again.

11. There are now nearly 6 million single mothers with children under 18 in the United States, and nearly 700,000 single fathers. They face many problems because they have to find some way of caring for the children while they are at work, and they are so constantly busy with the double responsibilities of job and parenthood that they often feel socially isolated and lonely. Single mothers in particular "face special and sometimes debilitating problems," one of which is financial pressure. Their median income is less than half that of married couples with children, and for many of them it is under the poverty level.

12. Middle age, which begins in the mid-40s and lasts about two decades, is a critical and difficult period of adjustment to declining physical vigor and jobs that have become dead-end or boring. Yet many people find that it is a "wonderful crisis" that brings a keener appreciation of life and the marriage relationship. A poll has shown that women over 50 are the most likely to report satisfactory and trouble-free marriages.

13. Old age is usually thought of as starting at 65. Increased life expectancy has raised the number of people over 65 to 26 million.

14. Although old age is popularly considered a period of loneliness, outmoded ideas, and forgetfulness, the fact is that old people are less likely to feel lonely than the young, and 87 percent of them are thoroughly satisfied with their circumstances and lifestyle. They are by and large better off financially than generally believed.

15. The 14 million elderly who are married and living with their spouse are better adjusted, in better health, and less likely to feel lonely than

the others; and their death rate is lower. A majority of them say their marriage has improved with age and is happier than ever before.

16. Retirement is the most difficult event the older family must face, and it seems to be harder on working women than on men. It is easier now than in traditional marriage, where the husband gained much of his satisfaction and self-esteem from being the provider and the wife feared that when he was home all day he would intrude into her domain of running the household.

17. Over half of all women over 65 are widows, who must cope with not only grief but in many cases "a total emotional, financial, and social reorganization of their lives." Most widows, however, eventually manage to deal with the difficult transition, make new friends, and establish a successful new lifestyle.

18. The nearly 2 million widowers experience considerably more problems and stress than widows and are less successful at adjusting. Their death rate is extremely high unless they remarry.

DISCUSSION QUESTIONS

1. Do you see a "corrosion" of many marriages that have lasted for twenty years and more? What indications have you observed?

2. Why do you think that companionship marriages fare better over time than traditional marriages?

3. What are the pros and cons of parenthood for you? What is your ideal family size?

4. What are the potential advantages and disadvantages of growing up as an "only child"?

5. Discuss the problems and the joys that middle-aged people you know are experiencing.

6. At what age do you plan on retirement from work? Why?

CHAPTER 11

The Fine Art of Parenthood

Being a parent, if you don't watch out, can make you a nervous wreck. A newborn seems such a frail and helpless creature—barely able to move, powerless to feed itself or speak its needs, at the total mercy of the adults around it. A conscientious mother and father are bound to feel an almost awesome sense of responsibility for this tiny package of humanity they have brought into a world it can hardly begin to comprehend.

In the United States today mothers and fathers worry more than most parents seem to have done in the past. A majority of them—including two-thirds of college-educated people—are convinced that how they treat a child will largely determine its future (Roper, 1974). They feel fully responsible for whether the child grows into a healthy, happy, successful adult or a neurotic and troubled misfit.

They have read about diets and the hazards of chemical additives in food products, and they worry about what to feed the infant. Later they worry about providing emotional security, intellectual stimulation, how to avoid being too strict or too lax in discipline, and above all how to avoid mistakes that, once committed, will forever doom the child to some kind of crippling psychological complex. In one study of a group of parents with above-average education, only 9 percent said they never worried (Geboy, 1981).

FICTION AND FACT ABOUT FORMULAS FOR PARENTS

Countless generations of parents, in societies all over the world, lived their lives without ever hearing about most of the matters that trouble today's college-educated parents. It was generally believed that a child would grow up just as nature intended, regardless of what parents did or did not do. The future lay in the hands of the gods or the mysterious workings of heredity.

It was the seventeenth-century philosopher John Locke who started heaping the burden of worry on parents with his bold declaration that the mind of the newborn was a *tabula rasa,* a "blank tablet" on which anything can be written through learning and experience. The modern science of psychology, in theories it generally accepted until recently, enlarged on Locke's idea and put the writing tool for the tabula rasa clearly in the hands of the parents. John Watson, founder of the influential behaviorist school of psychology, declared that he could take any dozen babies at birth and by controlling their "conditioning" turn them into anything he wished—doctor, lawyer, beggar, or thief. His theories implied that parents also controlled the future of their children, by intention or by accident.

Psychoanalysis, at least in the way it was generally perceived, added to the burden. Parents, it seemed, were responsible in one way or another for all the psychological ills that can trouble humanity, from inferiority complexes through sexual "fixations" and all the way to horrible mental disturbances like schizophrenia. In the many books and plays about unhappy people that were influenced by psychoanalysis, the problem always went back to some kind of unwholesome relationship with the mother, father, or both—or to that well-publicized event a *traumatic incident,* a single, searing psychological experience that left a festering lifetime scar.

A Nation of "Experts" on Children

During the long months of pregnancy, the mother-to-be is fed an unending diet of advice intended to relieve her worries. Her friends with children tell her in detail how they got marvelous results by feeding their growing child nothing but high-protein foods (or carbohydrates or nothing but fruit and nuts), cured restless sleeping by putting the child on a rigid bedtime schedule (or letting it sleep whenever it wished), cured thumb sucking by putting the hands in mittens the moment the sucking began (or simply waited for the habit to disappear of its own accord). They relate convincing stories of the tactics that induced their child to walk and talk at remarkably early ages, a toilet-training method that made diapers obsolete by the second birthday, a guaranteed cure for colic or the sniffles.

Parents, grandparents, and in-laws all join the well-meaning panel of "experts." So do kindly matrons met at the supermarket counter and neighbors up and down the street—even those whose own children are notoriously ill behaved and destructive. If the mother- and father-to-be want to supplement all this advice they can buy or borrow a book—any one of scores of books available in shops and on library shelves, some written by scholars who have devoted years of study to child development, others by professional writers who have never so much as held a baby in their arms.

The Trouble with the Advice

Some of the books are both helpful and reassuring. The best known is *Dr. Spock's Baby and Child Care,* which was first published in 1946, has been revised and reprinted many times since, and has sold more than 30 million copies. It begins with the comforting words "You know more than you think you do" and contains considerable useful guidance on the child's physical and emotional welfare, including advice on distinguishing between symptoms of illness that demand the care of a pediatrician from those that look much more serious than they are (Spock and Rothenberg, 1985).

A study of parents of above-average education showed that about two-thirds had read Spock's book. In all, 85 percent of the parents had read one book or another, and usually several books. About 97 percent had read magazine articles, often a half dozen or more (Geboy, 1981).

Unfortunately many of the opinions urged on parents-to-be by some of the books and articles and most relatives and friends have one basic flaw. They may have succeeded with one particular baby, but they will not necessarily work on all children. Any generalities about child care are much like advice on how to have a happy marriage or a glorious sex life, in that they ignore the wide range of individual differences among the people of the world. Even babies lying helpless in the crib display a vast variety of characteristics. They are already *individuals,* with their own widely varying preferences, temperaments, and needs. What makes one flourish may make another wither.

No one has ever discovered a sure-fire formula for bringing up a child. Jerome Kagan, a psychologist who has devoted many years to studying the development of children, has summarized his basic finding in these words:

> Children do not require any specific actions from adults to develop optimally. There is no good evidence that children must have a certain amount or schedule of cuddling, kissing, spanking, holding, or deprivation of privileges to become gratified and productive adults.
>
> *(Kagan, 1976)*

The Best Advice: Don't Worry So Much

Evidence for Kagan's statement comes from the diversity of ways to bring up children practiced around the world. Do babies need a great deal of physical contact with their parents? They certainly get it in some of Guatemala's Indian tribes, where they are held by an adult for more than six hours a day. But they get little of it in parts of the Netherlands, where they are held only at feeding time and spend the rest of the day alone in their room, tied down to a bed (Rebelsky, 1967). Most college-educated parents in the United States talk a lot to children and try to explain what they are doing. But in some Norwegian farm areas a mother whose 4-year-old is blocking her path simply picks up the child and moves it, without a word of explanation (Baldwin, 1976).

So it goes from one society to the next. Some societies assume, like most American parents, that children are rational creatures who thrive on affection and sympathy, others that children are little wild animals who must be taught to control their instincts. Some encourage children to assert their rights, but others frown on the slightest display of aggressive behavior (Briggs, 1970).

It might seem logical to believe that if one of these methods produces good results, then the opposite method must be wrong and harmful. Yet the children of all these societies, when examined later on, are remarkably alike (Kagan, 1976). By any measure of emotional health or intellectual performance, there are no apparent differences among 12-year-olds in Guatemala, the Netherlands, rural Norway, or the American suburbs.

The message for parents is comforting. No need to become a nervous wreck. You need not worry about finding, listening to, and heeding advice. *Nobody* knows any right way to bring up a child. True, there are some practices that will probably help, but they are simply common-sense procedures that most parents already follow. There is no magic formula that guarantees success, and nothing so clearly harmful as a traumatic incident that will doom you to dismal failure. Often, indeed, an event that parents fear may have been traumatic passes unnoticed by the child.

BABIES AT BIRTH: ALL DIFFERENT, BUT ALL DURABLE

Babies in the crib, though they may seem pathetically helpless, have a remarkable ability to adjust to the world, adapt to what it offers them, survive, and flourish. They are much tougher—rubbery, resilient, and capable of bouncing back from physical and psychological adversity—than they look.

A deprived childhood, of course, seriously hampers normal development, and at one time it was generally believed to produce lasting emotional problems. A number of cases have been reported, however, in which children who suffered extreme neglect and mistreatment managed to shake off the experience, once they were in a more benign environment, and seemed to recover completely.

One example was reported by a psychologist in Czechoslovakia, where 6-year-old twin boys were found living in the cruelest of circumstances. Their psychopathic mother and mentally retarded stepfather had confined them all their lives in a closet of the cellar. Nobody in the family was permitted to talk to them, and they lived in a dim world of silence and total isolation except for each other's company.

When they were found, looking like normal children just half their age, they appeared hopelessly retarded—barely able to walk or talk, so poorly developed mentally that it was impossible to test their intelligence. Yet they began to show improvement as soon as they were moved to a favorable environment. Five years later they had about average IQs and seemed to be normal in emotional and social development (Koluchova, 1972). Clearly children can sometimes overcome the most wretched early experiences.

Cheerful, Cranky, Patient, and Irritable Babies

Even newborns are aware of the world and capable of responding. Just a few hours after birth they can see well enough to follow a moving object with their eyes. They soon recognize the difference between a sweet taste and a sour or bitter one, and their sense of smell is so keen that they can distinguish their own mother's milk from any other (Werner and Lipsitt, 1981). In response to the environment they close their eyes as protection against light and pull away from a sharp object that hurts the sole of the foot.

They quickly display their individual differences. Some are especially sensitive to sights and sounds and show signs of distress at the slightest noise or a light that is only moderately bright. Some will adapt very quickly to noise or light and quit crying, and others are slow to adapt. Some are much more active than others. They move their arms and legs with considerable force and are big and vigorous eaters. Later on they are likely to bang their toys around, kick at the sides of the crib, and babble in loud tones. Some are unusually irritable. They are easily provoked to whine or cry and often have temper tantrums. Others are more patient and get upset less easily.

"Easy," "Slow-to-warm-up," and "Difficult" Babies

Perhaps the most striking difference of all is in what might be called temperament. Note the remarkable difference between the two babies in Figure 11–1, the girl in the top row of photos and the boy in the bottom row. The two children are a sister and brother born several years apart, photographed when both were 3 months old and having their first experience with a new kind of cereal. The girl seemed to welcome the new experience. The boy fought it off.

The girl was what is called an "easy" child—cheerful, quick to accept new foods and schedules, and inclined to regularity in habits of sleeping and eating. The boy was a "difficult" child—unfriendly, hard to please, easily upset by new experiences, erratic about sleeping and eating, and likely to cry a lot and have temper tantrums. A group

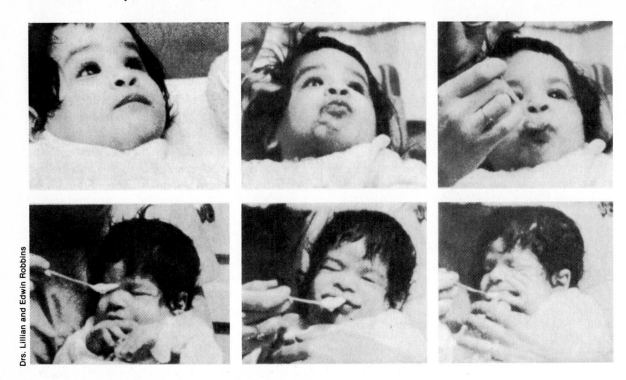

Drs. Lillian and Edwin Robbins

Figure 11–1
SISTER AND BROTHER—A CONTRAST IN TEMPERAMENT
These babies, sister and brother, were photographed when both were
3 months old and being introduced to a new kind of cereal. The difference
in their reaction and the reason for it are explained in the text.

of investigators of children's temperaments found that 40 percent of the newborn are easy babies and 10 percent are difficult (Thomas, Chess, and Birch, 1970).

A third group found by the investigators was the "slow-to-warm-up," who are less cheerful than easy babies but not nearly so negative as the difficult. Their first reaction to any change is to withdraw, and they need time to adjust. Their eating and sleeping habits tend to be irregular. About 15 percent of the newborn were in this group, leaving 35 percent who showed a mixture of the three types of temperament.

Parents who believe that all babies are alike and should be treated alike can get into real trouble, especially when, as in the case of the sister and brother shown in Figure 11–1, a first and easy child is followed by a difficult second child. The methods that worked beautifully on the first prove a frustrating failure with the other, because a difficult child simply does not react in the same way as an easy child. Indeed, children of all three types of temperament, the investigators concluded, really need very different treatment as infants and through the early years of school.

Easy children flourish as infants under any kind of care, but they adapt so quickly and well to the home environment that they often have trouble adjusting to the new demands of a schoolroom and teacher. The slow-to-warm-up, who shy from new experiences, need parents who are willing to be patient. They have to adjust at their own pace and will only back away more stubbornly if put under pressure.

Even more patience and a good deal of tolerance are demanded of the parents of difficult children. These youngsters are a thorny problem to everyone around them, in the home and later the school. Any attempt to force them into good behavior will only make them act worse. It takes them a long time to learn to obey rules and get along with other people, and there is no way to make the process go faster or less painfully.

An Encouraging Word for Troubled Parents: Time Is on Your Side

Although babies in the crib display many differences in temperament and other characteristics, they have one thing in common. Fortunately for parents who have difficult children or other problems, all babies change—often rapidly and to a spectacular degree. Easy, slow-to-warm-up, and difficult babies are very different in the cradle, but they seem much the same by the time they are 6 to 10 years of age. Many other traits displayed in early childhood disappear even faster.

One study of such characteristics as irritability, readiness to smile, activity level, and ability to pay attention found no significant relationship at all between children's behavior in their first year and at the age of 27 months. Some children had changed to an almost unbelievable degree. One boy, as an infant, seemed deeply troubled; he kept rocking his body and sucking on his arm. Two years later this habit was gone and he seemed perfectly normal (Kagan, 1971).

About the only early trait that seems likely to persist is shyness in children under 3, which has been found likely to continue throughout childhood and adolescence (Kagan, 1983).

Parents find it discouraging when a young child seems irritable, boisterous, or unable to pay attention. Often they are provoked into criticism and punishment. Yet it is very difficult to predict, from behavior in the early years, what a child will be like in elementary school, much less as an adolescent or adult. Inattentive babies often learn to concentrate and become excellent students. Noisy babies quiet down, and stubborn ones become more reasonable. Even those who seem to show signs of emotional problems may turn out to be perfectly normal.

With babies, time can cure a lot of ills. Perhaps the best advice to parents is to keep in mind that babies show many individual differences, but all of them thrive on warmth and love. If you can stay optimistic and manage to tolerate obnoxious behavior for a while, you will usually find your patience rewarded.

WHAT BABIES NEED WHILE BODY AND BRAIN MATURE

Within the tiny body of the newborn are all the physical and nervous structures ever needed to become a strong and intelligent adult. They need time to develop, however, and in the meanwhile the child depends on the adults in its world, usually the parents, for survival.

A baby lying on its belly in the crib cannot even lift its head. All the muscle fibers needed for any kind of movement are present, but they are only one-fortieth of their eventual size and weight, and they must grow and get stronger. It takes about two months for the baby to lift its chin from the bed, about six months to sit up in a high chair, about fifteen months to walk without help.

The skeleton at birth is mostly cartilage, softer and more pliable than bone, which only gradually hardens. The skull has gaps called fontanels that will close as the cartilage turns to bone and grows. The most noticeable of the fontanels, in the middle of the top of the head, is a tender spot where a blow is especially likely to cause damage to the immature brain. Indeed, the brain is vulnerable to any harsh jarring because it has not yet developed the supporting tissues and fluids that will eventually hold it firmly inside the skull.

The Rapid Growth of Mental Skills

The brain at birth contains most of the 10 billion nerve cells of full maturity (Greenough, 1982), but it weighs only about eleven ounces, less than a quarter of the three pounds it will eventually reach. Its growth is due chiefly to the development of new branches on the individual cells, which spread out, like a growing tree, and form connections with other cells. This branching out, rapid in the early years, slower thereafter, enables the cells to receive nervous messages from hundreds and sometimes thousands of other brain cells, with which it eventually becomes elaborately connected and interconnected.

As the brain grows and its interconnections multiply and become more efficient, the baby's mental powers increase at a dazzling rate. Children a month old can already recognize a word they hear often, but they will forget if a single day goes by without repetition of the word. Three months later

they can remember the word for a week or more.

By the time they are 6 months old they are aware of the difference between a toy seen now and a toy seen just previously. By the age of 1 they can remember where they have seen someone hide a toy. Often they are beginning to imitate actions, like dialing a phone, that they have seen their parents perform (Kagan, 1981a). Early in the second year they seem mentally ready to use language, though actual speech must wait until the age of 18 months to 2 years, when their vocal cords have matured enough to produce the words the brain orders (Bonvillian, Orlansky, and Novack, 1983).

Pushing the Child to Perform: Is It Wise?

Parents often try to speed up the maturation process, for both physical and mental skills. They work hard to persuade the baby to talk and later to write and recognize written words. They buy tricycles and junior-sized baseball bats and push the child to use them. But the development of the brain cells and muscle fibers cannot be hastened to any appreciable degree.

Mild encouragement sometimes helps to some extent. For example, infants whose parents talk to them a great deal often begin to speak well before others whose parents seldom bother. But deliberate and forceful attempts to push children beyond their level can only do harm (McGraw, 1943). Youngsters may get nervous and afraid of failure or soured on activities they would otherwise learn to enjoy.

Similarly, there is no need to worry if a child is slower to walk or talk than a previous baby, a neighbor's child, or the averages listed in books. Some children are just naturally slower than others to develop some of the skills. Unless there is something seriously wrong with the body or nervous system (as a pediatrician can readily determine), they eventually catch up. A child who is barely saying a word by the second birthday may be chattering a blue streak just a month or two later when the vocal cords are ready.

Being slow to mature in any respect is not necessarily a sign of below-average intelligence. In fact, no relationship whatever has been found between the way children behave when as old as 27 months and their scores on reading and intelligence tests when they reach 10 (Kagan, Lapidus, and Moore, 1978).

One Thing That May Help: An Enriched Environment

There is one exception to the general rule that maturation cannot be hastened. The growth and branching of the brain cells appear to be stimulated by learning, and therefore by objects and experiences that encourage curiosity and experimentation. Some examples that parents can supply for the baby in the crib are rattles that it can push or try to grasp, mobiles that it can watch and later try to move, or stuffed animals to be held in the arms—anything, in the crib and early childhood, that helps create an enriched, or varied, environment.

Like most of what is believed to be true of the human brain, the suggestion that learning opportunities stimulate growth of the brain cells comes indirectly, from experiments with animals. In one study a group of rats was raised from birth in ordinary cages, bare except for water and food dishes, and another group in cages that provided an enriched environment with various kinds of visual stimuli and toys. Examination after

death showed that animals from the enriched cages had heavier brains (Bennett et al., 1964). Another study showed that encouraging animals to learn resulted in a greater number of branches on the brain cells, indicating that the cells had formed more connections with other parts of the brain (Greenough, 1976).

Presumably what was true of these laboratory animals is also true of human babies. Thus it appears that development of the child's brain—and mental skills—is encouraged by a varied environment containing toys and other objects that can be pushed, shaken, rolled, hammered into holes, molded or built into new shapes, colored or scrawled on, ridden, or climbed on. For most parents this is not a problem requiring any special attention because most homes, particularly middle-class homes, provide ample variety without any thought to the branches on brain cells.

Absence of early stimulation is by no means fatal anyway, because the growth of new brain connections continues throughout life and the child can catch up later. The Netherlands children who spend most of their infancy bound in a bassinet have no mobiles or toys and experience almost no stimulation at all. Yet by the age of 5 they seem as bright as 5-year-old Americans. The real danger for many parents is just the opposite—that they will push the child by offering too much stimulation too soon. One study has concluded that

> presenting stimulation can be very frustrating and discouraging for the baby who is still unprepared to handle it. . . . Ideally, stimulation should challenge babies to reach just beyond their present level, but it should not demand something the child is not yet capable of. Supplying a 6-month-old with a violin to fondle is not going to

influence the child's musical skills—but the same "enrichment" at age 5 might make a big difference.*

(Segal and Segal, 1984)

THE CHILD'S EARLY MONTHS: THE IMPORTANCE OF ATTACHMENT TO AN ADULT

During the early months of life the baby matures rapidly from an inert package of tissue, lying helpless and almost motionless, into an active, thinking little human being. By 18 months babies can sit up, grasp things with their hands, stand, walk, and climb stairs. They can remember objects and what these objects can be used for, and they already understand the meaning of words that have frequently been spoken to them. Some of them have begun to speak a little. They imitate actions they have witnessed, and in their play they are capable of make-believe, like "feeding" a doll with a spoonful of sand.

So much has happened. So many skills have developed; so much has been learned. The miracle of growth still has a long way to go, but never again will it race forward with such dazzling speed.

Erikson's Stage of Trust versus Mistrust

Erik Erikson (1963), a psychoanalyst, has proposed that our entire lifetime, starting at birth, is a long series of stages in "psychosocial development." At each stage, he holds, development is pushed forward by a sort of dual thrust exerted by the changing human personality and society. That is to

say, our personality and the way we view ourself change along with the changing social relationships we form.

At each stage, the first of which occurs in the first year of life, we face a new social situation and thus a new set of problems, or what Erikson calls a "psychosocial crisis" that demands adjustment and growth. If we surmount the crisis we move along to the next stage equipped with greater maturity and new dimensions of personality. If we fail, our development is distorted or stopped.

The first crisis is what Erikson terms "trust versus mistrust." The favorable outcome is for the infant to develop faith in the environment and the future. The unfavorable outcome is suspicion and fear of future events. How the crisis will turn out is influenced strongly by what seems to be an inborn tendency of human babies to form a close relationship with the adult or adults who take care of them. Child experts call this *attachment* to the person on whom they depend for care, comfort, and security.

If all goes well, attachment meets the needs of babies for such essentials as food, water, warmth, and cleanliness; and it provides a safe and cozy haven that protects them against danger and distress. From it they can acquire trust in the world and the people in it and faith in what the future will bring. They develop confidence and optimism. If the security is denied them, or if their needs are met in only haphazard and unpredictable fashion, they can become cynical about the world and fearful and pessimistic toward the future.

Attachment and Courage to Explore

Even animals seem to be born with a tendency to attachment. Indeed, much of the emphasis placed on it by experts in child care

---

*Segal, J. and Z. Segal, *Growing Up Smart and Happy.* Copyright © 1984 McGraw-Hill Book Co. Reproduced by permission of the publisher.

has been influenced by studies Harry F. Harlow (1961) made years ago with newborn monkeys that he took from their mothers and moved in with the strange-looking figures shown in Figure 11-2, which he called "surrogate mothers."

One "mother," made of wire, was equipped with a bottle and nipple from which the baby could feed. The other was made of sponge rubber and covered with terrycloth, serving no purpose, but offering a soft and inviting place to cling. As is apparent in the photographs, the baby monkeys developed a strong sense of attachment to the terrycloth mother, to which they clung even while sucking on the wire mother's bottle of food.

Note particularly the photograph at the right in Figure 11-2. Here an unfamiliar object, just visible at the left edge of the photo, has been placed in the cage. The baby monkey, both curious and fearful, is making its first hesitant attempt to discover, by feeling with its foot, what this strange and at first frightening object may be. While gathering courage for this daring exploration, it stays close to the safety of its terrycloth mother.

A Start toward Becoming Self-Sufficient

Human babies also seem to need the security of attachment to begin exploring the world around them—an important first step to becoming self-sufficient and outgrowing total dependence on the caretaker. One study of child behavior arranged to place babies just under a year old and their mothers in an unfamiliar room containing a chair piled high with attractive toys. As long as the mother

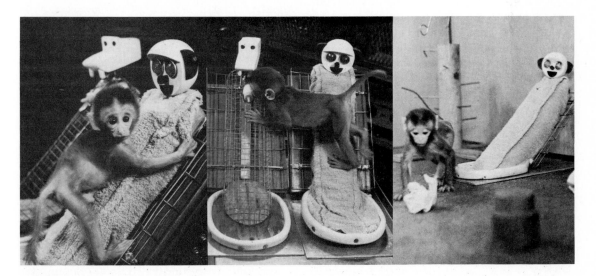

Figure 11-2
BABY MONKEY AND "SURROGATE MOTHERS"
The monkey in a cage with two mechanical figures serving as its substitute mother shows a clear preference for the soft, terrycloth one to which it can cling (left). Indeed it maintains its hold even while leaning over for the food provided by the wire figure (middle) and stays close while tentatively exploring the strange new object that has been placed in the cage (right). Left and Right: Courtesy of Harry S. Harlow, University of Wisconsin Primate Laboratory. Middle: University of Wisconsin Primate Laboratory.

was in the room, the baby took a good look at the toys, then approached them, and finally began touching them. If the mother left, the baby stopped exploring the toys (Ainsworth and Bell, 1970).

The relationship between attachment, exploration, and eventually standing on one's own two feet has been summarized in these comments:

> Babies who enjoy a solid relationship with the mother eventually feel more free to move out into the world, playing and exploring more independently—confident that Mom will be there, cheering from the sidelines and waiting for the prodigal's return. Children securely attached to their mothers as infants turn out to be more enthusiastic, persistent, and generally more competent than those who are not. . . . If the father plays an active role in caring for and teaching the child, he can help create the early bonds that have traditionally been reserved only for the mother. . . . How much and how well fathers interact with their infants can significantly affect the child's intellectual progress.
>
> *(Segal and Segal, 1984)*

The father's potential contribution has also been described in these words:

> Compared to children who are reared only by their mothers, preschoolers who also have attentive fathers tend to have a more positive self-concept, to feel better about being a boy or a girl, to get along better with other children and adults, and to function more effectively in achievement-oriented situations.
>
> *(Elkind and Weiner, 1978)*

The way one father established attachment with a baby—to the delight of both of them—is described in the box on *Opinions and Experiences,* which suggests a little game that any parent might try.

Teri Leigh Stratford

A toddler exploring the world: a first step toward becoming self-sufficient.

What Babies Seem to Need Most

During the burst of growth and development in the first year or so of life, the needs of babies are relatively simple. They require care and nurturance, as has been said, and an opportunity to satisfy their inborn tendency to become attached to the caretaker. For most rapid mental development they need "environmental variety that can be assimilated with moderate effort," though too much variety, like any attempt to push them into too much accomplishment too soon can "frighten the child and provoke withdrawal and inhibition" (Kagan, 1976).

They need the opportunity to practice their growing ability to use their muscles to

Opinions and Experiences

PLAYING "BUMPTY-BUMP" WITH AN 8-WEEK-OLD

An ingenious father discovers a way to delight his baby girl.

One father tried a game with his 8-week-old daughter. The infant sat on the father's knee while he held her hands and arms securely in his hands. Then, with a relatively expressionless face, he waited and waited and waited, until the little girl eventually sighed. Instantly, he bounced her gently on his knee, gave a broad smile, and said "Bumpty-bump." Then his face went blank, and he waited again, until his daughter produced another vocalization to which he responded in precisely the same way.

On the first day the game lasted for ten minutes, and the baby sighed and gurgled only three times. The next day, the pace quickened, and by the third day the 8-weeker was a veritable chatterbox. But the most important thing was that father and daughter literally fell in love with one another. In fact, when the father came home from work after a week of such games,

all he had to do was lean over the crib and his little girl would coo and smile at him. It made the mother rather mad, because she was spending her entire days caring for the infant but the father was getting all the smiles.

There are many lessons in this example. First, the father responded immediately to one particular behavior of the child—vocalizing. A swift response was necessary for the child to associate the father's behavior with her own vocalization. Next, the father made himself and his response as distinctive as possible. The blank face helped make the "bumpty-bumps" stand out; they were not lost in a stream of conversation and other facial expressions. And bouncing, smiling, and talking are behaviors babies "understand." Moreover, the father responded consistently, every time the infant vocalized. Finally, less than ten minutes a day for a few days was all that was required for that father and infant to become attached to one another.

From Robert B. McCall, *Infants*. Cambridge, Mass: Harvard University Press, 1980. Reprinted by permission.

crawl, walk, and manipulate objects with their hands. They gain both competence and emotional satisfaction from moving around, banging at mobiles, shaking rattles, cuddling stuffed animals, and playing with blocks. They also need what Kagan (1976) calls "regularity of experience"—not necessarily a rigid schedule but one that is reasonably predictable, because even by the age of 6 months babies establish cycles of activity, sleeping, and eating in accordance with the pattern they have come to expect. When "these expectations are not realized, anxiety grows and can disturb major aspects of functioning."

How to Foster Attachment and Security

Parents can probably provide the best possible atmosphere for the newborn's development not by following any set formula that is supposed to work with all children but by "listening" to what this particular infant is trying to tell them about its own individual requirements and desires. To a parent who is alert to the baby's behavior and tries to understand and adjust to it, a child has many ways of communicating: its facial expressions, the way it whimpers, cries, or gurgles. How an effective mother responds, as contrasted to treatment by a less skillful or attentive person, is described in the box titled *Being a good mother to the young child.*

A mother who has to divide her time between the baby and a job need not be any less helpful during this period than if she spent the entire day at home. The formation of close and affectionate emotional ties does not require twenty-four-hour-a-day devotion, as is explained in the box titled *How attachment and love grow.* A father busy at work all day can share in helping the baby flourish, provided he devotes some affectionate attention during his time at home.

In general, fathers are not nearly such unconcerned and remote figures as is often believed. McCall (1980) has said:

> Research shows that the birth of a child has a strong emotional impact on most fathers. . . . Moreover, when fathers are observed in the newborn nursery in the absence of the mother, they immediately perform both maternal and paternal caretaking duties quite naturally and competently. Babies in the first year will choose to go to their fathers just as often, and sometimes even more frequently, as to their mothers. . . . Fathers are not disinterested, incompetent, or unimportant.

THE PRESCHOOL YEARS: BECOMING A MEMBER OF SOCIETY

Toward the end of the second year, children encounter a totally new experience. They leave the confines of the crib, walk around the home, and start to become members of the community. For the first time they learn that life is not entirely geared to indulging and pleasing them. Instead it sets rules, which they must now learn to follow.

In the home they can now explore so energetically they find numerous articles that at first look like fascinating toys but in fact are not to be touched. Lamps are not made to be knocked over. Fragile dishes are not for dashing to pieces on the floor. Knives may look to 2-year-olds like new objects to be grasped and shaken, and electric cords like an invitation to chew; but they are dangerous and forbidden by the rules.

Eventually children face what is initially the most burdensome rule of all, which decrees that the elimination drive must be satisfied only in the bathroom and that they cannot always respond immediately to its bodily sensations. They encounter the strange new demands of toilet training. In all these ways they must learn, sometimes smoothly and sometimes only after a struggle, to become disciplined members of society.

The Parents' Dilemma and a Way to Resolve It

To parents the child's first brushes with discipline can be a difficult period. They are called on to walk a tightrope between jeopardizing the child's safety and sense of responsibility (if they are too lax in enforcing the rules) and repressing and inhibiting development (if they are too strict).

Many parents, with the best of intentions, are overprotective. Children of 2 and 3 still seem so small, vulnerable, and unaware of the world's dangers that it is all too easy to feel obliged to keep a constant wary watch over their every move, fear that every new activity will be dangerous, and thus keep youngsters "tied to the apron strings." Parents may also be tempted to be too rigid about their own standards of neatness and get upset when children make a mess, get their clothes dirty, or smudge the furniture with greasy fingers.

Opinions and Experiences

BEING A GOOD MOTHER TO THE YOUNG CHILD

A group of experts on parent-child relationships describes the basic difference between effective and ineffective mothering.

The sensitive mother is able to see things from her baby's point of view. She is tuned-in to receive her baby's signals; she interprets them correctly, and she responds to them promptly and appropriately. Although she nearly always gives the baby what he seems to want, when she does not she is tactful in acknowledging his communication and in offering an acceptable alternative. She makes her responses [in accordance with] the baby's signals and communications. The sensitive mother, by definition, cannot be rejecting, interfering, or ignoring.

The insensitive mother, on the other hand, gears her interventions and initiations of interactions almost exclusively in terms of her own wishes, moods, and activities. She tends either to distort the implications of her baby's communications, interpreting them in the light of her wishes or defenses, or not to respond to them at all.

From M. D. S. Ainsworth, S. M. Bell, and D. J. Stayton. Individual differences in strange-situation behavior of 1-year-olds. In H. R. Schaffer (ed.), *The origins of human social relations.* New York: Academic Press, 1971.

Parents who are overprotective or overneat, unfortunately, are likely to infect their children with their own anxieties. They are bound to show their concern, if not through punishment then in indirect ways of expressing disapproval. The children's fear of disapproval may inhibit attempts to try anything new and make them pull back from all the challenges that life presents.

The best formula for parents is to be permissive without being lax. The most successful parents know they have to put a stop to exploration that can lead the child to danger or destructiveness. They call a halt only when necessary, and they encourage other new activities that can safely promote a growing sense of control over the environment. Their children are likely to learn quickly that curiosity and experimentation are generally approved, and only some activities are forbidden. They are off to a good start to becoming confident and self-sufficient members of society.

Discipline, Reward, and "Inner Standards"

In learning the rules, children of 2 and 3 are influenced in part by reward and punishment. Their successes at toilet training bring them praise and a hug. Backing off when starting to reach for a knife and being told "no!" is rewarded with an approving smile. They may be punished, physically or with clear expressions of disapproval, when they knock over a lamp or start down a forbidden stairway.

Perhaps much more influential than reward and punishment is the fact that children begin, around the age of 2, to develop their own self-generated desire to do the right thing. Psychologists say they have acquired

Opinions and Experiences

HOW ATTACHMENT AND LOVE GROW

A psychologist describes the secret—and joy—of establishing a close relationship with the young child.

Whereas it once was thought that love grew out of the feeding situation, we now know this is not the case. Infants develop attachments with their fathers, who typically do not feed them or may not even spend a great deal of time with them. Children also develop attachments with the grandparents, who may not live in the same home or town.

Attachment appears to be based not on the amount of time spent with children but on how that time is spent. A sensitive, responsive relationship between parent and infant is especially important, one in which parents make their responses contingent to their infant's actions and respect their infant's desire to influence and control the social situation. This may take only a few minutes a day. But it does require some concentrated, undivided attention, and a few minutes of "infant-only" time may be worth hours of the casual time spent with the baby nearby. Special games may take place at any time—during and after feeding or changing, when the father gets home, or just when baby or parents feel like it. The most important sign that such games are going well is that parents and infant are having a good time.

Our notions of motherhood and fatherhood are changing. Care and feeding are necessary tasks, but they are not the materials of which love between parent and infant is made. Rather, infants and parents become attached to one another when they play, when one responds to the other in appropriate and consistent ways, when one allows the other to lead as well as follow, and when a parent takes time to care, to guide, and to share.

It is not so much the amount of time spent with the infant; it is the nature of what happens during this time that is important in causing love between parent and child, fostering the child's development, and creating the joy and fulfillment that can accompany family life.

"inner standards" and the desire to live up to these standards, which is regarded as one of the most powerful of human motives. They become aware that their behavior will be judged by the other people around them, and they very much want the judgment to be favorable. In other words, they sense what is expected of them and they expect it of themselves:

Children begin to set their own internal standards. They now begin to comprehend whether or not they can accomplish something, and so they set goals for themselves.

A smile of delight crosses their faces as they triumphantly fit the last piece of the puzzle into place. Or they may frown and cry if they are unable to fit the blocks into the right holes. At the end of the second year, children have a remarkable understanding of their conduct and their abilities—and the way these may or may not live up not only to what others expect of them but to their own standards of doing the right thing.

(Segal and Segal, 1984)

The ability to distinguish between right and wrong and the desire to live up to inner standards appear to develop even before children have learned to become concerned about possible punishment, and it seems to be an even more powerful influence on their behavior. Indeed, excessive punishment, instead of leading children to avoid dangerous or destructive actions, may actually succeed only in making them afraid of trying *anything* and thus interfere with the development of self-sufficiency and self-esteem.

What Children Need Most in the Preschool Years

To Erikson (1963) the psychosocial crisis of the second year in the child's life is "autonomy versus doubt." If all goes well, the outcome is a sense of self-control and adequacy. If not, the result is a feeling of shame and self-doubt. Children who have coped successfully with the crisis are confident that they can live up to their inner standards of behavior and competence and will meet society's expectations and gain its esteem. Children who have failed are unsure of their standards and dubious of their ability to meet them.

To acquire confidence, children need help in distinguishing between what is right and what is wrong. Their parents' expectations, which become their own inner standards, must be consistent from day to day. As Kagan (1976) has pointed out, small children cannot deal successfully with the confusion "produced by being punished for fighting on Monday but jokingly teased for the same violation on Wednesday." They also need further practice at exercising their growing physical and mental skills; and when they have developed to the point where they can talk, they need exposure to language as spoken by adults: "Evidence indicates that all children need is exposure—no special tutoring, books, television programs, or radio. The simple experience of hearing people talking—especially to them—seems sufficient."

Another important need is "actions, gestures, and communication" that clearly tell children they possess "virtue, value, and worth." Unfortunately it is difficult to suggest ways for parents to convey this message, or to define any specific actions that may make a child feel rejected instead of loved and esteemed. The children in Norway who seem ignored by their mothers do not show any signs of suffering from rejection. Nor necessarily do children elsewhere who receive little physical affection or get slapped across the face for being late to the table at meal time:

> Evaluation of a parent as rejecting or accepting cannot be answered by noting the parent's behavior, for rejection is not a fixed quality of behavior. Like pleasure, pain, or beauty, rejection is in the mind of the rejectee. It is a belief held by the child, not an action by a parent.
>
> *(Kagan, 1976)*

In sum, demonstrating to children that they are valued and esteemed, like many other aspects of human relationships, seems to be mostly a matter of attitude and spirit, on both sides.

THE WORLD OF THE SCHOOLROOM AND CLASSMATES

When children enter the first grade their parents cease to be the only significant influence on their development. Henceforth they will be more and more impressed by two important groups that have entered their life—their teachers and their classmates.

Later they will encounter many other influences—the newspapers, magazines, and

Ken Karp

Nursery school: for many children, their first encounter with an important new influence on development.

books they read, the highly varied people they meet on the college campus or at a job and are either attracted to or repelled by. They may fall into ''bad company,'' as parents like to put it, or be surrounded by ''good company.'' Their attitudes and tastes will be affected by what they see on a television or movie screen, even by the music they hear on the radio. This is why parents have far less control or responsibility for how their children ''turn out'' as adults than is generally believed.

What Schoolmates Do for the Child

Children at school begin to evaluate themselves on the basis of how their classmates regard them as well as what their parents think. Indeed their companions' opinions may seem more realistic and carry even more weight. For one thing, school pupils can make direct comparisons of their intelligence, strength, and other traits. For another, they regard the opinion of other children as more objective and honest than their parents' beliefs, and certainly easier to interpret. They can hardly avoid knowing for sure whether classmates regard them as likeable and competent or unpleasant and foolish.

The schoolmates also provide an outlet for the hostility children usually feel toward many aspects of the adult world. Around others their own age, they can freely express their hostilities, be noisy, make a mess, and do all the other things their parents forbid. Their rebelliousness is likely to gain them admiration rather than disapproval. Even if they do something that displeases the group, they do not necessarily suffer rejection. Children seem to have a system of ''idiosyncracy credits'' they grant to one another, allowing them to engage in a certain amount of unseemly behavior without losing respect (Fine, 1981).

In many ways children encourage each other to develop. They can provide examples that teach generosity and help, and they can assist in learning school work. At times they are more effective than any parents in relieving the turmoil and anxiety of growing up (Furman, Rahe, and Harrup, 1981).

The Push toward Being Dominant or Submissive

The group is also likely to have a strong influence on whether a child tends to be dominant or submissive in relation to other people—a trait that is likely to be well established by the age of 10 and often persists into adulthood. Some children develop a pattern of being leaders who actively try to influence and persuade their friends. Others become followers, passively conforming to suggestions.

Parents also play a part in dominance and submission. If they are permissive and grant full opportunity to explore and try new experiences, their children are likely to lean toward dominance. If the parents exercise strong control, and especially if they keep their offspring ''tied to their apron strings,'' their children are likely to become submissive.

The actions and opinions of classmates are even more influential. The children likeliest to become dominant are those who sense that they are admired by the others—often the largest and strongest boys and the most attractive girls. Those likeliest to become submissive are the ones who feel inferior because their classmates do not seem to have a very high opinion of them—often the smaller boys and less attractive girls.

SOME SPECIAL CONCERNS: TELEVISION, DISCIPLINE, AND TEENAGERS

Parents worry about their children at least through the high school years and sometimes long afterward. Their top concerns, it was found in one opinion poll, are giving in to their children too often, the feeling that the children are watching too much violence on television and eating too much junk food, their own insecurities about whether they are doing the right things as parents, and the problem of spending enough time with the children, all mentioned by about a third of the parents (Yankelovich, 1977a).

Another common concern, adolescence, is a difficult period both for children going through it and their parents, who may find their offspring in what appears to be violent rebellion against them and their standards just at a time when they themselves are going through a life crisis. They are becoming middle-aged and they often feel that ''the world is closing in on them,'' closing the door on their chances for a brilliant career and all their other dreams of youth (Conger, 1977). A parent-child relationship that was close and rewarding during the early years may suddenly freeze into arm's-length aloofness or flair into open hostility.

As with everything else about parenthood, there is no magic formula for relieving these concerns. The situation varies from child to child, parent to parent, and family to family. Parents can only try to understand what is happening, be aware of what child experts have found to be generally helpful in problem situations, and deal as best they can with their own children. When things are really going badly, they can console themselves with the thought that they are only one of the influences that have shaped the personalities of their children.

The Lure of Television

Many people with small children, especially when pressed for time, rely on the television set as a convenient and cost-free babysitter. Starting early in life, children are content to watch the screen for long periods of time and all the while be quiet, demand nothing else, and stay out of harm's way.

Are they really out of harm's way? An overwhelming majority of experts on child care think not, especially since watching the screen can get to be a habit for children.

On the average, children watch television for at least thirty hours a week (Moody, 1980)—more time, over the course of a year, than they spend in school. Those who spend the most hours in front of the set have often picked up the habit from parents who are "heavy watchers" (Singer and Singer, 1980). Some of what they see, like "Sesame Street," actually improves their learning skills and performance in school (Segal and Segal, 1984). There seems to be no question that children can "learn from watching television," which is "a potential force for good" (Pearl, 1982).

Television, Mayhem, and Murder

Unfortunately only a very few programs help educate children. The others, intended only to hold attention and entertain, present a staggering number of fights, beatings, stabbings, shootings, and murder. A study in the 1970s found that even kiddie cartoon shows, on the average, depicted twenty-one acts of violence an hour (Slaby, Quarforth, and McConnachie, 1976). The number appears to have remained at just about that level (Gerbner et al., 1980).

Television producers and their sponsors claim that violence is just make-believe that children never associate with real life, just as they never take seriously the idea that a talking wolf ate Little Red Riding Hood's grandmother. A good deal of evidence has piled up to the contrary.

A study of preschool children showed that heavy viewers of television violence were themselves more aggressive at play (Singer and Singer, 1980). Another study found that elementary school pupils who were heavy viewers were considered the most aggressive children in the class by the others, not only in the United States but in Finland and Poland (Eron and Houesmann, 1980). It was also found that physical aggression increased among children when television became available in their community for the first time (Granzberg and Steinbring, 1980).

A study sponsored by the National Institute of Mental Health surveyed all the available evidence and found "overwhelming" proof that television's excessive violence causes aggressive behavior. Dr. Spock (1976) has said, "I believe that parents should flatly forbid programs that go in for violence. . . . Young children can only partly distinguish between drama and reality. Parents can explain, 'It isn't right for people to hurt each other or kill each other, and I don't want you to watch them do it.'"

The Effect on Schoolwork and Diet

Just as television encourages violence, it also seems to distract children from their school work and cut down their level of performance, especially in reading. In elementary school the heavy viewers apply "much less effort" than light viewers. Sixth graders who watched less than an hour a day were found to make higher scores on various achievement tests than those watching four or more hours (Segal and Segal, 1984).

The advertising that accompanies children's television shows contributes to another of parents' common worries. A government report has noted that "almost all the choices advertised on programs aimed at children are pre-sweetened cereals, candy, and soft drinks," with a strong suggestion that this junk food is all that is "needed for a good life" (Federal Trade Commission, 1978). Children brain-washed into the notion that sugared goodies promote health may resist their parents' attempts to keep them on a more genuinely healthful diet.

The Quandary of Discipline: To Be Strict or Permissive?

Is it better to be a strict parent who sets firm rules, insists that they be followed to the letter, and punishes any infractions? Or a permissive parent who allows lots of leeway, sets as few rules as possible, and seldom or never uses any punishment even when a child misbehaves miserably?

This is a tricky question. Experts have persuasively argued both sides. Public opinion seems about equally divided. A poll found that 26 percent of parents consider themselves strict and not inclined to spare the rod, 23 percent permissive and skeptical of the effectiveness of spanking. The other 51 percent fell somewhere in the middle—neither very strict nor very lenient, or perhaps just undecided about which course is more successful (Yankelovich, Skelly, and White, 1977a).

The Split among Parents: "Traditionalists" versus "New Breed"

The pollsters concluded that parents are divided into two groups: (1) "traditionalists," who continue to accept the once-general beliefs about bringing up children under strict parental control, and (2) a "new breed," who are more permissive and exercise far less control.

The two groups differ in their lifestyle as well as their attitudes toward children. The traditionalists, numbering 57 percent, place a high value on religion, hard work, and saving money. They want their children to be successful and are prepared to make sacrifices to help. They also expect to be in full charge and to make decisions for the children. The new breed, 43 percent, are less concerned with religion, financial security, and success. They love their children but do not place the child's interests above their own. Many of them are not inclined to make any sacrifices, but at the same time they do not think the children have any future obligations to them. They do not push their children to be successful but let them make their own decisions.

The division into traditionalists and new breed seems to be another aspect of the mixture of attitudes about marriages and families that has been discussed frequently in this book, notably the preference for traditional or companionship marriage and masculine and feminine sex roles or more androgynous ones. Just as Americans today are torn between the old and new ideas on marriage styles, sex roles, and the way wife and husband should behave toward each other, so too are they pressured by conflicting opinions on whether to be strict or permissive, to spank or not to spank.

What Kind of Discipline Works Best?

To start answering the question of whether it is better to be strict or permissive, you need only take a careful look at the families you know. You will doubtless see parents who frequently yell at, slap, spank, and punish in numerous other ways—and whose children seem to be always misbehaving. Chalk one up against punishment. Doubtless you will also see parents who are patient, loving, and tolerant of anything the children choose to do—and whose children seem to grow more demanding and obnoxious by the day. Chalk one up against permissiveness.

On the other hand, you will see parents who keep strict control and have no hesitation about using punishment when it seems called for—and whose children behave beautifully and seem happy and affectionate. You will also find permissive parents who have never once punished a child—and whose children are an absolute delight, polite, thoughtful, and bubbling with joy. Score one for each side. Have the observations added up to a tie?

In a sense they have. The fact is that neither strictness nor permissiveness will necessarily work, nor will it necessarily fail. Children who feel loved and cherished can thrive under either kind of treatment; their own inner standards will impel them to behave. As Spock (1985) says, "They work hard, all by themselves, to be more grown-up and responsible." Children who feel rejected and unwanted will express their feelings by misbehaving. Neither punishment nor indulgence will make them act any better and will probably only make them worse.

Parents often repeat the pattern of their own childhood. If it was taken for granted in their family that infractions of the rules called for punishment, they too are likely to consider punishment a necessary part of teaching the rules. If they grew up in a family that managed to produce good behavior through guidance unaccompanied by punishment, they are likely to use this method. Either way, they may get good results—or bad ones.

Discipline's Happy Medium

What really creates good behavior, most child experts would agree, is neither strictness nor permissiveness, punishment nor refraining from punishment. Instead it is, as Spock (1985) says, "growing up in a loving family—being loved and learning to love in return." Punishment is "never the main factor in discipline—it's only a vigorous additional reminder that the parents feel strongly about what they say."

Being strict, even spanking at times, does no harm "so long as the parents are basically kind and so long as the children are growing up happy and friendly." It *is* harmful when the parents are "overbearing, harsh, chronically disapproving," and inconsiderate of the child's age and individuality. Being permissive works if the parents are at the same time "not afraid to be firm." It does not work if the parents never enforce any standards and let the children get away with murder. The result can only be spoiled, selfish, and basically unhappy children.

In other words, there is a happy medium between strictness and permissiveness. Finding it is another of the aspects of human relations that seem to be mostly a matter of attitude and spirit rather than specific actions.

The Crisis of Adolescence

Many people, looking back on their lives, say that adolescence was the period in which they were most confused and their morale was at its lowest. They mention such problems as striving desperately for recognition by their schoolmates, especially those of the opposite sex, being under pressure from their parents to succeed socially and scholastically, and trying to establish some kind of independence while still financially dependent on the family (Macfarlane, 1964).

Certainly adolescents, feeling suddenly grown-up and searching for their own identity, must struggle with many questions: Who am I? What am I? What do I want to do with my life? What do I believe? To what kind of work, of all the many options available in today's world, do I want to devote myself? They find themselves thinking about life's meaning, moral standards, and religion; and often they begin to doubt the values held by their parents. Some of them come to feel alienated from society—a possible explanation for the number of delinquencies and teenage suicides.

Even parents who have always had a warm and affectionate relationship with their children in earlier years experience a sudden chill. For one thing, their teenagers seem totally wrapped up in their own concerns, from their most philosophic speculations to such mundane matters as their physical appearance. Adolescents seem off in a world of their own, unconcerned about doing their chores, being reasonably polite, or even being on time. For another thing, their urge for independence may lead to open rebellion against the parents' authority and discipline.

Parents Who Have the Most Trouble—and the Least

Parents who are either extremely strict or extremely permissive have been found to have the most trouble getting along with adolescents. Those who continue to insist that their word is law and deny their suddenly grown-

Marc P. Andersen

Turning over the car keys: a ritual of adolescence.

up teenagers any right at all to make their own decisions are likely either to trigger the most bitter rebelliousness or create low self-esteem and total loss of confidence (Kandel and Lesser, 1972). Those who allow their teenagers to "do their own thing" no matter how outrageous it may be or where it may lead are likely to wind up with children who have no sense of responsibility whatever.

What if anything does work in this difficult period? The best answer seems to come from a study that examined the home backgrounds of high school students. The teenagers with the fewest problems, it was found, tended to come from very similar homes. Their mothers had fairly conservative values and were firm in enforcing rules about such matters as doing homework and getting home by a certain hour at night. They clearly expressed disapproval of drugs, lying, or stealing. At the same time they had a close and affectionate relationship with the teenagers and provided a considerable amount of support and independence (Jessor and Jessor, 1977).

Another case, one might say, of the happy medium. The most successful parents are neither overstrict nor overpermissive. Instead they are *firm*—and at the same time affectionate, understanding, respectful, reasonable, and fair.

SUMMARY

1. Of parents with above-average education, two-thirds believe that how they bring up a child will largely determine its future prospects. Only 9 percent never worry about bringing up their children. The others worry about diets, emotional security, whether to be strict or lax in discipline, and how to avoid "traumatic incidents" that might give the child a lasting psychological complex.

2. Parents are deluged with advice from relatives, friends, and experts (genuine or self-appointed) who write books and magazine articles. Much of the advice—especially if it suggests a sure-fire formula guaranteeing happy children—ignores the fact that even newborn babies are *individuals,* with their own varied characteristics and needs.

3. Children have a remarkable ability to adjust to the world and adapt to what it offers them. Child-rearing practices differ from one society to another, but they have much the same results. No specific method of treating children, whether in physical contact, displays of affection, or discipline, works best.

4. Among the individual differences displayed in the crib are variations in sensitivity to being upset by lights or noises, speed of adaptation to such matters, level of activity, and tendency to be irritable or patient.

5. Babies also display three different types of temperament:

   a. "Easy" children are cheerful, quick to accept new foods and schedules, and regular in their eating and sleeping habits. They readily adapt to almost any home environment, but they do this so well that they may have trouble later adjusting to the new demands of school.

   b. "Slow-to-warm-up" children shy at first from any change or new experience. They need time to adjust at their own pace and may back away even more stubbornly if put under pressure. They do best if their parents are willing to be patient.

   c. "Difficult" children are unfriendly, hard to please, easily upset by new experiences, and likely to cry a lot and have temper tantrums. They are a problem to their parents and later their teachers. They need time to learn to obey rules and get along with people, and any attempt to force them into better behavior will only make them act worse.

6. Time is on the parents' side because many traits displayed in the crib disappear later. Easy, slow-to-warm-up, and difficult babies all seem much alike by the time they are 6 to 10 years old. Noisy babies quiet down and stubborn ones become more reasonable. Even those who seem to show signs of emotional problems may turn out to be perfectly normal.

7. Babies at birth have all the muscle cells and nearly all the brain cells they will ever have, but these structures need time to mature. The brain will grow from eleven ounces to three pounds as the cells develop new branches that will connect and interconnect with other brain cells. The baby's mental powers increase rapidly along with this development, which apparently is encour-

aged by an enriched environment that provides opportunities to learn. Muscular development is encouraged by crawling and manipulating objects with the hands.

8. Deliberate attempts to push children beyond their level or ability, however, are harmful rather than helpful.

9. Erikson has suggested a lifetime series of stages in "psychosocial development," in each of which development is pushed forward by a mutual thrust exerted by the changing human personality and new social relationships and experiences. At each stage a new social situation creates a "psychosocial crisis" that demands adjustment and growth.

10. The psychosocial crisis of the first year of life is called "trust versus mistrust." The favorable outcome is for the infant to develop faith in the environment and the future. The unfavorable outcome is suspicion and fear of future events.

11. The first-year crisis is strongly influenced by *attachment,* the inborn tendency of babies to form a close relationship with the adult or adults who take care of them. A successful attachment to a loving and thoughtful caretaker provides a safe and cozy haven against danger and distress and a secure base from which the baby can start exploring the world.

12. Parents can help by being sensitive to the baby's needs and what it is trying to tell them and acting accordingly rather than trying to impose their own wishes and moods. Establishing a close and affectionate relationship need not be a full-time job because the way time is spent with the baby is more important than the amount.

13. In the preschool years children begin to move around and become members of the community, and for the first time they encounter discipline. They learn that life is not entirely geared to indulging and pleasing them, but that they must follow rules about destroying property, not getting into danger, and toilet training.

14. Preschool children learn discipline in part

through reward and punishment, but mostly through their own self-generated desire to do the right thing. Psychologists say they have acquired *inner standards* and the motive to live up to these standards.

15. Parents can help by providing consistent standards of what is right and what is wrong and "actions, gestures, and communication" that clearly tell children they possess "virtue, value, and worth."

16. Once they are in school, the influence of classmates and teachers becomes even more important than the parents, who will never again be in sole control.

17. Television, used by many parents to keep their children quiet, can be a dangerous baby sitter. There is clear evidence that the large amount of violence on tv, even in kiddie shows, encourages aggressive behavior; and much of the advertising is for junk foods. Moreover, children who watch a great deal apply less effort to their school work.

18. In discipline, parents are split between "traditionalists," who take full charge of children, make decisions for them, and are strict about enforcing rules, and the "new breed," who are more permissive and let children make their own decisions.

19. Both methods sometimes succeed and sometimes fail. Being strict seems to work if the parents are basically kind and loving, but not if they are distant, harsh, and constantly disapproving. Being permissive works if the parents also stand up for their own rights and are not afraid to be firm but not if they never enforce standards and let children get away with murder.

20. Adolescence is a difficult period both for the teenagers, struggling to establish their own identity, and the parents, who find their children aloof and often rebellious. It has been found that adolescents who display the fewest problems come from homes in which the mother is firm in enforcing rules about homework and curfews but

at the same time affectionate, understanding, and able to provide support and independence.

DISCUSSION QUESTIONS

1. What advice do you think your parents followed in raising you?
2. You have decided to create an "enriched environment" for your newborn. How would you do this?
3. Describe what you would do to develop your baby's sense of attachment.
4. Besides your parents, what were other powerful forces in your life as you grew up?
5. In what ways can television have negative impact on children? Did it have any negative impact on you?
6. Would you say that you are a "traditionalist" or a member of the "new breed" in your attitudes about child rearing?

CHAPTER 12

Divorce and Remarriage

About a half century ago a prominent Denver judge shocked the nation by publicly declaring himself in favor of what came to be popularly known as "trial marriage"—that is, a period in which a woman and man lived together before deciding to take out a license. If the trial did not work out, no marriage (Lindsey and Evans, 1927).

The judge never actually used the words "trial marriage" and what he advocated was considerably more formal than the term implies. The phrase got into the newspaper headlines, however, and the judge found himself generally regarded as not only eccentric but downright immoral. He suffered from being a little ahead of his time. If he were still alive he would find his once outrageous idea, even in the exaggerated form it took in the public imagination, vindicated by our society, though in a roundabout and hidden way.

Twenty million or more Americans have now been married, divorced, and married again—in some cases as many as two, three, or even more times (Spanier and Glick, 1980a). As one sociologist has pointed out, "There is nothing far-fetched about saying that what we've got in the United States—though we would never call it by its real name—is a nationwide system of trial marriage. You try being married to A for a while.

If it doesn't work out, you get a divorce and marry B" (Cumming, 1970).

Whether or not we choose to call the system trial marriage, there is no question that divorce and remarriage are a prominent part of the American scene. The divorce rate has risen rapidly throughout this century, as shown in Figure 12–1. Ever since 1975 our courts have been granting nearly 1.2 million

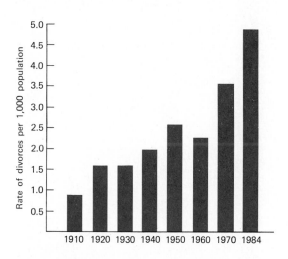

Figure 12–1
U. S. DIVORCE: UP, UP, AND UP
In this century the divorce rate has moved up by leaps and bounds—to a figure that is now more than five times higher than in 1910 (National Center for Health Statistics, 1985).

divorces a year (National Center for Health Statistics, 1985). This is a truly staggering number. If you started this chapter on a weekday when the courts are in session, you can figure that 20 divorces were granted somewhere in the nation just while you were reading up to this point. By the end of the day, around 4,000 will have taken place. Divorce has been called as big an industry as automobiles, employing a host of lawyers, judges and courtroom staff, social workers, and record keepers, plus the indirect services of all the real estate agents who provide new residences for the former wife and husband and the publishing people who produce books and magazine articles advising the divorced how to cope (Bohannon, 1985).

Although the more than 2 million who keep this industry astir are fleeing from one particular marriage, they are not necessarily fleeing from the idea of marriage in general. They may be temporarily disillusioned. They may swear never again. But what usually happens to them is illustrated by the case of the man quoted in the box on *Opinions and Experiences,* which explains why divorce and remarriage are two sides of the same coin and are discussed together in this chapter.

It should be noted that many of the facts presented here about divorce also apply to couples who live together without marriage, then eventually break up and go their separate ways. The end of any intimate relationship, whether in or out of marriage, is likely to stem from similar causes and create similar problems. Many couples who live together without marriage, when they come to a parting, find themselves faced with the same emotional turmoil and difficulties of readjustment as people who go through actual divorce. With this thought in mind, you can if you wish interpret the word *divorce* wherever it occurs in this chapter to mean the final and permanent rupture of any male-female living arrangement, or for that matter of a homosexual bond.

SOME FACTS ABOUT MODERN DIVORCE

Divorce, in the legal sense, was once not only a rarity but a scandal. A century ago the total number of divorces granted in the United States in any given year was only about 20,000. Even a half century ago the number usually ran under 200,000 a year (Jacobson, 1959). If public opinion polls had been taken in those years, they would no doubt have shown that a considerable majority of Americans opposed the very idea of divorce. The more ''respectable'' members of society spoke of it only in whispers, if at all. The man or woman who had been divorced was shunned or at least treated with suspicion.

Even as recently as 1970, a nationwide public opinion poll showed that only a bare majority of Americans—53 percent—believed that divorce was a suitable and acceptable solution for a marriage that had turned out badly. A similar poll four years later showed that the majority had grown to 60 percent (Roper, 1974). It is doubtless even higher today. Certainly great numbers of Americans—all the millions who have been through divorce—have cast the most convincing kind of ballot of all.

Divorce Now and through the Ages

Because of the rising figures—and because divorce was so rare in our nation's past—divorce is usually thought of as a new problem. It is often said to be related to industrialization, the concentration of population in big cities, and the generally impersonal

Opinions and Experiences

A DIVORCED MAN SURPRISES HIMSELF

A young man in New York talks about some of the reasons his marriage failed and the unexpected result of being divorced.

I'm not really the marrying type. I come from a family of four boys and I grew up as a man's man. I like to spend my evenings playing poker with the boys. On my days off, I like to round up a couple of other fellows and play golf or go to the races. I never danced a step in my life; I don't like the movies; and I hate parties.

Don't ask me why I ever got married. But everybody seems to do it, and I did too. My wife didn't like it much and I didn't like it at all. It went against my grain to be tied down. I like to go where I feel like, eat when I feel like it, and spend my money having fun. You can have that little house in the suburbs, with the mortgage payments and the lawn to mow.

So we broke up and my wife went to Nevada to get a divorce. When I got a letter saying the marriage was over, I spent the happiest day of my life just reading it over and over again and making plans for a glorious future on the golf course and at the race track. I felt free as a bird. How could I ever have been so foolish, I asked myself, as to tap a woman on the shoulder and say, "I like your looks, so I've decided to devote the rest of my life to you." Thank goodness that nonsense was over. Never again.

Three months and nineteen days later I got married again.

quality of modern life. But widespread divorce is far from a new invention. It has cropped up in various societies almost from the very start of history.

In ancient Greece divorce was what one social historian has called "an everyday event" (Westermarck, 1925). Indeed, Greek law decreed that a man could end his marriage whenever he pleased, simply by sending his wife and her dowry (the money and goods she brought to the marriage) back to her parents. In ancient Rome, at least among the more wealthy and prominent, it seems to have been considered bad taste to stay married to the same person too long. Among well-known Romans, Ovid was married three times, Julius Caesar and Mark Anthony four times, Pompey five times. A Roman author wrote that women were described as being not twenty or thirty years old but as being four or five marriages old. A horrified Roman journalist—somewhat like one of today's editorial writers deploring the modern statistics—complained that many marriages broke up before the wedding flowers had time to wither.

Even in the present century there have been places where marriage has been a frantic game of musical chairs. There have been well-authenticated cases of men in some Arab nations who have had more than fifty wives. In some primitive societies, at least until recently, a couple could get a divorce simply by appearing before the village elders and tearing a betel leaf in two. In such places changes in marriage partners have been known to come so thick and fast that people sometimes lost track and absent-mindedly remarried a mate they had already once divorced.

Were Our Great-grandparents Really So Faithful?

Even in the United States, the low divorce statistics of the past probably do not tell the full story. For one thing, living together without being married is not nearly so new as the couples who are doing it now like to think. Our ancestors did it too. The only difference was that they pretended to be married, though they had never been anywhere near the license bureau. The arrangement was called common-law marriage.

Our nation probably had hundreds of thousands of common-law marriages, especially in big-city slums and among the impoverished blacks on Southern farms. These marriages were never recorded. When they broke up, as they doubtless often did, they never became part of the divorce statistics.

For another thing, a husband or wife of the past could simply pack up, disappear, and start a new life somewhere else. There were no drivers' licenses, Social Security numbers, or credit cards to establish a person's identity. People could live where they wished under any name that struck their fancy. The temptation to end an unhappy marriage by moving away and becoming somebody else must have been especially strong among husbands. In all probability many thousands of them, fed up with their families and with working on the farms and in the shops of the East, quietly took off for the wide-open spaces of the frontier. The next time you see a Western movie, take a critical look at all those footloose cowboys and unattached sheriffs, shooting each other between drinks in the dance halls. If the truth were only known, how many of them do you suppose were deserters who had left an abandoned wife and broken home back east?

If desertions and break-ups of common-law marriages could be counted, we would find a good deal more divorce in the past than the official figures show, in the real if not the legal sense of divorce. Even so, the total was far lower than today's, for there has never before been a period in American history when it could be predicted that nearly half of all young couples will eventually be divorced, which is the current estimate based on Census Bureau figures (Glick, 1984).

The Strangest Fact of All about Broken Marriages

Yet the sharp rise in divorce figures conceals a startling fact about American marriage, past and present. Suppose that at the start of this year we had managed to round up 1,000 married couples whose experiences were destined to be more or less average. At the end of the year we look them up again. How many will still be married? How will this figure compare with what we would have found 25 years ago, or 50 or 100 years ago?

We would have to guess that far more of today's marriages would fall by the wayside—but we would be in for a surprise. We would find that out of the 1,000 original marriages, just about as many were still intact a year later as at any time in our nation's history (Davis, 1972).

How can this be? The answer is that the death rate has fallen during the past century just about as fast as the divorce rate has gone up. At the time of the Civil War, 32 marriages out of every 1,000 were ended each year by the death of one of the partners—often at an early age—for every marriage ended by divorce. Today this ratio has been reversed. Thus the total number of "broken marriages"—if a broken marriage is defined as one that ends for any reason—has remained about the same. In this sense marriage is just about as stable today as ever, though for different reasons.

The last two paragraphs on broken marriages, past and present, were offered chiefly as a curious sidelight; but they may account in part for today's high divorce rate. We can speculate that some couples can get along for a number of years—perhaps as many as they would have spent together in the old days before one or the other died—but not over the full range of today's lengthened life expectancy.

WHAT ARE *YOUR* CHANCES OF DIVORCE?

The various statistics, of course, do not tell us much about our own chances of divorce. Like so many other things, success in marriage depends on individual differences, and the range of individual differences is very great. Although nearly half the marriages performed today are expected to end in divorce, no given marriage has a fifty-fifty chance of proving a failure. A family expert watching two young people take their wedding vows, and knowing everything about them and their backgrounds, might estimate their particular chances of divorce at anywhere from almost zero to almost certain.

On Being "Divorce-prone"

There is a certain analogy between divorce and automobile accidents. As every insurance company knows, some accidents are unavoidable. The very best drivers may come to grief through mechanical failure, road hazards, or another driver's error. On the other hand, some drivers are accident-prone. This group includes a high proportion of young males, people who drive when drinking, and people who are just not very good drivers under the best conditions. Insurance companies take this into account by charging higher premiums for the accident-prone.

Similarly, some people are divorce-prone. The divorce rate in any given group of people has been found to vary with their personality traits, family background, education, income, age at marriage, and even where they live. If there was such a thing as insurance against divorce—which would not be a bad idea, since divorce usually causes financial problems—some couples would have to pay only a low premium, others a very high premium.

The Importance of Education and Income

The premium would be higher for blacks, since Census Bureau statistics indicate that 55 percent of today's young blacks will get divorces, compared with 49 percent of young whites (Glick, 1984). The number will be even higher for interracial marriages between a black and a white (Norton and Glick, 1976).

Whatever your race, however, your own premium would be reduced by the fact that you are a college student, because the number of people who get divorced goes down as educational level goes up. The prediction for college graduates is only about 40 percent, compared with well over 50 percent for people who never went to college. The number is especially high among dropouts from either high school or college (Spanier and Glick, 1981).

Another important factor in determining the risk of divorce is income. For men the figures are striking: There are three times as many divorces among people in the lowest income brackets as among those above the comfort level (Glick and Norton, 1971). Obviously a man's risk of divorce goes down dramatically as his ability as a breadwinner goes up. For women, on the other hand, the situation is just the opposite. Working wives who have jobs at the highest income and professional levels have unusually high divorce rates (Norton and Glick, 1976). We can speculate that this is because they are more independent economically and psychologically than the average, or perhaps many husbands find it difficult to be married to a highly successful woman.

Getting Married too Young

Early marriage is a serious hazard. Women who marry before the age of 18 are three times more likely to get divorced than women who wait until they are at least 20. Those who marry at 18 or 19 have a 50 percent higher failure rate. For men, those who marry in their teens are about twice as likely to get a divorce as those who wait until age 20 to 24 (Spanier and Glick, 1981).

These figures are probably not entirely due to age, because many of the teenagers who marry do so under the most unfavorable circumstances. Many of them are not so much eager for marriage as trying to escape from a miserable and conflict-ridden life at home. A large number have parents who are separated, divorced, alcoholic, or mentally disturbed. They lack job training and are unable to earn enough money to support themselves comfortably, and usually they have not learned to handle money anyway. They are already estranged from their parents, and marriage tends to pull them away from old friends who remain single. Thus

they have nowhere to turn for advice and support (Reiner and Edwards, 1974).

Even among the best-equipped young people, from the most advantageous kinds of homes, the divorce rate for those who marry in their teens is higher than for those who wait (Hong, 1974). One reason is simply lack of maturity. As Jessie Bernard (1972) has said, those who marry very young "are unformed, they have not achieved an identity, they really do not know who they are or what they want." They may choose each other for the wrong reasons: "The young man is attracted to a young woman for precisely the qualities—cuteness, flirtatiousness, flightiness—that will not make her a good wife. The young woman is attracted to the kind of young men—the rock singer, the motion picture star, the unconventional—who do not make the best husbands." When they get a little older and more mature, they are likely to find that they are not suited to each other at all.

Is Divorce Contagious?

The chances of divorce depend to a certain extent on the type of community and neighborhood. Divorce has always been less common in rural areas and small towns where many kinds of social pressure—close association with neighbors, the school, and often the pastor and the church—help hold marriages together. It has been much more common in big cities, where people lead more isolated lives and marriage finds few outside supports.

Divorce runs in families and in certain social circles. If your parents, uncles and aunts, older brothers and sisters, and closest friends have all stayed married, your own chances of staying married are better than average. If your parents and many of your other associates have been divorced, then your own chances of divorce are higher. It has been observed for a long time that divorce is contagious (Kirkpatrick, 1963). It seems to be catching, like the measles.

One reason is that being around divorced people makes divorce seem an easy and natural thing to do. To our great-grandparents, divorce was a form of deviant behavior. Now all of us know so many divorced people that we consider it perfectly normal. The more such people we have around us, the more likely we are to think of divorce from time to time as one of life's alternatives. This is particularly true because we often see that our friends and relatives are happy in second marriages and are unaware of the difficulties they went through at the time of divorce (see the box on *Opinions and Experiences*). We tend to think of divorce as a safety valve for marital unhappiness, and many of us have set it at a very low level of pressure: "When divorce looks easy, your boiling point goes down" (Bernard, 1964).

Like Parent, like Child

The experiences of our parents seem to be particularly influential. Many studies have shown that the divorce rate is higher among the children of divorced parents than among people whose parents have stayed married (Pope and Mueller, 1976). Indeed parents who have a bad marriage can increase our own chances of divorce even if they themselves have never been divorced or even separated. One study, indeed, has indicated that severe discord between parents is the worst possible kind of family background, worse even than separation, divorce, or financial insecurity in the home. Growing up in an atmosphere of discord seems particularly likely to reduce the chances of successful marriage for women, and especially young

women in their 20s (Overall, Henry, and Woodward, 1974).

Why should a tendency toward a conflict-ridden marriage be passed along from parents to children? The authors of the "severe discord" study believe that there are probably two reasons. The first is socialization. If as young children we observe our parents argue and bicker, we are likely to get the idea that this is the way men and women are supposed to treat each other. One might say that we tend to grow up not only expecting trouble but indeed asking for it. The other possible reason lies in workings of heredity. Parents who constantly fight may do so because they have psychological problems, and these problems may depend on characteristics that can be inherited, such as the workings of the glands and nervous system.

THE PSYCHOLOGICAL CAUSES OF DIVORCE

Psychological problems are almost as widespread as the common cold. Psychiatrists estimate as a rule of thumb that about a third of all Americans are neurotic, that is to say, suffering from irrational anxieties, fears, or other symptoms of stress, frustration, and conflict. Most neurotic people manage to get along despite their problems, but they cannot function as well or as happily as they should. As for serious mental disorders, it is estimated that they afflict about 15 percent of Americans in the course of a year (Regier and Taube, 1981).

Some Divorce-prone Personalities

Since most adults are married, it follows that many millions of wives and husbands suffer in one way or another from psychological

Opinions and Experiences

"WHAT MY POOR NIECE DOESN'T KNOW"

A woman in Colorado worries that she might have helped make divorce catching in her family.

Last week I went to the wedding of my 20-year-old niece. While I was helping her dress I said, "I suppose you're all nervous and excited." She just laughed and asked, "Why? Why should I be nervous? If it doesn't work out, I can always get a divorce and try again. Like you did."

What my poor niece doesn't know is that getting a divorce can mean going through hell. I'll never forget mine. It was the saddest time of my life, a horrible time. I don't know how I lived through it. There are no rules to tell you how to behave. It's hard to face your friends. You don't know what to say or do.

And the problems seemed to go on and on. I was unmarried for a long time, trying to bring up two sons without a father and feeling inadequate the entire time. The other children in the neighborhood teased and picked on the boys. They seemed to sense that the boys had no father to protect them.

This went on for three long years because, believe me, finding a second husband isn't as easy as my niece seems to think. There were lots of fellows who wanted to take me out, but they weren't thinking in terms of marriage. Or, if they were, they weren't the right kind of husband material. When you get a little older and have children, you can't settle for a man who would rather act the playboy than worry about his job. You know you have to find someone who will be a good father to your children. If not, it doesn't matter how charming he is. Forget it.

Things did work out eventually. We have a very happy family now. Probably my niece thinks of me as a person who proved that you can get divorced and try again, successfully. She's right about me, in a sense. I only wish I could convince her what a price I paid for that second chance.

problems that not only impair their own performance and happiness but may very well make life difficult for their spouses. Bernard (1972) has described the hazards in these terms:

> There are millions of mentally or emotionally crippled men and women rendering normal life impossible for their mates. There are many men and women who are marginal in mental health: mean, hostile, aggressive, punitive, suspicious, pugnacious, irresponsible, dependent, not always enough to warrant a diagnosis as abnormal or pathological or sick—the legally insane are forbidden to marry—but enough to make those about them suffer. There are no precise and accurate figures on the actual number of alcoholics in this country,

and estimates vary. A current estimate is about 9 million. Many of them are married and making their spouses—especially wives, since there are more male than female alcoholics—miserable. In addition, there is an indeterminate number of sociopaths* who are making life insufferable for an indeterminate number of spouses.

Psychology and Divorce

Does this last description of the psychological hazards to marriage sound too gloomy? Perhaps. Unfortunately all the evidence bears it out. Heavy drinking, for example,

---

*Sociopaths are people who seem to lack any normal conscience or sense of social responsibility, like criminals who experience no remorse for even the most brutal offenses.

is without doubt a frequent cause of marital problems and divorce. Among people who have been divorced, the proportion of alcoholics is significantly higher than among other people (Woodruff, Guze, and Clayton, 1972).

As for the various conditions that a psychiatrist would describe as mental illness, these too are more common among people who wind up in divorce. In one survey made in Missouri, the investigators managed to study men and women who had received divorce decrees in one particular month, then matched them against a control group of couples from the same neighborhoods who were still married. By the investigators' diagnosis, 68 percent of the divorced men and 78 percent of the divorced women were suffering from psychiatric disorders; only 34 percent of the still-married men and 18 percent of the still-married women were (Briscoe et al., 1973). The findings were even more striking in cases where the investigators were able to interview both partners. In fully 92 percent of these divorces, at least one partner had a psychiatric illness (Briscoe and Smith, 1974).

It can be argued, of course, that psychiatrists tend to see at least a little bit of mental illness in all of us. By their definition, a lot of us would be under treatment or locked up, even though we seem to ourselves and our friends to be behaving in at least a reasonably normal manner. Still, even if psychiatrists set higher standards for mental health than getting along in the world really requires, the figures on the people who got divorced and those who did not are impressive.

The People with No Talent for Marriage

In addition to the women and men whose psychological problems make them divorce-prone, there are many others who simply have no talent for marriage. Bernard (1972) has said:

> In addition to the sick and near-sick people, there is an indeterminate number who, with no diagnosable defect or deficiency, are just not suited for the discipline that living with another person in an intimate relationship calls for. . . . People who lack this aptitude are quite normal, indeed sometimes superior, in many ways. There is nothing intrinsically wrong with them. They just do not have the interests or the values demanded by marriage or the willingness to assume its responsibilities.

Some of them realize this and avoid marriage, or they are such obvious risks that no one is willing to marry them. But the social pressures toward marriage have been so strong in the United States that many people unsuited for it have been led to try it. Some of these people have made themselves and their spouses miserable for a lifetime. Others have kept getting married, divorced, remarried, and redivorced all their lives, engaging in one unsuccessful attempt after another.

Perhaps all these events will happen less frequently in the future, because the idea that everyone should be married seems to be losing its hold and more people may choose to remain single. As for the danger that we ourselves may make the mistake of marrying someone who wants to try despite a total lack of talent for living together, this can be avoided by applying the principles of selecting a mate that the book has discussed.

THE EMOTIONAL AND LEGAL PAIN OF DIVORCE

When marriage is ended by death, the widow or widower can usually count on sympathy, support, and assistance. Relatives and friends rally around. Grief can be expressed openly. Indeed the partner left behind is fully expected to mourn, be unhappy, have trouble adjusting to a new life, and need all the help that people can offer.

Divorce is a different matter. As commonplace as it has become in our society, we still have not found ways of dealing with it. It has been described as "a crisis most of us are not prepared to cope with," and we are even less prepared to offer any kind of moral support to someone else who is going through it (Herman, 1974). It causes grief just as surely as does the death of a mate. Yet divorced people must face the grief alone. Their friends and relatives hardly know whether to offer condolences or congratulations. Because of their embarrassment—and perhaps also their own mixed feelings about divorce—they often make the experience more difficult rather than easier.

Arthur Tress, Photo Researchers

Loneliness and pain—felt deeply by four out of five of the women and men who get divorced.

One study of people who had been through divorce showed that only 20 percent of the men and 13 percent of the women considered the experience relatively painless. Many of the others had found it stressful, though bearable; and 16 percent of the men and 27 percent of the women had found it "traumatic, a nightmare." As the author of the survey pointed out: "For the person who goes through a divorce, an entire life is often turned topsy-turvy. Intimate bonds with another individual are broken; relationships with children are changed; friendship patterns are disrupted; different living arrangements must be established" (Albrecht, 1980). Another social scientist has observed, "If, as the poets say, 'the course of true love never did run smooth,' it is nothing compared to the course of true divorce" (Kressel, 1980).

In a time when the chances are high that even the college educated will some day go through the experience of divorce, it is not pleasant to report these facts—but forewarned is forearmed. Divorce is painful. It hurts in many ways and often for a long time. In case you are ever divorced, you should know what to expect, lest you be not only hurt but amazed and bewildered, as so many people are. As one sociologist has pointed out, divorce is often even more shattering than it need be "because so many of us are ignorant of what it requires of us. . . . We have never been taught what we are supposed to do, let alone what we are supposed to feel" (Bohannon, 1970).

The Love-Hate Mixture

Part of the pain of divorce—or the breakup of any intimate relationship—is the mixed emotions it produces. Even the worst relationship was not always or altogether bad. The partners are bound to have shared some close and happy moments. They lived together. They shared many experiences and developed ties of attachment that tend to persist even when the relationship as a whole has turned sour.

The strength of these old ties, which often surprises people who separate, can best be understood by examining carefully the statements in the box on *Opinions and Experiences*. All the women quoted there were plagued by the strong attachment they still felt to their husbands, however unhappy the marriage had actually been. The thought of breaking the relationship frightened them, sometimes to the point of sheer terror. Nor is this uncomfortable feeling confined only to wives. Men seem to find a breakup just as distressing as do women (Weiss, 1976).

Along with the persistent and troublesome attachment go deep feelings of anger. People who reach the point of divorce feel betrayed by each other. They blame each other. Their strong resentment is compounded by the very fact that they do still have emotional ties. They are caught in all the agonies of a love-hate relationship. As one young woman has put it:

> In separating from someone you discover in yourself things that you had never felt before in your life. That's one of the things that really freaks you out. I've always used my mind to keep down anything I didn't like. And now I discover, wow, I can hate!
> *(Weiss, 1976).*

The Matter of Hating Oneself— and Getting Sick

People who get divorced are likely to be angry not only at their former mates but at themselves. They can hardly help thinking: "The marriage failed. It can't all have been his (her) fault. I must have been to blame, too." Many studies have shown that divorced people suffer from such feelings of

failure and guilt (Siegal and Short, 1974). Their own sense of self-esteem suffers, especially since they have probably listened to many attacks on it during the ultimate conflict that led to divorce (Herman, 1974). They are down on themselves and the world.

The world, as a matter of fact, may not treat them very well. The couple's friends may feel torn, not knowing whether to side with the husband or the wife (Miller, 1970). Because they have trouble deciding where their allegiance lies, they may drop both of the newly divorced people. Divorced women, in particular, often find themselves outcasts—at least rejected, if not actually treated with hostility and fear (Freund, 1974). As one divorced woman complained bitterly, "Friends? They drop you like a hot potato. The exceptions are the real ones you made before marriage, those who are unmarried, and your husband's men friends who want to make a pass at you" (Bohannon, 1970).

All in all, the problems are so great that many divorced people show signs of severe stress. A study in Britain found that 85 percent of divorced women reported physical symptoms, including migraine headaches, dizziness, skin rashes, falling hair, loss of appetite, and pains in the chest and stomach (Chester, 1971). A U.S. survey found that even more divorced men than women, by considerable numbers, suffered from high blood pressure, ulcers, and feelings of guilt and loneliness. About a fifth of the divorced people had thought of suicide—far more than found among the married or never-married (Cargan and Melko, 1982).

Pain and the Sex Roles

What kinds of people suffer the most? One study of men and women who had recently filed for divorce found many indications

Opinions and Experiences

YOU CAN'T WASH A MAN RIGHT OUT OF YOUR HAIR

How attachment to a husband can persist even after breaking up is described by five women who attended the series "Seminars for the Separated" conducted in Boston by Harvard's Laboratory of Community Psychiatry.

Woman No. 1. Maybe it is first love or whatever, but I'm still attracted to him. There is a basic something, and I can't seem to get rid of that. I do want a divorce and I don't want a divorce.

Woman No. 2. I wouldn't want to go back, but I hadn't expected to feel as bad as I do.

Woman No. 3. I don't like him. As a man I find him boring. If I met him at a party I'd talk with him for about two minutes and then I'd say, "I'll see you." But the emotional tug is still there. He is still attractive to me.

Woman No. 4. When the idea occurred to me that I could live without Dave and be happier, my immediate next feeling was just gut fear. It's really hard to explain. It was just terror.

Woman No. 5. When my husband left I had this panicky feeling which was out of proportion to what was really happening. I was afraid I was being abandoned. I couldn't shake the feeling. I remembered later that the first time I had that feeling was when I had pneumonia and my mother left me in the hospital, in a private room, in the winter. And this picture came back of this hospital and those old gray rooms, and it was winter and every night at five o'clock, when the shadows would come across my bed, my mother would put on her coat and say: "Goodbye, I will see you tomorrow." And I had such a feeling of panic and fear at being left.

From R. S. Weiss. The Emotional Impact of Marital Separation. Divorce and Separation: Context, Causes, and Consequences. George Levinger and Oliver C. Moles (ed.), Copyright © 1979 by the Society for the Psychological Study of Social Issues. Reprinted by permission of Basic Books, Inc., Publishers

that, in general, it is people who have played the traditional sex roles and are thus stunned by the problems of living alone: "Men with very traditional perspectives on married life may be quite unprepared for the new demands to cook, clean, and wash dishes. Traditional women may be equally unprepared or unwilling to assume responsibilities for servicing the car, repairing appliances, or providing an income" (Chiriboga and Thurnher, 1980).

Among young men, it was found, the least upset were those who had played a more androgynous role in their marriage. Instead of regarding themselves as boss, they had made joint decisions about their job and where to live. The best-adjusted young women were those who had been more assertive in the marriage, exercising considerable control over jobs and finances, and who had relied less on their husband to handle all the practical details of living. Another study of women who were getting divorces also found that those who had rejected the feminine role—or did so during the divorce process—"experience less distress, more well-being and personal growth, higher self-esteem, and a greater sense of personal effectiveness than women who maintain traditional sex role attitudes" (Brown and Manela, 1978).

Divorce and the Law

Until recently divorce created serious legal problems in addition to all the others. One party had to file suit, make charges, and prove that the other party was guilty of cruelty, "wickedness," bigamy, or some other such heinous offense. The state of New York, for example, once granted divorce only on proof of adultery. Even if husband and wife could agree more or less amicably that the marriage should be dissolved, one or the other had to go to the indignity of being caught and photographed in bed with a member of the opposite sex. Usually the so-called adultery was arranged by a friendly detective agency and the member of the opposite sex was merely paid to be present while the photographs were taken—never touched and indeed never seen before or after.

Divorce was at best humiliating and at worst marked by bitter charges and countercharges, with each spouse fighting to foist off the legal blame. This is now changing. In 1969 California adopted a new law providing for *no-fault* divorce, and this type of legal procedure has spread rapidly. A no-fault divorce can be granted whenever a husband and wife agree that the marriage has broken down and cannot be saved for any reason and without any implication that either party is to blame. Indeed, many states no longer even use the word *divorce*. Their legal term now is *dissolution* of the marriage, a neutral word that helps get rid of the old notions of misconduct, guilt, and legal hassling.

Almost all states now have the no-fault system, which has enabled many couples to get a divorce without the expense of lawyers and with less bitterness. Opponents once argued that it would increase divorce by making the process too easy, but this has not happened (Dixon and Weitzman, 1980). One drawback, from the wife's point of view, is that no-fault decrees seem to award alimony and child support to the wife slightly less often and in smaller amounts (Welch and Price-Bonham, 1983).

Mediation as an Alternative to Battling

Another recent attempt to make divorce less agonizing is *mediation,* or the use of an impartial arbiter who tries to help the two parties reach a mutually acceptable arrangement for custody of the children, child support and alimony, and dividing the couple's property. Mediation has been described as an effort to avoid a courtroom battle that, "by making the husband and wife legal adversaries, only reinforces [their] anger and discontent." The mediator seeks to "help the disputing couple become rational and responsible enough to cooperate toward making compromises acceptable to both," and thus replace "inherently stressful, competitive, and acrimonious court litigation with a low-stress, impartial, cooperative approach" (Coogler, Weber, and McKenry, 1979).

Trained mediators—usually psychologists, social workers, or lawyers—are now available in a number of cities,* and in California a state law requires that they be called on in all divorces where child custody is at issue. Sometimes the mediator helps draw up an agreement and then suggests that the wife and husband have their own lawyers present it to the court. Other mediators, if not themselves lawyers, work with a single attorney who handles the court procedure.

*One source of information is the Family Mediation Association, 5018 Allan Road, Bethesda, MD 20814.

Either way, a divorce obtained through mediation usually costs only about half as much as if the two parties started with separate lawyers. Some couples are so bitter toward each other, and so hopelessly at odds over such issues as property division, that mediation is futile. Mediation has led to agreements in many cases, however, and couples who have used it often report satisfaction with the results.

After the Pain, What?

With or without no-fault laws and mediation, divorce is emotionally painful and sometimes physically disabling; but it is not necessarily fatal. Most people manage to get over it, and often they profit from it. As one student of divorce has written, it is without doubt "a difficult and complex crisis," but it also "affords chances for emotional maturity, fosters independence, and reveals individual growth potentials" (Herman, 1974). For those who have been trapped in a bad marriage, it provides a chance to create a new and better life.

The same study that showed considerable numbers of divorced people who considered the experience "a nightmare" also found that a surprising number believed they were "better off" than before the divorce. Of the men, 91 percent took this position. Of the women, 93 percent agreed, though nearly two-thirds of the women reported having a lower income than before and nearly half said their income was "much lower."

Is Divorce Good or Bad?

If your own marriage gets into trouble, should you lean in the direction of staying married despite the problems and unhappiness? Or should you be quick to call it quits despite the pain that divorce is bound to produce?

This is not an easy choice to make. Kirkpatrick (1963) has called it an attempt to pick the lesser of two evils, "like deciding to retain an infected leg as compared with suffering an amputation " (Kirkpatrick, 1963). At any given time, more than a million Americans are probably spending gloomy days and sleepless nights agonizing over the decision.

As for the reasons marriages arrive at the brink of divorce, Table 12–1 offers some important clues. Note that the table reveals a considerable range of opinions. Not one of the thirteen items on the list was considered a sufficient reason to consider divorce by more than 57 percent of college-educated women. Yet even the two items that turned out to have the least support were considered sufficient grounds by 7 percent of the women. If a longer list had been used—or if the people in the survey had been asked to draw up their own lists—the poll doubtless would have shown that a great many other matters can be regarded as sufficient reason to contemplate divorce.

Obviously there are many individual differences in attitudes about what is so intolerable in a marriage that divorce begins to seem preferable. If you ever face the choice, only you can make it on the basis of your individual situation and personality, including whatever religious and moral attitudes you have toward divorce. The advice you get from friends and relatives is likely to be useless and perhaps even harmful because it is based on their own experiences and prejudices, not on knowledge and analysis of your particular feelings and problems. It takes a very good marriage counselor to provide any genuine guidance, and even a marriage

Table 12–1

What College Women Regard as Grounds for Divorce

Reason	Percentage of college-educated women who consider it sufficient cause for divorce
1. Lack of communication	57
2. Partner has severe drinking problem	54
3. Being in love with someone else	53
4. Partner's sexual infidelity	51
5. No longer being in love	44
6. Not liking the same kind of life, activities, friends (little in common)	36
7. Unsatisfactory sexual relationship	33
8. Having different views on whether to have children	28
9. Feeling that you have no real identity of your own, that you must be what spouse expects you to be	27
10. Conflict over how money should be handled	18
11. Very different ideas about how children should be raised	18
12. Feeling romance has gone out of marriage	7
13. Conflict over wife wanting to work	7

These thirteen possible grounds for considering divorce were listed in a public opinion poll, and people were asked to name all those they regarded as sufficient reason. Shown in the table are the responses of college-educated women, who mentioned lack of communication more than any other item. The five reasons chosen most often by men in the poll were, in order, (1) being in love with someone else, (2) partner's severe drinking problem, (3) no longer being in love, (4) lack of communication, and (5) partner's sexual infidelity. *Data from The Roper Organization, The Virginia Slims American Women's Opinion Poll, Vol. III. New York: The Roper Organization, 1974.*

counselor can only clarify the situation and then leave the decision up to you.

How a Marriage Counselor Might Answer the Question

The general attitude of marriage counselors toward divorce deserves mention. In the early days, most counselors took the position that every marriage was worth saving, that divorce, if not necessarily a sin, was a form of failure to be avoided if at all possible. Today the trend is to be concerned less with the success or failure of the marriage than with the individual welfare of the partners. As one psychiatrist has said, "No marriage should ever be held of more importance than one of its participants. Persons, not marriages, are worth saving" (Seidenberg, 1973).

Counselors believe (in general) that most marriages can be improved by assisting the two partners to grow along the lines suggested in Chapters 8 and 9 (fairness, reciprocity, communication, self-esteem, and mutual esteem) and to avoid the kind of conflict described in Chapter 7. In this sense, they continue to try to save marriages and they often succeed. They also believe (again in general) that some marriages have become so mired in misunderstanding and bitterness that they resemble a crippling physical disability or chronic illness, for which "divorce is probably the most effective remedy" (Renne, 1971).

Marriage counselors display as many individual differences as all the rest of us, but perhaps most would tend to agree with this statement by a therapist who has worked with many hundreds of families:

> I have seen so many couples who started out with love feelings, but became mixed-up, angry, and helpless. When they were helped to understand . . . love again became evident. On the other hand, there are some couples who have endured so much that they are literally dead to one another. Since I have not had much success in raising the dead, I think in these cases the best policy is to have a good funeral and start over.
>
> *(Satir, 1972)*

The problem for people contemplating divorce, of course, is this: Is the marriage dead? Or is it merely suffering from a headache that time or a little judicious medicine will cure? The answers will always have to be found on an individual basis.

REMARRIAGE: THE PROBLEMS AND THE SUCCESSES

Although divorce is almost always painful and often agonizingly so, it does not necessarily doom people to a lifetime of bitterness and misery. The man quoted earlier in the box titled *A divorced man surprises himself,* who was remarried within four months of his divorce, was by no means unusual except for his speed. About 85 percent of all divorced men and 75 percent of all divorced women remarry, about a third of them within two years and half of them within three years (Spanier and Glick, 1980a). Divorced people of all ages are more likely to get married than other people the same age who have remained single up to that time (Norton and Glick, 1976).

The men who remarry are of all ages and backgrounds. The women most likely to marry again are those who are under thirty,

Suzanne Szasz, Photo Researchers

Remarriage and the start of stepparenthood: How will it turn out?

were married young and for less than five years, and have only one child or none. Women college graduates are considerably less likely than average to marry again, probably because they are the best able to live independently (Spanier and Glick, 1980a). Indeed all college-educated people are less inclined to remarry than others. So are blacks, for reasons that are not known (Glick, 1984).

The remarriage rate for women would doubtless be higher except that the facts of life and death make marriage more difficult for older women. Men, being the weaker sex in life expectancy, begin to die off after their mid 20s, and soon become relatively scarce. There is a surplus of a million women between the ages of 25 and 44, two million between 45 and 64, and over four million 65 and older (Bureau of the Census, 1984b). Thus about seven million women in all aged 25 and older—divorced, single, or widowed—cannot possibly get married because no men are available.

The Divorced Man's Problems

The fact that so many divorced people get remarried would seem to be a great tribute to their abiding faith in marriage (or perhaps their need for it), for they face difficult obstacles. One, already mentioned, is that divorce leaves most people badly shaken, and they have to get over the anguish before they can even think of marrying again. Even if and when they surmount this hurdle, they face handicaps that never trouble single people seeking a mate for the first time,

The divorced man, theoretically, is footloose and fancy-free. He has a delightful opportunity to go out on the town and play the field. If he is seriously looking for a new wife, his opportunities are legion. So we might

think. The truth is somewhat different. Of all American women over 20, the majority are already taken. In the ages 25 to 34, over 70 percent are married (Bureau of the Census, 1984a). Thus, prospective brides are not so easy to find as the newly divorced man fondly imagines.

If the man is paying alimony, he may be so strapped for money that he has to wait until his ex-wife remarries and the payments stop. He may be viewed with suspicion by the single women he approaches or, if not by them, by their parents. Sometimes the ex-wife causes problems. For example, he may notice a strange coolness on the part of his old acquaintances, especially the women in whom he shows any interest. One student of divorce and remarriage has found that the reason, likely as not, is that his former wife is getting in a few parting shots. She has spread the word, not necessarily true, that he is given to all kinds of weird behavior, including cruelty and sexual kinkiness. Or the former wife may kill him with kindness. She may appear to be so unhappy—but so patient and forgiving about it—that he is almost bound to feel guilty if he even thinks of marrying again (Bernard, 1956).

The Divorced Woman's Problems

Remarriage is even more difficult for the divorced woman. She too has a limited field of eligibles, for nearly 65 percent of all men aged 25 to 34 are already married. A considerable number of others are the leftovers from the "bottom of the barrel." If the divorced woman is still young, say in her mid-20s, she may try to renew acquaintances with some of the men she knew in college or high school. Usually this merely teaches her the truth of the old adage that you can never go back. The man who was the life of the party when he was 20 is now a dedicated bookkeeper who likes to go to bed early and already shows all the symptoms of chronic bachelorhood. The man who was such a generous spender when he was on an allowance from his family now has trouble holding a job and making ends meet. Even if her old friends have not changed, she has. She no longer has anything in common with them.

A divorced woman with children usually has added problems. She may be in financial trouble, lacking the money for clothes, entertaining, or going to places where she might meet men. Even if someone asks for a date, she may have to turn it down for lack of funds to pay a baby sitter. Or she may have to wait for the rare man who is willing to help her feed the children, bathe them, and put them to bed before the date can really begin.

Q. Whom Do Divorced People Marry? A. Each Other.

Despite all the obstacles, the remarriage rate is remarkably high. One reason is the well-known tendency of birds of a feather. Divorced women and divorced men seem to have a natural affinity. Certainly they have at least one important experience in common. Often they are beset by the same kinds of problems. Somehow they meet, they feel a kinship, and they decide to face the problems together.

The majority of divorced men and women remarry someone who has also been divorced (Garfield, 1980), a remarkable fact considering that so few divorced people are available in comparison with single people. The divorced woman, for example, is nearly four times as likely to meet a single man aged

25 to 34 as a divorced man (Bureau of the Census, 1984b). Yet somehow it is the divorced man to whom she is usually attracted.

Starting with Two Strikes

If marriage in today's world is a hazardous undertaking at best, remarriage is even riskier. As one sociologist has observed, "The difficulties with which remarried families must wrestle may be tremendous," and in many ways "it is a miracle that any second marriage should survive at all" (Bernard, 1956).

The minor problems are endless. The remarried man may slip and call his new wife by his first wife's name. The woman who marries her old friend Mary's ex-husband may be tempted, the first time they have a serious quarrel, to utter those inflammatory words "No wonder Mary couldn't stand you." The more serious problems include money. Typically, couples in a second marriage have less of it than other couples, particularly if the husband is paying child support or alimony to his ex-wife.

The Stepparent's Woes

If one partner or the other brings children to the marriage—or both do and thus establish a blended family of yours, mine, and ours—the situation is particularly hazardous. Although millions of American children under 18 now live with a stepparent (Glick, 1979), our society has not yet established clear-cut standards of behavior for the people in these families. Everyone in the family—stepparent, natural parent, and children—is likely to be confused about what role to play and what to expect in return, and conflicts are almost bound to occur (Fast and Cain, 1966).

The role of a stepmother, it has been noted,"is much more difficult than that of the stepfather. . . . [She] must be exceptional before she is considered acceptable. No matter how skillful and patient a stepmother may be, all her actions are suspect . . . especially if the child perceives that the stepmother took the father away from the biological mother." She is likely to have the most trouble with girls of any age, and with children of both sexes who are in their teens (Jones, 1978). Teenagers, indeed, have disrupted many remarriages, and sometimes destroyed them. They have enough trouble of their own trying to establish an identity and gradually emancipate themselves from the family, and it is "disruptive to accept an added burden: a newcomer, a new family tie." They tend to be "distrustful, suspicious, and resentful toward a new parent," and "because of their bitterness, hatred, and vengefulness" they may try to "drive a step-parent out of the home" by manipulating their natural parent and any younger brothers and sisters.

There Are Advantages, Too

Yet if remarriage faces unusual obstacles, it also has some unusual advantages. For one thing, people who marry for a second time are older. They are well past the years when so many marriages fail because of immaturity, lack of identity, and the tendency to marry the wrong person for the wrong reasons. Often they have profited from the lessons of their unsuccessful first marriages:

> They have served an apprenticeship. They have acquired skills by practicing—not only in human relations but also in down-to-earth, practical matters. . . . An analysis of biographical sketches contributed by re-

married persons concluded that the majority had gained in maturity, wisdom, and tolerance. A minority found that their old personality differences persisted, but most of them believed that they had profited from their experience. Their first marriage had been, in effect, a preparatory school. . . . One man even said that if he had known as much about human relationships before his first marriage as he did when he married for the second time, his first marriage would have been just as successful as his second one was proving to be.

> (Bernard, 1956)

People who remarry are likely to be more realistic about themselves, their ambitions, and what to expect of a mate. They usually place fewer demands on each other; they ask less and appreciate more. They are less likely to commit the fatal error of trying to change each other. They are more likely to be willing to work at the job of being married, and their attitudes toward sex may be more casual and relaxed. They tend to share in making decisions and dividing the household chores and often have closer emotional ties (Weingarten, 1980). Thus, like the couple quoted in the box called *Easier the second time around,* they have many things going for them that they lacked in their first marriage.

How Remarriages Turn Out

How do the hazards and advantages balance out? In other words, how happy is remarriage likely to be?

Failure is frequent, with more than half of all remarriages ending in another divorce. The high rate is due in part to the confirmed "serial polygamists" who keep marrying and remarrying all their lives, as described in the box titled *The multiple divorcers.* There are not many such people. Only about 20 percent of today's young women and men

Opinions and Experiences

EASIER THE SECOND TIME AROUND

A New Jersey couple now in their 30s describe why they were better prepared this time than for their first marriages, which ended in divorce.

The Husband's Comments:

I was just starting out as an insurance salesman when I got married the first time. The job wasn't easy. Sometimes I went for months without making an important sale, and I'd get panicky and work my head off from morning until late at night. Or I'd have a run of good luck and get delusions of grandeur. I'd decide that I was born to be a high-salaried general agent and work even harder. My ex-wife never could make up her mind how she felt about all this. She was socially ambitious and wanted me to make more money. At the same time she resented the fact that I was away from home so much.

Now I'm more relaxed. I know I'm a good salesman and can make a living, but I also know that I'll never be a $40,000-a-year man. I don't worry or drive myself. I spend a lot of time just enjoying life with my family.

The Wife's Comments:

One thing wrong with my first marriage was me. I was terribly ambitious. I worked in the publicity department at a television station and had dreams of being a script writer, maybe even for the movies. My husband was a photographer who didn't like to work too hard, and I was always after him to be as ambitious as I was.

I got pregnant by accident but decided to have the baby and quit my job to take care of her. Life as a housewife and mother bored me; so I spent most of my time trying to write scripts. But I never once made a sale. You might say that I was no good at either one of the jobs I was trying to fill.

Sex was a problem too. I conceived my daughter without ever having had a climax. It wasn't until my first husband and I were finally on the verge of breaking up—and I guess I quit having such grand ideas of what sex was supposed to be like—that I began to discover that it had its possibilities.

This time everything is different. I've learned that I'm never going to be a writer. I just haven't got what it takes. I'm happy to divide my time between being a housewife, bringing up my daughter, and working part-time in the local library. I'd never think of nagging my husband about working harder; I knew when I married him just what he was earning and could expect to earn the rest of our lives. And I don't have any false illusions about sex. I know that it can be good, bad, or indifferent, depending on how things go—and, no matter which, the world isn't going to stop turning.

are expected to have two or more divorces, with the rate higher for whites than blacks (Glick, 1984). The multiple divorcers help swell the statistics without telling us much about the outcome of remarriages in general.

Among remarriages that last, the level of happiness seems in general to be as high as for any other kind of marriage. One study found that 65 percent of remarried people said the experience they had gained in the previous marriage helped them adjust, and 88 percent said the present marriage was much better (Albrecht, 1979).

Opinions and Experiences

THE "MULTIPLE DIVORCERS"

A sociologist describes the strange phenomenon of people who move from one unhappy marriage to another, often trying again with exactly the same kind of mate with whom they failed before.

All matrimonial lawyers have a few "regular clients." One lady lawyer who specializes in family matters told me about a woman for whom she had obtained five divorces—and she was not the lawyer who got this client her first one. Within a very short period after each final decree, the client calls the lawyer and says, "The most wonderful thing has just happened to me!" The lawyer always says, "All right, dear, bring him over." When the recently divorced client arrives with a new man . . . he is precisely the same type as all the others: short, stocky, unkempt, shirt open at the neck, loud sports coat. As the lawyer expressed it, "Her fourth husband was a little different. He was taller, had wavy blond hair, had a necktie, and a quiet sports coat. . . . It took her almost six months to make him beat her up."

. . . . I know another lawyer who obtained three divorces for a prominent businessman. The businessman always picks out the same kind of mousey, mother-ridden woman, and divorces her in about three years. His lawyer is his best friend—certainly he is the friend of longest standing. The lawyer says of him, in half-pity, half-mockery, that he is his most treasured client.

From P. Bohannon. Divorce Chains, Households of Remarriage, and Multiple Divorcers. In P. Bohannon (ed.), *Divorce and After.* Copyright © 1968, 1970 by Paul Bohannon. Reprinted by permission of the publisher.

What Does the Successful Remarriage Prove?

Unquestionably millions of Americans who failed at marriage the first time, got divorces, and eventually remarried are now perfectly happy. What does this tell us about marriage in general?

One thing it tells us is that many of the most divorce-prone people—the alcoholics, the seriously neurotic, those who simply lack the talent for living in an intimate relationship—become marriage dropouts. They try once, fail, and never try again. They join the ranks of the 20 percent of divorced people who do not attempt remarriage.

It also tells us that many first marriages have failed because husband and wife were not suited to each other. Somehow they failed at the process of finding a mate. They did not take full advantage of the process but instead fell into one or another of the pitfalls. Jessie Bernard (1970) has suggested: "There was nothing wrong with them in their first marriage except a team factor. They were neither psychotic nor neurotic; they were not lacking in marital aptitude; they were simply married to the wrong mates." In their second marriage, they made a wiser selection.

The final message of successful remarriage can be explained only by citing the strange fact that there are quite a few cases where husband and wife get divorced, live apart for a time, then eventually get married again to each other. There are perhaps 10,000 or more of these Xerox-machine remarriages every year. A sociologist once managed to track down 200 such couples and found that only about a quarter of them were again unhappy and another quarter dubious, but that the other half now regarded the marriage as happy (Popenoe, 1938). We have to assume that they were doing better the second time because they were older, wiser, and more tolerant—all the things that are advantages in any kind of marriage.

SUMMARY

1. Divorce has increased rapidly throughout this century, to the point where U.S. courts now grant nearly 1.2 million decrees a year.

2. Although actual divorce was a rarity in the 1800s, the official figures concealed a large number of marriages broken up through desertion and common-law marriages that were abandoned. Moreover, many marriages were ended by the death of one of the spouses at an early age. Thus about as many couples remain together today as 50 or 100 years ago.

3. The divorce rate is highest among blacks, couples who marry in their teens, and people who have a lower-level education and income, whose parents divorced or had conflict-ridden marriages, or who have psychological problems or simply ''just are not suited for the discipline that living with another person calls for.''

4. Only about 13 percent of women and 20 percent of men who go through divorce find it relatively painless. Most people find it stressful though bearable, and 27 percent of women and 13 percent of men find it ''traumatic, a nightmare.''

5. Contributing to the pain of divorce are (a) the fact that the partners, no matter how unhappy the marriage, have emotional ties that are difficult to break, and (b) feelings of failure and guilt over the breakup. People who have played the traditional sex roles are less prepared to start over on their own than people who have had a more androgynous relationship.

6. Some recent attempts to ease the pain are (a) no-fault divorce, now available in almost all states, in which a decree is granted whenever a wife and husband agree that the marriage has failed, without any implication that either is to blame, and (b) mediation, or use of an impartial arbiter who tries to help the partners reach a mutual agreement for division of property, child custody, child support, and alimony.

7. Although divorce is painful, it may lead to individual growth, maturity, and independence. Marriage counselors usually try to save a troubled marriage but recognize that ''divorce is probably the most effective remedy'' for a relationship that has become totally mired in misunderstanding and bitterness.

8. Most divorced people—75 percent of women and 85 percent of men—remarry, about half of them within three years. The majority marry someone who has also been divorced. Remarried couples face ''tremendous difficulties,'' and more than half of all remarriages end in divorce.

9. The remarriages that endure seem to be just as happy as any others. The partners are older and wiser than at the time of first marriage, which may have failed because of immaturity, lack of identity, and a tendency to marry the wrong person for the wrong reasons. In remarriage they are likely to establish closer emotional ties because they are less demanding and more realistic about themselves, their ambitions, and what to expect of a mate.

DISCUSSION QUESTIONS

1. How do you feel about divorce? Do you consider it a suitable and acceptable solution for a marriage that has turned out badly?

2. Based on factors such as personality traits, family background, education, income,

age, and race, what are *your* chances of divorce?

3. What do you think is the best way to react to couples who are going through a divorce? Why?

4. Why have most states adopted no-fault divorce laws?

5. What factors affect remarriage rates for women? Why?

6. Discuss some of the unique problems faced by those who remarry after divorce.

CHAPTER 13

Where Today's Trends May Be Leading

The next time you sit in a classroom take a good look around you and pause for a moment to marvel. You are seeing something unprecedented and extraordinary, one of the wonders of present-day America. College classrooms much like yours, spread across our nation, now have 12 million occupants. How many college students do you suppose there were at the start of the century?

Even if you guess as low as a million, you are still guessing too high. The actual number, though hard to believe, was fewer than a quarter of a million (Office of Education, 1900). A college education was the rare privilege of the highly advantaged and highly motivated few.

All those bright and shining (or perhaps reluctant) faces around you in today's classroom have a bearing on marriages because they illustrate the increased flexibility, mobility, and opportunity we now enjoy. Going to college, the privilege of about one young American out of every three, greatly expands your horizons. It opens up all kinds of possibilities, offering you a wide variety of lifestyles, of places to live and occupations to follow, of interests to pursue.

Americans in general, and the college-educated in particular, have far more options today than most people ever had in the past. Young men are not automatically channeled into the same job their father had. Young women do not necessarily have to think of themselves as destined to be a housewife just like their mother.

Socialization no longer pushes us permanently and irrevocably into playing the roles of masculine males and feminine females. Relationships between men and women are no longer stamped out, like mass-produced fortune cookies, in the rigid pattern of traditional marriages. Where once only a few people were aware of the possibilities, now millions are embracing companionship marriage, in one or another of all the various forms it can take.

YESTERDAY'S CHANGES, TOMORROW'S POSSIBILITIES

The question naturally arises: Where is all this leading us? Where do we go from here? But the question does not have a ready answer. Humanity's crystal ball has always been clouded, and even those best qualified to peer into it have made some spectacular mistakes.

At the start of every year economists and government officials predict what will happen to business conditions, unemployment rates, inflation, and interest rates, and every year as many of their predictions prove to be wrong as right. Sure cures for cancer, arthritis, acne, baldness, and obesity have been breathlessly hailed in the newspapers; and have quickly proved useless. Prophets have announced that the world was ending, yet the world still turns.

The recent changes in marriages and families have piled one atop another with breathtaking speed, making it difficult to say for sure exactly where we stand today, much less where we are headed. About all we can realistically attempt is to examine current trends and analyze where they may or may not be leading. We may find some possibilities that deserve attention, if not as an infallible blueprint of the future in general, at least as a guide to what we might best do about our own individual prospects.

Three Decades of Revolutionary Events

As indications of the rapid pace of change, note the following: Companionship marriage did not become widespread enough to attract attention until the 1940s. Serious questioning of the traditional masculine and feminine roles did not begin until the 1950s. The sexual revolution began rolling in the 1960s, reached its peak in the 1970s, and began to wane around 1980. The number of wives with jobs outside the home, now a clear majority, did not reach the 25 percent level until the 1960s. The divorce rate did not begin its big jump to present levels until about 1965.

Just since the early 1970s, public opinion about many issues that affect marriages and families has shifted radically. The following beliefs, for example, were held by only a minority of Americans in the recent past but

are now found in opinion polls to be the majority view:

> It is all right for a married woman to earn money even if her husband can support her.
>
> Premarital sex is not morally wrong.
>
> It is not morally wrong for unmarried people to live together or for single people to have children.
>
> Interracial marriages are not immoral.
>
> The fact that a woman remains unmarried does not mean that she is "sick," "neurotic," or "immoral."
>
> The ideal family size is no more than two children.
>
> Both sexes have the responsibility to care for small children. (Yankelovich, 1981)

The Continuing Pull of Tradition

Many people, however, still hold the traditional beliefs. The minorities who disagree with the views just listed range from 25 to 38 percent, meaning 42 to 63 million Americans aged 18 and over. Many other traditional beliefs continue to prevail. Overwhelming majorities of Americans disapprove of drugs, married men or women who have affairs, and mate swapping and agree that "a woman should put her husband and children ahead of her career." Indeed a 55 percent majority feel that "it's more important for a wife to help her husband's career than to have one herself" (Yankelovich, 1981).

Thus the new and the old exist side by side in today's society. Some traditional ideas still flourish. Others have shriveled into minority opinions. Millions of people embrace the traditional roles of masculinity and femininity; other millions have abandoned them for some kind of androgyny, and presumably the youngest generation is being socialized accordingly. Millions of couples have traditional marriages and millions have some form of companionship marriage. Though the sexual revolution has come and gone, it has left behind a vastly changed moral climate and a gamut of sexual beliefs and behaviors that have their own followers.

We are surrounded by people who hold different attitudes, play different roles, and have different lifestyles; and we have our choice of which to accept and which to reject. This difficult choice is further complicated by the way that many forces have contributed to our socialization, and we are pulled in many different directions at once. Our own feelings and preferences may be hazy and sometimes inconsistent. Like our society, we have swallowed too many changes too fast to digest them comfortably. We have so many choices that we despair at times of making the right one.

The Lure of the Peaceful Past

When we feel overwhelmed by the changes, the choices, and the conflicts they have created, it is only natural to long for what seems like the simpler, calmer, and less troublesome past. This longing for the good old days is by no means a new development in human history. Arlene Skolnick (1981) has written that almost every previous generation has also worried about the sad state of the family and believed that the past was a "Golden Age of family harmony."

Historians, Skolnick points out, have never managed to find such a Golden Age, because "adultery, illegitimacy, marital and parent-child conflict, and other deviations from family norms" are by no means "20th-century inventions." Until fairly recently,

indeed, life for most people was a meager and hazardous encounter with high death rates, especially among infants. Societies were plagued by "uncontrolled fertility and a food supply fluctuating above and below the subsistence level. Families faced conflicts unknown today. The husband's wish for sex vied with the wife's fear of death in childbirth. . . . In times of scarcity, families had to decide who would eat first and who would not; rationality demanded that the most productive ones be chosen, or the whole family would starve."

Even in the more recent past, say toward the end of the last century, the nostalgic picture of the serene and untroubled three-generation family, with grandparents, parents, and children all basking around the fireplace, is largely a myth because grandparents were rare until the recent sharp rise in life expectancy:

> Death in the family was more frequent than divorce is today. . . . The aged were not a problem because there were so few of them. Adolescents were not a problem during the era of child labor and few public high schools. Middle-aged men and women were not caught between the demands of adolescent children and aging parents, nor did they have to confront the issue of what to do with the rest of their years since they could not expect to have many more.
> *(Skolnick, 1981)*

The chief difficulty, says Skolnick, is that we live in a time of vast and rapid change "when old rules and accustomed patterns of behavior no longer apply. . . . We are no longer peasants, Puritans, pioneers, or even suburbanites" of the type so prominent in the 1950s. "We face conditions unknown to our ancestors, and we must find new ways to cope with them."

Even if today's society offers so many possibilities that we may despair at times of ever sorting them out, most of us seem to be aware of the possibilities and to welcome the opportunity to choose. A public opinion poll has shown that 73 percent of Americans feel they have ''more freedom of choice'' than their parents did. Most feel confident that they will manage to take advantage of the choices and live their life the way they ''truly want to live,'' and they believe they are happier or at least just as happy as their parents (Yankelovich, 1981).

Some Probabilities for the Future

What seems most likely to happen in coming years, according to many students of the changes and trends, is that the rapid-fire burst of new developments will slow. Indeed it seems to have been slackening since the mid-1970s. ''We may have entered a period in which American families can adjust to the sharp changes'' of the previous two decades (Cherlin and Furstenberg, 1983). If such a period of relative calm does occur, both our society and the individuals in it will have a breathing spell in which they can digest the recent changes and resolve some of the problems that are now still so new and difficult.

The rise in the divorce rate, which was one of the most dramatic of the recent developments, has begun to lose momentum; and probably any ''further rise in the rate will tend to diminish, if not cease, during the next several years'' (Spanier and Glick, 1981). Indeed the divorce rate reached its peak around 1980, as shown in Figure 13-1, and has since dropped slightly. The number of unmarried couples living together, which has grown even more rapidly than the divorce statistics to a present total of 2 million, will probably continue to rise, to as many as 3.6 million in 1990 (Glick, 1984).

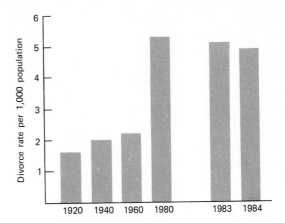

Figure 13-1
THE DIVORCE RATE:
IS IT STARTING BACK DOWN?
After rising slowly but steadily in the first half of the century, the divorce rate shot up to an all-time high of 5.3 around 1980. Since then it has dropped slightly to 4.9 in 1984— which may or may not mean that it has started a lasting decline (National Center for Health Statistics, 1985).

But living together has become not so much a substitute for marriage as ''either another stage in the process of courtship . . . or a transition between first and second marriages'' (Cherlin and Furstenberg, 1983).

The mass migration of wives and mothers into the work force may or may not continue. Some scholars believe that the move has approached the saturation point and will begin to level off. Other observers have concluded that the move will continue at a rapid pace and lead to new roles and relationships in the family. Men will be freed from the need to be the sole or chief earner, will have more leisure, and will spend more time sharing housework and child care. Working wives will be freed from their present overload of job plus household responsibilities (Insurance Information Institute, 1983).

As of now ''men do not participate a great deal in those tasks generally defined as household labor''—though many husbands *think* they do—and this is true at all ages and income levels. One reason seems to be that "the working wife is a new phenomenon" in our society and early sex-role socialization has not had time to adjust. Most of today's adults have grown up continuing to consider housework as part of the female role and foreign to the male role (Condran and Bode, 1982).

Two Big Problems: Working Conditions and Child Care

If sex-role socialization has lagged behind the rise in women workers, so has the marketplace itself. Fewer than one worker in five today is a man fully responsible for the support of his wife and children, yet most workers still have "full-time, five-day-a-week, regular-hour jobs, with pay and fringe benefits based on the assumption that the jobholder is the sole earner in the family" (Yankelovich, 1981). This poses special difficulties for working mothers, especially the 8 million who have children under the age of 6.

A number of changes have already been made for the convenience of two-worker families with children. Even in the 1970s some 300,000 workers were on "flexitime," an arrangement that enables them to set their own hours, arrive and leave when they please, even take a long lunch hour to be home with the children, as long as they put in the usual total number of hours (Stein, Cohen, and Gadon, 1976). Some companies are offering "paired" jobs to women and men who split the work, put in a half day each, and are home to take care of the children the rest of the time. Others permit employees to do some of their work at home. Some companies operate their own day-care centers, where parents can leave their children while they work.

As yet only small numbers of workers enjoy these new conveniences, and combining jobs and children continues to pose many problems. In a study made shortly before the start of the decade, a group of androgeny-minded parents who were trying to share the job of parenthood were asked to list their chief difficulties. Prominent on their list were job scheduling (matching husband's work schedules with wife's), inflexibility in number of working hours a week, and day care (DeFrain, 1979).

Most two-job parents have to find some way to provide care for the children during hours when it is impossible for either mother or father to be home. Making arrangements can be both difficult and expensive, even though various forms of child-care services have been increasing steadily to meet the demand. The number of children in nursery schools almost doubled from 1970 to 1980, to a total of 2 million, but only 15 percent of the small children of working parents were in these schools or other day-care facilities. Another 29 percent were supervised by hired caretakers within the home, and 47 percent in someone else's home (Bureau of the Census, 1982). In some cases the caretaker was another mother who had temporarily given up her usual job to take care of her own children and brought others into her home to provide income (Bane et al., 1979).

Although many working mothers worry that their absence from a child during even part of the day may be harmful, child psychologists have clearly established that a two-job family is not necessarily damaging in any way. Another competent and loving caretaker or a well-run day-care center can provide just as much emotional security and encouragement as a natural parent (Kagan, 1985). Our nation, however, does not have enough facilities for the present 8 million small children of two-worker families, much less the 2 million more who will probably be added by 1990. The Census Bureau has warned that child care "will no doubt be one of the most crucial social issues of the next decade" (Bureau of the Census, 1982). For some thoughts on these matters from the viewpoint of economics, see the box on *Opinions and Experiences*.

"EGALITARIAN MARRIAGE,": ITS HANDICAPS, AND ITS FUTURE

One important recent trend has been the rise of *egalitarian marriage,* that is, marriage in which the tasks of earning a living, keeping the home, and caring for the children "are shared equally by wife and husband," who also have equal power in the family and voice in making decisions. Egalitarian marriage, in a sense the most total form of companionship marriage, is as yet rare, but "more and more couples are moving in this direction" (Smith, 1980).

Almost all today's egalitarian marriages are also *dual-career* marriages, but they go even further. A dual-career marriage is simply one in which both wife and husband regard their work outside the home as not just a job, perhaps even merely a temporary job, but a permanent part of their lifestyle to which they are fully committed. Typically both dual-career partners are in the skilled crafts, managerial work, or professions. They are teachers, lawyers, accountants, and technicians and executives of various kinds.

Both partners in the typical dual-career marriage regard their careers as important and rewarding, and they may be equally dedicated and work equally long and hard, but they still run their home along more or less conventional lines, with the wife responsible for most of the housework, cooking, and child care. Generally the husband spends only a few hours a week at such tasks (Nichols and Metzen, 1982). The wife, suffering from the "overload" already discussed, winds up putting in seventy-one to eighty-three hours a week at her two jobs outside and inside the home (Ferber and Birnbaum, 1980).

The Egalitarian Marriage and Role Sharing

What distinguishes the egalitarian marriage is its "equal sharing of traditionally sex-segregated roles" (Haas, 1980). The wife and husband take equal responsibility for such traditionally feminine tasks as child care and housekeeping (cooking, cleaning, and laundry) as well as masculine tasks like repairs and work in the yard. They have equal influence on all decisions—both the major ones that have traditionally been made by the husband (where to work and live, which car and how much insurance to buy) and the minor ones that have traditionally been made by the wife (how much to spend on food, selection of a doctor).

In sharing tasks and decisions the egalitarian couple may assign areas of specialization. They may decide that the husband is more skillful and efficient at cooking and preparing tax returns, the wife at doing the laundry and balancing the checkbook, or vice versa. The tasks are never divided on the basis of what the traditional sex roles label women's work and men's work. The partners consider the sexes and each other as absolute equals in all respects, except insofar as any two individuals vary in specific talents.

Being Equal Isn't Easy

The egalitarian couple face numerous difficulties. All dual-career marriages, indeed, suffer "considerable stress and strain" from the conflicting demands of the career and a

Opinions and Experiences

WORKING WIVES, CHILD CARE, AND THE FUTURE OF MARRIAGE

The first comment is from an economist on the staff of the Bureau of Labor Statistics.

The family life and problems of working couples may have an increasing impact on society as a whole if, as expected, the number and proportion of wives in the labor force continues to grow. . . .

Child care is certainly a major problem for dual earner parents. . . . Currently the major caretakers of children are public schools and nuclear families, supplemented by a wide variety of other means, formal as well as informal. The amalgam of child-care methods evidently stems from the limited availability of institutional day care, the parents' financial considerations, and their desire to control as much of their children's upbringing as possible. . . . The nation may soon confront the necessity of formulating some sort of child-care policies which take dual-earner families into account. Many other areas of present concern such as accommodating work schedules to family needs . . . are also likely to become more pressing as the number of dual-earner couples increases (Hayghe, 1981).

Another economist looks at the problem from a historical perspective.

From V. Fuchs, *How We Live*. Harvard University Press. Copyright © 1983 by the President and Fellows of Harvard College. Reprinted by permission.

[In the traditional family] women typically specialized in home production, including child care, cooking, and cleaning, while men specialized in work in the market. . . . The earnings potential of men was higher than that of women for two principal reasons. First, the fact that women usually bore several children and were at risk of additional pregnancies sharply reduced their opportunity to successfully pursue a remunerative career. Second, physical strength was an asset in most jobs. . . . Although the economic power of the husband was usually greater than that of the wife, their consumption of goods and services was usually equal. Such marriages, therefore, were typically hierarchical rather than egalitarian. . . . The inequality in economic power resulted in deference of the wife toward the husband, a double standard with respect to sexual behavior, and other gender inequalities. . . .

Perpetuation of such inequality is morally indefensible. Fortunately . . . the economic opportunities available to women in postindustrial society are far better than they were previously, and women have much better control over their fertility. These . . . changes will reduce economic inequality, there will be less specialization, and male dominance is likely to diminish.

"rich family life." The overload of responsibilities leaves little time for socializing with relatives and friends, and often not fully as much time as the careers really demand (Skinner, 1980). In addition, the egalitarian marriage has its own built-in problems—so many that "it is not uncommon for couples starting out with egalitarian ideals to find themselves in a rather conventional marriage" in spite of their original hopes (Smith, 1980).

After considerable search, Linda Haas (1980) managed to find thirty-one egalitarian couples in the Indianapolis area and study their problems and satisfactions. The chief difficulty turned out to be the sharing

Ray Ellis, Photo Researchers

One aspect of egalitarian marriage: a husband who shares the care of the children.

of domestic chores. Many of the couples mentioned that "it was hard to break with the traditional pattern they had observed in their parents' households," which made one partner or both reluctant to do some of the necessary chores. Some couples found themselves at odds over their standards for housekeeping: "Husbands consistently felt wives were too finicky and wives regarded husbands as too sloppy." In many cases the problem was "the wife's reluctance to give up her traditional authority over many domestic chores." In some cases the partners lacked skill at various tasks—the husband in cooking and sewing, the wife in making repairs or taking care of the car.

Most of the couples were concerned that their careers might conflict—for example, if one of the partners had an opportunity for an attractive position in a different city. Another common problem was conflicts between jobs and family responsibilities. Because of job demands they found that "housework didn't get done, they lacked en-

ergy and patience to interact well with their children, or they did not have enough leisure time to spend with their families." Because of their family responsibilities they "had to cut down on over-time work, had trouble doing job-related work at home, had to rearrange their schedules when the children became ill, or had little time to attend job-related meetings in the evenings and on weekends" (Haas, 1980).

But Equality Does Have Its Advantages

Despite the problems, the couples in the Haas study seemed happy with their choice of egalitarian marriage. Sharing in decisions, which they found relatively easy to arrange, produced an unexpected blessing because "it called for a considerable amount of discussion, and this communicating in turn brought greater intimacy between husband and wife." Because both had jobs and shared housework and child care, they could "appreciate and sympathize with each other more." Their role-sharing also "gave them the opportunity to do more things together, increasing interaction and thus enhancing husband-wife closeness."

The couples with children found that role sharing also improved their parent-child relationships. A number of these wives "felt they had become better mothers because they worked outside the home and shared child-care with their husbands. They felt they were less bored, less hassled with managing two roles, and not resentful about the entire burden of childcare." Some of them had found that "children got to know their father better than they would in the traditional family" and "benefited by being exposed to more than just the mother's outlook on things."

Is egalitarian marriage likely to become more common in the future? Will more and more husbands become willing to move in that direction by playing a greater part in housekeeping and child care?

Many of the recent developments point in that direction. Because of the large number of wives who now work outside the home, it has been suggested, it is possible that the family will significantly change its pattern of dividing household chores (Condran and Bode, 1982), out of sheer necessity if for no other reason. In any two-worker family, even one that is far from egalitarian, there has to be a certain amount of sharing of roles and tasks. Thus it seems likely that many of today's children, brought up by parents who both work, will observe far different patterns of female and male behavior than those that prevailed in the past and will be socialized into far different attitudes toward sex roles in marriage. But egalitarian marriage is a radical change from the traditional, husband-dominated marriage that prevailed until recently and still has millions of adher-

ents. It will gain any widespread popularity only slowly, if at all.

THE SINGLE LIFE AS A COMFORTABLE ALTERNATIVE TO MARRIAGE

There is another recent trend, in a way the exact opposite of egalitarian marriage, that may also be an influence in the future. You and all today's members of our society are now free to make one choice—willingly, deliberately, and as a form of self-fulfillment—that was unthinkable to most people in the recent past. You can decide to avoid marriage and remain single, at least until you change your mind and possibly for the rest of your days.

If you make this choice you will meet with some difficulties, for our society still continues to view single people with a certain amount of suspicion and put pressure on them in various ways to join the ranks of the married majority. But being single is far more respectable than it used to be, and it shows every promise of growing more so. The single male is no longer branded as a poor old bachelor so eccentric or cranky or both that no woman would have him. The single female is not universally thought of as a poor, sex-starved old maid who just didn't have what it takes to catch a man.

"Marriage Pushers" of the Past

As recently as the decade of the 1950s, to be single was to be a member of a small minority—in a very real sense, a social freak. Almost everybody got married, usually as quickly as possible. More than half of all American men were married before their

23rd birthday, more than half of all women before they reached 21 (Bureau of the Census, 1977).

The pressure to marry was especially strong on women. Bernard (1972) has written:

> It was assumed that there must be something wrong with the unmarried. In the 1950s women [were] convinced that not to get married was indeed a fate worse than death, for without marriage one could not be completely fulfilled. College seniors were struck with 'senior panic' if they did not have some kind of marital commitment before they got their degrees.

So lonely and despised was the single life that people got married if they possibly could. One study of the unmarried in the 1950s found that they were mostly people with severe personal or social problems that disqualified them as possible mates (Kuhn, 1955). A study in the 1960s found that many were feeble-minded, mentally ill, or physically handicapped (Landis, 1965).

Ours was a nation of marriage pushers, selling the roles of wife or husband as the only appropriate ones. Many people were pressured into marriage even though they lacked any real desire or talent to play the roles. Too much marriage, among people unsuited for married life, may have been partly responsible for the rapid rise in divorce. Discussing the fact that the United States was one of the most married and most divorced societies of all time, Margaret Mead (1971) observed that:

> Ours is a terribly overmarried society, because we can't think of any other way for anybody to live except in matrimony, as couples. It's very, very difficult to lead a life unless you're married. So everybody gets married . . . We have, in a sense, overdepended on marriage in this country. We've vastly overdone it.

For Singles Today, Lots More Company

It is still easier to be married than not to be. As pointed out earlier in this book, most of us have a tendency to conform by behaving as other people behave; and to be single in our still much-married society continues to be nonconformist behavior. Single people may suffer feelings of guilt because of pressure from parents and married friends. They may also have other problems, some of which are mentioned in the box on *Opinions and Experiences*. Note particularly the comment of the young woman who worried about her behavior around the husbands in the married couples with whom she was friendly. This is a common difficulty: "Unattached people, especially women, are considered a threat to married people" (Duberman, 1975).

Despite the continuing problems, the number of single adults is far higher today than it was in the 1950s, or for that matter even at the start of the 1970s. The sharp rise in the number of people who remain unmarried in their 20s and early 30s is illustrated in Figure 13–2. Single women and men are now actually in the majority among those in their early 20s. After that age they are outnumbered, but they are not nearly so alone as they were just a few years ago. All told there are about 20 million single people in their 20s and 3 million in their early 30s.

These figures may or may not mean that more Americans are choosing to remain single as a permanent lifestyle. Paul Glick, who specializes in population trends, believes that in all likelihood about 10 percent of today's

Opinions and Experiences

PROBLEMS OF THE SINGLE

Some single people who were surveyed by sociologist Peter Stein describe the dark side of the life they have chosen.

A young woman employed as a computer programer

My boss couldn't, or didn't want to, understand why I was not married. He imagines all sorts of orgies going on. Two of the younger guys [in the office] said they felt sorry for me, that I was missing out on a lot of fun. When I told them that I was happy and that I neither wanted to marry nor be a mother, they looked upset. . . . They couldn't understand my position and I think they didn't believe me. I was pretty upset by it.

Another young woman

When I'm friends with married people, I have to be very careful in how I act around husbands. Either one or both might think I'm coming on to the husband, when I'm really not.

A man who was an assistant professor at a university

It was hard being the only single person in the department. I would be invited to social gatherings and would get pretty nervous about who my date should be. The men would get into shop talk and the women, in some other part of the house, would talk about their families, the school system, and summer vacations. My date and I would usually feel uneasy, not quite fitting in and yet feeling a bit guilty about not fitting in.

A woman of 28

When I tell people I'm 28 and not married, they look at me like there's something wrong with me—they think I'm a lesbian. Some just feel sorry for me. What a drag.

A man of 35

[I am under] a non-specific pressure, a sort of wonderment that I can still be alone. I sometimes feel pressure from my own confusion of how come I don't conform to the patterns of people who are in the same situation as I am in terms of career and age.

From Stein, P. J. Singlehood: an Alternative to Marriage. *Family Coordinator*, 1975, 24, pp. 489–503.

young men and 12 percent of young women may never marry—a sharp increase from the mere 3 or 4 percent of people who became adults in the 1950s (Glick, 1984). Certainly young women and men are at least waiting longer to marry, on the average, than their parents did. This means that the young singles have more company and are therefore under less pressure to join the ranks of the married. The more they postpone marriage, Glick has suggested, the more likely they are to remain single permanently.

Many observers believe that the result would be a net increase in human happiness.

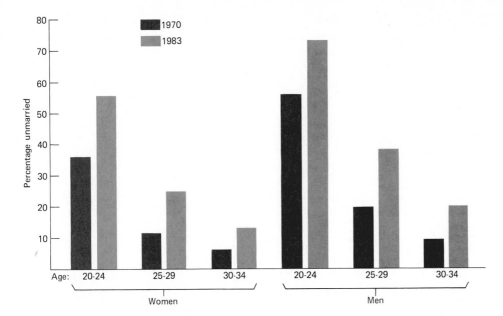

Figure 13–2
BEING SINGLE: ITS RISING POPULARITY
Since the much-married decade of the 1950s there has been a sharp
increase in the number of women and men who are single at all ages from
20 to 34. The big jump since 1970 is shown by the bars (Bureau of the Census, 1984a).

One psychoanalyst, for example, has suggested that "the stampede toward marriage" so pronounced during the 1950s was a "frantic attitude" that did "a tragic disservice" both to young people and to the integrity of marriage itself. "If, hopefully, the single state does gain respectability, marriage will cease to be the unalterable imperative. . . . With that pressure relieved, better and more equitable social contracts may evolve" (Seidenberg, 1973c).

The Case for Staying Single

Among the chief reasons more people are remaining single—at least for more years and possibly for a lifetime—are today's permissive sexual atmosphere and the great upsurge of women employed in the business

world. The effect of these changes has been to nullify what used to be two strong motives for marriage: "Men no longer [have to] marry to get sex and women no longer [have to] marry to get financial support" (Bird, 1972).

Among women an additional reason has been the liberation movement, with its emphasis on equal rights and independence (Glick, 1975). The movement has led many women to think for the first time about the possibility of being self-sufficient. Some of them have found that the "unmarried woman has greater freedom to take advantage of the exceptional opportunites offered by today's changing world." As they enter their 30s, still unmarried, they "are beginning to build up economic independence, an investment in work, and a . . . value system that allows them to identify and exploit major sources of personal and social satisfactions in other areas than marriage and the family'' (Adams, 1971).

Some people are single because they have looked at marriage and found it wanting. This is especially true of people who were once married, got divorced, and have made up their mind not to remarry. A survey has shown that many such people have decided, on the basis of their own experience or observations of relatives and friends, that marriage is ''a stalemated, boring situation'' that ''inhibits independence, experimentation, and learning'' (Stein, 1975). Others are not necessarily disillusioned with marriage but have decided that—for them—it has fewer advantages than single life. They have cho-

sen to give up ''the security and interdependence of a family relationship'' in return for ''independence, experimentation, social and psychological autonomy'' (Sussman, 1975).

Some of the advantages of being single, as reported by men and women who have chosen that lifestyle, are described in the box on *Opinions and Experiences*. These people have made their choice and they like it, especially the greater freedom to do what they please when they please, without responsibility for anyone else.

Lifestyles for Singles

As for how single people live—with what kinds of pleasures and joys and trials and

Michael Kagan, Monkmeyer

The "swinging" lifestyle: a singles bar in New York City.

Opinions and Experiences

ADVANTAGES OF BEING SINGLE

Some other people surveyed by Peter Stein describe the bright side of the single life.

A young man's comments

There aren't any conditions under which I would consider getting married. . . . I want freedom of choice, freedom to do what I want to do instead of being tied to just one person and doing the same . . . things over and over.

A young woman's comments

There are so many things I want to do. Now that I've completed school and am making a good living, there is fun to be had. I've started a dance class, learned pottery, and joined a women's group.

A man who is again a bachelor after two marriages

I am having an experience I never had before, since I was always answerable to some-

one—my family or wife. I never had the experience of being completely self-motivated, having to consider someone else's reaction to what I do—approval, disapproval, does the job pay enough? It makes me feel potent . . . and very responsible for what I do. Productive, capable of dealing with life's exigencies, and capable even of seeking friendly help when I need it. Whether you are self-realized or not cannot be blamed or credited to someone else.

Another man's comments

Clown, promoter, radical, friend, playboy, priest . . . you name it, the possibilities are there. I'm in a situation to discover my potentialities and act on them. It's an exciting process—sometimes frightening, but I like having alternatives to choose from.

Stein, P. J. Singlehood: Alternative to Marriage, *Family Coordinator,* 1975, 24, pp. 489–503.

tribulations—there are many legends. The magazines, movies, and television sometimes make it seem as if all unmarried people head right from work for a singles bar—to drink, dance, and generally make merry until pairing up for the night, with the only question being "Your place or mine?" There has been much publicity about swinging apartments run especially for the single, built around swimming pools where they can admire each other's physiques.

There is a certain amount of truth in this.

The nation does have its share of singles bars, especially in big metropolitan areas. And there are singles apartments where a good deal of partying goes on. In general single people spend more money than the married on entertainment, travel, and sports cars.

But single people come in all shapes and sizes (and for that matter ages). They display a wide variety of interests, tastes, personalities, and sexual behavior. There is no such thing as a lifestyle for singles but rather as many different lifestyles as there are people. A recent survey of 3,000 representative Americans living alone, either because they had never married or were divorced or widowed, concluded that "the single life . . . is neither the wild spree advertised by the sensationalists nor the dour state of loneliness many fear it to be" (Simenauer and Carroll, 1982).

The kind of swinging singles life emphasized in the magazines and movies, though it does have its adherents, probably attracts only a small minority of single people—and even the members of this minority do not necessarily stay with the life very long. A study of single people in the Chicago area found that they tended to visit singles bars less and less frequently as time went on. Indeed singles bars, singles apartments, and parties were considered by many of the people surveyed to be generally unsatisfactory ways to meet people and establish friendships—far less likely to be successful than meetings that took place in connection with jobs (Starr and Carns, 1972).

In the 1982 Simenauer-Carroll survey, the most frequently mentioned methods of meeting the opposite sex were those shown in Table 13-1. Although singles bars ranked high on the list, they had produced unhappy results for a number of women. About 2 percent had been robbed by men they met at a bar, 3 percent talked out of money or property, 3 percent raped, 5 percent physically mistreated, and 16 percent subjected to verbal or psychological abuse.

Happiness and Unhappiness among Singles

How happy are single people? Again there are too many individual differences to permit a definite answer. In public opinion polls fewer single than married people usually de-

Table 13-1

Where Single People Meet Each Other

Method	Percentage of Women	Men
Through friends	36	30
At bars	18	24
Social gatherings	18	22
Singles functions	18	14
At work	9	10

These are the ways most frequently mentioned in the 1982 survey discussed in the text. The term "singles functions" means clubs, dances, discussion groups, and group trips to sporting events, sponsored by organizations catering to single people—mostly older people. Some of the people surveyed mentioned two or even more of these methods. Only 1 percent of both sexes mentioned ads in newspapers or magazines. (Copyright © 1982 by J. Simenauer and D. Carroll. Reprinted by permission of Simon and Schuster, Inc. and the Julian Bach Literary Agency).

scribe their lives as very happy or very satisfactory—in one poll 48 percent as compared with 60 percent of the married (Roper, 1974). But this may be due to the fact that a number of people still remain single not by choice but because of physical or psychological problems, probably including a tendency to be chronically dissatisfied.

In the Simenauer-Carroll survey, 55 percent of the women and 50 percent of the men said that the lifestyle had been "wonderful" or "basically fine" despite the fact that there were "plenty of problems." But 46 percent of the women and 38 percent of the men were displeased with their lifestyle. The advantages they named most often are listed in Table 13-2, the disadvantages in Table 13-3. The study concluded that being single is in itself "neither more nor less productive of happiness than any other" arrangement (Simenauer and Carroll, 1982).

Table 13-2

Why People Like the Single Life

Reason	Percentage of singles	
	Women	Men
Mobility and freedom	49	49
Time to pursue personal interests	21	17
The social life (dating, entertainment, excitement)	12	15
Privacy	10	8

These are the four advantages of the lifestyle mentioned most frequently by single people *(Simenauer and Carroll, 1982).*

To put this in more personal terms, if you should ever find yourself torn between remaining single and getting married, the only solid advice anyone can give you is this: Being single is great if you like it—but considerably less than great if you don't. As one thoughtful bachelor said, after pondering himself and his friends, "Some single people

Table 13-3

What's Wrong with the Single Life

The problem	Percentage of singles	
	Women	Men
Loneliness	44	42
The "dating grind"	11	14
Restricted social and sexual life	10	12
A tendency to become rigid, self-centered, and selfish	8	14
Economic insecurity	16	2

These are the five most frequently mentioned disadvantages of being single *(Simenauer and Carroll, 1982).*

are happy and some aren't—just like married people" (Jacoby, 1974).

Single Women and Single Men

It was once a popular legend that men remain single by choice and women for lack of opportunity—and that the world is therefore full of happy-go-lucky bachelors and frustrated spinsters. Like many popular beliefs, this was contrary to the facts. The statistics show that single men, as a group, do not fare nearly so well as unmarried women.

Bachelors are considerably more likely to die in automobile accidents and from causes related to psychological stress, such as lung cancer and cirrhosis of the liver, as well as from that ultimate gesture of despair, suicide (Gove, 1973). A majority of studies have found that single men are more likely to suffer from various kinds of mental disorders. They are nearly 50 percent more likely to be patients in mental hospitals (Gove, 1972).

One public opinion survey produced findings summarized in these words: "Women get along without men better than men get along without women. . . . Single women of all ages are happier and more satisfied with their lives than single men. . . . [Contrary to the old legend] the truth is that there are more carefree spinsters and anxious bachelors" (Campbell, 1975). On the basis of this kind of evidence it has been suggested that today's typical single woman, far from being a neurotic and pitiable old maid, is in truth a pretty, sexy, prosperous career woman who enjoys life and "likes men and loves children . . . but mainly in small doses" (Hornig, 1970).

The differences between single women and single men seem to arise in part from differences in the kinds of people who are likely to remain single. Women are most likely to be unmarried if they make a good salary and hold a high-level professional or technical job, but men if they have low earnings at a low-level job (Havens, 1973). One study has indicated that the proportion of unmarried women seems to be highest among the most intelligent, especially those with a college education, and the proportion of unmarried men seems to be particularly high among those who had unsatisfactory relationships in childhood with their parents, brothers, and sisters (Spreitzer and Riley, 1974).

Again, however, individual differences prevail. Not all unmarried women are superior people who would be ideal mates if they so chose, and not all unmarried men are hopeless leftovers. Indeed some men who seem to be confirmed bachelors change their mind, marry late in life, and have a marriage that is successful by any standards. Some people are single because of homosexual preferences, which have little if anything to do with earning ability, education, intelligence, or most other personality traits. Some homosexuals, especially women, establish long-lasting one-to-one relationships that resemble marriages (Cotton, 1975).

ALTERNATIVES TO CONVENTIONAL MARRIAGE

Remaining single is perhaps the only clear-cut alternative to marriage. A number of other lifestyles, of various kinds and engaged in by varying numbers and kinds of women and men, are alternatives to marriage as it is usually thought of. Many of them reject the conventional pattern of sexual exclusiveness. Some, notably communes based on religion, are not so much an alternative to marriage, which they may continue to value,

as an attempt to establish a new kind of ideal community within the larger society.

Swinging (or Mate Swapping)

The most dramatic and widely publicized alternative is *swinging*, a form of organized infidelity. Most of the time swingers live like any other couple. They work, maintain a household, and often bring up children. But they frequently get together with acquaintances—sometimes just one other couple, sometimes several, at a meeting where everybody is free to make sexual advances to everyone else.

Most swingers carefully avoid any emotional attachment to the other people in their group. Often the couples do not meet socially except at their sexual parties. Because husband and wife both participate in the mate swapping, they do not regard themselves as unfaithful but as "having transcended the perceived pettiness, hypocrisy, immaturity, and dishonesty" of extramarital affairs conducted in secrecy (Varni, 1972).

They believe in the slogan: "The family that swings together clings together," in other words, that their sexual variety strengthens them as individuals and as married couples (Denfield and Gordon, 1970). But many couples who try this lifestyle drop out, often because they are "hurt and psychologically damaged" (Denfield, 1974).

Open-ended Marriage, or Permission to Be Unfaithful

Another alternative is known as *comarital sex* (Roy and Roy, 1968), or *open-ended marriage,* in which wife and husband agree that both are free to pursue any outside sexual activities they wish. The term *open-ended* was coined by Ronald Mazur (1973), who defines it as:

monogamous in the sense that it's based upon an intended lifetime commitment between two . . . but open-ended because it does not exclude freedom to have any number of intimate relationships with others. . . . [Its goal is] the possibility of a vibrant monogamy which embraces the being of any other human being who seeks the grace of human caring and touch.

Advocates of open-ended marriage maintain that sexual monogamy is an infringement on individual freedom and growth, which future generations may view as "a form of emotional and sexual malnutrition, a condition of sexual deprivation for both male and female rather than a sexual privilege" (Smith and Smith, 1974)

The open-ended arrangement is often confused with *open marriage,* which was the title of a popular and influential book of the early 1970s. The book was in fact merely a strong argument in favor of companionship marriage—even egalitarian marriage—as opposed to the traditional kind. Its authors summarized their message in these words:

> Open marriage is a relationship in which the partners are committed to their own and to each other's growth. It . . . is flexible enough to allow for change, which is constantly being renegotiated in the light of changing needs, consensus in decision making, in acceptance and encouragement of individual growth, and in openness to new possibilities for growth.
>
> *(O'Neill and O'Neill, 1972)*

The book did suggest that some people might prefer their marriage to include freedom for extramarital sexual experiences, "but such relationships are not necessarily an integral part of open marriage. It is another option that you may or may not want to explore." After making further studies,

one of the authors has reported finding very few couples who managed to cope successfully or for long with sexual permissiveness: "For most people a partner's infidelity elicits deep and upsetting emotions. The assurance of sexual fidelity is still an important and necessary attribute of most marriages and infidelity an extremely threatening situation" (O'Neill, 1977). For one of the interviews that helped convince the author, see the box on *Opinions and Experiences.*

Group Marriage, or Can Four or Six Live Better than Two?

Another highly publicized alternative, *group marriage,* sometimes called *multilateral marriage,* was the topic of a well-known 1973 study by Larry and Joan Constantine, family therapists. The Constantines themselves once engaged in a four-way marriage with another couple, which they described as "short-lived . . . turbulent and difficult but not without its joy and some profoundly intimate moments." They managed to find 104 people who had taken part in twenty-six group marriages, usually of two women and two men but sometimes of three people or five and in one case six. Each person was considered married not necessarily to everyone else but to at least two others.

By and large these people "were seeking growth, a better family for their children, a community, and sexual and intellectual variety." Some of them apparently found what they wanted, because two of the group marriages were still intact after three years, another two after five years. Most of the marriages had broken up, often very quickly. More than half of them lasted less than a year. Among the problems that proved fatal were personality clashes, failures in communication, personal "hangups," jealousy, and conflicts in lifestyle.

Opinions and Experiences

TO BE OR NOT TO BE FAITHFUL

A young wife who meets many men on her job describes to Nena O'Neill her feelings about fidelity.

There is a guy at work who is devastatingly attractive. If I were single, he would be someone I would want to have an affair with, and I know the feeling is mutual. Once there, for a moment, I was really tempted—and then decided, no.

If I did succumb, there would be that loss of innocence. Once it's done, it's like you put your finger in the cake and it's not going to look the same anymore, or feel the same either. I realized that I'd be attractive to a lot of people and be attracted to them, but I'm very attracted to my husband and very much in love with him.

Who needs to satisfy something that could be only sexual? My relationship with my husband is sexual but it's much more than that. It's affection; it's love.

Comments by "Maryanne," in N. O'Neill. *The Marriage Premise.* New York: M. Evans, copyright © 1977 by Nena O'Neill. Reprinted by permission of the publisher and the Sterling Lord Agency, Inc.

One sociologist has pointed out that group marriage "aggravates and highlights the problems of two-person marriage," for it requires each of the participants "to adjust to the idiosyncracies" of several people instead of only one (Bernard, 1972). In other words, it is difficult for any of us to establish a fully successful relationship with even one partner, much less two or three or more. At the height of the publicity about group marriages, in the early 1970s, the Constantines estimate that there were only about 1,000 of them in the nation.

Intimate Friendships

Somewhat akin to group marriage is the alternative of *intimate friendships.* These are like any other friendships among adults who live in their own households and get together frequently to share their social lives and recreation, except that they also include sexual intimacy. This is not considered essential to the friendship, nor even so important as other shared interests, but it is viewed as "appropriate" if and when desired.

A study of several hundred people engaged in intimate friendships (Ramey, 1975) found that most of them seemed to be seeking greater intensity and variety of intimacy, both emotional and sexual. They wanted a "deeper sharing" and feeling of "belongingness" with friends, which they believed might also lead to greater intimacy with their own partners. They felt that "the availability of sexual sharing among friends," even if never exercised, "greatly enhances the friendship."

Since the people in intimate friendships do not share a common household, they avoid much of the day-to-day friction that occurs in group marriages. They have their own problems, however, including lack of time, arranging schedules for getting together, and even finding babysitters to free them for their meetings. The friendships often break up for much the same reasons as group marriages. The participants find that their interests move apart, the attraction between members is too one-sided or "gets too close for comfort," or, in married couples, one partner or the other feels "left behind."

Communes: A "New Idea" That Goes Way Back in History

When communes were making headlines in the 1960s, many people thought they were a brand-new invention. Actually they have been traced to the years B.C. and have cropped up at many times and in many places ever since (Fairfield, 1971). In our nation a boom period occurred shortly before the Civil War and numerous communes of various kinds flourished, though later they gradually dwindled in membership or disappeared (Kanter, 1973).

Most communes throughout history have represented an attempt to create a new kind of community, free from the faults the members perceived in society as a whole. Many of them have been based on religious beliefs, for example the sixty Shaker communities that flourished a century ago. The Amish and Hutterite groups, whose community life resembles communes in many respects, are among today's examples. Most of the communes have demanded rigid standards of behavior, often including monogamy and sometimes even celibacy, which was considered the noblest life of all by the Shakers. As Jessie Bernard (1972) has said, communes "are a lifestyle, not . . . a form of marriage."

Many of the communes that appeared in the 1960s were conspicuously different. They were part of the rebellion against the constraints of society, often dedicated to complete sexual freedom and pursuit of the drug culture. Many of them made only haphaz-

ard efforts to support themselves, or no effort at all, and instead were financed by welfare payments, food stamps, and gifts from relatives (Berger, Hackett, and Millar, 1972). Many quickly ran out of money or broke up for other reasons, and somewhere between 85 and 95 percent of the members dropped out within three years (Sussman, 1975).

Today, besides the large religious groups, the nation has a considerable number of small communes, many of them in big cities and around college campuses. Most of them have been established by students or young wage earners as a way to share the cost of housing and the expense and work of preparing meals, though members may also be seeking the companionship and support of other people with the same interests.

A study of thirty-two such communes in the Chicago area found that the most successful and long-lasting ones tended to be conservative in such matters as financial prudence, getting the housework done regularly, and responsibility for the welfare of any children of members. They also arranged schedules so that members had sufficient time to be alone. A number of them set a definite time limit on the life of the commune, which members generally regarded as a temporary stage in their life and career (Cornfield, 1983).

THE SEARCH FOR SELF-FULFILLMENT: A PROMISE OR A THREAT FOR THE FUTURE?

The various alternatives to conventional marriage were widely publicized in the 1960s and 1970s, possibly because they were attuned to the search for self-fulfillment that became a significant force in those two decades. Many people, joining the move to fulfillment, decided that the customary form of marriage and the family was too constricting and would soon be replaced by arrangements offering individuals more opportunity to "do their own thing."

Of the people who actually entered into one or another of the alternatives, some found it fulfilling and some did not. None of the new suggestions ever really attracted a large following, however, and the publicity has since died down. A recent survey of people living without partners because they had never married or were divorced or widowed asked the subjects to check off any items they found attractive in a list of alternatives. Only

about 7 percent checked open-ended marriage, 4 percent a free-love society, and 2 percent group or communal marriage (Simenauer and Carroll, 1982).

How Many Are Engaged in the Search for Fulfillment? How Many Ignore It?

The 1960s and 1970s marked the height of the sexual revolution, rebellion against society, and experimentation with "consciousness raising" through encounter groups, Yoga, meditation, and mind-altering drugs. Books on discovering awareness through physical and psychological self-improvement

Laimute E. Druskis

The search for self-fulfillment: one of the Americans who "spend a great deal of time thinking about themselves."

abounded. The thirst for fulfillment was so intense that one popular writer called the 1970s the "me decade" and a historian said our society had become devoted to "the cult of narcissism" (Lasch, 1978).

Although many of the extremes of the 1960s and 1970s have long since lost their popularity, a desire for some kind of self-fulfillment continues to be a major factor in the lives of many Americans and will doubtless influence the future of marriages and families. Just how strong a force self-fulfillment has become was perhaps best demonstrated in a series of public opinion polls, made near the start of the 80s. These surveys, by the polling organization of Yankelovich, Skelly, and White, showed the following interesting facts about American attitudes (Yankelovich, 1981):

Twenty Percent of Adults remain untouched by the many changes that have taken place in our society in recent years. They are "totally uninvolved in the search for self-fulfillment." They accept the traditional masculine and feminine sex roles and the traditional pattern of marriage. "Their lifestyles and philosophy have not changed from the outlook that dominated America in the 1950s and earlier periods."

Seventeen Percent of Adults are totally dedicated to the search for self-fulfillment, which they place "high above all other concerns." Far more than other Americans, they describe themselves as "spending a great deal of time thinking about themselves" and "searching for ways and means to acquire a higher level of self-knowledge." They feel a need to be well educated and well read, find excitement and sensation, and "restore romance and mystery to modern life." They are more likely than other Americans to eat health foods, take up Yoga and meditation,

join psychological encounter groups, analyze their dreams, and seek psychotherapy. They believe that "satisfaction comes from shaping oneself rather than from home and family life."

Sixty-three Percent of Adults fall somewhere between the first two groups. These people have many concerns in life besides self-fulfillment—such things as "family obligations, work, inflation worries, health cares, kids with school problems, crime, what the Russians are up to, the football game." But they are well aware of the changes that have been taking place in our society and are raising questions about "what we should be giving to our family life and getting from it" and "what we should be getting out of our jobs and what commitments we should be making to them." They wonder whether society's "old rules still make sense." The pollsters describe them as "involved in the weak form of the self-fulfillment search" (Yankelovich, 1981).

A Pessimistic View of the Search

As the Yankelovich polls make clear, most people have been caught up in one way or another in the search for fulfillment, some of them to the exclusion of all other concerns. What is this trend likely to do to marriages and families of the future?

Some observers have concluded that self-fulfillment, if carried to its extreme, makes it impossible to establish a close and enduring relationship with anyone, especially the intimate and trusting commitment of marriage. For a forceful expression of this view, see the opinions of Edward Levine in the box titled *A pessimistic view of today's "unbridled individualism,"* which you should read before going on to the next paragraph.

Opinions and Experiences

A PESSIMISTIC VIEW OF TODAY'S "UNBRIDLED INDIVIDUALISM"

A sociologist maintains that the search for self-fulfillment raises serious doubts about the future of marriages and families.

Values have become weak, vacillating, and ambiguous. . . . The weakened influence of moral principles rooted in religion and tradition has led many people to consider them as useful when the situation is appropriate, rather than as standards with universal relevance and applicability. This change has made possible the ascendance of values and behavior that stress impulse gratification, self-centeredness, and an orientation to the present, in contrast with the traditional values that emphasize impulse regulation, regard for others, and an orientation to the future. This shift in standards and behavior has been extremely detrimental to the well-being of marriage and family, as well as to the socialization and emotional development of children. . . .

The inordinate emphasis that many husbands and wives give to the pursuit of their personal interests has eclipsed the needs of their marriage and distracted them from attending to these needs. This is partly evidenced by the remarkably high and unprecedented rate of divorce . . . a sign that many spouses were unwilling to devote the necessary efforts to resolving their marital problems. . . . The emphasis on self-fulfillment has tended to draw spouses away from each other. Personal preferences supersede the needs of keeping the marriage intact and gratifying. . . .

Although parents are best suited for rearing children, they have tended to shift much of the responsibility to others, such as baby sitters and day-care centers. More parents will probably do so in the years ahead, and the harmful effects this has on the emotional development of children will also become more widespread. . . .

When children develop inadequate self controls, as tends to occur when they are permissively, inattentively, or indifferently parented (more common than ever today) they often become dominated by their impulses. As a result, in the course of growing up, they are easily and frequently frustrated when they cannot satisfy their impulses. Their inability to resolve these conflicts creates further frustration which, in turn, generates anger and depression. . . . Those who marry are more likely than not to experience marital problems deriving from their emotional troubles. . . . Others may be unable to marry because of their emotional problems. . . .

The present state of marriage and the family is an ill omen for the balance of the decade and, perhaps, the years beyond. Unbridled individualism will continue to trouble and disrupt marriage and family life, and children will increasingly pay the emotional and behavioral costs of negligent and inadequate parenting.

One reason for Levine's pessimism, as the box makes clear, is his belief that "unbridled individualism" on the part of parents is especially harmful to their children. But he feels that today's young people, for all the psychological damage they suffer, may yet turn out to be the eventual salvation of marriage and the family:

Young people may find that their quest for identity and meaning in life can be realized by turning to marriage and family and the values on which they have rested. Surely this is a more meaningful alternative than drug use, religious cults, the loneliness and aimlessness of single people. Their dissatisfactions with family life as children and adolescents may induce them to restore and revive marriage and the family. At any rate the prospects for reversing the decline of the family during the past decade depend heavily on young adults, for their decisions will largely determine the state of the family in the 1980s and the decades to follow.

(Levine, 1981)

A Hopeful View

Levine's view can be summarized as the belief that marriage and the family are headed for disaster unless the nation's new generations rebel against today's trends and especially against "unbridled individualism." In sharp contrast to this pessimistic view of the future are the conclusions Daniel Yankelovich has drawn from his polls of opinions and attitudes. Yankelovich (1981) agrees that many of the recent changes in our society have produced serious problems, for example, "the breakup of families, a restless movement from job to job, an endless rumination about one's inner needs and unfulfilled potentials." He concedes that "the ethics of the search for self-fulfillment discard many of the traditional rules of personal conduct" and have led many people to abandon the "old self-denial ethic" and instead "refuse to deny *anything* to themselves—not out of bottomless appetite but on the strange moral principle that 'I have a duty to myself.'"

Yet he finds that the search for self-fulfillment is by no means just "an outpouring of self-centeredness and self-indulgence." He calls it, not "proof that the American character is changing for the worse," but "a transition phase from slavish rejection of the old rules to a synthesis of old and new," a synthesis that he believes will revolutionize and regenerate our society and create happier and more democratic families. Yankelovich's comments are summarized in the box titled *A hopeful view: Self-fulfillment as "a way toward a brighter future."*

WOMEN, THEIR ROLES TODAY, AND THE FUTURE

For a final glimpse of what the future may bring, a recent study sponsored by the National Science Foundation (Baruch, Barnett, and Rivers, 1983) is worthy of special attention. To examine what is happening to women in the various roles possible in today's society, the investigators made an in-depth survey of 300 women in the Boston area, using a number of tests and lengthy interviews to determine how they felt—and why—about their life. The findings add a new dimension to what has been said in the book about the choices and roles now available in our society and the pros and cons of being a housewife-mother or partner-wife or one of the divorced or single women who now make up substantial groups in our society.

All Kinds of People in All Kinds of Roles

The importance of individual differences was clearly apparent in the report. Some women, regardless of their role, felt very much in charge of their life and confident of their ability, but some others were anxious and self-questioning. Some gained a great deal of pleasure and self-esteem from the role they were playing, but others were unhappy and restless. In part this seemed to depend on

Opinions and Experiences

A HOPEFUL VIEW: SELF–FULFILLMENT AS "A WAY TOWARD A BRIGHTER FUTURE"

A public opinion pollster finds strong indications that today's problems are merely potholes on our journey to a "happy new phase of human experience."

For a brief period from the mid-'60s to the early '80s . . . the search for self-fulfillment expressed itself in language borrowed from pop psychology: the need to "keep growing," the urge to express one's "potentials," to be recognized for "oneself" as a "real person," etc. . . . [Some Americans have been placing] their personal self-fulfillment high above all other concerns—above money, security, performing well, or working at a satisfying job. . . . They speak the tongue of "need" language: they are forever preoccupied with their inner psychological needs. They operate on the premise that emotional cravings are sacred objects and that it is a crime against nature to harbor an unfulfilled emotional need. . . . They find their freedom exhilarating . . . but they embrace a theory of freedom that seems to presuppose that you are free only when you do not commit yourself. . . .

This psychological outlook grows out of a too-narrow conception of what a self is and how it should be fulfilled, a conception that now shows signs of fading. . . . Today's self-preoccupation neither reflects an enduring change in our culture nor is it what Americans are really looking for in their search for self-fulfillment. The preoccupation with self is a deflection, a false start in a journey toward a goal that is as important for our society as for the individual. . . .

The self-fulfillment search is a more complex, fateful, and irreversible phenomenon than simply the by-product of a shift in the national character toward narcissism. It is nothing less than a search for a new American philosophy of life. . . . It is a breeding ground for better times. It generates new energies to revitalize the economy and it seeks human goals broader than those measured solely by annual increments of the gross national product. It is not that the new philosophy of life rejects materialistic values: Americans are far too practical for that. But it broadens them to embrace a wider range of human experience. Under its influence, Americans may become less self-absorbed and better prepared to face the difficult choices that now confront our civilization. . . .

While a prognosis of our future based solely on our political/economic prospects may leave us pessimistic, even desperate, one based on our cultural prospects—our shared social values—may point the way to a brighter future. . . . The seekers of self-fulfillment pursued a false strategy in the '70s, and Americans of the '80s are learning to distinguish false and destructive strategies from valid ones adaptive to a world that is just beginning to emerge. . . .

I believe the struggle for self-fulfillment in today's world is the leading edge of a genuine cultural revolution. It is moving our industrial civilization toward a new phase of human experience.

whether they had chosen the role deliberately (and had made a choice that was suited to their own personality and tastes) or had been forced into the role (or had chosen unwisely).

For all groups of women, happiness also depended on a satisfactory sexual life and the size of the family income. A general threat to happiness was the fact that all the roles were found to be subject to what the authors of the study termed "out-of-step anxiety." As their report explains:

> They all were vulnerable, but in different ways. Never-married women can feel out of step because they are not married; divorced women can feel that way because they aren't married any longer. Childless women often feel different because they don't have children, and employed women who do have children often feel anxious because they have departed from the "proper" role they were socialized to play. And the one group of women that did follow the expected route of marrying, staying home, and raising children now find that the rules have changed—suddenly, society is questioning the value of what they are doing. It's nearly impossible to be a woman today and not feel out of step.
>
> *(Baruch, Barnett, and Rivers, 1983)*

All the women, at the time of the study, were 35 to 55 years old—meaning that many of the important developments that have created conflict and doubt about attitudes toward sex roles, marriages, and families took place while they were growing up. Those problems and pressures, however, still affect today's young women to at least some extent and often very strongly, and the authors of the study consider their findings "highly relevant" to today's younger people. Following is a summary of what the survey showed about the lives of women in the various possible role choices, especially their difficulties and their opportunities for self-esteem and satisfaction.

The Housewife-Mother

As a group, the women who were devoting full time to keeping a home and raising their children ranked very high in the amount of pleasure they found in life. The chief reason seemed to be that they enjoyed not just one but two "oases of intimacy": Their close relationships with their husband and their children. The women ranked very low, however, in what the report called "mastery," or sense of being in charge of one's own destiny. For both pleasure and self-esteem, the housewife-mother is dependent on the husband and therefore vulnerable. Her joys depend basically on how well the marriage is going and the husband's occupational prestige. To what extent she feels in charge of her destiny depends on whether the husband seems to approve of her decision to remain a housewife and how much he helps her with the housework and child care, help that she interprets as "proof that her job is a serious one and needs to be done."

Married, a Mother, and Employed

Many people assume that working mothers, because of their overload of responsibilities, suffer "high levels of stress and conflict." The survey found, on the contrary, that in fact they "are doing very well indeed." They ranked highest of all groups in the pleasure they found in life, and well above average in their sense of "mastery." Like the housewife-mothers, they had two oases of intimacy, their husband and their children. In

Michael Kagan, Monkmeyer

Success at a job: a source of both pleasure and a sense of mastery for women in many of today's professions.

addition they had their job. At times when their marriage was not going well, "good experiences" on the job helped "offset distress at home." A happy marriage helped them when there were problems at work. Thus they enjoyed "two distinct sources of pleasure: love and work."

Employed mothers, unlike housewife-mothers, are not dependent on their husband's income, occupational prestige, or approval. Nonetheless the survey found that the "quality of the marriage is crucial." The wife's relationship with her husband affects both her pleasure in life and her sense of mastery: If the marriage "is going badly, she

probably isn't getting that comforting assurance that helps her feel, 'I'm okay.' "

Married, Employed, but No Children

The working wives without children ranked very high in sense of mastery, but only a little above average in pleasure. How they felt seemed to depend in large part on whether they actually preferred being childless or had regrets because they were never able to have children or had "drifted into permanent childlessness by putting off their decisions."

The job was especially important to these women, affecting both the pleasure they found in life and their sense of mastery. If they enjoyed their work, they did not feel too dependent on the marriage; but "a bad work experience" was "especially risky." Also important was their sexual relationship with the husband, which was found to be "particularly critical when a couple is not held together by parental responsibilities."

The Housewife Who Is Not a Mother

This group now seems to be very small and composed mostly of older women, because nowadays younger wives without children almost always work outside the home. The group ranked at the very bottom in sense of mastery—"there's no doubt that this role is risky for a woman's feelings of self-esteem"—and near the bottom in pleasure. A woman in this role is totally dependent on her husband's "income, his attitude toward her being home, how well the marriage is going, sexual satisfaction, and how happy she is with the way decisions are made in the marriage." She is "extremely vulnerable to problems in the marriage'' and to loss of the husband.

The Single Woman

This group, which included only working women who had never been married, proved to be no testimonial to the single life. It ranked at the bottom in pleasure and below average in mastery. These low marks were probably due at least in part to the fact that all the women had grown up at a time when singlehood was still regarded with distaste. Today's younger single women probably have a different attitude toward the role and regard it as more rewarding.

For what the findings are worth to newer generations, they showed that the single women were dependent for all their satisfactions on their job—the higher the prestige the better—and their relationships with their parents, sisters, and brothers. Work was important as ''a source of enjoyment as well as of self-esteem.'' Also important was the woman's attitude toward the role:

> The woman who finds that her lifestyle suits her is better off than the woman who feels that her life was imposed on her because she was never ''chosen.'' . . . a never-married woman who really wants to be a married homemaker, who doesn't feel that she's working because she wants to, can feel particularly discouraged about herself and her life.

The Divorced Mother with a Job

These women, despite the pains of divorce and the difficulties of the single parent, proved to be getting along with surprising success. They ranked highest of all the groups in feeling in charge of their own destiny and just below average in the pleasure they found in life. The women had all been divorced for at least a year and for an average of seven years, and had ''for the most part been able to get their lives on track again after a very rocky period.''

Like working mothers, these women have two sources of satisfaction, their job and their children, but their relationship with the children is much more influential than in any other group: ''[Their] well-being seems linked to their children. How their children are doing, and how they are doing as mothers, constitutes a 'stamp of approval.' It is the one built-in intimate relationship. If the kids are doing well, they can feel they are doing well.'' On the other hand, ''problems with children present a major zone of vulnerability.'' In sum, divorced women must do well at both their jobs—the one in the marketplace and especially the other as single parent. Many of them manage to do it.

HOW THE FACTS AND OPINIONS ABOUT THE FUTURE ADD UP

As throughout history, the future will doubtless see much that is new yet much that reflects what has happened in the past. All the traditional attitudes toward marriage and the family will continue to influence some people very strongly and everyone to at least some extent. The new attitudes that have cropped up so rapidly in our recent hectic period of change will also shape the future, for some people powerfully, for others to a lesser degree.

In some ways our society is likely to become less pluralistic. The differences in family patterns between ethnic and religious groups and people in different regions of the nation, already waning in some respects, will probably continue to decline and may disappear. In other important ways, however, family patterns and roles are becoming more pluralistic than ever. The National Science Foundation study demonstrates the wide variety of roles now played by women, and the Yankelovich polls on self-fulfillment show how conflicting attitudes toward roles and family life now exist side by side, each with its own many adherents.

Changing Patterns of Socialization

How early socialization and childhood observation of parents' behavior continue to influence us all through life is apparent in many studies cited in this book. The Science Foundation study provides further evidence of how women are pressured in opposite directions by traditional views they acquired at an early age and the new standards they have since encountered, to the point where they find it nearly impossible to "not feel out of step" no matter which they choose. The reluctance of men to engage fully in household and child-care tasks, even if they have moved toward an androgynous attitude on sex roles, is another indication of socialization's power.

Yet the new attitudes have affected everyone. Even people who continue to accept the traditional sex roles and have traditional marriages do not behave the same way as their like-minded parents and grandparents did before them. Even in traditional homes, young children are likely to observe more discussion of family problems and sharing of decisions and tasks than was common in the past. This new brand of socialization experienced by today's youngsters will undoubtedly affect their attitudes and behavior as adults, though we cannot predict exactly how.

The Postrevolutionary Era of Marriage

Although the rapid march of new events in recent decades revolutionized thinking about marriages and families, the changes no longer seem so strikingly novel and baffling. The giant leap "from institution to companionship" occurred more than forty years ago, and companionship has since become the choice of many millions. The sexual revolution had its heyday in the 1960s and 1970s and is now subsiding into more conventional standards. The young women who were in the front lines of women's liberation are now middle-aged. We have entered a postrevolutionary era of what should be at least relative stability and calm.

One source of trouble in the recent past was that everyone was caught up in the revolution, but few people understood what was really going on. In fact it was almost impossible for *anybody* to keep up with all the changes, hold them in perspective, and separate the possible long-term trends from the mere passing fads that were hailed so ardently and optimistically by their supporters.

Now the changes are better understood, and analysis of what has been happening and why is widely available in courses like this one. If we are indeed entering an era more stable than the recent past, we should have the time as well as the tools we need to cope with the new problems and grasp the new opportunities.

SUMMARY

1. One of the most notable trends of recent years has been an explosive growth in the number of opportunities and choices we have in education, lifestyles, occupations, and places to live. In particular, we now have more freedom to choose our own sex role—from traditional masculinity or femininity to total androgyny—and our own marriage relationship, from the traditional husband-dominated pattern to the most extreme form of companionship.

2. The new ideas exist alongside the old, and we are surrounded by people who hold very different attitudes, play different sex roles, and have different lifestyles. The changes have come so fast that our society has not had time to adjust, and as Skolnick has said, we "face conditions unknown to our ancestors and must find ways to cope with them."

3. Although choosing from among the possibilities can be difficult and confusing, most Americans seem to welcome them. A poll has shown that 73 percent feel they have "more freedom of choice" than their parents did. Most are confident they will manage to take advantage of the opportunities and live their life the way they "truly want to live."

4. Some of the likely developments in coming years, according to many students of the changes and trends, are these:

   a. The rapid rate of new developments will slow, and we will have a period of relative stability "in which American families can adjust to the sharp changes" of recent decades.

   b. The rise in the divorce rate will slow and perhaps stop. The number of unmarried couples who live together will probably double again, to 3.6 million by the end of the decade. Living together has become not so much a substitute for marriage as "an-

other stage in courtship" or a transition between first and second marriages.

   c. The large number of wives and mothers who work outside the home, which some but not all observers think will continue to grow, will lead to increased help by husbands with housework and child care.

5. One major problem society faces is to remove some of the difficulties now faced by two-worker couples, especially those with children. This will require changes in working hours and conditions and increased facilities for child care, "one of the most crucial social issues of the next decade."

6. *Egalitarian marriage,* defined as "equal sharing of traditionally sex-segregated roles," is a new pattern of relationship. The egalitarian couple take equal responsibility for such feminine tasks as housekeeping and child care as well as such masculine tasks as earning a living, working in the yard, and making repairs. They have an equal voice in all decisions affecting the family. As yet egalitarian marriages are rare, but "more and more couples are moving in this direction."

7. Among the difficulties reported by egalitarian couples are the sharing of domestic chores, which most men have been socialized to avoid, and the conflicting demands of a career and a rich family life. Among the advantages reported are a greater intimacy, as the result of discussion of shared decisions, and improved parent-child relationships.

8. Many young people are deciding to remain single as an alternative to marriage, at least until later in life. The number of single people in their 20s has grown rapidly to 20 million, and in their early 30s to about 3 million. Paul Glick estimates that about 10 percent of today's young men and 12 percent of young women may never marry—a sharp jump from the 3 or 4 percent of people who became adults in the 1950s.

9. Among the reasons for the rise in single

adults are today's permissive sexual standards and increased opportunities for women in the business world. "Men no longer have to marry to get sex and women no longer have to marry to get financial support." Single people have chosen to give up "the security and interdependence of a family relationship" in return for "independence, experimentation, social and psychological autonomy."

10. Despite publicity about singles bars and swinging apartments, these are not typical of single people, who have as many different lifestyles as anyone else.

11. Satisfaction with the single life varies from one individual to another. "Some single people are happy and some aren't—just like married people."

12. Single men do not fare nearly so well as single women. "Women get along without men better than men get along without women. [Contrary to the old myth] there are more carefree spinsters and anxious bachelors."

13. Prominent among the alternatives to conventional marriage are the following:

Swinging, or organized infidelity. Wife and husband live an ordinary life most of the time but get together with others for mate-swapping parties.

Open-ended marriage, in which husband and wife agree that both are free to pursue any outside sexual activities they wish.

Group marriage, in which three or more people live together as if everyone was married to everyone else.

Intimate friendships, or groups of people who get together to share their social lives and recreation and consider sexual intimacy between any two of them to be appropriate if and when desired.

Communes, in which groups of people live together in the same residence or community. Their members seek to create a new kind of community, free from the faults they perceive in society. Many of them, past and present, have been based on religious beliefs and monogamy. Although some communes established in the 1960s substituted total sexual freedom for marriage, the majority throughout history have been "a lifestyle, not an alternative to marriage." Today the nation has a considerable number of small communes, particularly in big cities and around college campuses, whose chief purpose is to share the cost of housing and the expense and work of preparing meals, with the members also seeking the companionship and support of other people with the same interests.

14. The appeal of alternatives to conventional marriage was closely tied to another trend of the 1960s and 1970s—the search for self-fulfillment through such various forms of "consciousness raising" as encounter groups, Yoga, meditation, and mind-altering drugs. The desire for some kind of self-fulfillment will probably continue to influence our society. Public opinion polls show these facts about the form the search now takes:

Seventeen percent of adults are totally dedicated to finding self-fulfillment, which they place "high above all other concerns." Far more than most people, they spend a great deal of time thinking about themselves and seeking ways to "acquire a higher level of self-knowledge."

Twenty percent of adults remain unaffected by the search for self-fulfillment or other recent developments. Their attitudes, marriages, and lifestyles are like those prevailing in the 1950s and earlier.

Sixty-three percent fall somewhere between the other two groups. They are aware of the recent changes and are raising questions about marriage patterns and lifestyles but have many concerns and interests besides self-fulfillment.

15. The future effect of the various attitudes toward self-fulfillment is a matter of debate. Edward Levine believes they are leading toward selfish standards and behavior that have already been "extremely detrimental to the well-being of marriage and family." Daniel Yankelovich, the pollster, interprets his studies as showing that the narcissism of the 1960s was just a false start on "a search for a new American philosophy of life" that will enlarge and enrich human goals and create "a brighter future."

16. A recent study sponsored by the National Science Foundation explored how women, in the various roles now possible, have fared: the housewife-mother, the mother who works outside the home, the working wife without children, the dwindling group of housewives without children who do not work outside the home, the divorced mothers, and the single women. All groups were found subject to "out-of-step anxiety" because in one way or another they had departed from the role they were socialized to play or, in the case of housewife-mothers, had found the role seriously challenged by new attitudes. All groups also had many women who had adjusted well and achieved both pleasure and a sense of control over their life.

DISCUSSION QUESTIONS

1. What are some of the changes that companies have made for the convenience of two-worker families with children? Can you think of other changes that would be helpful?

2. What do you think would be the advantages and the difficulties of egalitarian marriage? Would you want an egalitarian marriage?

3. How does our society put pressure on people to marry?

4. Discuss the pros and cons of remaining single. Would the single life be a good option for you?

5. Would you say that you are totally uninvolved in the search for self-fulfillment, totally dedicated to the search for self-fulfillment, or somewhere in-between? Why have you taken the position that you have?

6. What do you think will be the three most difficult problems for marriages and families in the next ten years? What do you think will be the three most signficant opportunities?

Family Finances

These are hard times for any married couple, or for that matter single people, to decide whether to buy a house or rent and how to balance income and spending, carry enough insurance, prepare for emergencies, and save for the future—in other words, how to cope with the whole complex issue of handling finances. Even in the most stable periods, few people have enough money for everything they need or might like; so for most of us deciding to do or buy one thing always means giving up something else. The recent period has been spectacularly *un*stable, adding immensely to the difficulties.

For many years starting in 1973 the cost of living in the United States leaped higher and higher, and what cost $1 in 1973 cost more than $2 by 1981 (Economic Report of the President, 1985). At the start of the 1980s, the cost of living was rising by 13 percent a year, and many people were convinced that inflation would continue at that rate, or even worse, forever and ever. Then it settled back, and the cost of living rose by less than 4 percent a year through the first half of the decade. What will it do in the future? Ask six financial experts and you will get six answers.

Interest rates rose to an all-time peak at the start of 1981, making it almost prohibitively expensive to take out a loan for a car purchase or a mortgage on a house. Then

they dropped quickly, to more manageable levels. On the other hand taxes fell through the first half of the 1980s, adding to the wage earner's take-home pay. Where taxes and interest rates will go in the future is anybody's guess.

COPING WITH THE NEW ECONOMY

In this rapidly shifting and unpredictable economy, many of the old attitudes toward family finances no longer apply. Your grandparents probably believed, and perhaps also your parents, that it was wise to have a savings account in the bank for emergencies, carry as much life insurance as you could and never borrow against it, buy a house, and if at all possible start on the day you were married to save 10 percent of your pay for your old age. All these things are now either questionable, downright unwise, or impossible.

How then are we to cope? The best answer, in a period like this, is with flexibility and hope. There is no way of knowing where the cost of living, interest rates, and taxes will stand even a year from now, much less ten or twenty or fifty years. Past predictions by the most eminent of the experts have disagreed widely, and sometimes all of them have turned out to be wrong.

All any of us can do is try to understand the problems, recognize that there is no guaranteed formula for solving them, and be prepared to adjust to whatever happens. These pages will present some of the possible choices you are likely to face, the advantages and disadvantages of the possible solutions, and how to avoid the financial pitfalls into which many people stumble.

Attitudes toward Money and Husband-Wife Conflict

People somehow grow up, perhaps by copying or rebelling against their parents, with two totally opposite attitudes toward money. Some people are grasshoppers, who like to spend for the enjoyment of living for the day. Some are ants, who like to hoard their assets for the coming of winter. Many are grasshoppers in some respects and ants in others. They are happy to spend money for some things (say newer and better cars) but think that buying others (say clothes) is an extravagance.

Partners in marriage are seldom likely to agree about every possible use of money, and a dedicated grasshopper and a dedicated ant are likely to disagree about almost everything. No wonder conflicts over money, as stated earlier, are one of the most common complaints heard by marriage counselors. Yet the conflicts are usually just a sign that something else is wrong with the relationship. If the partners are basically affectionate, respectful, and happy to have each other, disagreements over spending and saving are usually resolved, through compromise and mutual adjustment.

Even the extreme ant and the extreme grasshopper may not only live with their differences but actually profit from them. There is something to be said, they discover, for both sides of the argument. The one who likes to hoard against the future may learn that it can be a relief to escape at times from rigid self-denial and indulge oneself a bit. The one who prefers to live for the moment may learn that a certain amount of security can also be rewarding.

A Sensible View of Spending and Saving Money

A psychiatrist once offered these useful suggestions for a sound and healthy attitude toward money and spending:

1. Money is not an end in itself. Rather, it should be regarded as a way of acquiring the things you really want. Making more money should never be allowed to interfere with health, love, contentment, hobbies, or recreation.
2. Spending for necessities and a certain number of luxuries should be taken for granted. It is abnormal to let hoarding money become life's chief goal.
3. It is also abnormal to worry constantly that people will take advantage of you in money matters. Naturally you want to be careful not to get cheated—but don't let the actual threat get blown out of proportion. The words ''can't afford it'' are properly used only to state a clear fact. Don't use them to punish yourself or your partner.

(Bergler, 1970)

These suggestions are valid regardless of whether the economic climate is stable or rapidly shifting. The things that people want to use their money to acquire, of course, will vary from family to family. People may put priority on their house and neighborhood, their recreational interests, their children's schooling, or any of dozens of other possibilities. For some, indeed, security is more meaningful than anything else. You have to go along with your own—and your partner's—tastes and preferences.

KEEPING A FAMILY BUDGET: A BOTHER BUT A BLESSING

To many people the word *budget* has an ominous ring. It suggests drastic discipline, penny pinching, and enough joyless bookkeeping to take all the fun out of life. Many, indeed, refuse to keep one. A public opinion poll once found that Americans are split equally between people who operate on a budget and people who do not (Yankelovich, Skelly, and White, 1975). In all probability, however, even the nonbudgeters usually have some informal system of gearing their spending to their income, for failure to do so is an invitation to bankruptcy (where some people without financial discipline do in fact wind up).

A budget of one kind or another is recommended by all family experts, and establishing one is less burdensome than it may sound. The budget need not and should not be a straitjacket. It should allow for whatever kind of recreation the partners prefer, give both partners some spending money for their own personal needs, and permit an occasional indulgence. Instead of being regarded as a lifetime commitment to a rigid schedule, it should be revised from time to time to take account of changes in income, taxes, the cost of living, and the partners' notions of what they prefer their money to buy.

How to Start Setting Up a Budget

Although a budget is in essence a plan for the future, the first step in establishing one is to examine the past. You will need a detailed record of *everything* the family spends out of pocket over a three-month or four-month period on major items like food all the way down to the casual purchase of a newspaper or a package of chewing gum. You probably will not remember absolutely every single impulse purchase, but at least you will get a good idea where most of the cash on hand is going.

The second step is to list all your fixed expenses: rent or mortgage payments, telephone bills, electric and gas, water, heating oil if you use it, and any taxes that you usually have to pay in addition to what is withheld from paychecks. Other fixed expenses are your automobile and any other transportation you use to get to work, as well as the premiums on all the insurances you carry and all the payments due each month on your debts (credit cards, installment purchases, and automobile loans). All these are obligations that you have to meet, and the money must come right off the top of your earnings.

Just undertaking these two steps often proves to be an eye-opener. The fixed expenses, when listed one after another, may add up to a frightening total, especially if you have a lot of debts. But you have to know how big they are to do any realistic planning.

The list of where the out-of-pocket money goes may reveal some previously unsuspected leaks in the pocketbook. Do the occasional flyers you both take on the state lottery add up to $10 a week, or $520 a year? Have you got into the habit of buying magazines on impulse but then never getting around to reading them? Do you often spend money on expensive food items that you do not really enjoy all that much?

Asking these questions should not become an austere exercise in eliminating any trace of self-indulgence. Rather it should be viewed as a calm appraisal of money spent and value received. If those lottery tickets give you $10 worth of pleasure, why not buy them? On the other hand, you may decide that you can get more fun out of $10 spent some other way. The whole idea of a budget is to channel your income in whatever ways bring you, considering your own tastes and preferences, the most satisfaction. You may find, indeed, that you are spending not too much but too little on things you greatly enjoy.

Balancing Outgo and Income

The next step is to list all income: your family paychecks plus any extras you may be able to count on, such as earnings on money you have put aside, year-end bonuses from the employer, or cash gifts from your parents at Christmas. Once you have reached this point, you know or have a pretty good idea how much money is coming in and how much has been going out. Somehow, of course, the two must now be balanced.

Your income minus your fixed payments is what you have left over for everything else: food, all the various items needed to keep the household running, clothing, medical expenses, recreation and vacations, personal care (haircuts and cleaning bills), tobacco and alcohol if you use them, gifts to church and charities, new purchases of appliances or a car, and savings. If your fixed expenses are large, as they are for most families, you may find that a distressingly small amount is left for all these matters—but you have to make it do or go into debt.

Some Common Mistakes in Spending: Too Much House

Marriage counselors find that many couples have trouble making ends meet because they have let their fixed expenses get too high. Frequently they have bought a home that was far more expensive than they could really afford, and by the time they meet the mortgage payments and pay for the upkeep they have little left for anything else. One counselor reports the case of a couple who found, when they sat down to examine their records, that 42 percent of their take-home pay was drained off by their house (Phillips, 1985).

This is an easy mistake to make now that the median price has reached $74,500 for an existing house (National Association of Realtors, 1985) and an even higher figure for a new home. You find that for just an extra thousand or two—which seems negligible considering what you have to pay anyway—you can get some extra room, or a bigger yard, or a more convenient neighborhood. The extras, plus all the interest on them during the twenty- or thirty-year life of the mortgage, can make the difference between being able to handle the cost and being broke.

Too Much Car

Automobiles are a good deal more expensive than generally realized, especially since they can be bought on the installment plan for monthly payments that may seem easily manageable. But the monthly payment is just the tip of the iceberg. A car also needs gasoline, insurance, maintenance, and repairs, and eventually it must be replaced. At the middle of this decade it was estimated that even a compact car, driven 10,000 miles a year for five years, costs nearly $5,000 a year (Hertz, 1985). Owning a bigger car, or trading it in oftener, costs considerably more.

The expense can be reduced by driving less and keeping the car longer. Driving the same 50,000 miles over a period of about six and a half years, for example, will cut the cost to around $4,000 a year. Buying a used car—especially if you get it checked by an independent mechanic before signing the papers or buy it from an acquaintance who you know has treated it well—can save money. The total family expense can be lowered by avoiding the purchase of a second car if at all possible. Even if one car is not quite enough at times, you may be able to save considerable money by using taxis or rented cars on those occasions.

Too Much Debt

Government statistics show that at the middle of this decade Americans owed $594 billion on installment purchases, $580 billion on personal loans, and $1,347 billion on home mortgages (Federal Reserve Board, 1985). Most of the money was owed by younger people.

Thus being in debt is not unusual. But some people dig themselves into a hole. What with their mortgage, balance due on their credit cards, and time payments on their car, refrigerator, and kitchen range, they are so deeply committed that their fixed expenses drain off almost their entire income. The debt goes unpaid, and the interest digs the hole deeper by the month.

In these times of "easy credit," the pitfall of too much debt is especially treacherous. Buying on credit is never really "easy." At mid-decade the interest rate on most unpaid balances was around 18 percent. This means that if you keep using your credit cards or making time payments on your purchases, never reducing the total amount you owe, you are in effect paying nearly a fifth more for everything than you think you are.

A couple whose list of income and outgo reveals too much debt must face the facts. They have been living beyond their means and paying an 18 percent penalty for it, and they must now stop short, no matter how

painful the jolt. The only escape is to undertake an austerity program: no more use of credit cards, no major purchases except when absolutely necessary, a bare-bones budget for daily expenses. They can take consolation from knowing that their austerity period will someday end, after accomplishing its goal of a long-term improvement in their lifestyle and especially their peace of mind.

Other Frequent Mistakes

Some people fall victim to a hobby that refuses to stop growing. Buying a cheap camera may lead eventually to an expensive one, a whole array of lenses and other accessories, and darkroom equipment. Hitting a few golf balls at a driving range may lead to buying more and better clubs, professional lessons, and membership in a costly country club. An afternoon or evening at the race track may lead to an addiction. Nothing wrong with these or any other hobbies, of course—provided you are aware of what they cost, can afford them, and get your money's worth in real enjoyment.

Some people who when single spent a large part of their income on clothes carry the habit over into marriage, continuing to buy bigger and better wardrobes than they now really need or enjoy. Some spend a disproportionate share of their income overindulging their children. They buy expensive baseball gloves, football padding, skin-diving equipment, and fishing tackle and provide the best in clothing and lessons in music, dancing, and horseback riding—for much of which the children could hardly care less.

Another common error is reacting to good fortune by going on a splurge. One counselor was consulted by a couple who never had financial problems until one partner found a new job at a big increase in salary. They celebrated by hastening to redecorate and refurnish their house and buy everything that struck their fancy, including a boat. When the splurge ended, they had committed all their extra income for years to come—in fact overcommitted it.

SOME WAYS TO STRETCH YOUR DOLLARS

In contrast to the mistakes that can waste a large part of your income are a number of ways to make your dollars go further. They take some time and study, and none of them makes a spectacular difference just in itself, but they can add up to a great deal of money over a year and a lifetime. By applying them carefully and consistently a family can live just as well, in real value and enjoyment, as a less prudent family with a considerably larger income.

The methods all deal with how you spend your money, especially how you go about making your purchases of housing and major appliances (the biggest item in every budget), food (second biggest), transportation, and clothing, plus one other important item that is not usually thought of as a form of spending. This item is credit, which is closely akin to other purchases in that it can be bought cheaper at some sources than others. The chief suggestions of experts on family money management are summarized in the following sections.

Housing: To Buy or to Rent?

During the rapid inflation of the 1970s there seemed to be no doubt about the wisdom of buying your own house if at all possible. The price of a new home tripled from 1967 to 1979, making it the best possible invest-

ment. Even if you had to move within a year or two you could quickly find a buyer and almost always make a profit. Of course you had to pay real estate taxes and interest on the mortgage, but much of this money came back in the form of reduced income taxes.

Some of the advantages may not always continue. The rise in prices leveled off in the first part of the 1980s and actually declined in many areas, sometimes sharply. Some members of Congress have been talking about changing the income tax laws to remove local taxes, and possibly even mortgage interest payments, from the list of deductible items. Finding a buyer is not always as easy as in the boom years.

Thus the question of whether to buy or rent is not easily answered at the moment. Authorities on family finances have found that there is not much difference in expense; generally speaking it costs about as much to rent an apartment as to buy and maintain a house in the same kind of neighborhood with the same number of bedrooms (Stillman, 1984). Owning a house, even if its value never rises, means that the portion of the mortgage payment that goes to pay off the debt (small in the early years, larger later on) is an investment. Renting has the advantage of mobility: Unless you are stuck with a long-term lease with no excuse for leaving, you can readily move to a career opportunity in a different community or to better or less expensive housing as your income changes.

Making the Decision and Buying a House

What you decide will have to be based partly on your guess about the future and to an even greater extent on your own finances and the cost and availability of housing in your community, plus the size of the down payment and monthly mortgage payments that a purchase would require. Because houses are expensive, the decision may be made for you, at least until your family income rises.

If you decide to buy, the best advice is to make some firm decisions before you even start to look at any houses. Exactly how big a house do you need, either now or in the foreseeable future? What is the price range you can handle comfortably? What kind of neighborhood do you prefer? Is it important to be near schools and stores? How big a yard and garden are you prepared to take care of?

Once you have considered these questions, stick to your answers. Looking at an available home, it is all too easy to get carried away by a single desirable feature like built-in kitchen appliances or a bed of roses in full bloom and ignore the fact that the house does not meet more essential requirements. Above all, do not let enthusiasm trap you into buying too much house.

The Purchase of Major Appliances

If you own a house, and in many cases even if you rent, you will probably have to buy at least a refrigerator and range, and you may also want a clothes washer, dryer, dishwasher, and other costly appliances. The total expense is formidable, especially when you add the cost of the repairs all of them will need from time to time and replacements when they wear out.

As in buying a house, the specialists in family finance advise deciding in advance exactly what you need and what features you consider most useful. Your own experience and the advice of friends will help, and you can pick up a variety of brochures from appliance dealers listing the advantages of their machines. The simplest appliances, with the fewest frills, are the cheapest and need the fewest repairs, but you may consider some of the added features worth the extra cost.

Prices on exactly the same item vary from dealer to dealer, often by considerable amounts, and it pays to shop around. Most retail stores advertise sales from time to time, but beware of the many dealers who have a "sale" almost every day of the year, yet always charge more than you would have to pay elsewhere. Besides the initial cost, consider the warranty offered with the machine and the availability and price of repairs.

Buying Furniture: A Lifetime Investment

In selecting furniture, price does not much matter. Good furniture will last a lifetime. Indeed, as you can see at any exhibition of antiques, it may last for many lifetimes. If you divide the purchase price by say thirty years to determine the annual cost, you will find little difference between paying $500 for a sofa or $750. Spending too little may in fact cost money in the long run, because a cheap sofa will probably have to be thrown out in a few years. The important thing is *quality*.

Unless you have studied furniture, you cannot see or feel quality. An established furniture or department store that has always stood behind its merchandise, or the label of a highly regarded manufacturer, is your best assurance.

How to Choose an Automobile

Although the automobile is one of the largest items in any family budget, many people buy for the wrong reasons. They have a strong prejudice for a certain brand name, or favor a racy-looking car, or have been impressed by an advertising campaign. None of these matters has much to do with how well a car will behave in general or meet your individual needs.

The questions to ask yourself in advance, say specialists in family finance, are these: How many people will ordinarily ride in the car—in other words, how big must it be? How much trunk space will you need? How many miles a year will you drive, for how many years? (This determines how important durability is to you.) How essential to you are easy parking, gasoline mileage, quick acceleration and stopping, and a "hard" ride or a "soft" ride? Since accessories can drive up the purchase price, which ones are truly valuable to you?

The cheapest time to buy a new car is in late summer, just before the new models come out and dealers are trying to clear out their present supply. But the price is a bargain only if you plan to keep the car five years or more, because it will be a year old, for sale or trade-in purposes, a few weeks after you buy it. At all times of year, different dealers set different prices at which they will sell without a trade-in, or they will offer differing prices on the car you do trade in. For help in determining how much leeway a dealer actually has in setting a reasonably profitable price, there is a publication that lists the current cost of new cars to the dealer.*

A used car, if you get one that has been treated well and is in good condition, can save a lot of money. The best way to buy is from an acquaintance known to have taken good care of the car. If you buy from a dealer, it is important to know how long the firm has been in business and learn as much as you can about its reputation. Buying from

an unknown individual who has advertised in a newspaper may save the middleman's profit, but ordinarily you will have no way of checking why the car is no longer wanted. Whichever method you use, you need the help of knowledge about the going prices of used cars* and an independent mechanic to make a careful check of the car before you buy.

Shopping for Food

The trips you make to the grocery store or supermarket seem hardly worth considering, compared with the large outlays for housing, appliances, and a car, but they add up. The average family spends between a fifth and a fourth of its income on food (Stillman, 1984). A few dollars saved here and there on groceries can make a considerable difference over a year.

Advance planning is again the key. Prudent buying demands a shopping list, prepared after consulting the specials advertised in newspapers or on radio and tv. Without a list, you are at the mercy of impulse buying, encouraged by the artful way stores arrange attractive displays of their wares—and sometimes by your own appetite, unless you have heeded the old warning never to shop when you are hungry.

One trip a week, purchasing as much as you will need, is better than more frequent shopping. It saves time and gasoline. For many items, the largest package is a better value than a small one, as you can readily determine by looking at the "unit price" listed on the shelf. This figure, which tells you how much you will pay for each ounce or pound of the product, is the only way you

*The publication is *Edmund's New Car Prices,* distributed monthly by Dell Publishing Company of New York City. It is available in many libraries.

*See the *Official Used Car Guide* published by the National Automobile Dealers Association, 8400 West Park Drive, McLean, VA. Also available in libraries.

can tell the real cost, because the larger look-ing of two boxes or cans may actually con-tain less than the smaller-looking one. Some stores, in addition to well-known brand names, carry "house brands" that are cheaper per unit and often, though not al-ways, of equal quality and taste.

Shopping for Credit

Buying on credit or borrowing money, as has been said is always expensive, but it is less expensive in some places than others. On a home purchase, you may find that different banks and insurance companies set some-what different interest rates—and even a .5 percent difference in the rate adds up over the twenty or thirty years of paying off the mortgage. Rates on time payments for new automobiles also vary, and auto companies sometimes offer special low rates to attract customers. The cheapest way to borrow cash is usually at a bank. The most expensive way is from a personal loan company, which will charge around 24 percent and sometimes much more.

It pays to shop around. Even more val-uable, if you have the patience and disci-pline, is avoiding the use of credit altogether on anything but buying a house, for which very few people ever have enough money in hand. Some specialists in family finance sug-gest this approach: Think only about the first of the many large expenditures you will make in your lifetime on such items as au-tomobiles and appliances. Instead of buying it immediately, on credit that will cost 16 percent or more, wait until you have saved enough to pay cash, meanwhile keeping the money in a savings account that will pay you 5 percent or more. After this first purchase, start saving for the second. The inconveni-ence of waiting for the first item will be re-paid by a "startling" amount of saving over

a lifetime (Gross, Crandall, and Knoll, 1980).

How Much Insurance and What Kind?

Some types of insurance are an absolute ne-cessity in this world of possible misfortunes. If you drive a car, you need liability insur-ance to protect against the risk of losing all your life savings if sued for injuries in an ac-cident. The more you have the better, and it does not cost much more to buy $100,000 of coverage than $10,000. If you own a house, you need fire insurance or risk hav-ing everything you have paid and still owe burn up with the building. Especially if you have children or debts, you need life insur-ance to protect your family from financial disaster if you die.

Many other types, though less essential, can be very valuable. Disability insurance is protection against an illness or accident that leaves you unable to work. Health insurance is a cushion against high medical and hos-pital expenses in case of major illness. Col-lision insurance protects against an accident that seriously damages your car. Other types cover other financially crippling events. Life is so full of possible hazards, however, that you cannot possibly pay for enough insur-ance to cover them all; so you have to pick and choose—and hope for the best about the other dangers. Some suggestions follow.

Life insurance   The rule of thumb is to have enough to keep the family income at its pre-sent level for a minimum of three years. If you are the sole wage earner, making $20,000 a year, you need at least a $60,000 policy. In a two-paycheck family, each part-ner should be insured for at least three times annual income, and preferably more if there are children whose care may cost more if either partner dies. You may get considerable help from insurance paid for by the company you work for. Social Security provides payments to a widow, though not a widower, with a child under 18 years old. You will have to determine the amount in your own case from information available at libraries or Social Security offices.

Whatever the amount of life protection you need, over and above any coverage provided by an employer or Social Security, the cheapest and usually most appropriate kind is *term insurance.* This is in essence a bet that you will die before the term, usually five years, is up. If you lose the bet, as you hope you will, whatever premiums you have paid are a total loss and you have to bet again on the next five years, paying more because the rates go up for older people. Other policies, variations on the well-known type called *ordinary insurance,* keep the same premium rate for a lifetime and gradually build up a cash value against which you can borrow. They represent a combination of insurance protection and saving—but you can do much better by getting term insurance, at a much lower premium especially in your younger years, and taking care of your own savings program as a cushion against old age when renewing a term policy gets too expensive.

Car insurance is horribly expensive, especially in metropolitan areas where accidents are more frequent. Yet you have no choice but to buy liability insurance, and you may want theft and collision insurance, at least as long as the car is fairly new and would be costly to replace. On an older car of low value you may want to take your chances.

In buying collision insurance, you can save considerable money with a deductible clause requiring you to pay the first $50 to $500 of damage. For maximum savings, set the deductible amount as high as you dare risk. If everyone who uses the car is a good driver, you may even want to forget collision insurance, on the theory that what you would pay for it over your lifetime will be much more than the cost of repairing collision damage. Even the best drivers can have accidents, of course, but some people have driven for a half century with no more than about $500, or $10 a year, in repair bills.

Shopping for insurance   On all kinds of insurance, different companies have different premium rates, and it pays to shop around. You cannot choose on the basis of price alone, however, because you need absolute assurance that the company will remain in business and be able to pay its obligations. For unbiased information on company ratings, you can consult two books published annually by the Alfred M. Best Company, one for life and health insurance, the other for property and accident insurance. They can be found in many libraries.

SAVINGS, PENSIONS, AND INVESTMENTS

Saving for the future, especially as an umbrella against the rainy days it may bring and the time when retirement means no more paychecks, is an attractive idea. So is the dream of having savings to put into investments that will add to future income and—just possibly—make you wealthy. An old rule of thumb held that the young family should squirrel away 10 percent of income for possible emergencies and another 10 percent for future purchases and eventually old age.

Unfortunately the old formula, though still laudable, is no longer possible for most people. Barring the way is the high cost of setting up and maintaining any kind of modern residence, the expense of an automobile, and the fact that each child now absorbs 15 percent or more of family income.

Most couples go into debt to set up their home and remain in debt, or barely out of it, for many years. Not until they are in their 50s are they likely to become savers instead of borrowers. Then the children have grown up, the mortgage is paid off, and a new financial era begins.

Saving for Emergencies

Even in the lean years, many couples manage to keep some money aside, if only on a temporary basis, to tide them over an emergency—an expensive illness or an unexpected repair bill—or to buy a costly item they will probably need in the future. The question is where to keep the money and have it earn interest while remaining instantly available for use.

In the past, the standard method was a *savings account* at the nearest bank or savings and loan company. This still has its advantages. You can deposit more money in the account or make a withdrawal at any time. Having the account may improve your credit rating and make it easier to get a loan should you need one. But the rate of interest—recently a little over 5 percent at most banks, a fraction of a point higher at most savings and loan institutions—is less than you can get in the following alternatives:

A certificate of deposit requires you to leave the money in the bank for the life of the certificate—from a week to six years or more—or lose all or a big part of the interest. Therefore you have to be sure you will not need the money in the meantime. The longer the time you choose, the higher the rate, which was as much as 11 percent at mid-decade.

Credit unions, run by the employees of many companies, act much like banks, taking deposits and making loans. Only those who work for the company can be customers, and usually no other banking services are provided. The credit unions therefore have almost no expenses, especially since they are usually staffed by unpaid volunteers. A well-run credit union with a proven record is a good place both to keep money, at an interest rate somewhat higher than bank rates, and to borrow, at a lower rate than you could get elsewhere on a personal loan.

Money market funds are available at many banks and brokerage firms, as well as from other financial organizations that advertise frequently in newspaper business sections. Big-city papers list the largest ones every week, along with the interest rate they have been paying, which is always higher than the return on savings accounts.

Money market funds take in money by selling shares to their customers and invest it in short-term paper, that is, loans that borrowers agree to repay in thirty to ninety days. Some funds lend mostly to corporations, others solely to the government. They hold no long-term investments whose value may go up or down as the prevailing interest rate changes. Thus, they always receive interest at the rate dictated by the market conditions of the moment and distribute it to their shareholders as "dividends" that are in fact interest payments.

The value per share always stays at $1, but the dividends rise and fall as prevailing interest rates shift. You can withdraw money at any time by selling shares back to the fund at their $1 price. Some funds provide checks that you can use like any other checks, but usually with the requirement that each check must be written for at least $500. Most funds also require a minimum amount, usually $500 or more, for opening a new account.

The large sum you need to start and the fact that your account is not insured are the only disadvantages.

Bank "Christmas Funds" are an odd and unprofitable way of making sure you will have money to buy presents the following December. The bank requires a set payment into the fund every week starting early in the year, at a figure that will add up to the amount you want available just before Christmas, when you collect it in a lump sum. For many years the funds paid no interest at all. Now some of them do offer a small return, less than on a savings account. The funds are strictly for people who need the discipline of forced savings to be sure of money for the holidays.

Retirement and Social Security

The idea of saving 10 percent of pay for old age is one old financial rule that almost everybody still follows, often without realizing it. Know it or not and like it or not, over 7 percent of your pay, at almost any job you are ever likely to have, will come right off your check and go into Social Security funds, there to remain untouched until you are at least 62 years old. Your employer must contribute an equal amount, meaning that you are in effect saving not just 10 percent of your earnings but closer to 15 percent. When you retire you start receiving Social Security in the form of "benefits" paid on the first of every month. The amount depends largely on how much you have put in and for how many years, but it is also subject to any changes that Congress may make in the meantime to allow for swings in the cost of living—as well as all the many factors that can affect the Social Security Administration's ability to pay. Thus there is no way of knowing how much you can expect to receive or how well the monthly check will meet your needs.

Company Pension and Savings Plans

Many companies also provide pensions for their employees, in an amount based on years of service and salary in the period just before retirement. If you work for such a company, you will have a valuable supplement to Social Security—provided the company stays in business, its pension fund remains solvent, and you stay there long enough to qualify. The number of years you must work for the company varies from one plan to another, but is always a potential problem because many Americans change jobs for one reason or another, in some cases many times before they retire.

Instead of a pension plan, or sometimes in addition, some companies have a savings plan to which employees can contribute a percentage of their earnings, which the company then matches in whole or in part. Any money you contribute to your account is tax-exempt, and so is the money earned by the account from investments that the company makes in your behalf, often in the company's own stock. Nothing is taxed until you start drawing from the account after retirement age. Because of this tax-free feature, and the fact that the company adds as much as a dollar for every dollar you contribute, these plans are extremely attractive.

An IRA—Your Own Best Pension Plan

The best way to set up your own retirement fund, if your employer does not provide one or as an additional source of funds, is with an Individual Retirement Account, popularly known as IRA. Any portion of your income that you put into it is taxfree until you start withdrawals, and so is all the interest or dividends earned by the money in your account. You can put in up to $2,000 a year, or $2,250 if your spouse has no earnings.

Because an IRA account is taxfree until used, any money put into it grows rapidly, as can be seen in Table A–1. Indeed if both marriage partners set up IRAs in their mid-20s, contribute the maximum $2,000 a year, and get as much as an 8 percent return on their money, they can retire with over $2 million. Even a smaller contribution, as little as $25 a month, can provide a sizeable nest egg. The only disadvantage is that you cannot touch any of the money, for any reason, until you reach the age of $59\frac{1}{2}$. If you do, you become liable for taxes on the entire amount and pay a 10 percent penalty besides.

IRAs can be set up at banks, savings and loan institutions, mutual funds, or brokerage houses. Probably the best way is a *discretionary,* or self-directed, account with a discount broker who charges no fees as custodian or for opening and closing the account. In a discretionary account you can decide for yourself where to invest the money. An ideal investment combining safety and a good return is zero-coupon U. S. Treasury bonds or notes. These pay no annual interest, but at maturity they are redeemed for their face value, always considerably higher than the amount you paid for them. The original cost to you depends on the prevailing rate of interest at the time on government securities and the number of years to maturity. A bond maturing in twenty years might cost anywhere from $100 to $200, or perhaps more than that in coming years if interest rates decline sharply.

The Opportunities and Booby Traps of Investing

If you are one of the fortunate few, you may find yourself with extra money, over and above what you set aside for retirement and a readily available emergency fund, that you can invest. You may simply want to add to your income, build a sizeable estate that you can eventually leave to your children, or even take a flyer in the hope of getting rich. Whatever your motive, and whatever

Table A–1
How an IRA can brighten your retirement days

| | Value at age 65
Amount contributed | | | |
| Age at start
of account | $25 a month
Interest rate, compounded semiannually | | Maximum of $2,000 a year | |
	8%	10%	8%	10%
25	$82,687	$145,634	$584,336	$1,044,663
30	54,844	88,279	386,091	633,027
35	35,699	53,038	252,163	380,318
45	14,254	18,120	100,564	129,933

An IRA account, because of its taxfree feature, mounts up to a surprising sum at age sixty-five—especially if you start the account as soon as possible, get the highest interest rate available with safety, and contribute as much each year as you possibly can.

Opinions and Experiences

A LIST OF INVESTMENT DON'TS

These are cautions against the most common pitfalls that await the careless investor. Many people who should have known better, as well as beginners, have fallen into them, with disastrous results.

1. Never put money into a "chance-of-a-lifetime" investment peddled by an unknown salesperson who calls on the phone. These salespersons work out of so-called boiler rooms run by a never-ending succession of fly-by-night companies that offer impossible bargains on precious metals, cattle ranches, oil wells, or anything else that happens to be in fashion. What they sell through their nonstop telephoning usually does not even exist; and after enough checks have poured in they quietly disappear without a trace, taking the money with them.

2. If someone offers you a "guaranteed" interest return far higher than any going rate— say 30 or 40 percent a year—head for the nearest exit. If the investment was legitimate, the promoter could get money much cheaper. Such offers are clearly and obviously swindles, yet naive investors lose millions of dollars a year on them.

3. Leave trading in commodities and options to the professional traders. These are legitimate investments that play a useful role in the business world, but they are deadly to amateurs. Over the years 80 to 90 percent of investors who ventured into commodities have gone broke. Options trading is newer but will probably show similar results. Yes, they sound like a cheap way to buy a chance for immense profits. No, you won't have any profits.

4. Don't act solely on the basis of an opinion you find in a financial program on tv or in the business section of a newspaper. The person venturing the opinion may have impressive credentials and sound convincing, but you can be sure that on the same day another equally qualified and impressive expert is saying exactly the opposite. Even the best-informed investment advisers are often wrong.

5. Beware of bandwagons. Perhaps the most common mistake of all is to invest in something merely because it has been jumping in value. There seems to be a natural tendency to assume that rare coins will make you rich because they have doubled in value for a friend, or that a fast-food stock that has tripled in price over the past two years will triple again in the next two. The past, unfortunately, is not necessarily a guide to the future. You may jump on the bandwagon just as it is slowing to a stop and starting to roll backward downhill. Polaroid stock was a great investment in the 1960s and skyrocketed to 149½ in 1972. Two years later it sold below 15.

amount you have available, you are now in a complex field where no brief discussion can possibly guide you.

Many people have devoted long hours of study, sometimes even a lifetime, to seeking the best path. They have invested in real estate, stocks, bonds, mutual funds, commodities, cattle, race horses, gold, silver, old coins and stamps, art works, antiques, and oil-drilling ventures. Some have succeeded, to a degree ranging from modest to spectacular. Some have gone broke.

Investing's Obvious *Don'ts* and Dubious *Do's*

It is easy to describe the pitfalls that await the investor, like the common ones described in the box called *A list of investment don'ts*. It is much more difficult to suggest any sure pathways to success. There are dozens of ways to invest money, all of which require considerable study before you can determine how appropriate they may be in your own particular case, considering your income, assets, aims, and even temperament. (Some people seek maximum security and hate to take risks. Others like to take their chances and can shrug off a loss.)

At one end of the investment spectrum are gilt-edged securities like U. S. Treasury bonds and notes. You know you will continue to get the interest rate specified on the document and will get your original investment back at maturity, though how much your money will be worth at that time de-pends on what has happened to the inflation rate in the meanwhile. At the other end are outright gambles, like purchase of a stock option entitling you to buy 100 shares of the stock at a specified price on the date the option expires. If the price of the stock has risen sharply, you make a nice profit. If the stock has not moved higher, you tear up the option and say goodbye to the money you paid.

To invest wisely you need a good deal of education in at least some of the various possibilities. The education demands time and effort—but if you are like most people, who must wait years before they get out of the red and finally have some extra money, you have plenty of time.

Sexual Anatomy, Pregnancy, and Birth Control

The human body's provisions for keeping the species alive are one of nature's miracles: A complex and ingenious arrangement designed to perform the impossible task of taking a single cell from the mother, another from the father, and persuading these two fragile bits of living matter—one no bigger than a pencil dot, the other visible only under a powerful microscope—to find each other, unite, and grow safely into a new human being.

Creating the female egg is a marvelous accomplishment in itself, and so is the formation of the male sperm cell. The two must then somehow make a hazardous journey to a place where they can meet and the fertilized egg can find a safe haven to multiply into two cells, then four, and finally the billions of cells of the newborn child. Getting them there is a dangerous exercise in traffic engineering, requiring a cunning arrangement of anatomical structures and a delicate balance of hormones. The task is impossible—yet it gets done.

THE MALE SEX ORGANS

The sexual anatomy of the male is illustrated in Figure B–1, to which you should refer while reading the rest of this section. The external organ, the *penis,* is composed of spongy tissue full of blood vessels, beneath a surface rich in sensitive nerve endings. The nerves are especially numerous at the *glans,* or rounded head, the *corona,* or ridge around the head, and *frenum,* a thin strip of skin connecting the head and the surface covering of the penis. (These three structures are mentioned in the box on premature ejaculation.) When the interior of the penis becomes engorged with blood, it elongates and hardens.

Beneath the penis is another external structure, the pouch-like *scrotum,* that holds the chief sex glands, the two egg-shaped *testicles.* These glands produce both the male hormone, *testosterone,* and the sperm cells of reproduction. When the sperm cells are fully mature, they travel up the duct called the *vas deferens* to the *prostate gland,* where they are mixed with copious amounts of *semen,* a milky fluid that provides the alkaline environment they need for survival. They are then held in *seminal vesicles* until ejaculation, when a series of sharp, rhythmic contractions expels them through the penis. The two *Cowper's glands,* just below the prostate, produce a clear, gummy fluid that flows through the penis during sexual arousal and appears as tiny drops at the tip. The fluid helps provide a safe environment for the passage of the semen and sperm cells.

372

A REMEDY FOR PREMATURE EJACULATION

Masters and Johnson report that they have successfully treated many complaints of premature ejaculation, defined as a man's inability to delay long enough for his partner to have an orgasm at least 50 percent of the time, by applying an old method known as the "squeeze technique."

Basically, the technique requires a training period in which the woman stimulates her partner manually. At a signal, when he feels that orgasm is about to occur, she then stops, places her thumb on the frenum and her forefinger on the top of the glans just in front of the corona, and squeezes with considerable force for about four seconds. This immediately ends the desire to ejaculate. After a few minutes' rest, the process can be repeated, and the man gradually learns to control the timing of orgasm himself.

The technique can also be used to interrupt and prolong intercourse, if a powerful urge to ejaculate occurs too quickly. It requires the assistance of a partner, because it does not work if the man attempts to apply the pressure himself.

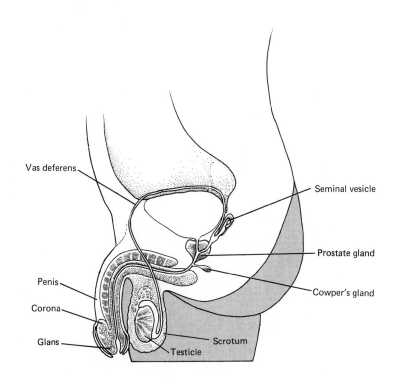

Figure B-1.
THE MALE REPRODUCTIVE SYSTEM.

THE FEMALE SEX ORGANS

The sexual anatomy of the female is illustrated in Figure B–2. The only visible structure is the *vulva*, or entrance to the *vagina*, which is a long, flexible tube that expands to hold the length of the erect penis or permit delivery of the baby at birth. The vulva is made up of three structures. The *mons* is a fatty pad of tissue, covered with pubic hair, at the fork of the groin. Below the mons, and surrounding the vaginal opening, are two sets of protective lips: the *labia major*, or large outer folds of fatty flesh, and *labia minor*, or small folds of membrane lying inside the larger lips. The labia minor are rich in nerve endings and blood vessels, which become engorged during sexual excitement, enlarging and reddening the folds.

At the very top, where the two labia minor join, the lips have a hood-like extension that covers the *clitoris*, which lies just below the surface. The clitoris, which is the center of sexual sensations, is also rich in blood vessels as well as sensitive nerve endings. When stimulated it enlarges and hardens and can be felt as a small lump often resembling an elongated pencil eraser, though it varies in size.

Near the top of the vagina, and just to the front of it, lies the *womb* or *uterus*, a pear-shaped, thick-walled chamber where a fertilized egg grows into a baby. The narrow end of the womb, called the *cervix*, projects slightly into the vagina and has a small opening. The other sex organs are the left and right *ovaries*, which are glands that produce both eggs and the two female hormones, *estrogen* and *progesterone;* and the *Fallopian tubes*, which have passageways just about big enough to hold a broomstraw leading from the ovaries to the womb.

HOW A NEW LIFE BEGINS

The complex process of reproduction begins with an event that occurs in one of the ovaries roughly every 28 days. Even at birth the ovaries contain their lifetime supply of eggs—about 40,000 of them—but the eggs are not yet mature and ready for fertilization. Starting at puberty, when menstruation begins, an egg in one of the ovaries begins to ripen, at about the midpoint between the start of one menstrual period and the start of the next. A small blister forms on the surface of the ovary and eventually bursts, discharging the mature egg cell.

At this point the egg's chances of survival seem dim. It is covered by a thick, rough coating of other smaller cells that have become attached to it while it was ripening. No tiny sperm cell could possibly penetrate that tough coating, and the egg will die and be washed away within about 24 hours unless it is fertilized and finds shelter and nourishment from the inner wall of the womb. As yet it merely lies motionless at the surface of the ovary, still about four inches away from the womb and unable to travel under its own power.

To the rescue comes the fallopian tube that waits nearby. The end of the tube, shaped like a half-opened tulip, extends toward the ovary like a hand prepared to grasp the newly ejected egg, and it also has the suction power of a tiny vacuum cleaner. Gently it pulls in the egg cell and starts it down the journey to the womb, propelled by contractions of the fallopian tube and the lashing movements of little hair-like structures lining the passageway. As the egg progresses on this slow trip—four inches in three to four days—much of its impenetrable coating of other cells is gradually brushed away. It is now ready to be fertilized and to start a new

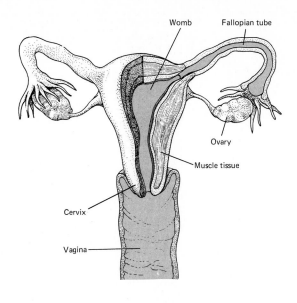

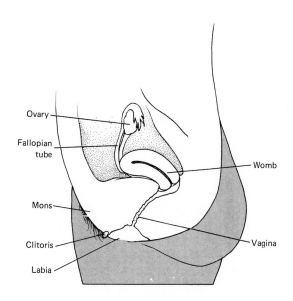

Figure B-2.
THE FEMALE REPRODUCTIVE SYSTEM.

life—*if* it happens to meet up in time with a male sperm, deposited in the vagina just a little earlier or later.

HOW SPERM—AGAINST ALL ODDS—FINDS EGG

No single sperm cell ejaculated into the vagina has much chance of meeting up with the egg. Though the sperm moves rapidly as it lashes its long tail, it has no sense of direction. It simply swims blindly in whatever direction it happens to be aimed. It may go in the right direction, at a right angle to the proper path, or even in reverse, as if fleeing from its task.

The bodily fluids in the vagina are slightly acid, and acid kills sperm. The male cell can survive only if by chance it happens on the opening in the cervix and thus finds the passageway to the womb, where the fluids are alkaline and provide safety. But the passageway is an inch long and its sides are folded and wrinkled. If the sperm swims into one of the wrinkles, it is stranded there or thrown back. The cell may get tired and stop swimming. If it does reach the womb it must still travel further and find the tiny hole that is the doorway to the fallopian tube that holds the egg.

For any given sperm cell, the odds are about 250,000 to 1 against its ever reaching the right tube. But nature has its own way to beat the odds. The male ejaculation contains an amazing 500 million sperm, and about 2,000 of them manage to reach the tube. There they begin to swim rapidly upward, as the egg cell moves slowly down. Like a tennis ball thrown into a swarm of bees, the egg is about to have a collision.

THE FERTILIZATION PROCESS

The first sperm that bumps into the egg never makes it to the inside. The egg is still coated with some other cells, even after the brushing it has received, that are fastened tight with a gluelike substance. The first sperm is stopped short. All it can do is secrete a chemical it contains, which starts to dissolve the glue. Other sperm bump, stop, and attack with more of the chemical. Finally the egg's entire outer membrane is stripped clean. The next sperm to strike bores right through the membrane. It too may still fail to reach the crucial center of the egg, but sooner or later some sperm cell may make it.

Fertilization is a joining of the chromosomes, powerful little packages of the complex chemical that is the key to heredity. A complete cell of the human body contains 46 chromosomes, arranged in pairs. But in forming the cells of reproduction, the pairs split. In men a set of 23 chromosomes goes into one sperm cell; the other set of 23 into another. In women, one set goes into the egg and the other is simply cast aside.

When a sperm cell fertilizes an egg, the chromosomes pair up again, forming the total of 46 necessary for growth. One pair, in which the chromosomes may not be exactly alike, determines the sex of the baby. A so-called X-X pair, of two similar chromosomes, dictates a girl. An X-Y pair, with unlike partners, means a boy. The mother's egg, of course, always contains the X member of the pair. But about half of the father's sperm cells have the X and the other half the Y. Whether the egg will become a girl or a boy depends entirely on which sperm cell does the job of fertilization.

THE ROLE OF THE MENSTRUAL CYCLE

The menstrual cycle, though always a nuisance and sometimes upsetting or painful, is nature's neatly timed method of preparing the womb to welcome and nurture a fertilized egg. The cycle begins when an egg cell starts to ripen in one of the ovaries. The ripening process stimulates production of the hormone *estrogen,* which works directly or indirectly to perform three tasks: It 1) prevents ripening of any other eggs, 2) causes the inner walls of the womb to thicken, and 3) starts getting the milk-producing glands of the breasts prepared for feeding a baby.

The flow of estrogen reaches its peak in about 11 days, setting off two more events. The opening of the cervix, which is ordinarily blocked by a thick mucouslike substance, is cleared out. Another hormone, produced in response to the estrogen, triggers the release of the ripe egg, which soon starts its slow journey down a fallopian tube.

Once the egg has burst loose, the generous flow of estrogen slows, and the ovary starts producing the hormone *progesterone.* The change stimulates the thickened walls of the womb to become engorged with blood and start secreting bodily fluids essential to receive an egg. Everything is now ready for sperm cells to arrive at the opening to the cervix.

If pregnancy does not occur, the ovary cuts down its production of hormones. Without this stimulation, the thickened wall of the womb starts to break down and is flushed away in the form of the menstrual flow, which lasts about five days. On the third day of the flow, another egg starts to ripen slowly—and another cycle is under way.

If the egg has been fertilized, it has already split into two cells, then four, and so on before it reaches the womb. There it floats aimlessly for a day or two, until it bumps against the wall. It immediately starts to burrow in and puts forth a tiny network of roots, which anchor it firmly and begin soaking up nourishment from the mother's blood stream. The roots gradually enlarge and lengthen into the umbilical cord, through which the mother's blood circulates into and out of the growing baby.

BIRTH CONTROL

Attempts at *contraception,* or the prevention of fertilization, are as old as written history. They were discussed in a Chinese medical text 1,300 years ago, in India 1,600, and in an Egyptian papyrus nearly 4,000 years ago. They could hardly have been mentioned much before then, because our earliest ancestors had no idea that there was any connection between sexual intercourse and pregnancy or indeed that the father had anything at all to do with the birth of a child.

When a primitive woman did not want children she presumably prayed to the various gods believed to control her fate, or wore some kind of magic charm to keep away the spirit believed to enter the body. Even the women of ancient Greece and Rome, and of Europe in the Middle Ages, often relied on magic charms made of such things as a cat's liver, a child's tooth, or a salamander.

The father's role was not completely established until about 300 years ago, when the newly-invented microscope revealed the living sperm cells in semen. It was suspected much earlier and is mentioned in the Bible and in the writings of Aristotle. Birth control began to take the form of attempting to prevent the semen from entering the womb. One early method, *withdrawal,* or *coitus interruptus,* is still used at times. The Egyptians began the use of plugs inserted in the vagina, a primitive version of the modern *diaphragm.* The Greeks used a forerunner of today's *spermicides* in the form of honey, ground pomegranate seeds, or other substances. Many societies adopted the equivalent of the modern *rhythm method,* but made the natural mistake of assuming that the "safe days" were between menstrual periods.

Contraception in the U. S. Today

Of today's American couples in their childbearing years, a great majority practice some form of contraception. Recent surveys found that over 33 million women used one method or another to limit or space childbirth, and only about 3 million did not (Forrest and Henshaw, 1983). The most widely-used methods are listed in Table B–1.

A considerable number of women also rely on *abortion,* or surgical removal of the embryo, if an unwanted pregnancy occurs. Abortion has been practiced in all known societies. It was illegal in the U. S., though widely performed in secret, until 1973. It is still a matter of controversy, but a majority of Americans now favor it. An opinion poll found 56 percent in favor of legalized abortion in the first three months of pregnancy, with 41 percent opposed and the rest undecided (Harris, 1981). Catholics were the only group with a majority against the practice, by a margin of only 49 to 48 percent.

The most common methods of contraception are described in the following sections:

Sterilization is a surgical technique that permanently prevents conception, though

Table B–1

Contraceptive Measures Used in the U.S.

Method	Millions of United States women who use it
Sterilization	11.6
Pill	10
Condom	4.5
IUD	2.3
Diaphragm	2
Spermicide	1.5
Withdrawal	1
Rhythm	.5
No method	3

Owing to a decline in popularity of the pill, sterilization has become the most widely-used form of birth control in the early years of this decade. The pill had dropped to second place, with other methods well behind (Forrest and Henshaw, Reprinted/adapted with permission from *Family Planning Perspectives,* 1983, 15, 4.

the operation is sometimes reversible. For a woman, the fallopian tubes are cut or tied so that no egg cell can reach the womb. In men, the passage of sperm cells from the testicles is diverted from the prostate gland to the blood stream and afterward the male semen contains no sperm. For both sexes, the operation is relatively simple and can usually be performed on an out-patient basis. A total of 11.6 million Americans—6.8 million women and 4.9 million men—had been sterilized by 1982 (Forrest and Henshaw, 1983), making this the most widely-used of all methods. Most of the women and men had already become parents and decided that their families were as large as they wanted them to be.

The pill, taken by 10 million women near the start of the decade, manipulates the menstrual cycle through a small daily dose of synthetic progesterone and estrogen, thus preventing the release of a ripe egg while creating a minimum of unpleasant side effects. The pill has had considerable adverse publicity linking it to cancer and heart disease, and many women are afraid of it. In fact it seems to discourage rather than cause cancer, and for women under 35 years of age most medical authorities consider it as safe as any other method. It increases the risk of heart disease and strokes for women over 35 who smoke, and all women over 40 (Ory, 1983).

Condoms, on which 4.5 million women relied in the early 1980s, are sheaths of synthetic rubber worn by the man to catch the semen and prevent it from getting into the vagina. The idea dates back at least to the 16th Century, but early versions were unsatisfactory because no suitable material was available, and condoms were not widely used until the manufacture of rubber began about 150 years ago. They are most effective if used along with a spermicidal jelly in case any semen leaks from the sheath or around the edges or is accidentally deposited on the outer surface while it is being put into place; this is a strong possibility because the fluid from the Cowper's glands often contains sperm.

Intrauterine devices, or IUDs, used by 2.3 million women, are devices inserted by a physician into the womb, where they remain until removed or accidentally expelled during menstruation. They are made of plastic or a combination of plastic and copper, and come in various shapes and sizes. They are highly effective in preventing pregnancy, though it is not known how or why they work. Among users of some types of IUDs that are no longer manufactured, there has been an unusually high number of acute pel-

vic infections, and the popularity of the devices has declined as a result (Forrest and Henshaw, 1983). Many women have worn them for years with no ill effects.

The diaphragm, used by 2 million women, is the sophisticated modern version of the old "plugs" invented by the Egyptians. It is a shallow cup of synthetic rubber, two to four inches wide, with a flexible metal outer ring to hold the device in place over the entrance to the womb. A physician or other trained person has to make the initial fitting, determine the proper size, and instruct the user how to put it in place by feeling for the bump of the cervix on the upper wall of the vagina. The diaphragm must be inserted before every act of intercourse, with contraceptive jelly inside the cup and rubbed around the edge, and for extra protection more jelly is usually injected nearby in the vagina.

Diaphragms have a high failure rate (National Center for Health Statistics, 1984), but probably because they are not used every time, are inserted improperly, or are not left in place for the necessary six hours afterward. They may also be dislodged during intercourse.

Spermicides, on which 1.5 million women rely, are jellies, creams, or foams injected into the vagina before intercourse. They contain mild acids that kill or immobilize sperm cells on contact and also form a coating that helps prevent the passage of sperm into the womb. In general they are not very reliable and have one of the highest failure rates of all methods.

Withdrawal, that old standby of our ancestors, is still the method on which 1 million women rely. It has several disadvantages and a very high failure rate. It is difficult for the man to practice and reduces his sexual satisfaction and often the woman's as well. If the withdrawal is even an instant late, large numbers of sperm cells get into the vagina, and even if it is timed correctly, sperm may be deposited in the fluid from the Cowper's glands.

The rhythm method, although the only one approved by the Catholic Church, is practiced by only a half million women. It relies on the fact that a female egg cell is released into a fallopian tube only once a month and remains alive for only 24 hours unless fertilized. The release of the egg ordinarily occurs about 14 days before the start of the next menstrual flow, and conception can take place only if intercourse occurs during or around the 24 hours of the egg's lifetime.

Male sperm cells, once they have reached the womb, usually remain active for 48 hours but sometimes survive for several more days. Thus conception can usually occur on only three days of the month, or at most about seven days. The other days of the menstrual cycle are "safe days." But exactly when the unsafe days occur, unfortunately, is difficult to predict. Few women have menstrual cycles that are invariably 28 days long, and even these women may suddenly change as they get older. Usually the cycle ranges anywhere from 21 to 38 days, often in totally irregular fashion. Release of an egg may also be triggered at odd times by physical or emotional stress. Therefore the rhythm method fails more often than any other except possibly withdrawal.

References

ABERNATHY, T. J. JR., et al. "A Comparison of the Sexual Attitudes and Behavior of Rural, Suburban, and Urban Adolescents." *Adolescence*, 1979, 14, 289–95.

ABRAVANEL, E. A. "A Psychological Analysis of the Concept of Role." Master's thesis, Swarthmore College, 1962.

ADAMS, B. N. *The Family: a Sociological Interpretation*. Chicago: Rand McNally, 1974.

———, and R. E. CROMWELL. "Morning and Night People in the Family: a Preliminary Statement." *Family Coordinator*, 1978, 27, 5–13.

ADAMS, M. "The Single Woman in Today's Society." *American Journal of Orthopsychiatry*, 1971, 42, 776–86.

AINSWORTH, M. D. S., and S. M. BELL. "Attachment, Exploration, and Separation." *Child Development*, 1970, 41, 49–68.

AINSWORTH, M. D. S., S. M. BELL, and D. J. STAYTON. "Individual Differences in Strange-situation Behavior of 1-Year-Olds." In H. R. Shaffer (ed.) *The Origins of Human Social Relations*. New York: Academic Press, 1971.

ALAN GUTTMACHER INSTITUTE. Report on international teenage pregnancy and abortion rates, 1985.

ALBERT, G. "Needed: a Rebellion against Romance." *Journal of Family Counseling*, 1973, 1, 28–34.

ALBRECHT, S. L. "Correlates of Marital Happiness among the Remarried." *Journal of Marriage and the Family*, 1979, 41, 857–67.

———. "Reactions and Adjustments to Divorce: Differences in the Experiences of Males and Females." *Family Relations*, 1980, 29, 59–68.

ALEXANDER, L. K. Personal communication, 1981.

ALLEN, G. "How Your Daughter Grows Up to Be a Man." *Humanist*, 1980. 40, 34–38.

AMMONS, P., and N. STINNETT. "The Vital Marriage: a Closer Look." *Family Relations*, 1980, 29, 37–42.

ANDERSON, F. Personal communication, 1981.

ANDERSON, M. "The Relevance of Family History." In M. Anderson (ed.) *Sociology of the Family, 2nd ed.* New York: Penguin, 1980.

ATCHLEY, R. C. *The Social Forces in Later Life*. Belmont, CA: Wadsworth, 1972.

———. "Selected Social and Psychological Differences between Men and Women in Later Life." *Journal of Gerontology*, 1976, 31, 204–11.

———. *The Social Forces in Later Life, 2nd ed.* Belmont, CA: Wadsworth, 1977.

AYOUB, D. M., W. T. GREENOUGH, and J. M. JURASKA. "Sex Differences in Dendritic Structure in the Preoptic Area of the Juvenile Macaque Monkey Brain." *Science*, 1983, 219, 197–98.

AZRIN, N. H., B. J. NASTER, and R. JONES. "Reciprocity Counseling: a Rapid Learning-based Procedure for Marital Counseling." *Behavior Research and Therapy*, 1973, 11, 365–82.

BACH, G. R. *Therapeutic Aggression*. Chicago: Human Development Institute, 1973.

BAHR, S. J., C. E. BOWERMAN, and V. GECAS. "Adolescent Perceptions of Conjugal Power." *Social Forces*, 1974, 52, 356–67.

BALDWIN, A. I. Observations cited in J. Kagan, "The Psychological Requirements for Human Development." In N. B. Talbot (ed.) *Raising Children in Modern America: Problems and Prospective Solutions*. Boston: Little, Brown, 1976.

BALSWICK, J. O., and C. W. PEEK. "The Inexpressive Male: a Tragedy of American Society." *Family Coordinator*, 1971, 20, 363–68.

BALWIN, A. L. Personal communication, 1975.

BAMBERGER, J. "The Myth of Matriarchy." In M. Z. Rosaldo and L. Lamphere (eds.) *Woman, Culture, and Society*. Stanford, CA: Stanford University Press, 1974.

BANE, M. J. *Here to Stay: American Families in the Twentieth Century*. New York: Basic Books, 1976.

——, et al. "Child-care Arrangements of Working Parents." *Monthly Labor Review*, October 1979. 50–56.

BANKOFF, E. A. "Social Support and Adaptation to Widowhood." *Journal of Marriage and the Family*, 1983, 45, 827–39.

BARDIS, P. D. "Family Forms and Variations Historically Considered." In H. T. Christensen, (ed.) *Handbook of Marriage and the Family*. Chicago: Rand McNally, 1964.

BARDWICK, J. M. *Psychology of Women*. New York: Harper and Row, 1973.

BARRY, H. T., M. K. BACON, and I. CHILD. "A Cross-cultural Survey of Some Sex Differences in Socialization." *Journal of Abnormal and Social Psychology*, 1957, 55, 327–32.

BART, P. "The Loneliness of the Long-distance Mother." In J. Freeman (ed.) *Women: a Feminist Perspective*. Palo Alto, CA: Mayfield, 1975.

BARTEL, G. D. *Group Sex: a Scientific Eyewitness Report on the American Way of Swinging*. New York: Wyden, 1971.

BARTON, K., G. KAWASH, and R. B. CATTELL. "Personality Motivation and Marital Role Factors as Predictors of Life Data In Married Couples." *Journal of Marriage and the Family*, 1972, 34, 474–80.

BARUCH, G., R. BARNETT, and C. RIVERS. *Lifeprints: New Patterns of Love and Work for Today's Women*. New York: McGraw-Hill, 1983.

BAUMRIND, D. "From Each According to Her Ability." *School Review*, February 1972, 161–95.

BEACH, F. A. "Hormonal Control of Sex-Related Behavior." In F. A. Beach (ed.) *Human Sexuality in Four Perspectives*. Baltimore: Johns Hopkins Press, 1976.

BECK, D. F. "Research Findings on the Outcome of Marital Counseling." *Social Casework*, 1975, 56, 153–81.

BECKMAN, L. J., and B. B. HOUSER. "The More You Have, the More You Do." *Psychology of Women Quarterly*, 1979, 4, 160–74.

BELL, I. P. "The Double Standard." *Trans-action*, 1970, 8, 75–80.

BELL, R. R., and P. L. BELL. "Sexual Satisfaction among Married Women." *Medical Aspects of Human Sexuality*, Dec. 1972, 136, 141–44.

BELL, R. R., and K. COUGHEY. "Premarital Sexual Experience among College Females, 1958, 1968, and 1978. *Family Relations*, 1980, 29, 353–57.

BEM, D. *Beliefs, Attitudes, and Human Affairs*. Belmont, CA: Brooks/Cole, 1970.

BEM, S. L. "The Measurement of Psychological Androgyny." *Journal of Consulting and Clinical Psychology*, 1974, 42, 155–62.

——. "Beyond Androgyny: Some Presumptuous Prescriptions for a Liberated Sexual Identity." In A. S. Skolnick and J. H. Skolnick, *Family in Transition, 2nd ed.* Boston: Little, Brown, 1977.

BENEDICT, R. *Patterns of Culture*. Boston: Houghton Mifflin, 1959.

BENNETT, E. L., et al. "Chemical and Anatomical Plasticity in the Brain." *Science*, 1964, 146, 610–19.

BENNETT, E. M., and L. R. COHEN. "Men and Women: Personality Patterns and Contrasts." *Genetic Psychology Monographs*, 1959, 101–55.

BENTLER, P. M., and M. D. NEWCOMB. "Longitudinal Study of Marital Success and Failure." *Journal of Consulting and Clinical Psychology*, 1978, 46, 1053–70.

BERGER, B., B. HACKETT, and R. M. MILLAR. "The Communal Family." *Family Coordinator*, 1972, 21, 419–27.

BERGLER, E. *Money and Emotional Conflicts*. New York: International Universities Press, 1970.

BERLAND, T. "Maintaining the Male." *Generation in the Middle*. Chicago: Blue Cross, 1970.

BERNARD, J. *Remarriage*. New York: Dryden, 1956.

——. Personal communication, 1964.

——. "No News, but New Ideas." In P. Bohannon (ed.) *Divorce and After*. Garden City, NY: Doubleday, 1970.

——. *The Future of Marriage*. New York: World, 1972.

——. Personal communication, 1973.

——. "Comments on Glenn's Paper." *Journal of Marriage and the Family*, 1975, 37, 600–601.

BERSCHEID, E., and E. C. WALSTER. *Interper-*

sonal Attraction, 2nd ed. Reading, MA: Addison-Wesley, 1978.

BEUF, A. "Doctor, Lawyer, Household Drudge." Journal of Communication, 1974, 24, 142–45.

BIRCHLER, G. R., R. L. WEISS, and L. D. WAMPLER. "Differential Patterns of Social Reinforcement as a Function of Degree of Marital Distress and Level of Intimacy." Paper presented to the Western Psychological Association, Portland, OR, April 1972.

BIRD, C. "The Case against Marriage." In L. K. Howe (ed.) The Future of the Family. New York: Simon and Schuster, 1972.

BLAKE, J. "Family Size and the Quality of Children." Demography, 1981, 18, 421–42.

BLAU, P. Exchange and Power in Social Life. New York: Wiley, 1964.

———, C. BEEKER, and K. M. FITZPATRICK. "Intersecting Social Affiliations and Intermarriage." Social Forces, 1984, 62, 585–606.

BLOCK, J., A. VON DER LIPPE, and J. H. BLOCK. "Sex-role and Socialization Patterns: Some Personality Concomitants and Environmental Antecedents." Journal of Consulting and Clinical Psychology, 1973, 41, 321–41.

BLOOD, R. O. JR., and D. M. WOLFE. Husbands and Wives. New York: Free Press, 1960.

BLOOM, D. E., AND J. TRUSSELL. What Are the Determinants of Delayed Child-bearing and Voluntary Childlessness in the United States? National Bureau of Economic Research, working paper no. 1140, 1983.

BLUMSTEIN, P. and P. SCHWARTZ. American Couples. New York: Wm. Morrow, 1983.

BOHANNON, P. "The Six Stations of Divorce." In P. Bohannon (ed.) Divorce and After. Garden City, NY: Doubleday, 1970.

———. All the Happy Families: Exploring the Varieties of Family Life. New York: McGraw-Hill, 1985.

BONNEY, M. E. "Relationships between Social Success, Family Size, Socio-economic Home Background, and Intelligence among Children in Grades 3 to 5." Sociometry, 1954, 7, 26–39.

BONVILLIAN, J. D., M. D. ORLANSKY, and L. L. NOVACK. "Early Sign Language Acquisition and its Relation to Cognitive and Motor Development." In J. G. Kyle and B. Woll (eds.) Language in Sign: an International Perspective on Sign Language. London: Croom, Helm, 1983.

BOOTH, A. "Does Wives' Employment Cause Stress for Husbands?" Family Coordinator, 1979, 28, 445–49.

BORLAND, D. C. "A Cohort Analysis Approach to the Empty-nest Syndrome among Three Ethnic Groups of Women: a Theoretical Position." Journal of Marriage and the Family, 1982, 44, 117–29.

BOSSARD, J. "Residential Propinquity as a Factor in Marriage Selection." American Journal of Sociology, 1932, 38, 219–24.

BRICKMAN, P. (ed.) Social Conflict. Lexington, MA: Heath, 1974.

BRIGGS, J. Never in Anger. Cambridge, MA: Harvard University Press, 1970.

BRIM, O. "Selected Theories of the Male Mid-life Crisis." Paper presented to the American Psychological Association, New Orleans, 1974.

BRIM, O. "Theories of Male Mid-Life Crisis." Counseling Psychologist, 1976, 6, 2–9.

BRISCOE, C. W., et al. "Divorce and Psychiatric Disease." Archives of General Psychiatry, 1973, 29, 119–25.

———, and J. B. SMITH. "Psychiatric Illness—Marital Units and Divorce." Journal of Nervous and Mental Disease, 1974, 158, 440–45.

BRODBELT, S. "College Dating and Aggression." College Student Journal, 1983, 17, 273–77.

BRODERICK, C. B., and S. E. FOWLER. "New Patterns of Relationships between the Sexes among Preadolescents." Marriage and Family Living, 1961, 23, 27–30.

BROOKS, J., and M. LEWIS. "Attachment Behavior in Thirteen-month-old, Opposite-sex Twins." Child Development, 1974, 45, 243–47.

BROVERMAN, I. K., et al. "Sex-role Stereotypes: a Current Appraisal." Journal of Social Issues, 1972, 28, 59–79.

BROWN, P., and R. MANELA. "Changing Family Roles: Women and Divorce." Journal of Divorce, 1978, 1, 315–28.

BROWN, R. W. Social Psychology. New York: Free Press, 1965.

BUREAU OF LABOR STATISTICS. "Number of Working Mothers Now at Record Level." News Release, July 26, 1984.

BUREAU OF THE CENSUS. "Money Income of Families and Persons in the United States." Current Population Reports, 1975, Series P-60, No. 105.

———. Marital Status: March, 1976. Current Population Reports, 1977, Series P-20, No. 306.

———. "Fertility of American Women." Current Population Reports, 1979, Series P-20, No. 341.

———. "Families Maintained by Female Householders." *Current Population Reports,* 1980a, Series P-23, No. 107.

———. *1980 Census of Population,* Supplementary Report, 1980b, Series Pc-80, No. S1-9.

———. "Households and Family Characteristics: March 1981." *Current Population Reports,* 1982, Series P-20, No. 380.

———. "Fertility of American Women." *Current Population Reports,* 1983a, Series P-20, No. 379.

———. "State of Residence in 1975 by State of Residence in 1980." *Current Population Reports,* 1983b, Supplementary Report No. PC-80, No. S1-9.

———. "Marital Status and Living Arrangements: March 1984." *Current Population Reports,* 1983c, Series P-20, No. 389.

———. "Households, Families, Marital Status, and Living Arrangements: March 1984." *Current Population Reports,* 1984a, Series P-20, No. 391.

———. "Estimates of the Population of the United States, by Age, Sex, and Race: 1980 to 1983." *Current Population Reports,* 1984b, Series P-25, No. 949.

———. "Money Income of Households, Families, and Persons in the United States: 1983." *Current Population Reports,* 1984c, Series P-60, No. 145.

———. "School Enrollment—Social and Economic Characteristics of Students: October 1983." *Current Population Reports,* 1984d, Series P-20, No. 394.

———. *Statistical Abstract of the U.S., 1985.*

BURGESS, E. W., and H. J. LOCKE. *The Family: from Institution to Companionship.* New York: American Book, 1945.

———, and P. WALLIN. *Engagement and Marriage.* Philadelphia: Lippincott, 1953.

BURKE, R. J., T. WEIR, and R. E. DuWORS JR. "Work Demands on Administrators and Spouse Well-Being." *Human Relations,* 1980, 33, 253–78.

BURSTEIN, B. "Life History and Current Values as Predictors of Sexual Behavior and Satisfaction in College Women." Paper presented to the Western Psychological Association, April 1975.

BURTON, A. "Marriage without Failure." *Psychological Reports,* 1973, 32, 1199-1208.

CALIFORNIA COMMISSION ON CRIME CONTROL AND VIOLENCE PREVENTION. *An Ounce of Prevention: Toward an Understanding of the Causes of Domestic Violence,* 1981.

CAMERON, C., S. OSKAMP, and W. SPARKS. "Courtship American Style: Newspaper Ads." *Family Coordinator,* 1977, 26, 27–30.

CAMMALLERI, S. Personal communication, 1984.

CAMPBELL, A. "The American Way of Mating: Marriage, Si; Marriage, Only Maybe." *Psychology Today,* May 1975, 39–42.

———. *The Sense of Well-being in America.* New York: McGraw-Hill, 1981.

CARGAN, L., and M. MELKO. *Singles.* Beverly Hills, CA: SAGE, 1982.

CARNS, D. E. "Talking about Sex: Notes on First Coitus and the Double Standard." *Journal of Marriage and the Family,* 1973, 35, 677-88.

CARTER, H., and P. C. GLICK. *Marriage and Divorce: a Social and Economic Study.* Cambridge, MA: Harvard University Press, 1970.

CENTERS, R. "Marital Selection and Occupational Strata." *American Journal of Sociology,* 1949, 54, 530–35.

———, B. H. RAVEN, and A. RODRIGUES. "Conjugal Power Structure: a Re-examination." *American Sociological Review,* 1971, 36, 264–78.

CHADWICK, B. A., S. ALBRECHT, and P. KUNZ. "Marital and Family Role Satisfaction." *Journal of Marriage and the Family,* 1976, 38, 431-40.

CHERLIN, A., and F. F. FURSTENBERG JR. "The American Family in the Year 2000." *Futurist,* 1983, 17, 7–14.

CHESTER, R. "Health and Marriage Breakdown: Experience of a Sample of Divorced Women." *British Journal of Preventive Social Medicine,* 1971, 25, 231.

CHICO, N. Unpublished study, California State College at Hayward, 1985.

CHILMAN, C. S. "Habitat and American Families: a Social-psychological Review." *Family Coordinator,* 1978, 27, 105-11.

CHIRIBOGA, D. A., and M. THURNHER. "Marital Lifestyles and Adjustment to Separation. *Journal of Divorce,* 1980, 5, 379–90.

CHRISTENSEN, H. T., and C. F. GREGG. "Changing Sex Norms in America and Scandinavia." *Journal of Marriage and the Family,* 1970, 32, 616–27.

CLARK, H. H., and E. V. CLARK. *Psychology and Language.* New York: Harcourt Brace Jovanovich, 1977.

CLINCH, T. A. "The Professional Woman and Her Family." *Humanist,* 1975, 35, 14–16.

COHEN, J. F. "Male Roles in Mid-life." *Family Coordinator,* 1979, 28, 465–71.

COLLINS, R. "A Conflict Theory of Sexual Stratification." *Social Problems,* 1971, 19, 3–21.

COMMISSION ON POPULATION GROWTH IN

AMERICA. *Population and the American Future.* New York: New American Library, 1972.

CONDRAN, J. G., and J. G. BODE. "Rashomon, Working Wives, and Family Division of Labor: Middletown, 1980." *Journal of Marriage and the Family,* 1982, 44, 421–26.

CONGER, J. J. *Adolescence and Youth.* New York: Harper and Row, 1977.

CONSTANTINE, L. L., and J. M. CONSTANTINE. *Group Marriage.* New York: Collier, 1973.

COOGLER, O.J., R. E. WEBER, and P. C. McKENRY. "Divorce Mediation: a Means of Facilitating Divorce and Adjustment." *Family Coordinator,* 1979, 28, 255–59.

COOKERLY, J. R., "The Outcome of the Six Major Forms of Marriage Counseling Compared: a Pilot Study." *Journal of Marriage and the Family,* 1973, 35, 608–11.

COOLEY, C. H. *Social Organization.* New York: Charles Scribner's Sons, 1910.

COOMBS, R. "Value Consensus and Partner Satisfaction among Dating Couples."*Journal of Marriage and the Family,* 1966, 28, 166–73.

CORNFIELD, N. "The Success of Urban Communes." *Journal of Marriage and the Family,* 1983, 45, 115–26.

CORRALES, R. "The Influence of Family Life's Cycle Categories upon Marital Satisfaction in the First Six Years of Marriage." Doctoral dissertation, U. of Minnesota, 1974.

COTTON, W. L. "Social and Sexual Relationships of Lesbians." *Journal of Sex Research,* 1975, 11, 139–48.

COWAN, P. and C., and L. and J. COIE. "The Impact of Children upon Their Parents." In L. Newman and W. Miller (eds.) *The First Child and Family Formation.* Chapel Hill: University of North Carolina Press, 1978.

CROSBIE, P.V. "The American Family: a Question of Change." *Humboldt Journal of Social Relations,* 1976, 4, 25–35.

CROSBY, J. F. "The Death of the Family—Revisited." *Humanist,* 1975, 35, 12–14.

CUBER, J. F., and P. B. HARROFF. *The Significant Americans: a Study of Sexual Behavior among the Affluent.* New York: Appleton-Century-Crofts, 1965.

CUMMING, E. Personal communication, 1970.

D'ANDRADE, R. G. "Sex Differences and Cultural Institutions." In E. E. Maccoby (ed.) *The Development of Sex Differences.* Stanford, CA: Stanford University Press, 1966.

DAVIDS, L. "North American Marriage." *Futurist,* 1971, 5, 19–94.

DAVIDSON, K., R. B. GINSBERG, and H. H. KAY. *Sex-based Discrimination.* St. Paul, MN: West, 1974.

DAVIS, E. "The Mental and Linguistic Superiority of Only Girls." *Child Development,* 1937, 8, 130–43.

DAVIS, J. A. *General Social Surveys, 1972–83: Cumulative Codebook.* Chicago, National Opinion Research Center, 1983.

DAVIS, K. "The American Family in Relation to Demographic Change." In C. F. Westoff and R. Parke Jr. (eds.) *Demographic and Social Aspects of Population Growth.* Washington: Commission on Population Growth and the American Future, 1972.

DeFRAIN, J. "Androgynous Parents Tell Who They Are and What They Need. " *Family Coordinator,* 1979, 28, 237–43.

DeMARIS, A., and G. R. LESLIE. "Cohabitation with the Future Spouse: Its Influence upon Marital Satisfaction and Communication." *Journal of Marriage and the Family,* 1984, 46, 77–84.

DENFIELD, D. "Dropouts from Swinging." *Family Coordinator,* 1974, 23, 45–49.

——, and M. GORDON. "Mate-swapping: the Family that Swings Together Clings Together." *Journal of Sex Research,* 1970, 7, 85–89.

DEPARTMENT OF HEALTH, EDUCATION, and WELFARE. Report on the health of the U.S. population, 1978.

DEPARTMENT OF LABOR. *Time of Change: 1983 Handbook on Women Workers.* Washington, DC: Government Printing Office, 1983.

DIEPOLD, J. JR., and R. D. YOUNG. "Empirical Studies of Adolescent Sexual Behavior: a Critical Review." *Adolescence,* 1979, 14, 45–64.

DITKOFF, G. S. "Stereotypes of Adolescents toward the Working Woman." *Adolescence,* 1979, 14, 277–82.

DIXON, R. B., and L. J. WEITZMAN. "Evaluating the Impact of No-fault Divorce in California." *Family Relations,* 1980, 29, 297–307.

DOWD, M. "Many Women in Poll Value Job As Much As Family Life." New York *Times,* Dec. 4, 1983.

DREIKUS, R. "Determinants of Changing Attitudes of Marital Partners toward Each Other." In S. Rosenbaum and I. Alger (eds.) *The Marriage Relationship: Psychoanalytic Perspectives.* New York: Basic Books, 1968.

DUBERMAN, L. *The Reconstituted Family.* Chicago: Nelson-Hall, 1975.

DURBIN, K. "On Sexual Jealousy." In G. C. Clanton and L. G. Smith (eds.) *Jealousy.* Englewood Cliffs, NJ: Prentice-Hall, 1977.

DUVALL, E. M., and R. HILL. *Being Married.* New York: Association Press, 1960.

ECONOMIC REPORT OF THE PRESIDENT, 1985. Washington, DC; Government Printing Office, 1985.

EHRMANN, W. *Premarital Sexual Behavior.* New York: Bantam, 1960.

——. "Marital and Nonmarital Sexual Behavior." In H. T. Christensen (ed.) *Handbook of Marriage and the Family.* Chicago: Rand-McNally, 1964.

ELKIND, D., and I. B. WEINER. *Development of the Child.* New York: John Wiley, 1978.

EPSTEIN, J. *Divorced in America.* New York: Dutton, 1974.

ERICKSEN, J. A., W. L. YANCEY, and E. P. ERICKSEN. "The Division of Family Roles." *Journal of Marriage and the Family,* 1979, 41, 301–13.

ERIKSON, E. H. *Childhood and Society, 2nd ed.* New York: Norton, 1963.

ERON, L. D., and L. R. HOUSEMANN. "Adolescent Aggression and Television." *Annals of the New York Academy of Sciences,* 1980, 347, 319–31.

ESLINGER, K. N., A. C. CLARKE, and R. R. DYNES. "The Principle of Least Interest, Dating Behavior, and Family Integration Patterns." *Journal of Marriage and the Family,* 1972, 34, 269–72.

ETZIONI, A. "Science and the Future of the Family." *Science,* April 29, 1977, 487.

——. In *Hearings of the White House Conference on Families.* Washington: Government Printing Office, 1978.

FAIRCHILD, H. P. *Dictionary of Sociology and Related Sciences.* Paterson, NJ: Littlefield, Adams, 1964.

FAIRFIELD, R. *Communes, U.S.A.: a Personal Tour.* Baltimore: Penguin, 1971.

FALK, G., U. FALK, and G. V. TOMASHEVICH. *Aging in America and Other Cultures.* Saratoga, CA: Century Twenty One, 1981.

FARRELL, M., et al. Unpulished paper, State University of New York at Buffalo, 1975.

FAST, I., and A. CAIN. "The Stepparent Role: Potential for Disturbances in Family Function. *American Journal of Orthopsychiatry,* 1966, 36, 485–90.

FEDERAL RESERVE BOARD. *Flow of FUNDS Accounts, Fourth Quarter 1984,* 1985.

FEDERAL TRADE COMMISSION. *FTC Staff Report on Television Advertising to Children.* Washington, DC: Government Printing Office, 1978.

FELDBERG, R., and J. KOHEN. "Family Life in an Anti-family Setting: a Critique of Marriage and Divorce." *Family Coordinator,* 1976, 25, 151–59.

FELDMAN, H. "The Effects of Children on the Family." In A. Michael (ed.) *Family Issues of Employed Women in Europe and America.* The Netherlands: E. J. Brill, 1971.

——. Personal communication, 1975.

FELDMAN, K. A., and T. M. NEWCOMB. *The Impact of College on Students,* Vol. I. San Francisco: Jossey-Bass, 1969.

FENGLER, A. P. "Attitudinal Orientations of Wives toward Their Husbands' Retirement." *Journal of Aging and Human Development,* 1975, 6, 139–52.

FENTON, N. "The Only Child." *Journal of Genetic Psychology,* 1928, 35, 546–56.

FERBER, M., and B. BIRNBAUM. "Economics of the Family: Who Maximizes What?" *Family Economics Review,* summer/fall 1980, 13–16.

FERREE, M. M. "The Confused American Housewife." *Psychology Today,* September 1976, 76–80.

FIDELL, L., D. HOFFMAN, and P. KEITH-SPIEGEL. "Some Social Implications of Sex-choice Technology." *Psychology of Women Quarterly,* 1979, 4, 32–42.

FIGLEY, C. Personal communication, 1978.

FINE, G. A. "Friends, Impression Management, and Preadolescent Behavior." In S. R. Asher and J. M. Gottman, *The Development of Children's Friendships.* London: Cambridge University Press, 1981.

FLEISCHMANN, K. "Marriage by Contract: Defining the Terms of Relationship." *Family Law Quarterly,* 1974, 8, 27–49.

FOOTE, N. N. "Sex as Play." *Social Problems,* 1954, 1, 159–63.

——, and L. S. COTTRELL. *Identity and Interpersonal Competence.* Chicago: University of Chicago Press, 1955.

FORREST, J. D., and S. K. HENSHAW. "What U.S. Women Think and Do about Contraception." *Family Planning Perspectives,* 1983, 15, 157–66.

FOSTER, B. G. "Self-disclosure and Intimacy in Long-term Marriages." In N. Stinnett, et al. (eds.) *Family Strengths 4: Positive Support Systems.* Lincoln: University of Nebraska Press, 1982.

FRANK, E., C. ANDERSON, and D. RUBIN-STEIN. "Marital Role Ideals and Perception of Marital Role Behavior in Distressed and Non-distressed Couples." *Journal of Marriage and Family Therapy*, 1980, 6, 55–63.

FRANK, J. D. "General Psychotherapy: the Restoration of Morale." In D. X. Freedman and J. E. Dyrud (eds.) *American Handbook of Psychiatry, 2nd ed.*, Vol. V. New York: Basic Books, 1975.

FREEDMAN, J. L., J. M. CARLSMITH, and D. O. SEARS. *Social Psychology*. Englewood Cliffs, NJ: Prentice-Hall, 1970.

FREUND, J. "Divorce and Grief." *Journal of Family Counseling*, 1974, 2, 40–43.

FRIEZE, I. H. "Women's Expectations for and Causal Attributions of Success and Failure." In M. T. Shuch Mednick, S. S. Schwartz Tangri, and L. Wladis Hoffman (eds.) *Women and Achievement*. New York: Halstead, 1975.

FRUMKIN, R. M. "Sexual Freedom." In *Encyclopedia of Sexual Behavior*. New York: Anderson, 1973.

FUCHS, V. R. *How We Live*. Cambridge, MA: Harvard University Press, 1983.

FURMAN, W., D. F. RAHE, and W. W. HARRUP. "Rehabilitation of Socially-withdrawn Preschool Children through Mixed-age and Same-age Socialization." In E. M. Hetherington and R. D. Parke (eds.) *Contemporary Readings in Child Psychology, 2nd ed.* New York: McGraw-Hill, 1981.

GAGNON, J. H. (ed.) *Human Sexuality: an Age of Ambiguity*. Boston: Educational Associates, 1975.

GALLAGHER, B. J. III. "Attitude Differences Across Three Generations: Class and Sex Components." *Adolescence*, 1979, 14, 503–16.

GALLUP, G. *Women in America*. Princeton, NJ: Gallup Public Opinion Index, Report No. 128, 1976.

———. *Gallup Youth Survey*, 1977.

———. *Growing Numbers of Americans Favor Discussion of Sex in Classroom*. Princeton, NJ: Gallup Poll, 1978

———. *American Families*. Princeton, NJ: Gallup Organization, 1980.

———. *Survey on Preferred Family Size*. Princeton, NJ: Gallup Poll, 1985.

GARFIELD, R. "The Decision to Remarry." *Journal of Divorce*, 1980, 4, 1–10.

GARFIELD, S. L. *Clinical Psychology*. Chicago: Aldine, 1974.

GASS, G. Z. "Equitable Marriage." *Family Coordinator*, 1974, 23, 369–72.

GEBHARD, P. H. Personal communications, 1980, 1981, and 1982.

GEBOY, M. J. "Who is Listening to the 'Experts'? The Use of Child-care Materials by Parents." *Family Relations*, 1981, 30, 205–10.

GECAS, V. "The Influence of Social Class on Socialization." In W. R. Burr et al. (eds.) *Contemporary Theories about the Family*. New York: Free Press, 1979.

GEERTZ, C. "The Concept of Culture and the Concept of Man." *Social Education*, 1965, 32, 147–52.

GELLHORN, E., and A. D. MILLER. "Methacholine and Noradrenalin Tests." *Archives of General Psychology*, 1961, 4, 371–80.

GERBNER, G., et al. "The 'mainstreaming' of America: Violence Profile No. 11." *Journal of Communication*, 1980, 30, 10–29.

GERRARD, M. "Sex, Guilt, and Contraceptive Use." *Journal of Personality and Social Psychology*, 1982, 42, 153–58.

GERSON, M. "The Lure of Motherhood." *Psychology of Women Quarterly*, 1980, 5, 208–17.

GESCHWIND, N., and W. LEVITSKY. "Human Brain." *Science*, 1968, 161, 186–87.

GIL, D. G. *Violence against Children: Physical Child Abuse in the United States*. Cambridge, MA: Harvard University Press, 1970.

GILMARTIN, B. G. "Sexual Deviance and Social Networks: a Study of Social, Family, and Interaction Patterns among Co-marital Sex-Participants." In J. R. Smith and L. G. Smith (eds.) *Beyond Monogamy*. Baltimore: The Johns Hopkins Press, 1974.

GLASGOW, R. E., and H. ARKOWITZ, "The Behavioral Assessment of Male and Female Social Competence in Dyadic Heterosexual Interactions." *Behavior Therapy*, 1975, 6, 488–98.

GLENN, N. D. "The Contribution of Marriage to the Psychological Well-being of Males and Females." *Journal of Marriage and the Family*, 1975a, 37, 594–600.

———. "Psychological Well-being in the Post-parental Stage: Some Evidence from National Surveys." *Journal of Marriage and the Family*, 1975b, 35, 105–10.

———, and S. K. HOPPE, "Only Children as Adults: Psychological Well-being." *Journal of Family Issues*, 1984, 5, 363–82.

———, and S. McLANAHAN. "Children and Marital Happiness: a Further Specification of the Relationship." *Journal of Marriage and the Family*, 1982, 44, 63–72.

GLICK, P. C. "A Demographer Looks at American Families." *Journal of Marriage and the Family,* 1975, 37, 15–26.

———. "Updating the Life Cycle of the Family." *Journal of Marriage and the Family,* 1977, 39, 5–13.

———. "Children of Divorced Parents in Demographic Perspective." *Journal of Social Issues,* 1979, 35, 170–82.

———. "Marriage, Divorce, and Living Arrangements." *Journal of Family Issues,* 1984, 5, 7–26.

———, and A. J. NORTON. "Frequency, Duration, and probability of Marriage and Divorce." *Journal of Marriage and the Family,* 1971, 33, 307–17.

GOLDBERG, S., and M. LEWIS. "Play Behavior in the Year-old Infant: Early Sex Differences." *Child Development,* 1969, 40, 21–30.

GOLDSEN, R., et al. *What College Students Think.* Princeton, NJ: Van Nostrand, 1960.

GOODE, W. J. *After Divorce.* Glencoe, IL: Free Press, 1956.

———. *World Revolution and Family Patterns.* New York: Free Press, 1963.

———. *The Family.* Englewood Cliffs, NJ: Prentice-Hall, 1964.

GOODSTEIN, R. K. "Inextricable Interaction: Social, Psychologic, and Biological Stresses Facing the Elderly." *American Journal of Orthopsychiatry,* 1981, 51, 219–29.

GORDON, M. (ed.) *The American Family in Social-historical Perspective.* New York: St. Martin's Press, 1973.

GORDON, S. "The Egalitarian Family is Alive and Well." *Humanist,* 1975, 35, 18–19.

GOVE, W. R. "The Relationship between Sex Roles, Marital Status, and Mental Illness." *Social Forces,* 1972, 51, 34–44.

———. "Sex, Marital Status, and Mortality." *American Journal of Sociology,* 1973, 79, 45–67.

———, and J. F. TUDOR. "Adult Sex Roles and Mental Illness." *American Journal of Sociology,* 1973, 78, 812–15.

———, et al. "The Family Life Cycle: Internal Dynamics and Social Consequences." *Sociology and Social Research,* 1973, 57, 182–95.

GRANZBERG, G., and J. STEINBRING. "Television and the Canadian Indian." Department of Anthropology, University of Winnipeg, 1980.

GRAY, R. "The Changing Role of Women and Adolescent Girls in America." *Adolescence,* 1979, 14, 439–50.

GREENBERGER, E., AND L. D. STEINBERG. "Sex Differences in Early Labor Force Experience: Harbinger of Things to Come." *Social Forces,* 1983, 62, 467–86.

GREENOUGH, W. T. "Enduring Brain Effects of Differential Experience and Training." In M. R. Rosenzweig and E. L. Bennett (eds.) *Neural Mechanisms of Learning and Memory.* Cambridge, MA: M.I.T. Press, 1976.

———. Lecture to the Developmental Psychology Research Group, Estes Park, CO, June 1982.

GREVEN, P. J. JR. "Family Structure in 17th Century Andover, Mass." *William and Mary Quarterly,* 1966, 3, 234–56.

GROSS, I. H., E. W. CRANDALL, and M. M. KNOLL. *Management for Modern Families, 4th ed.* Englewood Cliffs, NJ: Prentice-Hall, 1980.

GRUVER, G. G., and S. K. LABADIE. "Marital Dissatisfaction among College Students." *Journal of College Students Personnel,* 1975, 16, 454–58.

GURIN, G., J. VEROFF, and S. FELD. *Americans View Their Mental Health.* New York: Basic Books, 1960.

GUTMANN, D. "Developmental Issues in the Masculine Mid-life Crisis." Paper delivered to the Boston Society for Gerontologic Psychiatry, May 1975.

HAAS, L. "Role-sharing Couples: a Study of Egalitarian Marriages." *Family Relations,* 1980, 29, 289–96.

HABAKKUK, H. J. "Family Structure and Economic Change in 19th Century Europe." *Journal of Economic History,* 1955, 25, 1–12.

HALEY, J. *Strategies of Psychotherapy.* New York: Grune and Stratton, 1963.

HANSEN, S. L., and M. W. HICKS. "Sex Role Attitudes and Perceived Dating-mating Choices of Youth." *Adolescence,* 1980, 15, 83–90.

HARLOW, H. F. "The Development of Affectional Patterns in Infant Monkeys." In B. M. Foss (ed.) *Determinants of Infant Behavior.* London: Methuen, 1961.

HARRIMAN, L. C. "Families in the 1980's: Issues and Concerns." *Journal of Home Economics,* 1982, 74, 31–35.

HARRIS L. and ASSOCIATES. "Change Yes—Upheaval No." *LIFE,* 1971, 70, 23–30.

———. Study commissioned by National Council on the Aging, 1975.

———. Survey of Attitudes toward Abortion, 1981.

HARRISON, J. B. "Men's Roles and Men's Lives." *Journal of Women in Culture and Society,* 1978, 4, 324–36.

HART, R. *Children's Experience of Place.* New York: Irvington, 1978.

HARTMAN, L. M. "Effects of Sex and Marital Therapy on Sexual Interaction and Marital Happiness." *Journal of Sex and Marital Therapy,* 1983, 9, 137-51.

HAVEMANN, E. *Birth Control.* Time-Life Books, 1967.

HAVENS, E. M. "Women, Work, and Wedlock: a Note on Female Marital Patterns in the United States." *American Journal of Sociology,* 1973, 78, 975-81.

HAWKE, S., and D. KNOX. "The One-child Family: a New Lifestyle." *Family Coordinator,* 1978, 27, 215-19.

HAWKINS, J. L., C. WEISBERG, and D. RAY. "Marital Communication and Social Class." *Journal of Marriage and the Family,* 1977, 39, 479-90.

——. "Spouse Differences in Communication Style: Preference, Perception, Behavior." *Journal of Marriage and the Family,* 1980, 42, 585-93.

HAYGHE, H. "Husbands and Wives as Earners: an Analysis of Family Data." *Monthly Labor Review,* 1981, 104, 46-59.

HEER, D. M. "Husband and Wife Perceptions of Family Power Structure." *Marriage and Family Living,* 1962, 24, 65-67.

—— "The Measurement and Bases of Family Power: an Overview." *Journal of Marriage and the Family,* 1963, 25, 133-39.

HEILBRUN, A. B. JR., and H. L. SCHWARTZ. "Sex-gender Differences in Level of Androgyny." *Sex Roles,* 1982, 8, 201-14.

HELSING, K. J., M. SZKLO, and G. W. COMSTOCK. "Factors Associated with Mortality after Widowhood." *American Journal of Public Health,* 1981, 71, 802-9.

HENTON, J. Personal communication, 1982.

HENZE, L. F., and J. W. HUDSON. "Personal and Family Characteristics of Cohabiting and Non-cohabiting College Students." *Journal of Marriage and the Family,* 1974, 36, 722-27.

HERMAN, S. J. "Divorce: a Grief Process." *Perspectives in Psychiatric Care,* 1974, 12, 108-12.

HERTZ CORP. Report on cost of driving an automobile, 1985.

HESSELLUND, H. "On Some Sociological Sex Differences." *Journal of Sex Research,* 1971, 7, 263-73.

HEY, R. N., and E. H. MUDD. "Recurring Problems in Marriage Counseling." *Marriage and Family Living,* 1959, 21, 127-29.

HILL, C. T., Z. RUBIN, and L. A. PEPLAU. "Breakups before Marriage: the End of 103 Affairs." *Journal of Social Issues,* 1976, 32, 147-68.

HILL, E. A., and L. T. DORFMAN, "Reactions of Housewives to the Retirement of Their Husbands." *Family Relations,* 1982, 31, 195-200.

HILTZ, S. R. "Helping Widows: Group Discussions as a Therapeutic Technique." *Family Coordinator,* 1975, 24, 331-36.

——. "Widowhood: a Roleless Role." *Marriage and Family Review,* 1978, 1, 1-10.

HINDS, M. D. "The Child Victim of Incest." New York *Times,* June 15, 1981.

HOFFMAN, L. W. "The Value of Children to Parents and the Decrease in Family Size." *Proceedings of the American Philosophical Society,* 1975, 119, 430-38.

——, and F. I. NYE. *Working Mothers.* San Francisco: Jossey-Bass, 1974.

HOLMES, T. H., and R. H. RAHE. 'The Social Readjustment Rating Scale.' *Journal of Psychosomatic Research,* 1967, 11, 213-18.

HOLMSTROM, L. L. *The Two-career Family.* Cambridge, MA: Schenkman, 1973.

HONG, L. K. "The Instability of Teenage Marriage in the United States: an Evaluation of the Socioeconomic Status Hypothesis." *International Journal of Sociology of the Family,* 1974, 4, 201-12.

HORNIG, R. "See Aunt Debbie...First-grade Symbol of Swinging Single." *Washington Evening Star,* March 28, 1970.

HORNUNG, C. A., B. C. McCULLOUGH, and T. SUGIMOTO. 'Status Relationships in Marriage: Risk Factors in Spouse Abuse." *Journal of Marriage and the Family,* 1981, 43, 675-92.

HOUSEKNECHT, S. K. "Childlessness and Marital Adjustment." *Journal of Marriage and the Family,* 1979a, 41, 259-65.

——. "Timing of the Decision to Remain Voluntarily Childless: Evidence for Continuous Socialization." *Psychology of Women Quarterly,* 1979b, 4, 81-96.

HOWELL, S. "Recent Advances in Studies of the Physical Environments of the Elderly." Lecture at the CUNY Graduate Center, New York, 1976.

HUDSON, J. W., and L. L. HOYT. "Campus Values in Mate Selection: Forty Years Later." Unpublished study, 1978.

HUSTON, T. L. *Foundations of Interpersonal Attraction.* New York: Academic Press, 1974.

INSTITUTE FOR SOCIAL RESEARCH. "Women

Work Longer, Harder on the Job than Men Do." *ISR Newsletter,* 1977, 5, 8.

——. Report on Attitudes toward Marriage, 1980.

INSTITUTE OF LIFE INSURANCE. *Youth—1974.* New York, 1975.

INSURANCE INFORMATION INSTITUTE. *Plan 2000,* 1983.

JACOBSON, P. H. *American Marriage and Divorce.* New York: Rinehart, 1959.

JACOBY, S. "49 Singles Can't Be All Right." New York *Times Magazine,* February 12, 1974.

JESSOR, R., and S. L. JESSOR. *Problem Behavior and Psychosocial Development.* New York: Academic Press, 1977.

JONES, S. M. "Divorce and Remarriage: a New Beginning, a New Set of Problems." *Journal of Divorce,* 1978, 2, 217–27.

JORGENSEN, S. R. "Social Class Heterogamy, Status Striving, and Perceptions of Marital Conflict." *Journal of Marriage and the Family,* 1977, 39, 653–61.

——. "Socioeconomic Rewards and Perceived Marital Quality: a Re-examination." *Journal of Marriage and the Family,* 1979, 41, 825–35.

——, and J. C. GAUDY. "Self-disclosure and Satisfaction in Marriage: the Relation Examined." *Family Relations,* 1980, 29, 281–87.

JOURARD, S. M. *The Transparent Self: Self-disclosure and Well-being.* Princeton, NJ: Van Nostrand, 1964.

KAGAN, J. *Change and Continuity in Infancy.* New York: Wiley, 1971.

——. "The Psychological Requirements for Human Development." In N. Talbot (ed.) *Raising Children in Modern America.* Boston: Little, Brown, 1976.

——. *The Second Year: the Emergence of Self-awareness.* Cambridge, MA: Harvard University Press, 1981a.

——. Personal communication, 1981b.

——. "Stress and Coping in Early Development." In N. Garmezy and M. Rutter (eds.) *Stress, Coping, and Development in Children.* New York: McGraw-Hill, 1983.

——. Personal communication, 1985.

——, D. R. LAPIDUS, and M. MOORE. "Infant Antecedents of Cognitive Functioning." *Child Development,* 1978, 49, 1005–23.

KALMUSS, D. S. "The Intergenerational Transmission of Marital Aggression." *Journal of Marriage and the Family,* 1984, 46, 11–19.

——, and M. A. STRAUS. "Wives' Marital Dependency and Wife Abuse." *Journal of Marriage and the Family,* 1982, 44, 277–86.

KANDEL, D. B., and G. S. LESSER. *Youth in Two Worlds.* San Francisco: Jossey-Bass, 1972.

KANIN, E. J., K. R. DAVIDSON, and S. R. SCHECK. "A Research Note on Male-female Differentials in the Experience of Heterosexual Love." *Journal of Sex Research,* 1970, 6, 64–72.

KANTER, R. M. "Commitment and Social Organization: a Study of Commitment Mechanisms in Utopian Communities." *American Sociological Review,* 1968, 33, 499–517.

KANTER, R. M. *Communes:* Creating and Managing the Collective Life. NY: Harper and Row, 1973.

KEENEY, B. P., and R. E. CROMWELL. "Temporal Cycles and Sequences in Family Systems." *Journal of Comparative Family Studies,* 1979, 10, 19–33.

KEITH, P. M., and T. H. BRUBAKER. "Male Household Roles in Later Life: a Look at Masculinity and Marital Relationships." *Family Coordinator,* 1979, 28, 497–502.

——, and E. A. POWERS. "Household Roles and Wellbeing of Older Men." Paper presented to the Society for the Study of Social Problems, Boston, 1979.

KELLER, S. "Does the Family Have a Future?" *Journal of Comparative Family Studies,* 1971, 2, 1–14.

KELLY, E. L. "Consistency of the Adult Personality." *American Psychologist,* 1955, 10, 654–81.

KEMPE, C. H. "Child Abuse and Neglect." In N. B. Talbot (ed.) *Raising Children in Modern America.* Boston: Little, Brown, 1976.

——. "Incest and Other Forms of Sexual Abuse." In C. H. Kempe and R. E. Helfes (eds.) *The Battered Child, 3rd ed.* Chicago: University of Chicago Press, 1980.

KEMPE, R. S., and C. H. KEMPE. *The Common Secret: Sexual Abuse of Children and Adolescents.* New York: W. H. Freeman, 1984.

KERCKHOFF, R. K. "Marriage and Middle Age." *Family Coordinator,* 1976, 20, 5–11.

KIMLICKA, T., H. CROSS, and J. A. TARNAI. "A Comparison of Androgynous, Feminine, Masculine, and Undifferentiated Women on Self-esteem, Body Satisfaction, and Sexual Satisfaction." *Psychology of Women Quarterly,* 1983, 7, 291–94.

KINSEY, A. C., W. B. POMEROY, and C. E. MARTIN. *Sexual Behavior in the Human Male.* Philadelphia: Saunders, 1948.

——, et al. *Sexual Behavior in the Human Female.* Philadelphia: Saunders, 1953.

KIRKENDALL, L. A., and R. W. LIBBY. "Interpersonal Relationships: Crux of the Sexual Revolution." *Journal of Social Issues,* 1966, 22, 45–59.

KIRKPATRICK, C. *The Family as Process and Institution, 2nd ed.* New York: Ronald, 1963.

KNOX, D. "Conceptions of Love at Three Developmental Levels." *Family Coordinator,* 1970, 19, 151–57.

——. *Marriage Happiness: a Behavioral Approach to Counseling.* Champaign, IL: Research Press, 1972.

——. "Trends in Marriage and the Family—the 1980s." *Family Relations,* 1980, 29, 145–50.

——, and M. J. SPORAKOWSKI. "Attitudes of College Students toward Love." *Journal of Marriage and the Family,* 1968, 30, 628–42.

——, and K. WILSON. "Dating Problems of University Students." *College Student Journal,* 1983, 17, 225–28.

KNUPFER, G., W. CLARK, and R. ROOM. "The Mental Health of the Unmarried." *American Journal of Psychiatry,* 1966, 122, 842–44.

KOENIG, E. R. Unpublished Notes, 1962.

KOGAN, B. A. *Human Sexual Expression.* New York: Harcourt Brace Jovanovich, 1973.

KOLLER, M. R. "Some Changes in Courtship Patterns in Three Generations of Ohio Women." *American Sociological Review,* 1951, 16, 366–70.

KOLUCHOVA, J. "Severe Deprivation in Twins." *Journal of Child Psychology and Psychiatry,* 1972, 13, 107–14.

KOMAROVSKY, M. *Blue-collar Marriage.* New York: Vintage, 1967.

——. "Cultural Contradictions and Sex Roles: the Masculine Case." *American Journal of Sociology,* 1973, 78, 873–84.

——. *Dilemmas of Masculinity: a Study of College Youth.* New York: Norton, 1976.

KOTLAR, S. "Instrumental and Expressive Marital Roles." *Sociology and Social Research,* 1962, 46, 186–94.

KOVAR, M. G. "Problems of Retirement." *American Demographics,* 1980, 2, 18–19.

KRESSEL, K. "Patterns of Coping in Divorce and Some Implications for Clinical Practice." *Family Relations,* 1980, 29, 234–42.

KUHN, M. "How Mates Are Sorted." In H. Becker and R. Hill (eds.) *Family, Marriage, and Parenthood.* Boston: Heath, 1955.

KYLE, J. G., and B. WOLL. *Language in Sign: an International Perspective on Sign Language.* London: Croom, Helm, 1983.

LAMKE, L. K. "Adjustment and Sex-role Orientation in Adolescence." *Journal of Youth and Adolescence,* 1982, 11, 247–59.

LAMSOM, H. D. "Marriage of Coeds to Fellow Students." *Marriage and Family Living,* 1946, 8, 27–28.

LANDIS, P. H. *Making the Most out of Marriages.* New York: Appleton-Century-Crofts, 1965.

LANDY, D., and H. SIGALL. "Beauty is Talent: Task Evaluation as a Function of the Performer's Physical Attractiveness." *Journal of Personality and Social Psychology,* 1973, 28, 218–24.

LANE, R. E. *Political Life.* New York: Free Press, 1959.

LARSON, L. E. "System and Subsystem Perception of Family Roles." *Journal of Marriage and the Family,* 1974, 36, 123–38.

LASCH, C. *The Culture of Narcissism.* New York: Norton, 1978.

LAZARUS, A. *Behavior Therapy and Beyond.* New York: McGraw-Hill, 1971.

LAZARUS, R. S. "The Stress and Coping Paradigm." Paper delivered to the University of Washington conference on *The Critical Evaluation of Behavioral Paradigms for Psychiatric Science,* 1978.

LEAR, M. W. "Is There a Male Menopause? *New York Times,* 1973.

LEDER, K. "Women in Communes." *Women, a Journal of Liberation,* 1969, 1, 34.

LEDERER, W. J. "Videotaping Your Marriage To Save It." *New York Magazine,* February 19, 1973, 38–41.

LEE, G. R., and E. ELLITHORPE. "Intergenerational Exchange and Subjective Well-being among the Elderly." *Journal of Marriage and the Family,* 1982, 44, 217–24.

LEIN, L. "Male Participation in Home Life: Impact of Social Supports and Breadwinner Responsibility on the Allocation of Tasks." *Family Coordinator,* 1979, 28, 489–95.

LeMASTERS, E. E., and J. DeFRAIN. *Parents in Contemporary America.* Homewood, IL: Dorsey, 1983.

LeSHAN, E. J. *The Wonderful Crisis of Middle Age.* New York: David McKay, 1973.

LESTER, G. W., E. BECKHAM, and D. H. BAUCOMB. "Implementation of Behavioral Marital Therapy." *Journal of Marital and Family Therapy,* 1980, 6, 189-99.

LEUBA, C. *The Sexual Nature of Man.* Garden City, NY: Doubleday, 1954.

LEVENSON, E. A. *The Fallacy of Understanding: an Inquiry into the Changing Structure of Psychoanalysis.* New York: Basic Books, 1972.

LEVINE, E. M. "Middle-class Family Decline." *Society,* 1981, 18, 72–78.

LEVINGER, G. "Sources of Dissatisfaction among Applicants for Divorce." *American Journal of Orthopsychiatry,* 1966, 36, 803–07.

LEVINSON, D., et al. "Periods in the Adult Development of Men Ages 18–45." *Counseling Psychologist,* 1976, 6, 21–28.

LEVITAN, S. A., and R. S. BELOUS. *What's Happening to the American Family.* Baltimore: Johns Hopkins University Press, 1981.

LEVY, J., and R. MUNROE. *The Happy Family.* New York: Knopf, 1959.

LEWIS, M., and H. R. ALS. "The Contribution of the Infant to the Interaction with His Mother." Paper presented to meeting of the Society for Research in Child Development, Denver, 1975.

LIBBY, R. W., and G. D. NASS. "Parental Views of Teenage Sexual Behavior." *Journal of Sex Research,* 1971, 7, 226–36.

LINDSEY, B. B., and W. EVANS. *The Companionate Marriage.* New York: Boni and Liveright, 1927.

LINGREN, H. S., et al. "Enhancing Marriage and Family Competencies Throughout Adult Life Development." In N. Stinnett, et al. (eds.) *Family Strengths 4: Positive Support Systems.* Lincoln: University of Nebraska Press, 1982.

LINTON, R. *The Study of Man.* New York: Appleton-Century-Crofts, 1936.

LOCKSLEY, A. "On the Effect of Wives' Employment on Marital Adjustment and Companionship." *Journal of Marriage and the Family,* 1980, 42, 337–46.

———. "Social Class and Marital Attitudes and Behavior." *Journal of Marriage and the Family,* 1982, 44, 427–40.

LOPATA, H. Z. *Occupation: Housewife.* New York: Oxford University Press, 1972a.

———. "Role Changes in Widowhood: a World Perspective." In D. Cowgill and L Holmes (eds.) *Aging and Modernization.* New York: Appleton-Century-Crofts, 1972b.

LORD, E. "Emergent Africa." In G. H. Seward and R. C. Williamson (eds.) *Sex Roles in Changing Society.* New York: Random House, 1970.

LOWRIE, S. H. "Dating, a Neglected Field of Study." *Marriage and Family Living,* 1948, 10, 90–91.

LUCKEY, E., and G. NASS. "A Comparison of Sexual Attitudes and Behavior in an International Sample." *Journal of Marriage and the Family,* 1969, 3, 364–79.

LYDON, S. "Understanding Orgasm." *Ramparts,* 1968, 7, 59–63.

LYNCH, C., and M. BLINDER. "The Romantic Relationship: Why and How People Fall in Love, the Way Couples Connect, and Why They Break Apart." *Family Therapy,* 1983, 10, 91–104.

LYNESS, J. L., M. E. LIPETZ, and K. E. DAVIS. "Living Together: an Alternative to Marriage." *Journal of Marriage and the Family,* 1972, 34, 305–11.

MacDONALD, M. L., et al. "Social Skills Training: Behavior Rehearsal in Groups and Dating Skills." *Journal of Counseling Psychology,* 1975, 22, 224–30.

MACE, D. R. "What I Have Learned about Family Life." *Family Coordinator,* 1974, 23, 189–95.

———. "The Outlook for Marriage: New Needs and Opportunities." *Foundation News,* November/December 1975, 16.

———, and V. C. MACE. *Marriage East and West.* New York: Doubleday, 1960.

———, and MACE. *We Can Have Better Marriages If We Want Them.* New York: Abingdon Press, 1974.

———, and MACE. "Marriage Enrichment—Wave of the Future?" *Family Coordinator,* 1975, 24, 131–35.

MACFARLANE, J. W. "From Infancy to Adulthood." *Childhood Education,* 1963, 39, 336–42.

———. "Perspectives on Personality Consistency and Change from the Guidance Study." *Vita Humana,* 1964, 7, 115–26.

MACKE, A. S., G. W. BOHRNSTEDT, and I. N. BERNSTEIN. "Housewives' Self-esteem and Their Husbands' Success: the Myth of Vicarious Involvement." *Journal of Marriage and the Family,* 1979, 41, 51–57.

MACKLIN, E. D. "Heterosexual Cohabitation among Unmarried College Students." *Family Coordinator,* 1972, 21, 463–72.

MADSEN, C. H. JR., and C. K. MADSEN. *Teaching/Discipline: Behavioral Principles toward a Positive Approach.* Boston: Allyn & Bacon, 1970.

MAINARDI, P. "The Politics of Housework." In R. Morgan (ed.) *Sisterhood Is Powerful.* New York: Vintage, 1970.

MAKEPEACE, J. M. "Courtship Violence among College Students." *Family Relations,* 1981, 30, 97–102.

MARCIANO, T. D. "Male Influences on Fertility." *Family Coordinator*, 1979, 28, 561–68.

MARIN, P. "A Revolution's Broken Promises." *Psychology Today*, 1983, 17, 50–57.

MARSHALL, D. S. "Sexual Behavior in Mangaia." In D. S. Marshall and R. C. Suggs (eds.) *Human Sexual Behavior*. Englewood Cliffs, NJ: Prentice-Hall, 1972.

MARTINSON, F. M. *Marriage and the American Ideal*. New York: Dodd Mead, 1960.

MASLOW, A. H. *Toward a Psychology of Being, 2nd ed*. New York: Van Nostrand, 1968.

MASTERS, W. H., and V. E. JOHNSON. *Human Sexual Response*. Boston: Little, Brown, 1966.

———. *Human Sexual Inadequacy*. Boston: Little, Brown, 1970.

———. Personal communication, 1972.

———. *The Pleasure Bond*. New York: Bantam Books, 1976.

MATHEWS, V. D. and C. S. MIHANOVICH. "New Orientations on Marital Adjustment." *Marriage and Family Living*, 1963, 25, 300–304.

MATTHEWS, W. J. "Violence in College Couples." *College Student Journal*, 1984, 18, 150–58.

MAZUR, R. *The New Intimacy*. Boston: Beacon Press, 1973.

McCALL, R. B. *Infants*. New York: Random House, 1980.

McGRAW, M. B. *The Neuromuscular Maturation of the Human Infant*. New York: Columbia University Press, 1943.

McKILLIP, J., and S. L. RIEDEL. "External Validity of Matching on Physical Attractiveness for Same and Opposite Sex Couples." *Journal of Applied and Social Psychology*, 1983, 13, 328–37.

McMILLIN, M. R. "Attitudes of College Men toward Career Involvement of Married Women." *Vocational Guidance Quarterly*, 1972, 21, 8–11.

MEAD, M. *Sex and Temperament in Three Primitive Societies*. New York: Dell, 1935.

———. "Future Family." *Trans-action*, 1971, 8, 50–53.

MELVILLE, K. "Changing the Family Game." *Sciences*, 1973, 13, 17–19.

MENDELSOHN, R., and S. DOBIE. "Women's Self-conception: a Block to Career Development." Unpublished study, Detroit Department of Mental Health, 1970.

MILL, J. S. *Three Essays*. London: Oxford University Press, 1966. Originally published in 1869.

MILLER, A. "Reactions of Friends to Divorce." In P. Bohannon (ed.) *Divorce and After*. Garden City, NY: Doubleday, 1970.

MILLER, B. C., and D. L. SOLLIE. "Normal Stress during the Transition to Parenthood." *Family Relations*, 1980, 29, 459–65.

MILLER, P. Y., and W. SIMON. "Adolescent Sexual Behavior: Context and Change." *Social Problems*, 1974, 22, 58–76.

MILLER, S. "Minnesota Couples Communication Program (MCCP): Premarital and Marital Groups." In D. H. Olson (ed.) *Treating Relationships*. Lake Mills, IA; Graphic, 1976.

———, D. B. WACKMAN, and S. R. JORGENSON. "Couple Communication Patterns and Marital Satisfaction." *Visiting Scholars Seminars, 1973–74*. Home Economics Center for Research, University of North Carolina at Greensboro, 1974.

———, R. CORRALES, and D. B. WACKMAN. "Recent Progress in Understanding and Facilitating Marital Communication." *Family Coordinator*, 1975, 24, 143–52.

MONEY, J., and A. A. EHRHARDT. *Man and Woman, Boy and Girl*. Baltimore: Johns Hopkins Press, 1972.

MONEY, J., and D. MATHEWS. "Prenatal Exposure to Virilizing Progestins: an Adult Follow-up Study of Twelve Women." *Archives of Sexual Behavior*, 1982, 11, 73–83.

MOODY, K. *Growing Up on Television*. New York: Times Books, 1980.

MOZDZIERZ, G. J., and T. J. LOTTMAN. "Games Married Couples Play: Adlerian View." *Journal of Individual Psychology*, 1973, 29, 182–94.

MUDD, E. H., and S. TAUBIN. "Success in Family Living: Does It Last? A Twenty-year Follow-up." *Journal of Family Therapy*, 1982, 10, 59–67.

MURDOCK, G. P. *Social Structure*. New York: Macmillan, 1949.

MURSTEIN, B. I. "Interview Behavior, Projective Techniques, and Questionnaires in the Clinical Assessment of Marital Choice." *Journal of Personality Assessment*, 1972, 36, 462–67.

———. "Sex Drive, Person Perception, and Marital Choice." *Archives of Sexual Behavior*, 1974, 3, 331–48.

MYRDAL, A., and V. KLEIN. *Women's Two Roles: Home and Work*. London: Routledge, 1956.

NAISBITT, J. *Megatrends*. New York: Warner, 1982.

NATIONAL ASSOCIATION OF REALTORS. Report on home sales, 1985.

NATIONAL CENTER FOR HEALTH STATISTICS. *Use of Contraception in the U.S.*, 1984.

———. *Monthly Vital Statistics Report*, 1985, 33, 1–3, and earlier reports.

NATIONAL INSTITUTE OF MENTAL HEALTH. *Television and Behavior: Ten Years of Scientific Progress and Implications for the Eighties.* Washington, DC: Government Printing Office, 1982.

NAVRAN, L. "Communication and Adjustment in Marriage." *Family Process,* 1967, 6, 173-84.

NEUGARTEN, B. L. (ed.) *Middle Age and Aging.* Chicago: University of Chicago Press, 1968.

——, and K. K. WEINSTEIN. "The Changing American Grandparent." *Journal of Marriage and the Family,* 1964, 26, 199-204.

NEWCOMB, T. M. "Persistence and Regression of Changed Attitudes: Long-range Studies." *Journal of Social Issues,* 1963, 19, 3-14.

NICHOLS, S., and E. METZEN. "Impact of Wife's Employment upon Husband's Housework." *Journal of Family Issues,* 1982, 3, 199-216.

NORDAU, M. *Die Conventionellen Lugen der Kulturmenscheit.* Leipzig, Germany, 1884.

NORTON, A. J. "Family Life Cycle: 1980." *Journal of Marriage and the Family,* 1983, 45, 267-75.

——, and GLICK, P. C. "Marital Instability: Past, Present, and Future." *Journal of Social Issues,* 1976, 32, 5-20.

NYE, F. I. "Values, Family, and a Changing Society." *Journal of Marriage and the Family,* 1967, 29, 241-48.

——, and F. M. BERARDO. *The Family: its Structure and Interaction.* New York: Macmillan, 1973.

O'BRIEN, J. E. "Violence in Divorce-prone Families." *Journal of Marriage and the Family,* 1971, 33, 692-98.

OFFICE OF EDUCATION. *Annual Report of the U. S. Commissioner of Education,* 1900.

OGBURN, W. F. "The Family and Its Functions." In *Recent Social Trends in the U. S.,* Report of the President's Research Committee on Social Trends, 1933.

OLLISON, L. "Socialization: Women, Worth, and Work." Unpublished paper, San Diego State University, 1975.

O'NEILL, N. *The Marriage Premise.* New York: M. Evans & Co., 1977.

——, and G. O'NEILL. Paper presented to the American Psychological Association, Honolulu, 1972.

——, and G. O'NEILL. *Open Marriage.* New York: Avon, 1973.

ORTHNER, D. K. "Leisure Activity Patterns and Marital Satisfaction over the Marital Career." *Journal of Marriage and the Family,* 1975, 37, 91-102.

ORY, H. W. "Mortality Associated with Fertility and Fertility Control: 1983." *Family Planning Perspectives,* 1983, 15, 57-63.

OTTO, H. "The New Marriage: Marriage as a Framework for Developing Personal Potential." In H. Otto (ed.) *The Family in Search of a Future.* New York: Appleton-Century-Crofts, 1970.

OVERALL, J. E., B. W. HENRY, and A. WOODWARD. "Dependence of Marital Problems on Parental Family History." *Journal of Abnormal Psychology,* 1974, 83, 446-50.

PAGELOW, M. D. "Secondary Battering and Alternatives of Female Victims of Spouse Abuse." In L. H. Bowker (ed.) *Women and Crime in America.* New York: Macmillan, 1981.

PARELIUS, A. P. "Emerging Sex-role Attitudes, Expectations, and Strains among College Women." *Journal of Marriage and the Family,* 1975, 37, 146-53.

PARSONS, T. "The American Family: its Relations to Personality and to the Social Structure." In T. Parsons and R. F. Bales (eds.) *Family Socialization and Interaction Process.* Glencoe, IL: Free Press, 1955.

PATTERSON, G. R., H. HOPS, and R. L. WEISS. "Interpersonal Skills Training for Couples In Early Stages of Conflict." *Journal of Marriage and the Family,* 1975, 37, 295-303.

PEARL, D. *Television and Behavior: Ten Years of Scientific Progress and Implications for the Eighties,* Vol. I, Summary Report. Washington, DC: Department of Health and Human Services. 1982. Publication ADM82-1195.

PEARLIN, L. I., and J. S. JOHNSON. "Marital Status, Life Strains, and Depression." *American Sociological Review,* 1977, 42, 704-15.

PETERMAN, D. J., C. A. RIDLEY, and S. M. ANDERSON. "A Comparison of Cohabiting and Noncohabiting College Students." *Journal of Marriage and the Family,* 1974, 36, 344-54.

PHILLIBER, S. G. "Socialization for Childbearing." *Journal of Social Issues,* 1980, 56, 30-44.

PHILLIBER, W. M., and D. V. HILLER. "A Research Note: Occupational Attainments and Perceptions of Status among Working Wives." *Journal of Marriage and the Family,* 1979, 41, 59-62.

PHILLIPS, C. Personal communications, 1980, 1982, and 1985.

PICKETT, R. S. "The American Family: an Embattled Institution." *Humanist,* 1975, 35, 3.

PIERSON, E. C., and W. V. D'ANTONIO. *Female*

and Male: Dimensions of Human Sexuality. Philadelphia: Lippincott, 1974.

PIETROFESA, J. K., and N. K. SCHLOSSBERG. "Counselor Bias and the Female Occupational Role." In N. Galzer-Malbin and H. Y. Waehrer (eds.) Woman in a Man-Made World: A Socioeconomic Handbook. Chicago: Rand McNally, 1972.

PLACE, D. M. Unpublished dissertation, University of California at San Francisco. Partially reported in "The Dating Experience of Adolescent Girls." *Adolescence,* 1975, 10, 157-74.

PLECK, J. H. "Men's New Roles in the Family: Housework and Child Care." Paper presented at the Merrill-Palmer Institute, Detroit, 1975.

———. "Men's Family Work: Three Perspectives and Some New Data." *Family Coordinator,* 1979, 28, 481-88.

POLATNICK, M. "Why Men Don't Rear Children: a Power Analysis." *Berkeley Journal of Sociology,* 1973-74, 18, 45-86.

POLIT, D. F., R. L. NUTTALL, and E. V. NUTTALL. "The Only Child Grows Up: a Look at Some Characteristics of Adult Only Children." *Family Relations,* 1980, 29, 99-106.

POLLIS, C. A. "Dating Involvement and Patterns of Idealization: a Test of Waller's Hypothesis." *Journal of Marriage and the Family,* 1969, 31, 765-70.

POLLOCK, J. C. *Aging in America: Trials and Triumphs.* New York: Research and Forecasts Inc., 1980.

POPE, H., and C. W. MUELLER. "The Intergenerational Transmission of Marital Instability: Comparisons by Race and Sex." *Journal of Social Issues,* 1976, 32, 49-66.

POPENOE, P. "Remarriage of Divorcees to Each Other." *American Sociological Review,* 1938, 3, 695-99.

POTTS, M., P. DIGGORY, and J. PEEL. *Abortion.* England: Cambridge University Press, 1977.

PRATT, W. F., and C. A. BACHRACH. "Preliminary Estimates of the Population 'At Risk' of Pregnancy and of Those Using Contraception: Findings from Cycle III of the National Survey of Family Growth." Paper presented to the American Public Health Association, 1983, updated by Pratt, 1984.

PRESIDENT'S COMMISSION ON MENTAL HEALTH. *Report of the Commission.* Washington: Government Printing Office, 1978.

PROGREBIN, L. C. "Down with Sexist Upbringing." *Ms. Magazine,* spring 1972, 18 et seq.

QUINN, W. H. "Personal and Family Adjustment in Later Life." *Journal of Marriage and the Family,* 1983, 45, 57-73.

RAINWATER, L. "Marital Sexuality in Four 'Cultures of Poverty.'" In D. S. Marshall and R. C. Suggs (eds.) *Human Sexual Behavior.* Englewood Cliffs, NJ: Prentice-Hall, 1972.

RAMEY, J. W. "Intimate Networks: Will They Replace the Monogamous Family?" *Futurist,* 1975, 9, 175-81.

———. "Multi-adult Household: Living Group of the Future?" *Futurist,* 1976, 10, 78-83.

RAPOPORT, R., and R. N. RAPOPORT. "Working Women and the Enabling Role of the Husband." Paper presented to the International Sociological Association, Moscow, 1972.

———. "Men, Women, and Equity." *Family Coordinator,* 1975a, 24, 421-32.

———. *Leisure and the Family Life Cycle.* London: Routledge and Kegan Paul, 1975b.

RATHS, O. N., et al. "The Counterphobic Mechanism as a Force in Mate Selection and Marital Stability." *Family Coordinator,* 1974, 23, 295.

RAWLINGS, S. "Perspectives on American Husbands and Wives." *Current Population Reports,* Census Bureau, December 1978, Series P-23, No. 77.

REBELSKY, F. "Infancy in Two Cultures." *Nedralns Ti jdschrift vor de Psychologie,* 1967, 2, 379-85.

REGIER, D. A., and C. A. TAUBE. "The Delivery of Mental Health Services." In S. Arieti and H. K. H. Brodie (eds.) *American Handbook of Psychiatry,* 1981, 7, 715-33.

REINER, B. S., and R. L. EDWARDS. "Adolescent Marriage—Social or Therapeutic Problem?" *Family Coordinator,* 1974, 234, 383-90.

REISS, I. L. "Toward a Sociology of the Heterosexual Love Relationship." *Marriage and Family Living,* 1960, 22, 139-45.

———. *The Social Context of Premarital Sexual Permissiveness.* New York: Holt, Rinehart & Winston, 1967.

———. *Family Systems in America.* Hinsdale, IL: Dryden, 1976.

RENNE, K. S. "Correlates of Dissatisfaction in America." *Journal of Marriage and the Family,* 1970, 32, 54-66.

———. "Health and Marital Experience in an Urban Population." *Journal of Marriage and the Family,* 1971, 33, 338-50.

RICHARDSON, J. G. "Wife Occupational Superiority and Marital Troubles: an Examination of the Hypothesis." *Journal of Marriage and the Family,* 1979, 41, 63-72.

RIGGS, K. *The Battered Woman: What Makes Her Tick?* Report for the Women's Crisis and Shelter Services of Santa Cruz County, 1981.

ROBERTSON, I. *Sociology.* New York: Worth, 1974.

ROBERTSON, J. F. 'Grandmotherhood: a Study of Role Conceptions." *Journal of Marriage and the Famly,* 1977, 39, 165-74.

ROBINSON, I. E., and D. JEDLICKA. "Change in Sexual Attitudes and Behavior of College Students from 1965 to 1980: a Research Note." *Journal of Marriage and the Family,* 1982, 44, 237-40.

ROBINSON, J. *How Americans Use Time: a Social-psychological Analysis.* New York: Praeger, 1977.

ROBINSON, N. H., and ROBINSON, J. "Sex Roles and the Territoriality of Everyday Behavior." Unpublished study, University of Michigan, 1975.

ROGERS, C. R. *Client-centered Therapy.* Boston: Houghton-Mifflin, 1953.

ROLLINS, B. C., and H. FELDMAN. "Marital Satisfaction over the Family Life Cycle." *Journal of Marriage and the Family,* 1970, 32, 20-28.

ROPER ORGANIZATION. *The Virginia Slims American Opinion Poll.* New York: Roper Organization, 1974.

———. *The Virginia Slims American Women's Poll.* New York: Roper Organization, 1980.

ROSEN, B. C. "The Achievement Syndrome: a Psychocultural Dimension of Social Stratification." *American Sociological Review,* 1956, 21, 203-11.

ROSENBERG, M. *Society and the Adolescent Self-image.* Princeton, NJ: Princeton University Press, 1965.

ROSS, H. L., and V. SAWHILL. *Time of Transition.* Washington, DC: Urban Institute, 1975.

ROSS, S., and J. WALTERS. "Perceptions of a Sample of University Men Concerning Women." *Journal of Genetic Psychology,* 1973, 122, 329-36.

ROTH, J., and R. F. PECK. "Social Class and Social Mobility Factors Related to Marital Adjustment." *American Sociological Review,* 1951, 16, 478-87.

ROY, D., and R. ROY. *Honest Sex.* New York: American Library, 1968.

ROY, R., and D. ROY. "Is Monogamy Outdated?" *Humanist,* 1970, 30, 19-26.

RUBIN, Z. "Measurement of Romantic Love." *Journal of Personality and Social Psychology,* 1970, 16, 265-73.

———. *Liking and Loving: an Invitation to Social Psychology.* New York: Holt, Rinehart, and Winston, 1973.

———, F. J. PROVENZANO, and Z. LURIA. "The Eye of the Beholder: Parents' Views on Sex of Newborns." *American Journal of Orthopsychiatry,* 1974, 44, 512-19.

——— et al. "Self-disclosure in Dating Couples; Sex Roles and the Ethic of Openness." *Journal of Marriage and the Family,* 1980, 42, 305-17.

RUSHING, W. A. "Marital Status and Mental Disorder: Evidence in Favor of a Behavioral Model." *Social Forces,* 1979, 58, 540-56.

RUSSELL, D. E. H. "The Incidence and Prevalence of Intrafamilial and Extrafamilial Sexual Abuse of Female Children." *Child Abuse and Neglect,* 1983, 7, 133-46.

RYDER, R. G. "Dimensions of Early Marriage." *Family Process,* 1970, 9, 51-68.

SADKER, M., and D. SADKER. "Sexism in the Schoolroom of the '80s." *Psychology Today,* March 19, 1985, 54-57.

SAEGERT, S., and G. WINKEL. "The Home: a Critical Problem for Changing Sex Roles." Paper presented to the American Sociological Association, San Francisco, 1978.

SAFILIOS-ROTHSCHILD, C. "The Story of Family Power: a Review, 1960-69." *Journal of Marriage and the Family,* 1970, 32, 539-52.

———. *Women and Social Policy.* Englewood Cliffs, NJ: Prentice-Hall, 1974.

———. "A Macro and Micro Examination of Family Power and Love." *Journal of Marriage and the Family,* 1976, 38, 355-63.

———. *Love, Sex, and Sex Roles.* Englewood Cliffs, NJ: Prentice-Hall, 1977.

SATIR, V. *Conjoint Family Therapy.* Palo Alto, CA: Science and Behavior Books, 1967.

———. "A Goal of Living." *Etcetera,* December 1970.

———. *Peoplemaking.* Palo Alto, CA: Science and Behavior Books, 1972.

SCANZONI, J. "Sex Roles, Economic Factors, and Marital Solidarity in Black and White Marriages." *Journal of Marriage and the Family,* 1975, 37, 130-44.

———. "Gender Roles and the Process of Fertility Contol." *Journal of Marriage and the Family,* 1976, 35, 315-32.

———, and M. McMURRY. "Continuities in the Explanation of Fertility Control. *Journal of Marriage and the Family,* 1972, 34, 315-22.

SCHELLENBERG, J. A. "Homogamy in Personal Values and the 'Field of Eligibles.'" *Social Forces,* 1960, 39, 157-62.

SCHLESINGER, B. *The One Parent Family.* Toronto, Can.: University of Toronto Press, 1980.

SCHRAM, R. W. "Marital Satisfaction over the

Family Life Cycle: a Critique and Proposal." *Journal of Marriage and the Family*, 1979, 41, 7–12.

SCHWARTZ, B. K. "Easing the Adaptation to Parenthood." *Journal of Family Counseling*, 1974, 2, 32–39.

SCHWARTZ, P. Personal communications, 1979 and 1980.

SCOTT, J. W. "The Sentiments of Love and Aspirations for Marriage and Their Association with Teenage Sexual Activity and Pregnancy." *Adolescence*, 1983, 18, 889–97.

SEGAL, J., and Z. SEGAL. *Growing Up Smart and Happy.* New York: McGraw-Hill, 1984.

SEIDENBERG, R. "Psychosexual Adjustment of the Unattractive Woman." *Medical Aspects of Human Sexuality*, 1973a, 7, 60–81.

———. *Marriage between Equals.* New York: Anchor Press, 1973b.

———. "For the Future—Equity?" In J. B. Miller (ed.) *Psychoanalysis and Women.* Hammondsworth, England: Penguin, 1973c.

SERBIN, L. A., et al. "A Comparison of Teacher Response to the Preacademic and Problem Behavior of Boys and Girls." *Child Development*, 1973, 44, 796–804.

SHANAS, E. "Older People and Their Families: the New Pioneers." *Journal of Marriage and the Family*, 1980, 42, 9–15.

———, et al. *Old People in Three Industrial Societies.* New York: Atherton, 1968.

SHAPIRO, A. "The Relationship between Self-concept and Self-disclosure." *Dissertation Abstracts International*, 1968, 39, 1180–81.

———, and C. SWENSEN. "Patterns of Self-disclosure among Married Couples." *Journal of Counseling Psychology*, 1969, 16, 179–80.

SHAVER, P., and J. FREEDMAN. "Your Pursuit of Happiness." *Psychology Today*, August 1976, 26–32.

SHERESKY, N., and M. MANNES. "A Radical Guide to Wedlock." *Saturday Review*, 1972, 55, 33–38.

SHOSTRUM, E. L. *Man, the Manipulator: the Inner Journey from Manipulation to Actualization.* New York: Abingdon Press, 1967.

SIEGAL, B., and J. SHORT. "Post-parting Depression." *Marriage and Divorce*, 1974, 1, 77–83.

SILVERMAN, P. R., and A. COOPERBAND. "On Widowhood: Mutual Help and the Elderly Widow." *Journal of Geriatric Psychiatry*, 1975, 8, 9–27.

SIMENAUER, J., and D. CARROLL. *Singles: the New Americans.* New York: Simon & Schuster, 1982

SIMMEL, G. *The Sociology of Georg Simmel.* Edited by K. Wolff. New York: Free Press, 1950.

SIMON, W., A. S. BERGER, AND J. H. GAGNON. "Beyond Anxiety and Fantasy: The Coital Experiences of College Youth." *Journal of Youth and Adolescence*, 1972, 1, 203–22.

SIMONS, R. G., and F. ROSENBERG. "Sex, Sex Roles, and Self-image." *Journal of Youth and Adolescence*, 1975, 4, 229–58.

SINDBERG, R. M., A. F. ROBERTS, and D. McCLAIN. "Mate Selection Factors in Computer Matched Marriages." *Journal of Marriage and the Family*, 1972, 34, 611–14.

SINGER, J. L., and D. G. SINGER. *Television, Imagination, and Aggression: a Study of Preschoolers.* Hillsdale, NJ: Erlbaum, 1980.

SINGH, B. K. "Trends in Attitudes toward Premarital Sexual Relations." *Journal of Marriage and the Family*, 1980, 42, 387–93.

SKINNER, D. A. "Dual-career Family Stress and Coping: a Literature Review." *Family Relations*, 1980, 29, 473–81.

SKOLNICK, A. *The Intimate Environment.* Boston: Little, Brown, 1973.

———. "The Family and Its Discontents." *Society*, 1981, 18, 42–47.

———, and J. H. SKOLNICK. *Intimacy, Family, and Society.* Boston: Little, Brown, 1974.

SLABY, R. G., G. R. QUARFORTH, and G. A. McCONNACHIE. "Television Violence and Its Sponsors." *Journal of Communication*, 1976, 26, 88–96.

SLEVIN, K. F., and C. R. WINGROVE. "Similarities and Differences among Three Generations of Women in Attitudes toward the Female Role in Contemporary Society." *Sex Roles*, 1983, 9, 609–24.

SMITH, A. D. "Egalitarian Marriage: Implications for Practice and Policy." *Social Casework*, 1980, 6, 288–95.

SMITH, J. R., and L. G. SMITH. *Beyond Monogamy.* Baltimore, MD: Johns Hopkins University Press, 1974.

SNYDER, D. K. "Multidimensional Assessment of Marital Satisfaction." *Journal of Marriage and the Family*, 1979, 41, 813–23.

SOLOMON, E. S., J. E. CLARE, and C. F. WESTOFF. "Social and Psychological Factors Affecting Fertility." *Milbank Memorial Fund Quarterly*, 1956, 34, 160–70.

SPANIER, G. B. "Married and Unmarried Cohabitation in the United States: 1980." *Journal of Marriage and the Family,* 1983, 45, 277–88.

——, and P. C. GLICK. "Paths to Remarriage." *Journal of Divorce,* 1980a, 3, 283–98.

——. "The Life Cycle of American Families: an Expanded Analysis." *Journal of Family History,* 1980b, 5, 97–111.

——. "Mate Selection Differentials between Whites and Blacks in the United States." *Social Forces,* 1980c, 53, 707–25.

——. "Marital Instability in the United States: Some Correlates and Recent Changes." *Family Relations,* 1981, 31, 329–38.

SPENCE, D., and T. LONNER. "The 'Empty Nest': a Transition within Motherhood." *Family Coordinator,* 1971, 20, 369–75.

SPOCK, B. *Baby and Child Care, 5th ed.* New York: Wallaby, 1976.

——, and M. B. ROTHENBERG. *Dr. Spock's Baby and Child Care, 6th ed.* New York: Simon and Schuster, 1985.

SPREITZER, E., and L. E. RILEY. "Factors Associated with Singlehood." *Journal of Marriage and the Family,* 1974, 74, 533–44.

SPRENKEL, D. H., and B. L. FISHER. "An Empirical Assessment of the Goals of Family Therapy." *Journal of Marital and Family Therapy,* 1980, 6, 131–39.

SPUHLER, J. N. "Assortive Mating with Respect to Physical Characteristics." *Eugenics Quarterly,* 1968, 15, 129–34.

SROLE, L., and Associates. *Mental Health in the Metropolis: the Midtown Manhattan Study.* New York: McGraw-Hill, 1962.

STAFFORD, R., E. BACKMAN, and P. JiBONA. "The Division of Labor among Cohabiting and Married Couples." *Journal of Marriage and the Family,* 1977, 39, 43–58.

STAKE, J. E., and E. LEVITZ. "Career Goals of College Women and Men and Perceived Achievement-related Encouragement." *Psychology of Women Quarterly,* 1979, 4, 151–59.

STANNARD, U. "Commentary on Article by R. Seidenberg." *Medical Aspects of Human Sexuality,* 1973, 7, 77.

STARR, B. D., and M. B. WEINER. *Sex and Sexuality in the Mature Years.* New York: Stein & Day, 1981.

STARR, J. R., and D. E. CARNS. "Singles in the City." *Society,* 1972, 9, 43–48.

STEIN, B., A. COHEN, and H. GADON. "Flexitime: Work when You Want To." *Psychology Today,* July 1976, 40–44.

STEIN, P. J. "Singlehood: an Alternative to Marriage." *Family Coordinator,* 1975, 24, 489–503.

STEINBACHER, R. "From Here to Fraternity." In C. C. Gould (ed.) *Beyond Domination.* Totowa, NJ: Rowman and Allanheld, 1984.

STENCEL, S. "The Changing American Family." In H. Gimlin (ed.) *Editorial Research Reports on the Changing American Family.* Washington, DC: Congressional Quarterly, 1979.

STEPHENS, W. N. *The Family in Cross-cultural Perspective.* New York: Holt, 1963.

STERN, M. Personal communication, 1983.

STEUER, F. B., J. M. APPLEFIELD, and R. SMITH. "Televised Aggression and the Interpersonal Aggression of Preschool Children." *Journal of Abnormal Psychology,* 1971, 88, 152–61.

STEVENS, B. "The Sexually Oppressed Male." *Psychotherapy,* 1974, 2, 16–21.

STILLMAN, R. J. *Guide to Personal Finance, 4th ed.* Englewood Cliffs, NJ: Prentice-Hall, 1984.

STINNETT, N., L. M. CARTER, and J. E. MONTGOMERY. "Older Persons' Perceptions of Their Marriages." *Journal of Marriage and the Family,* 1972, 34, 665–70.

STOLLER, R. J. "The 'Bedrock' of Masculinity and Femininity—Bisexuality." *Archives of General Psychiatry,* 1972, 26, 207–12.

STRAUS, M. A. "Leveling, Civility, and Violence in the Family." *Journal of Marriage and the Family,* 1974, 36, 13–39.

——. *Violence in the American Family.* Garden City, NY: Doubleday Anchor, 1978.

——. "Stress and Child Abuse." In C. H. Kempe and R. E. Helfes (eds.) *The Battered Child, 3rd ed.* Chicago: University of Chicago Press, 1980.

——. Comment at the Conference on Violence, 1981.

——, R. J. GELLES, and S. K. STEINMETZ. *Behind Closed Doors.* Garden City, NY: Anchor Books, 1980.

STRONG, J. R. "A Marital Conflict Resolution Model." *Journal of Marriage and Family Counseling,* 1975, 1, 269–76.

STUART, R. B. "Operant Interpersonal Treatment for Marital Discord." *Journal of Consulting and Clinical Psychology,* 1969, 33, 675–82.

SUELZLE, M. "Women in Labor." *Trans-action,* 1970, 8, 50–58.

SUSSMAN, M. B. "Family Systems in the 1970s: Analysis, Policies, and Programs." *Annals of the American Academy of Political and Social Science,* 1971, 396, 40–56.

——. "The Four F's of Variant Family Forms and

Marriage Styles." *Family Coordinator,* 1975, 24, 563-76.

SYMONDS, A. "The Liberated Woman: Healthy and Neurotic." *American Journal of Psychoanalysis,* 1974, 34, 177-83.

TANFER, K., and M. C. HORN. "Contraceptive Use, Pregnancy, and Fertility among Single American Women in Their 20s." *Family Planning Perspectives,* 1985, 17, 10-19.

TARG, D. B. "Toward a Reassessment of Women's Experience at Middle Age." *Family Coordinator,* 1979, 28, 377-82.

TARNOWIESKI, D. Survey for the American Management Association, May 1975.

TAVRIS, C., and C. OFFIR. *The Longest War.* New York: Harcourt Brace Jovanovich, 1977.

THOMAS, A., S. CHESS, and H. G. BIRCH. "The Origin of Personality." *Scientific American,* 1970, 223, 106-7.

THOMAS, E. J., C. I. WALTER, and K. O'FLAHERTY. "A Verbal Problem Checklist for Use in Assessing Family Verbal Behavior." *Behavior Therapy,* 1974, 5, 235-36.

THOMPSON, G. "Intelligence and Fertility: the Scottish 1947 Survey." *Eugenics Review,* 1950, 41, 163-70.

THORNTON, A. *Study of American Families: 1980 Report to Respondents.* Survey Research Center, University of Michigan, 1980.

———, D. F. ALWIN, and D. CAMBURN. "Causes and Consequences of Sex-role Attitudes and Attitude Change." *American Sociological Review,* 1983, 48, 211-27.

TARNDWIESKI, D. Survey for the American Management Association. May 1975.

TROST, J. "Married and Unmarried Cohabitation: the Case of Sweden, with Some Comparisons." *Journal of Marriage and the Family,* 1975, 37, 677-82.

UBELL, E. "Sex in America Today." *Parade,* October 28, 1984, 11-13.

UNGAR, S. B. "The Sex Typing of Adult and Child Behavior in Toy Sales." *Sex Roles,* 1982, 8, 251-60.

U. S. GOVERNMENT. Departments, Bureaus, and other agencies. Listed by name—e.g. Bureau of the Census, Department of Labor.

VANEK, J. "Time Spent in Housework." *Scientific American,* November 1974, 231, 116-20.

VAN VELSOR, E. and L. BEEGHLEY. "The Process of Class Identification among Employed Married Women: a Replication and Reana-

lysis." *Journal of Marriage and the Family,* 1979, 41, 771-78.

VARNI, C. A. "An Exploratory Study of Wife-swapping." *Pacific Sociological Review,* 1972, 15, 507-22.

VERBRUGGE, L. M. "Marital Status and Health." *Journal of Marriage and the Family,* 1979, 41, 267-85.

VEROFF, J., E. DOUVAN, and R. A. KULKA. *The Inner American.* New York: Basic Books, 1981.

VINCENT, C. E. "Social and Interpersonal Sources of Symptomatic Frigidity." *Marriage and Family Living,* 1956, 18, 355-60.

———. "Familia Spongia: The Adaptive Function." *Journal of Marriage and the Family,* 1966, 28, 29-36.

———. "An Open Letter to the 'Caught Generation.'" *Family Coordinator,* 1972, 21, 143-50.

———. *Sexual and Mental Health.* New York: McGraw-Hill, 1973.

———. "Prerequisites for Marital and Sexual Communication." In E. A. Powers and M. W. Lees (eds.) *Process in Relationship, 2nd ed.* St. Paul, MN: West, 1976.

WAKE, F. "Attitudes of Parents toward Premarital Sexual Behavior of Their Children and Themselves." *Journal of Sex Research,* 1969, 5, 1777.

WALKER, K., and M. WOODS. *Time Use: a Measure of Household Production of Family Goods and Services.* Washington, DC: American Home Economics Association, 1976.

WALKER, K., A. MacBRIDE, and M. L. S. VACHON. "Social Support Networks and the Crisis of Bereavement." *Social Science and Medicine,* 1977, 2, 35-41.

WALLER, W. "The Rating and Dating Complex." *American Sociological Review,* 1937, 2, 727-34.

———. *The Family: a Dynamic Interpretation.* New York: Dryden, 1938.

WALSHOCK, M. L. "Sex Role Typing and Feminine Sexuality." Paper presented to the American Sociological Association, 1973.

WALTERS, J., and N. STINNETT. "Parent-child Relationships: a Decade Review of Research." *Journal of Marriage and the Family,* 1971, 33, 70-111.

WAMPLER, K. S., and D. H. SPRENKLE. "The Minnesota Couple Communication Program: a Follow-up Study." *Journal of Marriage and the Family,* 1980, 42, 577-84.

WARD, C. D., M. A. CASTRO, and A. H. WILCOX. "Birth-order Effects in a Survey of Mate

Selection." *Journal of Social Psychology,* 1974, 94, 57–64.

WEINGARTEN, H. "Remarriage and Social Effects: National Survey Evidence of Social and Psychological Effects." *Journal of Family Issues,* 1980, 1, 533–59.

WEISS, R. L. *Marital Separation.* Springfield, MA: G. and C. Merriam, 1953.

———. "The Emotional Impact of Marital Separation." *Journal of Social Issues,* 1976, 32, 135–45.

———, H. HOPS, and G. R. PATTERSON. "A Framework for Conceptualizing Marital Conflict: a Technology for Altering It, Some Data for Evaluating It." In L. A. Hamerlynck, L. C. Hardy, and E. J. Mash (eds.) *Behavior Change: Methodology, Concepts, and Practice.* Champaign, IL: Research Press, 1973.

WEITZMAN, L. "Legal Regulation of Marriage: Tradition and Change." *California Law Review,* 1974, 62, 1169–1288.

———. "To Love, Honor, and Obey? Traditional Legal Marriage and Alternative Family Forms." *Family Coordinator,* 1975a, 24, 531–48.

———. "Sex-role Socialization." In J. Freeman (ed.) *Women: a Feminist Perspective.* Palo Alto, CA: Mayfield, 1975b.

WELCH, C. E. III, and S. PRICE-BONHAM. "A Decade of No-Fault Divorce Revisited: California, Georgia, and Washington." *Journal of Marriage and the Family,* 1983, 45, 411–18.

WELLS, C. *Idle Idylls.* New York: Dodd Mead, 1900.

WELLS, J. G. "A Critical Look at Marriage Contracts." *Family Coordinator,* 1976, 25, 33–37.

WERNER, J. S., and L. P. LIPSITT. "The Infancy of Human Sensory Systems." In E. S. Gollin (ed.) *Developmental Plasticity.* New York: Academic Press, 1981.

WERTHAM, F. "Battered Children and Baffled Adults." *Bulletin of the New York Academy of Medicine,* 1972, 48, 887–98.

WESTERMARCK, E. *The History of Human Marriage.* London: Macmillan, 1925.

WESTOFF, C. F. "Coital Frequency and Contraception." *Family Planning Perspectives,* 1974, 6, 136–41.

WHALEN, R. E. "Brain Mechanisms Controlling Sexual Behavior." In F. A. Beach (ed.) *Human Sexuality in Four Perspectives.* Baltimore: Johns Hopkins Press, 1976.

WHITEHURST, C. A. *Women in America: the Oppressed Majority.* Santa Monica, CA: Goodyear, 1977a.

———. "Youth Views Marriage: Awareness of Present and Future Potentials in Relationships." In R. Libby and R. Whitehurst (eds.) *Marriage and Alternatives: Exploring Intimate Relationships.* Glenview, IL: Scott Foresman, 1977b.

WHITEHURST, R. "Violence in Husband-wife Interaction." In S. Steinmetz and M. Straus (eds.) *Violence in the Family.* New York: Dodd Mead, 1974.

WIEMAN, R. J., D. I. SHOULDERS, and J. H. FARR. "Reciprocal Reinforcement in Marital Therapy." *Journal of Behavioral Therapy and Experimental Psychology,* 1974, 5, 291–95.

WILENSKY, H. "The Moonlighters: a Product of Relative Deprivation." *Industrial Relations,* 1963, 3, 105–24.

WILL, J., P. SELF, and N. DATAN. Paper presented to the American Psychological Association, 1974.

WILLIAMS, M. J. "Personal and Family Problems of High School Youth and Their Bearing upon Family Education Needs." *Social Forces,* 1949, 27, 279–85.

WILLIAMS, R. J. *Biochemical Individuality.* New York: Wiley, 1956.

WILLOUGHBY, R. R. "The Relationship to Emotionality of Age, Sex, and Conjugal Condition." *American Journal of Sociology,* 1938, 43, 920–31.

WILLS, T. A., R. L. WEISS, and G. R. PATTERSON. "A Behavioral Analysis of the Determinants of Marital Satisfaction." *Journal of Consulting and Clinical Psychology,* 1974, 42, 802–11.

WINCH, R. *Mate Selection.* New York: Harper and Brothers, 1958.

WINTER, D. G., and A. J. STEWART. "The Power Motive." In H. London and J. E. Exner (eds.) *Dimensions of Personality.* New York: Wiley, 1978.

WOODRUFF, R. A. JR., S. B. GUZE, and P. J. CLAYTON. "Divorce among Psychiatric Outpatients." *British Journal of Psychiatry,* 1972, 121, 289–92.

WYNNE, L., et al. "Pseudo-mutuality in the Family Relationships of Schizophrenics." *Psychiatry,* 1958, 21, 205–20.

YANKELOVICH, D. *New Roles: Searching for Self-fulfillment in a World Turned Upside Down.* New York: Random House, 1981.

YANKELOVICH, SKELLY, and WHITE. *The General Mills American Family Report, 1974–75.* Minneapolis: General Mills, 1975.

———. Poll commissioned by *Time Magazine,* published in issue of November 21, 1977a, 111 et seq.

———. *Raising Children in a Changing Society.* Minneapolis: General Mills, 1977b.

———. *The Yankelovich Monitor,* 1983.

YLLO, K. Personal communication, 1985.

———, and M. A. STRAUS. "Interpersonal Violence among Married and Cohabitating Couples." *Family Relations,* 1981, 30, 339–48.

YOUNG, M., and P. WILLMOTT. *The Symmetrical Family.* New York: Pantheon, 1974.

ZALBA, S. R. "Battered Children." *Trans-action,* July/August 1971, 58–61.

ZELNICK, M., and J. F. KANTNER. "Sexual Activity, Contraceptive Use, and Pregnancy among Metropolitan-area Teenagers: 1971–1979." *Family Planning Perspectives,* 1980, 12, 230–37.

———, and F. K. SHAH. "First Intercourse among Young Americans." *Family Planning Perspectives,* 1983, 15, 64–70.

ZINBERG, N. E. "Changing Stereotyped Sex Roles: Some Problems for Women and Men." *Psychiatric Opinion,* 1973, 10, 25–30.

ZUBE, M. "Changing Behavior and Outlook of Aging Men and Women." *Family Relations,* 1982, 31, 147–56.

ZUCKERMAN, D. "The Aspirations, Values, and Self-concepts of Men and Women Attending Seven U. S. Colleges." Paper presented to International Conference on Women, the Netherlands, April 1984.

Name Index

Subject Index